DATE DUE

DISCARD

FEB 1 4 2017	

EQUAL

EQUAL

Women Reshape American Law

FRED STREBEIGH

W. W. NORTON & COMPANY
NEW YORK   LONDON

For information about permission to reproduce
selections from this book, write to Permissions,
W. W. Norton & Company, Inc.,
500 Fifth Avenue, New York, NY 10110

For information about special discounts for bulk purchases,
please contact W. W. Norton Special Sales at
specialsales@wwnorton.com or 800-233-4830

Manufacturing by RR Donnelley, Harrisonburg, VA
Book design by Helene Berinsky
Production manager: Anna Oler

Library of Congress Cataloging-in-Publication Data

Strebeigh, Fred.
Equal : women reshape American law / Fred Strebeigh. — 1st ed.
p. cm.
Includes bibliographical references and index.
ISBN 978-0-393-06555-8 (hardcover)
1. Trials—United States. 2. Sex discrimination against women—
Law and legislation—United States. 3. Women's rights—
United States. I. Title.
KF226.S77 2009
342.7308'78—dc22

                                        2008044463

W. W. Norton & Company, Inc.
500 Fifth Avenue, New York, N.Y. 10110
www.wwnorton.com

W. W. Norton & Company Ltd.
Castle House, 75/76 Wells Street, London W1T 3QT

1 2 3 4 5 6 7 8 9 0

To women shaping law

CONTENTS

PROLOGUE

————+————

Toward Equality
(1968)

For a woman who wanted to become an American lawyer, the time
before 1968 was a time of inequality. If you entered Harvard Law
School before 1950, for example, you were male. Although some
American law schools had admitted a trickle of women for decades,
prior to 1950 Harvard practiced perfect discrimination: no women
need apply.

By 1967, the proportion of women in the nation's law schools
had reached only about 5 percent. 1968 changed American law. The
U.S. government announced plans to take away men's draft exemptions for attending law school. Harvard feared the worst. Testifying
before Congress to oppose the change, President Nathan Pusey of
Harvard predicted that his law school's entering class of 540 would
be "reduced by close to a half." Harvard Law might stay full only by
compromising on "quality or something." Moments later, Congressman John Erlenborn tried to help Harvard's president spell out that
compromise. Graduate programs like Harvard's, the congressman
said, seemed pushed toward "a policy of admitting women, the halt,
and the lame."

To that list, Harvard's president added "the foreign born." The
congressman repeated: "And the foreign." Half of Harvard Law

would need filling, they seemed to predict with a sniff of xenophobia, by women and others they viewed as outsiders.

The prediction to Congress proved partly true. Low on men, law schools opened the gates of the law to women. In 1968, the number of women entering American law schools jumped by 50 percent. Within a decade, the number of women entering law schools increased 1,000 percent, from fewer than 1,200 in 1967 to almost 12,000 in 1977. In 2001, law schools admitted 22,000 women, more than 49 percent of all entering law students. Women made the fastest advance in the history of America's elite professions.

As women entered the law, the law resisted. Judges would not hire women. Law firms asserted a right to discriminate against women. Judges permitted discrimination against pregnant women. Courts viewed workplace harassment as, one judge said, "a game played by the male superiors."

Young women lawyers, armed with new degrees, began to tackle the old ways of male-shaped law. The law began to change as law sometimes does—one story at a time, one case at a time, and one precedent at a time. Women lawyers went to court to tell the stories of Paula Wiesenfeld in 1972 (constitutional discrimination), Sally Armendariz in 1972 (pregnancy discrimination), Diane Blank in 1975 (employment discrimination), Mechelle Vinson in 1978 (sexual harassment), Christy Brzonkala in 1994 (violence against women), and many other women along the way. This book, drawing on interviews with and documents from participants in those cases, tells the stories behind the cases that propelled American law toward equality. And it tells tales of resistance from on high.

Part One

———————✦———————

SCRUTINY

(1970–1975)

1

The Story of Paula Wiesenfeld

Late in 1972 a new professor at Columbia Law School, Ruth Bader Ginsburg, heard the story of Paula and Stephen Wiesenfeld. Immediately she knew that their sad tale offered the legal case she needed. By taking their story to the Supreme Court of the United States, she could accomplish her greatest professional goal: to eliminate what she called "gender lines in the law." Ginsburg in the early 1970s was making the most profound attack on sexist law in the history of the American legal system.

The Wiesenfelds' story began as a romance. When Paula Polatschek first met Stephen Wiesenfeld, she had the looks of a Disney Mouseketeer. She had mahogany eyes and black hair with a tint of persimmon, turned up at her shoulders in a slight flip that almost matched the upturn of the corners of her mouth when she smiled—a sassy smile that formed her cheeks into hemispheres, like half-apples.

Stephen Wiesenfeld was slender with a hawklike nose and a reddish beard and a madcap look that made him resemble a young Gene Wilder. They had met in late 1969, and soon they were spending much of their time together, entertaining friends, fooling around, and photographing their antics. Stephen lived and worked in New Jersey; Paula lived in Manhattan and taught in White Plains, just north of New York City. After Paula's teaching ended in the spring of 1970, she drove down to New Jersey and stayed with Stephen through the summer.

As fall approached, with a couple of weeks remaining before school would start, Paula asked Stephen if she should go back to her apartment in Manhattan. The conversation was light as usual, more fooling than planning.

Paula asked, What if I get a job in New Jersey? Stephen knew Paula hadn't been looking for jobs. Mostly fooling, he proposed a sort of bet: "If you can get a job in New Jersey, we can get married." It was a bet he supposed he couldn't lose.

What Stephen couldn't fully know was how good a teacher Paula was, or how much her credentials put her in demand. As well as her undergraduate degree in math, she had a master's in education and had begun studying for her PhD in education. Within a week, Paula had two job offers. She took a job teaching mathematics at Edison High School, right in Stephen's hometown. They married in November.

Soon they were building a life together and, to go with it, a dream house. It was larger than most of their friends' houses, three thousand square feet, big enough that Stephen, in a moment of euphoria, was able to describe it as a fourteen-room house—a number that came from counting every walled-in space, including the entry hall and all the bathrooms. But whatever its room-count, it was theirs—built on land they chose, to their specifications. And Stephen, being something of a perfectionist, played a hands-on role. Many evenings, after the builders had left, he would go to the house to scout for substandard lumber or workmanship. If a piece of work fell far below his standards, he would simply remove it—leaving the builders to do the job better the next day. When the builders finished, the price tag was $32,000 and the job was all that Paula and Stephen had hoped. On the day they moved in, Paula said to Stephen, "I never dreamed I'd live in a house like this." For years he would remember how proud it made him to help Paula attain her dream.

At about the time Stephen and Paula moved into their new home, they discovered Paula was pregnant. So they began wallpapering a baby's room, choosing a pattern with blue elephants and pink camels and green palm trees. As they prepared the walls, they painted messages to each other like "I love you" and "Stephen loves Paula"—signals to the future about their love in the present.

As they went to doctors and childbirth classes, they made another preparation: how to organize their working lives. Paula's teaching was earning more money than Stephen's computer consulting, and more to the point, she had planned some demanding years. She wanted her PhD, and she needed it soon in order to meet her goal of becoming a school administrator and, if possible, a school principal.

Back when Stephen was a student at Taft High School in the Bronx, he had made his own plan: he wanted to become the president of a major corporation. Such professions didn't run in his family: his father had worked for years in the post office and later for a military arsenal. Seeking corporate presidents to emulate, Stephen looked up the career paths of industry leaders. He noticed some commonalities: many had a master of business administration, or a law degree, or some technical training in a field like math. So he decided to gather all three: an MBA and a master's in math from Fairleigh Dickinson University and, for good measure, a nonpracticing law degree through a program run by La Salle University.

As Stephen gathered his education, he found himself losing interest in what he thought of as the world of gray suits. He took a computer job with UNIVAC, which hired him on a day when he dropped by wearing sneakers and corduroys. UNIVAC put him to work as a mathematician with a team working toward an early antiballistic missile system.

The more Stephen learned, the more he wanted to become his own boss. So he founded the first of a series of small companies, called Eval-U-Metrics, an early form of computerized-accounting company designed to do payrolls for companies throughout the Northeast. From a small office with a primitive computer setup, he created the records and printed the checks for hundreds of workers in small factories, makers of clothing and handbags and paintbrushes.

Stephen's business didn't skyrocket. But it made money, and soon he was shifting from renting time on someone else's computer to owning his own mini-computer, back in the days when they could cost as much as a house—more than $30,000.

With Stephen plowing money into the business and struggling to make it go, his income stayed far lower than Paula's, which had passed $10,000. Furthermore, Stephen worked his own hours, often at home. Even when Stephen worked at his office, there was no reason why a young child could not play in a playpen there.

As the baby's arrival neared (a June birth seemed likely, perfect for a schoolteacher on summer leave), Stephen prepared to become their child's primary caretaker. Paula had bet well in her choice of a husband. But their luck didn't hold.

EARLY ON THE FIRST MONDAY in June of 1972, Paula felt labor-like pains. She and Stephen went to the hospital, where she gave birth to a son, Jason Paul, a few hours later. Jason's melding of Paula's broad face with Stephen's sharp features would create a boy so photogenic that before his tenth birthday he would be appearing as a television model for products like toothpaste and designer jeans. His combining of their intellects would create a student who, all through college, would mostly get As.

But within moments of Jason's birth, the doctor realized Paula was showing symptoms of an amniotic embolism, a rare backup of amniotic fluid into the lungs, creating conditions not unlike drowning. He began preventive measures immediately, and Paula fought for her life for four hours. But she lost, as had, the doctor told Stephen, every woman before her known to have the same type of embolism.

Stephen was devastated. Before he could begin to enjoy Jason's birth, he had to plan Paula's funeral. The funeral came the next day, and then Stephen had his first real contact with at least one of America's attitudes toward single fatherhood. As he sat in their dream house after the funeral, Paula's mother began redesigning his life. As for the house, she told him: sell it. As for Jason, she said: put him up for adoption. Her message was: wipe the slate clean.

Stephen listened with fascination as Paula's mother plotted out his child-free life. But as soon as Jason was old enough to leave the hospital, Stephen went and picked him up "like a sack of potatoes" and took him home. Stephen's parents stayed to help—easy enough for his father, who was retired, but much harder for his mother, who had to quit her job at a department store a few months' short of being fully vested for a pension. Stephen's sister offered to raise Jason herself, but Stephen wanted to raise his own child.

Soon after Stephen received his lesson in American attitudes toward single fatherhood, he got another lesson: in American problems finding good childcare. Unable to support Jason on earnings from his slow-growing consulting business, Stephen quickly found a well-paying job for $18,000 a year, with a small computer firm called Cyphernetics, and set out to find a good live-in babysitter. Problems arose.

First he hired a nurse from a nearby city. But soon Stephen got the sense that she wanted not so much to be Jason's nurse as Jason's stepmother. Then, at the suggestion of a Norwegian friend, Stephen made arrangements to bring an au pair from Norway. When changing diapers, she poked Jason with pins. When off duty, she tossed cigarette butts and banana peels out of her window onto the patio. Stephen had requested a clean, nonsmoker, someone familiar with children. He helped her find other work.

At about the middle of his nanny failures, Stephen Wiesenfeld encountered a wire-service article in his local paper, the *New Brunswick Home News*, on November 16, 1972, about the difficulties faced by single fathers trying to raise young children. For a long time, he had been stewing over an incident early in his widowerhood. Soon after Paula's death, Stephen's father (who, having just retired, had been reading up on Social Security benefits) had led him to the local Social Security office in New Brunswick. At the office, they had applied for two benefits that Stephen's father knew were available: a death benefit (about $200, which would help cover Paula's funeral expenses) and a child's benefit (about $200 per month, which would help raise Jason). Both were granted.

Stephen's father also asked about a third benefit: an extra $200 a month, the benefit for a parent whose spouse had died. The office said no, Stephen could not receive that benefit. It was available to help women—but not men—care for children. It was a "mother's insurance benefit." That extra $200 a month would have allowed Stephen to care for Jason himself, rather than rely on a cavalcade of nannies.

After that visit to the Social Security office, and as nannies continued to fail him, Stephen kept wondering if there was something he could do. But he had a sense that "you can't fight city hall." Or at least you can't fight without lots of money on your side. He didn't know how much money it would take, but it didn't demand graduate degrees in math and business to do rough calculations. He supposed a case against the federal government might cost more than $100,000. He calculated his potential return (about $200 per month for eighteen years—the limit on how long the insurance would be paid): a bit less than $44,000. He wasn't willing to invest tens of thousands of dollars above his best possible return.

So when he read an article about widowers in the newspaper, a bell went off. What if he wrote a letter to the editor, apparently responding to the article but mostly telling his story? Hoping to reach someone who could help make his case, he wrote to the *Home News*:

> Your article about widowed men last week prompted me to point out a serious inequality in the Social Security regulations.
>
> It has been my misfortune to discover that a male can not collect Social Security benefits as a woman can.
>
> My wife and I assumed reverse roles. She taught for seven years, the last two at Edison High School. She paid maximum dollars into Social Security. Meanwhile, I, for the most part, played homemaker.
>
> Last June she passed away while giving birth to our only child. My son can collect benefits but I, because I am not a WOMAN homemaker, can not receive benefits.
>
> Had I been paying into Social Security and had I died, she would have been able to receive benefits, but male homemakers can not. I wonder if Gloria Steinem knows about this?

One person who read the *New Brunswick Home News* was Phyllis Zatlin Boring, a professor of Spanish at Rutgers University and founder of the New Jersey branch of a new organization called the Women's Equity Action League (WEAL). The same day that she read Stephen Wiesenfeld's letter, on November 27, she wrote to him.

To his quite inscrutable final question, Professor Boring answered that she suspected Gloria Steinem did indeed "know about Social Security's inequities." Professor Boring suggested those inequities could be addressed by introducing legislation in Congress, but, she continued,

> of course, waiting for legislative reform can take a long time. In reading your letter the thought occurred to me that a legal test of the Social Security Law might be faster.

Professor Boring said she was not a lawyer, but she offered to put him in touch with lawyers at the American Civil Liberties Union (ACLU) who might be able to "handle such a case with a volunteer lawyer and, I believe, no expense to you." She did not mention that the most important of lawyers at the ACLU's Women's Rights Project was formerly a colleague on the Rutgers faculty, an ally in pushing Rutgers to admit women as students, and still a board member of WEAL: Ruth Bader Ginsburg.

On December 26, 1972, after he responded to Boring that he would indeed appreciate the assistance of the ACLU, Ginsburg called Stephen Wiesenfeld. She impressed him powerfully, mostly with the precision with which she laid out the responsibilities he would be accepting and, if he did accept them, the sequence that would ensue.

Three "facts," he would recall years later, she told him were crucial: Paula had to have been paying Social Security payroll taxes. Stephen had to be still unmarried. Jason had to be in Stephen's care. To the last he replied, "My son is in my care . . . , and I intend to keep it that way."

Other than Stephen's responsibility to confirm those facts, he would face only one demand on his time: to go to Newark, with a lawyer provided by the ACLU, to answer questions about his case for a legal deposition, a preparatory document for the court. That court would be a three-judge panel of the United States District Court for the District of New Jersey, located in Trenton. Ginsburg told Stephen that he need neither attend the district court argument nor pay anything for legal counsel.

In the same phone call, Ginsburg made sure that Stephen Wiesenfeld realized that though he was paying nothing, neither was he likely to gain anything. Since his yearly salary had jumped from about $2,600 while self-employed to $18,000 at Cyphernetics, he had soared past the annual income cutoff (approximately $8,400) for receiving mother's benefits.

Undeterred by his lack of reward, Wiesenfeld went on to imagine the plight of other single fathers—some less able than he, with his three graduate degrees, to find well-paid work; some whose efforts to raise a child could force them onto welfare. For them, his suit could indeed bring relief.

And reforming the law for other fathers seemed actually within reach. Ruth Bader Ginsburg explained that his case permitted use of a legal route toward reform that was rare in the law. Most cases that go to a district court must be appealed, if a loser wishes, to a court of appeals, in a process that can take years. But Stephen Wiesenfeld's case embodied a rare combination. It had undisputed facts, and it raised a constitutional question: Had the federal government, by offering mother's benefits but not parent's benefits, created a gender line that was clearly *irrational*? This rare combination could put Stephen's case on a fast track. The effect was, as Ginsburg told him and as he would repeat often, in astonishment: No matter who wins in district court, the loser will appeal straight to the Supreme Court of the United States.

As for Ginsburg, by the time she had finished her call with Stephen Wiesenfeld, she could tell this was the case she had been seeking for years.

GINSBURG IN THAT FIRST CONVERSATION did not tell Stephen that his case epitomized what she was coming to call the "double-edged sword" of sex discrimination, the sword that, though it might seem to cut with a single edge against a single gender—males, in this case—in reality cuts down both men and women. And she did not tell him that his was the first gender discrimination case that she would control from start to finish. Nor did she tell him that the route of Stephen

Wiesenfeld toward championing women's rights at the Supreme Court was only slightly more unlikely than her own.

Joan Ruth Bader was born on March 15, 1933, in the Flatbush section of Brooklyn, a neighborhood full of immigrant families (Italian, Irish, Jewish) and full of dreams: the sons would become doctors and lawyers; the daughters would marry sons. At home with the Baders, however, the dream differed slightly.

For one thing, Nathan and Celia Bader had no sons, just two daughters, Marilyn and Ruth. And then suddenly, at age eight, Marilyn died of meningitis, leaving her little sister to grow up as an only child. Nathan Bader, a shy man, soldiered on as a manufacturer of low-priced furs, making enough money that his daughter could own the cello she played in the school orchestra, could buy the black satin jacket with gold lettering that she wore while twirling her baton as a high-school "Go-Getter," and could even attend summer camp in the Adirondacks.

Ruth's mother was smart, lively, a constant reader who passed a love for books to her daughter by taking her often to a public library above a Chinese restaurant in Brooklyn. (As a result, Ruth would come to associate the joys of reading with the aromas of Chinese food.) But Celia was also an emblem of women's constricted opportunities.

Right after she graduated from high school at the precocious age of fifteen, Celia went to work in New York City's garment district to achieve her family's goal: putting her eldest brother through college at Cornell. Later, after she married, Ruth's mother would give up any hope of professional employment. Her own education abandoned at a young age, Celia Bader struggled to save enough money from her husband's earnings to send her daughter to college.

During Ruth's first year in high school, the family learned that Celia Bader was gravely ill with cervical cancer. Ruth often sat at her mother's bedside to do her studies because that gave her mother pleasure. The day before Ruth graduated as one of the top students in her high school at age seventeen, her mother died. Ruth had kept her mother's illness secret from most of her high-school friends, and few knew that Ruth had been growing up, as she put it later, "with the smell of death."

After her death, her mother's longing for Ruth's success became clear. In small bank accounts, saved for Ruth's education, she had gathered $8,000. Ruth would go, as had her mother's eldest brother, to Cornell.

IN THE AUTUMN OF 1950, Ruth Bader arrived at Cornell, where she quickly won a reputation for her intellect. She was, one classmate would say, "scary smart." In a time when women were not supposed to seem too studious, she discovered a distinctive strategy: she studied while hiding in various campus bathrooms.

In her freshman year, friends made a date for Ruth Bader that would end the days of solitary study. Martin Ginsburg—a star on the college golf team, the son of a well-to-do department store executive from Long Island—soon made Ruth forget that she still had a boyfriend from her Adirondack summer camp. In Ruth, Martin found a woman who shared many of his interests, with an intellect that engaged wide-ranging topics. Soon, they were imagining careers they could share. Discarding choice after choice, they settled on one that fascinated them both: the law.

Graduating a year before Ruth, in 1953 Martin Ginsburg enrolled in Harvard Law School. Ruth then graduated with the highest average among women in the Cornell class of 1954 and also won admission to Harvard Law, which before 1950 had never admitted a woman. They married in June, and then when Martin was called into military service from the reserves, Ruth gave up her admission to Harvard and joined him with the Army in Oklahoma. In July of 1955 she gave birth to their first child, Jane Carol Ginsburg. Once Martin had served his two years in the military, Harvard automatically welcomed him back. Ruth needed to win admission again, and she did, entering as one of nine women in the fall of 1956. They found a woman whom Ruth thought of as a "New England grandmother type" to care for Jane during the day.

During their second year enrolled together at Harvard Law, the scent of death returned. Martin was diagnosed with quickly spreading testicular cancer. He underwent massive surgery but was told that no one had ever survived once the disease had advanced so far.

As when her mother was dying, Ruth put her strength into studying—but now she was studying for two people (and raising a young daughter as well). Ruth collected notes taken by students in Martin's classes and then typed those notes for him; later, she typed his papers as he dictated to her. And while he slept, she did her own schoolwork—displaying the stamina that, in later life, would permit her to work full days on one to three hours of sleep each night. Ruth won high grades and a place on *Harvard Law Review*. Martin finished his degree on schedule and, defying the fatal diagnosis, recovered completely. He was hired as a tax lawyer by a prominent law firm in New York.

To keep the family together, Ruth Bader Ginsburg left Harvard. As a transfer student, she entered Columbia Law School, where an old classmate from high school, seeing her arrive at his law school, recalls thinking, "God, it's Ruth, and she's gonna be first again." He was right. She made law review at yet another law school and graduated from Columbia in a tie for first in the class of 1959.

From there, with the help of one of her Columbia professors, she obtained a one-year clerkship with a federal judge, and then, thanks to another professor who admired her work, she received an invitation to take on a scholarly project on a grant from the Carnegie Foundation to study a topic and country about which she knew almost nothing, the legal system of Sweden. And so she found herself pulled back toward academe. (Not for years would she let on to any but her closest friends the mischances—the denied interviews, the unoffered jobs—that made a university perhaps her only chance for professional advancement.)

IN 1963, WITH THE RESULTS OF HER research in Sweden en route to publication as her first book, Ginsburg won a job as assistant professor of law at Rutgers, making her one of the first twenty women to teach in an American law school and distinguishing Rutgers as a rare law school with two women professors (the first, Eva Hanks, was asked by a male colleague if she would be upset to cease being the school's lone woman).

In her early years at Rutgers, her scholarship followed the path begun by her research grant—writing books and articles on civil and judicial procedure in Sweden. Her teaching at first stayed close to her scholarship: civil procedure and conflict of laws (the tensions that arise between the laws of different states or countries). And her teaching, at least to some students, seemed scholarly in another sense: dry and formal, engaged but not engaging, delivered in an old-fashioned European style, as if Professor Ginsburg were lecturing from another time and place.

In 1970, a series of events changed her life. First, a group of Rutgers students asked Professor Ginsburg to teach a course on "women and the law." When Ginsburg had studied law, feminism never entered her conversations with classmates or teachers. Until the last months of 1969, no law school in America offered such a course. The request that she teach one had taken an odd route.

The idea came from the other side of the Hudson River and was carried to New Jersey by two law students traveling on the PATH train from New York City. It originated in Greenwich Village, at New York University (NYU) School of Law, in early September of 1968. A first-year law student, Janice Goodman, who not long before had been organizing against discrimination in Mississippi with the Freedom Democratic Party and the Student Nonviolent Coordinating Committee (SNCC), was standing in a bookstore line next to a second-year law student, Susan Deller Ross. They got talking about scholarships, and Ross told Goodman that the law school's most generous scholarship was closed to women. The prestigious Root-Tilden Scholarship provided tuition, room and board, dinners with famous people, paid summer internships, and a living stipend in a package worth about $10,000 a year—at a time when many starting legal jobs paid little more—to twenty male students. As they talked about this blatant discrimination, Ross said, Don't you think we should do something about that? Quickly they created one of the first women's groups at any law school, the Women's Rights Committee, and then they were in for a fine battle: to desex Root-Tilden.

They were battling at a fine time. Brand new in America was *women's liberation*—a phrase coined about fifteen months earlier, apparently, in June 1967 at a conference of Students for a Democratic Society (SDS). There, women's calls for "full participation" in SDS were greeted by male mockery and heckling. Within months, Women's Liberation groups were forming in Chicago and then New York. A further impetus came from women's efforts to take a role beyond the menial in battling segregation in the South—an effort narrated superbly by Susan Brownmiller in her memoir, *In Our Time*. Brownmiller had gone south with Janice Goodman (then running an urban program for Girl Scouts) in 1964 to volunteer with SNCC during Freedom Summer. On their first night in Mississippi, when they raised their hands to report for work, the local organizer replied, "Shit. I asked for volunteers and they sent me white women." As the summer ended, two women staffers of SNCC wrote a memo to present at a staff retreat near the Gulf Coast. Anonymously, they suggested that men restricted women to second-class status within the civil rights movement in part because of a crippling "assumption of male superiority." Their memo might have sunk without ripples but for the quick wit of one SNCC leader, Stokely Carmichael. One evening, down near the shoreline, Carmichael mused about the role of women in his organization and then announced, "The position of women in SNCC is prone."

One position that looked better than prone was that of lawyer. As her friend Brownmiller would later document, Goodman was among many women who began fighting for civil rights in Mississippi and later extended their efforts to a fight for the civil rights of women. Another was Eleanor Holmes, a third-year law student who would later become an ally to Goodman. When Holmes volunteered for SNCC in the summer of 1963, she arrived the day her supervisor in the field, Medgar Evers, was shot dead. Nearby at about the same time, a woman named Fannie Lou Hamer was caught using a bathroom in a bus station, thrown in jail, and beaten. When a staffer for SNCC named Lawrence Guyot rushed to free her, he got beaten nearly naked and added to the jail. Less than a day after arriving, Eleanor Holmes, thanks to her status as law student, had the task of retrieving Hamer and Guyot. Phoning a local police chief, she told him that she was going to the jail to get her people. And "let me tell you something," she continued, "I go to the Yale Law School, and I have called everybody to tell them where I will be going." It worked. She got her battered allies out of jail, months before she got her law degree—which led to her next job with SNCC, writing a legal brief for the Freedom Democratic Party to challenge the all-white delegation that planned to represent Mississippi at the 1964 Democratic Convention.

(Eleanor Holmes, later Eleanor Holmes Norton and delegate for the District of Columbia to Congress, had applied in 1959 for a Root-Tilden Scholarship at NYU because it was the nation's richest for legal training and her family had little money to pay tuition. She received a letter back saying that the scholarship, designed to support "future public leaders," was reserved for men. She accepted a lesser scholarship from Yale.)

Goodman's effort to open the Root-Tilden funding to all future public leaders hit NYU law school at a good time. In the late 1960s, it was one of the first law schools where the numbers of women were beginning to exceed the national average of four or five for every hundred men. In 1967, women accounted for more than 12 percent of its entering class.

Then, in 1968, all law schools received an incentive to admit more women: America's draft law changed, eliminating the deferment for men enrolled in law schools. Men averse to Vietnam found themselves headed into teaching (where the deferment remained) or into conscientious objection or even into Canada. Suddenly, law schools had new places for women.

In 1968, for the first and last time in history, the ratio of women to men attending law schools jumped more than 50 percent in a single year—from five to almost eight women for every hundred men. (NYU law school, ahead of the nation, admitted twenty for every hundred.) As if it might not rise again, the national ratio of women to men stayed at eight to one hundred for one more class. Then in 1970, another shock hit law schools almost as hard as the draft. It came after a lone scholar named Bernice Sandler, who had not seen herself as a feminist, was surprised to hear that she had been rejected for a teaching position because she was, according to a male colleague, "too strong." A bit of research led her to two more surprises. First, in 1968 President Lyndon Johnson had added sex discrimination to the forms of discrimination that were proscribed for contractors that accepted federal funds. Second, the director of the office in the Department of Labor that oversaw contracts had been hoping for a call like hers. He invited her to his office, where he taught her how to file complaints and make sure they would be noticed by members of Congress. Sandler filed her first one in early 1970, under the auspices of a recently founded group called the Women's Equity Action League (WEAL), and the federal government began delaying payment of millions of dollars in federal contracts to a number of universities. Law schools responded. The ratio rose almost 50 percent again, and every one hundred men were facing more than eleven women. And the next classes brought in almost fourteen women (1971), and then nineteen (1972), and then more than twenty-five (1973), thirty (1974), and then almost thirty-seven women (1975) for every hundred men.

By then it would not make sense to count women in measures of parts per hundred, for the scale of the ratio had changed. Now just three men were looking at each incoming woman. (And indeed, by 1978, a decade after the first big jump, American law schools would be admitting only two men for each woman. By century's end the ratio would reach almost exactly one to one.)

But in 1968, at the moment of the first big jump, the women of NYU could not know whether they had reinforcements coming—and indeed, so long as law schools discriminated against women in awarding scholarships like the Root-Tilden one, perhaps the reinforcements would never come.

When the NYU Women's Rights Committee began circulating a petition, some of the scholarship holders—known as "Roots"— argued against including women. The future public leaders described pleasures women could not share, such as building male camaraderie by throwing water balloons at each other while running nude through the all-male Root-Tilden residence. The importance of Root nakedness arose again, when Goodman was called in to meet with Professor Russell Niles, who as a dean of NYU Law in 1951 helped create the scholarship. Niles told Goodman that the scholarship had been given as a "sacred trust" that limited it to men. (He also endorsed letting Roots run nude; Goodman left giggling.)

As the Women's Rights Committee prepared to present its argument to a faculty meeting on November 22, close to that year's deadline for scholarship applications, Goodman took the task of researching legal tactics that permit breaking a trust. The challenge was tough but possible, she learned, in situations that involve important public policies such as ending discrimination.

Soon, Goodman received a surprise from an ally on the faculty, Professor Daniel Collins. Responding to her inquiries, he sent her a brief memo explaining that the faculty had voted two years earlier to let women be Roots. "It is the sense of the faculty that women be admitted to the Root-Tilden Program," said a resolution of the faculty from the fall of 1966, "on the same basis as men." Furthermore, Professor Niles had visited the scholarship's donor, the Avalon Foundation, evidently hoping it would oppose admitting women. The foundation's director replied that NYU could go ahead and "admit women if we want to." (Collins' memo to Goodman withheld Niles' reasons for opposition: Niles did not see sufficient need to "encourage bright young women.")

The story from two years before started to emerge in the law school newspaper, the *Commentator*. Professor Niles had insisted, when the faculty met in 1966, that it would be inappropriate to award the foundation's funds to women students. Niles lost. So the faculty had already voted to let women become Roots. But it never followed its vote with "administrative action." Collins told Ross, as she recalled later, that "nobody cared enough" to open the scholarship to women candidates.

When Ross rose to address the faculty on November 22, 1968, she warned that if the faculty did not take administrative action, the Women's Rights Committee would take legal action: NYU students would sue their own law school to open the scholarship. After the students threatened litigation, Goodman recalls, a professor turned to Russell Niles at the meeting to ask what the trust said. In response, Goodman recalls, Niles had to admit there was no trust document, only some letters between NYU and the foundation. In the meeting room, Goodman recalls stunned silence from the faculty. The students were told that they could leave the room.

Within days, outgoing mail from NYU—as demanded by the women's rights organization—carried notices to all major colleges and special letters to all women's colleges that women were welcome to apply to be Roots. The year's scholarship deadline was extended.

Having won their first battle and wanting to know more about women and the law, the NYU law women asked for a course. They met resistance. A male professor suggested the school's next step down would be to teach the law of the bicycle. But they persisted, creating their own syllabus. And to teach them their syllabus, the law school agreed to hire a part-time teacher, Diane Schulder, and pay her $500 to preside over the course that the students were designing. And so the first course on women in law began at NYU in the fall of 1969.

Once they had their course started, the students took their idea on the road. Jan Goodman and a friend named Mary F. Kelly headed for Rutgers in Newark, just a few stops on the PATH train out of Manhattan and one of the first law schools to begin admitting women in significant numbers. And Rutgers had something that NYU lacked: two tenured women law professors, including Ruth Bader Ginsburg, who found the idea worth exploring.

Thorough as ever, Professor Ginsburg set out to study all that had been written on the subject of women and the law. This, she found, "proved not to be a burdensome venture." She needed only a few weeks, for legal scholarship barely acknowledged women. To be sure, one widely used text on property law observed provocatively that "land, like woman, was meant to be possessed," but it did not examine the implications. As her study progressed, Ginsburg found the law filled with unexamined gender lines and her consciousness awakened. "How have people been putting up with such arbitrary distinctions?" she wondered. "How have I been putting up with them?" And so, responding to the urging of her Rutgers students and the emissaries from NYU, she decided to study and teach the law's treatment of women.

• • •

THE VERGE OF THE 1970S was a good time to challenge how the law handled women. In 1963, Congress had enacted the Equal Pay Act, which tried to end underpayment of women in the workplace and was the first federal law to address women's inequity since the Nineteenth Amendment gave women the right to vote in 1920. The next year, Congress took a far larger step: Congress included women within the protections of the Civil Rights Act of 1964. It thus apparently protected women against discrimination in hiring, firing, and what the Act called "all terms and conditions of employment." This new legislation led to new legal challenges for the 1970s: to convince the courts to interpret the new laws in a way that gave them meaning. In creating her Rutgers course, Ginsburg reviewed all the cases then making their way through the courts that involved discrimination against women. One that particularly appalled her was a case originating in Idaho about a woman named Sally Reed who had been denied the right to administer her deceased son's estate solely because she was a woman. The law's discrimination against Sally Reed was absolutely not *rational*—a key word, as Ginsburg knew, from the vantage of constitutional law. And so, in the spring of 1970, Ginsburg taught her first course on women and the law, including Sally Reed's case.

One day in the last week of July in 1970, after the spring term's teaching had ended, Ginsburg received a phone call from a stranger. Stephen Nagler, executive director at the New Jersey branch of the ACLU, wanted her to take a legal case to help a woman who had a problem with the military. Letters from a woman named Nora Simon had been bounced around by ACLU offices, from Washington (wrong region?) to New York (not a national case?), and had finally wound up in New Jersey (at times Nora Simon's home state). For years Ginsburg, who had never argued a case, wondered why Nagler called her.

The reason would have been no surprise. Working at the New Jersey ACLU that summer was a Rutgers law student, Diana Rigelman, who had just taken Ginsburg's first-year course in civil procedure. Rigelman had been impressed with her professor, whom she saw as an "ice woman"—precise, scholarly, and professional. Rigelman had also been one of the Rutgers students urging Ginsburg to teach about women and the law. After reading Simon's letter, Rigelman immediately thought of Ginsburg as someone the military would see as "a female lawyer with clout."

Nora Simon's letter to the ACLU told a sad story. Both she and her husband had been serving in the Army. She was a nurse and he a lieutenant. In 1969, they had a child. Soon after, their marriage ended, and they put the child up for adoption. Although both were now single and childless, Nora alone was now jobless. Her husband was permitted to continue as an Army officer. She was banned from all military service.

Neither the ACLU legal director nor the ACLU intern knew how much Simon's story resonated for Ginsburg. Five years earlier, then still an untenured professor at Rutgers, Ginsburg had become pregnant in midwinter. What if, she worried, her colleagues saw this as unprofessional and didn't renew her contract? Was it possible, Ginsburg worried, to lose your profession even if your pregnancy had no impact on your work? So Ginsburg kept quiet about her pregnancy through the spring term, quietly left for the summer, gave birth to her son James on September 8, and returned almost immediately to continue teaching. As far as her work went, all was unchanged.

For Nora Simon, all had changed. Although her Army work had been exemplary, although the Army at the height of the Vietnam War needed nurses like her, although she wanted to "serve her country," and although she was a single, childless nurse, because she *had* been pregnant she was banned from the military. Ginsburg agreed to help her.

It looked like an easy case, and Ginsburg approached it with her usual efficiency. At the end of July, she sent a long letter to the director for Equal Opportunity in the Armed Forces at the Pentagon. In this, her first legal assault on sex discrimination, she offered simple logic: When Nora Simon had sought to rejoin the Army after her marriage ended, she learned that "under Army regulations a discharge for pregnancy renders a person ineligible for re-enlistment." With the help of her congressman, she had learned that an exception did exist: she would have been eligible for reenlistment if her child had died. Ginsburg extended the principle of this exception to argue that Simon should, logically, also be eligible for the same exception:

Since Miss Simon is no longer married, and has effectively relinquished her parental right to the child to whom she gave birth, it seems clear that her current situation meets the concern evidenced in the exception recognized by the Army: she has no child dependent upon her for care or support. Her legal status is in all respects that of a single woman without issue.

But Ginsburg did not ground her case only on common sense and law. Looking for compassion, she went on to quote from Nora Simon's unpolished letter to the ACLU:

"I feel I would be of greater assistance to my country, which I love and respect, to make a career in the service. I know from experience that they need more [nurses]. . . . I am fully aware of Title VII of the Civil Rights Act, forbidding sex discrimination of either sex, if they are qualified for the job. . . . I am supposed to get equal Rights to a job for which I am qualified, but because of being a female, I am discriminated by the military service. . . . I definitely want to serve my country, whether it is in the Navy or the Army."

Ginsburg then moved to the law, adding that "Miss Simon's view that 'the Army should not have this out of date regulation still in effect' is supported by the consistent position of the Federal government since 1964 with respect to equal opportunity for women."

In this first letter, on her Rutgers law school stationery, Ginsburg created what would become her trademark blend of legal precision with compassionate concern. For a month and a half she received no reply from the Pentagon.

For Ginsburg this delay, while Nora Simon waited in limbo, was unconscionable. In a few days, while she and her family were holidaying in Hawaii, she turned her letter to the Pentagon into what she called a "zippy" legal complaint. But she did not take it to court. Instead, in late September and early October, she simply mailed her original letter to the offices of a number of people, including the secretary of defense and, most important, a general counsel for the U.S.

Army, who would be able to tell that she had a solid discrimination case against the armed forces.

That was all it took. In mid-October, the Pentagon informed Ginsburg that Simon was welcome to rejoin the Army. But if a strong letter was all it took, a single job for Nora Simon was all it got. The Army, though willing to make one exception in response to one smart law professor, was not ready to alter its policy. Ginsburg's efforts had made no change in American law.

Two weeks after the Army relented in the narrow case of Nora Simon, Ginsburg got her chance to try for broader impact. It arrived even more oddly than the case of Nora Simon—with an interruption by her husband. Near the end of October in 1970, in their large apartment on East 69th Street in Manhattan, Martin and Ruth Ginsburg were working as usual in their two separate offices. At nine o'clock at night, Martin walked into her office.

Although the Ginsburgs had chosen law school long ago to give them a profession they might share, their specializations had diverged: he was practicing tax law in Manhattan while she was teaching legal procedure in Newark.

"You've gotta read this," he said. Martin had been reading the tax advance sheets, part of his regimen as what he liked to call "a poor insular tax lawyer." On this occasion, he thought, he had a tax case for her.

"Marty," she said, tired from nighttime work for her law school teaching, "you know I have no time to read tax cases."

He just repeated himself: "You've gotta read *this*."

This was the case of Charles E. Moritz. What it offered was, as Martin Ginsburg had seen immediately, an instance of gender discrimination that was absolutely irrational. Moritz was a single man whose eighty-nine-year-old mother lived in his home. So that he could earn money to support them both, he hired a daytime caretaker for her. When he applied for a routine $600 deduction for "household help for invalid mother," he was denied the deduction. The reason: he was male. Had he been female, he would have been permitted the deduction.

Moments after the tax advance sheets had been dropped on her desk, Ruth Ginsburg came back to the room where her husband was working. It's a great case, she said. We ought to try to take it. And he thought, What a great idea. It would be their one case arguing as a team.

To start, Martin Ginsburg called Charles Moritz at his home in Denver. Moritz responded that he did not like getting crank calls: New York lawyers do not propose to travel two thousand miles to argue cases worth a few hundred dollars.

Martin responded, Let me write you a letter on my best stationery, saying who we are and why we think your case is important. The letter made only one demand of Moritz: when the government offered to settle for a lower tax payment, as Martin Ginsburg guaranteed it would, the only settlement Moritz could agree to was the full amount of the tax—a 100 percent concession—and only if the concession would be entered in federal court. The Ginsburgs would not go through a case like that of Nora Simon, which helped merely one person. This case must have national impact. Moritz agreed.

Seeking national impact, the Ginsburgs sought support from the national ACLU. And in requesting the support of ACLU headquarters to fly them to Denver and pay other costs, Ginsburg chose to avail herself of a remarkable bit of serendipity.

IN EARLY FALL OF 1970, as Ruth Bader Ginsburg was beginning her teaching term at Rutgers and pushing the case of Nora Simon to completion, at her office door appeared, from her distant past, the cheery face of Melvin Wulf. Wulf had been following Ginsburg's career since their childhood days at summer camp in the Adirondacks, where he remembered her as "Kiki" Bader.

Kiki—pronounced "Kicky"—was a twelve-year-old with big blue eyes. Mel was the sixteen-year-old waiter at her table all summer—affable in groups, handy in a canoe, and glamorous on stage singing the role of Richard Dauntless ("valorous is he") in Gilbert and Sullivan's *Ruddigore*. Young Kiki was a somewhat private child, and outgoing Mel Wulf was far too caught up in the life of the older girls to spend much time with her. That summer would stay with him, as the ultimate teenage idyll, particularly since Mel (graduate of a nearby boys' camp) was one of only six boy-waiters at Camp Che-Na-Wah with 140 slightly younger girls.

Even though he didn't know Kiki well, Wulf kept hearing about her, because his sister Harriet, the camp's waterfront counselor, kept in touch with Ruth's older cousin. During the same years, Mel was moving to legal prominence, becoming the legal director of the ACLU. Early in his work there, he had helped develop the legal concept of a right to privacy—crucial for defenders of birth control and later of a woman's right to have an abortion. He pushed the ACLU toward increased advocacy, taking a lead in supporting civil rights demonstrators in the South and then, against great resistance within the ACLU, urging his organization to attack the Vietnam War as a violation of the Constitution.

So one day in the fall of 1970 at Rutgers law school, where he had been invited to speak with students, Mel Wulf knocked on the office door of the professor that he still called "Kiki." For years he would recall this visit as the start of the process by which he "plucked Ruth Ginsburg from obscurity."

They mostly chatted: he talked about the ACLU; she about her expertise, including Swedish legal procedure. But she also told him about what he would later recall vaguely as "some down and dirty women's rights work in the New Jersey Civil Liberties Union." To Ginsburg, that work meant saving Nora Simon's professional future. To Mel, *down and dirty* work meant litigating far below his preferred pinnacle: "the lofty aeries" of the United States Supreme Court.

A few weeks after Wulf dropped by, Ginsburg believed she had a case for the aeries. *Moritz* offered, also, a twin to the case of Sally Reed. And *Reed*, which Ginsburg knew from teaching about women in the law, was then being appealed to the Supreme Court by the ACLU. In the *Moritz-Reed* combination, Ginsburg saw a male-female pair, each as irrational as the other in the line drawn between women and men. Moritz was a man who could not get a tax deduction for supporting his mother because he was male; Reed was a woman who could not administer an estate for her son because she was female. The symmetry was as perfect as the irrationality, and with it Ginsburg hoped to teach the lesson that sex discrimination hurts everyone, male and female.

She wrote Mel Wulf, asking for ACLU support and funding to cover the thousands of dollars in costs she and her husband were about to shell out to defend Charles Moritz's $600 tax deduction. Recalling Mel in his valorous *Ruddigore* role, singing about a ship that was a "tight little, light little, trim little, slim little craft," she told him that *Moritz* would be "as neat a craft as one could find to test sex-based discrimination against the Constitution." She and her husband would gladly make their case before federal court in Denver, and if not glorious there, she continued, they would "make a valorous try at the Supreme Court." Wulf agreed to support them. In midwinter the Ginsburgs went away for a two-day work-trip in order to draft the argument, a "docketing statement," that would become the kernel for most of her future work.

When Wulf saw the initial six pages, at the start of February, he was impressed. He wrote back to Ginsburg:

> Dear Ruth/Kiki:
> Your proposed docketing statement meets the high standards to be expected of one who was early exposed to the rigorous discipline of Che-Na-Wah. . . .
> Mel

Similarly impressed by those six pages was the U.S. government. It offered to settle for a dollar. Moritz declined. As agreed with the Ginsburgs, he held out for zero dollars and a legal precedent. The government declined, and the Ginsburgs began expanding the six-page kernel into a longer brief, ready for trial that summer in Denver. It would be Ruth Ginsburg's first court argument in her life.

When Ruth Ginsburg read a notice in *U.S. Law Week* that the case of Sally Reed, to which they hoped to link *Moritz*, was going to the Supreme Court, she immediately wrote Wulf asking what the ACLU had argued in its statement that convinced the Supreme Court to take jurisdiction in that case. Wulf's response brought surprising news. "I am the lawyer," said Wulf, "who both wrote the jurisdictional statement and who is handling the case." He invited her to call him to discuss tactics.

As she read the jurisdictional statement Wulf sent her, Ginsburg could see both enormous potential and clear shortcomings in strategy. Soon she proposed not merely to serve as discussant but to play a significant role. In early April, she sent Wulf the copy of their just-completed thirty-four-page brief in *Moritz*, which contained the type of arguments she wanted to see the ACLU making in *Reed*. Along with the *Moritz* brief, she sent a message designed to push Wulf's decision:

> Dear Mel: Some of this should be useful for *Reed v. Reed*. Have you thought about whether it would be appropriate to have a woman co-counsel in that case???

For perhaps the first and last time in her life, and quite emphatically, Ginsburg asked for special consideration as a "woman." Wulf did not respond immediately.

As part of her quest for a role in the *Reed* battle, she mailed the *Moritz* brief to friends throughout the New York legal community. Perhaps the most important of these mailings went to Norman Dorsen, professor of law at NYU and a highly regarded volunteer general counsel of the ACLU.

Dorsen wrote back immediately, calling the brief "one of the very best presentations" he had seen in a long time and saying he found it difficult to imagine she would lose—significant praise, since she was attempting an utterly new challenge to the Constitution. As a grace note, Dorsen sent a copy of his letter to Wulf. Within three days, Wulf called Ginsburg and asked her to work with him on *Reed*.

As Ginsburg would remember, seeking a role in *Reed* was one of the key decisions of her life. As Mel Wulf would eventually remark, "Damn, maybe I didn't pluck her from obscurity. Maybe she plucked herself from obscurity."

2

Old Law Meets a New Case—*Reed*

As Ginsburg and Wulf prepared to take the *Reed* case and the rights of women to the Supreme Court, they were facing a long history of inequity. For a century, the Supreme Court had consistently refused to extend to women what the Constitution called, in its Fourteenth Amendment, "the equal protection of the laws." Every woman who had come before the Supreme Court with a gender-equality plea had lost her case. As of 1970, pleas seemed futile. When the Court encountered legal obstacles to women's equality, it turned a blind eye. It declined to examine them or, in its language, to subject them to "scrutiny."

The Supreme Court's first refusal to extend equal protection of the laws to women came in 1873 in the case of Myra Bradwell. An expert on legal topics, founder and editor of an influential nineteenth-century legal journal, *The Chicago Legal News*, Bradwell in 1869 took and passed the Illinois bar exam, which should have qualified her to become a practicing attorney. Before she could practice law, however, the law stopped her. Under statutes created by the Illinois legislature at the dawn of statehood, no person could practice as an attorney without also obtaining a license from two justices of the Illinois Supreme Court. Whom to admit was left to the discretion of the justices, with one limitation that, in the unprecedented case of Myra

Bradwell, they found significant: the state supreme court "should not admit any person or class of persons who are not intended by the legislature to be admitted."

As it happened, the Illinois legislature in the first years of statehood in the early 1800s did not oppose admitting women to the bar. This legislative silence allowed the Illinois Supreme Court to look for guidance back to what it saw as the originating year of Illinois law: 1607, when Britain founded its first American colony in Virginia at Jamestown. "It is to be remembered," the justices wrote, "that at the time this statute was enacted we had, by express provision, adopted the common law of England." Looking back across centuries and overseas, the justices were able to assert that in 1607, "female attorneys at law were unknown in England." Seventeenth-century Britons "regarded as an almost axiomatic truth," the justices insisted, "that God designed the sexes to occupy different spheres of action, and that it belonged to men to make, apply, and execute the laws."

Thus, it seemed, worked the law: as the twentieth century looked to the nineteenth, so the nineteenth looked to the seventeenth, and the seventeenth looked all the way back to God's intentions at the creation.

Myra Bradwell had one last chance: the United States Constitution. The Fourteenth Amendment of 1868 guaranteed that

> no State shall make or enforce any law which shall abridge the privileges or immunities of citizens of the United States; nor shall any State deprive any person of life, liberty, or property, without due process of law; nor deny to any person within its jurisdiction the equal protection of the laws.

Enacted in the wake of the Civil War, this sweeping language seemed to extend equal protection of the law and equal privileges of citizenship to all Americans. And so Myra Bradwell's attorney contended that for someone such as Bradwell, possessed of legal learning and fine character, the practice of law was surely a privilege guaranteed under the law for a U.S. citizen.

For months, Bradwell awaited the word of the Court. The day

before her decision came down, she heard another decision, in the ominously named *Slaughter-House Cases*. Although that case involved a group of male butchers and had nothing to do with race or sex, the *Slaughter-House* decision prepared the ground for Bradwell. In a 5–4 decision, the justices ruled that "the one pervading purpose" of the Fourteenth Amendment had been to secure rights for black Americans—and thus the amendment did not increase the rights of white butchers. Then considering the clause that says no state shall deny "equal protection of the laws," the justices declared,

> We doubt very much whether any action of a State not directed by way of discrimination against the negroes as a class, or on account of their race, will ever be held to come within the purview of this provision.

Discrimination against women as a class, or on account of their sex, seemed beneath constitutional scrutiny.

The next day, April 15, 1873, Myra Bradwell learned that she could not become a lawyer. Writing for the U.S. Supreme Court, Justice Samuel Freeman Miller declared in few words that admission to practice in the courts of a *state* was not a privilege "belonging to citizens of the United States."

Three of Justice Miller's colleagues chose not to leave Bradwell with his few words. In a far longer concurring opinion written by Justice Joseph P. Bradley, they looked back to ancient law with a vision that outdid their brethren in Illinois. They found that

> the civil law, as well as nature herself, has always recognized a wide difference in the respective spheres and destinies of man and woman. Man is, or should be, woman's protector and defender. The natural and proper timidity and delicacy which belong to the female sex evidently unfits it for many of the occupations of civil life.

From their meditation on the common law, Justice Bradley and his allies did not fail to take the next step back toward the dawn of legal time. "The paramount destiny and mission of woman are to fulfill the noble and benign offices of wife and mother. This is the law of the Creator."

IN THE HUNDRED YEARS from the day Myra Bradwell was forbidden to practice law to the day Ginsburg became involved with the *Reed* case, remarkably little change had taken place in the Supreme Court's response to appeals for the rights of women. (Change had of course taken place outside the court, as when women won the right to vote in 1920. But to such change the Court's role was primarily as a remote spectator.)

By 1971, when Ruth Bader Ginsburg first walked into ACLU headquarters on lower Fifth Avenue in Manhattan, the Supreme Court's unresponsiveness to women's rights had become codified in a test that defined "standards of review" or, as they were sometimes called, "levels of scrutiny." The key question had become, If women claimed to the Supreme Court that they had been denied "equal protection" of the laws, did their claim need to be *scrutinized*? Put another way, if the Court encountered charges of discrimination against women, did it have to look closely? The answer, simpler than the question, was *no*.

Ruth Bader Ginsburg's goal in 1970, as it would remain through the next quarter century, was both simple and radical: turn *no* to *yes*. The case of Sally Reed, like that of Myra Bradwell a century earlier, had roots before the dawn of American nationhood. Sally Reed's desire seemed reasonable: Her young son had died without a will, and she wished to be considered to administer his estate. After Sally Reed separated from and later divorced her husband, her son Richard remained in her care through his early years (under what was known in the law as "tender years" doctrine). Those years passed, and his custody shifted to his father, Cecil. Their son eventually got into trouble with the law and wound up in a juvenile home. When he returned to live with his father, he was depressed, and after a short while, in 1967, at age nineteen, he committed suicide. Sally Reed blamed her former husband for their son's death.

After Richard's death, Sally Reed petitioned an Idaho probate court to name her the administrator of his estate, which contained little of value—clothes, a clarinet, a small record collection, and a $495 savings account. A few days later, her former husband objected to her appointment and requested, instead, that he be named administrator.

Their qualifications seemed equal. Nonetheless, the Idaho Probate Court had no choice. By law, Sally Reed could not be considered to serve as administrator. If two people were equally entitled to administer an estate, Idaho law said, "males must be preferred to females." As it became an American territory in 1864, Idaho had copied those words from California. Earlier, as it became a state in 1851, California had copied them from New York, which had apparently drawn them from some still earlier source.

The ACLU's involvement in challenging Idaho's old law had begun in early 1970. Looking through a copy of the newspaper *Law Week*, an ACLU volunteer attorney named Marvin Karpatkin noticed what seemed to be Idaho's final rejection of the appeal of Sally Reed. The Idaho Supreme Court had rejected her request, commenting that "nature itself has established the distinction" between men and women.

Mel Wulf called Sally Reed's attorney, Allen Derr, to offer help. When Derr accepted, Wulf began one of his specialties at the ACLU, a "jurisdictional statement"—the argument to the U.S. Supreme Court to take Sally Reed's case on appeal. Wulf's argument continually attacked Idaho's preference for men by calling it *irrational*, contending that it lacked a "rational basis," that it joined in a pattern of "irrational classification" of women's role in society.

When Ginsburg received Wulf's jurisdictional statement in March of 1971, she saw that his strategy was less radical than what she and her husband had been trying in *Moritz*. Although Wulf's approach would suffice for the case of Sally Reed, Ginsburg believed that it would not suffice for the cause of women's equality, for which she wanted a more radical strategy.

Ginsburg knew that the Supreme Court, in its recent decisions concerning equal protection of the laws, was settling on two levels of "scrutiny"—what might be called *strict scrutiny* and *slight scrutiny*, in effect a tough test and an easy test. Most discrimination encountered only slight scrutiny, the Supreme Court's easy test. Often the Court was asked to review a state law that discriminated—that drew lines—between two groups. Many state laws discriminated, for example, between those allowed to drive (people sixteen and over) and those prohibited to drive, or between those allowed to practice law (people who had passed bar exams) and those prohibited. Almost always, when asked to assess such discrimination, the Court used its easy test: did the state law have a "rational" relationship to a "legitimate" governmental objective? *Yes* was usually the Court's answer to the easy test, and it looked no further.

The Court looked harder, however, if it saw a state making a distinction that it considered "suspect." And when looking hard, it applied its tough test: did the state law reveal a "substantial" (more than just *rational*) relationship to an "overriding" (more than just *legitimate*) governmental objective? One Florida law that failed this test in the 1960s, for example, had prohibited a negro man from spending the night with a white woman. Florida claimed that it sought to protect sexual decency. The Supreme Court in 1964 asked whether a law that punished the sexual behavior of "one racial group and not that of another" had a strong relationship to any "overriding" state objective? The court said *no* and overturned the state law, consistent with the Court's view that the Fourteenth Amendment applied to "discrimination against the negroes."

Almost without exception, the Court flunked laws that faced the tough test but passed those that faced the easy one. From Mel Wulf's jurisdictional statement to the Supreme Court, Ginsburg could see that the ACLU had found in Idaho a rare law: one that would fail even the easy test. But flunking one very dumb law did little to help women in general. She decided that the *Reed* case should become the start of a larger strategy: to change the test. If Ginsburg could succeed, all discrimination against women would face not the easy test but the hard test—a test that, as of the spring of 1971, as the ACLU was planning its strategy, had been used only against discrimination by race (or a closely allied category, ancestry). If her strategy succeeded, Ginsburg would force the Supreme Court to see not just race but also sex as a "suspect classification." Compared to the modest goal of Mel Wulf's jurisdictional statement, Ruth Bader Ginsburg's strategy was utterly radical.

BY LATE SPRING OF 1971, Wulf and Ginsburg had assembled a team to draft the *Reed* brief to the U.S. Supreme Court. Since the Supreme Court hears arguments in primarily two forms (the written brief and the oral argument), and since Wulf had failed to convince Reed's lawyer, Allen Derr, to let anyone from the ACLU argue before the justices, the brief was crucial. It represented the ACLU's only chance to present its ideas to the Court.

The drafting team included Wulf, Ginsburg, and four women students from nearby law schools. Diana Rigelman, just graduated from Rutgers, had already been key in Ginsburg's work for Nora Simon. Ann E. Freedman, from Yale, had played a key role in spreading the idea of legal courses on women. Mary F. Kelly and Janice Goodman were the two NYU students who had first gone to Rutgers and helped originate Ginsburg's course on women and the law. When it came to action, these students saw themselves as radicals. They were proud to be the sort of feminists who, when a professor in class said something sexist, would stand up to him, calling out, "BOO, BOO."

The students knew that Ginsburg's goal was to argue for strict scrutiny. Goodman and Kelly set out to write a brief that would, in Goodman's words, "educate the court on everything." They wanted to produce a brief in the tradition of the legendary Louis D. Brandeis, who in 1908 had won a case at the Supreme Court with a brief that famously contained just two pages of law and 110 pages of social science.

The students created a draft laden with evidence of the "kinship between race and sex discrimination." In their footnote-filled draft, they noted Dolley Madison's avowal that in postcolonial America a woman was seen as the "chief slave of the harem." They cited the *New York Herald* of 1852, which argued that woman, "by her nature, her sex, just as the negro, is and always will be, to the end of time, inferior to the white race, and therefore, doomed to subjection." They quoted sociologist Gunnar Myrdal, exploring the legal status of American slaves:

> In the earlier common law, women and children were placed under the jurisdiction of the paternal power. When a legal status had to be found for the imported Negro servants in the seventeenth century, the nearest and most natural analogy was the status of women and children.

What Professor Ginsburg would do with all this, the students did not know. Surely, they presumed, she would fix their footnotes, for in quoting Madison and Myrdal and others, they had left them full of blank spaces and question marks and notes to Ginsburg that said, "Check source."

"We just dumped it on her," recalls Goodman, telling her they "didn't have time to check the citations." The students did not see themselves as "little law students." After all, they had desexed university scholarships, they had introduced the idea of courses on women and law, and they were the "leaders of the field." When the students next saw their brief, they did not recognize it, and not just because Professor Ginsburg had fixed their footnotes (as she had). The brief was unrecognizable because Professor Ginsburg had added to their student screed what the brief needed: the law. One thing the students realized later was how much they, and the ACLU also, had underestimated Ginsburg—not her evident intellect, but her hidden radicalism.

None knew about her first work experiences, after graduating at the top of her class at Cornell, in the surroundings of Fort Sill, Oklahoma, where her husband was posted after being called into the Army. They did not know that after qualifying for GS-5 level work on a civil service exam, she learned that she would have to settle for a GS-2 job, typing, because she had become pregnant; her boss told her that a pregnant woman could not travel to get the training for a GS-5 job.

They did not know that her job in Oklahoma gave her the chance to see discrimination against others as well. When Native Americans came to her office to request Social Security, Ginsburg's coworkers often demanded to see birth certificates—though Indian births had previously been considered not worth documenting. Seeing inequity, Ginsburg quietly accepted a driver's license or a hunting permit.

Nor did she mention that when she first applied to Harvard, she was admitted with strong financial aid, based on her own financial need. When she reapplied two years later, she was admitted with no aid. Why? Harvard had a policy that married female students received little aid if their husbands' parents had money. A needy male married to a wealthy woman, she and Martin gathered, would have received aid. The Ginsburgs had made little fuss, for they quickly learned that, as Martin later put it with a laugh, "Nobody could see anything wrong with it, except us."

Nor could the students imagine the experiences of being one of only nine women at Harvard Law School in 1956. Each year, Dean Erwin Griswold, who had apparently told the first entering class of women in 1950 that he had opposed their admission, invited the handful of recently admitted to a reception at his home. There the women mingled with numerous lions of Harvard's tenured and visiting law faculty (Ruth Ginsburg sat next to Herbert Wechsler), and Dean Griswold asked them, as a matter of ritual, the same question: What was each doing in law school, occupying a seat that could be held by a man? Ginsburg would always remember her diffident answer: that her husband was a year ahead and she hoped study would help her understand his work. And she would always esteem the wonderful classmate who had the nerve to answer the dean with her own question: with five hundred Harvard men and only nine women, "what better place to catch a man?"

Nor did the students know that after making law review at both Harvard and Columbia law school, and gaining grades among the top ten students at each, Ruth Ginsburg could get neither a job at a Manhattan firm nor an interview for a clerkship with a Supreme Court justice. She came closest to consideration of the latter by the legendary Justice Felix Frankfurter. Urged to consider her by the Harvard professor who usually selected his law clerks for him, Frankfurter responded by worrying that he might not like how she dressed. "I can't stand girls in pants!" he reportedly said. "Does she wear skirts?" Yes, she wore skirts. Still, he declined to offer her a position, saying he would feel uncomfortable. (Had he accepted her, she would have been the second woman to clerk for a Supreme Court justice.)

Another legendary judge who refused to hire her was Learned Hand, a judge she revered far above Frankfurter or the other justices on the Supreme Court. Hand refused to consider women because, he explained, he used strong language and did not want to be inhibited by their presence. Finally one of her law professors gave her name to a district court judge, Edmund L. Palmieri, who always let that professor choose his clerk without explanation. The judge balked: He sometimes worked late! What would his wife think? The professor managed to place Ginsburg on a trial basis as Palmieri's clerk only by arranging a backup clerk—ready to give up another job and replace Ginsburg if the judge disliked her. By coincidence, Judge Palmieri often drove the elderly Judge Hand home from work at the federal courthouse in New York City. Often Ginsburg rode along in the car's back seat, while in the front Judge Hand cursed freely. Ginsburg asked why he felt so free before a woman passenger but not a woman clerk? "Young lady," Hand replied, "here I am not looking you in the face."

NOW IN 1971 AS SHE PREPARED THE BRIEF for *Reed*, Ruth Bader Ginsburg was looking discrimination in the face. She believed that *Reed* could help teach the Court that sex discrimination really hurt people. Without such help, she supposed, the justices were men who thought, as she later put it, "What is this sex discrimination? What are you talking about? I'm so good to my wife and my daughter."

Briefs, often more than oral arguments, win cases at the Supreme Court, and her years of legal work had prepared her well. Ginsburg settled on two primary tasks: first, to knock down what appeared to be key precedents that might hurt her case, and, second, to plant the argument that, as much as race, sex should be regarded as a "suspect classification," and thus classification by sex should be critiqued with "strict scrutiny."

Her attack on precedent took on some of the most vital decisions against women's rights, ranging from 1908 (a case saying women deserved special protection) to as recent as 1961 (a case saying women need not serve on juries). Of these cases, her fullest attack came on a decision written in 1948 by the justice who worried that a female clerk might arrive wearing pants: Felix Frankfurter.

In that case the Supreme Court refused to declare unconstitutional a Michigan law banning women from working as bartenders but not from working in the lower-paying job of waitress. That law had made it impossible for a wife and daughter to keep running their family business, a bar, after the death of their husband and father. Frankfurter, upholding the ban and the women's deprivation, affirmed any state's right of drawing "a sharp line between the sexes." In support, he asserted that "the Constitution does not require legislatures to reflect sociological insight, or shifting social standards." He even seemed to question the morals of mother and daughter, commenting that the Court was dealing with what he called the profession of the "alewife, sprightly and ribald."

To beat Frankfurter, Ginsburg used Frankfurter. "Only six years" after the bartending case, she pointed out, Frankfurter had joined a unanimous Court in the landmark racial discrimination case *Brown v. Board of Education*, which had explicitly relied on "sociological insight" and contemporary "social standards." *Brown* might have led Justice Frankfurter to reconsider his position in the bartender case, she suggested, but in any event, by 1960 his mind had evidently changed. In an opinion of that year concerning the status of women, she wrote, Frankfurter

> buried the historic common law notion that husband and wife are legally one person. Writing for the Court, he declared, "we . . . do not allow ourselves to be obfuscated by medieval views regarding the legal status of women and the common law's reflection of them."

Ginsburg, having in effect pulled from her bag of tricks a reformed Frankfurter, next pulled forth, more remarkably, the inspiration for his reformation—as quoted approvingly by Frankfurter in his 1960 decision—the great Justice Oliver Wendell Holmes. "It is revolting," said Holmes, "to have no better reason for a rule of law than that it was laid down in the time of Henry IV. It is still more revolting if the grounds upon which it was laid down have vanished long since, and the rule simply persists from blind imitation of the past."

Frankfurter, like Holmes, surely would have realized, Ginsburg suggested, that the time had come for the extinction in America of "the law-sanctioned subordination of wife to husband, mother to father, woman to man." No longer could the law permit, as Frankfurter once argued, drawing "a sharp line between the sexes."

As illuminated by Ginsburg, Frankfurter had apparently seen the light. But did she believe this? No. His reasoning had been so bad, so glib—talking, as he did at one point in his bartending opinion, "about a merry old alewife," as she would later say, "and here's a mother and daughter who can't carry on their business, because there's no man in the house." Nonetheless, reshaped by the formidable drafting of Ginsburg, even Felix Frankfurter appeared ready to embrace change.

While Ginsburg's drafting was at the printers, in June 1971, suddenly another whiff of change reached her. To her utter surprise, a decision came down from the California Supreme Court, explicitly denominating sex as a suspect classification and thus demanding that sex discrimination receive strict scrutiny and the tough test. Though this was the decision of a single state, Ginsburg hastily spliced into her brief the new words from California: "Sex, like race and lineage, is an immutable trait, a status into which the class members are locked by the accident of birth."

Here was exactly the sort of legal opinion Ginsburg wanted, apparently written by a judge from California named Raymond Peters. (A few months later Ginsburg would meet that opinion's real author: Wendy Webster Williams.)

ON ITS FACE, GINSBURG'S BRIEF looked straightforward, but her craft made looks deceptive—much as a wily angler, baiting a hook, conceals its barb. Part one of her argument called for strict scrutiny. Part two, if the Court would not apply that tough test, called for an "intermediate test," what could be called intermediate scrutiny. Part three argued that even if the Court refused to apply the tough or intermediate test, it must decide for Sally Reed and declare unconstitutional Idaho's 1864 law.

None of the three arguments was as straightforward as it seemed. Ginsburg summarized her primary argument as follows: "The sex line" drawn by the Idaho legislature in 1864, because it subordinated women to men without regard to individual capacity, "creates a 'suspect classification' requiring close judicial scrutiny." Such legislative discrimination "grounded on sex, for purposes unrelated to any biological difference between the sexes, ranks with legislative discrimination based on race, another congenital, unalterable trait of birth, and merits no greater judicial deference." This argument, smoothly imbedding all the work the students had done to link sex to race, represented Ginsburg's ultimate goal: to win strict judicial scrutiny, and thus sure judicial defeat, for virtually any law that drew lines by sex.

Appearances aside, Ginsburg had no expectation of winning strict scrutiny. She introduced the topic merely to lay a foundation for future cases. Her plan drew its model from the work of the Legal Defense and Educational Fund of the National Association for the Advancement of Colored People (NAACP), two decades earlier. Led at the time by Thurgood Marshall, since 1967 a justice on the Supreme Court, the NAACP had brought a series of cases that had slowly educated the Court to see the evil of racial segregation and of the "separate but equal" standard. What Marshall had done with race, she would do with sex—one case at a time, step by step.

Ginsburg's second argument, for the intermediate test, received only a few lines. The essence of this test was that when any statute gives a preference to men over women, the Court should force lawmakers to prove it rational. The deception here, as Ginsburg knew, lay in calling this test "intermediate," for in practice it would prove virtually as tough as a test involving "strict scrutiny."

Having offered a second test that was still tough, Ginsburg was positioned to play her best trick: to offer a third one that sounded easy but was intermediate. She used the key words of the easy test, *reasonableness* and *rationality*, to provide the bait. Beneath the bait, she could conceal a hook.

Ginsburg reached back a few months to the work she and her husband had done in *Moritz*—work that had reached back decades, to an obscure tax case before the Supreme Court in the 1920s, known as *Royster Guano* (for a fertilizer company of that name). However odious its name, the *Royster Guano* decision contained phrasing that offered Ginsburg both bait and hook. When a state law makes a classification that draws a line, the justices declared, that classification "must be reasonable, not arbitrary, and must rest upon some ground of difference having a fair and substantial relation to the object of the legislation, so that all persons similarly circumstanced shall be treated alike."

But could Ginsburg use this language? *Royster Guano* had problems, quite beyond the fact that its *classification* drew lines not between men and women but between in-state and out-of-state fertilizer making. Its key phrasing had been quoted only once since the 1930s. Indeed, the doctrine on which it had been decided (that the Court could use the due process clause of the Fourteenth Amendment to invalidate states' economic laws) had been repudiated by the 1940s—and rightly repudiated, Ginsburg believed. As she and her husband worked on *Moritz*, *Royster Guano* became a joke at home: that the best case they could find reeked of millions of birds, defecating on everything in sight. They would say to each other, This is what we've got? The case just smelled wrong. But foul smelling or not, *Royster Guano* was the best she could find, so Ginsburg used it. The question remained, Would the Supreme Court go for it?

ONCE RUTH GINSBURG HAD FILED the brief in late June, the ACLU team awaited the opposing brief, written by a lone lawyer in Boise, Idaho: Charles S. Stout. When it arrived, it contained mostly predictable arguments: The constitutionality of Idaho's statute had "never before been questioned." If the Court followed Ginsburg's suggestion that sex lines receive strict scrutiny, "chaos would result." What Idaho's legislators knew in 1864 remained true today, that "men were as a rule more conversant with business affairs than were women." In all species "nature protects the female," and thus women must be treated differently from men "if the race is to be continued."

But along with much that was predictable, Stout's brief delivered a shocker: Idaho in 1971 had adopted a new probate code which eliminated the old sections that preferred men to women. This allowed Stout to make his most convincing argument against the case being heard by the Supreme Court: the case involved no "substantial federal question." Though the old law still applied to the Reeds and the new law would not take effect until mid-1972, the Court was now being asked to rule on a law that had been abandoned and that seemed to affect only a single estate worth less than $1,000.

Ginsburg immediately realized that the Court might dismiss *Reed*, wasting all their effort. Mel Wulf wrote to Allen Derr, upbraiding him for not warning the ACLU that the statute had been repealed and asking, with apparent sarcasm, "Have you given any thought to the consequences of the repeal upon the case?" Wulf initiated his last effort, in a series begun half a year before, to wrest the oral argument from Derr. Now Wulf argued—in letters not just to Derr but also to Sally Reed and to others—that *Reed* should be argued by a woman.

On his mind, as on Ginsburg's, was a recent case, *Phillips v. Martin Marietta*, in which a young male lawyer for the NAACP had been unable to divert what Wulf called "the kind of locker-room humor that some of the justices indulged themselves in." Some banter seemed revealing. In one question, Chief Justice Warren Burger grilled the young lawyer about whether a statute that forbade discrimination in hiring by large businesses would, if extended to federal judges, affect their choices of law clerks. What if, the chief justice asked, a judge refused to hire a young mother as "a lady law clerk" but willingly hired young fathers "whose wives had infant children"? Would that judge be discriminating illegally against women?

Yes, said the NAACP attorney, *if* the statute applied. But judges remained exempt.

"Are you sure," continued the chief justice, "it doesn't apply to Federal Judges?"

The courtroom filled with laughter. Few in the room knew the depth of Burger's interest in discrimination. Earlier, in private conference with his fellow justices, he had voted not to hear this case at all and thus to permit companies to discriminate against mothers who had pre-school-age children. Furthermore, he had told some of his own clerks that he would never hire a woman as clerk, and soon he would be telling the president of the United States not to nominate a woman as justice.

Ruth Ginsburg did not need inside knowledge to hear sexism running through the banter of the chief justice. He believed, she pointed out, that *wives* have children but fathers don't. Had he been speaking to a woman attorney, Ginsburg believed, his banter might not have sunk so low.

Wulf's worry about the Court's sexism and about Derr's judgment led him to make a final push to gain control over the case. Warning Derr that he was "going into the big leagues with a big league brief" and that he could make a "damn fool" of himself in oral argument before the Court, Wulf urged Derr to cede oral argument to a woman attorney for the ACLU: Wulf's former assistant, recently named head of the New York City Commission on Human Rights, Eleanor Holmes Norton.

Perhaps, as Janice Goodman, one of the NYU students, remarked later about Ginsburg at that stage, "The ACLU underestimated her. Everybody underestimated her. You know: she was a 'brief writer.'" In any event, Allen Derr stood his ground, with the support of Sally Reed: Derr would argue *Reed* before the Supreme Court.

As Allen Derr entered the last stages of preparing for the oral argument, Ginsburg offered him an opening analogy: that the case of Sally Reed could become as significant a turning point for sex discrimination as the case of Linda Brown—the great school desegregation case of 1954, *Brown v. Board of Education*—had been for race discrimination. Derr told her he liked the analogy and would use it, in his own words. A few weeks later at the Supreme Court, Ginsburg would have the chance to hear her idea emerge reshaped from Derr's lips.

Hoping to establish the significance of the moment, Derr began by telling the Court that "we are here today to ask you to do something that this Court has never done"—not the most auspicious beginning in a Court that honors precedent. Then, moving to Ginsburg's suggestion, somewhat haltingly he pushed on: "We feel that the case could have as [a pause]—at least as significant [another pause]—significance for women somewhat akin to what *Brown v. Board of Education* had for the Colored people." Sitting in the audience, hearing Derr's argument that the case had "significant significance" and his reference to "Colored people," Ginsburg was appalled.

As the phrase "Colored people" left his mouth, less than a minute into his allotted thirty minutes for oral argument, Derr was stopped short by the morning's first interruption—from one justice, asking about the Michigan case that prohibited women from serving as bartenders. Derr, aiming to get back to his prepared argument, managed to deflect that question and begin his attack on the easy, "rational relationship test." He continued for a minute before his next question: could the Idaho court have simply appointed both Mr. and Mrs. Reed as joint administrators? The answer should have been an easy *no*.

Instead, Allen Derr began, "There is a serious question on my mind. . . ." He would never get back to his prepared argument. For the rest of the argument, justices posed questions so quickly that Derr could rarely string sentences together. Afterward, Mel Wulf wrote Allen Derr that his argument, fulfilling Wulf's fears, "may have been one of the worst in the history of the Supreme Court." Wulf was not alone in his displeasure. Justice Harry Blackmun routinely gave grades to attorneys in Court, as if they were students presenting in seminar. He gave Derr a D, the opposing attorney a D+, and concluded his notes with this description: "perhaps the worst argued case I have heard up here."

IN THE AFTERMATH of the oral argument, Wulf believed all hope hung on Ginsburg's brief. Would it suffice? The answer came quickly. Within five weeks of oral argument, on November 22, 1971, Chief Justice Burger presented the decision he had written for a unanimous court. At first it seemed an ill omen that the decision would come from Burger, appointed not long before by Richard Nixon in an effort to make the Court more conservative. However ominous, Burger's decision was short, only six printed pages, and it found for Sally Reed. Idaho's preference in favor of males, it ruled, was unconstitutional: it violated the equal protection clause of the Fourteenth Amendment.

But Wulf and Ginsburg had never doubted the Court would invalidate Idaho's preference (which, as the chief justice noted, was already repealed). The key question remained which test he would apply. Burger made clear he intended to apply the familiar, easy test. "The question presented by this case," he stated, was whether Idaho's preference "bears a rational relationship" to Idaho's purpose. Burger wrote as if his decision left the law unchanged, still judging sex discrimination by its old, easy test.

To Mel Wulf, the decision was disappointing, and he took out some of his frustration on Allen Derr, telling him that "the bland and very narrow opinion of the Supreme Court reflects the quality of the argument made on behalf of Mrs. Reed." Ginsburg, in contrast, was delighted with the decision. The *Reed* decision, after all, marked the first time in history that the Court had invalidated a law as unconstitutional sex discrimination. More than that, it gave her the first step she needed for her step-by-step campaign.

She never would have expected, even from a "more liberal bunch" than this current Court (as she wrote to a friend right after the decision), what she thought of as the "giant step": declaring sex a suspect classification. For that step she could wait. *Reed*, she wrote, had provided "the turning point case."

Ginsburg could see that the chief justice had accepted her test as his own. Straight from her brief, as he explained that Idaho's law deserved "scrutiny," the chief justice wrote the old language of *Royster Guano* into new law: "A classification," he wrote, picking up the words planted by Ginsburg in her brief,

> must be reasonable, not arbitrary, and must rest upon some ground of difference having a fair and substantial relation to the object of the legislation, so that all persons similarly circumstanced shall be treated alike.

Not arbitrary. Fair and substantial. Treated alike. Those words, which led to Justice Burger's conclusion that Idaho's "dissimilar treatment for men and women who are thus similarly situated" violated the equal protection clause, created Ginsburg's solid first step. Against the odds,

Burger had taken the hook she had baited with *Royster Guano*. Soon he would feel the barb.

IMMEDIATELY AFTER THE *REED* VICTORY, in late 1971 Ruth Ginsburg presented the ACLU board with a proposal to create the "Women's Rights Project," dedicated to litigation that would press the strategy begun with *Reed*. The board agreed, with a beginning commitment of $50,000, which was 1 percent of the ACLU's $5 million in annual membership fees. The ACLU also committed to seek further grants, and one of the earliest, partly to cover mailing costs, came from the Playboy Foundation. (As a result, early mailings for the Women's Rights Project went out with a machine stamp that imprinted each envelope with the Playboy Bunny.)

Even before the project was announced, Ginsburg began working on two Supreme Court cases on sex discrimination, both involving women in the military and both likely to provide Ginsburg and the ACLU with a new high-water mark for the rise of "strict scrutiny." With Ginsburg in charge of sex litigation for the ACLU, Mel Wulf gladly stepped to the side (though, as legal director, he continued to sign off on all litigation). As he generously put it years later, "I knew when I was outclassed."

Ginsburg in the fall of 1972 was moving to Columbia Law School, becoming its first tenured woman professor of law. To Ginsburg, the invitation to teach where she had earned her law degree was welcome and slightly comic. In that year, Congress extended its two most formidable antidiscrimination statutes (Title VII and the Equal Pay Act) to cover academic employees. Magically, from Ginsburg's vantage, 1972 became what she called "the year of *the* woman"—every law school suddenly wanted *one*.

Columbia, fearful she might accept an offer from Harvard, agreed to appoint her on her own terms: she would join the law school as full professor but would spend half of her first year creating the Women's Rights Project. Thanks to this arrangement, Ginsburg had the time to guarantee that her project did not become a stepchild of the ACLU.

She linked her ACLU litigation to her Columbia teaching by creating an "Equal Rights Advocacy Seminar" whose students would do research to assist the Women's Rights Project. By this canny move, Ginsburg could now gather team after team of sharp students, like those she had worked with in *Reed*, hungry to take the lead in changing the law. Ginsburg planned to teach them mastery of procedure and attention to detail. Never again would students drop their drafts in Ginsburg's lap, telling *her* to fix the footnotes.

3

Frontiero Brings Hopes

Ginsburg's new role as head of the Women's Rights Project of the ACLU meant that she could now search for ideal cases. But she also inherited cases that the ACLU already had played some role in. At the same time that she first heard about the Wiesenfeld case, two ACLU cases were approaching their climactic moments in the Supreme Court.

Both cases concerned discrimination against women in the military, but Ginsburg gave priority to the case of Susan Struck. As an Air Force nurse serving in Vietnam in 1970, Struck had become pregnant at a time when an automatic rule required discharge of pregnant service members. This rule evidently could hurt women more than men.

Although the government encouraged her to have an abortion (before the Supreme Court's affirmative ruling of 1973 in *Roe v. Wade*), Struck refused: she was Roman Catholic. Instead, she told her superiors, she would bring her baby to term, using leave time that she had accumulated to give birth. She would immediately put her baby up for adoption. Although Struck's pregnancy seemed sure not to damage her work, the Air Force ordered Struck discharged for "moral or administrative reasons."

The ACLU in the state of Washington, where Struck was based after leaving Vietnam, challenged the Air Force's pregnancy rule as discriminatory but lost in both the district court and the court of appeals. Despite these losses, the ACLU won court orders to keep Struck from being discharged, and she proceeded as she had planned with the pregnancy and adoption.

As the case approached the Supreme Court, Ginsburg was prepared to attack the Air Force rule on both its "moral" and "administrative" grounds. If the ground was moral, Ginsburg wanted to know, why wasn't the father discharged? And if the ground was administrative, what was gained by discharging Struck, who had not asked the Air Force to grant her more time than it already owed her? Other service members who needed medical treatment, for such conditions as alcoholism and drug addiction, were routinely granted special medical leaves, often for absences far lengthier than Struck's.

Struck's case seemed ideal to Ginsburg, the next step in educating the Court about prejudiced views of women. In her less restrained moments, Ginsburg considered opening her brief as follows: "Captain Struck indulged in the wrong form of recreation in Vietnam. Had she been a drug addict . . . , or an alcoholic. . . ."

In *Struck*, Ginsburg saw utter irrationality. But after she filed her brief, disaster hit. The Air Force, although it had won each battle so far, received instructions not to fight this last one. It was told to make a one-person exception (much as the Army had made an exception for Nora Simon and much as the IRS had hoped to make an exception for Charles Moritz) and thus avoid facing Ruth Ginsburg. It waived Susan Struck's discharge and allowed her to continue work, thus making the case, in legal language, *moot*: since Struck would have no complaint, the controversy would die.

The Air Force's attorneys had little choice but to retreat from this battle, because the instruction came from the commanding officer of all attorneys in the government: the solicitor general of the United States. This particular solicitor general, already legendary, had by 1972 served as solicitor general under Lyndon Johnson, who appointed him, and Richard Nixon, who, unable to do better, kept him. He was on his way toward making more arguments before the Supreme Court than any man alive.

This solicitor general apparently saw that his office and the Air

Force, combined, would lose to Ruth Bader Ginsburg. He knew her. He was Erwin Griswold, legendary also as dean for decades of Harvard Law. He was the man who in 1956 had invited her to his home to ask her why she was taking a man's place in law school.

WITHOUT *STRUCK*, GINSBURG HAD just one chance to influence the Court in its 1972 term. Sharron Frontiero was a woman in the military facing clear discrimination, but her case lacked emotional pull. At issue was not a baby but money.

A lieutenant in the Air Force, Frontiero was supporting her husband while, with the help of the GI bill, he attended college near her military base in Montgomery, Alabama. Under Air Force regulations, she would have been automatically entitled to extra pay for their housing had she been a married man. But for a married woman, military rules awarded extra pay for housing only if her husband could prove he was "dependent" on her—which Sharron's husband was by most common-sense definitions, since her $8,200 a year provided more than three-quarters of their household income. But the military definition demanded that a husband be dependent on her for over one-half of his support. Since both Frontieros were thrifty and since the GI bill gave him a bit more than $200 a month, his monthly expenses of $354 failed to reach the military's cutoff for dependency. Thus Lieutenant Frontiero did not meet the standard for an extra housing allowance—a standard no male lieutenant would have needed to meet because the military assumed that a wife was "dependent."

With the help of antidiscrimination lawyers from the small-but-famous Southern Poverty Law Center in Alabama, Sharron and Joseph Frontiero challenged the Air Force in federal district court, alleging that it denied them the "equal protection of the laws" and thus violated the Constitution of the United States. They lost. The military's different treatment of men and women, said the court, had a "rational basis." This military rule passed the easy test.

When the center decided to appeal *Frontiero* to the Supreme Court, its caseload was being handled by a single lawyer, Joseph Levin. To ease his load, he asked Mel Wulf for ACLU help in trying to get the

Supreme Court to hear the case. Wulf agreed, with an understanding that the ACLU would have primary responsibility for *Frontiero* in the Supreme Court and that any oral argument would be handled by Ruth Ginsburg.

After Ginsburg's jurisdictional statement convinced the court to hear *Frontiero*, she began work toward a brief and oral argument intended to push the next step toward strict scrutiny. Then, three months before *Frontiero* would be heard in the Supreme Court, Levin announced a change of mind: he wished to argue the case. For him and his colleagues at the Southern Poverty Law Center, it was a first chance to argue before the Supreme Court; they had "grown very attached to this particular case."

Ginsburg answered Levin with one of the least characteristic letters of her life. She viewed herself, she made clear, as "not very good at self-advertisement," and her letter proved it. Nonetheless, she insisted, the ACLU had done its work in *Frontiero* with the "express under-standing" that the Women's Rights Project would supervise the case at the Supreme Court and that Ginsburg would argue it.

As Ginsburg continued, her attempt at self-advertisement foundered on her modesty. She tried to state her claims through the opinions of others: Levin must know, she said, that she had developed "some understanding of the knowledge of the women's rights area." Even male colleagues who once resisted the idea that men might not make the best sex-discrimination attorneys now appreciate "the importance of argument by a woman attorney in a case of this significance."

Levin was not swayed. He had agreed, he conceded, that Ginsburg would handle the oral argument. But now he reneged—though not, he insisted, from any "chauvinistic" desires.

THE LATE LOSS OF CONTROL left Ginsburg and the ACLU to prepare an *amicus* brief, making her argument that sex like race was a "sus-pect classification" and deserved the Court's "strict scrutiny." This new brief was the direct descendant of what she saw as the parent briefs that she had written for *Moritz* and *Reed*. But the *Frontiero* brief possessed one enormous advantage: thanks to Chief Justice Warren Burger, it could now cite the language of her *Reed* brief, even the language of *Royster Guano*, now enshrined as law.

The split between Levin's and Ginsburg's briefs, which called attention to disagreement even among *Frontiero*'s supporters, would become still more evident at oral argument when the team would split again: Levin would get twenty minutes to argue about rationality, and Ginsburg would then add ten minutes of her theory.

When the day arrived for oral argument at the Supreme Court, Levin was ready. Clearly an experienced advocate, he proved more than adequate to the sort of questioning that had derailed Allen Derr in *Reed*. For the first four minutes he sustained his argument unbroken before encountering his first interruption, a query about the relation of "earnings levels" to "dependency." Deftly turning the question to his advantage, Levin reminded the court that Sharron Frontiero brought in $8,200 and her husband only $2,800—numbers that, regardless of military definitions, revealed who depended on whom. In the next few minutes, questions came often: Did the Frontieros' case apply only to civilian spouses? Did Levin's income figures come from a "median head count of Armed Forces males"? Was the military 98 to 99 percent male? Was Sharron Frontiero's claim about equal rights or just about extra money? Such interruptions inevitably broke the flow of Levin's argument, but he artfully steered his answers back to the main line of his argument: that the tough test of strict scrutiny was appealing but unnecessary for his case; that an intermediate test would suffice; and that given such a test, the military's preferential treatment of men would surely flunk. Then late in his section of the argument, as he was getting into a rambling answer to yet another question, Levin suddenly realized he was squandering Ruth Ginsburg's promised minutes. "I have used more time than I should have," he announced abruptly, and cutting off his ramble, he introduced "Professor Ginsburg."

She stood at the counsel table, just before two o'clock on the afternoon of January 17, 1973, to make her first argument before the Supreme Court. For the shy Ginsburg, in only the second courtroom argument of her life, this was an uneasy moment. At lunchtime she had been so nervous she had not eaten; she feared she would throw up.

"Mr. Chief Justice, and may it please the Court," she began, in the traditional formalism of oral argument, "*Amicus* views this case as kin to *Reed v. Reed.*" With *Reed* in play, Ginsburg was on her home field. She could now make her case for *Frontiero* with the language of *Royster Guano*, the language that Chief Justice Burger injected from Ginsburg's brief into his *Reed* opinion: the preferential treatment of men lacked "a fair and substantial relation to the object of the legislation, so that all persons similarly circumstanced shall be treated alike." This was the language of her test that sounded easy but was, in fact, intermediate. Thanks to its articulation of that test in *Reed*, she continued, the Court could now proceed to the tough test—the test that subjected sex discrimination to strict scrutiny—without making any "giant step."

In the *Harvard Law Review* two months earlier, she reminded the justices, Professor Gerald Gunther, the eminent constitutional scholar and author of a renowned law school casebook on constitutional law, had commented that Burger's decision in *Reed* had begun legitimating an intermediate test. Burger's decision, said Gunther, could not be explained without imputing to the Court "some special sensitivity to sex as a classifying factor," without "importing some special suspicion of sex-related means." Put another way, the Court's "special suspicion" prepared the way for declaring sex a "suspect classification" and thus subjecting it to "strict scrutiny." (She did not mention that Gerald Gunther, by then at Stanford, had been the professor at Columbia who fought to get Ginsburg her first clerkship after judges such as Frankfurter and Hand had refused to consider a woman.)

As she advanced into her argument for strict scrutiny, her early nervousness faded. She turned her attack to her principle opposition, the brief defending the military's sex discrimination, filed for the government of the United States by Solicitor General Griswold. That brief conceded, she said, that the principle characteristic invoking strict scrutiny was present as much in sex as in race: a "visible and immutable biological characteristic," in the words of the solicitor general's brief, "that bears no necessary relation to ability."

(In quoting this concession, Ginsburg was referring to the work of her old dean. A few weeks before, however, without so much as a note of warning, Griswold had heard via the radio that Richard Nixon had replaced him by appointing, as his new solicitor general, a conservative but relatively unknown Yale professor named Robert Bork.)

But this generous concession was mere preface to the government's argument against strict scrutiny for sex discrimination, to which she now turned. The Fourteenth Amendment, the government had argued, had a historic purpose: to respond to discrimination not by sex but by race. But "suspect classification," Ginsburg noted, had since been extended to discrimination on the basis of national origin and alien citizenship. The Court had been able to extend strict scrutiny even to the new immigrant to America, she continued, although surely "the newcomer to our shores was not the paramount concern of the nation when the Fourteenth Amendment was adopted."

As Ginsburg continued her argument, her listeners pondered the odd silence of the justices. Seated next to her at the counsel table, an ACLU colleague named Brenda Feigen began to wonder why the Court had asked no questions. Seated far behind her in the packed gallery of the court, Martin Ginsburg began to worry if the justices were just letting her go through the motions in a direction that held no interest.

Still uninterrupted, Ginsburg swung to attack other arguments that sex discrimination did not deserve close scrutiny. To the government's allegation that women are a majority, she responded that numerical majority may not confer political force, since "the numerical majority was denied even the right to vote until 1920." To its allegation that classification by sex does not imply women's inferiority, she ran through a history of such discriminations that the Supreme Court had upheld in past years: excluding women from professions as various as lawyering or bar-tending, from overtime pay, and from such basic responsibilities as jury service. Such discriminations have a common effect, she said: "They help keep woman in her place, a place inferior to that occupied by men in our society." Ginsburg had done what her students, including the radicals from NYU, had noticed long before. In her quiet way, because she always had her facts in place, she could sound utterly logical and reasoned while, in fact, making the most radical statements.

Still uninterrupted by any of the Court's nine brethren, Ginsburg concluded by quoting Sarah Grimke, the nineteenth-century abolitionist and advocate for women's rights, choosing words that might have been applicable to her own precise but somewhat unpolished speaking style: "She spoke, not elegantly, but with unmistakable clarity. She said, 'I ask no favor for my sex. All I ask of our brethren is that they take their feet off our necks.'"

For almost ten uninterrupted minutes Ginsburg had made her case to the Supreme Court. Leaving the Court with Brenda Feigen at her side, Ginsburg asked, Had something gone wrong? Her young colleague could only insist they were mesmerized. She would have been less sure had she seen the notes of Justice Blackmun, who gave Ginsburg a grade of C+ followed by the words "very precise female."

WHEN THE JUSTICES GATHERED two days later in conference, the highly secretive gatherings to which not even law clerks are admitted, Ginsburg's concept of strict scrutiny apparently played no part. The key question, as always, was whether to affirm or reverse the lower court. Thus the main discussion focused on whether this case was indeed "kin to *Reed*"? If it was close kin, the Court should affirm, but if it was essentially unrelated, the Court could reverse.

As always in conference, the chief justice began the discussion, to be followed by the associate justices in descending order of seniority. Chief Justice Warren Burger opened by telling his brethren that *Frontiero* had "nothing to do with" *Reed* and that *Frontiero* had "enormous" implications for the armed forces. The military, insisted Burger, perhaps imagining a day when women might wish to end their exclusion from military combat, "has the right to draw lines" between men and women. The chief voted to deny benefits to the Frontieros, affirming the lower court.

Speaking second, William O. Douglas, the famous liberal, then in his thirty-fourth year on the Court, portrayed this as an issue of "equal protection," a case in which the word *his* should be understood, generically, "as including '*her.*' "Arguing as usual against the new and conservative chief, he voted to reverse. Third, William Brennan, Douglas's ally in many equal protection cases over the years, argued that *Reed* and *Frontiero* were undistinguishable, nearly twins in legal terms, and that thus the Court's decision for Sally Reed mandated a similar decision for Sharron Frontiero. He too voted to reverse, making the vote 2–1 for Frontiero.

Fourth came Potter Stewart, appointed by President Eisenhower and a powerful vote at the center of the Court (neither predictably so conservative as the chief nor so liberal as Brennan and Douglas). On *Frontiero*, he weighed in with the liberals. "This provision on its face," he said, "is grossly discriminatory" and "constitutionally invalid." He would vote to reverse. Byron White, more conservative than Stewart but also at the Court's center, then introduced a new notion: discrimination against men. The provision, he said, "discriminates against men married to women in the service." He also voted to reverse. At this point, the vote stood 4–1 for Frontiero, with one more vote needed for victory (but still no votes for strict scrutiny).

Next came one of the Court's great liberals, Thurgood Marshall, who just two decades before as a litigator had led the NAACP to its landmark antidiscrimination victory in *Brown v. Board of Education*. But Marshall was far from a sure vote for Frontiero's allegation of sex discrimination. Months earlier when the justices considered whether to hear Frontiero's case at all, Marshall had voted to affirm the lower court and reject her appeal. But now, after hearing oral argument, Marshall was inclined to switch his vote and, albeit tentatively, to reverse.

The next three justices—all appointed by Richard Nixon as part of his effort to make the court more conservative—seemed likely to join their chief in voting against Frontiero. Harry Blackmun, however, inclined with some uncertainty toward reversal. Lewis Powell, like White seeing a form of "discrimination against men," voted for reversal. That left only William Rehnquist, the formidable new conservative presence on the Court—added to the Court after Nixon feinted toward nominating a woman in a move resisted fiercely by Chief Justice Burger and described by Nixon at the time (recorded on White House tapes that stayed unavailable for three decades) as merely a "screen." Closing the discussion with an argument closely allied to the chief's opening—that this was not really an equal protection case, since the government was entitled to treat different claims differently—Justice Rehnquist voted against Sharron Frontiero.

One significance of the 7–2 vote in conference was that it had gone not just for the Frontieros but also against the chief justice. Whenever the chief was with the majority, he assigned the writer; when the chief was in a minority, however, the assignment was made by the senior justice in the majority, Justice Douglas.

Throughout the conference, Douglas had been scribbling notes about everyone's views and votes. At no point had he made any notation of the phrases that mattered so significantly to Ginsburg—no mention of "suspect classification" or "strict scrutiny." Ginsburg's unbroken argument seemed to have gone unheard.

Douglas assigned the opinion to his frequent ally, Brennan, and within a month Brennan had circulated a draft opinion following what he understood to be his instructions from the conference: to rule for the Frontieros for the reasons stated in *Reed*, and to do so, as he wrote in a memo to his colleagues, "without reaching the question whether sex constitutes a 'suspect criterion' calling for 'strict scrutiny.'" But Brennan had been strongly influenced by Ginsburg's argument. And as he circulated his memo, he suggested the *Frontiero* case might just offer what he called "an appropriate vehicle for us to recognize sex as a 'suspect criterion'"—to accord it strict scrutiny.

Brennan had been counting votes, and he supposed that besides his own, he could get at least three votes for "strict scrutiny." Thurgood Marshall had begun arguing that, much as Ginsburg had claimed in oral argument, the *Reed* decision went beyond the easy "rational basis" test, and Byron White was inclined to agree, as was William O. Douglas. Brennan needed just one more vote, and he wanted it from Potter Stewart, who had just sent around a memo on equal protection that Brennan found hopeful.

Two weeks after his initial draft opinion, Brennan circulated a revision. In bold terms it made an announcement:

We hold today that classifications based upon sex, like classifications based upon race, alienage, or national origin, are inherently suspect, and must therefore be subjected to strict judicial scrutiny.

Douglas, White, and Marshall joined his opinion immediately.

But would Potter Stewart become, in the argot of the Court, a "fifth vote"? While Brennan waited for Stewart's response, he received instead a strong counterattack from Lewis Powell. Powell had planned to vote for Frontiero so long as the decision went no further than *Reed*. But for him this new draft, in which he told Brennan, "You have now gone all the way," was an unjustifiable giant step.

In a memo to all the justices, Powell laid out an argument tuned to its time. Then on the minds of the nation was the most important women's rights legislation since the granting of the vote in 1920: the proposed equal rights amendment, the ERA, passed overwhelmingly by Congress in 1972 and under consideration by the legislatures of the states—thirty-eight of which were required to adopt it to make it an amendment to the Constitution. Its key language was simple and direct: equality of rights under the law shall not be denied "on account of sex." Some legal experts opposed it on the grounds that its passage was unnecessary—an argument made by William Rehnquist while serving as assistant attorney general for the Nixon administration. In contrast, a majority of state legislatures by 1973 supported the ERA, as did Ruth Bader Ginsburg. She viewed it as a step beyond an original and discriminatory understanding of the framers of the Constitution: "Were our state a pure democracy there would still be excluded from our deliberations women"—as Thomas Jefferson had put it, she pointed out. She viewed the ERA also as a rejection of the sort of "sharp legislative lines between the sexes" that she continued needing to fight in cases such as *Frontiero*.

The national debate, argued Powell's memo, should limit the Court:

> My principal concern about going this far at this time . . . is that it places the Court in the position of preempting the amendatory process initiated by the Congress. If the Equal Rights Amendment is duly adopted, it will represent the will of the people accomplished in the manner prescribed by the Constitution. If, on the other hand, this Court puts "sex" in the same category as "race" we will have assumed a decisional

responsibility (not within the democratic process) unnecessary
to the decision of this case, and at the very time that legislatures
around the country are debating the genuine pros and cons of
how far it is wise, fair and prudent to subject both sexes to
identical responsibilities as well as rights.

Thus Powell turned the existence of ERA legislation into a weapon
against Ginsburg's argument for equal rights. Using the fact that Congress had acted, Powell sought to recast Brennan's opinion—even
though it aligned with congressional intent—as a failure of judicial
restraint, a preemption of the role of Congress, and an attack on
the separation of powers as constructed by the Constitution. If only
Congress had not initiated an amendatory process, his argument suggested, then the Supreme Court might have felt free to make amends:
to correct long-standing discrimination.

Powell admitted that he had doubts about strict scrutiny because,
as he enigmatically said, "Women certainly have not been treated
as being fungible with men (thank God!)." But for now all that he
insisted was that a congressional move toward equal rights precluded
a similar judicial move: the existence of the ERA (not yet approved
by thirty-eight states) precluded the court from going "all the way"
to strict scrutiny.

Three days later, Stewart's long-awaited memo reached Brennan. It
agreed generally with Powell but left room for Brennan: it committed
Stewart, as yet, to no opinion.

Brennan, still hoping, drafted a strong response to Powell and sent
it to all the justices. It argued that what Powell called the "will of the
people" was already expressed: the ERA had won overwhelmingly
in Congress and had won a majority of state legislatures. The fact
that resistance in merely thirteen state legislatures could kill the ERA
should not stop the Supreme Court from correcting what most of the
nation saw as a century of injustice. Furthermore, as Brennan's proposed opinion made clear, Supreme Court justices had helped create
that injustice one hundred years earlier when they opined that restrict-
ing women meant following the "law of the Creator." Now is the time
and this is the case, Brennan argued to Powell, for the Supreme Court

to correct its long-standing error by taking "the 'suspect' approach" to discrimination against women.

Justice Potter Stewart, Brennan's target, stood apparently unmoved. (Or perhaps, as would be reported a few years later by Bob Woodward and Scott Armstrong in *The Brethren*, he had failed to talk Brennan into a compromise: if Brennan would hold back from strict scrutiny in the *Frontiero* case, Stewart would join him in the next such case. In any event, no compromise emerged.) The next day Stewart circulated a memo saying that though he would vote for Sharron Frontiero, he would not step beyond the decision in *Reed*.

What exactly the decision in *Reed* meant would remain unclear. The same day that Brennan lost Stewart's vote, he received the first memo on *Frontiero* from Chief Justice Burger. After watching what Burger called the "shuttlecock" memos flying back and forth about what *Reed* meant, Burger finally chimed in: "The author of *Reed*," he said, referring to himself, "never remotely contemplated such a broad concept" as strict scrutiny. "But then," he added, "a lot of people sire offspring unintended."

Whatever *Reed* did mean, it ruled. Brennan's push for haste had won no gains and brought clear costs: it hastened Stewart's commitment against strict scrutiny (or at least so Ginsburg supposed), and it led Powell to publish his argument (joined by Burger and Blackmun) that the Court must, in deference to "the will of the people," watch from afar as the ERA met its fate.

The politicking within the Court remained mostly hidden from Ginsburg, but she could tell how close she had come. She heard rumors that Stewart had wavered. She heard also that Stewart, speaking with Harvard students in March, in the same weeks that Brennan was trying to win his vote, sounded disinclined to strict scrutiny, whether originating in the Court or the ERA. As reported by the *Harvard Law School Record*, after wondering aloud why women pushed for the ERA, Stewart argued that under existing law "the female of the species has the best of both worlds. She can attack laws that unreasonably discriminate against her while preserving those that favor her."

When the Court's opinions appeared in May, Ginsburg saw that the only explicit dissent came from Justice Rehnquist, whom Nixon had added to the Court the same day as Powell. Powell's published response to Brennan was labeled a "concurrence"; it agreed that the Indiana law was unconstitutional, but only on the limited grounds established in *Reed*. In that concurrence, Ginsburg saw strong evidence that Brennan once had imagined he could win Stewart's fifth vote for strict scrutiny.

The evidence appeared in what amounted to a typo that slipped through unrevised. Powell's published response attacked not just an opinion of Brennan but the opinion of "the Court"—which, as Powell put it, "has assumed" the responsibility "to preempt by judicial action a major political decision." Ginsburg's sharp eye saw where this evidence pointed: Powell had written in opposition to what he thought would be a Brennan victory.

What Ginsburg could not know, because she did not have access to the internal memos between the justices, was that the key weapon against her effort for equal rights had been, ironically, the existence of the equal rights amendment. Its passage by Congress in 1972 now provided a rationale in 1973 for Supreme Court justices to resist ending legal discrimination against women.

THE CASE GINSBURG HOPED would bring the Supreme Court to her side was *Wiesenfeld*—the case of Paula and Stephen and Jason. Only three weeks before her Supreme Court argument in *Frontiero*, she had first talked to Stephen. To her, *Wiesenfeld* was the perfect case: discrimination against both woman as wage earner and father as parent, and discrimination that even harmed a baby, who was left with greater hardship if the parent lost was female rather than male. But before she could get *Wiesenfeld* to the Court, she had to face a disaster: the case of Melvin Kahn.

Ginsburg's goal had been a well-planned litigation campaign. Indeed *Reed* and *Frontiero*, though they reached the ACLU by chance, gave the appearance of deftly orchestrated first steps. Meanwhile, the ACLU's network of affiliates across the nation—such as the Washington Civil Liberties Union, which originated *Struck*—searched to help the ACLU find cases addressing issues that were, in Ginsburg's phrase, "ripe for change." Equally important, the ACLU worked to avoid cases that were likely to fail and, worse, make bad law. As a result, the ACLU had an ironclad rule. Although ACLU affiliates could bring cases independently, ACLU rules forbade bringing a case to the Supreme Court without first checking with the national office.

In the autumn of 1973, while Ginsburg's Columbia students were preparing the case of Stephen Wiesenfeld, Ginsburg learned that the Supreme Court had decided to hear a case that she thought could make very bad law. She heard not through any of the ACLU's special channels, but through the newspaper of the legal community, *Law Week*. When she called the attorney who was bringing the case, he shocked her. "You're from the ACLU?" he said, as she later recalled. "I did this as an ACLU case." The case involved Melvin Kahn, a Florida widower who opposed a Florida law that gave a tax break worth about $15 a year to widows but not to widowers. His argument superficially resembled *Wiesenfeld*: a government was denying a benefit to a man based on sex rather than on need. But *Kahn* sought only to help men.

A few days later the Florida attorney, Bill Hoppe, sent his short jurisdictional statement to Mel Wulf. As Wulf skimmed through the short statement, next to one paragraph he wrote, "Egad!":

> Today a woman is fully emancipated; Amendment XIX, U.S. Constitution. Their ability to enter all aspects of community life is virtually complete. A man's loss at the death of his spouse is equal to that of a woman although the woman's loss may move us more.

What to say? That the Nineteenth Amendment gave the vote, not *emancipation*?

As it happened, Hoppe asked for help. His enclosed letter reported that his Supreme Court brief was due in forty-five days, that he didn't know what it needed beyond what he put in his jurisdictional statement, and that he "would appreciate any help and advice you can give me on this matter." For Ginsburg, the *Kahn* problem was now her problem.

Among the flaws in Melvin Kahn's case, some were less obvious than others. For one, it was a state tax case, and many Supreme Court decisions had granted states "large leeway" in shaping their tax systems. Less obviously, the tax break sought to help poor widows, a group with special resonance for a member of the Court whose vote Ginsburg needed: William O. Douglas, one of Brennan's four votes in *Frontiero* for strict scrutiny. At age six, Douglas saw his mother left destitute by the death of his father, a rural preacher. Douglas and his slightly older sister tended yards, washed store windows, and picked fruit to earn the dimes and nickels that they brought home to their mother and that, as he recalled, "often meant the difference between dinner and no dinner." Douglas was unlikely to deny leeway to a state that wanted to give special help to widows.

Bringing a case that looked like a loser, Ginsburg sought to avoid back stepping from whatever point *Reed* and *Frontiero* had reached. She decided not to discuss sex as a suspect classification and not to urge strict scrutiny.

From the moment Ginsburg stepped to the Supreme Court lectern to open her oral argument for Kahn, she could tell things were going badly. The lectern was too high; she had to lower it.

When she had barely begun, she was hit with her first question from the bench, a quibble about what had or had not been alleged by Kahn's attorney in his Florida trial. Skillfully she steered back to her main argument: that a tax exemption to only widows fails the test articulated by Chief Justice Burger in *Reed*. "For," she continued,

> if need is the concern, then sex should not be a substitute for an income test. And if widowed state is the concern, then it is irrational to distinguish between taxpayers based on their sex.

Hearing Ginsburg arguing that the Court should ask only if Florida's sex discrimination was rational and not apply "strict scrutiny" apparently confused the Court. Halfway through her presentation, one perplexed justice interrupted. "Excuse me," he began, "I'm not too clear. You are arguing that sex ought not to be treated as a suspect classification?"

Ginsburg, unable to make her best argument with a bad case, could not put the confusion to rest. In the give-and-take that followed, one justice fumbled to a key question: was Ginsburg saying that she wanted no such tax exemption for women, no such preference for women, "even if it helps"? After more fumbling, and after questioning whether a preference "ever does help," she came as close as she could to an answer. She had not yet found any sex line in the law, she told the justices, "that genuinely helps. From a very shortsighted viewpoint, perhaps. . . . But the long run, no."

At the end-of-week conferences of the justices, the votes quickly went against Ginsburg. Scribbling notes as usual, Douglas jotted that he would affirm Florida's law. He then added, apparently mindful of his mother's nips and tucks to pay the real estate taxes, that "women as widows are largely destitute."

In his opinion for the Court, which the fast-writing Douglas had drafted within ten days, Douglas followed his jottings. "There can be no dispute," he wrote, for the Court, "that the financial difficulties confronting the lone woman in Florida or in any other state exceed those facing the man." He went on in similarly broad fashion. "Gender has never been rejected as an impermissible classification in all instances. Congress has not so far drafted women into the Armed Services." From there, he went on to affirm implicitly the Supreme Court case of 1908 that had upheld minimum-hour laws for women—precisely the sort of "protective" labor legislation that Ginsburg believed had the damaging effect of keeping women from earning as much as men. The lone consolation for Ginsburg was that Douglas grounded the Court's opinion only on *Reed* and its version of the rational-basis test, thus leaving possible affirmation of strict scrutiny to another day.

But though Douglas did not explicitly reject strict scrutiny, clearly he was not applying it. Of the four voters for strict scrutiny in the *Frontiero* case, only Brennan and Marshall still argued for it. With the loss of Douglas, the coalition supporting strict scrutiny had splintered. The progression by small steps that Ginsburg had sought to guide had taken a giant step backward.

4

Wiesenfeld Brings Reality

Back in the days before *Frontiero*, when Justice Brennan failed to get his fourth vote for "strict scrutiny," and back before *Kahn*, when Douglas led the majority backward to what she saw as "bad precedent," Ginsburg had a sure view of *Wiesenfeld*: "if ever there was a case to attract suspect classification for sex lines in the law," *Wiesenfeld* was that case. Legally, it had everything.

Unlike Reed and Frontiero, Stephen Wiesenfeld was Ginsburg's client, and he had entered the case not for personal gain (since he did not expect to receive any money) but for the principle that a woman's work should be worth as much as a man's (or, in this case, that a woman's insurance payout should be worth as much as a man's). Unlike *Struck*, this case would not go moot. *Wiesenfeld*, she wrote to an associate in early 1973, "presents no possibility of settlement short of a declaration that the law is unconstitutional."

And crucially unlike *Kahn*, Ruth Bader Ginsburg believed, *Wiesenfeld* did not attack a law that seemed to help women. Melvin Kahn had appeared to make a claim of reverse discrimination, to fire a salvo on behalf of what the media was beginning to call "men's lib." Only at first glance, Ginsburg believed, could Stephen Wiesenfeld be seen as another man using the rise of equal rights to get himself a bonus. By forcing judges to look closely at *Wiesenfeld*, Ginsburg hoped to show that discrimination against either sex ultimately hurt both. For years, Ginsburg had fought against the thinking behind such phrases as *men's lib* and *women's lib*. She wanted to fight for a broader liberation that freed society from such categorizing by gender. As *Wiesenfeld* moved to the Supreme Court, she would have her chance.

FOR THE CASE OF THE WIESENFELDS, the route to the Supreme Court would run, as Ruth Bader Ginsburg told Stephen Wiesenfeld in their first phone call, via district court in New Jersey. Because *Wiesenfeld* was a federal case (it challenged the federally funded Social Security program) and because it raised a constitutional question (did that program violate the equal protection clause?), it would be heard by not one but three judges. From there, since either party would appeal if it lost, the case could be expected to go to the United States Supreme Court.

To get the case ready, Ginsburg turned to the students in her Equal Rights Advocacy Seminar at Columbia Law School. At the start of each term that Ginsburg taught the seminar (its initials, like the amendment, ERA), students chose from among a menu of cases that Ginsburg might be taking to the Supreme Court. Students had worked on briefs for the wonderful *Struck*, the near-miss *Frontiero*, the hapless *Kahn*, and now *Wiesenfeld*.

At Columbia, Ginsburg teamed with unusual students. Few were fresh from college; one had been an art historian, another had a doctorate in French literature, and a third had worked as a journalist until she brought a sex discrimination case against her magazine. Many were ready to rumble; one class prided itself on getting the law school's main women's bathroom expanded by taking away part of the main men's room. Ginsburg's ERA seminar gave her students the chance to test themselves against major law. Taking on the federal courts felt like "breaking new ground"—in the words of Sandra Grayson, who took the assignment to write the *Wiesenfeld* brief for the district court—like an "uphill battle" in which you could never know whether you would succeed.

For each student and document, the pattern was much the same: a student would write; Professor Ginsburg would rewrite. Mary Elizabeth ("M.E.") Freeman, one of the bathroom liberators who signed up for the chance to write the *Wiesenfeld* brief for the Supreme Court, remembered that case, with its compelling facts, as manna from heaven. "I mean," Freeman would say years later, the youthful energy of those days bubbling up in her words,

> to pick a man whose wife died in childbirth, something that doesn't happen a lot in the latter part of the twentieth century, with a BABY—a child in arms that has, as its only parent left, a father who wants to take care of his kid! I mean, WIDOWS AND ORPHANS—you can't get any better than that!

Brief drafting was fun. Students like Freeman would go overboard, filling early drafts with sarcasm and sometimes venom. Then "Ruth," as all the students called her, would cut and polish. She would transform sarcasm to irony, venom to law. And sometimes Ruth would add one of her legal jabs—what students thought of as her *zingers*, so sharp that students would cry out, "OH, YES YES," laughing aloud. For her classmates, Freeman thought, challenging the Court felt like their version of going to war—only two or three years out of a life, but a time of bonding and achievements to talk about for a lifetime. And unlike war, this was fun! It had no downside.

Working with Ruth also brought a shocking change from the rest of law school classes, where the abstract could crowd out the human. Clients like Stephen and Jason Wiesenfeld became part of the students' lives. Students saw letters Stephen wrote and letters Ruth wrote back, advising him, for example, about his nanny woes: "Having gone through more helpers and housekeepers than I care to count over the past seventeen years," she told him, with her mix of optimism and realism, "I know that eventually the right person does appear, and then you are set for a few years."

The students in Ginsburg's seminar came to realize that the story of the Wiesenfelds offered a window into Ginsburg's vision of an ideal society: one in which fathers cared for and helped raise kids, in which gender lines blurred toward invisibility. Freeman, looking back years later, saw the case as "illustrative of what Ruth has been saying her whole life, about children and parents and childcare. She has always emphasized the need to bring fathers into the picture and make them fully responsible. And here Stephen was stepping up to the plate and doing it."

To GET *WIESENFELD* READY for the Supreme Court, in the spring semester of 1973 (in the months after she argued *Frontiero* but before she received the opinion and learned that Brennan had failed to win five votes for strict scrutiny), Ginsburg challenged her ERA seminar to go, in the period of one semester, from startup to a hearing before a three-judge panel of a district court. The students sprinted to draft and file all the papers: the legal complaint, the application for a three-judge court, and various motions and depositions.

The law school term had just ended when a three-judge panel in Trenton heard the case. The government's attorney argued that the law acknowledged a "natural basis" for widows to be more protected than widowers. Ginsburg argued for strict scrutiny. Either way, the decision of the district court seemed unimportant since, no matter how the case was decided, it was going next to the Supreme Court. But during the argument in the district court, Stephen Wiesenfeld heard the government make an argument he was not expecting: because he now had a good job, the case should be dismissed.

The government's argument was strong: to be eligible for full "mother's insurance benefits" of just under $250 per month, which were apparently designed by Congress to help a widow stay at home and care for a child, Stephen's own income could not exceed $200 per month. Since he was now earning $1,500 a month at Cyphernetics, his case seemed to involve no money. Under federal law, to bring suit Stephen had to prove that the amount of money in controversy reached at least $10,000.

After all the time and effort from Ginsburg and her students, Stephen worried that his job might cost them their case. Before the district court could decide, and without describing his scheme to Ginsburg, Stephen Wiesenfeld made a decision. To save the case, he gave up his job at Cyphernetics.

The law's criteria forced Stephen to apply his MBA skills to choosing a new line of work, one that had to meet tricky specifications:

1. He needed the ability to control his income. That meant he should again become a sole proprietor of a business, into which he could reinvest any profits while paying himself a salary small enough to qualify for Social Security.

2. He needed a place for Jason to play while he worked. That suggested he should run a retail shop near home.

3. He didn't want to commit himself and Jason to long hours in a store. That mandated he make rapid sales of a few high-margin items.

He needed, in order to keep his hours short and margin high, a product about to experience a jump in demand. Choosing that product posed the biggest challenge. To determine where demand might jump, Stephen read the newspapers with new acuity. In the news in the summer of 1973, the big drama was far away: tension in the Middle East. This settled him on his choice, one not obvious to everyone: from a small storefront near the Rutgers campus, from 1:00 to 5:00 p.m. daily, he would sell high-grade bicycles.

Stephen's MBA had served him well. In October, he opened a store with just enough room to hold ten Fuji bikes (a well-made product otherwise unavailable nearby) and tucked a playpen for one-and-a-half-year-old Jason in a corner. Late that month, Arab nations announced an oil embargo. As fuel prices soared, Americans rediscovered the bicycle. Into Stephen's store came young doctors and lawyers and Rutgers students. His income again would have quickly disqualified him for Social Security if he had not invested his profits back in the business. He bought bicycles galore, jamming them into his garage.

As soon as Wiesenfeld told Ginsburg he was out of his $1,500-a-month job, she saw the legal gain. He was, she wrote to one of her former Rutgers students who was assisting her as co-counsel on the case, "back in the situation he was in just before the complaint was filed—jobless and unquestionably qualified for benefits, apart from his sex." She asked her former student to put together an affidavit to inform the court.

Wiesenfeld never told Ginsburg that he left his well-paid job to preserve her case. Certainly she had never asked him for that sacrifice. "She was the kind of person," he would say years later, "you knew would not ask you to alter your lifestyle or what you want to do in order to keep her going."

In December of 1973, just as Stephen's bicycle shop was beginning to boom, the district court issued its opinion in *Wiesenfeld*. It devoted two pages to what it called the government's "strong argument for dismissal": Stephen's Cyphernetics salary had meant that his case involved no money, and surely less than $10,000. To Stephen's relief, on the grounds that "he is now unemployed," the court ruled not to dismiss the case.

The district court then proceeded to give Ginsburg an unprecedented victory. Not only did it rule in Stephen's favor, it went beyond precedent by citing what Justice William Brennan had asserted in *Frontiero*—that sex was "inherently suspect" and thus deserved strict scrutiny. Astonishingly, the district court chose to ignore the Supreme Court majority, which had rejected Brennan's argument. The stage was set for a battle at the Supreme Court.

THE GOVERNMENT COUNTERATTACK came under the direction of the solicitor general of the United States, Robert Bork. Despite the powerful role of the solicitor general in shaping American law, for years it had remained a somewhat obscure position, little noticed by the public. Two months before the district court's decision in favor of the Wiesenfelds, however, Bork had briefly lifted the role of the solicitor general into the public glare. At that point, in October of 1973, Archibald Cox of Harvard, who had himself served as solicitor general under President Kennedy, was acting as a government-appointed special prosecutor, charged with deciding what indictments, if any, should be brought against Nixon and his associates in conjunction with the combination of burglary and cover-up that had become known as "Watergate."

Three months before, when the nation first learned that President Nixon had been secretly taping his phone conversations and White House meetings, Cox had subpoenaed key conversations. Nixon resisted; Cox persisted. Finally, in what became known as the "Saturday night massacre," on October 20, 1973, Nixon ordered Attorney General Elliot Richardson to fire Cox. Refusing, Richardson resigned. Richardson's deputy attorney general, William Ruckelshaus, given the same order, also resigned. Next in line was Bork, who, thanks to two resignations, had risen to acting attorney general. Bork fired Cox.

The national outrage swelled so fast that within a week, Nixon had relinquished his tapes, and soon after, Bork, as acting attorney general, had appointed a new Watergate special prosecutor. Not long after, with the appointment of a new attorney general, Bork returned to focus again on his role as solicitor general.

One of the many cases then before his office was *Wiesenfeld*, and in February the Office of the Solicitor General notified the Supreme Court that, as Ginsburg had anticipated, it opposed the district court's ruling. Its appeal contended that precedent in *Kahn*, which declared a constitutional preference for widows, governed *Wiesenfeld*. Courts should focus on the government-created advantage (to widows) and not on any government-created disadvantage (to female wage-earners).

Ginsburg responded not just by rebutting the government's arguments but also by reversing their sequence. Her argument began by focusing on (and attempting to see through the eyes of) one particular female wage-earner. Ginsburg's brief commenced its argument with Paula Wiesenfeld, who

> contributed to Social Security on precisely the same basis as an insured male individual. Upon her death, however, her family received fewer benefits than those paid to similarly situated families of male breadwinners. The sole reason for the differential was Paula Wiesenfeld's sex. As a breadwinning woman, she was treated equally for Social Security contribution purposes,

but unequally for the purpose of determining family benefits
due under her account.

Standing before the court, in oral argument, she extended this line
of attack, condemning this law that, because "the deceased worker is
female," subjected her family's protection "to a 50 percent discount."
Because the law classified people not by their work but by their sex,
she told the justices,

> Paula Wiesenfeld, in fact the principal wage earner, is treated
> as though her years of work were of only secondary value to
> her family. Stephen Wiesenfeld, in fact the nurturing parent, is
> treated as though he did not perform that function. And Jason
> Paul, a motherless infant with a father able and willing to pro-
> vide care for him personally, is treated as an infant not entitled
> to the personal care of his sole surviving parent.

Repeating each of the Wiesenfelds' names in turn, Ginsburg made the
entire family part of the case. She always used both of the infant boy's
given names, as if the claim of Jason *Paul* kept alive as well the claim
of his mother *Paula*. Also present, not just nominally, was Stephen
Wiesenfeld. Ginsburg sat him directly beside her and directly before
the justices at the counsel table. She had not done this before with a
client and never would again at the Supreme Court. She would never
know if the justices knew that the man sitting at her side was Stephen
Wiesenfeld. But she did know that judges worry about made-up cases,
and she wanted to send a signal that "this was as genuine as any case"
and that "this sort of sex stereotyping hurt many people, everyday
people, people like Stephen Wiesenfeld." And she wanted—and for
this it mattered that Stephen was a man—the justices to be able to see
themselves in his situation.

Throughout his case, Ginsburg had made Stephen feel close to this
extraordinarily public presentation of his life. The night before they
would appear in Court, she had called him to discuss her strategy for
oral argument. She had expressed her fears: only three votes would
come easily, a fourth (Potter Stewart) would be wavering, and four

more would likely be opposed. With William O. Douglas incapacitated and absent for this argument, she might do no better than a 4–4 tie, and could easily do worse.

Now, seated beside her as she spoke, Stephen heard not her recent fears but her enduring assurance. The experiences of his family, she told the Court, epitomized the reality that most laws which purport to give special help to women in fact strike against those women like Paula Wiesenfeld who "choose to be wives and mothers and, at the same time, to participate as full and equal individuals in a work-centered world."

For years, Ginsburg had been arguing that such double-edged damage typified the effect of laws that allegedly favor women. Now standing before the Court, in oral argument she admitted to the justices (as she had tried to avoid the year before in *Kahn*) that the gift of a $15 tax break to widows represented a rare single-edged law that gave an advantage to some women but did not, with a second edge, strike directly against others. But *Wiesenfeld* was not a case of a man grasping after a woman's benefits.

Paula's unacknowledged labor represented both the norm and the archetype of the double-edged law—an insurance benefit that, although it gave to the family of a nonworking mother who survived, took away from the family of a hard-working mother who died. American law's devaluation of Paula Wiesenfeld's labor, wrote Ginsburg in one of the zingers in her brief, "presents a classic example of the double-edged discrimination characteristic of laws that chivalrous gentlemen, sitting in chambers, misconceive as a favor to the ladies." Ginsburg's oral argument made clear that any Supreme Court justice was following chivalric code, rooted in the Dark Ages, if he voted to support Social Security regulations that had taken Paula Wiesenfeld's money and then, *because* she was female, gave nothing back.

PRECISELY TWO MONTHS after he and Ginsburg walked away from the counsel table, Stephen Wiesenfeld was sitting at home when a neighbor called. News had come over the radio: victory at the Court.

Minutes later the phone rang again. Ginsburg was calling him, from a phone booth next to her parked car just off a roadway. She too had been listening to the radio. She sounded ecstatic, rambling, far from her normal self. She asked Stephen, What was the decision? How did the justices vote? She wanted to know, in essence, what have we won? He had no idea.

The decision was unanimous. Justice Brennan's opinion was joined by all the justices but Rehnquist. And even he—the lone dissenter in *Frontiero* and an opponent in *Kahn*—did not dissent. The Court's opinion criticized the government (and, implicitly, the solicitor general). "The Government seeks to characterize," it said, the payment of widows' benefits rather than parents' benefits as an effort to compensate women for economic difficulties "which still confront women who seek to support themselves and their families." But the Court dismissed this argument, responding that "the mere recitation of benign, compensatory purpose is not an automatic shield" that prevents the Court from asking why a law exists. By looking closely at the history of the law, the opinion revealed that its purpose was to permit a surviving parent to stay at home to care for a child. To discriminate between surviving parents based on their gender, the Court ruled, was "entirely irrational."

Hidden from Ginsburg's view was a last burst of discrimination against women that had played a role in her victory. She received a hint of it a few weeks later from a former student, Lynn Hecht Schafran, now clerking with the judge, Edmund L. Palmieri, who had welcomed Ginsburg after other judges refused to hire a woman. Replying to an invitation to celebrate the *Wiesenfeld* victory with the Ginsburgs, Schafran added a story she had heard about one of Brennan's clerks:

> This was Justice Brennan's year to have a clerk from Berkeley and when he wrote inquiring as to the name of their best candidate, they replied with the name of a woman. Brennan wrote back saying no, no, he wanted the name of their best male candidate. Berkeley replied that this was the only candidate they had any intention of recommending and that Brennan had better shape up, which is why he has a female clerk this year.

Schafran had the story basically right, although it remained murky even to Brennan's clerk, Marsha Berzon. In her last months at Berkeley, Berzon heard she had got the clerkship, then wouldn't get it, then got it again. From Professor Stephen R. Barnett, who phoned her at each reversal, she heard the rumor that opposition came from Brennan's secretary; but when Berzon arrived at his chambers, everyone got along well. Another rumor suggested the justice liked to curse in chambers, but Berzon never heard cursing. Around her the justice had the manner, she recalled later, of "an older gentleman." But he had, she gathered, earlier turned away another woman nominated by her law school.

When *Wiesenfeld* arrived, as neither Ginsburg nor Schafran could know, Brennan involved Berzon before the justices met in conference, where votes split badly. Burger, Rehnquist, and apparently Blackmun planned to vote against Ginsburg's case. Looking to gather support as she drafted an opinion for Brennan, Berzon followed a cue that she felt Ginsburg had planted with a footnote in her brief: dig into the history of the law from the 1930s that created mother's insurance benefits. Berzon found what she needed. She wrote what became the climactic section of the opinion by Brennan, a historical discussion showing that Congress had written its law not to aid wives whose husbands had died but to aid children whose parents had died. Given the goal of aiding children, the opinion argued, a law must be overturned as entirely irrational if it "discriminates among surviving children solely on the basis of the sex of the surviving parent."

Berzon's historical analysis apparently lifted *Wiesenfeld* to unanimity. Most surprising, Rehnquist concurred. Writing separately, he too praised the opinion's legislative history and joined its attack on the irrationality of a law that discriminated against a child merely because "the only parent remaining to it" is male. Decades later Ginsburg would marvel that for once she had won Rehnquist's vote in a case involving equal protection. *Wiesenfeld* "had to be the perfect case, or we couldn't have got Rehnquist," she remarked years later. "Rehnquist was caught by the baby." He was also caught by the research of a clerk who had almost lost her chance to work at the Supreme Court because she was a woman.

But the perfect case produced an imperfect victory. Gone, as if forgotten, was the long-running argument that Ginsburg had been building since her first Supreme Court case on behalf of Sally Reed: that classification by gender deserved the Court's "strict scrutiny," that sex was a "suspect classification," that discrimination against a woman was as significant as discrimination against someone from a racial minority.

After the failure to win strict scrutiny in *Frontiero*, and after the outright loss in *Kahn*, and after other disappointments that suggested a growing hostility from Justice Stewart—all entwined with the arrival on the Court of new conservatives—Ginsburg had dropped her claim for full equality of the sexes. She knew Brennan could not muster the votes. Instead of insisting that sex discrimination face the hard test of "strict scrutiny," she had decided to argue merely that it face some form of test, what she viewed as " 'heightened scrutiny' without further labeling."

Her reasoning was simple. After *Kahn*, she could not afford another loss, particularly in a case that she had once believed was her best. She could not afford to let what she believed was the right claim lead the court to a wrong decision. And never again as a litigator would Ginsburg push the Court to give strict scrutiny to the claims of women. Throughout the next generation, whenever women asked the Supreme Court to enforce the Constitution's promise of "equal protection of the laws," they would have to accept that the Court saw discrimination against women as merely second-class discrimination. Not until Ginsburg became a justice of the Supreme Court was she able to nudge the Court's language higher—to what she called "skeptical scrutiny" in her 1996 Court opinion that ended exclusion of all women from Virginia Military Institute, but never to "strict scrutiny."

STEPHEN WIESENFELD, after Ginsburg won his case and the Social Security Administration granted him parent's benefits, wanted the victory to be not just principled but practical. Making use of the Social Security benefits of $248 a month awarded by the Supreme Court, he decided to raise Jason at home. He sold his bicycle shop, a year and a half after opening it, at a $22,000 profit. He then moved from New Jersey to Florida, seeking a location with low taxes and good public schools, where he lived from 1975 to 1982 on Social Security benefits and raised Jason. "I wanted to make sure that I qualified for the benefit for a while," Wiesenfeld later explained, "so that all her work would have some value." In 1982, his latest at-home entrepreneurial venture, writing accounting software for nonprofit institutions, became suddenly so profitable that he had to return that year's Social Security benefits and once again began making considerable amounts of money. In 1993, Stephen Wiesenfeld testified to the Senate Judiciary Committee in support of Ruth Bader Ginsburg's nomination to the Supreme Court. In 1998, Justice Ginsburg presided at the wedding of Jason Paul Wiesenfeld, who had just graduated from her alma mater, Columbia Law School.

Part Two

———————◆———————

PREGNANCY
(1972–1978)

5

What Happened to Sally Armendariz Could Not Happen to a Man

By 1978, Ruth Bader Ginsburg was commenting that the law had reached the stage where it could help a woman so long as whatever harmed her could also "happen to a man." What happened to Sally Armendariz could not happen to a man—or at least not exactly. What happened to her would lead to the most infamous decision in the Supreme Court's early years of groping with sex discrimination.

In early May of 1972, Sally Armendariz was driving near her home, among the farm fields of Gilroy, California, when she was rear-ended by another car. She was not easily slowed by hard knocks. She had been born twenty-nine years earlier into a Mexican-American family that had worked in California for generations, usually in the fields picking. Every time she looked at her mother, she thought of the hardship of the fields. Working before Sally was born, on one brutally hot day her mother had lain down in a field and fallen asleep, exhausted, facing up into the California sun. She woke up blind.

Looking for a route away from fieldwork, Sally Armendariz became the second child and the first daughter in her extended family to graduate from high school. At age nineteen, she found work as a secretary. For ten years she never took a sick day. No car accident, she resolved, could keep her from working.

But though her rear-ender was an accident that could "happen to a man," its effect could not: when Sally Armendariz was hit from behind, she was four months pregnant. The afternoon after the accident, back at work, she suddenly felt ill. Her doctor told her to go home and get rest. Late that night she went into labor; an ambulance arrived to rush her and her husband to the hospital, and in the early morning she lost her child to a miscarriage.

The pain following the car accident and miscarriage became so severe that for two weeks Armendariz could not even wash dishes. Her doctor told her to stay away from her office for three weeks. At that point, in May of 1972, Sally's husband had just become unemployed, making her the sole support for him and their eight-month-old son. Fortunately, she knew, for the past ten years she had paid 1 percent of her $394 monthly salary to California's State Disability Insurance program, and she had never asked for a penny. The program's purpose was to protect workers who became temporarily disabled. Assuming she could receive back some part of what she had paid out, she went to the local unemployment office in Gilroy to file a request for benefits.

The office denied her request. Had she been a man hurt in a crash, she learned, the office would have paid gladly. But the State Disability Insurance program had one significant loophole: it refused to pay benefits for any disability "arising in connection with pregnancy." She was denied benefits because what happened to her could not, to repeat Ruth Bader Ginsburg's words, "happen to a man."

SALLY ARMENDARIZ WAS A FIGHTER, as she had been since high school. She and some classmates, gathered by their Catholic priest, had formed a group called the Young Christian Workers that tried to identify social problems and then work to fix them. And here she was, in the middle of a classic social problem. She demanded an appeal.

In midsummer Sally Armendariz stood before a referee for the state's Unemployment Insurance Appeals Board. He denied her claim. He said the state's denial of pregnancy-related disabilities allowed no exception. When she pressed him, he explained what he supposed was the state's reasoning: unlike most disabilities, becoming pregnant was *voluntary.*

She asked, Missing work was voluntary? Getting hit by a car was voluntary? And being pregnant was voluntary? Did he, she asked, want the human race to come to an end? And then she told him, If he didn't grant her three weeks of benefits, less than $100, she would sue the state of California for discrimination against women.

What he said next, she would recall for years. The referee turned off the tape recorder that had been running through their meeting. You sound serious, he told her. He said he went through this "all the time," turning down pregnant women because the law gave him no choice. And if Sally Armendariz was gunning to bring a lawsuit, he added, in words she would always remember, "I hope you follow through. And I hope you win."

For a worker aiming to sue the state, Armendariz had dream employers. She worked for the Gilroy office of California Rural Legal Assistance, a federally funded law firm whose purpose was to end the exploitation of California's farm-worker community. Her office had half-a-dozen young lawyers, whom she called "the guys." To her, they were a strange and adorable band of eastern Jewish boys, crusaders who had come west to right the wrongs with which her family lived. She had introduced them to Mexican cooking and teased them about supporting baseball teams from places like Chicago. When it came to challenging the state of California, she thought, nobody was more gung-ho than "the guys."

One of the first guys to hear the story of Sally Armendariz was Peter Weiner, two years out of Yale Law School and one year past his clerkship with a liberal justice of the California Supreme Court. And while he was clerking, one of his fellow clerks had pounced on a case that, Weiner thought, could help Armendariz.

The clerk was Wendy Webster Williams, then fresh out of Boalt Hall, the law school of the University of California at Berkeley, class of 1970. While working in their judge's office, she became one of Weiner's best friends. After clerking, they both won federal fellowships that sent them to work for two years on poverty law: he with California Rural Legal Assistance and she with the Legal Aid Society, located an hour north in San Mateo. So after hearing Sally Armendariz tell her story, he phoned Wendy. His call would shape the next half-decade of her life.

WENDY WEBSTER WILLIAMS had grown up the eldest of seven children, a tall child who mixed effervescence and eloquence. After finishing her undergraduate work at the University of California at Berkeley, she went on to study English literature. Her then husband enrolled in Hastings College of the Law in San Francisco to study law. Soon she too enrolled in law school—so that she could talk to him about his work, she told friends—becoming one of the few women law students at Boalt Hall.

Williams encountered a law school where professors became known for asserting that women belonged at home, or for asking female students to justify the placement of women on juries, or for scolding female students for wasting spaces that could hold young men. Sometimes the challenge to women reached a constitutional level. Throughout her life, Williams would recall one moment in a law class, near the end of her studies, when she and some other women raised the issue that would soon—but had not yet—come to dominate the efforts of Ruth Bader Ginsburg before the Supreme Court. In a discussion concerning the "strict scrutiny" that the Court used to probe and consequently forbid discrimination against African-Americans, they made the obvious extension: shouldn't the Court subject discrimination against women also to the rigors of "strict scrutiny"?

Williams' professor laughed. He called her argument absurd. He proclaimed that for the Supreme Court, such serious scrutiny of discrimination against women would come "not in our lifetimes."

Fortunately for young women fighting old laws, one professor stood out from the mostly male ranks of Berkeley's Boalt Hall law faculty in the 1960s. She was Herma Hill Kay, a formidable but slightly reserved specialist in family law. When Berkeley appointed her in 1960, Kay became only the fourteenth woman appointed by an American law school to a tenure-track position, one that could lead to a permanent professorship. The first woman in America with such a position, Barbara Nachtrieb Armstrong, had been appointed at Berkeley in 1922. In 1957, as Professor Armstrong approached retirement, she remained Boalt's one woman professor. That number, she insisted, must not fall to zero. It did. Three years later, Boalt hired Kay.

The only child of a Methodist minister and a schoolteacher, Kay first heard she should study law during a sixth-grade civics class in her native South Carolina. Alone among her classmates, she contended that the South deserved to have lost the Civil War. After listening to this contrary and feisty youngster, her teacher made an obvious suggestion: become a lawyer.

Kay did. After graduating from the University of Chicago Law School in 1959 as one of only three women in her class, she clerked at the California Supreme Court before going to Berkeley. To Kay, the potentially tame specialty of family law proved slowly radicalizing. It was, she found, "rife with discrimination" against women, and by the late 1960s, she had begun to work toward laws liberalizing abortion and divorce in the state of California. But to many on the faculty, her sharpest sign of distinction was that, inspired by Amelia Earhart, she flew a private plane.

Although Kay was working against sex discrimination, no organization at Boalt Hall shared that work or even met to discuss the status of women. For years, however, there had been one association intimately linked to women's status: the Boalt Hall Law Wives Club. When the law school held institutes and conferences, the Law Wives acted as hostesses and served coffee. At the entire University of California at Berkeley in the late 1960s, so far as Kay could tell, no group gathered university women for purposes beyond the social. Then in the spring of 1969, Herma Hill Kay received a memo from someone in the president's office, inviting female faculty and staff to gather for a discussion. Kay went. Although the organizers had no plans beyond community outreach, Kay returned to the law school with a notion. She invited all her female students to convene, perhaps as a step toward some useful organization. Her memo began, "Dear Boalt Hall Girl."

The women who gathered, Kay thought, seemed a new breed: not passive consumers of legal education but seekers of fundamental change. They had spent summers registering voters in Mississippi or had taken part in early efforts at raising women's consciousness of discrimination. Now together in a room, they told familiar stories: the law professor who questioned whether women should serve on juries, law firms and judges who refused to interview women for jobs, and so on. On the spot, the women decided to form a new group, the Boalt Hall Women's Association. They would help plan a course on women in the law to be taught by Professor Kay. They would begin the "rooting out of anti-woman discrimination" in law firms. They coined a slogan: "Wanted by the Law: Women!"

Among the students who showed up, a tall woman stood out, at least to Kay, for her urgency and energy. She seemed to epitomize a phrase that showed up on bumper stickers: "Question Authority!" Wendy Webster Williams was approaching graduation. Before the Boalt Hall Women's Association had organized its first course, she had her degree and a job, beginning in mid-1970, as law clerk for Justice Raymond J. Peters of the California Supreme Court. Immediately, Williams became caught up in the life that made law clerk in America's upper-level courts probably the most exciting job for any recent law school graduate: providing research and information directly to the men who would decide the most important legal issues of the day.

IN THE CHAMBERS OF JUSTICE RAYMOND PETERS, Wendy Webster Williams had been working for only a few weeks when a case arrived in a memo from another justice, urging that the California Supreme Court "deny review." The justice wanted to uphold, without scrutiny or a hearing, a decision of California's Department of Alcoholic Beverage Control to revoke the liquor license of a few bars that had broken a California law that forbade the hiring of women to work as bartenders.

When Williams realized that the California Supreme Court was likely to uphold this decision and the law behind it, she saw travesty. She went "scooting right in to my judge," as she put it later, and said, This won't do! This can't be! This is sex discrimination! Justice

Peters, a formidable man then in his midsixties, looked at his young law clerk. All he said, in his gruff voice, was, Well, write me a memo, and we'll see.

So Williams just "killed myself," as she recalled, writing a memo saying why the California Supreme Court had to hear this bartender case. And in it, she made the case that discrimination against women demanded scrutiny—indeed, demanded *strict* scrutiny, the very claim Ginsburg was about to make at the U.S. Supreme Court in *Reed*. Justice Peters liked the memo and circulated it to his colleagues. After their conference, Peters called his young clerk. "Well," he said, "we're gonna review the case."

When the brief defending the bars arrived, Williams read it and thought it was terrible. It would not help Judge Peters rule that the bars engaged illegally in sex discrimination.

The bar owners' case lacked some luster. If ever a case was designed to bring forth judicial caricatures of women "sprightly and ribald" (in the words of Justice Felix Frankfurter from the Michigan case in the 1940s), it was this: Sail'er Inn was a topless bar. It had run afoul of the law when it tried to promote women from working as topless waitresses to working as topless bartenders.

The nudity was incidental, Williams believed; the case was about opening jobs to women. Williams needed someone to make arguments in an *amicus* brief that would lead not to issues of obscenity but to issues of equal protection under the Constitution. Then she could rely on that brief in her draft opinion. So Williams did something that, she later thought, might have been a bit improper. She called Boalt Hall and reached Herma Hill Kay and described the case and said, "An *amicus* brief HAS TO COME IN." And Professor Kay said, An *amicus* brief will come in.

Professor Kay, always the teacher, didn't sit down and write the brief. She called on the students of the Boalt Hall Women's Association. The association had been working on its first women-in-the-law course, following the lead of the early course at NYU. Taking a course was different from taking a case, and Kay saw *Sail'er Inn* as a great opportunity for the students to learn how to make an argument. But some had doubts about making this argument.

The students saw this case as "the smarmiest thing," one recalled: A group of guys wanted to look at topless women? Would half-bare bartending at Sail'er Inn advance women's equality? After holding a debate, the Boalt Hall Women's Association resolved that what mattered most was not the medium but the message: discrimination against women was unconstitutional. Professor Kay gave guidance on some constitutional issues, and then two of the law students, Mary Dunlap and Margaret Kemp, wrote the brief. They dug back to 1915 to find a U.S. Supreme Court case which declared that the "right to work for a living" was guaranteed by the Fourteenth Amendment to the Constitution. Forced to confront Justice Frankfurter's ruling from the 1940s that restricted the right of women to tend bar in Michigan, they tried a tactic similar to Ginsburg's in her brief for Sally Reed: by the 1950s, they insisted, the Court had begun to move past Frankfurter's dismissal of "shifting social standards" and sociological insights. As for here and now, the state of California had recently declared that the opportunity to work for a living was guaranteed to women, without discrimination, as a "civil right." The brief reached the supreme court of the state of California in December of 1970, submitted by Kay as sponsor of the Boalt Hall Women's Association.

The brief was so good, Williams remembered, that when the Sail'er Inn lawyers arrived for oral argument, they used the Boalt Hall brief and made a fine constitutional argument in favor of letting women tend bar. Then Justice Peters and his fellow judges gathered to vote on the fate of the hard work by Williams, Kay, and the women of Boalt Hall.

WAITING ANXIOUSLY IN HER OFFICE, Wendy Williams heard the phone ring. She grabbed it. A voice barked, "Hi! This is Ray Peters." Her heart stopped. She waited. And then he barked again: "Women's Lib is gonna love me!"

Williams made her voice sweet and asked, "What happened, Judge?"

We voted, he told her. It's unanimous. We're gonna do it.

Williams was now set to draft the first decision in which any state's supreme court declared that sex discrimination violated the Constitution. Better yet, its decision could announce that sex discrimination violated the equal protection guarantee of two constitutions: the Constitution of California and the Constitution of the United States. For both constitutions, Williams' key challenge was the old problem of standard of review: minimal scrutiny or strict scrutiny? Although the decision in *Sail'er Inn* had to acknowledge that the U.S. Supreme Court had not yet "designated classifications based on sex as 'suspect classifications' requiring close scrutiny," it could go on to rule that suspicion was emerging that "sex, like race and lineage, is an immutable trait, a status into which the class members are locked by accident of birth."

These were the words that, to her delight, Ruth Bader Ginsburg only a few weeks later could splice into her *Reed* brief as it went to the U.S. Supreme Court. "The pedestal upon which women have been placed has all too often, upon closer inspection, been revealed as a cage," the *Sail'er Inn* opinion continued, adding with finality: "We conclude that the sexual classifications are properly treated as suspect."

Furthermore, the ringing language of *Sail'er Inn*—its analogizing of sex to race, its understanding of pedestal as cage, its finding of strict scrutiny—would be quoted throughout the nation in judicial opinions and law reviews and legal texts. To students of law, this opinion spoke to issues of the country and the Constitution, not just to local issues and urban bars. No one reading the California Supreme Court opinion of May 27, 1971, would ever know that this case arose from a bar's desire to offer martinis shaken by naked women.

6

The First Pregnancy Case: *Aiello*

When Wendy Webster Williams heard the story of Sally Armendariz from her friend Peter Weiner at California Rural Legal Assistance, she got excited. Here was a case that, building on her drafting in *Sail'er Inn*, could strengthen women's claim to equality under California law. As she and Weiner worked together and talked to friends, other women with similar stories started appearing, broadening their case.

First from Marin County, north of San Francisco, came Elizabeth Johnson, a single mother with a five-year-old child, who was proud to be escaping the need for welfare thanks to an $1,800-a-year job with a phone company. Then in May of 1972, she was forced to leave work by a sudden disability: leg swelling, stomach and back pain, fever and nausea. After a few days, doctors finally diagnosed the problem. Her fallopian tubes had ruptured and she was bleeding internally. To save her life, they operated immediately. Forbidden to return to work for the next six weeks, she applied for disability benefits under the California Unemployment Insurance Code. She was turned down. Her hemorrhaging had been caused when a fertilized egg had lodged in her fallopian tubes. Though not a pregnancy in any normal sense, since no child could be born and since the mother if untreated would die, this medical emergency was known as a "tubal pregnancy." Thus Johnson was denied disability benefits.

Third among potential clients was Jacqueline Jaramillo, from Oakland, California. Her pregnancy was the result of a failed intrauterine device (IUD). She abhorred abortion because she had been raised Catholic. She was working to put her husband through law school but planned to have her child, so she applied for insurance to carry her through the six weeks that her doctor had told her to expect to be disabled after giving birth. Jaramillo thus represented a routine pregnancy for a working woman, and a routine denial of benefits by the state, so Williams added her to the case.

JUST BEFORE WILLIAMS COULD GET all her cases assembled and ready to file in the summer of 1972, she took her scheduled, two-week holiday away from San Mateo Legal Aid. When she got back and learned what had gone wrong, she swore that would be her last vacation.

On her answering machine, she had calls from another lawyer telling her he had another case like that of Sally Armendariz. In San Francisco a woman named Carolyn Aiello was forced out of work by an ectopic pregnancy (of which a tubal pregnancy is one type), which cannot lead to childbirth because it occurs outside the womb. The lawyer's message added that he had just filed Aiello's case, on the last day of July, in federal court.

Williams wanted to stay away from federal courts, where Ginsburg had just fallen short, in *Reed*, of winning strict scrutiny for sex discrimination. Williams wanted to fight in the state courts, where her own work had won strict scrutiny. Although she and Weiner filed suit as planned in state court, she knew the progression was unstoppable: the state of California, facing suits in both state and federal courts, requested that her cases be removed to federal court, where they would be consolidated with the case of Carolyn Aiello, whose original lawyer soon decided to leave the case.

The federal case would be called *Aiello*, with Williams as lead lawyer, leading toward a destination she wished not to reach: federal court. Worse, because she was bringing a constitutional challenge to a state law, *Aiello* would slip onto what amounted to the federal fast track. This was the same fast track that Ginsburg, with cases she had chosen carefully, wished to take: to a three-judge district court followed by immediate appeal to the United States Supreme Court.

The shock waves from *Aiello* spread fast, reaching an attorney in Washington, DC, Ruth Weyand. In nine arguments before the Supreme Court, Weyand had not lost a case. In the first half of 1971, she had begun laying the groundwork for a case similar to that of Sally Armendariz but designed to take advantage of the few American laws that limited discrimination against women. In the summer of 1972, Wendy Webster Williams knew nothing about these better-laid plans on the other side of the continent.

As *AIELLO* MOVED ONTO ITS FAST TRACK, the next worry for Williams came with the selection of the three-judge panel in district court. Judge Ben C. Duniway sounded promising. He was great nephew to a famous feminist from the state of Oregon. Judge Spencer Williams, not long before, had served under Governor Ronald Reagan as head of the department that enforced the law that Williams was attacking. Ever ready to question authority, she tried to get him disqualified from the case. She failed. He seemed a sure vote against her.

That left Judge Alfonso J. Zirpoli, whom Williams knew best. They met when he refused to hire her as his clerk. Williams understood she was the first woman he had ever interviewed for a clerkship, and during the interview she said to him that she heard he didn't hire women.

What followed she would recall as a peculiar interchange. His hand went over his face. He started muttering about how long his secretary had been with him. Eventually, Judge Zirpoli hired one of Williams' friends, a male law school classmate at Berkeley with lower academic standing. And when Williams' friend tried to sort out the problem, what he reported back was that Judge Zirpoli rejected women applicants because his secretary didn't want to work with female law clerks. The odds in the case were not looking favorable.

Williams' big problem was not gauging the judges but making a federal case. Indeed, when she drafted her initial complaint, she based two of her four claims on the Constitution of the state of California, which she could no longer use. But she also based two claims on federal law. The first foundation was obvious: the equal protection clause of the U.S. Constitution, the same clause used by Ruth Bader Ginsburg in *Reed*. Indeed, Ginsburg's partial victory in *Reed* gave Williams her only hope of gaining any help from the equal protection clause.

The second federal foundation was more recent. As her final cause of action, Williams invoked a new document, the revised sex discrimination guidelines of the U.S. Equal Employment Opportunity Commission (EEOC). On April 5, 1972, the month before Armendariz's car crash and miscarriage, the EEOC had issued, for the first time, guidelines covering pregnancy discrimination. The guidelines declared that "classifications based upon physical characteristics unique to one sex are sex-based classifications."

Although Williams did not know at the time, publication of these guidelines broke a years-old logjam at the EEOC. The breakthrough had come partly thanks to one new lawyer there, Susan Deller Ross, who in 1968 at NYU had helped set in motion the creation of the first law school course on women in the law. Williams hoped the agency's imprimatur would carry weight. She used the EEOC guidelines to argue that a state that denied disability insurance to Armendariz based on pregnancy (a physical characteristic unique to one sex) was making a sex-based denial—an argument she hoped could apply under the Constitution's equal protection clause.

IN LATE FEBRUARY OF 1973, Williams appeared at the U.S. courthouse in San Francisco to make her case: pregnancy discrimination was sex discrimination that violated the Constitution of the United States. Sally Armendariz, sitting in the courtroom, thought Wendy did a great job—loading her argument with good examples. Williams knew, however, that good stories don't win against bad law. After the argument ended, she awaited rejection by the federal court system.

On May 31, 1973, the three-judge district court issued its opinion,

written by Alfonso Zirpoli. The first question he addressed, as so often
in equal protection cases, was the level of scrutiny that a court should
use. After much discussion of Ginsburg's victory in *Reed* (and citation
of the chief justice's parroting of *Royster Guano*), the court decided to
apply what it called a "slightly altered 'rational basis' test"—scrutiny
that was far from strict and yet "slightly, but perceptibly, more rigorous" than the slight scrutiny that had for years permitted states to
discriminate freely on the basis of sex.

The court dealt at length with California's claim that it was protecting the solvency of its insurance program by excluding pregnancy-
related disabilities, which the state claimed were expensive. "If the
state wishes to prevent or limit large claims," the court replied, it
should limit "all claims in excess of certain amounts." But even if covering pregnancy added as much cost as California claimed, the court
calculated that the increase could be met easily. Each worker's pay-in
might rise from 1 percent to 1.37 percent of income. Furthermore,
continued Judge Zirpoli, cost alone cannot justify discrimination.

The court pounced hard on California's argument that pregnancy
is largely voluntary and thus "would make it possible for a woman
not interested in a career to abuse the disability insurance program
by working a short period, becoming pregnant, and collecting a substantial award." The state had worked up a hypothetical situation:
a woman could work for one year, contribute $85, and then col-
lect $2,730—*assuming* she could convince a doctor to certify that
her pregnancy created twenty-six weeks of disability. Judge Zirpoli
treated the state's assumption with scorn. He condemned as irrational
an insurance program that paid for voluntary disability due to plastic
surgery but excluded involuntary disability such as Armendariz's miscarriage caused by a car crash. Such irrationality led Judge Zirpoli,
joined by Judge Duniway, to find that the California Unemployment
Insurance Code embodied discrimination against women that violated
the Constitution of the United States.

Wendy Williams, thanks in good part to the litany of irrationalities
that she presented in her argument to the district court, had won. But
Judge Williams dissented. *Reed* invoked no more than rational relationship test, he said, and the state's wish to limit insurance costs was

rational. To the extent that the California law "discriminates against women," he concluded, "it does so reasonably." He was speaking less to his two colleagues than to the audience at the next stop on *Aiello*'s fast track: the Supreme Court of the United States.

GOING STRAIGHT TO *THE SUPREMES*—as Wendy Webster Williams' friends in law school used to call the men on the high court—was bad enough. Then, worse, California changed the terms of her case.

In a sense, that change represented a victory for Williams and women throughout California. A few months before Sally Armendariz's car crash led to her miscarriage, another California woman had run afoul of the state's irrational insurance plan. Like Carolyn Aiello, this other California woman suffered an ectopic pregnancy. Similarly, she and her lawyers decided to challenge the rules of California Unemployment Insurance in state court. But they made a simpler attack: not a constitutional challenge but a definitional challenge. They argued that ectopic pregnancies, since they occur where no fetus can survive, differ from true "pregnancy."

The state opposed the definitional challenge. In the first tier of California's three-level system of courts, the state won. But in the second tier, the state lost—precisely a week before the state lost *Aiello* in federal court. (The entire battle in state courts was unknown to Williams and, the state's lawyers in *Aiello* claimed, unknown to them also.)

The state's defense of an insurance plan that discriminated against women had become suddenly embarrassing in both state and federal courts. Rather than appeal two losses to two different supreme courts, the state shifted tactics. Cutting its losses, the state surrendered to the definitional challenge. It issued directives to pay benefits, designed to compensate "in part" for wage loss, to anyone who had an "abnormal pregnancy with involuntary implications." That meant paying off Carolyn Aiello, Elizabeth Johnson, and Sally Armendariz. For the state, the price was right. Armendariz, for example, received $84.

A few such payouts would not destroy California's insurance program. But the payouts could destroy Williams' case by eliminating the state's worst irrationality. Although the change represented a victory for three of Williams' four plaintiffs, it raised the odds against Williams at the Supreme Court. Gone were the utterly irrational stories: the car crash that didn't count as disabling because its victim was also pregnant; the debilitating surgery that did not count as a "disability" because an egg had been present.

As California appealed to the Supreme Court of the United States, it could argue that only one case remained—the lone complainant who had experienced a "normal pregnancy and delivery," Jacqueline Jaramillo. Jaramillo was, however, hardly *alone*. Some two hundred thousand working women in California gave birth each year. And Jaramillo's story illustrated women's need to be protected against loss of income due to a few weeks of disability associated with childbirth.

WHEN JACQUELINE JARAMILLO'S IUD FAILED and she found herself pregnant with her first child, the timing was bad. She and her husband, Louis, had met while working with farm workers in central Colorado. Teamed with them was a law professor from the University of Colorado who became so impressed with Louis that he convinced him to apply to law schools. When Louis won admission to a law school in San Francisco, the professor's family offered to pay Louis's tuition, and the Jaramillos gladly accepted.

Since free tuition did not provide food or rent, Jacqueline's salary carried the family. And then her IUD failed. Her doctor instructed her to arrange for six weeks of leave after childbirth. Her employer hoped to pay her salary to someone temporarily to cover her responsibilities, and encouraged her to apply for disability insurance.

When California Unemployment Insurance turned her down, she and Louis seemed to face hard choices: Would he drop out of law school for a term in order to work? Not possible, they felt, since the fast pace of legal training discouraged skipping a term. Would she consider an abortion? Although Jaqueline had been raised as what she called a "cradle Catholic," she had reason to worry that abortion might be her only chance to keep Louis on schedule and not waste the once-in-a-lifetime gift of free tuition. Before she had to ponder abortion, her employer found a solution: Louis could do her work for six weeks without dropping out of law school. Her paycheck stayed in the family. But for the Jaramillos, a few weeks of disability had come close to causing a family crisis. Though her case had been added only at the last minute to the others, Jacqueline Jaramillo represented a reasonable stand-in for hundreds of thousands of working women in California.

IN LATE 1973 WHEN THE SUPREME COURT announced it would hear the case that had begun with Sally Armendariz, Williams was technically ineligible to argue at the Court. She had passed her California bar exams in January of 1971. The Supreme Court had rules against arguments by novices. Someone who has been a lawyer for less than three years will not be admitted to the Bar of the Supreme Court. Fortunately, the Court scheduled oral argument for March in 1974. With two months to spare, Williams gained permission to address the Court.

A day before leaving for Washington, while walking down the front steps of the state court building in San Francisco, Williams slipped and badly twisted her ankle. It ballooned. Her doctor told her to keep her leg elevated and motionless for three days, and then he would put on a cast. When she told him she had to go to Washington the next day, he built the cast immediately and gave her painkillers and crutches. Finally she looked, she said, like an expert on disabilities.

Weiner and Williams arrived in DC in late March. To prepare for oral argument, they met with Washington-area litigators in the once-grand dining room of a townhouse that served as headquarters for a small group of public-interest attorneys called the Center for Law and Social Policy. The attorneys at the center included Marcia Greenberger, who had been working on another pregnancy-insurance case, with Ruth Weyand, that had been designed for federal rather than California courts. Strategizing proceeded with knowledge that

Aiello had been an imperfect case—its oddity suggested even by its new name at the Supreme Court, *Geduldig v. Aiello.* The case that had begun with Sally Armendariz and then carried the name of Carolyn Aiello now involved neither of them. What had transformed into the case of Jacqueline Jaramillo on behalf of many thousands of women would become known in the Court's one-name shorthand as *Geduldig,* for Dwight Geduldig, the man who directed California's Department of Human Resources Development and opposed paying unemployment-insurance benefits to pregnant women.

As oral arguments began for *Geduldig v. Aiello* at the Supreme Court, Joanne Condas, a deputy attorney general for the state of California, spoke first. (Justice Blackmun, who liked to depict attorneys appearing before him, scribbled "redhead" and "B+" atop his page of notes on her argument.) The district court decision, she estimated, would cost California workers $120 million a year. Male and female workers already paid out 1 percent of their salaries for protection against disability, and California wished to protect these workers from paying more. California's program, Condas said, would go bankrupt if forced to hand out $120 million—a third of its current costs—to pay for the pregnancies of a few women.

When Condas addressed the key argument against the state's position, that the California plan denied equal protection to women, her argument remained fundamentally economic: Women contributed only 28 percent of the money going to the California plan but drew 38 percent of its benefits. Thus she asserted, citing Judge Williams' dissent in the lower court, women already derived more benefit from the program than men. Worse, in any given year any new pregnancy benefits would go to only 2 percent of the workforce: the roughly 5 percent of women who are pregnant in any year. That female 2 percent would get all of the newly added $120 million, "the lion's share of the benefits." As her final comment, Condas added the suggestion, based not on California figures but on those provided by individual corporations, that half of those newly enriched women would then choose not to return to their jobs.

. . .

ON CRUTCHES IN LATE MORNING, Williams hobbled to the microphone. Although she had found sleeping difficult, no one could take her place. If any justice inquired about her injury, she readied her joke that crutches made her a disability expert. None asked. (Blackmun scribbled "B–" next to her name in his notes and then "long stringy hair, tall.")

Although Williams did not want to focus on cost, she had answers to most of California's economic arguments. Speaking to the figure of $120 million a year, for example, Williams showed that California assumed pregnant women would stay disabled for fifteen weeks, but America's leading association of obstetricians estimated that women's disability leave would average half as long. As to California's provocative "lion's share" argument—that men already "pay in more and get out less," as one justice put it during oral argument—Williams had an answer: The major predictor of disability rates is not sex but income. Low-income men and women in California, for example, took disability leaves of similar length; high-income workers of both sexes took disability leaves of far shorter length than did low-income workers. What might look like a sex difference was instead—since the average income of California women was only 60 percent of men's—really an income difference. Still, Williams conceded during oral argument, in California "women filed 44 percent of the claims, and they are 40 percent of the workforce."

After spending precious minutes battling the claim that women get the lion's share, Williams turned to her primary point: California's law hurt women, the "only group" excluded from its protection. "Nowhere is the economic discrimination against women," she told the Court, "more apparent than in the rules and practices surrounding the reality that women are the bearers of children." From that reality had emerged the "stereotyped notions that women belong in the home with their children, that women are not serious members of the work force, and that women generally have a male breadwinner in their families to support them." And from those notions had emerged a body of law which forces

able-bodied women off the job, which denies them unemployment insurance once they've gone on mandatory maternity
leave, denies them sick leave when their disability results from
pregnancy, . . . which does not permit them to return to work
at the time when they become physically able, often denies them
seniority and other benefits which accrue to workers normally
disabled, and finally—when they try to return to the job—often
the jobs themselves are denied.

Here was the real answer to California's many points. Not getting
insurance, not receiving high incomes, not being allowed to return
to their old jobs, not getting promoted—these disadvantages were
encouraged by legal stereotyping and legal discrimination. The law
created what it claimed to respond to.

The centrality of pregnancy to discrimination led to Williams'
climactic point: "So long as classifications based upon pregnancy are
thrust outside the bounds of judicial scrutiny, so long will women
suffer unwarranted and arbitrary discrimination because they are
women." Discriminating against the pregnant meant discriminating
against women. Pregnancy discrimination was sex discrimination.

Chief Justice Burger, ending the oral argument as usual with
thanks to opposing counsels, concluded on a rare phrase: "Thank
you, ladies." Although the first woman to argue before the Supreme
Court had done so in 1880, not until 1971 had two women contended
at the Supreme Court. They had met in a landmark case, *Doe v.
Bolton*, when Georgia's attorney general sent a female assistant to
argue against another female attorney, who was trying to establish
that women had a right to abortion. Now again in 1974 in *Geduldig
v. Aiello*, two women attorneys offered the Supreme Court opposed
visions of what women wanted.

MEETING PRIVATELY, SOON AFTER the oral argument, the Supreme
Court justices gathered in conference to consider *Geduldig v. Aiello*.
The justice most likely to approve the call for *scrutiny* was William
Brennan. Ten months before, in response to Ginsburg's arguments in

Frontiero, he had written for a plurality of four justices that sex discrimination deserved the strict test that any state law like California's would surely fail. In that opinion he had quoted, as if they were his own views, Williams' words from the opinion that she wrote, while still a law clerk, in *Sail'er Inn*: "The pedestal upon which women have been placed has all too often, upon closer inspection, been revealed as a cage."

In the conference for discussion of *Geduldig v. Aiello*, Justice Brennan could not win a majority of his colleagues. His only allies were Thurgood Marshall and William O. Douglas. White, his fourth vote in *Frontiero*, now inclined against Brennan. And Potter Stewart, the pivotal vote supporting Brennan's decision (though not his call for strict scrutiny) in *Frontiero*, turned decisively against Brennan. Stewart, the swing vote, now could draft an opinion for the majority.

Stewart's draft opinion devoted much effort to blurring the line dividing men from women. Williams had argued that women were the "only group" harmed by California's exclusion of coverage. So long as California's law seemed to divide women whom it harmed from men whom it did not, the law evidently discriminated against women.

Although Justice Stewart acknowledged that the case was brought by women, in order to blur the dividing line he sought others whom the law harmed. He pointed to California law's exclusion from disability coverage of any individual under court commitment as a "dipsomaniac, drug addict, or sexual psychopath"—even though California's lawyer had stated that such court commitments were too archaic to constitute "valid exclusions." Stewart pointed also to the exclusion of disabilities that were short term (fewer than eight days) or long term (beyond twenty-six weeks)—even though such exclusions seemed not to make distinctions between one population "group" and another. After those exclusions, he mentioned "certain disabilities that are attributable to pregnancy." Thus grouped with court-identified dipsomania (rare) and the common cold (short term), pregnancy seemed just another weakness of the flesh.

By acknowledging no harm that affected a single group, Stewart avoided the strict scrutiny question. In his draft opinion's last dozen lines, seeing no evidence that California discriminated against "any definable group," he reached this conclusion: "There is no risk from which men are protected and women are not. Likewise, there is no risk from which women are protected and men are not." By his formula, only if a state started protecting pregnant men could discrimination law force it to protect pregnant women.

Within the body of his draft opinion, only those two sentences acknowledged the case's tension between men and women. By crafting an almost gender-free draft, Stewart avoided the question dominating earlier equal protection cases: why did this case not deserve scrutiny? His omission sent ripples around the Court. One law clerk, remarking to Justice Blackmun that Stewart's draft had "skirted discussion of sex discrimination," added, "I would think that this can't go on forever." Justice White, after reading Stewart's draft, replied that he wanted to read Brennan's dissent before joining either side.

A month later, Brennan circulated a draft of his answering dissent. Based on *Reed* and *Frontiero*, he argued that California's program failed to pass the scrutiny it deserved. Unlike Stewart, Brennan mentioned *sex* and saw discrimination against *women*:

> In my view, by singling out for less favorable treatment a gender-linked disability peculiar to women, the State has created a double-standard for disability compensation. . . . [S]uch dissimilar treatment of men and women, on the basis of physical characteristics inextricably linked to one sex, inevitably constitutes sex discrimination.

Having identified the discrimination, Brennan challenged the opinion drafted by Stewart for not "satisfactorily explaining what differentiates the gender-based classification employed in this case from those found unconstitutional in *Reed* and *Frontiero*."

Apparently stung by Brennan's challenge, Potter Stewart appended, near the end of his draft, a twenty-four-line footnote. Arguing that this case was "a far cry" from *Reed* and *Frontiero*, Stewart belatedly explained how he could separate pregnancy from women. The California program, he explained, "does not exclude anyone from benefit eligibility because of gender." Instead, it "merely removes one physical condition—pregnancy—from the list of compensable disabilities." Thus California's exclusion, because based on pregnancy rather than gender, could legally discriminate against "anyone" who was pregnant. Having explained that California's pregnancy exclusion did not discriminate between groups of men and groups of women, for the first time Stewart defined the two groups at issue: "The program divides potential recipients into two groups—pregnant women and nonpregnant persons."

By crafting *nonpregnant persons*, which included women, Justice Stewart solved his problem. The opposed groups were not women and men; the opposed groups were pregnant women and all others, including women who were not pregnant. If women stood on both sides of a line, that line could not be a line *between* the sexes. If California was not drawing a gender line, Stewart saw no need to engage in serious scrutiny.

Justice Stewart's footnote number 20, the only major addition to his draft, completed his opinion. Brennan's dissent won him no converts among the other justices. The Supreme Court had ruled: the United States Constitution permits discrimination against pregnant persons.

7

The Second Pregnancy Case:
General Electric

The loss for pregnant persons was a bad loss for women, but *Geduldig v. Aiello* had become a bad case the moment it shifted from state to federal courts. Waiting in the wings was another case aimed to attack pregnancy discrimination. In contrast to *Geduldig*, at each point this case seemed right: the right litigator with the right plaintiffs engaging the right law in the right courts. The case would become known as the *General Electric* case, and the attorney preparing it, though little known to most Americans, was one of the most successful women lawyers in the history of Supreme Court litigation: Ruth Weyand.

As of the day in 1973 when Williams first heard of Armendariz and thus began her first trip to the Supreme Court, Ruth Weyand had already served as counsel—writing briefs as well as delivering nine oral arguments at the Supreme Court—in more than 140 cases before federal courts in a career spanning more than four decades. And in those oral arguments before the Supreme Court, tackling controversial discrimination and labor issues, Ruth Weyand had never lost.

By the time she was seven years old, Ruth Weyand knew she wanted to be a lawyer. All through her childhood, court decisions in labor and constitutional law had been part of family dinner conversations, often injected by her father, a sociology professor at Grinnell College in Iowa. By age ten she was preparing for the law by winning local debate contests; at the age of fifteen, she enrolled at the University of Chicago.

When she came home from college for her first midyear holiday, an event occurred that she would retell for decades and that a colleague would retell in the pages of the *National Law Journal*: It was Christmas morning, 1928. Her father turned on the family's brand-new console radio. On came the voice of a radio announcer, describing preparations being made by a lynch mob to burn a black man. Hearing those words, Weyand became so angry, she recalled to a colleague years later, that "I wanted to go right out and be a 'Joan d'Arc.'" Weyand's father, wanting not to upset the family, just shut off the radio. Incensed, sixteen-year-old Ruth called him a hypocrite and challenged him to go with her and stop the mob. All he could say was, "If I could stop it from happening I would, but I can't. The place for your Joan d'Arc act is in the courtroom."

She agreed. By age seventeen, her undergraduate work finished at a time when most students were still aiming for college, Ruth Weyand was aiming for the University of Chicago Law School. It seemed a good choice, particularly since in 1870 Chicago had become the first school in America to award a law degree to a woman. In 1930, however, it rejected Ruth Weyand. The registrar told her, she later recalled, that "the faculty was not keen on admitting women because they knew we only came to find husbands."

Seemingly dissuaded from law, Weyand enrolled in Chicago's graduate school of social service—a field more welcoming to women. That school permitted its students to take courses in law, and in her first term Weyand enrolled only in law school courses. Her grades exceeded those of all two hundred of Chicago's first-year law students. Convinced, the University of Chicago responded by returning her first-term tuition in social services and admitting her to its law school with a full scholarship. In 1932, she graduated with honors at age twenty.

She then went looking for a job. No law firm, including the ones that employed Weyand's lower-ranked classmates, would hire her. Six months of rejections led Ruth Weyand back to her law school dean, asking him to make her record look like a man's. She said she would go to interviews smoking a cigar and wearing a man's suit. Instead, the dean got on the phone to law firms. Although she eventually found work with a Chicago firm, it strove to keep clients ignorant that a woman was doing their legal work. "I kept submitting briefs with my name reading 'Ruth Weyand,' and they kept coming back 'R. Weyand,'" she told a colleague years later. "If a client saw me, the partners would say 'Oh, well she just walks the briefs over to court.'"

In 1938, Ruth Weyand escaped the sexism of private practice by moving to Washington and the National Labor Relations Board (NLRB). She rose rapidly to become the attorney in charge of NLRB litigation before the United States Supreme Court. Two of the landmark labor cases she won established that a union selected by a majority of workers may speak for all workers in a unit and that employees may solicit others for union membership while on company property. In addition, as a brief writer she played a part in key race-discrimination cases. Her briefs helped to outlaw discrimination by race in collective bargaining and to outlaw discrimination by race in real estate sales.

And then in 1950 Ruth Weyand began to experience race discrimination firsthand. During the late 1940s, years when she was working along with Thurgood Marshall of the NAACP against racially restrictive real estate covenants, she had fallen in love with another NAACP lawyer, Leslie S. Perry. When they married in 1949, Perry urged her to keep the marriage secret. He worried they would cause controversy, since he was black. In 1950, when word of their marriage became public, his prediction proved true. Multiple articles appeared in major newspapers after Perry's former wife, from whom he was divorced, sued Weyand for alienating her husband's affections.

Interracial marriage remained illegal in most states. An *Ebony* magazine article in 1949 quoted a psychologist's speculation that "a successful negro male tends to demonstrate his success, maybe unconsciously by seeking a light or white female." When time came for the birth of their first child, Weyand chose not to use anesthesia out of worry that her son might be at risk because of the surrounding tension. After he was born, someone set fire to Weyand and Perry's home in Washington while their infant son was inside.

Despite Weyand's undefeated record arguing at the Supreme Court for the NLRB, it fired her. A front-page article in the *Washington Post* said that the general counsel of the NLRB "was reported to feel that Miss Weyand's value to the board has been impaired by the publicity" surrounding her marriage.

Her labor law career continued, however, first with a private law firm and then in 1965 with a union that represented electrical workers and had a particularly large percentage of women workers. There Ruth Weyand played a major role in introducing to America the concept of pay equity or "comparable worth": the concept that women should be paid as much as men not only for "equal work" (as mandated by the Equal Pay Act of 1963) but also for comparable work. And in the same years at the electrical workers' union, she won a major victory against what unions saw as the arrogance of a company that bargained with a "take-it-or leave-it" negotiating policy, a tactic that became known as *Boulwarism*, for that company's vice president, Lemuel Boulwar. The company was General Electric.

THE IDEAL CASE FOR RUTH WEYAND, involving discrimination by General Electric against pregnant women, began in 1971. That spring, a few workers for General Electric in Salem, Virginia, a small city in the Roanoke valley, read in a newsletter called *Keeping Up with the Law*, produced by Weyand for her union, that the Equal Employment Opportunity Commission had just issued a decision against a small company that, like big GE, had a disability plan for its workers. That company, also like GE, refused to cover workers whose disabilities arose from childbirth or pregnancy. Such a refusal, the EEOC had ruled, was illegal discrimination.

For decades, the women's union had tried through bargaining to argue that General Electric's disability coverage should not exclude, alone among all disabilities, pregnancy disability. Now a part of the U.S. government, the EEOC, seemed inclined to agree with the union.

As a first step, a few women working for GE in Salem who were pregnant went to file for disability claims. General Electric refused to give them claim forms. They eventually got the forms and filed claims, which GE then denied.

These women's stories had the straightforward sound of workers who wanted to work. Barbara Hall, for example, a young woman with dark hair worn in a flip, had been working with General Electric for five years before she learned she was pregnant in March of 1971. Her doctor told her she could work as long as she "felt good." And, indeed, she continued to feel good enough to work right up until the time her baby was born. But GE's nurse, following the GE employee handbook, told Barbara Hall that she had to stop working at the end of her sixth month of pregnancy and thus give up her next three months of income. Hall spent five days in the hospital after childbirth and soon afterward applied to return to work. GE told her to wait until six weeks after childbirth. When she called again to begin work, GE told her to wait two more weeks. All told, GE had forced her to lose at least four months of work and income.

When Hall heard that the EEOC had ruled she was entitled to disability payments for the time when General Electric had prohibited her from working, she wanted to apply for them. If they were granted, GE would pay her 60 percent of her regular weekly wage. The other Salem women told similar stories—wanting to work as long as they felt fine, but willing to accept 60 percent disability payments from GE if the company forced them off the job.

To supplement these straightforward but undramatic tales, Weyand and her legal colleagues sought out other stories. As a tale of readiness to work, they found Erma Thomas in Texas. Because her doctor told her that she could stay on the job until she went to the hospital to have her baby, she convinced her GE plant to let her work. She finished her usual shift on a Friday afternoon and gave birth that night. Thomas' story showed that some women could work even through the entirety of a normal pregnancy.

As a tale of irrationality, they found Emma Furch, also in Texas, who was disabled by a blood clot in her lung. General Electric refused to pay disability benefits because at the same time Furch was also pregnant. Furch's story showed that pregnancy was used to exclude women from otherwise-earned benefits.

Perhaps most dramatically, as a tale of hardship, they found Sherrie O'Steen. In 1972, O'Steen was working for General Electric in coastal Virginia when she found out she was pregnant, and at about the same time, her husband abandoned her, leaving her to take care of their two-year-old daughter. Sherrie O'Steen had no money to spare. She convinced her foreman to let her work, despite GE's rules, to the end of her seventh month of pregnancy. When GE "put me out without pay," as she said, she couldn't pay her bills. Her electric company cut her off in November just before her son was born, leaving her to raise two children in winter in an unheated and unlighted house with an unusable stove and refrigerator. She and her children endured their cold house for a month and a half until she received a state welfare check in midwinter. As soon as GE let her return to work, six weeks after her child was born, she returned to her job on the assembly line.

With General Electric, which employed one hundred thousand women, Weyand had found a significant target. GE had been a pioneer in the concept of employee benefits, and in the process had created ample evidence that it viewed women as second-class employees. Early on, GE had excluded women from a newly created disability benefit plan on the grounds that "women did not recognize the responsibilities of life," in the words of a GE president, Gerard Swope, "for they probably were hoping to get married soon and leave the company."

Discrimination against women, Weyand was able to demonstrate, showed in wage differentials at General Electric. At the end of World War II, for example, the War Labor Board had ordered General Electric to raise women's wages. The Board's goal was to reduce "long-standing differentials between rates for women's jobs and men's jobs which, it was proven, cannot be justified on the basis of comparative job content." The differential had been explicitly codified by General Electric: Starting pay for a man in a typical job was 71 cents and for a woman 57 cents. At the end of six months, the man's pay rose to 92 cents and the woman's to 74 cents. On this basis, Weyand could argue that GE's exclusion of women from pregnancy benefits represented merely another part of GE's systematic wage discrimination against women.

But the biggest advantage of the *General Electric* case over *Geduldig v. Aiello*, the California case unwillingly brought to the Supreme Court by Wendy Webster Williams, was not a more experienced litigator or more carefully chosen plaintiffs or a better target for litigation. The big change, one of huge consequence for all cases involving women and discrimination, was a better law, known in legal shorthand simply as *Title VII*.

TITLE VII HAD TAKEN ITS FINAL FORM in one of the oddest bursts of legislative game-playing in the history of American feminism. And no understanding of what would happen, in not just the *General Electric* case but in almost all legal battles for women's rights, could begin without tracing its origins.

Title VII was the employment section of the landmark Civil Rights Act of 1964—introduced by President John F. Kennedy five months before he died and signed by President Lyndon B. Johnson on the one-year anniversary of its introduction. Kennedy had introduced the bill to combat national discrimination against African-Americans and to respond to specific events in the spring and early summer of 1963: "Bull" Connor, the police commissioner of Birmingham, Alabama, sending police dogs on Good Friday to end a march led by the Rev. Martin Luther King Jr.; and Governor George Wallace of Alabama announcing that he would ignore a federal court's instruction to permit two black students to enter a summer program at the University of Alabama.

Kennedy went on television to proclaim that the nation faced a moral issue "as old as the Scriptures" and "as clear as the Constitution." Recalling that a century had passed since President Lincoln had ended slavery, he challenged the nation:

> If an American, because his skin is dark, cannot eat lunch in a restaurant open to the public; if he cannot send his children to the best public school available; if he cannot vote for the pubic officials who represent him; if, in short, he cannot enjoy the full and free life which all of us want, then who among us

would be content to have the color of his skin changed and stay in his place?

Noting, at the height of the cold war, that we preach freedom to the world, Kennedy continued:

> But are we to say to the world—and much more importantly to ourselves—that this is the land of the free, except for the Negroes; that we have no second-class citizens, except Negroes; that we have no class or caste system, no ghettoes, no master race, except with respect to Negroes?

Kennedy's answer, introduced a week later, was his civil rights bill. It sought sweeping federal power to end discrimination in America. It sought to eliminate the exclusion of blacks from hotels and restaurants, to eliminate segregation in restrooms and schools, and to eliminate barriers to voting. And, under what would become "Title VII," it sought to end discrimination in employment and create a federal commission to foster equality in the realm of employment opportunities.

Kennedy's bill met enormous resistance and legendary support, including, two months after the bill's introduction, a march on Washington that brought two hundred thousand people to the mall, where they heard, among other speeches, Martin Luther King Jr.'s "I Have a Dream." Despite fierce opposition to that dream from many congressmen, particularly from southern states, Kennedy's bill was destined to become national law, banning many forms of racial discrimination.

Drafters of the president's civil rights bill did not seek, however, to reduce discrimination against women, despite the fact that women's earnings had declined relative to men's. On average, a woman who worked full-time earned 63.6 percent of a man's salary in 1957 but only 60.6 percent in 1960.

Such disparities had already led to lobbying by women, during Kennedy's first years as president, on behalf of what became the Equal Pay Act of 1963. That law had also met powerful counterlobbying by industry groups. Much compromised in its final form, the Act forbade paying a man more than a woman if both did "equal work." But it allowed an employer to continue paying men more if their higher pay was based on

(i) a seniority system;
(ii) a merit system;
(iii) a system which measures earnings by quantity or quality of production; or
(iv) a differential based on any other factor other than sex.

An employer could also pay men more by claiming that women's work was not "equal work." Although much constricted, the Equal Pay Act seemed a major achievement to its hard-working female advocates, many of whom President Kennedy gathered for a signing ceremony in his office on June 10, 1963. Nine days later he introduced his far more sweeping civil rights bill.

In late November of 1963, two days before the death of the president, the new civil rights bill crossed a major legislative hurdle, winning the support of the House Judiciary Committee. Its language attacked many forms of discrimination based on "race, color, religion, or national origin." It said nothing about sex.

The specter that a great advance in American civil rights would do nothing for women led to mobilization by the National Woman's Party, for years a leading supporter of an equal rights amendment to the U.S. Constitution—an amendment opposed by the Kennedy administration. The civil rights bill, protested the Woman's Party (using language that may have served both tactically and as a display of the party's conservative slant), "would not even give protection against discrimination because of 'race, color, religion, or national origin,' to a *White Woman*, a *Woman of the Christian Religion*, or a *Woman of United States Origin*." The party sent every member of Congress a resolution calling for an amendment that would add *sex* to the categories covered by Title VII.

Adding *sex* suited at least one powerful and conservative congressman, Representative Howard Smith of Virginia, an ERA supporter but an attacker of Kennedy's civil rights bill. If civil rights legislation had to pass, Smith had been arguing since the 1950s, it should at least protect white women. And although he apparently lacked the votes, he would be happy if adding *sex* could kill the bill. Seeing an opportunity, two congresswomen decided to endorse the addition of *sex* to Title VII, as part of an odd strategy: Howard Smith would introduce the amendment. His endorsement, they supposed, could win southern and conservative votes that women otherwise would not get.

On February 8, 1964, Smith rose on the House floor to propose an amendment to Title VII of the civil rights legislation: to enlarge its protection against discrimination in employment, he proposed adding the word *sex*. Much banter followed. Smith read a letter from a woman complaining that many women were cheated out of husbands because too few men could be found. He instructed his colleagues to take note of such "real grievances." Representative Emanuel Celler, who had introduced the civil rights bill originally in the House, joked that in his house full of women he usually had the last words: "yes, dear." He then raised a variety of possible problems, many of them unconnected to employment and most of them familiar from long-expressed opposition to the long-proposed equal rights amendment: possible disadvantages to women in alimony payments, custody agreements, and the military draft.

When Celler finished opposing the addition of *sex*, eleven of the twelve women members of the House rose to support it. They had prepared well. Most articulate, Representative Martha Griffiths of Michigan, a key supporter of the ERA, noted that the laughing responses to the amendment revealed that American women remained second-class citizens. She went on to argue that unless the sex amendment passed, a white woman turned away from a job where only whites work—perhaps washing dishes in a restaurant or teaching politics in a university—would have no recourse. But "if a colored woman shows up and she is qualified," Griffiths continued, "she is going to have an open entree into any particular field."

At the end of two hours, a vote was called. An odd coalition aligned briefly—including women from both parties opposed to sex discrimination, Republican men sympathetic to women's rights, and southern Democrats interested in killing the civil rights bill—in a vote

of 168 to 133 to add *sex* to Title VII's prohibitions against employment discrimination. Only two days later, the amended bill passed
the House, 290 to 130. In a move that would taint Title VII for years,
all but one of the men who had spoken for the sex amendment voted
against the full bill. And years later, according to Griffiths, Smith told
her that he had offered his sex amendment "as a joke."

Emerging with a surprise vote from one part of Congress did not,
however, make the bill law. In the coming months, many women
lobbied aggressively to win similar language in the Senate and to
overcome major opposition there. Finally the Senate passed a bill
that included *sex* but differed in other terms from the House bill,
forcing the House to vote yet again on the sex provision. The House
affirmed overwhelmingly, and President Johnson signed the bill that
same day, July 2, 1964. Suddenly, at least in certain types of employment, discrimination against women was illegal. But what kinds of
discrimination? And who would decide?

To make such decisions regarding discrimination by "race, color,
religion, sex, or national origin," the Kennedy administration proposed creating a commission, on the model of the National Labor
Relations Board, to be called the Equal Employment Opportunity
Commission, which could issue orders instructing employers to "cease
and desist" from discriminatory practices. Before the civil rights bill
passed, opponents in the House and Senate managed to strip the commission of most of its proposed powers. Not only could the EEOC not
issue orders to ban discriminatory practices; it could not even initiate
litigation on behalf of employees who had suffered discrimination.
Its limited powers amounted to these: It could receive complaints of
discrimination and try to conciliate between employee and employer;
if conciliation failed, it could give the employee a right-to-sue letter
and could file a brief in the courts on behalf of the employee; it could
recommend that the U.S. attorney general prosecute a case that was
particularly grave. And, separate from individual cases, it could issue
guidelines, which were less powerful than orders and whose legal
weight was untested.

• • •

THE NEED TO PONDER SEX FREQUENTLY came as a surprise to the EEOC. In its first year, more than a third of all complaints, far more than expected, came from women. To such complaints, the responses of a majority of the early commissioners, according to the one woman among the five EEOC commissioners, ranged typically from "boredom" to "virulent hostility."

The commissioners' unease transmitted to their staff. The commission's first executive director told the secretary of labor that "the Commission is very much aware of the importance of not becoming known as the 'sex commission.'" His successor expressed his opposition to the idea that men might be forced to hire male secretaries and stated publicly that the sex amendment to Title VII was a "fluke" that had been "conceived out of wedlock."

Wary of playing sex commission for a bastardized law, the EEOC did not always help women. In one of its earliest decisions, the EEOC ruled that advertisements for jobs could not be segregated by race: the *New York Times* could not run an ad whose job description announced that "no blacks need apply." But the EEOC's five commissioners ruled, by a vote of 3–2, that want ads for jobs could be segregated by sex. Newspaper columns could continue to announce, "Help Wanted—Male" or "Help Wanted—Female."

Pregnancy seemed the toughest issue for the EEOC to tackle. Not until 1971 could the commission formulate a clear position, thanks in part to the work of two young women lawyers.

The first woman lawyer to join the EEOC was Sonia Pressman Fuentes. Fuentes had graduated Phi Beta Kappa from Cornell and first in her class at the University of Miami School of Law, and she began work as the third lawyer hired in the general counsel's office at the EEOC, four months after it opened its doors. She had joined the agency to expand civil rights, which to her meant the rights of blacks. But soon she found herself encountering charges of discrimination against women, and *sex* was right there in Title VII along with *race*. Because she behaved as if Title VII applied to sex, the general counsel who hired her began calling her a "sex maniac."

When Fuentes began to ponder pregnancy, she encountered two theories. One said pregnancy was special, since only women could bear children, and thus pregnant women deserved special protection. This first theory connected to a long history of laws designed specially to protect women, such as ones to keep them from working too many hours or too late at night. The second theory said that, as Fuentes and one of her colleagues explained in a 1968 summary, "disability due to pregnancy ought to be treated like any other temporary disability." Early opinions by the EEOC reflected its perplexity. Issues remained knotty: Could a company terminate a woman when her pregnancy started to show? (Probably not.) Did seniority accumulate during pregnancy leave? (Unclear.)

Such piecemeal opinions on pregnancy could not be used to formulate policy. At the start of the 1970s, five years after the EEOC was founded, Sonia Fuentes was still trying to get the EEOC to endorse a set of guidelines on pregnancy. At that point, she leaned personally toward special treatment. She had traveled to Europe, where some countries guaranteed women a pregnancy leave. Similarly the EEOC, she supposed, should require companies to give women a special paid leave for pregnancy, perhaps for six weeks or so. When she became pregnant with her own daughter in 1971, six weeks sounded about right.

In the fall of 1970, the general counsel's office of the EEOC made a new hire, Susan Deller Ross. Fresh out of NYU law school, she was arguably the first of the NYU activists. Ross had proposed opening NYU's Root-Tilden Scholarship to women, a proposal that led to the creation of NYU's Women's Rights Committee. Leaving law school, she was delighted to find work at what she believed was the best place in the country to engage with women's issues: the EEOC.

Ross was in for a surprise. On her first day at the EEOC, one woman said to her, with disapproval in her voice, "I hear you're one of those feminists." Soon after, by way of opening banter, a male lawyer with whom Ross would be working launched into a law-school-type hypothetical: What if you have a construction company that has only male workers, and the company has Porta Potties for its male workers? What if it costs a lot of money to get a Porta Potti for a woman? Shouldn't the cost of getting a new Porta Potti be a reason why the construction company shouldn't have to hire women?

Ross was stunned. At what should be the best place in the country to promote equal opportunity for women, this male lawyer was arguing that women's hopes for high-paying jobs should be outweighed by the price of Porta Potties. Ross did not know how her reputation had reached the EEOC ahead of her, but evidently the place hadn't been looking for feminist attorneys. Now it had one. While at NYU, she interned at the ACLU. When Ross arrived at ACLU offices, she found that two of the ACLU's women board members were hopping mad. A key committee of the ACLU had just voted, as the entire ACLU had been voting for years, to continue to oppose the equal rights amendment. The ACLU's grounds were that the ERA might lead to overruling so-called protective labor laws for women. So Ross took on, as an ACLU research project, the task of evaluating these special-treatment laws.

What Ross found was twofold. First, the recently passed Title VII of the Civil Rights Act of 1964 was leading courts to invalidate many such protective labor laws. Second, those invalidations meant good riddance to bad rubbish. Protective labor laws had served for years to "protect" women out of good jobs. A typical provision of such a law might limit the total number of hours women could work, thus allowing women to get home to their children and housework. But many good jobs, such as supervisory jobs, required employees to work—even if only occasionally—for long stretches. Protective labor laws guaranteed that many supervisors must be male. No woman need apply. Other kinds of protective labor laws had subtler effects. If laws made women less efficient or less available for work, for example, employers avoided hiring women altogether.

As Ross's critique of protective labor laws became known, she was sought out by a number of women in Washington, including Catherine East, the executive secretary of the federal Citizens' Advisory Council on the Status of Women, a group appointed as advisors by the president of the United States. East, a covert ally of Betty Friedan and (also covertly) Sonia Fuentes in creating the National Organization for Women (NOW), by 1970 had drafted a simple approach to pregnancy that followed theory two: treat it not as something different but as something similar.

When Ross arrived at the EEOC and found the commission back-logged with complaints from pregnant women who were getting fired or were not getting disability insurance, Ross turned to East's similar-treatment approach. Although at first Fuentes argued for six weeks of guaranteed leave, based on a European model, eventually Ross convinced her and also the commissioners that the EEOC should take an equal-treatment approach to pregnancy. In March of 1972, seven years after the EEOC first began grappling with pregnancy, the commission issued official guidelines:

> Disabilities caused or contributed to by pregnancy, miscarriage, abortion, childbirth, and recovery therefrom are, for all job-related purposes, temporary disabilities and should be treated as such under any health or temporary disability insurance or sick leave plan available in connection with employment.

Put simply, the guidelines said that employers had to treat pregnancy disability the same as they treated any other "temporary disability." If a company provided sick pay or covered hospital costs for a man during an operation and subsequent recuperation, that company must provide sick pay or cover hospital costs for a woman during child-birth and subsequent recuperation. This concept, which came to be known as the "equal treatment" approach to pregnancy, had two clear advantages: First, practically, it could provide grounds to win money for women who were excluded by many disability insurance plans, like California's and General Electric's, that refused to help them when their disability was linked to pregnancy. Second, it could guide judges, for it fit pregnancy into existing categories of discrimination. The concept was familiar to the law since the time of Aristotle: likes should be treated alike. So long as the disabling effects of childbirth resembled the disabling effects of men's medical conditions, women had to be treated as well as men.

BECAUSE THE EEOC WAS CREATED with no power to initiate litigation, from its earliest days the task of convincing judges that an employer was discriminating had fallen to lawyers outside the EEOC. After the group of General Electric women from Virginia read about the EEOC's ruling, the next step had been for Ruth Weyand to begin planning a case under Title VII, which seemed a far better law for the *General Electric* case than the Constitution of the United States had been for *Geduldig v. Aiello.*

Furthermore, under Title VII, Weyand could try her case in the right court. Thanks to a provision created to prevent victims of discrimination from having to bring cases in their hometowns, where they might face entrenched prejudice, she could select among a range of district courts. She chose the court for the Eastern District of Virginia, in Richmond, where Judge Robert R. Merhige Jr. had already ruled that a pregnant schoolteacher could not be forced to leave her job at the end of her fifth month of pregnancy. Judge Merhige's opinion in that case, *Susan Cohen v. Chesterfield County School Board,* used language that suited Weyand perfectly: "The maternity policy of the School Board denies pregnant women such as Mrs. Cohen equal protection of the laws because it treats pregnancy differently than other medical disabilities." Those words, written in May of 1971, perfectly anticipated not only the argument Wendy Webster Williams would soon be making in the case of Carolyn Aiello but also the language Susan Deller Ross would soon be writing into the EEOC pregnancy guidelines. This judge, Ruth Weyand felt sure, saw that pregnancy discrimination was sex discrimination.

THE GENERAL ELECTRIC TRIAL in district court lasted three days. In late July of 1973, Judge Merhige heard testimony from numerous General Electric women, including Erma Thomas and Emma Furch, who came from Texas; Sherrie O'Steen, who came from her new home in Kentucky; and Barbara Hall and Doris Wiley, from the original group of seven at the GE plant in Salem, Virginia. Surrounding their short and clear stories, Judge Merhige heard extensive expert testimony on relevant questions: How did the EEOC first treat pregnancy? How do the government agencies now treat pregnancy? How do physicians view work during pregnancy? How many women do not return to General Electric after pregnancy? How much cost would pregnancy coverage add to disability plans? (To this issue, Judge Merhige expressed "serious doubts that costs mean anything when you are talking about discrimination.")

Judge Merhige's behavior left Weyand thinking he was the "friendly judge" she sought. Then for months he issued no decision. As she waited, Weyand supposed he was watching the progress of his earlier *Cohen* opinion—pregnancy must not be treated "differently than other medical disabilities"—which had battled through a turbulent series of wins and losses in higher courts.

Eleven days after a three-judge panel at the court of appeals affirmed him in *Cohen*, Merhige agreed to hear the *General Electric* case. Then in early 1973 the entire court of appeals, its judges sitting *en banc*, overruled him in *Cohen*. The court's chief judge, Clement Haynsworth, announced that no man-made law "can relieve females from all of the burdens" of motherhood.

Three months later, the Supreme Court said it would hear *Cohen*. Long before that oral argument at the Supreme Court, Ruth Weyand and her GE case reached Merhige's courtroom.

Finally, his *Cohen* decision won, in a sense. The Supreme Court overruled the court of appeals in early 1974, and Susan Cohen won— albeit on grounds that differed from Merhige's original opinion. But a win was a win, and within three months, Judge Merhige issued his long-delayed *General Electric* opinion, which could now cite, as apparent support, the Supreme Court's decision.

Despite his months of delay and the trial's "voluminous records and endless motions," Judge Merhige's *General Electric* opinion announced that the key issues revealed underlying simplicity. Merhige focused his greatest attention on GE's claim that pregnancy was "voluntary." To this he gave little credence, remarking that GE covered male employees for such voluntary disabilities as those caused by elective cosmetic surgery and, in an extreme case of voluntary disability, by attempted suicide.

This theme of voluntariness had led General Electric to detailed discussion of the ease of contraception. GE apparently gained boldness from the Supreme Court's decision in the bitterly divisive abortion case, *Roe v. Wade*, announced only a few months earlier, that had legalized abortion. At one point during the trial, arguing that women could now control pregnancy, GE's lawyer suggested that abortion had been reduced to a mere "lunch-hour treatment."

Responding to such cavalier portrayals of abortion, Judge Merhige reached the essence of what Ruth Weyand had been arguing. He refused to accept GE's implication that Congress wished, as he put it, that female employees "forego a fundamental right, such as a woman's right to bear children, as a condition precedent to the enjoyment of the benefits of employment free of discrimination."

This was a surrender, Judge Merhige continued, that General Electric asked from women only. "While pregnancy is unique to women, parenthood is common to both sexes," he remarked, and "yet under G.E.'s policy, it is only their female employees who must, if they wish to avoid a total loss of company induced income, forego the right and privilege of this natural state." Merhige found no difficulty agreeing with the EEOC and with Ruth Weyand that pregnancy discrimination was sex discrimination. Recalling the experience of Sherrie O'Steen, who had been forced to raise her newborn without heat or refrigeration, he continued that only women "are required to undergo the economic hardship of the disability which arises from their participation in the procreative experience."

Convinced of the case's "underlying simplicity," Judge Merhige found numerous other issues not relevant. He refused, for example, to admit Ruth Weyand's argument about General Electric's alleged discrimination in years prior to 1964, when Congress enacted Title VII. Further, he declined to consider GE's arguments that forcing the payment of pregnancy disability benefits would dramatically increase GE's costs.

Merhige drew his decision from the "great mass of expert testimony," as he put it, that confirms the obvious: Pregnancy for a time can be physically disabling. Males receive full disability coverage; females do not. General Electric's male employees and women employees, though "similarly situated," face "disparate treatment." From such disparity, Judge Merhige reached his conclusion: "That this is sex discrimination is self evident." He ruled fully for the female employees of GE, affirming both Weyand's arguments and the EEOC's guidelines: pregnancy discrimination is sex discrimination.

Weyand felt delighted. Then two months later the Supreme Court issued its *Geduldig v. Aiello* decision, declaring that a state insurance program that discriminated against pregnant women was not engaging in unconstitutional sex discrimination, because the state was discriminating not between men and women but between "pregnant women and nonpregnant persons." Weyand felt doomed.

WHEN THE COURT OF APPEALS AGREED to GE's request that it review Judge Merhige's opinion for the district court, Ruth Weyand gained a new ally. Although Weyand was undefeated before the Supreme Court, her experience did not compare to that of her new ally, Beatrice Rosenberg. A high-school classmate of William J. Brennan (now Justice Brennan), Rosenberg had joined the criminal division of the U.S. Justice Department in 1943. In her career there, Rosenberg argued more than thirty cases before the Supreme Court—more cases than any other woman. Then in 1972, she joined the EEOC, where she became a mentor to young lawyers.

To help Ruth Weyand with oral argument at the court of appeals, Rosenberg sent Linda Dorian, who had joined the EEOC right after law school. Dorian found Weyand in her well-worn union offices, low on funding and overflowing with files, and set to work going through piles of documents.

While preparing, they kept worrying which judges would sit before them in the appeals court's three-judge panel. They least wanted to face Clement Haynsworth, who not only believed that no law could "relieve females" from the burdens of motherhood but also had become notorious five years earlier when Richard Nixon tried to appoint him to the Supreme Court as part of a so-called southern strategy. His past opinions met opposition from civil rights groups and labor unions. Ethics questions ultimately led to his defeat by the Senate in the first rejection of a Supreme Court nominee in four decades.

Eventually Weyand and Dorian learned that they would argue their case to Haynsworth and two of his allies in that earlier pregnancy decision. GE's lawyers appeared jubilant.

In argument before the court of appeals on January 8, 1975, Weyand and Dorian took turns making parts of the oral argument. One moment that stood out for Dorian came near the end when the GE lawyers had their chance for rebuttal. Dorian, who had given birth to her daughter just before joining the EEOC, felt acutely aware that other women were forced by their employers to choose between a job and a family. GE's lawyer returned to one of the arguments he had used in district court, telling the court of appeals that women were guaranteed the right to abortion and could eliminate any pregnancy by going to a clinic for a "lunch-hour" treatment. A look of horror, Dorian thought, passed across the judges' faces. In her own last chance to speak, feeling sure that the judges saw her as a young woman who might have an infant at home, Dorian struck back. Congress when passing Title VII, Dorian insisted, would never have intended to force a woman to choose between her right to be employed and her right to bear a child.

Despite Dorian's strong finish, Ruth Weyand feared those three judges would hand her a loss, forcing her to appeal. Months passed. While Weyand waited, another shock arrived: the Supreme Court agreed to hear the same legal issue that Weyand had worked so hard to develop in her *General Electric* case. It would hear a case concerning an insurance company called Liberty Mutual, which, like GE, excluded pregnant women from coverage by its disability insurance.

To Weyand, the *Liberty Mutual* case had terrible shortcomings. Unlike the GE case, *Liberty Mutual* reached the Supreme Court with very few details. Based on a single undisputed fact, that Liberty Mutual excluded only pregnancy from its disability coverage, lower courts had ruled that Liberty Mutual had committed sex discrimination in violation of Title VII.

The lawyers for GE shared Ruth Weyand's distaste for this low-fact case. They knew that Liberty Mutual's lawyers had, as one lower court pointed out, offered no "evidentiary facts that could arguably give rise to a defense." If the Supreme Court ruled against Liberty Mutual in this fact-free case, that ruling would probably mean defeat for GE. Hoping that their case could be added to consideration of *Liberty Mutual* by the Supreme Court, GE's lawyers wrote to the court of appeals to ask for a quick decision. Instead, the appeals court announced that it would delay deciding *General Electric* until the Supreme Court decided *Liberty Mutual*.

One of GE's attorneys then went to Weyand with a suggestion that, so far as he knew, had no precedent. Because all attorneys in the GE case wanted their facts before the Supreme Court, they should unite in an effort to leapfrog the indecisive court of appeals. Both sides should file a joint petition to the Supreme Court asking that their case be heard.

Weyand felt sure that her case had better facts than *Liberty Mutual*. Bea Rosenberg at the EEOC agreed. Twenty days after the Supreme Court decided to hear *Liberty Mutual*, and eight days after the court of appeals refused to decide the GE case, a joint petition reached the Supreme Court asking that it hear the GE case in order to gain detailed evidence about the impact of excluding pregnancy.

Apparently stung by this move to bypass it, the court of appeals changed its plan and, within ten days, announced its delayed decision: by a vote of 2–1, with Chief Judge Haynsworth in the majority, it agreed with Ruth Weyand, Linda Dorian, the EEOC guidelines, and the women of GE. Further, the court ruled that the loss in *Geduldig v. Aiello*, Wendy Williams' case, did no damage to Ruth Weyand's GE case. In discussing what the court called "a well-recognized difference of approach in applying constitutional standards under the Equal Protection Clause as in *Geduldig v. Aiello* and in the statutory construction of the 'sex-blind' mandate of Title VII," the court seemed to lecture GE's lawyers on the difference between Williams' problem under the Constitution and Weyand's advantage under Title VII. To escape constitutional condemnation, pregnancy discrimination

need only be "rationally supportable" and that was the situation in *Aiello*. . . . Title VII, however, authorizes no such "rationality" test in determining the propriety of its application. It represents a flat and absolute prohibition against all sex discrimination in conditions of employment.

The decision made a flat condemnation of pregnancy discrimination under Title VII and an absolute distinction between the *General Electric* case and *Geduldig v. Aiello.*

Weyand's case, carefully developed over years, seemed the perfect case to take to the Supreme Court. The justices agreed. They voted to combine *Liberty Mutual* with *General Electric*, to be argued in sequence and considered together.

RUTH WEYAND ROSE TO BEGIN her Supreme Court argument on January 20, 1976, as the last in a two-hour succession of litigators that spanned two days. First had come the attorney for Liberty Mutual, who began and ended by hammering home a simple point: this Court's decision two years before in *Geduldig v. Aiello* settled this case.

The lawyer for Liberty Mutual, Kalvin M. Grove, relied on Justice Stewart's *nonpregnant persons* footnote to make the argument that Ruth Weyand dreaded, following a track laid down by the judge whom Weyand and Linda Dorian had not convinced when they argued at the court of appeals. As Liberty Mutual's lawyer insisted, all discussion hinges, in the words of that judge,

> on whether the exclusion of pregnancy related disability from the disability benefits plan is sex discrimination. If it is not sex discrimination, then . . . there is no Title VII violation.

The lawyer for Sandra Wetzel and the other women suing Liberty Mutual, Howard A. Specter, had little answer to Liberty Mutual's claim that pregnancy discrimination was not sex discrimination. He spent much time reminding the Supreme Court that the record of his case contained few facts and that Liberty Mutual had offered few defenses other than what he called the "very troublesome" case of *Geduldig v. Aiello.*

When he searched for evidence against Liberty Mutual's case, he turned to sections of Ruth Weyand's ever-expanding brief (which he called the "fat yellow one") against GE—now 266 pages long, bound in the traditional yellow cover of plaintiffs' briefs but dwarfing most others in the files of the Supreme Court. He urged the justices to consult Weyand's pages 121–128 (for a history of the Equal Pay Act of 1963) and then to turn back to pages 106–119 (for a history of EEOC statements on pregnancy since 1965). Nothing he said seemed to make *Geduldig v. Aiello* less troublesome.

The attorney for General Electric, Theophil C. Kammholz, rose to address the Court late in the afternoon. He faced only eight justices. Harry Blackmun, who had absented himself from the *Liberty Mutual* case owing to what was understood to be a connection between that insurance company and his former law firm, also chose not to hear the GE case. Kammholz, following Liberty Mutual's strong showing and acknowledging what he called his own "lack of modesty," seemed unworried by the need to win five votes from a shorthanded court. Moving quickly to his *lunch-hour* argument, he declared that modern pregnancies can be reliably planned and readily aborted in what he now called "an in-and-out noon-hour treatment."

If any justices felt offense that GE was offering lunch-break abortion as its answer to workplace pregnancy, their questions showed none. GE's lawyer and the justices moved to a discussion of how much women cost to insure and how much longer women live than men, a discussion that led to easy banter. Female longevity brought women a long return on retirement annuities, which, said one justice, is "one of the good things women have going for them, isn't it?"

"Yes," said Kammholz, "among others, Your Honor."

Laughter filled the court, and GE's lawyer followed his advantage to point to his strongest card, already in play thanks to *Liberty Mutual*: *Geduldig v. Aiello* meant that the Supreme Court had already decided that pregnancy discrimination was not sex discrimination— a company could discriminate legally against the pregnant without discriminating illegally against women.

Ruth Weyand, slight in build, standing before the eight justices of the Court, may have appeared to be standing in something of a hole, dug craftily by the preceding hour of argument by corporate attorneys. Among other problems, she needed to establish that her GE case, which had arrived as a caboose behind *Liberty Mutual*, could add to the Supreme Court's deliberation. To do so, she piled on facts from her voluminous record on pregnancy discrimination and its harm to women who worked at GE and elsewhere: GE's long-ago president believed that women hoped to get married and leave the workforce rather than "recognize the responsibilities of life." GE's disability plan, though excluding pregnancy disability, paid for "anything a man was ever disabled for" including voluntary hair transplants and voluntary cosmetic surgery. GE's women, such as Emma Furch and Sherrie O'Steen, suffered when deprived of disability benefits—losing disability payment for a pulmonary embolism that followed closely after a pregnancy, for example, and waiting in an unheated house for the birth of her child.

Weyand's argument represented the surface of her fat yellow brief. Her case gained depth also from *amicus* briefs by allies who amounted to a who's who of women attorneys working on pregnancy and sex discrimination. Many had written already against GE in the court of appeals in 1975, and then against Liberty Mutual when its case rose ahead of GE's to the Supreme Court, where now their arguments again allied with Weyand's. For the Women's Rights Project of the ACLU, Ruth Bader Ginsburg had teamed with Susan Deller Ross (seven months' pregnant when they filed their brief) to deliver a defense of the EEOC guidelines (which Ross had written) on pregnancy discrimination—and to insist that Title VII demanded that pregnancy discrimination receive rigorous scrutiny rather than the slight scrutiny used by the Court when it ruled that the Constitution did not forbid California's discrimination against the pregnant in *Geduldig v. Aiello.* Wendy Webster Williams, still smarting from losing the Aiello case, teamed with her friend Peter Weiner to deliver a brief that condemned employers who forced women to choose between the chance to work and the right to procreate.

The most valuable brief siding with Ruth Weyand was a short one, just thirty-three pages. It represented the labors at the EEOC of Bea Rosenberg and Linda Dorian. Although Dorian was not arguing in tandem with Weyand, as she had at the court of appeals, she and Rosenberg strove to put the government's arguments behind Weyand at the Supreme Court. Rosenberg had apparently worked, also, to win permission to file any brief supporting Weyand. Solicitor General Robert Bork, whose name would appear as lead author on their brief for the United States and the EEOC, at first, Dorian gathered from Rosenberg, "didn't want the government to participate." Not long after Solicitor General Bork had leapt to national attention in 1973 for firing the special prosecutor investigating President Nixon in Watergate, Bork opposed Ruth Bader Ginsburg's sex discrimination argument in *Wiesenfeld*.

Rosenberg wanted the government to provide a sharper brief than Weyand's fat yellow one. The more Weyand's grew, the more Rosenberg pressed Dorian to "tighten your brief again." What emerged was taut: (1) Title VII forbids excluding pregnancy-related disabilities from a plan that protects employees against other disabilities. (2) The *Geduldig v. Aiello* decision stating that the Constitution permits pregnancy discrimination does not prevent the Court from ruling that Title VII forbids pregnancy discrimination.

Beyond all the briefs in her support, Ruth Weyand had another crucial body of opinions helping her at the Supreme Court. All six courts of appeals that had considered pregnancy benefits under Title VII had ruled that pregnancy discrimination violated Title VII's prohibition on sex discrimination. The many judges of those other federal courts, as Weyand made clear in her brief and in her oral argument to the Court, agreed with her central point: pregnancy discrimination equals sex discrimination.

FOLLOWING HER ORAL ARGUMENT to the Supreme Court, Weyand prepared to wait for the justices' ruling. Two months afterward, she received a surprise: a unanimous Supreme Court threw out *Liberty Mutual*. During oral argument, Justice Rehnquist had asked about procedure in the lower courts. Two months later, answering his own questions, he ruled that the judges in both the district court and the court of appeals, misunderstanding a federal rule, had permitted an appeal to proceed prematurely. The district court needed to do more than rule against Liberty Mutual, as it had; it also needed to decide how much Liberty Mutual must pay in compensation to its female employees. Without that ruling, the decision of the district court could not be appealed. Now Ruth Weyand's GE case, no longer a caboose, had to take the lead against pregnancy discrimination. Another two months later, the Supreme Court finally released its GE opinion. In one sentence, it announced that *General Electric* would be "restored to calendar for reargument."

The need to reargue, the attorneys knew, sent them into little-charted territory. Although a few watershed cases—school desegregation (*Brown v. Board of Education*, argued 1952 and reargued 1953), for example, and liberalized abortion (*Roe v. Wade*, argued 1971 and reargued 1972)—had led the Court to ask attorneys to argue a case again on a subsequent year's calendar, rearguments were uncommon. Further, the reasons had seemed clear for those famous rearguments. When the Court asked for reargument in the school desegregation cases of the 1950s, the justices provided lengthy questions to guide attorneys. The first abortion argument occurred before a severely shorthanded Court that was awaiting the arrival in early 1972 of Justices Powell and Rehnquist. For *General Electric*, however, the attorneys received no guidance.

Speculation among attorneys focused on the absence of Justice Blackmun from the first oral argument. If he skipped the GE argument because of a conflict of interest involving Liberty Mutual, they guessed he would take part at a new argument.

Blackmun's notes, hidden until the release of his Supreme Court papers in 2004, showed the impact of, if not the reason for, his missing vote. At the justices' conference, he tallied the votes of a split court: four voting with Weyand (Stevens, Brennan, Marshall, and Powell), three voting with GE (Burger, White, and Rehnquist), and Potter Stewart seemingly so torn that Blackmun marked his vote as "pass." On the one hand, Stewart believed his own opinion in *Geduldig v. Aiello* meant that women had suffered "no discrimination." But he noted that the Court had ruled in 1971 that EEOC guidelines deserved "great deference." As long as Stewart wavered, Weyand held her lead.

As the second oral argument approached, Blackmun continued to ask himself (with no further explanation in his papers), "Do I recuse"? He was convinced by late summer that the Court was split "4 to 4" on the GE case, suggesting his vote would decide. He expressed long-standing doubts about Potter Stewart's nonpregnant-persons opinion in *Geduldig v. Aiello*, which he resented as "a bit of strong-arming in typical PS fashion." As he mulled, Blackmun wound up jousting with one of his clerks, Donna Murasky—only his second woman clerk among the seventeen clerks who had worked with him on the Court. In a bench memo she typed in preparation for the new GE argument, she called the company's history of benefits "male-oriented." Blackmun penciled, in her memo's margins, "oh, come now?" To her comment that GE had a policy of forcing pregnant women to stop work, he penciled, "so—". Arguing that Blackmun should side with Weyand, she stated that "I have no idea why Congress bothered to include the sex discrimination provision of the Act" if that provision did not protect pregnant women. Blackmun penciled, "Donna overstates, methinks."

At the EEOC Bea Rosenberg, unaware that Weyand had a young ally in the chambers of the Court's pivotal justice, sought to assure Weyand that she did not stand alone at reargument. When Rosenberg urged the U.S. government to join Weyand in oral argument, the Office of the Solicitor General agreed but did not send one of its own attorneys. Instead, Rosenberg got an odd substitute. From within the Justice Department came an assistant attorney general for civil rights, Stanley J. Pottinger. "OK, Linda, here's the deal," Rosenberg explained, as Dorian recalled later. "You write the brief, and Stan Pottinger is arguing the case, and it's our job to get together any materials he needs."

Stanley Pottinger, articulate and charismatic, was developing a reputation for making sex discrimination a priority in the Civil Rights Division. He had pressed to end discrimination against women in universities, helping to make 1972 what Ruth Bader Ginsburg called "the year of *the* woman," and by 1976 had begun a multiyear romance with Gloria Steinem, the editor of *Ms.* magazine. Although Pottinger believed that pregnancy discrimination constituted discrimination against women, in his role as assistant attorney general he rarely argued a case. Baffled when invited to join the reargument with Weyand, he asked representatives of the solicitor general for their reasoning.

He was being offered a "doomed mission," Pottinger learned from the solicitor general's office. He need not take the offer. But if he argued, the advantages included these: he would make a case that he believed in; the Court would see that the government stood with Weyand; and the staff of the solicitor general would avoid arguing a loser. Pottinger accepted.

IN OPENING THE REARGUMENT at the Supreme Court on October 13, 1976, GE's lawyer was able to move smoothly over his well-paved arguments. Women plan pregnancies. Pregnancy is unique. Women cost more to insure than men. To give disability payments for pregnancy would be to provide "special severance pay to women only" because many pregnant women plan not to return to GE after childbirth. (In an error that the justices did not catch, he stated women's return rate as only 40 percent. In fact, 40 percent was the figure for those who did *not* return, and as Weyand often pointed out, 40 percent equaled GE's annual turnover rate for all employees.) Continuing almost unchallenged by questions, Kammholz hit his key points. Congress in 1964 and the EEOC in 1965 believed that Title VII did not cover pregnancy. Most important, thanks to Justice Stewart's famous footnote 20 in *Geduldig v. Aiello*, GE's pregnancy discrimination could not be called sex discrimination and so "there is . . . no sex discrimination in our case."

One justice who challenged Kammholz was Blackmun, who, aware his vote was crucial, pressed hard. His questions confirmed that GE excluded medical disabilities that arose as complications of pregnancy, that GE excluded no medical condition other than pregnancy, that GE covered hospitalization for such voluntary procedures as cosmetic surgery, and that GE did not exclude diseases such as sickle-cell anemia that could be suffered disproportionately by a distinct racial group.

Ruth Weyand opened her fifteen minutes of oral argument with efforts to follow the Court's apparent interest. Taking an opening provided by Justice Blackmun, she pointed out that "there is not a single thing that a man gets disabled by that GE does not cover fully." She drew also on old themes, such as Sherrie O'Steen awaiting childbirth in an unlighted and unheated house. She corrected GE's erroneous claim that most women leave work after pregnancy, and then, with time short to challenge claims made by GE in a new "reply brief" that answered her ninety-five-page "supplemental brief," Weyand asked permission to file yet another brief. At this late point she hit her first major challenge, from a bad direction. Justice Blackmun said he had already been asked to read some 250 pages of her briefing. Did she, he challenged her, "expect that we can absorb that"?

As Ruth Weyand backpedaled, expressing regrets, Blackmun pressed: "Are you going to file another 100 pages?" More backpedaling led to his next question: Did she think that her "61 pages of facts" met the Supreme Court requirement for a "concise statement"? After stating more "regret that you haven't found the brief helpful," Ruth Weyand concluded her argument, turning red in the face, struggling to pull her papers together, saying only, "I'm sorry."

The task of pulling the case together now fell to Stanley Pottinger. Opening his oral argument, Pottinger managed six words: "Mr. Chief Justice, and may it . . ." Justice Byron White interrupted. What rule, he demanded, permitted Pottinger to argue this case "without an order of the Court?"

Dumbfounded, Pottinger began babbling: He said he had not addressed any rule. He understood he was permitted to argue. The government had interpreted the rules of the Court "by indirection." Pottinger bluffed. He had no idea—and never would—what rule or order White cared about. Attacked upon opening his mouth, Pottinger thought to himself, as he recalled years later, "Boy this is just exactly what everyone predicted." The justices were signaling, thought Pottinger, "we don't want you here, and we're going to blow you out of the water with our opinions. But you just keep on truckin'."

So he did. Taking aim at the weakness identified by Justice Blackmun's question about why GE paid for disability from planned cosmetic surgery but not planned pregnancy, he began defining the purpose of Title VII.

Now Justice Stewart cut Pottinger off, raising Stewart's much-discussed opinion in *Geduldig v. Aiello*—and then, for some reason, veering to discuss not interpretation but pronunciation. Carolyn Aiello's last name stumped him, said the justice. He added extra syllables. He pronounced it *eye-lee-able*.

Pottinger offered *eye-yellow* as a solution to Stewart's problem. Then Pottinger tried to say why the Aiello case did not doom his case. Stewart offered little chance. *Geduldig v. Aiello* made clear, the justice asserted, that a "pregnancy exclusion was not a sex discrimination." Trucking on, Pottinger reminded the justices of *Griggs*, the 1971 case urging great deference to EEOC guidelines. Questions came fast. Justices seemed unconvinced. Pottinger sat down feeling he had accomplished his doomed mission.

The argument's twists confused Linda Dorian, who left the courtroom thinking that Weyand had lost her poise but Pottinger had kept his. Why, she asked Rosenberg, had Pottinger's first words faced such a blistering attack from Justice White? "Linda," Bea replied, as Dorian recalled, "he didn't want the government involved. He wanted to be free to rule against us, for the plaintiffs, without having to rule against the government." White seemed a lost vote, along with Stewart. Blackmun, who chastised Weyand about padding her briefs but also probed GE about covering cosmetic surgery, remained a hope. Scribbling notes during oral argument, he had scored Weyand worse than both men, calling her "pretty bad." But he had listened closely to Pottinger, taking more notes on his argument than on those of the other two attorneys combined.

THE *GENERAL ELECTRIC* DECISION followed oral argument by only two months. On December 7, 1976, the Supreme Court announced its decision.

Justice Rehnquist had emerged from the justices' conference in October with the chance to draft for an unsure majority. Powell, while inclining against the women in conference, said he was "still not firm." Stewart, swinging away from deference to the EEOC, was now opining that his *Geduldig v. Aiello* opinion "still is correct." But Justice Brennan, preparing to dissent along with Marshall and Stevens, was going to work on a draft that seemed designed to lure Stewart back by arguing that years of careful EEOC study "culminated" in the 1972 EEOC guidelines against pregnancy discrimination. And although Blackmun seemed ready to vote against the women, he faced new opposition in his chambers. Diane Wood, the third woman clerk he ever hired, went to work on him—opposing Rehnquist's draft and proposing mitigating changes. Allied with her and convinced that Rehnquist did not yet have five votes, another Blackmun clerk, William Block, drafted similar changes, which Blackmun proposed to Rehnquist with a hint that Blackmun's vote depended on them. Stewart urged Rehnquist to follow Blackmun's softening proposals.

Rehnquist rebuffed them all. Apparently he had his votes. Rehnquist's unmitigated opinion, in final form as in draft, defined the court's task as straightforward: rule that the decision in *Geduldig v. Aiello* guaranteed General Electric's win. To meet this task, he set out to show that the intent of Congress in 1964 was misrepresented by the EEOC pregnancy guidelines of 1972 and well represented by the Supreme Court's *Geduldig* decision of 1974.

Discrediting the EEOC proved easy. In his opinion, Rehnquist reprinted letters (dug up by GE) from the mid-1960s when the EEOC feared becoming known as the "sex commission." In 1966, the EEOC general counsel had written that Title VII permitted companies to cut off salaries to disabled workers when their disabilities "result from pregnancy and childbirth." This was the same general counsel, Charles Duncan, who had labeled Fuentes a "sex maniac" for urging the commission to fight sex discrimination. Similarly, Duncan had written for the EEOC that a corporate insurance plan could, without violating Title VII, "simply exclude maternity as a covered risk." Surely, insisted Justice Rehnquist, the intent of Congress in 1964 finds truer representation in EEOC interpretations of 1966 than in revisions of 1972.

Rehnquist sought to align that intent with his majority on the current Supreme Court. What Congress in 1964 intended by *discrimination* was left unclear, he contended, because Congress left *discrimination* undefined in Title VII. Faced with that congressional lapse, where should the Supreme Court look for congressional intent concerning the meaning of *discrimination* under Title VII—and whether Title VII proscribed pregnancy discrimination? Why not look, Justice

Rehnquist suggested, to the Court's own decisions construing the equal protection clause of the Fourteenth Amendment? After all, the contexts—by which he presumably meant the Fourteenth Amendment and Title VII—were "not wholly dissimilar."

That double negative (*not . . . dis-*), plus softening (*not wholly dis-*), sufficed for Justice Rehnquist. It blurred distinctions between law shaped by constitutional amendment and by congressional legislation, and distinctions between the 1860s and the 1960s. His next sentence leapt to *Geduldig v. Aiello* and his Court's decision that California had a constitutional right to discriminate against pregnant women. Since the Aiello case had analyzed a "strikingly similar" exclusion of pregnancy benefits in the "not wholly dissimilar" context of the Fourteenth Amendment, that case seemed relevant. The Court's *Geduldig v. Aiello* decision in 1974 could help the Court determine in 1976 what Congress intended in 1964 when it forbade companies "to discriminate . . . because of . . . sex."

Justice Stevens resisted. "Of course," he wrote in dissent, "when it enacted Title VII of the Civil Rights Act of 1964, Congress could not possibly have relied on language which this Court was to use a decade later."

His dissent did not suffice. Five other justices—Burger, Stewart, White, Powell, and Blackmun—joined Rehnquist in favor of General Electric. They confirmed that Stewart's footnote 20 in *Geduldig v. Aiello* expressed the intent of Congress: American law permits discrimination that favors nonpregnant persons and hurts pregnant women. Case closed.

8

***

The Final Pregnancy Battle:
Beyond the Supreme Court

The decision's date felt apt—Pearl Harbor Day in 1976, the anniversary of a day of infamy. "Women's Rights Movement Is Dealt Major Blow," said the *New York Times'* headline atop page one. Women's groups, said a subhead, felt "shock and anger."

Ruth Weyand, as losing attorney, had to meet the press. She did not mope. She laid a plan. Listening as her GE defeat neared, Weyand had heard opposing lawyers and even judges telling her that she didn't belong in court. Long ago, the lone dissenter on the court of appeals had started a pattern. Although federal courts could not help Weyand, he insisted (since the Supreme Court said pregnancy discrimination is not sex discrimination), Congress could. If it wished, Congress could "legislate in favor of pregnant women." After all, he jabbed, "legislatures have made less rational classifications for centuries."

As Weyand awaited the start of her first *General Electric* case at the Supreme Court, an opposing lawyer for Liberty Mutual also acknowledged that Congress could legislate to protect pregnant women—but "Congress did not so choose." Within an hour, Weyand heard a similar nod to Congress from GE's lawyer. Responsibility to help pregnant women should fall not on the Court, he insisted, but on "the folks" in Congress. And Justice Blackmun nine months later, while privately mulling what he thought would be his deciding vote, had been dictating and scribbling to himself a reminder: "if we are wrong, Congress can change."

As she read Justice Rehnquist's *General Electric* opinion, Weyand saw the capstone. Just as his brethren in *Geduldig v. Aiello* had left California's lawmakers constitutionally free to discriminate against pregnant persons, Rehnquist said, his *General Electric* decision left other lawmakers free to do the opposite. But the lawmakers in Congress, he insisted, "did not intend" with Title VII to outlaw pregnancy discrimination.

Weyand, though beaten in court, handed reporters a hastily typed press release and a new plan: she and her allies would "move to get Congress to enact legislation making discrimination because of pregnancy equally as illegal as other discrimination because of sex, race, nationality, or religion." The scheme, like the phrasing, sounded rough. No women's group had ever asked (much less "moved to get") Congress to pass a statute to reverse a Court decision.

Newspaper reporters nonetheless followed Weyand's lead. A *New York Times* subhead read, "Congress Free to Act." An Associated Press wire story, emerging from Teletype machines into newsrooms around the nation, gave half its space to Weyand's press release and its supporters.

Hidden from the news was some long-term planning. At EEOC headquarters, Linda Dorian, Sonia Fuentes, and their so-called pregnancy working group had already decided that a loss at the Supreme Court would force them to try Congress. At the Civil Rights Division of the Justice Department, Stan Pottinger understood that he had made his doomed mission to the Court as a self-sacrificing pawn. He took a "dive," as he recalled later, to show Congress that the Supreme Court was rebuffing not just the clients of Ruth Weyand but also the government of the United States.

Within days of the defeat at the Supreme Court, Ruth Weyand and Susan Deller Ross became co-chairs of a new organization: the Campaign to End Discrimination Against Pregnant Workers. Within a week they had gathered congressional staffers and representatives of women's groups for a meeting that the *New York Times* reported under the headline "Feminist Leaders Plan Coalition for Law Aiding Pregnant Women."

Within two months of the Supreme Court defeat, Ruth Bader Ginsburg (writing as professor of law at Columbia) and Susan Deller Ross (as staff attorney at the ACLU) had published an op-ed article in the *New York Times.* "If it is not sex discrimination to exclude pregnant women from standard fringe-benefit programs," they challenged the Court, "is it sex discrimination to fire pregnant women" or to "refuse to hire them"? Fortunately, they concluded, Congress could protect America from the Supreme Court's answers because "legislative overruling is available when the Court misconceives Congressional purpose." They challenged Congress to reverse the Court and thus to demonstrate "the nation's current commitment to achievement of genuinely equal opportunity for women."

Within four months of the Supreme Court defeat, Susan Deller Ross and Wendy Webster Williams (now an assistant professor of law at Georgetown University) were testifying before a committee of the House of Representatives. Working as a team, they had stayed up most of the night before their testimony. Williams was typing her speech with a recently broken wrist—not so disabling as the ankle injury that forced her to argue *Geduldig v. Aiello* on crutches at the Supreme Court. They were testifying on behalf of congressional legislation that they, Weyand, and the Campaign had drafted. Just introduced by a group of U.S. representatives and senators, their bill's language would amend Title VII, overturn the Supreme Court's decision against Weyand, and "prohibit sex discrimination on the basis of pregnancy."

To the Congress, Williams restated part of her argument in *Geduldig v. Aiello* and went beyond it to describe a national embarrassment: The plight of America's working women like Sherrie O'Steen—sent away by GE without pay to bear her child—put Americans "alone among working women in the industrialized countries of the world." Anywhere in Europe, for example, a working mother, disabled briefly while giving birth, would have received some portion of her salary.

Susan Deller Ross defended the pregnancy guidelines of the EEOC, largely drafted by her and rebuffed by the Court. Because the Court's logic could extend to any discrimination against pregnant women, including firing them, the Supreme Court had "virtually nullified the sex discrimination provisions of Title VII." The bill before Congress, she explained, would correct the Supreme Court's error and would restore the original intent of Congress when it passed Title VII: that "all sex discrimination be eliminated, root and branch, from the marketplace."

Congressmen proclaimed their agreement with Ross and their outrage at Rehnquist's claim about what they "did not intend." Representative Augustus Hawkins of California, one of the new bill's hundred congressional cosponsors, made clear that he aimed to "overturn" the Court's decision in order to fix its mistake. "I know that when I cast my vote for Title VII" in 1964, he announced to Congress, "I understood that protection to include pregnancy." In roll call votes, Congress made its intent clear: 75 votes to 11 in the Senate, 376 to 43 in the House.

Less than two years after the Supreme Court's decision against Ruth Weyand and the women of General Electric, Congress passed and President Jimmy Carter signed the Pregnancy Discrimination Act of 1978. In few words, it stated the obvious: pregnancy discrimination is illegal sex discrimination.

Through years of fighting, women won in the Justice Department and in the Equal Employment Opportunity Commission. They won in all the courts of appeals that heard their case. They won in eighteen district courts. They won in Congress. Only the Supreme Court had blocked their way.

Part Three

LAWYERING

(1968–1984)

9

———+———

A Problem in the Profession

In 1968, Diane Blank wanted to be a lawyer, and her road ahead seemed clear. She had won admission to New York University School of Law.

Blank arrived at NYU and in *Bride's* magazine at the same moment. In the fall 1968 issue of *Bride's*, there she was, a recent graduate of Barnard College. While her new husband-the-law-student beamed, she hugged him, with both their wedding bands prominent in the foreground. While he sat at the kitchen table, in what a caption called their tiny apartment "furnished with castoffs," she stood at a stove. While he showed her a typed page, she smiled with appreciation. While he strode with briefcase and tweed jacket down the front steps of their apartment building, apparently off to a day at Fordham Law School, she reached to hold his hand; she stepped gingerly and looked—as shot from below by the *Bride's* photographer—like a very leggy blonde.

"SUCCESS AS A STUDENT'S WIFE" proclaimed the *Bride's* headline, larger than any of the article's photos. Beneath it, Blank and a few other brides told stories of working so a husband could get a college degree, study full-time, or become the lawyer that he had dreamed of being "since he was a little boy." But small print in one caption revealed a challenging story not told by the headline: Diane Blank told *Bride's* that she would "never be satisfied just being a housewife." She wanted success as a lawyer. She was starting on a path that would change the behavior of some of America's most powerful law firms.

While still in college at Barnard, Blank began taking courses in business and constitutional law at Columbia Law School. She liked law. She did well. Grading at Columbia Law, she thought, was easier than at Barnard College. And compared to the infinite vagaries posed by art and literature, law seemed knowable, she thought, "finite."

At NYU, she went right to work, making dean's list in her first year. She planned a series of second-year courses that would be heavy with business law: accounting, corporations, taxation, securities. For the summer before that second year, she won a job at a prestigious New York law firm. It had both a venerable name—Cadwalader, Wickersham & Taft—and a premiere address, One Wall Street. It called her a "law clerk"—a fancy name, she knew, for work in the steno pool. But it was the first step toward getting hired for a second internship as a "summer associate" and then after graduation as a full-time "associate"—the title that most law firms give a young lawyer who has not ascended to the exalted position of "partner" in the firm.

Diane Blank's route via Barnard and NYU to Wall Street was carrying her far from her hometown, on the "wrong side of the tracks," as she said, in Pawtucket, Rhode Island, and at East Providence Senior High School. Her father had died when she was young. Her mother, who had just a high school education, got work as a bookkeeper at a dairy. At home, money was scarce.

Cadwalader occupied a richer realm. The firm worked its law clerks hard but also introduced them to the social life ahead. Some gatherings took place at private country clubs, where Blank started learning games like tennis. At one of these social events another Cadwalader summer clerk took her aside to ask, How could women ever expect to be equal? Weren't women out of commission five days a month?

But he was just a young clerk talking. What surprised her came from the firm's partners. Because she had secretarial skills and could do legal citation, she began to get pulled from the steno pool to substitute for the secretaries who worked directly with the partners. The first partner Blank worked with sat her down to talk. Did her husband, he wondered, want her to be a lawyer? And who would cook her husband's dinner?

She had answers: Her husband's father had urged her toward law. Her husband ate late at night. But her answers felt glancing. The partner had doubts that a wife should be a lawyer.

WORKING WITH DIANE BLANK that summer at Cadwalader was a classmate, Mary F. Kelly, who, a few months later, would help introduce courses on women in the law to Rutgers and to Ruth Bader Ginsburg. Like Blank, Kelly began encountering odd reactions at Cadwalader, particularly from the one partner with whom she worked most often.

Kelly had gone to law school to escape being a secretary. She had graduated with honors in 1965 from the College of New Rochelle, whose self-proclaimed mission was to produce "valiant Christian women." She quickly won jobs that created an impressive resume: executive director of the New Jersey Americans for Democratic Action and caseworker and later fiscal auditor for welfare departments in New York. But in all these jobs, she mostly typed. Kelly was a great typist, and employers wanted her to be their great secretary.

Law, she thought, offered the chance to do serious work in areas she cared about: politics generally and, perhaps, even the legal and political struggle to stop the Vietnam War. With backing from an attorney with whom she had worked at Americans for Democratic Action, Kelly won admission to his alma mater, the NYU School of Law.

Arriving in the fall of 1968 with Blank, Kelly joined the first large class of NYU law women—accounting for 20 percent of the entering students. She quickly grasped that NYU had admitted women because men were bound for Vietnam. Faculty members sent clues, Kelly sensed, that women didn't belong. One well-known NYU professor of civil procedure had his "ladies day" when he grilled only women students. Other professors used sexually charged legal cases, full of abortion and rape and sexual imagery, to pique the interest of male students.

Crucial to Mary Kelly, who was struggling to put herself through

law school, NYU had long excluded women from its richest scholarship. The battle in the fall of 1968 to open the prestigious Root-Tilden
Scholarship to women, against resistance by some law professors,
became the hook that pulled Kelly into the newly formed Women's
Rights Committee. But most professors responded well, she thought.
Quickly the faculty voted to open the scholarship to women. Law
schools seemed ready to change.

But were law firms ready? At Cadwalader with Blank in their first
summer after law school, Kelly found herself working mostly again
as a secretary. She was amused, thinking, This is exactly what I went
to law school not to do. Late that summer, as Kelly was preparing to
return to NYU, the law partner she had worked with most took her
aside. He made her an offer. Would she stay at Cadwalader, Wickersham & Taft? Would she continue with him? He said she would be
a wonderful secretary. The partner meant well. So did Diane Blank's
partner, who thought a wife should cook for her husband.

EARLY IN THEIR SECOND YEARS, most law students began interviewing for the next summer's job. In late September, Blank requested an
interview with the firm Shearman & Sterling, of 53 Wall Street. A
few days later, a list posted at NYU's placement office told her the
firm had chosen not to interview her. She walked off feeling personal
rejection but, she later insisted, nothing more. After running into
a few of her female classmates who had also missed the cut for an
interview, she began to wonder if their rejection was merely personal.
The women got together in their usual place: the women's lounge at
the ladies' bathroom at the law school. For months it had been the
unofficial meeting place of the Women's Rights Committee—a place
where notices could be posted, where young mothers could nurse
babies, and where everyone could talk.

She and four classmates decided to return to the placement office to
look closely at the list. From sixty-seven students who applied for interviews, Shearman & Sterling had selected forty. Three were women,
all in Diane Blank's class. Looking closely at her class, she saw that
forty-four men and nine women had applied; for interviews, the firm

chose half the men but a third of the women. The three chosen women shared a single qualification: all had been elected to the same honor, membership in the *NYU Law Review*. A closer look showed that if Shearman & Sterling had asked to interview only men who were on the *Law Review*, it would be interviewing almost exactly the same proportion of men as women: a third of those who applied. But to that list of *Law Review* students, the firm added seven more men and no more women. Blank noticed that three of those seven additional men worked for another legal review, the *Annual Survey of American Law*. But so did she, as an articles editor, and those three men worked as writers under her. Blank and her fellow students started to wonder if Shearman & Sterling was discriminating in favor of men.

By now it was October 2—the day before the firm's interviewers would arrive on campus. Blank and four of her classmates asked for a meeting with C. Delos Putz, an assistant dean who was in charge of placement. Meeting at four o'clock in his office, the five women described to Dean Putz what they thought was sex-based discrimination and told him they expected something to be done. Putz immediately phoned Shearman & Sterling. He described the accusations and asked one of their attorneys to stay at the offices until he could check the accusations more fully. He then gave the five students the resumes of all NYU students who had applied to Shearman & Sterling. For an hour, the women scoured the data. Finally, they decided, the evidence was "equivocal." The resumes showed too many variables to make a strong case of discrimination.

Dean Putz phoned Shearman & Sterling, relayed the students' opinion, and explained that the women applicants nonetheless would appreciate the chance to confer with members of the Shearman & Sterling hiring committee. It agreed. The firm would give a courtesy interview the next day to Diane Blank, as a representative of the five women. Four days later, the chairs of the hiring committee would meet with concerned NYU law students in the office of Dean Putz.

The night after that first meeting with Dean Putz, Blank stayed up late looking again through all the resumes. She drew up pages of charts to compare credentials. In column after column with neatly printed headings such as *Law Review* and *Dean's List* and *Moot*

Court, she checked off obvious credentials for all fifty-three of her classmates, whether granted or denied interviews. In further columns called *Work Experience*, *College & Major*, and *Other*, she looked for further strengths such as "criminal law intern," "Harvard," or "fluent in French."

When she tallied her results, the "whole situation looked equivocal." Given the "small numbers involved," as she recalled a few months later, "it seemed difficult to prove any clear-cut discrimination in the interview selection process." But the key disparity remained: after deciding to interview all the women and men who had made law review, Shearman & Sterling found reasons to interview extra men but no more women. Why?

The next day, before the interviews of the job candidates from NYU law, Blank was ushered in to meet a Shearman & Sterling interviewer, R. Bruce MacWhorter. This was not a job interview. Although Blank did not pretend she hoped for a job with Shearman & Sterling, she did ask the question that had dominated her late-night chart-making: what did Shearman & Sterling look for in a resume? MacWhorter, according to Blank's memo notes taken at the meeting, said that Shearman & Sterling "looked first for Law Review experience."

Blank knew that. But what else did the firm look for? Next, said MacWhorter, came evidence of maturity and responsibility. What sort of evidence? "A position of command in the military," he suggested. Blank, in all her charts, had not made a column for *military*—a bastion of discrimination in favor of males and utterly legal.

Four days later, Blank was able to continue the conversation in Dean Putz's office with MacWhorter and two chairmen of the hiring committee. One of the chairs added yet another column that Blank had not created on her chart: *emissary*. In selecting second-year students to work for the summer, he said, they sought students who would act as emissaries by praising Shearman & Sterling to other students at NYU. The hiring committee chair then explained, as Blank recalled later, that "this emissary role could best be filled by a single (not married) male who lived in the school dormitories and who participated in extracurricular activities so that he had a great deal of contact with his fellow students." Blank countered that women were outnumbered by men at NYU law by about four to one. Surrounded by NYU men hungry for the company of women, Blank explained, NYU women had lots of contact with fellow students.

That day's conversations revealed still more about Shearman & Sterling. An NYU student asked why seven of the firm's nine women attorneys worked in a single part of the firm's practice—Trusts and Estates. One of the hiring-committee chairs explained that women are specially suited for such work because they work well with widows and orphans. Also, whereas no corporate client ever requested a woman attorney, some women were requested by clients in Trusts and Estates.

Earlier, MacWhorter had told Blank that an opening might be found for a woman in litigation, the high-profile work that usually culminated in oral arguments before judges and sometimes juries. Shearman & Sterling would welcome a woman in this mostly male specialty because, according to Blank's record of their conversation, a woman could be hired with the confidence that "a woman would never have to appear in court"; she could write briefs and stay unseen.

Another NYU student asked why no woman attorney at Shearman & Sterling, even those employed for more than two decades, had ever become a partner. An attorney explained that these women had special technical drafting abilities, but did not say why such special abilities did not lead to partnership. Another NYU student asked whether the firm let a woman do work that required travel. One of the chairs said no. The concern, Blank gathered, was adultery. Lawyers' wives might object if husbands traveled for work with female attorneys. When asked whether women attorneys were invited to join men at the firm's summer outing to a Long Island country club, a chair said they were not. "But," a chair added, "the ladies have their own little luncheon party on that day, have a few drinks, and enjoy themselves thoroughly."

SUCH PREJUDICE WAS NOT NEWS, of course, to women who had struggled to enter the law in years gone by. Ruth Bader Ginsburg could not, when she graduated from law school in 1959, get an interview for a Supreme Court clerkship. Sandra Day O'Connor, in her only law firm interview after she graduated in 1952 near the top of her class at Stanford Law, was told that good typing might win her a job as a legal secretary—an offer she did not receive. And Ruth Weyand, after graduating from the University of Chicago Law School in 1932, was forced to sign her work "R. Weyand" and prohibited from showing herself in court.

To the administration of NYU law school in the late 1960s, discrimination against women remained familiar. A year earlier, in the student newspaper, one of Dean Putz's colleagues in the placement office had discussed what he called "the prejudice encountered by girl students seeking employment." Fortunately, this dean thought he saw an answer, for at least a year or two. With the Vietnam War growing worse, men were being drafted. With men unavailable, the dean predicted, "more female students will be hired." But law (unlike war) seemed to offer no answer to discrimination against women by lawyers. Law firms discriminated legally.

But what about the Civil Rights Act of 1964? Its pivotal section, Title VII, declared illegal an employer's refusal to hire any individual because of her sex. (Employers also could not refuse because of race, color, religion, or national origin.) Did Title VII make a difference in the battle against law firm discrimination? Was law firm discrimination illegal? Did firms' treatment of women amount, as Shearman & Sterling apparently supposed, to the way of the world? Or could that treatment generate, as NYU's young law women wondered, a federal case? In the fall of 1969, five years after the passage of the Civil Rights Act, no one knew.

In late October, a Shearman & Sterling interviewer at the University of Chicago collided with another law student, Nancy Grossman. Giving her only a brief interview (according to a memo she typed that afternoon), he expressed doubt whether his firm that year would "have an opening for a woman." Such openings depended, she gathered, on the needs of Trusts and Estates, where he said the firm's few women "are traditionally placed." Grossman's experience led the university's director of placement, Nicholas J. Bosen, to write (in a letter that he circulated to the placement offices of Yale, Harvard, and Columbia) to Shearman & Sterling asking if her account was correct and, if so, "when do you plan to change the terms of hiring and conditions of employment for women?"

One of the hiring-committee chairs from Shearman & Sterling who had appeared at NYU now had another fire to put out. Replying to the Chicago dean, he denied discrimination but not the claims about where his firm had placed women attorneys, except to add that one now worked on taxes. His strongest defense came via his portrayal of the NYU incident: At a law school (which he left unnamed), he said, allegations against a number of New York firms (unnamed) had led three Shearman & Sterling partners (unnamed) to appear before a group of "female activists." As a result, he concluded, "the charge of discrimination against this firm was found" (by someone unnamed) "to be unsubstantiated."

Chicago's placement dean quickly backed down, sending out letters saying that the "allegations in this case are unwarranted." To the interviewer from Shearman & Sterling, the dean wrote a lengthy apology. He referred to his law school's "most vocal" women and to the "enormous pressures from students." He hoped his school's dealings with Shearman & Sterling had "not suffered irreparable damage."

Unsatisfied, Chicago students sent Nancy Grossman's memo to placement offices at other law schools, including NYU, and filed a charge of discrimination with the EEOC. They charged their law school with operating "a patently discriminatory hiring service." It had "actively supported the discriminatory practice of law firms" by inviting them to use law school placement facilities. When the women of NYU started receiving copies of the Chicago Law correspondence, they were surprised to read that Shearman & Sterling was offering its meeting at NYU as evidence that a charge of discrimination had been "found" unsubstantiated.

WOMEN FROM DIFFERENT LAW SCHOOLS needed to exchange their stories and their findings. One fall day in 1969 in Diane Blank's kitchen, Blank and Jan Goodman (who had played a key role in opening the Root-Tilden Scholarship to women) had an idea: Let's get

women together. Let's gather stories. Let's hold a national conference
of women law students. They set the date: April 1970. Place: NYU
School of Law.

Just as the idea for an NYU-hosted conference of women law students was forming, another legal conference came to New York: the
annual conference of the Association of American Law Schools. Each
December the association gathered hundreds of law school teachers and
administrators from around the nation to discuss issues in legal education. At this year's conference, Dean Robert McKay of NYU urged
the association to create a committee on women and the law in order
to investigate, as his students wished, sex-based discrimination in the
legal profession. The Association of American Law Schools refused.

Spurred by this refusal, the NYU Women's Rights Committee
decided to conduct its own study. Using addresses it could gather
from sources including women's organizations and the New York
City phone book, it mailed 700 questionnaires to women practicing
law in New York. By February, it had 77 answers. The responses
were skewed in predictable ways: More than 50 percent (39) of the
respondents had graduated from NYU or Columbia law school, and
almost 50 percent (38) had received law degrees in the past decade.
But they were skewed in at least one surprising way, toward academic
excellence: almost a third (24) reported graduating in the top tenth of
their law school classes or making law review (or both).

From a mix of experience and lore, the Women's Rights Committee
had offered a series of questions about what women might have heard
when interviewing for work as lawyers. Of the seventy-seven women
who answered the questionnaire, nine reported being told in law firm
interviews that women do not become partners at the firm. Thirteen
heard a version of "we just hired a woman and couldn't hire another."
Fifteen heard that "we hire some women, but not many." Twenty-two
recalled being asked, "Are you planning to have children?" Twenty-
six women—more than a third of those responding—heard "we don't
like to hire women" (or at least not "many" women).

The overall data aligned with anecdotes offered by the respondents.
A woman who graduated magna cum laude from her law school in
1969 was turned down for jobs by two federal judges because "they or

their male law clerks did not wish to work for extended periods with a woman." A woman who graduated in 1967 recalled being turned away by several law firms because she would "distract men from their jobs." Other reasons for job refusals included:

> Clients wouldn't like it.
> Partners' wives wouldn't like it.
> Secretaries won't take orders from a woman.
> You won't have anyone to eat lunch with—the only other women
>   we have are secretaries.

If the study had a bright side, it revealed that women who obtained legal work found that on-the-job discrimination seemed less formidable than job-hunting discrimination.

Still, a number said they had encountered daunting law firm policies. Of the seventy-seven respondents, seven had been excluded from professional meetings because they were women. Ten had been excluded from their employer's social events because they were women. Eight had been urged away from specific work, and nine had been urged toward such specialties as trusts and estates. Fourteen understood that their firms had lower salary scales for women than for men. Sixteen—more than 20 percent of the respondents—understood that their employers would not promote women to partnerships or top administrative posts.

Many anecdotes, which the Women's Rights Committee grouped under "humiliation on the job," described collisions of the social with the professional. A woman attorney who attended a meeting at the "men-only" dining room of the Harvard Club was asked—"since you're here"—to switch to an inconspicuous seat at the table. A woman going to a meeting at another university club was stopped by a guard, who separated her from her male colleagues. He insisted that she use the "women's staircase" instead of the men's. She invited her colleagues to continue their conversation by joining her on the women's staircase, as permitted by club rules. They blushed but would not walk with her. A number of stories surfaced about exclusion of women from social events, such as Shearman & Sterling's country club outings. One respondent told a story about being excluded from the firm's annual affair, a gambling evening. Instead of inviting her to join her law partners, her firm gave her a free night on the town with her husband. Other anecdotes narrated head-on, professional collisions. At a bar association meeting, a male judge told a woman lawyer that "women don't belong at bar association meetings." A judge who wanted to exclude women attorneys from the professional meetings of their field seemed to judge women unready to join the ranks of lawyers.

At about the time in early 1970 that the Women's Rights Committee was compiling its "Pilot Study of Sex Based Discrimination in the Legal Profession," it hosted two prominent women attorneys for speeches to the law school. Doris Sassower, former president of the New York Women's Bar Association, offered comparative statistics concerning women's work as attorneys. In a 1968 issue of the journal *TRIAL*, she had compared professional representation among women and minority groups: "One out of every 7300 Negroes has managed to become a lawyer," she reported, "but only one of out every 12,500 women has been able to achieve this status. On the statistics, it could be argued that it is even harder for a woman to become a lawyer than for a Negro." For the NYU law women, she added some international comparisons. In Russia, for example, women accounted for 36 percent of all lawyers—compared with America's 3 percent.

The second speaker was Eleanor Holmes Norton, assistant legal director of the ACLU, who would soon play a crucial role in the drive to open New York firms to women. Norton reported that she got fewer cases brought by women than by members of any other group. The barriers that kept women from organizing, she said, seemed to be cultural in nature. A few days later at the ACLU, Norton announced that she was beginning a sex discrimination lawsuit on behalf of forty-six women employees at *Newsweek*—with whom, as she later put it, she had "needed to do group therapy" to convince a significant number of them to bring a case.

For the Women's Rights Committee of NYU law school, a mix of personal experience, data from their study, and the counsel of experienced attorneys made bringing a case seem far from unimaginable.

10

Taking Action

In early April of 1970, women from seventeen different law schools, as far west as Berkeley and as far south as Duke, gathered at NYU. For two days they discussed issues affecting women law students, particularly hiring discrimination. The discussion led to a series of resolutions, which Diane Blank and Jan Goodman typed up. Most ranged from tame to mildly bold: Law students would visit colleges near their campuses to urge women to apply to law schools. Students from New York law schools would pressure the New York Bar Association to add an antidiscrimination statement to the interview guidelines provided to New York law firms. During the next year's interview season, law students would report incidents of discrimination by law firms to a πdesignated student at each school. Because stories from multiple law schools had already led students to view Shearman & Sterling as one of the "worst offenders" among New York firms, students agreed to demand that law school placement offices prohibit that firm from using school facilities to conduct interviews in the coming academic year.

Buried in the middle of these resolutions was the major one. Women's groups at all the law schools agreed they would "join a Title VII action to be initiated through the Equal Employment Opportunity Commission (EEOC) against five to ten large New York firms." These aspiring lawyers planned to charge a handful of the nation's most powerful law firms with sex discrimination. In the coming interview season, women would interview as much as possible. They would inquire about areas of employment, such as litigation, from which firms seemed to exclude women. They would listen for evidence of what Title VII called a pattern or practice of discrimination in law firm hiring.

During the summer after the first national conference of law women, most of the NYU students continued to add distinction. Blank and Kelly both won promotions at their Wall Street firm, Cadwalader, from summer secretary to summer associate, the first rung up the ladder to real lawyering. Kelly, after she and her teammate Edie Barnett won NYU's "moot court" contest, what amounted to the law school's competition for top litigators and speakers, began preparing to represent NYU in the nationals. Susan Deller Ross, just graduated from NYU, got her first full-time legal job, as an attorney at the EEOC. In late June, Congress invited Blank and Ross to give testimony at hearings on discrimination against women, where they retold part of the difficulties at NYU, including the origins of the Women's Rights Committee in the battle to open scholarships to women. (Less visibly, but partly as a result of the NYU activism, in July Professor Ruth Bader Ginsburg began work on her first sex discrimination case, on behalf of an Army nurse named Nora Simon, whom no one else seemed willing to assist.)

WHEN INTERVIEW SEASON BEGAN in the fall of 1970, stories began filtering back from women law students. Jane Dolkart, a Columbia student with a young child who hoped to become a litigator, was appalled by her interview with Cravath, Swaine & Moore. A hiring partner sat her down, looked at her resume, and then asked, Isn't motherhood the greatest goal for a woman? He spent the rest of the interview, as she recalled, telling her why she should not pursue litigation. Litigation involved travel, and she would not want to travel with a young child. He asked, Had she considered trusts and estates? Dolkart was shocked. She was not what she would later call "politically educated." She wasn't much of a feminist, and she had not gone to the interview to collect information for a lawsuit, so she just sat through the interview feeling horrible. (Soon afterward, she found a firm that seemed to take women seriously, which hired her and where she worked happily.)

Another Columbia student, Margaret Kohn, interviewed at Royall, Koegel & Wells. After discussing her resume, the firm's recruiter surprised Kohn by introducing the topic of women lawyers. His firm, he said, had only one—in trusts and estates. "For some reason women are really good at trusts and estates; they love the detail work and they're competent at it," he continued (at least according to her memory, which he would later partly dispute). Kohn tried to turn the conversation toward work she wanted. "Your firm does a lot of litigation work," she recalled asking, "doesn't it?" Litigation also, she suggested, required mastering detail. But he countered, she recalled, by explaining that litigation sometimes involved "bigger issues"—away from which, she inferred, he hoped that she could be steered. Late in the interview he returned to possibilities for women working with trusts and estates. Kohn eventually took a job with another firm.

One of the strongest stories of alleged discrimination came from Diane Blank. In mid-October, she had interviewed with Sullivan & Cromwell. In a firm of more than 130 attorneys, she learned that three were women. All worked in female ghettoes: one with trusts and estates and the other two doing repetitive paperwork mandated by securities laws. Blank's suspicion that Sullivan & Cromwell did not wish to hire many women sharpened when the firm decided not to interview five women whose grades had won them places on either a law review or the *Annual Survey of American Law*, while interviewing a number of men whose qualifications seemed lower. Perhaps most simply, according to Blank, the Sullivan & Cromwell partner who interviewed her said, in words she jotted down immediately after on a note card, "some of the partners have prejudices against women."

When Mary Kelly interviewed with the firm of Carter, Ledyard, she encountered mildly dismissive comments, which carried a tone, as she later recalled, of wondering why a nice lady like you would want to do this job. She was urged not to do litigation—remarkable in Kelly's case because she had won her law school's moot court contest. Kelly wound up choosing between offers from Cadwalader (the firm where she had worked as law clerk and associate) and another Wall Street firm, Willkie Farr & Gallagher, which hired her as a litigator.

Kelly, meanwhile, had teamed up with Professor Daniel Collins of NYU to create a summary of discrimination experienced by law students. Partly in response to NYU's urging, the Association of American Law Schools in mid-1969 agreed to create the Special Committee on Women in Legal Education, with Professor Collins as chair. The committee sent a questionnaire to major American law schools. Of the seventy-six schools that replied, more than one-third reported complaints of discriminatory incidents linked to students' interviewing for jobs. Taken together, they showed discrimination by law firms nationwide—in Maine, Massachusetts, New York, Pennsylvania, Georgia, Kentucky, Texas, Minnesota, Colorado, and California.

To turn the stories of discrimination into a lawsuit, the women of NYU and Columbia needed an attorney. At this point two brilliant women attorneys, who would become mentors to the New York law women, joined their circle: Eleanor Holmes Norton and Harriet Rabb.

MANY NYU WOMEN HAD FIRST HEARD Eleanor Holmes Norton, a 1964 graduate of Yale Law School, when she addressed them in March of 1970 about the paucity of cases brought by women to the ACLU. Within weeks, at age thirty-two and pregnant with her first child, Norton became chair of the city's Commission on Human Rights. Before Mayor John Lindsay swore her in, she told reporters that she planned to do all she could to fight discrimination against women. When NYU soon afterward asked her to take over as teacher for the course on women and the law, she accepted because, as she later recalled, she was excited that students wanted to engage in rigorous study of sex discrimination.

She was also aware of an irony. Years earlier when NYU turned her down for its Root-Tilden Scholarship, she presumed it was reserved for men by a bequest and made no protest. She had begun law school, she later reflected, with "almost no feminist consciousness."

One collaboration between Norton and her students in the spring term of 1971 began as a symposium on the equal rights amendment, scheduled for the meeting hall of the Association of the Bar of the City of New York—an organization that had recently issued a report opposing the ERA. The association invited an impressive panel of participants, including Norton, Betty Friedan, and Gloria Steinem—all of whom had spoken a few months earlier during a week of public hearings, initiated by Norton at her commission, that she believed were the first such hearings on women's rights in America. But when the NYU women received the association's invitation, they were shocked. In its largest type, the invitation wondered, "Has 'Women's Liberation' Liberated Anyone?" It went on to describe the event as a symposium not on the equal rights amendment but on "the 'Women's Rights Amendment' and Kindred Matters."

The NYU women deduced that the bar association planned "to make feminists look like idiots," as Blank put it. They called one of their many meetings, with invitations put up in the women's bathroom stalls. At a meeting that Blank recalls as filled with women hanging "from the rafters," they told Ellie Norton, as they had come to call her, that they were furious. At another meeting soon after, which included both Norton and Steinem, the law women hatched a plan to surprise the association.

Soon after the symposium began on the evening of March 25 in the filled-to-capacity hall of the mostly male Association of the Bar, Gloria Steinem rose to address an audience of some fifteen hundred—at least half of them women. Speaking briefly, Steinem advised the august association that it needed a new kind of lawyer. To assist, she announced, she had entered its walls as a "Trojan horse"—making it sound as if these new women lawyers were waiting, within her, to be released onto the world. She then let loose the young law women of NYU, who had been documenting discrimination by New York lawyers and their firms.

First, accepting the floor from Steinem, came Mary Kelly. Speaking from scrawled notes, she accused the bar of issuing—and then refusing to change—a trivializing invitation. She suggested that the association would never have dared distribute invitations asking, for example, "Has the anti-defamation league liberated any Jews?" or "The NAACP—has it liberated any blacks?" A discussion of women's liberation, she continued, might well begin with an examination of the bar. To this end, she and her NYU colleagues had examined the association's record and found it "seriously lacking." She noted that "the association has no women lawyers among its present officers and has 46 committees without a single woman lawyer." Since this "unbroken history of male domination and male orientation" has led the association to ignore discrimination against women, Kelly introduced a series of colleagues—none of them the invited speakers—to illustrate "some of the areas where the association had done nothing."

Jan Goodman stepped to the microphone to denounce the bar for opposing the ERA based on the deliberations of its "Federal Legislation Committee," which did not contain women or invite testimony from women. Diane Blank described patterns of discrimination in hiring, including shuttling women to work on trusts and estates or simply refusing to hire them. Emily Goodman, a young practicing attorney, told stories of a committee within the New York bar association designated to screen applicants for the bar that had, she said, treated women "obscenely." One divorced woman lawyer who sought admission to the bar was asked, said Goodman, "What kind of lawyer would you make if you would breach a sacred contract," her marriage contract?

At this point the chairman of the symposium had heard enough. Cutting off the uninvited speakers, he turned to his invited ones. With only a slight change in tone, Betty Friedan called for "a whole new body of law" that would be "written by and for women." The evening's most detailed legal critique came from Eleanor Holmes Norton. She attacked the association for advocating that Congress create an anemic substitute for the ERA: a new antidiscrimination statute. "The virtually impossible technical difficulties of drafting such a statute would relegate women's rights to future centuries," she said. "Fast and effective remedies to inequality are the only ones worth offering."

Norton's call for fast and effective remedies to sex discrimination came at a crucial juncture in the development of discrimination law. Just three weeks earlier, the Supreme Court had announced a major decision in a race discrimination case, *Griggs v. Duke Power.* The court ruled that, in the words of Columbia law professor George Cooper, who had contributed to the brief, "the effects of employment practices rather than their intent" would determine whether an employer was practicing illegal discrimination. Put another way, the *Griggs* case made clear that no employer could say he *intended* to help blacks but refused to hire them.

PROFESSOR GEORGE COOPER OF COLUMBIA LAW rightly saw *Griggs* as a "startling breakthrough" for the law. To push the law further, Cooper had another idea: get the EEOC to fund a clinic to train law students to bring lawsuits against employers who discriminated. The need for a clinic arose from the compromised genesis of the EEOC. Because the EEOC had received no power to initiate litigation, the work of enforcing Title VII's ban on workplace discrimination often fell to idealistic attorneys: George Cooper of Columbia Law volunteering with the NAACP in the case of Willie Griggs, Ruth Bader Ginsburg of Rutgers volunteering with the ACLU in the case of Sally Reed, and so on. To assist with these time-consuming cases, Cooper proposed that the EEOC give Columbia Law School a few thousand dollars, what he called a "peanuts grant," to train young law students as discrimination fighters. Thus EEOC money could teach law students to bring the suits that the EEOC could not bring.

Cooper got his grant and, with the support of the dean of Columbia Law School, Michael Sovern, went looking for a lawyer whom Columbia could hire to run its new Employment Rights Project. Though Cooper did lots of interviewing, he found his attorney by relying—ironically, as he saw it—on what he called "the old-boy network." The perfect attorney in Cooper's view turned out to be Harriet Rabb, a Columbia Law grad of 1966 and a family friend of the dean. Rabb was someone, Cooper thought, with "the balls for the job"—someone whose legal career had started with the activist lawyers Arthur Kinoy and William Kunstler, and who had assisted

Kinoy in his teaching of constitutional litigation at Rutgers School of Law, where Kinoy was a professor. As Cooper later reflected, "I had enough awareness of categories of Title VII to realize" that this attorney was "a member of a protected class"—protected against discrimination by Title VII.

HARRIET RABB'S ROUTE TO HER JOB at Columbia included intersections of the personal with the political. Growing up the daughter of two Jewish physicians in Houston, Harriet Rachel Schaffer encountered discrimination early. Her high-school hopes to become a cheerleader, for example, went nowhere. "The idea of having a Jewish cheerleader" at her school, she later explained, "wouldn't have passed the laugh test down there." Once when she phoned the house of a boy named Harry whom she was dating, his father called him to the phone by yelling loud enough for Harriet to get the message: "Harry, it's that nigger girl calling."

Heading north for college, she enrolled in Barnard and then in Columbia Law, where she experienced minor variations on the familiar challenges to women. One Columbia law professor's hazing took the form of a "Valentine's Day massacre." On that day, he insisted that all women stand up as the class began and remain standing throughout. He would then call only on women, asking what Rabb recalled as "all the embarrassing and difficult-to-discuss problems."

Embarrassing questions continued as she began to seek work as an attorney. Interviewers asked her how she would practice law if she had children, and what she would do if, in some legal negotiation, her adversary got nasty. What if he swore? What if he took a punch at her? (She heard of similar questions aimed at her friends: What were their husband's jobs? What method did they use for birth control?)

Rabb found work with a law firm that did not ask such questions: the pioneering civil rights firm headed by William Kunstler and Arthur Kinoy, where she had interned. Within two weeks of her arrival in 1965 for a summer job at Kunstler, Kunstler & Kinoy, three young civil rights workers disappeared in Mississippi, killed by the Ku Klux Klan. The family lawyer for one of the dead activists was Arthur

Kinoy. Rabb, who would later say that her only political act during her Texas childhood was drinking from black water fountains—and whose physician father in Houston had maintained segregated waiting areas for blacks and for whites—suddenly found herself working with litigators at the cutting edge of civil rights law.

After graduating from Columbia Law in 1966, she stayed on that edge, working with her mentor Kinoy. At his newly formed public-interest law firm, the Center for Constitutional Rights, she worked with him through 1969, facing the ongoing challenge of what she later called "saving the world from reactionaries." During her years lawyering with Kunstler and Kinoy, she represented many of the antireactionary icons of the day: H. Rap Brown of the Black Panther Party; Jerry Rubin, who was arrested for leading a march on the Pentagon; and the Students for a Democratic Society (SDS), the organization that symbolized campus resistance to the Vietnam War. All were radical, like Rabb, and not outspokenly feminist, like the center itself.

At the moment when feminists were first proclaiming that the personal was political, Rabb was heading toward a perverse encounter with that dictum. After law school, she began dating—in a Manhattan-to-Washington romance—one of her Columbia Law classmates, Bruce Rabb. Like Harriet, Bruce had also moved quickly to a position in the great civil rights battles of the era: he worked on civil rights with the Domestic Council of the White House staff of President Richard Nixon, a position to which Bruce had risen partly on the basis of a tradition of family service. His father had held the staff position of secretary to the cabinet under President Eisenhower (and would later be appointed an ambassador by President Reagan).

Their jobs seemed headed for a collision. Harriet's work attracted the attention of the FBI. On one occasion, when the SDS lost a conference venue on short notice, she phoned Bruce to discuss SDS's difficulty. As Harriet's FBI file grew, her legal mentors, Kunstler and Kinoy, presented her with a problem. Given the political sensitivity of what she and Bruce worked on, their romance was creating the risk that neither of their employers would totally trust them. Harriet quit her job, married Bruce, and moved to Washington.

In Washington, the collision of personal and political turned professional: Republicans in the capital do not hire Democrats; Democrats do not hire wives of prominently placed Republicans. At this low point, however, Harriet Rabb received an offer from on high. It came from Judge David Bazelon of the United States Court of Appeals for the District of Columbia Circuit, who knew her as an impressive litigator before his court and knew her husband's family. He offered her a job as clerk for the court.

The offer stood for only a week. Bazelon called her to his office and told her that her FBI file had reached him and his colleagues. "My dear," he said, "I propose you withdraw your application for this job. You have been to some very strange meetings." Two of his colleagues had resisted her appointment—one saying he would lock his chambers to prevent her entry and both threatening to "contact the White House." Rabb recalled that Bazelon had tears in his eyes.

Bruce kept his job, and Judge Bazelon helped Harriet find work with a newly formed community law firm, where she specialized in consumer safety litigation under, for example, the Child Protection and Toy Safety Act. It was a far cry from battling for civil rights with Kunstler and Kinoy.

MEANWHILE, EARLY IN 1971 at Columbia Law School, legal alma mater to both Bruce and Harriet Rabb, Professor George Cooper needed an attorney to take on his new challenge: to create an employment rights clinic, using the grant from the EEOC. Not only did Harriet Rabb already have many valuable contacts in New York, including Kunstler, Kinoy, Norton, and Michael Sovern, the Columbia dean whose wife had been a classmate of the Rabbs at Columbia Law; she also had extensive experience with one of the country's leading civil rights firms, the Center for Constitutional Rights. What happened next caught George Cooper by surprise.

Even before Harriet Rabb began working for Columbia, the New York law women felt sure she would be an ally. Rabb "was like a gift," one of her first students recalled—even if "to the faculty, she was just a salaried employee." Since Rabb was appointed only as director of the project, she was not a tenured professor with job security. In 1971

Columbia Law still had no women professors, and as fast as Rabb had been hired, she could be fired. Nonetheless, women law students began consulting with her about the cases they hoped to bring against major New York law firms.

While Columbia was appointing Rabb, the New York law women were looking for an attorney who could eventually represent them. They conferred with Eleanor Holmes Norton, law teacher for some of them, including Diane Blank, in their women-in-the-law course at NYU. Though Norton had done much litigating in her many years at the ACLU, she could not bring a case from her new position as chair of the NYC Commission on Human Rights, so she introduced Blank to Rabb.

Blank and her fellow students had already done much of the legal work. Under the complicated procedural rules of Title VII of the Civil Rights Act, they needed to file complaints before they could bring lawsuits in federal court. Ironically, because they were bringing cases within the jurisdiction of New York City, which had its own laws forbidding discrimination, they needed to file charges, in advance of EEOC consideration, with the Commission on Human Rights, run by Norton.

Complaints flowed to the commission. For Norton, the students' suits fit the sort of cases she wanted her commission to support. Margaret Kohn's, which arrived in May of 1971, described the interview during which a partner in Royall, Koegel & Wells seemed to steer her away from litigation and toward trusts and estates, which he said "women are really good at."

Another complaint arrived in late June from Diane Blank, against Sullivan & Cromwell, detailing a dearth of women attorneys at the firm. Among more than 140 attorneys, the firm had only three women. Among approximately fifty partners, the firm had no women. The complaint alleged that "anti-female bias" showed in the firm's refusal to interview NYU women with strong credentials. It quoted a comment by Diane Blank's interviewer that some of his partners were "prejudiced against women."

Although the complaints by Kohn and Blank would eventually emerge as the most significant, they were far from alone in alleging discrimination. The large number of charges by young women attorneys made their experiences hard to ignore. In a press release they included a count of partners in New York City's largest firms: 9 women among 1,409 partners, a ratio of 1 to 156. The release also alleged that interviewers had said, "We would give you an offer on the spot if it weren't for your sex" or "Your problem is that you're wearing a skirt."

The women's complaints broke into the open on July 1, 1971—just as Harriet Rabb took up her position at Columbia Law. The headline atop a page in the *New York Times* read, "13 Women Law Students Here Accuse 10 Large Firms of Bias." The list of firms in the *Times* was a who's who of powerful New York firms: Aranow, Brodsky, Bohlinger, Einhorn & Dann; Carter, Ledyard & Milburn; Cravath, Swaine & Moore; Gilbert, Segall & Young; Roth, Carlson, Kwit, Spengler, Mallin & Goodell; Royall, Koegel & Wells; Shea, Gallop, Climenko & Gould; Shearman & Sterling; Sullivan & Cromwell; and Winthrop, Stimson, Putnam & Roberts.

A partner in one, Charles Goodell, a former U.S. Senator, said that his firm would investigate the charges and added that he was a "strong advocate of women's lib." The *Times* then noted that his firm employed no women as attorneys and that one of its interviewers had been accused of saying that it "did not like to hire women lawyers because they would go off and get married especially if they were pretty."

WHILE HARRIET RABB WAS SETTING UP her office at Columbia Law School, and before she could begin litigating in women's lawsuits against New York firms, the young law women suddenly brought her another battle—an urgent one. In mid-July of 1971, those women who had just graduated from NYU, Columbia, and other law schools were studying for the most important test of their legal careers, the New York State Bar Exam, which, if they passed, would give them the right to practice law. As they received letters assigning them a location to take the test, they realized they had all been sent to a single test location: the Commodore Hotel. In contrast, most of their male classmates had been assigned not to a hotel but to rooms at local law schools: NYU, Fordham, and Columbia.

Soon they received more surprises. First, because all women's tests would carry numbers in a narrow range, #1200 to #1600, graders might be able to identify tests taken by women. Second, being tested with these women at the Commodore were a large proportion of the male test-takers whom the bar association termed "repeaters," typically men who had flunked the test before. While their male classmates would be tested at local law schools, the women would be sent to a hotel for flunkies and women—two groups that, the women feared, exam graders might conflate.

On July 16, 1971, Mary Kelly phoned the office of the State Board of Law Examiners in Albany to inquire about the test locations. A clerk explained that the board had employed only "one female matron" who could escort women to restrooms and that she would be working at the Commodore. That same day, sixty law women met to discuss what to do.

They saw at least two problems if they proceeded to take the tests: (1) Given the numbering of examination books, graders might, even unintentionally, expect below-average work from the Commodore group. (2) If groups that tested together were graded together (as Kelly had been led to believe by an instructor at a bar review course), then women faced another sort of problem. "We want to be sure we're not being graded against each other," one woman explained, "because even male chauvinists in law school will admit that women on the whole do statistically better than men."

Their fears may have been ungrounded, but what should they do to find out? The sixty women faced a related problem. How could a would-be lawyer dare to challenge the State Board of Law Examiners? What if the challenge itself brought reprisals—perhaps in the committees that consider the "character and fitness" of a would-be lawyer? Given the risks, Mary Kelly was among a handful of women who decided to protest the sex-segregated bar exams. Kelly called Rabb and said, It sounds like the old story with blacks and "administrative convenience." Rabb decided to take the case.

Operating not through her program at Columbia but through the

New York Civil Liberties Union as a "cooperating attorney," a volunteer position, Rabb initiated a federal suit on behalf of eight women against the New York State Board of Law Examiners. Again headlines sprouted. The *New York Daily News* article of July 20, 1971, carried the headline "Fem Students Sue the Bar Examiners."

The battle was short and sweet. The next day's headline in the *New York Post* read, "Testing Board Invites Gals: Join Men at Bar (Exams)." In less than an hour in a U.S. district court before Judge Marvin E. Frankel, Rabb and her students had won. The chairman of the State Board of Law Examiners agreed to end sex segregation in bar examinations. That segregation had been caused, he explained, only by "administrative convenience" and efforts to avoid hiring female restroom proctors. He agreed to go to the Commodore Hotel to tell the law women not that their exams would be desegregated but that they would be the last to take segregated bar exams in New York. The board, he insisted, had not intended "to discriminate." Then he explained safeguards to ensure that the women's tests this year would be assessed equally with the men's.

In response to his capitulation, Rabb and the law students agreed to withdraw their lawsuits. But as newspaper accounts made clear, the law women had sued a powerhouse in the legal establishment and had emerged victorious.

Other discrimination cases began flowing to Harriet Rabb. In early 1970, women employees at *Newsweek*, represented by Eleanor Holmes Norton while still an attorney for the ACLU, had filed a class-action lawsuit that led to a nondiscrimination agreement with management. When the women found the agreement produced unsatisfactory results, they returned to Norton, who could no longer represent them because of her appointment as chair of New York's Commission on Human Rights. Rabb took Norton's place, becoming the attorney for the *Newsweek* women, whose legal case became the first for Rabb and the Employment Rights Project that Cooper had hired her to run. Eventually, Rabb and the project worked out a new settlement with *Newsweek*. Success in those negotiations led, in turn, to Rabb and her project team representing aggrieved women employees of *Reader's Digest* and then of the *New York Times*. Meanwhile,

Rabb was preparing the law women's cases against such firms as Sullivan & Cromwell. Rabb and her team, which still included George Cooper, were becoming, at least for litigation under Title VII, the most visible gender-discrimination lawyers in America.

George Cooper had never dreamed this would happen. He had not hired Rabb to work on sex. His own work had attacked race discrimination, and he came out of a milieu that accepted sex discrimination as normal. When he graduated from Harvard Law School in 1961, he went to a big Washington law firm that every year, as he recalled, would hire a dozen or more associates and "always one woman—no more, no less." She was hired, he understood, not on the partner track but on the "associate track." Women were hired for their competence but, unlike men, were not expected to stay—although, Cooper observed, "a few quirky women would stay," would never marry, and would remain forever associates but not partners. His first legal experience taught Cooper this arrangement was "the way things were."

Now, using a program that Cooper had masterminded, Rabb and her students were aiming to change the way things were, partly by litigating against firms that gave money to Columbia or were led by Columbia Law graduates. Although Cooper stood behind them, he needed to talk to his dean, Michael Sovern. The dean told him to go for it. Cooper warned, "Shit may hit the fan." The dean said he would handle it. Rabb found that Dean Sovern backed her whenever she needed him.

THE NEW YORK CITY COMMISSION ON HUMAN RIGHTS, under Norton, eventually reviewed ten different complaints produced by the Columbia and NYU law women. It winnowed away the weaker ones, tossing out five for lacking "probable cause." Among those that won support from the commission were the cases of Margaret Kohn and Diane Blank.

Reporting in April of 1972, the Commission on Human Rights related a series of thirteen results from its investigation of possible discrimination by Royall, Koegel & Wells, the firm about which Kohn

had complained. Of the firm's eighty-six permanent attorneys, for
example, only one was a woman. In the preceding decade, however,
women had represented 5 percent of its "applicant flow" but only 2
percent of its job offers (and less than 1 percent of its offers for permanent jobs). Even rejected applicants were treated differently. Unlike
rejected female applicants, rejected males sometimes received letters
inviting them to continue to seek work at the firm. After employment,
different treatment continued. The firm paid the initiation fees of
several partners in a club that excluded women from membership. Perhaps most surprising was a finding based on a commission conversation with the partner who had interviewed Kohn for a job. According
to the commission's report, although Kohn was not hired, the partner
admitted that she "was the second best applicant he interviewed at
Columbia for 1971 summer employment." The investigation led the
commission to find "probable cause" that the firm had discriminated
against both Kohn and other women attorneys because of their sex.
Soon afterward, the EEOC issued Kohn a letter that gave her "permission to sue" the law firm of Royall, Koegel & Wells.

Reporting in January of 1974, on the complaint of Diane Blank
against Sullivan & Cromwell, the Commission on Human Rights
related brief but similar results. It found that though she was not hired,
her *curriculum vitae* indicated "performance equal to if not better
than that of males hired" by the firm. It found that the firm showed
a "tendency toward sex-segregated job classifications," indicated by
an absence until 1971 of women in its tax and litigation groups. It
reported that the firm used social clubs that excluded women from
membership, "thereby depriving women associates of equal conditions
of employment." It found that the firm had never had a woman partner. In Blank's case, as well as in Kohn's, the Commission on Human
Rights made a finding of "probable cause" that Sullivan & Cromwell
had engaged in sex discrimination.

As a next step, Blank took the commission's findings to the New
York office of the EEOC. There Blank's case hit difficulties. The
EEOC's district director ruled, for example, that Blank's credentials
were below that of the man whom Sullivan & Cromwell hired from
her NYU class after its interviews in the fall of 1970. The director also

made note of new statistics provided by Sullivan & Cromwell: from 1970 to 1974, Sullivan & Cromwell's percentage of women among its associates had risen dramatically, from about 1.4 to 12.5 percent of all associates. The director concluded that the EEOC did not see "probable cause" to believe that Sullivan & Cromwell had illegally discriminated against Blank. However, following standard procedure, the EEOC informed Blank that she still had the "right to sue" Sullivan & Cromwell, if she wished, in a U.S. district court.

11

A Young Woman Takes an Old Wall Street Firm to Court

In January of 1975, Harriet Rabb submitted a complaint for a class-action suit alleging a "pattern and practice of sex discrimination" by Sullivan & Cromwell, against Diane Blank and against other women whom the firm might have refused to hire, in the United States District Court for the Southern District of New York. To defend against the charges, the firm made a surprising decision. It did not assign one of its lawyers to defend itself. Instead Sullivan & Cromwell, widely viewed as an establishment firm, selected a New York lawyer known for his attacks on the establishment.

Ephraim London, a partner in the small firm of London & Buttenwieser, came from a family of progressive lawyers. His uncle, Meyer London, won election to Congress in 1914 as one of a few Socialist Party congressmen. After graduating from NYU School of Law in 1934, Ephraim joined the firm started by his father and his uncle, which defended the rights of garment workers on the lower east side of Manhattan.

Ephraim London became known as an anticensorship lawyer. For decades, he argued and won Supreme Court cases establishing the principle that constitutional protection of free speech extended to film. Thanks to cases argued by London, Americans won the right to see such films as *The Miracle* from Italy (Supreme Court, 1952), *Lady Chatterley's Lover* from France (1959), and *Language of Love* from Sweden (1971). In arguing before the Supreme Court, often defending films called obscene, Ephraim London had never lost.

Other credentials made London a sharp choice to challenge allegations of discrimination. He was familiar with women attorneys. His mother, who had met his father when she joined the law firm as a typist, later trained at night school to become a lawyer herself. His law partner was Helen Lehman Buttenwieser. She too showed antiestablishment flare. In the 1960s she raised $60,000 bail to win temporary freedom for a convicted Soviet spy, Robert Soblen, whom their firm was representing. (The spy fled bail, which was forfeited.)

Furthermore, London knew about the NYU law women and was positioned to learn more. He taught constitutional law at NYU. He had even hosted some of the women, including Kelly, in his townhouse on Washington Mews, near the heart of the NYU campus, when they needed training for moot court competition. For Rabb and Blank, London was poised to prove a canny and formidable opponent.

AT THE FILING OF DIANE BLANK'S COMPLAINT, the district court, following its usual practice, drew a name of a judge from a drum. Out came Judge Constance Baker Motley, the only woman among the court's twenty-seven judges. During the same decades that Ephraim London was winning obscenity cases before the Supreme Court (all nine of the cases he argued), Constance Baker Motley had been winning race discrimination cases (she won nine out of ten). Despite their similar records, her path to the law had been less direct than London's.

Constance Baker was born in 1921, the daughter of a cobbler and a seamstress who had emigrated from Nevis in the West Indies to New Haven, Connecticut. Her father became a dishwasher in a hotel opposite Yale University and later a chef for Yale's elite secret society, Skull and Bones. "When I was growing up," she recalled in her autobiography, *Equal Justice under Law*, "all of my male relatives seemed to work at one Yale eating club or another."

She grew up in a family and a public school system that talked little about race and lots about getting a good education. No one mentioned that both her parents were descended from slaves. No one explained that the mural she passed each day in junior high school depicted the leader of a slave revolt against the crew of a Spanish slave ship, the *Amistad*. "We black students," she recalled, "never raised sensitive questions about race and color, and the white students never did either."

Although her parents urged their children to study hard, as they themselves had in the English Standard Schools on Nevis, neither parent offered young Constance much guidance toward a career. Yet soon after entering New Haven High School, located near Yale Law School, she began to imagine her future. She engaged in discussions of politics and race. She attended meetings of a local black women's group, the Women's Civic League. She read works by James Weldon Johnson, W.E.B. DuBois, and Abraham Lincoln—who, she learned, once said that the most challenging of all professions was the law. So at age fifteen, following Lincoln, Constance Baker Motley decided to become a lawyer. She received no encouragement. (Her mother suggested that she try hair dressing.) She came to realize that she was someone who would not, as she wrote years later, "be put down. I rejected the notion that my race or sex would bar my success in life." She did, however, see a serious obstacle: poverty.

Her thrifty father had worked throughout her life to start a business. Just as she was entering high school, he bought that business: a small restaurant where he made lunches for local laborers. But he made the error of buying his restaurant in the late stages of the Great Depression of the 1930s. The restaurant failed. It took his savings, leaving nothing to send a daughter to college.

When Constance Baker finished high school, having completed her college prep courses (as well as three years of Latin) and graduating with honors, she had to settle for a job as a trainee in a federal program called the National Youth Administration. It paid her $50 a month to refinish old wooden chairs—the same work, she learned, being done by prisoners in a nearby jail.

In her second year on the job, she was asked to speak, in her role as president and founder of the New Haven Negro Youth Council, at a public meeting about the lack of activity at a local community center. It had been built by a local businessman and Yale trustee, Clarence Blakeslee. Standing out in a series of noncontroversial speakers, Constance Baker explained that the dominance of Yale people on the center's board had alienated the black community. The next day she heard that Blakeslee wanted to meet her. Soon afterward, in his office, he quizzed her about why she was not in college. Her family, she explained, had no money. If she went to college, he asked, what would she do? She said she would become a lawyer. "Well, I don't know much about women in the law," he replied. "But if that's what you want to do, I'll be happy to pay your way for as long as you want to go. I am sending my grandson to Harvard Law School. I guess if I can send him to Harvard, I can send you to Columbia."

So Columbia Law School is where she went. On the way, she did undergraduate study at Fisk and then New York University, and Blakeslee paid her way. At her graduation in 1946 from Columbia, Blakeslee, then age eighty-three, came to offer still more help. He wanted to give her the name of a partner in a New York law firm who was a "fine man"—his code, she had come to realize, for a man who was not racist—whom he believed would hire her. But, she told Blakeslee, she had found her dream job.

Months earlier, she had begun work as a clerk to a young attorney, Thurgood Marshall, counsel to the Legal Defense and Educational Fund (LDF) of the NAACP. In a few years she became one of the principal trial attorneys for the LDF. She worked on briefs for *Brown v. Board of Education*, which in 1954 declared unconstitutional America's long history of segregated and "separate but equal" public education. In 1961 she argued the case that won admission for Charlayne Hunter-Gault to the still-segregated University of Georgia. In 1962 she took the lead in arguing in court and directing the massive effort that desegregated the University of Mississippi, "Ole Miss," by winning admission for James Meredith. In 1963 she helped represent Martin Luther King Jr. when he protested segregation in Birmingham, Alabama. As she worked, she learned to take in stride the behavior that she encountered as a black attorney (a judge, for example, who made a practice of closing his eyes when a black person argued in his court) or as a woman attorney (a judge in 1949, unable to call her *Attorney Motley* or even *Mrs. Motley*, became the first person who ever addressed her as *Ms.*).

After Thurgood Marshall left the LDF, Motley became probably (Supreme Court historians remain unsure) the first black woman to argue a Supreme Court case. Beginning with victory in a case concerning the right to adequate counsel (for a black man sentenced to death in Alabama for breaking and entering with "intent" to ravish), she went on to win Supreme Court cases that helped desegregate American restaurants, parks, and schools. Her last case before the court in 1964, an attempt to desegregate juries, led to her one loss, 6 votes to 3. (Two decades later the Court reversed itself, allowing Motley to remark that she was ultimately, belatedly, undefeated at the Supreme Court.)

In 1966, President Lyndon Johnson—after hearing praise from his attorney general for Motley's skill in presenting Supreme Court oral arguments and, as he said, after hearing praise for her from every civil rights leader in the country—appointed her a federal judge. When she moved into her chambers in the U.S. District Court for the Southern District of New York, a short walk from City Hall, she joined a federal trial court with twenty-four male judges. She became its first woman judge and its first nonwhite judge. She also became America's fifth woman to serve as a federal judge and its first black woman.

Her judicial colleagues in New York did their sometimes-awkward best to make Constance Baker Motley welcome. They even made sure she could attend their traditional dinners in the famously all-male Century Club. Not for years did she learn that she had attended only because her chief judge had lied to help her. He told the Century Club that she was attending the dinners as a secretary, a woman brought along to take notes on what the male judges said.

IN EARLY 1975, DOCUMENTS FOR THE CASE of *Diane Blank v. Sullivan & Cromwell* began to arrive in Judge Motley's chambers. In the formal language of Title VII litigation, the complaint filed by Harriet

Rabb stated that Blank, as plaintiff, "seeks a declaratory judgment . . . to restrain defendants [Sullivan & Cromwell] from maintaining practices, policies, customs and usages which discriminate against plaintiff and members of her class because of their sex with respect to hiring and conditions of employment." The complaint repeated many of the findings of the Commission on Human Rights, including the fact that the firm had never promoted a woman to the rank of partner.

In early April, Ephraim London filed his first crucial document on behalf of Sullivan & Cromwell. Formally but without detail, it denied most of Blank's allegations. Following the string of denials, London advanced a series of "affirmative defenses"—any of which might, if accepted by Judge Motley, defeat Diane Blank's case. London challenged, for example, whether Blank had filed charges quickly enough with the EEOC. And he challenged her standing to bring a class action on behalf of other women whom Sullivan & Cromwell might have discriminated against.

Buried within these challenges, familiar to any judge or attorney working on this sort of discrimination case, came a surprising one. Blank, London alleged, had come to Court with "unclean hands." Blank, he claimed, had applied for an interview with Sullivan & Cromwell not because she wanted a job but because she wanted to file a complaint for sex discrimination. To this end, he continued, she had lied when she claimed that a partner in the firm told her that "some of the partners are prejudiced against women." Furthermore, London asserted, in order to attack other firms, she had urged other women to lie about discrimination.

The charge of "unclean hands" surprised Harriet Rabb. She had expected the usual defenses, but not that Blank was suborning perjury. When she phoned Blank the next day, Rabb said this was the "ugliest case" she had worked on since she defended H. Rap Brown.

Soon the case took another surprising turn. In mid-April, Judge Motley received a letter from Ephraim London, with a copy sent to Harriet Rabb, in which he suggested that Motley should "ask to be relieved" from the case. Although he mentioned no specific incident, he wrote, "I believe you have a mind set that may tend, without your being aware of it, to influence your judgment."

Characterizing her mindset, he told Judge Motley that when appointed a decade earlier, she had "identified with women lawyers who suffered discrimination in employment." Lest he seem illiberal, he added that he hoped that she still felt identification with sufferers of discrimination. Nonetheless, urging her to leave Blank's case, he quoted in support the words of Justice Felix Frankfurter:

> Unconscious feelings may operate in the ultimate judgment, or may, not unfairly, lead others to believe they are operating. . . . The guiding consideration is that the administration of justice should reasonably appear to be disinterested as well as be so in fact.

Despite his turn to Frankfurter, London did not pretend that he had legal grounds for Motley's removal. And he assured her that he did not plan to ask for her disqualification.

After receiving London's letter, Motley did not reply immediately. A decade earlier, when she had joined the court, she had expected lawyers to "misbehave," as she put it, because she was a woman. After all, when she was appointed, only four other women in the country served as federal judges—so lawyers might be surprised when they drew her as a judge. But from 1966 to 1975, no lawyer had ever tried to get her to leave a case until now.

While Motley delayed replying, Rabb fired back at London. Immediately she replied to him and Motley that, if his reasoning were followed,

> there would not be any judge in this court who could hear this case. Indeed all judges would be disabled because each would appear other than open-minded or disinterested because each judge in the District is an attorney, of a sex. . . .

Further, Rabb pointed out, many judges had previously worked for mostly-male law firms. Fearing that London might pressure Judge Motley to leave the case, Rabb asked the judge not to depart without giving her a chance to argue that Motley should stay. Disputing

Rabb's logic, Ephraim London sent a second letter to Motley, again pressing her to leave.

While his effort to remove Judge Motley hung unresolved, London took a legal deposition, a formal interrogation of Blank at his offices with Rabb present. Blank had been dreading this grilling session. "I feel like this horrible inevitable thing," she wrote in her journal, "is going to happen to me over which I can have no control."

London began by asking Blank if she was now practicing as an attorney, which she was. After graduating from law school in 1971, Blank had moved to a clerkship, for Judge Charles H. Tenney, in the very court where her case was now being tried. Then, in 1973, she had teamed up with a group of friends and their friends to create her own law firm: Bellamy, Blank, Goodman, Kelly, Ross, and Stanley. Most of the partners had already done significant legal work. Carol Bellamy was a New York state senator and had been an attorney for a high-powered firm, Cravath, Swaine & Moore (later she would head UNICEF). Jan Goodman had teamed with Mary Kelly to help write the brief with Ruth Ginsburg in *Reed v. Reed* that led the Supreme Court to rule sex discrimination unconstitutional. Susan Deller Ross and Nancy Stanley had worked at the EEOC.

After ascertaining that Blank still practiced law, London asked her to name her law firm. Since the lawsuit concerned Sullivan & Cromwell—a firm that turned Blank down rather than a firm that had accepted her—Rabb, as legal counsel, intervened to ask what made the question relevant. London explained that he hoped to show that "Ms. Blank has embarked on a career of a certain kind" that was "consistent with the bringing of this action for certain purposes." He did not call the career or its purposes *feminist*. But he added that he planned to "inquire into the question of whether or not Ms. Blank or her firm discriminates against men."

With this sally, London proceeded to elicit the names of the other attorneys who worked for the firm. After asking if the firm employed any men, he learned that it had employed three: Christopher, Bruce, and Bill (Blank could recall only their first names), who had all worked as temporary secretaries. Pressing on, London pushed Blank to agree that her firm—which she said conducted a "general civil practice" of law—was in fact specializing in the "protection of women's rights." When she would not agree, he asked one of his simplest questions: "How is your telephone answered?"

"Feminist Law Firm," Blank replied. She explained that receptionists had objected to answering repeatedly with the name of all six partners, so they agreed on this shorthand. Working from this fact, London quickly succeeded in winning an acknowledgment that, indeed, being a female attorney gave her a "certain perspective" and that her firm conducted test cases intended to be "helpful to women."

Later in his questioning, London turned to the spring of 1970 and the first National Conference of Law Women. He asked if Blank had attended. At this point, Harriet Rabb objected—more strenuously than before—to the relevance of the question. "Do you intend," Harriet Rabb inquired, "to ask her about every conference she went to?" London said that he might, and pressed on. When Rabb pressed back, he advised her that she was "not a judge" and suggested that Judge Motley would instruct Blank to respond to his questions about the conference.

When Blank replied readily that she had attended, London asked if she went as a "representative" of the NYU women. No, said Blank, but she and Jan Goodman had organized it. London also devoted much time to finding out about meetings of the NYU Committee on Women's Rights, and how Blank had encouraged women to write down experiences during employment interviews that seemed discriminatory, collected complaints about those interviews, and passed them along to Harriet Rabb. Throughout this line of questioning, Rabb objected that such details seemed irrelevant in a case about discrimination by Sullivan & Cromwell.

At this point, hours into a deposition that would consume most of two days, the actors' positions in the drama were clear: London wanted to demonstrate that Blank was the ringleader of a conspiracy that hoped to use what he called "guerilla tactics" against Wall Street law firms. Blank wanted to give credit to her colleagues in the women's movement and to deny that anyone had lied. Rabb wanted to object that conferences and committees had nothing to do with the case, which should address one key question: did Sullivan & Cromwell's hiring practices discriminate against women?

By late in the second day, tensions rose to a peak. When London began to focus on one of Blank's weak points—her less-than-stellar grades, which had not qualified her to serve on NYU's law review but instead on the less-esteemed *Annual Survey of American Law*— Rabb objected to his repeated use of the phrase "isn't it a fact." Her objection to the form of his questions, London insisted, showed that Rabb never learned how to conduct a deposition. "I cannot believe," he told her, "that anyone who passed the bar exam could be as obtuse as you pretend to be."

As the ordeal neared completion, London tried to show that Blank, too, was either obtuse or obfuscating. Most tellingly, he challenged Blank on her claim that when she was looking for a job, Sullivan & Cromwell "hired male applicants whose qualifications were less than or equal to the plaintiff's." London asked Blank if she could name one of those applicants. "No," she said. Then, London asked, on what facts did she rely for making her complaint? When Blank responded that the complaint grew out of the findings of the NYC Commission on Human Rights, London could not contain himself. Those findings, he suggested, grew out of her own earlier complaint. He began yelling at her. When Rabb upbraided him, he caught himself. "I apologize for shouting at the witness," he said. "I know that is not proper conduct in an examination."

In his closing line of questioning, London turned yet again to the presence of Blank—and, he seemed to hope, also of Rabb—at national conferences of law women. At the second such conference, he asked, did Blank recall an agreement to launch a "consolidated attack on Wall Street firms?" Did she recall an accord at that conference on the use of "guerrilla tactics"?

With Rabb objecting repeatedly to his efforts to discover a conspiracy, London strove to add Rabb to his list of conspirators. Was Rabb present at the first National Conference of Law Women in 1970? (Blank could not recall her there.) Was Rabb present at any meetings of the NYU Women's Rights Committee? (Blank could not recall.) Had Rabb helped Blank prepare questionnaires that were distributed at such meetings? (No.) Did Rabb meet or confer with Blank about complaints against other law firms?

At this point, Rabb's objections stopped London's conspiracy probe by directing Blank not to answer. When London pushed, on a related front, to learn what Blank knew about Rabb's "connection" to such organizations as New York's Civil Liberties Union or Columbia's Employment Rights Project, Rabb again blocked his path and directed Blank not to answer.

A reader of the deposition could sense that London was gunning not just for Diane Blank. He was trying to paint Blank and Rabb as co-conspirators in a guerrilla attack on Wall Street law firms. But a critical reader could also see that Blank's case had major weaknesses. She seemed unable, albeit four years after her job interviews, to name a single male student hired by Sullivan & Cromwell who had qualifications that she could match. And she seemed not to recognize the problem.

IN THE CHAMBERS OF JUDGE MOTLEY, receiving all these documents, was just such a critical reader: a law clerk named Sara Steinbock. Steinbock had graduated in 1974 from NYU School of Law, where she too had been a member of the Women's Rights Committee. And she could recall Diane Blank as a student. Now, Steinbock had her first legal job, as one of two clerks to Motley.

To Steinbock, who understood that Blank had not made law review, Blank's case looked not great. Furthermore, Steinbock believed that Sullivan & Cromwell had made a wise choice of London as attorney. Rather than defend itself with one of its own corporate partners, who might have the Waspy style that would confirm stereotypes about the all-male partnership, it had gone to someone who was Jewish and a well-known liberal.

Whatever London's background, however, Steinbock thought that he had written an odd letter: asking a judge to recuse herself based on a "mindset." But Steinbock was, as she thought, "a kid," just learning how to comport herself as a lawyer. And London was a "lion of the bar" from whom she could learn.

Then in May of 1975 another odd letter from Ephraim London reached Judge Motley's chambers and Steinbock's desk. Apparently London was not getting along with Rabb. In a letter copied to the judge, he told Rabb he would not sign a minor agreement, a so-called stipulation, because Rabb had behaved like a "yahoo" during her client's deposition.

Soon after the "yahoo" letter reached her chambers, Judge Motley replied to London's letter from weeks earlier that had asked her to leave the case. She construed his letter, she informed him, as an attempt to remove her from the case. If so, she suggested that he follow full procedure: file a "timely and sufficient affidavit setting forth the facts on which you rely." Steinbock got the impression that the judge handled it as a matter of business, taking nothing personally. Quickly London replied that Motley had misunderstood. He had no intention, he reiterated, to ask for her disqualification.

With that confrontation averted, all parties proceeded to a crucial issue in the case: could Blank bring it as a class action on behalf of other women against whom Sullivan & Cromwell might have discriminated? Motley instructed Rabb to submit her written argument for Blank and London to submit any opposition no later than August 5, 1975. All sides understood that the future of the case hung in the balance. If Diane Blank represented a class, she could demand answers to questions about how Sullivan & Cromwell had treated all women who applied to work there.

WHEN JUDGE MOTLEY CALLED ALL PARTIES into her courtroom, on June 2, 1975, for the first pretrial conference, none of the participants could guess its purpose. "All right ladies and gentleman," Judge Motley said, welcoming them to her courtroom and stating that she had called the conference to deal with the flood of paper that had been descending on her chambers. First, Motley turned to Blank's motion for certification of the case as a class action. Rabb's written argument on behalf of Blank, which had arrived a few days earlier, pointed out that class certification had recently been granted in a similar case in the same court: *Kohn v. Royall, Koegel & Wells*. In the case for Margaret Kohn, which Rabb was also arguing, Judge Morris E. Lasker had ruled that Kohn could bring her suit as a class action. He had cited well-established case law, including a 1969 ruling by the Court of Appeals for the Seventh Circuit: "A suit for violation of Title VII is necessarily a class action as the evil sought to be ended is discrimination on the basis of a class characteristic" such as race or sex.

Motley noted that earlier she had given London five further weeks to oppose Rabb's motion. However, after reviewing Rabb's documents, Judge Motley said that she concurred with Judge Lasker's arguments and that, as she put it, Diane Blank's case "is the usual and normal type of action which is brought as a class action on behalf of persons similarly situated." Thus, she announced, "I don't see any real need for belaboring this point." Unless London right now could raise some new question about class certification, she said, she would certify the class today—five weeks ahead of schedule.

Watching from the jury box, Steinbock was shocked. Evidently shocked also, the tall, silver-haired attorney for Sullivan & Cromwell burst out, "Your honor, I am not prepared to—"

Before he could finish, Motley cut in, asking, "What is your name, sir?"

It was London, of course. He was not yet prepared, he said, to argue against class certification. Indeed, he made clear, he hoped never to discuss class certification. To avoid that issue, he wished to hold an entirely "separate trial." That trial, which he claimed would be short, would consider a different question: whether Diane Blank had filed her papers late with the EEOC. By showing that her papers had arrived late, he could end this matter quickly.

London's claim about late papers would require him, in his separate trial, to show that Sullivan & Cromwell's discrimination against women (if it ever existed) had ended—was not ongoing. To support this claim, London could offer the statistics that had apparently swayed the New York district office of the EEOC: that the firm's percentage of women among its associates had recently risen from about 1.4 to 12.5 percent. Further, though he did not articulate this motive, London had designed his short trial to put Rabb at a disadvantage. Rabb would be unable to show that Sullivan & Cromwell continued to discriminate because she would not yet have the information that London refused to give her (and that London would not be forced to give her until after Judge Motley certified the class action).

But Motley viewed the argument about ongoing discrimination, which might include a probe of those statistics, as the heart of the case. Determining whether Sullivan & Cromwell still discriminated was not work for a short trial preceding a full trial. She was not going to let London try this case twice.

With the goal of moving the case ahead, Motley stated, "I am going to rule now that it is a class action." She told London that he could still write a memo to explain why this was not a usual and normal class action and that, if he came up with something new, she would reconsider.

"May I remind your Honor," London asked in a last attempt, about the earlier order giving him five further weeks before she would certify the class. "Yes," she replied, "I have just countermanded it."

Still in the jury box, Sara Steinbock sat thinking, "Oh my god." It would be her job to draft Motley's memorandum opinion. Inevitably, Steinbock would need to justify the judge's change of plan. But to Motley the reasons were clear. Until she certified the class action, London could resist giving information in depositions and interrogatories. She was beginning to think that London's "job was to stall."

Motley then turned to his motion to require Blank to answer questions about her attendance (and Rabb's also) at conferences of law women. "The Court's ruling," she declared, "is that those questions are irrelevant to the merits of this case and the plaintiff is not required to answer any question relating to any conference that she attended regarding women's rights." Blank's challenge in this lawsuit was straightforward: to prove that Sullivan & Cromwell discriminated against women.

London agreed. But he had asked about the law conferences for a different reason. Blank's case, he believed, should be thrown out for lying, for "unclean hands." London wished, he told Judge Motley, to show evidence that at these conferences Blank and other participants had decided that they would sue law firms and, further, "where it was necessary, there would be falsification of the facts." This strategy was typified, he believed, by Blank's false claim that a partner in Sullivan & Cromwell said that "some of the partners have prejudices against women." He would reveal that Blank and her friends had conspired in what he called a "barratrous and champertous plan."

A BARRATOR, ACCORDING TO BLACKSTONE'S COMMENTARIES of the 1700s, was someone who engaged in "frequently exciting" harassing lawsuits and, according to *Black's Law Dictionary*, was a "maintainer of suits . . . a disturber of the peace who spreads false rumors and calumnies." In these reference works, *champerty* was worse. It meant making a bargain to pursue someone's legal claim in order to profit from the proceeds (*Black's Law Dictionary*). Lawyers who practiced *champerty* were "pests of civil society" (Blackstone's *Commentaries*). To Steinbock, just past law school, the odd terms made London sound archaic.

To Motley, they echoed her recent past. After the Supreme Court had ruled in 1954 that segregated education was unconstitutional, the NAACP encouraged black students to apply to all-white schools and colleges. Southern states responded by attacking the encouragement as illegal. They tried to paint the NAACP's civil rights lawyers as violators of a legal canon that forbade *barratry* and *champerty*.

Taking antibarratry laws that had long been used to combat "ambulance-chasing" by lawyers who profited from others' pain, southern states added language aimed at the NAACP. Virginia, for example, revived an old law that had prohibited lawyers from snagging business by paying a "runner" (an employee who chased after accident victims to get business) or a "capper" (a decoy who helped work a swindle); onto that law, the state grafted a clause permitting prosecution of any "individual or organization which retains a lawyer in connection with an action to which it is not a party and in which it has no pecuniary right or liability." Not coincidentally, the NAACP retained lawyers for just such an action: helping black students win admission to white schools.

Virginia's highest court ruled that the NAACP was violating the state's new antibarratry statute, which the court endorsed as a "valid police regulation." With other states enacting similar antibarratry traps, the NAACP appealed in federal court. Motley joined in writing the brief in support of her NAACP colleagues. Over a string of years, her allies making oral arguments against Virginia's barratry tactic included Spottswood W. Robinson III, Thurgood Marshall, and Robert L. Carter—all of whom would eventually, like Motley, become federal judges. In the climactic case, Carter argued for the NAACP before the United States Supreme Court. He lost.

Writing the decision in early 1962 for a 5–4 majority was Justice Felix Frankfurter, who wanted to steer the Court away from appearing "to discriminate as partisans in favor of Negroes." Virginia's antibarratry and anti-NAACP statute provided his chance. No state, Frankfurter wrote, needed to exempt the NAACP from its antibarratry laws simply because NAACP lawyers were "moved not by financial gain but by public interest." Motives that replaced venality with virtue would not shield NAACP lawyers from indictment as barrators. Ancient antibarratry law trumped emergent public-interest law.

The decision never appeared. After suffering a stroke, Justice Frankfurter, along with another justice in the five-vote majority, resigned from the court. Robert L. Carter went back to argue the case a second time. Again the vote was 5 to 4. But the NAACP won. Its lawyers, including Constance Baker Motley, could continue fighting discrimination.

LONDON'S ATTACKS ON RABB, Judge Motley grasped, went beyond charges of *barratry*. During his interrogation of Diane Blank, he had upbraided Rabb for lacking the training of an attorney. When Rabb objected to the form of his questions, he countered by calling her "obtuse." Now, in a different form of insult during the pretrial conference, London claimed Rabb had acted improperly by trying to "whisper advice" to her client. As Motley ruled against London, stating that Blank was permitted to consult counsel before answering a question, London's string of insults reminded Motley of his letter calling Rabb a *yahoo*. Asking for a copy, she read it aloud in court:

Dear Ms. Rabb, don't bother to send the stipulation. I won't sign it. There is no reason to accommodate you so long as you ignore your commitments and behave like a yahoo—as you did during your client's examination.

What, Judge Motley wanted to know, did he have in mind? For that matter, what was a *yahoo*?

"A *yahoo*, your Honor, is a word that comes from Swift's *Gulliver's Travels*." Explaining Jonathan Swift's eighteenth-century allegory, he went on to say that *yahoos* were a "very crude kind of people who behaved in an uncontrolled manner" and that he had intended—

The judge cut him off. In front of Motley sat his written complaint, which excerpted what he viewed as Rabb's moments of unlawyerly obstruction. In it he attacked Rabb with yet another epithet: *puerile*— a term, he added, that "may now be applied to a woman's conduct" though it originally applied to the mischief of young boys.

Rereading these excerpts, Motley saw no grounds for calling Rabb's defense crude or for calling Rabb a *yahoo*. In Motley's nine years as a federal judge, she told London, she had seen no case "in which a lawyer has addressed his opponent with any such language." She had doubts he would try such tactics before a male judge. In her courtroom, she said, "We don't conduct any cases like that."

In the courthouse cafeteria at midday, judges sat together and talked about their work. "You know how everybody talks about their business at lunchtime," Motley recalled years later. "And we obviously talked about lawyers who were ridiculous." Her colleagues who knew London began volunteering opinions. He wasn't a member of Sullivan & Cromwell, they reminded her. The firm had hired an outsider to do what it knew was improper, they suggested, and so that no lawyer from Sullivan & Cromwell risked being held in contempt of court for charging an attorney with *barratry* and a judge with prejudice. The white-shoe firm had hired London, Motley gathered, to do its dirty work.

THE WORK GOT DIRTIER. On July 24, 1975, London filed an "Application for Disqualification." Reversing his repeated statements that he would not seek her removal from the case, London now formally pressed Motley to disqualify herself. Her past actions showed, he argued, that she "identified with those who suffered discrimination in employment because of sex or race."

Not waiting for an answer, London went over Motley's head. Writing to the court of appeals, he requested that it overturn her ruling on class certification, informing them that he had asked Motley to disqualify herself. Facing this probably unprecedented attempt to disqualify a federal judge on the basis of sex and race, Motley went looking for courage and for precedent. She found both in the work of Judge Leon Higginbotham, serving since 1964 on the district court in Philadelphia.

Only the year before, in a case involving charges of racial prejudice by white workers, Higginbotham had been pressed to disqualify himself based on news reports of a speech which he, a black judge, had made about ending racial injustice. To a gathering of black historians, he urged that blacks look beyond federal court as they sought to end discrimination. The pressure to disqualify included the assertion that in speaking to blacks about ending discrimination, he used the pronoun *we*. To this, he replied,

> Defendants assert that my use of the term "we" indicates an emotional identification with my audience which requires my disqualification. Perhaps defendants would have wanted me to say "You black people must pursue your options for equal justice in other forums." Maybe that approach would have been permissible. Perhaps, on the Fourth of July, they would want orators to say "You hold these truths to be self evident, that all men are created equal . . . ," but never declare that "We hold these truths to be self evident." If defendants' rationale is accepted, whenever an orator says "we" in such a context, he is involved in a conspiracy which precludes his capacity to judge thereafter with impartiality.

Higginbotham proceeded to pick apart each segment of the attack on his impartiality with care.

Only late in his reply did he suggest why white litigants might try to disqualify him. Their pressure might arise in part from the fact that until 1961

> no President had ever appointed a black as a United States District Judge. If blacks could accept the fact of their manifest absence from the federal judicial process for almost two centuries, the plain truth is that white litigants are now going to have to accept the new day where the judiciary will not be entirely white and where some black judges will adjudicate cases involving race relations.

As he reached his conclusion, he made clear where he stood. "In a nation which," he said,

> had a revolution theoretically based on the declaration that "we hold these truths to be self-evident, that all men are created equal," a judge should not be disqualified if two centuries later he believes that the rhetoric must be made real for all citizens.

Judge Higginbotham stayed on the case.

His words gave courage to Judge Motley. Since London was already going over her head to the court of appeals, she needed to reply quickly. Over a weekend, Motley produced her answer to London's challenge, a memorandum opinion that she finished on Monday, August 4, 1975. The opinion addressed each of London's charges, holding the most personal for last.

To his charge that she had not let him hold a brief trial to show that Diane Blank's papers were late, she countered that the papers could not be deemed late if discrimination was continuing—a question at the heart of the main trial. She wrote that London was withholding information that was needed for the main trial to move forward and would not be brought out in a brief trial. To his charge that she had certified the class without giving him a chance to reply, she countered that she remained willing to read any reply.

Near the end of her response, she turned to London's more personal charges, including what he called her identification with people who had faced discrimination "because of sex or race." According to him, she once deplored employment discrimination for tending "to make its victims social and economic cripples, hopeless victims of warped and reactionary social custom." He alleged also that she once said that her nomination to the federal court was significant to Negroes and women lawyers who were suffering discrimination. "I hasten to add," he continued, that both he and the firm of Sullivan & Cromwell "are in agreement with the quoted statements"—for which he gave no source, and which he introduced as evidence that she would not be "objective."

Replying to London's charge that she identified with people who suffered sex discrimination and race discrimination, she pointed out that Ephraim London

offers as support for this "identification" an eloquent quote, attributed to me, on the crippling effects of discrimination. Mr. London offers, however, neither evidence of this alleged "identification" nor citation for the direct quote.

Though questioning his quotations, Motley did not hide from her decades of lawyering for the NAACP. It was beyond dispute, she said, "that for much of my legal career I worked on behalf of blacks who suffered race discrimination. I am a woman, and before being elevated to the bench, was a woman lawyer." But the fact that a judge had engaged in civil rights litigation or was the same sex as a possible victim of sex discrimination should not prove sufficient to force her disqualification. Elaborating on a point made by Harriet Rabb immediately after London's first letter urging Motley to leave the case, she continued that if, indeed, the

background or sex or race of each judge were, by definition, sufficient grounds for removal, no judge on this court could hear this case, or many others, by virtue of the fact that all of them were attorneys, of a sex, often with distinguished law firm or public service backgrounds.

Although Motley had little contact with the nascent feminist theory of the 1970s, London's challenge had turned her opinion toward a crucial realization that was emerging about man-made law: Male lawyers like London supposed (and in this case had the nerve to argue, on behalf of an all-male partnership) that the standard for unbiased judging was white and male. If a judge diverged in sex (female) and race (colored), a male lawyer could try to remove her for embodying "bias" not common in judicious white males.

As Motley concluded, her opinion tweaked London, recalling that in early letters he had asked her to disqualify herself but twice stated that he had no grounds to move formally for disqualification. Despite the fact, noted Motley,

> that he previously specifically declined to make such a motion on the ground that it was baseless, Mr. London now nonetheless includes the factors of my background, race and sex, which have not changed during the pendency of the litigation.

Though London may have changed his tune, Judge Motley had not. She refused to disqualify herself.

Almost immediately, the all-male court of appeals replied: Judge Motley would not be disqualified. Ephraim London had lost his gamble.

LONDON'S FAILURE TO ELIMINATE Judge Motley did not mean failure in his defense of Sullivan & Cromwell. From her vantage as clerk, Sara Steinbock supposed that Blank might still lose when her case went to trial. Steinbock's impression remained that Blank and Rabb had a case that was "not so strong"—even if it was a case that London "made stronger each time he showed up." Steinbock also sensed no note of triumph in Motley as she rebuffed London, and surely no levity.

Steinbock herself had indulged in a bit of light irony—a sign, she realized, that she was becoming outraged by London. In the bits of phrasing that Steinbock drafted toward Motley's refusal to disqualify herself, she was the one who slipped in the wisecrack that Motley's

race and sex had "not changed during the pendency of the litigation."
It was Steinbock's favorite line—clever, she thought, but likely to be
cut by the judge. When Motley signed off on it, Steinbock had hoped
to see her smile or even chuckle. Motley did neither. Steinbock realized
that Motley was treating the case professionally, not emotionally—as
a mature judge, not as a kid clerk.

At about this time, the visibility of the case increased sharply.
Although well covered in New York's legal press, the battle between
Rabb and London had mostly escaped the national media. An article
in the *Wall Street Journal*, however, managed to gather information
from both Rabb and London that had not surfaced in court. London,
after what the *Journal* reporter called a bit of arm twisting, revealed
that his *yahoo* letter had been prompted merely by a flare-up about
rescheduling a deposition, which he admitted to the *Journal* "wasn't
so all-fired important." Rabb admitted that she had been introduced
to Blank and her allies by Eleanor Holmes Norton—who, the *Journal*
noted, was head of the city Commission on Human Rights, "before
which many of the complaints were filed"—a revelation that probably came closer to suggesting a conspiracy than anything London
had managed to elicit.

Blank heard immediately that Rabb was upset, calling the article
scurrilous. Then Rabb got a call from a friend in the investment
banking firm Lehman Brothers. He said the article was the "talk of
Wall Street." To investment bankers this was a story, as Blank put
it, about "a law firm that can't win its own lawsuit, and on top of
that goes out and hires a buffoon for a lawyer." The partners at Lehman Brothers, he told Rabb, were calling up partners at Sullivan &
Cromwell to tease them.

Still, the article left Blank's credentials looking far from strong.
Blank did not enjoy reading in the *Wall Street Journal* that she had
received mediocre grades in law school and edited "a sort of second
string law review." Weaknesses in Blank's individual case made it
crucial to show that Sullivan & Cromwell had discriminated against
women as a class. From the start, London had fought against handing
over data from the firm that might strengthen that claim. The statistics that Sullivan & Cromwell guarded most fiercely concerned its

partners—a weak spot, since the firm had never promoted a woman to partner. Among Rabb's questions were fairly simple ones that could combine to reveal a pattern, if it existed, of discrimination: For those men who arrived as associates and were invited to join the partnership, how long on average had they remained associates? For those women who arrived as associates and did not receive invitations to partnership, how long had they remained associates? For those women whose years as associates exceeded the average for the men who made partner, why was each woman not offered the opportunity to become a partner?

As the case moved forward in the spring of 1976, London fought hard against providing the data about partnership. Refusing to answer Rabb's questions, he argued that they were irrelevant because "Title VII does not require an offer of partnership to any person or employee. Any construction of the law that requires an offer of partnership to an employee or class of employees would, we believe, violate Constitutional guarantees." Behind this resistance lay a pivotal claim: that the U.S. Constitution, with its guarantee of due process and freedom of association, trumped Title VII and protected partnerships, which invite members to join rather than hire employees to labor. This claim represented the ultimate effort to keep the legal profession free to discriminate by sex or race.

In support, London submitted a fourteen-page affidavit, almost a legal brief in itself, from one of Sullivan & Cromwell's most senior partners, John F. Cannon. At length Cannon described the burdens that he and his fellow partners would endure if they were required to sort through mounds of confidential matter relating to each candidate who had been considered for partner. "I personally," he said, "expect that I would have to spend the major portion of my time over several weeks in the effort." Moreover, Rabb's questions about "why we do or do not invite lawyers to join our partnership are irrelevant and improper," he asserted. Congress "did not in Title VII confer upon the federal judiciary the responsibility to review the membership practices of law partnerships."

Judge Motley sided with the firm. Rebuffing Rabb, Motley ruled that partnership information was irrelevant. Because Blank sought to become only an associate, Sullivan & Cromwell could refuse to explain why it had invited no women associates to join its partnership.

Undeterred, Rabb applied to Judge Motley for a rehearing, and she did so with the help of a powerful new ally: the national office of the EEOC. Although the EEOC's New York office had found in 1974 that Blank probably had not been discriminated against by Sullivan & Cromwell, now in June of 1976 the national office decided to support her request for information about women's efforts to become partners at Sullivan & Cromwell. The EEOC was unwilling to concede to Sullivan & Cromwell's claim that "partners and partnerships are not within the purview of Title VII of the Civil Rights Act of 1964." The EEOC argued in a brief to Judge Motley that large law firms must not succeed in insulating themselves from antidiscrimination law merely by "choosing to do business in the partnership form."

This argument came from an invigorated EEOC, one strongly engaged with women's rights and no longer dreading, as it had in the 1960s, being denigrated as a "sex commission." Authors of the brief included the legendary Bea Rosenberg, who directed litigation for the EEOC's effort to convince the Supreme Court that pregnancy discrimination was sex discrimination. They included also Charles Reischel, the EEOC attorney who had tested Susan Deller Ross with a hypothetical about Porta Potties and who had since married Nancy Stanley, a member of Blank's law firm.

Sullivan & Cromwell did not shrink from this new assault. Replying to the EEOC brief, London relentlessly defended the firm's contention that "Title VII did not make it unlawful for a partnership to discriminate on the basis of sex" in the selection of partners. He cited the partnership laws of New York State to argue that joining a partnership must be voluntary. He cited the due process guarantee of the U.S. Constitution to argue that partners could not be commanded to admit new partners.

Judge Motley, watching the incoming fusillades—EEOC versus a major New York firm, Title VII of the Civil Rights Act versus the Fifth Amendment of the Constitution—chose to step out of the line of fire. She found it "unnecessary," she wrote in her reconsideration of whether the firm must provide partnership information, "to reach the difficult issue" of whether Title VII made it "unlawful for a partnership to discriminate." But whether or not Sullivan & Cromwell had the right to discriminate in hiring partners, she agreed with Rabb and the EEOC that any such discrimination might offer evidence of a "similar pattern in the selection of associates, where it would be illegal."

In reaching this conclusion, Motley drew on a case recently heard in her own circuit, that of Margaret Kohn. In that case alleging discrimination in the hiring of female law associates, Judge Morris Lasker had endorsed the following argument made by a magistrate:

> It is difficult to conceive of anything more telling with respect to whether or not these associates are being subject to employment discrimination than whether they proceed on to partnerships in the firm in the same manner as male attorneys with similar capabilities.

Here was precisely the ruling that Sullivan & Cromwell had been dreading. Providing partnership information would demand significant time, as Joseph Cannon had earlier advised Motley. More important, though he did not say so, such information might reveal a multidecade pattern of prejudice against women in his firm and the legal profession. The time had come to settle.

12

Time to Settle

By late spring of 1977, a proposed settlement had been signed by all parties. When it became available at the courthouse for reading, in advance of a final hearing, the press reported it with alacrity. The *New York Law Journal* announced in bold type that the "Sullivan & Cromwell Sex-Bias Accord Is Latest Triumph for Harriet Rabb." In the article, which explained that she had turned down a position as an attorney in President Jimmy Carter's administration in order to continue sex-discrimination litigation, the headline called Rabb "The Ms. Who Keeps Picking on the 'Boys'."

The headline writers of the *Wall Street Journal* showed restraint: "New York Law Firm Accepts Conditions in Hiring-Bias Case." Its reporter showed less. "Two women lawyers and a woman judge," he wrote, "have brought Sullivan and Cromwell, one of the most prestigious and conservative old-line Wall Street law firms, to its knees."

Press coverage may have contributed to the truculence shown by London at the final settlement hearing before Judge Motley. Within minutes, he was repeating his old assertions about bad faith and a weak case. Amid his claims, a new one seemed to slip out: the firm would not discriminate in the future, as it "has not certainly in the past several years." If this hinted at concern for past discrimination, thanks to the settlement no details would emerge. London's protestations aside, the settlement gave Diane Blank, Harriet Rabb, and the Employment Rights Project what amounted to a culminating victory. Sullivan & Cromwell's agreements included the following:

> *Recruiting women.* Every year the firm would send Rabb its recruiting materials so that she could warn them against any discriminatory language. The materials would list the number of women associates working for the firm. The firm committed to interview at law schools with high percentages of women.

> *Interviewing women.* A partner would instruct all his interviewers not to ask "irrelevant" questions about marital status, family plans, and childcare. He would tell interviewers not to assume that women cannot travel, work long hours, or manage tough negotiations.

> *Hiring women.* The firm would expect to offer jobs to women at a percentage comparable to the applications it received from women. Near the end of each hiring year, the firm would give Rabb a report with exact numbers of women interviewed and offers made.

> *Paying women.* Every year, the firm would give Rabb a table showing whether any women associates were receiving less pay than men. If Rabb objected to any woman's low pay, a firm partner would explain its rationale. If Rabb still objected, the firm would hand the woman a form saying that Rabb wanted to talk to her— permitting Rabb to inform her that the firm might be underpaying her because she was a woman.

> *Socializing with women.* The firm was required to invite women to its social events, which could not occur in clubs that excluded women.

If Harriet Rabb did not like what she learned about the firm's recruiting, interviewing, hiring, payment, or treatment of women, she could take her complaints to an arbitrator (a lawyer from another firm, agreed to in advance by Rabb but paid for by Sullivan & Cromwell). And if Rabb disliked any decision made by the arbitrator, she could appeal the decision back to Judge Motley.

On top of providing data, and paying an arbitrator if Rabb disliked what the data revealed, Sullivan & Cromwell also agreed to pay the Employment Rights Project $30,000 as fees for the hours that its lawyers had devoted to suing the firm. Of that total, Blank received $2,000, which she understood was a fee for her legal work on her own behalf.

Whether or not Sullivan & Cromwell felt brought to its knees, as the *Wall Street Journal* suggested, the firm could not feel alone. The firm of Rogers & Wells (successor to Royall, Koegel & Wells) had entered into a similar settlement in its case with Margaret Kohn, paying fees of $40,000 and agreeing to a hiring quota (which Sullivan & Cromwell had avoided).

All told, of the ten complaints that Diane Blank and her classmates brought in 1971 to the NYC Commission on Human Rights, half led to settlements. Although settlements in the three that did not go to court were kept confidential, news reporters learned that one covered recruitment policy and two resembled Kohn's settlement, which established quotas for job offers to women.

The signs of a changing legal culture were showing at Sullivan & Cromwell. When the firm interviewed Blank in 1970, it had no women partners and only three women associates (roughly 3 percent of all associates). When Sullivan & Cromwell settled with Blank in 1977, it had twenty-six women associates (more than 22 percent) but still no women partners. When the *Wall Street Journal*'s canny reporter asked whether some women would eventually make partner, a spokesman for Sullivan & Cromwell replied with one word: "Obviously."

But how soon? How many? Sullivan & Cromwell had not conceded that antidiscrimination law controlled invitations to become partners. Some seven years later, when that issue finally reached the Supreme Court, Sullivan & Cromwell would have only one woman among its seventy-five partners.

13

The Chief Justice's Second Draft

When the claim that law firms could discriminate against women in their partnership decisions reached the Supreme Court in the 1980s, the firm making that claim was arguably more high powered than Sullivan & Cromwell. Griffin Bell, one of the senior partners in the firm, King & Spalding of Atlanta, Georgia, was both a former federal judge and a former attorney general of the United States.

Bringing the case against them was a young attorney named Elizabeth Anderson Hishon, known to her friends as Betsy. In the first year that Harriet Rabb worked at Columbia, and shortly before Ruth Bader Ginsburg arrived there, Hishon finished her law degree, graduating in 1972. Few if any of the women's rights leaders at Columbia recalled her playing an activist role in their law school days. She saw herself as someone who did not wear armbands or march in demonstrations. She distinguished herself not with activism but scholarship, and she graduated as a Harlan Fiske Stone Scholar.

Before she arrived at King & Spalding, the firm had hired one woman attorney, as an associate, back in about 1944, and then promoted dozens of men to partner while that woman remained an associate for over three decades. She worked for the firm, still not as a partner, when it hired Hishon in 1972.

Seven years after the firm hired Hishon, it passed her over for partnership and forced her to leave. She believed it had failed to meet one of the promises it made when it recruited her out of Columbia Law School: "fair and equal" consideration with men in competition for partnership. Arguing that she had been discriminated against by the firm, which still had never promoted a woman to partner, she filed papers in federal court charging Atlanta's most powerful law firm with discrimination.

The firm chose not to argue that it did not engage in discrimination. Instead it made a counterargument that followed the path set by Sullivan & Cromwell in its replies to Diane Blank. King & Spalding argued that its partnership decisions could legally discriminate against women. And it argued not just that Title VII did not cover partnerships, but further that the First Amendment of the Constitution granted law partners the right to freedom of association and expression that would be violated if they were forbidden to apply whatever selection criteria they chose—even if this meant engaging in sex discrimination or, incidental to this case, race discrimination.

The law firm won first in federal district court and again before a three-judge panel in a court of appeals, which ruled that "Title VII does not apply to decisions regarding partnership." The reach of Griffin Bell and his firm extended so pervasively in that southern court that, according to Hishon's attorney, "nine of the twelve active judges of the Eleventh Circuit may have disqualified themselves" to avoid potential conflicts of interest. When the case seemed likely to go to the Supreme Court, the head of the Civil Rights Division in the Office of the Attorney General, William Bradford Reynolds, let his staff know that he sided with the firm. Undefeated in court, supported in the Office of the Attorney General, and known for having among its partners a previous attorney general of the United States, the firm stood poised for a victory that would declare that law firms, in the selection of partners, were exempt from antidiscrimination law and could legally discriminate against women.

Some lawyerly fun in the summer of 1983, before argument in the Supreme Court, may have hurt the firm's case in the court of public opinion. For a summer outing, King & Spalding planned originally to hold a wet T-shirt contest featuring a few of the women among its associates. When soaking the women's shirts seemed impolitic, the firm instead held a bathing-suit contest. It gave a prize to a summer intern, then entering her third year at Harvard Law, who, in the words of one partner, had "the body we'd like to see more of." This story spread, with help from the *Wall Street Journal*.

ORAL ARGUMENT ON HALLOWEEN in the case of Betsy Hishon brought sustained insistence by King & Spalding's attorney, Charles. J. Morgan Jr., that "lawyers are entitled to the highest degree of First Amendment associational freedom" and that the Constitution protected them from Title VII. Further, although no congressman during debates had suggested exempting lawyers from Title VII, he argued that congressmen had intended the exemption. His reason: many congressmen were lawyers and, in passing Title VII, "certainly had in their minds that they were lawyers." Justices resisted, insisting that lawyers in Congress "knew full well how to write exemptions." Morgan asserted also that law partnerships' freedom from Title VII meant partners could force women to work more years than men before being considered for partnerships. Arguing against him, Emmett J. Bondurant II—a family friend of the Hishons who at first urged Betsy not to sue, on the grounds that she would "get over" the pain of injustice—contended that the special position of lawyers in society, and the importance that minorities advance within the legal profession, "advocates for and not against coverage of Title VII."

In conference on November 2, 1983, all nine justices voted against King & Spalding and apparently in favor of applying Title VII to partnerships. Chief Justice Burger took the opinion for himself. For the rights of women, he seemed inauspicious. While Diane Blank had been seeking jobs with law firms in late 1970, Burger—during oral argument in a Title VII case—had sought reassurance that federal judges could, "as a matter of general policy," refuse to hire a "lady law clerk" if she had an infant child. (Privately in the fall of 1971, he was resisting so strongly the possible appointment of a woman to the Supreme Court that he delivered to the White House a letter of resignation.)

The chief made a last effort to protect partnerships. His draft opinion, which remained hidden from public view, stunned fellow justices. Apparently recognizing its historical worth, Justice Blackmun scrawled atop his copy a tall exclamation point and then, in script far larger than his usually small handwriting, "Do not Destroy." Burger devoted much of the first half of his opinion to suggesting that partners of King & Spalding might not be "employees" for the "purposes of Title VII" and thus might be exempt from Title VII.

Then the chief justice explained that Betsy Hishon's chances would depend on her claim that King & Spalding had made a "contract"—unusual among law firms—that specified she would be reviewed for partnership on a "fair and equal" basis. Burger's opinion offered her the chance to bring "evidence" showing the firm "indeed made such a contract." After extended discussion suggesting that partnerships might be protected by the Constitution against intrusion by civil rights law, he said, "The question is not whether Congress intended Title VII to intrude on partnership decisions but whether Title VII provides a federal court remedy when a partnership has made the kind of contract that petitioner alleges." Put another way: Only when a partnership is so generous or foolish that it contracts to make hiring "fair and equal" can Title VII enforce its prohibition against hiring that is unfair or unequal. Any partnership smart enough to avoid such explicit contracts would be unaffected by *Hishon*. And King & Spalding would be unaffected if it could convince a lower court that it had not made such a contract.

The chief justice's last effort to protect law partnerships brought instant opposition. On the day the draft appeared, in a letter to all justices, William J. Brennan attacked Burger's effort to limit Title VII. Two days later, Justice Stevens rebuked the chief justice for not following the unanimous vote in conference. That day also, Justice Brennan circulated a full draft attacking the chief justice's "novel theory of Title VII under which petitioners must prove the existence of a common law contract in order to receive the protections of a federal statute." Congress would not have bothered to create what Brennan called "the elaborate scheme" of the Civil Rights Act of 1964 merely to "afford a federal forum to enforce common law contracts to pro-

vide a 'fair and equal' treatment." In short, Brennan argued, King &
Spalding's "obligation to treat its employees equally does not derive
solely from its voluntary promise to do so. It is, instead, a mandate
of federal law."

Under attack, and with other justices including Thurgood Marshall and Sandra Day O'Connor opposing his contract theory, Chief
Justice Burger surrendered. He wrote to his fellow justices that "there
seems to be considerable feeling that the case should not turn on the
contract" and "I will try my hand at another run." Next to "not turn
on the contract," Justice Blackmun penciled, "*Of course!*"

The chief justice's next run went slowly. In May he delivered an
opinion with new twists. After again discussing the alleged "contract," in a footnote he conceded that Title VII made such contracts
unnecessary. After quoting a Court opinion from 1973 that "private
discrimination may be characterized as a form of exercising freedom
of association protected by the First Amendment," within a few words
he also quoted that opinion's comment that such discrimination "has
never been accorded affirmative constitutional protections"—leaving
open whether constitutional protection might yet be accorded to discrimination. The chief justice's writhings could make full sense only
to the few readers who saw his first-draft efforts to help King &
Spalding. Finally, if reluctantly, he overruled the lower court decision
that had exempted partnerships from Title VII and thus freed them
to discriminate.

Having missed the chief justice's contortions, the press reported the
decision's straightforward impact. The *New York Times* announced
on its front page that the Court had "ruled unanimously today that
law firms may not discriminate on the basis of sex, race, religion or
national origin in deciding which young lawyers to promote to the
status of partner." The *Washington Post* pointed to the case's broad
effect, reaching other partnerships such as "advertising agencies and
architecture, engineering and accounting firms."

Now that law firms could no longer claim a legal right to discriminate against women or blacks or Jews, the ruling seemed obvious.
As George Will wrote in the *Washington Post*, the Supreme Court's

decision said to King & Spalding, "Give me a break." This was a law firm, Will added, "from which a sophist could take a correspondence course in sophistry." Hidden from all but a few justices and clerks was the fact that, only months before and trying to deliver an opinion of the Supreme Court, the chief justice of the United States had been writing on the side of the sophists.

Part Four

———————◆———————

HARASSMENT
(1974–1986)

14

No Law

For nineteen-year-old Mechelle Vinson, coming from her family home among the battered bungalows of a one-block street in northeast Washington, in a neighborhood wedged between railway lines, it was all uphill, two miles uphill along Rhode Island Avenue to the bank where she found her first professional opportunity. Capital City Federal Savings & Loan sat at the crest of the broad street. Looking left from the front door of the bank, a teller could see the red-brick walls and white-doric columns of the National Bank of Washington and, looking right, the blocky red brick of a union headquarters. Straight across from the bank stood the imposing Romanesque columns and arches of St. Frances de Sales School and, to its right, the church of St. Frances de Sales, home to the oldest Catholic congregation in the District of Columbia.

To Mechelle Vinson, Capital City Federal was more than a bank. It was her family bank and her neighborhood bank, "a very small, black bank," she would later call it, in what felt to her like a very small, black neighborhood—one of those close-knit and steady urban communities of Washington where everyone knew everyone else. Vinson had wanted a job at this bank, and she had gone after it, she let people know, because she was young and willing to learn and because she felt a struggle to "be something."

One day in September of 1974 she saw the bank's manager, whom she knew as Mr. Taylor, walking down the street, and she asked if he had any job openings. He gave her an application, and within a few days she was a teller trainee. She had been working jobs since she was twelve, and by age fifteen she had started a marriage that was now having problems, and she saw the bank as her chance finally to advance. Her job evaluations, over the months and years ahead, were described by the bank as "outstanding." She rose quickly from trainee to teller to head teller to assistant branch manager. Sidney Taylor evaluated her, on a scale of 1 to 10, as a "9 plus," and by late 1978 she was holding the positions of head teller and assistant branch manager simultaneously. People noticed her cheerful voice and dramatic looks—most strikingly her bronze-colored skin, her high forehead, and her prominent nose that gave her the look of a Mayan princess. She was ambitious and skilled, a fine manager who, as Taylor would tell her and others, could "go far" with Capital City.

Sidney Taylor seemed a fine manager—dapper, gentlemanly, and, most inspirational for Mechelle Vinson, self-made. Not many years before, he had come out of military service and taken a job as a janitor with this very bank. Through hard work, he had risen to become not just manager of the branch but also the bank's first assistant vice president who was black and, he believed, the first black assistant manager for any major savings association in DC. He had made a home for his wife and seven children only a few minutes' walk from his bank, and he walked the streets often to build his business. He was proud that the branch had grown in size under his care. He was proud, also, that as a bank vice president he could help his community and create jobs for young black employees with potential, like Vinson.

When she arrived at the bank, Vinson wanted to prove to Mr. Taylor, as she always called him, that she had potential. But even during her initial ninety-day probationary period, she would later say, she began to wonder about how Mr. Taylor treated his workers—or at least, how he treated the one other teller working at the bank, Christine Malone. Christina, as Vinson called her, was training Mechelle in day-to-day bank work, and together with Taylor they would become a close-knit unit. Some days he would bring them flowers, what she called "prettying up" their teller windows. Some evenings he would even treat the two of them to an early dinner, according to Vinson, at a neighborhood Chinese restaurant.

At times Mr. Taylor handed out, Vinson recalled, something new to her in the world of business: overtime pay for hours she had not worked. When she asked if there had been a mistake, she remembered that he would respond, "You all have worked so good, that is the reason why I gave you the overtime." Vinson remembered exclaiming, "Oh Christina, we have the greatest boss," to which Christina replied, Vinson recalled, "Oh you just don't know."

Occasionally, Vinson sensed she had entered a less-than-happy work environment. She thought she noticed Mr. Taylor brushing Christina's bottom, or touching her breasts, or chasing her in the back of the bank where the typewriters were kept. Christina seemed not to appreciate Mr. Taylor's behavior, but she was a bashful girl, thought Vinson, who didn't know how to keep a man at bay. To Vinson, Christina seemed to have been raised by parents like her own, who didn't teach girls how to communicate about sex or how to keep men from getting their way. Vinson remembered a little ditty Christina would use:

> Your eyes may shine, your teeth may grit,
> But none of this, you shall get.

Perhaps the ditty was too playful. Vinson thought it did not help Christina.

Then one day when Mechelle and Christina were in the ladies' bathroom, as Vinson remembered, Mr. Taylor barged in on them. Vinson recalled that he took his penis, pulled it up inside his pants, pulled his pants back in order to show it against the cloth of the pants, and seemed to shake it at Christina. Vinson recalled that when Mr. Taylor realized Mechelle was in the bathroom too, he said, "Excuse me." Vinson felt that whatever was going on between Mr. Taylor and Christina was between the two of them. Perhaps they had once had a relationship, she thought, and it had gone bad. Vinson had been raised to believe that when it's not your business, "you see and you don't say."

One Friday, according to Vinson, Christina and Mr. Taylor had a fight over Christina's trouble counting money—"settling her sheet," which was required before they could all leave for the weekend. Mr. Taylor was saying, "You're gonna settle this goddamn sheet, bitch," as Vinson recalled, Christina was saying, "I'm not gonna settle this damn sheet," and Mechelle was in the middle trying to keep them from fighting. Then Christina said she'd had enough and stormed out the door. Next week, Christina didn't have a job.

WITH CHRISTINE MALONE GONE, a new saga began—at least as recalled by Vinson. Without Malone, Vinson would have no one to vouch for her story, and Sidney Taylor would deny most of it. Indeed, the stories have never been verified.

In Vinson's narrative, Taylor continued his generosity, even giving her $120 when she was short on money to begin renting an apartment. Then, a couple of weeks after she had moved, he invited her to join him for dinner. While they were sitting there, she recalled, he said to her, "Mechelle, I have been good to you." When she said she appreciated it, he said he didn't want her to say thank you, she recalled: he wanted her to go to bed with him. And he warned her, according to Vinson, that "just like he hired me, he would fire me."

After dinner, she said, she got in his car, and they drove to a nearby hotel, where he got them a room. There, she recalled afterward, he told her to take her dress off, but she said no. He said she was a grown lady now, he wouldn't hurt her, and she should take her clothes off. Again she said no. He went to take a shower. She waited, sitting on the bed. He came back wearing no clothes and told her to undress, she recalled, and when she said no, he unzipped her dress and took it off and began kissing her and, as she would eventually tell a courtroom, "he put his penis in." In a courtroom years later, she would retell these events precisely but without drama, and she would insist that she never consented to sex. But though she claimed she said "no," she didn't otherwise resist. She gave in, she said.

Years later in court, he insisted that "there was never a time that I indulged in sex with Ms. Vinson," and he denied all of her assertions about having sex.

As Vinson recalled, after they left the hotel Mr. Taylor drove her back to her apartment. At least, after giving in to sex this time, she would later say, "I felt I didn't owe him anything—it was over." But the next morning at work, she said, he touched her buttocks and breasts. In the afternoon, when customers thinned out, she said, he touched her again. She felt sick inside. He told her that he was her supervisor, that he gave her her paycheck, and that she had to do what he wanted.

In the coming months, she recalled being forced to have sex many times, always in the bank, even once on the floor of the bank's walk-in vault. She had stayed late at Taylor's instructions, to prepare for an inspection the next day by federal auditors. As she was working there, she later testified,

> the vault door closed, and Mr. Taylor grabbed me and said, "You are going to fuck me this evening." I said, "Mr. Taylor, only thing I want to do is do my work and leave here." He said, "You are going to fuck me before you leave here." We got to tussling on the floor. He knocked me down on the floor and took my panties off and he forced his penis in me.

After that, she found her vagina was torn, she said, and she bled for weeks.

When he wasn't forcing her to have sex, she later remembered, some days he would put his hands on her body, even from behind while she was working with customers. At times he would follow her into the ladies' bathroom, she recalled, showing her that his penis was erect or asking her if she knew where he could get his "dick sucked" or telling her, "You are going to fuck me this evening." When she told him he should stop, she recalled, sometimes he would respond, "I give you a paycheck."

Vinson believed Taylor's sexual affairs extended beyond herself, for one of her regular jobs as teller became to hand money to one of his "outside women," as she put it, a woman who often visited the bank. After she had become assistant branch manager, she said, two junior bank employees came to her to request that she, as their superior, intercede for them with their boss; they said they were "tired of Mr. Taylor touching them." When she carried their complaint to Taylor, she would later recall, he told her that he was just "relaxing" his employees and the ones who didn't like it could "get the hell out." Vinson stayed. In years to come, after she finally told her story, many people asked her a one-word question: "Why?"

"Because he had told me this is what I had to do—I owed him," she would say. "Just like he hired me, he would fire me. So that was going in my head. This man would fire me. My God. I need my job."

MECHELLE VINSON TOLD HER STORY TO ALMOST NO ONE, until one day in September of 1978. Having decided that she needed to divorce the husband whom she had married when she was about fifteen years old and with whom she was having problems, some violent she said, when she began work at the bank in 1974, she went to an office that ran a TV ad for "low-cost divorces—$275." There she met an easy-to-talk-to young lawyer named Judith Ludwic, and within a few meetings they had arranged the divorce.

When the divorce was almost final, the usually immaculate Vinson came by Ludwic's office, looking wretched. Her hair was falling out, with bald spots showing. Ludwic told her that when a relationship comes to an end, people are often upset, and she asked Vinson, Is that what's bothering you? Vinson said no: "I have a boss that's bothering me." Then, speaking in her matter-of-fact voice, Vinson finally told someone part of her long story. It went late into the night. Ludwic had the impression that Mechelle had never intended to divulge any of this information. Mechelle couldn't stop crying. Throughout, Ludwic noted, Mechelle was always very respectful of her boss, calling him Mr. Taylor.

But Ludwic was horrified. "What locked in my mind," she said later, was the vault. She imagined the door closing with a steel wheel and being sexually assaulted in a stainless-steel place. It was like being raped in a morgue.

Ludwic, just out of law school, had passed the bar less than a year before. She had gone to the University of Detroit at night while earning a living teaching high school. She hadn't entered the legal profession to defend the rights of women and hadn't ever called herself a feminist. She couldn't remember law books explaining anything that would help Vinson. Still, Ludwic was outraged, and she told Mechelle, speaking as her lawyer, that she did not have to have sex to keep a job.

Unfortunately, as Ludwic would later recall, "On what legal ground I stood, I did not know." As it happens, that ground was thin. In the spring of 1975, when Vinson was first caught in what she recalled as a mix of sexual advance and coercion by her boss, there was, for all practical purposes, no law to help her.

In the years that Mechelle Vinson was feeling "bothered" by her boss, American law was beginning to hear stories remarkably like hers. Other women were starting to tell their stories in court, even though there was no law to address their dilemmas.

In Washington, DC, in the early 1970s, an administrative assistant named Paulette Barnes, who worked for the Environmental Protection Agency's director of equal employment opportunity, reported that soon after she was hired, her boss began going after her for "sexual favors" and telling her that "if she cooperated with him in a sexual affair, her employment status would be enhanced." Barnes found a coworker willing to support her story because she too had experienced his unseemly behavior. Her coworker, a secretary, testified that on a business trip to Puerto Rico, the boss had arranged to book them both into the same hotel room. She learned of his plan only when he walked into what she thought was her room and began undressing. Both the secretary and Barnes reported that, after they rebuffed their boss, he began to retaliate against them at work.

In another case, in Arizona in late 1973, Jane Corne and Geneva DeVane, two clerical workers employed by Bausch & Lomb, found themselves repeatedly subjected to "verbal and physical sexual advances" by a supervisor. Once his treatment became unbearable, they resigned and filed legal complaints.

At about the same time that the Arizona women were resigning from their jobs, Adrienne Tomkins, a secretary for an electric company in New Jersey, was being asked by her new boss to dine at a hotel restaurant to discuss a promotion. Over lunch he revealed that, as she later recalled, he "wanted to lay me." He told her that he couldn't walk around the office with a hard-on all the time and that unless they had sex they could not have a "working relationship." When she tried to leave the restaurant, he "restrained me physically" and said she wasn't going anywhere but the executive suite on the hotel's thirteenth floor. She refused. She was transferred to another department and later fired.

Also in the early 1970s, at a bank in California, a teller named Margaret Miller claimed that her boss pressured her to give in sexually, to be "cooperative." Perhaps because he was white, Miller's boss told her he had never before "felt this way about a black chick." She refused and soon lost her job.

And in Washington in early 1972, Diane Williams, a young aide in the public information office of the Justice Department—of all places—reported that she was subjected to advances by her supervisor. She asserted that he sent her a note: "Seldom a day goes by without a loving thought of you." When she rejected his advances for a sexual relationship, she alleged, his treatment of her shifted from adoration to "harassment and humiliation." In late 1972, he fired her.

When women took their grievances to court, they left further aggrieved. In Washington, a judge told Paulette Barnes that her story involved not law but "the subtleties of an inharmonious personal relationship." In Arizona, a judge told the two women who worked for Bausch & Lomb that federal law could not get involved "every time any employee made amorous or sexually oriented advances toward another." He added that the "only sure way an employer could avoid such charges would be to have employees who were asexual." In New Jersey, a judge advised Adrienne Tomkins that the law could not get involved for a simple reason: "if an inebriated approach by a supervisor to a subordinate at the office Christmas party could form the basis of a federal lawsuit for sex discrimination if a promotion or a raise is later denied to the subordinate, we would need 4,000 federal trial judges instead of some 400." And in California, a judge told Margaret Miller that law could not get involved because her story concerned merely "a natural sex phenomenon"—the attraction of males to females. He added that her case could lead to lawsuits arising from "flirtations of the smallest order." (The judge later told Miller's attorney that his "gal" clerks, as he called them, refused to write the opinion he wanted, leaving him to do his own work.)

Taken in sum, these early responses of American law said to women: This problem is not legal but personal. This problem is yours.

15

Naming Sexual Harassment

Not only did the problem that Mechelle Vinson faced have no law. It also had no recognition, no politics, no movement, and no awareness in the nation. Perhaps most remarkably, it had *no name*. But events in early 1975 would soon give Vinson's problem a name: sexual harassment.

The term *sexual harassment* apparently first appeared publicly in print in a letter of late March in 1975, written on the stationery of the Human Affairs Program of Cornell University and designed for wide distribution. It began, in the tone of grassroots organizing, with "Dear Sisters":

> Two weeks ago an Ithaca woman came to the Women's Section of the Human Affairs Program for assistance. The woman, who is the sole support of her two children, was denied unemployment benefits because it was ruled that her reasons for leaving her job were "personal" and "non-compelling."
>
> She was forced to leave after eight years of service because of a pattern of sexual harassment by a male superior which caused her tension and anxiety so severe that she developed painful physical side effects. Her complaints concerning this behavior

were treated lightly by her department and she was told that a
mature woman should be able to handle such situations.

The naming of the problem and the Cornell letter marked the start
of a movement. But the movement, even as it started, was on thin
ground.

The Human Affairs Program was an odd annex of Cornell University. It had emerged as a curricular response by Cornell to the radicalism of the late 1960s. The program taught courses in such topics
as prison reform, bank red-lining, and, in a new course developed in
the fall of 1974 by a young teacher named Lin Farley, women and
work. The letter that introduced the term *sexual harassment* had been
drafted and signed by Farley and two of her fellow teachers in the
program, Susan Meyer and Karen Sauvigné, both young and committed to social change.

The letter had originated, albeit indirectly, from the program's
teaching and particularly from the opening days of Lin Farley's course.
While readying her classes on the topic, Farley had found preparation
difficult. Data seemed thin, and analysis even thinner. Frustrated,
Farley decided to turn, as she put it, to "consciousness-raising," the
emergent women's movement strategy of asking women to talk about
their lives, a strategy that Farley viewed as "a remarkable tool for
unlocking that vast storehouse of women's own experiences."

This turn to consciousness-raising—C-R in the abbreviation of
the day—meant that Farley and her students devoted one early class
to telling their stories about what had happened to them in past jobs
because they were women. For students at an Ivy League university,
they were a diverse group: in race, an almost equal mix of black and
white; in class, a range from rich to poor. By the time the conversation ended, Farley believed she had heard something absent from the
scholarship on women and work: "Each one of us had already quit
or been fired from a job at least once because we had been made too
uncomfortable by the behavior of men."

To discover whether a pattern existed, Farley began asking around
among working women. Then in March of 1975, Carmita Wood

came to Farley with her story, too complicated to record in a one-page letter.

Wood's story, which she would eventually spell out in legal documents but would never be able to prove conclusively, went briefly as follows: The lone support of two children, she had begun working eight years earlier, in 1966, in a lab at Cornell. She received one promotion in 1968 and another in 1971, making her the first woman to hold the post of administrative assistant for the lab. In recognition of her new-found stature, she became the second woman ever admitted to the Ithaca Management Club and, feeling a new level of security, she took out a $10,000 loan to remodel her home.

Soon, however, her sense of security began to fade. Her new job moved her to a new building and put her in frequent contact with the lab's director. Although Wood did not know her new boss well, she had already had one worrying experience. In the fall of 1970, at a faculty cocktail party, she had walked to a patio where her boss was standing with his wife. When Wood said, "Good evening," he replied by saying the same and also by reaching behind her and putting his hand on her bottom. Embarrassed, Wood quickly stepped away.

Wood's promotion in 1971 meant that her boss would now begin making frequent business visits to her office. When he visited, she would later report, he would sometimes lean against her while she was seated at her desk. While he discussed business, he would press against her in a way that pinned her between his body and her desk, and he would peer at her body and clothes. At other times, as she recalled (and as two other lab employees eventually confirmed in sworn testimony), he would "stand with his hands shaking in his pockets and rock against the back of a chair, as if he were stimulating his genitals." He also, as a number of employees observed, seemed to enjoy peering through a glass partition that allowed him to watch Wood and other women working in her vicinity. Wood's worry increased after another employee, a maid, reported that during a Christmas party in 1972, Wood's boss caught the maid alone in an elevator, put his arm on her shoulder, and tried to kiss her.

Wood's difficulties with her boss reached their nadir, according to her story, at the next year's Christmas party, which she was in charge of organizing. In mid-afternoon, her boss arrived along with about forty other party-goers. When he asked her to dance, she refused. He asked again. She refused again—partly because she was busy running the party. Then, after asking her yet again, she recounted, "he grabbed my arms and pulled me to the area where a few couples were dancing."

What happened next she would eventually describe in sworn testimony:

> During the course of the dance, he placed his hands under my
> sweater and vest which, when not so disturbed, extended well
> below my waist. He proceeded to place his hands up my back
> toward my shoulders. This raised my sweater and vest in such
> a manner that my back was exposed. He then rubbed his hands
> up and down my bare skin on my back.

One of her coworkers could see the anguish in Wood's face: she seemed, the coworker thought, "about to cry."

Wood felt publicly humiliated. After the dance she complained to at least two coworkers that her boss had a lot of "nerve" to embarrass her before all their colleagues. Less specifically, she complained also to her direct supervisor, who recalled that on several occasions during her employment Wood had mentioned that their boss had "looked at her and made her feel uncomfortable." But what she recalled as complaints, he heard as humorous and casual comments that he "dismissed" (as he said in an affidavit) as "a diversion she enjoyed." Her supervisor, who had praised her skills in working with others, did not recall hearing about the incident at the Christmas party (he was taking his son to a hockey practice at the time). In any event, his view was that both Wood and her coworkers were "very capable women," as he put it, who were "capable of taking care of themselves, so to speak." To take care of themselves, he suggested that they "try not to get into those situations."

Not long after the Christmas party, Wood began intensifying her efforts to transfer to another part of the university. Also not long after the Christmas party, she began experiencing pain in her hand and arm, which became excruciating. Trips to several doctors provided no relief. Finally, in June of 1974, at about the time her boss was due to return to her building after a leave of absence, Wood resigned from her job. She had decided to go to Florida, hoping the warmer climate would ease her physical pain. But leaving her job was risky, particularly at that moment—the United States was in the midst of a recession, with unemployment running at high levels.

Almost immediately after Carmita Wood left her job at Cornell, the pain in her arm and hand disappeared. It never came back. Later, a psychotherapist told her that her pain had been a physical reaction to emotional stress on the job.

Blessed with no pain but cursed with no work, Wood tried to find a job. For a while she worked as a real estate agent but lost money. Finally, in late 1974, she decided to apply for unemployment insurance from the New York State Department of Labor. At a hearing there, she described quitting her job "for health reasons," the real estate job at which she "didn't sell a thing," and her need, with two children to feed, for unemployment benefits.

Four days later, on December 30, 1974, she received a rejection from the hearing officer of the New York State Department of Labor, penned on a printed form in almost illegible scrawl. "You quit your job without good cause," the official wrote, and continued on that she had quit "for personal non-compelling reasons" rather than health reasons and that she had failed to apply "for a leave of absence which would be available to" her.

Unless Wood could prove that she was compelled to leave, she could not receive benefits. She decided to appeal to a referee of the New York State Department of Labor. This time she came with two coworkers as witnesses to the events that had led to her distress. She also came with her direct supervisor, who made clear he viewed her not just as a satisfactory employee but as one he unsuccessfully had tried to help obtain a leave of absence and one he would recommend for further work at the university.

At this hearing, for the first time, Carmita Wood tried to tell her full story. The state government's referee seemed to see the story as a chance for humor. After Wood described her disabling symptoms, the referee responded, "So you're saying, in effect," that her boss "was a pain in the neck"? When she explained that he treated women as second-class citizens, he asked, "Oh, so he's one of these Male Chauvinist Pigs?" After hearing that one of Wood's coworkers had threatened to resign if her boss did not stop touching her and that her boss was fifty-seven years old, the referee kept the tone jocular: "Well, he's young enough to be interested, anyway."

Given the referee's tone, and the difficulty it created for telling her story, Wood could not have been surprised when she received another rejection. Dated March 7, 1975, it reiterated the earlier judgment, this time not scrawled but typed: Wood had left her job for "personal non-compelling reasons." She had no claim. Her last chance, if she had one, would be to go to court.

A few days later, Wood went to the Women's Section of the Human Affairs Program for assistance, where she met Farley and then Susan Meyer and Karen Sauvigné. Wood told them she was no feminist activist—"not a bra burner," she said, as Meyer later recalled. But she had heard that the Women's Section was interested in this type of problem.

Farley, Meyer, and Sauvigné decided to help Wood: to find her a lawyer, hold a rally, gather support, and start a movement. They decided to draft the letter that began "Dear Sisters." But before they could write about the problem, it needed a name.

SEEKING A NAME FOR THIS PROBLEM, Farley, Meyer, and Sauvigné gathered a small group in their office. Should they call the problem "sexual coercion"? "Sexual intimidation"? "Sexual blackmail"? "Your boss propositioning you"? None rang true. But one phrase had the right sound. It was not too forceful and not too petty: *sexual harassment*.

Although it contained the spark of a new idea, it contained oddly little tinder. The letter did not say what the superior had done. The letter left everything to the powers of suggestion: this problem was about the sort of *situations* that society expected could be handled by a *mature woman*.

Despite its lack of detail, the letter continued—with typographical errors that made its haste apparent—to suggest that this woman was not alone:

> We understand that this situation is one in which working women continually find themselves and that forcing a woman to make a choice between self-respect and economic security is impossible—whichever choice she makes she will loose [*sic*]. A woman's role in any kind of work situation should be based soley [*sic*] on her ability to perforn [*sic*] her job—not on whether she maintains a sexual rapport with the boss.

Beyond the typos, the letter's haste showed also in a claim that was more tentative than it sounded: "this situation is one in which working women continually find themselves." In fact, the authors of the letter were writing with anecdotal evidence from a small group and their own experience.

Hearing stories like Wood's had brought back their stories. Karen Sauvigné found herself recalling an experience from a few years earlier in graduate school: She had been offered a five-nights-a-week waitressing job in the restaurant downstairs from her apartment. Soon, she found her boss assuming he could just pop upstairs to visit her. She was *mature* enough to keep him out, but he cut her work to one night a week.

Susan Meyer remembered her first real job, working as a "girl Friday" in an office with five men in the Chrysler Building in New York, and knowing she was supposed to be a good sport about all the sexual jokes aimed at her, jokes she knew she was supposed to join but that made her feel awkward. She remembered particularly the time she was alone in the office with one man, who began joking, then leaning against her, with his arms on both sides, pinning her against a wall. She couldn't escape. She thought, If I were more sophisticated, I could handle this.

Part of the letter's goal was to invite more memories, more stories, perhaps even more legal cases. Stretching a bit, the letter continued: "Women are organizing to fight this kind of exploitation both by legal and political means." Aptly, the letter reached its climactic plea for help:

> We know of no precedent for this sort of action and we would deeply appreciate your passing on to us any information you may have about similar cases and/or about the physical and psychological effects of prolonged stress upon women. The women we are working with are trying to build a strong organizing campaign and a strong legal case—they need alot of input from other women to do this effectively.

Farley, Meyer, and Sauvigné sent their plea to about a hundred progressive lawyers around the country. The names of these "Dear Sisters" had been gathered by Sauvigné during her work as a legal staffer for two previous employers. One was the Women's Rights Project of the ACLU, where she worked for Ruth Bader Ginsburg, then a professor of law at Columbia University. The other, which had offices in the same building as the ACLU, was the Law Students Civil Rights Research Council—abbreviated LSCRRC and pronounced "liskrik"—a hotbed for young law students, often interns who wanted to change the world.

In response to their plea, only one lawyer wrote back. But a letter came back from a twenty-eight-year-old graduate student in political science at Yale University who had spent a year in a law school program. Her name was Catharine Alice MacKinnon, and she had come to the Upstate Women's Center in Ithaca earlier that year as a singer and guitar player in a duo that traveled the Northeast to play at weddings, events, and coffeehouses. She put her name on a list for a newsletter, and Sauvigné, who had heard MacKinnon's name through LSCRRC in New York and met her when she sang in Ithaca, added her name to the list for the "Dear Sisters" letter. When MacKinnon received that letter, she would always recall, it "just exploded in my mind." This, she thought, is what the situation of women is really about—and everything that the law of sex discrimination made it difficult if not impossible to address. She wrote back to the Human Affairs Program at Cornell, saying she wanted to help. But as of the spring of 1975, MacKinnon's hopes to become a lawyer battling sex discrimination were being frustrated by Yale Law School, which kept refusing to admit her for a degree that would let her practice law.

WHEN MACKINNON WAS BORN, in October of 1946, her father was a young lawyer involved in electoral politics. Already a Minnesota state legislator, George E. MacKinnon was then fighting the last weeks of a political campaign that would win him a seat in the U.S. Congress. There he became friends with another first-term congressman, Richard M. Nixon. Sitting side by side as Republican members of the House Labor Committee, they worked together drafting the Taft-Hartley Act, which protected employees from being forced to join unions. Nixon and MacKinnon also collaborated on an investigation of Alger Hiss for allegedly passing U.S. secrets to the Soviet Union.

Just after his daughter's second birthday, Congressman MacKinnon lost his bid for re-election. With his wife and daughter, he returned to the Lake Minnetonka area to become a local lawyer in the rural district that he had represented. More than twenty years would pass before his return to long-term work in Washington, as a judge appointed to the Court of Appeals for the District of Columbia in 1969 by newly elected President Richard Nixon.

Catharine MacKinnon lived for sixteen years in that farming community, attending public schools and imbibing a sense of heartland values. When discussion arose that his bright daughter "Kitty" (as they called her) should go to a private school to put her on a fast track, her father was adamant: the public school that was good enough for the local kids was good enough for his kids, and he didn't want any child of his growing up to think she was better than anybody else.

From her mother and grandmothers, Catharine developed a sense of women's work and worth. Even her name represented a women's tradition. She was named for her maternal grandmother, Alice S. Davis, and her grandmother's best friend, Catharine ("Kitty") Pierce, head tutor in art history at Radcliffe College. From her paternal grandmother, beginning at age six, Catharine MacKinnon learned knitting and quilting. When her family visited Minnesota state fairs, as they often did, she admired the embroidery and the appliqué, the scalloping and cross-stitching, as art. When her maternal grandmother made a complex quilt of blue cornflowers and yellow daisies as a gift for her daughter, she called it her "life's work." And Smith College, which Catharine MacKinnon, her mother, and both her namesakes attended, set a context for believing, as she would later put it, "that women were real."

Catharine's father often took her to the offices where he worked. By the time she was entering grade school, that was the office of the federal prosecutor in Minneapolis. His best-known investigation became a classic battle against gangsters and racketeering. He was known widely in the state as the prosecutor who "put Kid Cann in jail." When he took her to work, he never gave her the sense that she could not become whatever she chose, although he assumed that she would marry and have children. In the fall of 1958, when she was twelve, she went out with him on the campaign trail after he had been drafted by Republicans to run for governor—a race he lost.

At Smith College, where Catharine MacKinnon enrolled in 1964, she majored in government. Studying with the inspirational professor Leo Weinstein, who taught both constitutional law and classical political theory, MacKinnon wrote a paper in which she discussed the First Amendment theories of a professor at Yale Law School, Thomas Emerson, whom Thurgood Marshall of the NAACP had enlisted in the battle against race discrimination. After she mailed her paper to Emerson, he invited her to meet with him at Yale Law where, as she later recalled, "he took me seriously. We discussed all the issues. And he was warm and great." Her admiration for Emerson's work, which combined theory with practice, made MacKinnon want to study with him. She applied to Yale, wanting to study both law and politics. After Yale's highly competitive law school turned her down for admission for the fall of 1969 (its enrollment was 87 percent male), she won admission to Yale's graduate program in political science.

In 1970 and 1971, Yale Law again rejected MacKinnon for its three-year degree program. Deans at the law school, in conversations that she recalls, gave various reasons. "By the time you applied" in 1969, she was told in a sentence she remembers verbatim, "we had already accepted all our women." Her 1970 turndown was linked to a grade of B at Smith College in graphic arts. In 1971, a dean told her that Yale Law was offering places particularly to black women and to men returning from Vietnam.

In 1972 Yale Law admitted her to a new one-year program, the Master of Studies in Law or MSL, designed for nonlegal professionals. As that year ended, MacKinnon still wanted to enroll for a three-year law degree. The school's recently named dean for admissions, James Thomas, urged her not to apply immediately because, as she recalled later, "it's in opposition to the whole purpose of the MSL— that somebody will use it as a back door into the law school." She needed a formal waiver to permit her to apply. Then, to her surprise, Dean Thomas told her that her previous applications had not received a full review by the school's admissions committee because a committee chair had taken her file out of the process multiple times and prevented it from circulating. MacKinnon later heard that the reason was opposition to her feminism. Following the guidance of the new admissions dean, and the permission from a new chair of admissions to apply after she completed the MSL year and a hiatus year, she applied for the fall of 1975. Considered by a full committee, she was accepted, six years after her first application.

The years that Yale Law held MacKinnon at bay, and while she began work toward her doctorate in political science, were intellectually dynamic. In the early 1970s, New Haven, much as any university city, was a place of intellectual ferment. For MacKinnon, the shift from Smith to Yale involved a shift from listening to acting. She arrived at Yale not long before the New Haven trial of Bobby Seale, national chairman of the Black Panther Party, for the alleged murder of another Panther suspected of being a police informer—a trial that led Yale's president, Kingman Brewster, to express skepticism whether a black revolutionary could get a fair trial in America. Politics became a question not only of what you thought but also of what you were going to do.

To consider what actions to take, MacKinnon and her friends in the political science cohort met once a week for dinner. They discussed supporting the Panthers, unionizing Yale workers, advancing class struggle. In early 1970, a male student gave MacKinnon an issue of *Rat*, a radical New York newspaper. It was created entirely by women—including Robin Morgan, who was then working on her anthology *Sisterhood Is Powerful*—who had taken over the newspaper after its usual male editors produced their own special issue, on sex and porn. To MacKinnon, the liberated *Rat* was the "first feminist anything I ever saw." Also among MacKinnon's friends, mimeographed copies began to circulate from an unknown writer's incomplete book: Kate Millett's *Sexual Politics*.

From this fusion of politics and feminism, MacKinnon was beginning a long graduate project that would become her equivalent of the quilt that her grandmother called "life's work." She would use Marxism and feminism to critique each other—and central to her critique would become Marxism's failure to take into account the inequality of the sexes. It would eventually become both her 1987 doctoral dissertation for Yale and her 1989 book for Harvard University Press, *Toward a Feminist Theory of the State*.

16

Women and the Law

Despite her outsider status at Yale Law School through most of the early 1970s, MacKinnon remained part of the community of law students—attending law classes, whether registered or not. In the spring of 1975, she became part of a course on sex discrimination taught by a young professor named Barbara Underwood, who assigned a new textbook: *Sex Discrimination and the Law: Causes and Remedies*. Almost no one called it by that title. Using the names of its authors, students called it *Babcock, Freedman, Norton, and Ross*. The authors were well known to Underwood and many others, particularly at Yale and New York University, for the book's origins lay in the earliest courses on women and the law—courses originated at NYU in the fall of 1969 by Susan *Ross* and later taught by Eleanor Holmes *Norton*, whose Yale Law roommate, Barbara *Babcock*, had been the first instructor to teach a women-in-the-law course at Yale after its initiation in the spring of 1970 by Yale students including Ann *Freedman*. The courses had evolved into a casebook two inches thick that made it possible for all law schools to offer instruction on gender issues.

What MacKinnon encountered in her 1975 course troubled her. The key analyses of *Sex Discrimination and the Law*, like many analyses of Professors Ruth Bader Ginsburg and Herma Hill Kay in their *Text, Cases, and Materials on Sex-Based Discrimination* of 1974, depended on one crucial starting point: a fundamental similarity between women and men, a presumption that men and women are "similarly circumstanced" (the words from *Royster Guano* that Professor Ginsburg dug up for the *Reed* case at the Supreme Court) or "similarly situated" (from the closing lines of the *Reed* opinion). But MacKinnon believed that the crucial starting point could not be similarity; it had to acknowledge women's second-class status, which often led to what she called their "disadvantagement" because of sex. The summer before MacKinnon enrolled in Underwood's course, the Supreme Court had delivered the fiasco of *Geduldig v. Aiello*, the pregnancy case in which the classification of "pregnant women" and "nonpregnant persons" had allowed the Court to deny women health benefits. For MacKinnon, this legal discrimination would come to represent women's sex-based subordination and disadvantagement.

When MacKinnon received the "Dear Sisters" letter of March 1975, she thought, as she would recall for years, that what happened to Carmita Wood was "about everything the situation of women was really about" but that the existing law of sex discrimination made difficult or impossible to address. She sent a copy of the letter to Underwood, suggesting it might make a good exam question—one that asked, "How is this sex discrimination?" since the harassment described in the letter involved "*conditions of work*, not hiring, firing, promotion and other clear thresholds."

At about the same time that law students were preparing for exams, in Ithaca a group calling itself Working Women United, growing from the work of Farley, Meyer, and Sauvigné to help Carmita Wood, was preparing what would become the first large-scale discussion of "sexual harassment."

THE WORKING WOMEN UNITED speak-out in Ithaca, on May 4, 1975, brought 275 women together on folding chairs in a local gymnasium, beneath battered basketball hoops, to listen as about twenty women, including Carmita Wood, retold experiences with sexual harass-ment. Although galvanizing for the organizers of the new institute, the speak-out itself did not reach far beyond the gym walls. Some women had spoken with no agreement for making their testimony public, and in any event the institute would not manage for half a year to complete a transcript.

Word spread thanks largely to a reporter for the *New York Times*, Enid Nemy, whose interest was piqued thanks to an initiative of Elea-nor Holmes Norton. As soon as Norton moved from the ACLU to the rights commission in 1970, and as she was preparing to teach her first course on women and the law at NYU, she began to organize a gov-ernmental hearing on women's rights, probably the first in America. For a new set of hearings in late April of 1975, Norton's commis-sion invited Lin Farley to give testimony on sexual harassment. That caught the attention of Nemy, who in her years as a reporter doing interviews had heard, "continually but peripherally," women's stories of being grabbed in offices or denied promotions after declining to go on dates with supervisors, usually from women who viewed it as one of the "penalties you paid for being a woman in the workplace."

During the summer after the speak-out, Nemy conducted follow-up interviews, and her article of late August in 1975 quoted numer-ous women describing sexual harassment. A Cornell student spoke of being pawed while working as a waitress to put herself through college, explaining that because you need the tips, "you aren't in any position to say 'get your crummy hands off me.'" An employee in the personnel department of Ithaca College said that she had encountered problems in every job she had held, beginning with babysitting when "husbands taking me home would make passes at me." A nurse at a university hospital called sexual harassment "a working condition between doctors and nurses." A woman who had trained briefly in commercial real estate told of being propositioned by a superior who, after she refused him, told her she would be "sorry" and worked to end her training as a realtor. Nemy's retelling in the *New York Times* broke new ground, for, as she heard from the president of the National Association for Women, "sexual harassment is one of the few sexist issues that has been totally in the closet."

Nemy's reporting also showed that it was coming out of the closet. Eleanor Holmes Norton told her that the Commission on Human Rights was working on sexual-harassment language to be included in all the city's affirmative-action agreements. Early drafting read as follows: "respondent agrees to afford protection to male and female employees alike against unfair abuse of sexual privacy." If Norton's legal pioneering made her actions unsurprising, the same could not be said for the director of the Unemployment Division of the New York State Department of Labor—the division whose hearing officer had refused unemployment benefits to Carmita Wood on the grounds that she had quit her job for "personal non-compelling reasons." Did the Department of Labor indeed believe that someone who quit her work in response to sexual harassment had quit "without good cause"? Speaking to Nemy of the *New York Times*, the boss of the hearing officer declared that sexual harassment, if proven, was "good cause for leaving a job."

Although Nemy's article went a long way toward giving sexual harassment a national name, it indicated how far sexual harassment remained from gaining a clear place in the law. The article did not appear with the legal news of the *Times*. It appeared in the "family/style" section. The only legal case Nemy mentioned, involving the two women in Arizona who charged that their boss had subjected them to sexual advances, was thus far a loser. Legally, what could turn the tide from losses toward victories? The New York labor director sounded sympathetic about sexual harassment, for example, but he wanted proof. Nemy's article showed that much legal work lay undone.

In the fall of 1975, as MacKinnon re-enrolled in Yale Law School—this time for a full law degree—she read Nemy's article and read also the first issue of a newsletter from Working Women United, called *Labor Pains*, which arrived in her Yale mailbox. Its headline announced, "Speak Out Draws Tears and Anger." Inside the newsletter an article by Carmita Wood described poignantly what she had experienced when she decided to "become a public figure involved in an issue that has only been whispered about." In words suggesting she had not imagined what she was getting into, she acknowledged, "It's rough," and continued,

Inside myself there was fear, self-doubt, and insecurity. I asked myself if I really had the courage to go through with it. Would it affect my family and friends? Would people look at me with disgust and scorn? Would they think I had made the whole thing up for some obscure reason of my own? Would it affect any future employment I might try to get? Would anyone else support me in this issue except my closest friends and the immediate group of women I was already working with?

To all the questions above, Carmita Wood continued, the answer was yes.

In law school, MacKinnon decided to begin an independent project ("supervised analytic writing," as Yale called it, working with the guidance of Professor Thomas Emerson) that would attempt to develop a legal theory of sexual harassment as sex discrimination. Although MacKinnon hoped that her law school paper might directly help Carmita Wood, when MacKinnon called Karen Sauvigné in the fall, she learned that the final attempt by Working Women United to help Wood get unemployment benefits had been rejected. Wood could still appeal to federal courts, but at Working Women United there was, as MacKinnon penned in her copy of *Labor Pains*, "not energy to appeal."

In the paper that she titled "Sexual Harassment of Working Women: A Case of Sex Discrimination," MacKinnon set out to tackle the two halves of the title in sequence. First, through dozens of pages, she depicted the harassment, drawing on information from Working Women United, from Enid Nemy's article in the *New York Times*, and from her own interviewing of women around her. Second, she began to argue the case that such harassment—far from constituting "a natural sex phenomenon" or revealing "the subtleties of an inharmonious personal relationship"—was illegal discrimination. MacKinnon's challenge was to shape the law of sex discrimination to address the facts of sexual harassment. To make her case, MacKinnon devoted much early effort to a version of the challenge that Ruth Bader Ginsburg had taken on in her brief for Sally Reed: reveal the linkages between illegal racism and still-legal sexism. But MacKinnon re-entered that old discussion with a new insight, which would emerge as her drafting proceeded: that forms of discrimination the Supreme Court had treated as neutral and ruled legal led, in fact, to what MacKinnon called women's "disadvantagement."

The law against discrimination, she pointed out, "has emerged as a response, however inadequate, to the demands by black people for legal equality as a means to social equality." In the process of creating that law, she continued, "courts have been brought to see that many practices are unquestionably racist, practices which they allow to persist in their corresponding sexist forms." As an example, MacKinnon proposed a corporation that "hired only blacks for positions which, as a persistent side-component, required personal services such as making coffee for the white superiors" or running personal errands for white superiors. No court, she argued, would hesitate to condemn this hiring pattern as racially discriminatory. Similarly, no court would hesitate to condemn a corporation that, for aesthetic reasons, dressed blacks—and only blacks—in busboy uniforms. But, she continued,

> How many employers, by contrast, hire women for their "aesthetic" appeal in Playboy bunny-type outfits? To further unpack these "aesthetics," should it be all right if employers just find women behind typewriters "prettier to look at" than they would men?

"Does this mean," MacKinnon asked, "that being looked at (for a start) by the boss (male) is part of what many women are hired for?" The courts' current acceptance of sexism, she pointed out, paralleled their older acceptance of racism.

Like Ginsburg and her students, MacKinnon found a stunning resemblance between old legal racism and enduring legal sexism. On one page, MacKinnon juxtaposed three legal opinions that showed remarkable continuity in phrasing:

Old sexism (from *Bradwell*, Illinois, 1869):
That God designed the sexes to occupy different spheres of

action, and that it belonged to men to make, apply, and execute the laws, was regarded as almost axiomatic truth.

Old racism (from a miscegenation case, Virginia, 1959):

Almighty God created the races white, black, yellow, Malay and red, and He placed them on separate continents. . . . The fact that He separated the races shows that He did not intend for the races to mix.

Modern sexism (from a public assistance case, Oregon, 1970):

The Creator took care of classifying men and women differently, and . . . we are not prepared to say that the classifications thus made were without good reason.

A continuity stood out in the minds of judges: that God had separated men from women, just as he had separated whites from blacks. But a discontinuity was also clear—judges had decided to act against racism. MacKinnon's goal was to pose a primary question: why had judges dropped the language of divinely ordained spheres in matters of race but not sex? Put another way, what permitted judges, now repudiating old racism, to persist in modern sexism?

These questions recalled early efforts by Ruth Bader Ginsburg. What led judges to refuse to scrutinize sex discrimination with the same level of suspicion that they directed at race discrimination? What led the Supreme Court to reject Ginsburg's arguments that sex, like race, be a "suspect category," and thus that sex discrimination be subject to "strict scrutiny"? The questions also recalled the pregnancy fiascoes experienced by Wendy Webster Williams and Ruth Weyand. What led the Supreme Court to decide that discrimination against pregnant women was not discrimination against women? MacKinnon was setting out, in part, to find a way to address the problem that had stopped Ginsburg from reaching her goal.

What began to emerge in MacKinnon's law school paper was a complex argument about what judges saw when they saw *discrimination*. Because discrimination law "emerged as a response . . . to the demands by black people for legal equality as a means to social equality," that law became in origin, MacKinnon argued, "a substantive law on blacks: shaped by their social experience, tailored to the effects of racism and the history of slavery, and applied only in a limited way to other groups." *Substantive law*, a key phrase in MacKinnon's paper, meant law that saw not just form but substance, law that saw not just discrimination (which could seem neutral, as when one discriminates vanilla from chocolate) but *disadvantagement*.

As a classic example in which the Supreme Court saw discrimination without disadvantagement, MacKinnon pointed to the famous *Plessy* case of 1896, in which the Court upheld as constitutional the segregation of blacks and whites into "separate but equal" railroad cars. The Court's nineteenth-century majority refused to recognize that separation was a badge of disadvantage, that *separate* might mean not *equal* but *subordinate*. It argued that a law which makes "merely a legal distinction"—that is, which merely discriminates or merely separates—"has no tendency to destroy the legal equality of the two races." *Plessy*'s argument, the opposite of *substantive*, asked not about substance but about form. Seeing only form, the Supreme Court saw no inequality.

But in race cases, eventually, such arguments for formal equality failed. Even in *Plessy* in 1896, the failure was prefigured in Justice Harlan's famous dissent, which MacKinnon quoted:

> Everyone knows that the statute in question had its origin and purpose, not so much to exclude white persons from railroad cars occupied by blacks as to exclude colored people from coaches occupied by or assigned to white persons. . . . No one would be so wanting in candor as to assert the contrary.

As MacKinnon recognized, Harlan was rebuffing the formal argument: the argument that each side is merely discriminated between, that neither is discriminated against. Harlan answered with a substantive argument: socially, everyone knows that being black has meant being excluded, and such exclusion is part of what the Thirteenth Amendment to the Constitution sought to prohibit when it forbade practices that impose "badges of servitude."

Although the Supreme Court had long refused to apply the Thirteenth Amendment to women, women could use—and had used, beginning with Ginsburg in *Reed*—the Fourteenth Amendment's guarantee of equal protection of the laws. Under the Fourteenth Amendment, MacKinnon argued, the concept of "suspect classification" had functioned as a substantive classification for blacks. Because race was a "suspect classification," judges scrutinized lines drawn by race with the suspicion that they should be illegal. Had Ginsburg succeeded in her efforts to make sex also a suspect classification, women would have benefited from the Court's helpful *suspicion*— a perspective that carried a sense of substance. But the courts had rebuffed Ginsburg, leaving the law with a neutral presumption about sex discrimination—a presumption not of suspicion but of rationality. Discrimination against women was acceptable if it was, to use the most common test, not "arbitrary."

The word *arbitrary* had come to pervade the law of sex discrimination. Like the notion of "similarly situated," it had arrived when Chief Justice Burger, in the *Reed* case, took the hook that Ginsburg had baited with *Royster Guano*. Following the language she had given him from that obscure fertilizer case from the 1920s, the chief justice had ruled that when a government makes a classification that draws a line between men and women, that classification

> must be reasonable, not arbitrary, and must rest upon some ground of difference having a fair and substantial relation to the object of the legislation, so that all persons similarly circumstanced shall be treated alike.

Thanks to Ginsburg's ingenious introduction of *Royster Guano* into Supreme Court decisions on sex discrimination, the low-level standard of what is *reasonable* had been defined and thus raised toward what eventually became called "intermediate-level" scrutiny. But when the Court rejected Ginsburg's effort to raise the level as high as she wished, to strict scrutiny and suspect classification, the law of sex discrimination was left with the language of *Royster Guano*, and particularly two concepts: *similarly circumstanced* and *not arbitrary*.

WOMEN AND THE LAW   239

And quickly those concepts had become crucial to all cases of sex discrimination.

Combined, those two concepts meant that a woman who complained of sex discrimination had to prove she was treated less well than *similarly circumstanced* men; if she was a typist, to use an example of MacKinnon's, she needed to prove she was treated worse than male typists (if her company employed male typists). And once she had proved her treatment was worse, she must prove it was also *arbitrary*—not based on, say, the fact that she typed eighty words per minute while the company's average (or only) male typist could type eighty-five. No court would rule unlawful a company's desire for faster typists. But what, MacKinnon asked, if the company's bosses desired to look at "pretty/attractive" typists? Would this mean, as MacKinnon asked, "that being looked at" by a boss "is part of what many women are hired for?"

MacKinnon's question about a starting point for sexual harassment became far from hypothetical when combined with Paulette Barnes' experience with her government supervisor and then with the district court. Making the first federal court decision on sexual harassment (but not using that term), the court ruled in effect that Barnes' problem arose from being attractive. It ruled that she was discriminated against "not because she was a woman, but because she refused to engage in a sexual affair with her supervisor" whom she had attracted. Though the court judged his behavior inexcusable, it judged his behavior was not sex discrimination because it did not "evidence an arbitrary barrier to continued employment based on plaintiff's sex." That crucial formulation imbedded both key components—*arbitrary* and *similarly situated*—of what MacKinnon was critiquing as a search for equality in form but not in substance, a search for "formal equality." Losing her job (what the judge called hitting "an arbitrary barrier to continued employment") was not *based on sex*, thought the judge, because no man was similarly situated to Barnes: no man had attracted her male boss and then refused the boss's advances. And losing her job was not *arbitrary* because the barrier to her employment was purposeful, created not for all women but for one woman, by her boss, for the purpose of getting that woman into bed (or out of a job)—and she could choose.

Sex discrimination law, as analyzed by MacKinnon, seemed ridiculous. To bring a claim of sex discrimination, a woman must prove she is situated similarly to some man but treated differently—and *arbitrarily* differently. The worst joke came in pregnancy cases which,

> because of the physical impossibility of men getting pregnant, make clear the inadequacy of "arbitrariness" logic to comprehend that disadvantagement of pregnant people is disadvantagement of women.

Here emerged MacKinnon's answer to questions about the Supreme Court's blindness to both pregnancy discrimination and sexual harassment. Question: What had led the Court to decide that discrimination against pregnant women was not discrimination against women? Answer: Because no men were *similarly situated* to women, no discrimination existed between *similarly situated* men and women— between, that is, pregnant men and pregnant women. Question: Why had the Court failed to see that sexual harassment was a form of sex discrimination? Answer: So long as only women were attractive to male bosses, no discrimination existed. Using its arbitrariness approach, typified by Justice Stewart's "pregnant women" and "nonpregnant persons," the Court could see sexual harassers as merely distinguishing between attractive women and nonattractive persons. (Don't we all, a judge might wonder, make such distinctions?)

As an improvement to this *arbitrariness* approach—and as the goal of her paper on sexual harassment—MacKinnon advanced a method to scrutinize sex discrimination that she called a *disadvantagement* approach (and in later years would call a *dominance* approach). The disadvantagement approach was not formal but substantive. As MacKinnon saw it, the *arbitrariness* approach turned on whether a practice (excluding, for example, pregnant women from health benefits) differentiated *arbitrarily* between citizens who were *similarly situated* (women who were pregnant and men who were similarly pregnant). Pushing beyond such absurdity, and pointing to other substantive recognitions in the law such as Justice Harlan's vision that discrimination imposes "badges of servitude," MacKinnon proposed a *disadvantagement* approach that "turns upon whether the practice or rule disadvantages one sex and not the other."

Using this approach, a court would ask simply, If pregnancy benefits are denied to women, "will any man himself ever be disadvantaged?" The answer would be clear: men did not suffer but women did. Under MacKinnon's approach, an instance of disadvantage because of pregnancy or sexual harassment in the workplace, if proven, would become illegal discrimination under Title VII. Judges would scrutinize sex discrimination (including harassment) that, like race discrimination (including harassment), for too long had both sustained and relied upon a workplace hierarchy that MacKinnon condemned, as she concluded her law school paper, as "separate and subordinate, not equal." Without such a major change in thinking, however, the law's support of sex discrimination would leave judges where they had once been with race. Although what MacKinnon called "judicial participation in the subordination of blacks" had been recognized and repudiated, what remained alive and well was judicial subordination of women.

JUDICIAL CONSIDERATION OF on-the-job harassment of women remained in its early stages in the autumn of 1975 as Catharine MacKinnon, in her first term studying for a JD at Yale Law, continued working on her draft. No federal court opinion had used the term *sexual harassment*. In the same months, lawyers for Paulette Barnes, using the term *sexual blackmail*, were preparing for oral argument in the first harassment case to reach a court of appeals. MacKinnon kept working on her paper during Yale's Thanksgiving and Christmas holidays that year, even when she traveled to her parents' home in Washington and to her father's chambers in the Court of Appeals for the District of Columbia, where, although at first she had not realized it, *Barnes* had been scheduled for argument.

Researching a paper on a topic unrecognized by law posed problems. To find federal cases on a legal topic such as *assault*, a law student could go to shelves of fat books called *West's Federal Practice Digest*. Because *West* assigned "Key Numbers" to key terms such as *assault and battery*, a student flipping through pages could find hundreds of cases. But *sexual harassment* had no West Key Number. One day that fall, Judge MacKinnon told his daughter that his courthouse had received a new and expensive machine, called Lexis, which could search for any words that appeared anywhere in legal opinions.

Catharine MacKinnon could imagine the possibilities of Lexis. On a day when almost no one was working in her father's courthouse, perhaps the Friday after Christmas in 1975, he led her out the back door of his chambers. Carrying her law school draft, she entered the back door of the court's library, which was being remodeled. In a closet-sized room with its floor still torn up and its lights incompletely wired, she found a just-installed Lexis terminal.

On December 17, *Barnes* was argued. It had been screened in advance and assigned to the court's summary calendar—used for cases that the screening judge felt were less important and deserved less time than cases on the regular calendar—by Judge Spottswood Robinson III. After the argument, Catharine MacKinnon heard that its three-judge panel, not announced in advance, included her father. When he led her to Lexis, he knew that she was doing research on issues related to *Barnes* and harassment but, as she recalled years later, "that was all he knew" about her paper.

Although she had never used a computer, MacKinnon started to figure out how this machine could help her find cases she might have missed. When she typed in *sexual harassment*, nothing came back. So MacKinnon tried phrases like *sexual advances and employment*. She tried *sexual abuse at work* and other variations.

Suddenly a young woman in a dark suit appeared, standing in front of her. To MacKinnon she looked professional, with soft dark curls, prominent eyes, and beautiful skin, pinkish in the cheeks. The woman said she worked with Judge Robinson. MacKinnon guessed she was a law clerk.

Then she said, as MacKinnon recalled, We understand you've written something on this subject that nobody around here knows anything about—this sexual byplay at work, when the woman doesn't want it.

Neither MacKinnon nor the clerk mentioned *Barnes*. MacKinnon remembers the woman asking, If somebody is making sexual advances to a woman at work, can that be sex discrimination?

Yes, said MacKinnon, I think it is.

The young woman asked, Do you have anything written? We can't find anything on it.

MacKinnon would always remember what happened next. She picked up her only copy of her paper, a sheaf an inch or two deep, thinking, If she loses it, I don't have a copy. MacKinnon said the draft was only partially done.

Whatever it is, the young woman said (in words MacKinnon would long recall as verbatim), "it's got to be more than we've got." The woman said she would make a copy and return the paper. To Mac-Kinnon, handing over her paper felt like giving away her baby to a stranger.

MacKinnon had not started writing her paper just for school. She was writing it for the real world. "This is my shot," MacKinnon thought. "I'm taking it." The young woman carried off the paper. MacKinnon never saw her again. The paper came back in an envelope, handed to her by her father. They didn't discuss it, and he seemed to have received it without explanation via his secretary. As for the views of Judge Spottswood Robinson, whom her father and other colleagues on his court often called "Spotts," Catharine MacKinnon would wait many months before hearing his opinion about sexual harassment and Paulette Barnes.

JUDGE SPOTTSWOOD W. ROBINSON III was the child of a successful lawyer and businessman in Richmond, Virginia, who enrolled in Howard Law School in 1936, planning to get his degree and return to legal practice with his father. Those modest goals paled beside those of his dean: Charles Houston, graduate of Amherst College and Harvard Law, one of approximately a hundred black lawyers in America who had a degree from a first-rank law school. Appointed a decade earlier to give new life to Howard Law, Houston had dropped the number of degrees granted by the school from fifty-eight in the early 1920s to eleven in 1933 and raised the school's level. Houston drove his students ferociously, and with a goal beyond making them great lawyers. He had taken over at Howard in an era when the law continued to discriminate shamelessly against blacks, when state laws still restricted Negro voting, when courts could exclude blacks from sitting on juries, and when federal courts still endorsed segregated schools, restaurants, and trains. In the words of one Howard graduate, the new goal of Howard Law under Houston was "to learn how to bend the law to the needs of blacks."

Robinson arrived at Howard Law a year after Charles Houston moved from his deanship to become special counsel to the NAACP while remaining the law school's behind-the-scenes inspiration. The day Robinson put his foot in the door of Howard Law, he would later realize, was the turning point in his life. Charles Houston became his idol. At Howard, Robinson showed the habits of hard work and attention to detail that would stay with him the rest of his life. He would graduate in 1939 with the highest grade-point average in the history of Howard Law.

After briefly joining his father's law practice, he returned to Howard Law to teach and to join the effort to end segregation in America. With another Howard graduate, in 1943 he created a Virginia firm devoted to fighting for civil rights. By the early 1950s, as *Brown v. Board of Education* was heading toward the Supreme Court, perhaps only Thurgood Marshall, as head attorney for the NAACP, had spent significantly more time working for school desegregation than Spottswood Robinson.

Robinson had also become a brilliant legal writer, full of passion that may have been heated at least slightly by the experience of getting turned away from segregated lunch counters as he traveled for legal work in the South. When the time came in late 1953 to give a final polish to the NAACP's 235-page brief to the Supreme Court in the pivotal segregation cases that became *Brown*, Robinson provided that polish. And when a series of NAACP attorneys went before the Supreme Court to make the winning arguments in the *Brown* case, Robinson presented the first argument.

In 1964, after spending four years as dean of Howard Law, Robinson became the first black judge on the United States District Court for the District of Columbia. In 1966 he became the first black to serve on any federal court of appeals—the court for the DC circuit, on which he distinguished himself for the extraordinary scholarship of his opinions and came to be known as "Mr. Footnote."

So when Catharine MacKinnon handed over her draft, full of linkages of legal racism to legal sexism, to someone she understood worked with Judge Robinson, she was apparently sending it to the judicial chambers of one of the most brilliant advocates in the history of the American battle against race discrimination.

17

Mechelle Vinson Goes to Trial

At about the time that feminist organizers began laying the groundwork for sexual harassment law, out on the West Coast another feminist lawyer—"Born a feminist," said one admirer—was completing her legal training and heading toward a collision with the development of sexual harassment law.

Patricia Barry, born in Omaha and raised on the California coast in Los Angeles County, graduated from California State University, Los Angeles, and started teaching high school in one of the poorest school districts in the state. But she wasn't happy teaching English; she had loved political science, and she thought she might like law. In 1970 she won admission as one of the few women students to the law school of the University of California at Los Angeles. Among her fellow students, men outnumbered women ten to one, and Barry thought the men set the tone. The legal world, she came to think, turned women into male imitators. Barry hardly went to class. Though she nearly flunked out, she got her law degree.

Barry was tall, blonde, broad-shouldered, glamorous, and defiantly Irish-Polish. When people got her angry, as they often did, she would say they had got her Irish up. If movie studios in the early 1970s had wanted another Rita Hayworth, they might have looked to Patricia

Barry. After law school, one of her first employment rejections came from a judge who told her she "looked like a starlet"—despite her tied-back hair and navy blue dress. She knew she still looked twenty-one. After the judge said he couldn't hire someone with her looks, she went home and cried.

Eventually Barry found work with another California judge. That job went sour after his secretary asked her, and Barry agreed, to defend the judicial secretaries who were trying to organize a union. Looking for new ways to be a lawyer, she decided to head for Washington, DC, which she saw as her way station en route to Paris. Barry wanted to travel; she wanted to become fluent in French; she had heard that the American Bar Association in Washington had a placement service that could help a lawyer find work in France.

On the road east, Barry's old Volkswagen Beetle blew a rod in Utah, limped to Omaha, and died. Almost penniless, she reached DC. Hoping she could save enough money to move on to France, she began waitressing and applying for lawyers' jobs.

For legal inspiration, Pat Barry would go down to the Supreme Court. One day in the autumn of 1974, she heard an oral argument by Ruth Bader Ginsburg for the Women's Rights Project of the ACLU. Ginsburg was urging the Court to overturn a Louisiana law that effectively excluded women from juries. To do so, she needed to fend off challenges by numerous justices, including one who accused her of treating "cavalierly" a Supreme Court decision, *Hoyt v. Florida*, which had upheld a similar law only thirteen years earlier. Ginsburg proceeded to dismember that problematic decision so deftly that after her time for argument expired, Chief Justice Warren Burger took a moment to praise her. Her argument had been "much less cavalier toward *Hoyt*," he remarked, than the opinion of three lower-court judges who had dismissed *Hoyt* as mere "sterile precedent."

Hearing Ginsburg slice through bad law, Barry thought to herself that some day she too would argue at the Supreme Court. Who knows where that thought came from. Barry was a waitress with a law degree. Then a friendly administrator whom she had met at the referral service of the District of Columbia bar association called Barry, offering the chance to take a case. Since Barry had no lawyers in her family, she couldn't tell if the call was strange or standard procedure. She thought, as she said later, "Oh, is this is the way you practice law in DC? They just call up and give you cases?"

The referral was a long shot, litigating against the U.S. Army in a case of employment discrimination—one of many topics Barry had not really studied while skipping classes at UCLA. On behalf of a chemist from India who believed he had been discriminated against by the Army because he had born outside the United States, she went to the Law Library Reading Room of the Library of Congress and buried herself in the fine points and legislative history of Title VII.

To type court papers, she borrowed an old typewriter. It needed work. Whenever Barry typed to the end of a line, the typewriter flung its carriage off its tracks and onto the desk. Barry persisted. She argued in a hearing against the Army. Then she argued in district court and the court of appeals for the District of Columbia. Eventually she won damages for her client and lawyer fees for herself. At an early stage a hearing officer told her, as she would recall years later, "You're the best attorney I've ever seen." So, that was it: Pat Barry *was* a lawyer. And she had a specialty: employment discrimination.

Other cases followed, and she rented office space in the National Press Building. In the summer of 1979, Barry got a call from an attorney named John Marshall Meisburg who had been briefly representing a young bank teller named Mechelle Vinson. On a referral from Judith Ludwic, in whom Vinson had confided, Meisburg began representing Vinson—interviewing some of her coworkers and starting to build her case. But Meisburg, who had spent most of his career in government rather than private practice, soon decided to move to Florida to work for the government. Vinson felt stunned. "He had said," she later recalled, "he was gonna be here for me—has these great laws, and he's gonna fight for me." When he introduced Barry, Vinson thought, Here was a lawyer with a totally different style. Vinson also learned that here was a lawyer with no money. To save a few dollars, for example, Vinson would have to help Barry by having friends serve their side's subpoenas.

∙ ∙ ∙

VINSON'S CASE LOOKED EASY TO BARRY, who had not yet litigated on the emerging issue of sexual harassment. Needing information, Barry looked for a book. She found the only law book on the subject— *Sexual Harassment of Working Women*, published that year, 1979, by Yale University Press—the final product of repeated rewriting begun years earlier in law school by Catharine MacKinnon.

MacKinnon's paper for Professor Tom Emerson had grown dramatically since the day in late 1975 when she carried her only copy to the Lexis terminal in her father's courthouse. In late summer or early fall of 1976, some of it went to Professor Nadine Taub of Rutgers to assist in litigating the sexual harassment case of Adrienne Tomkins. At about the same time, MacKinnon had handed it in to Professor Emerson, who returned it with suggestions but no theoretical opposition.

MacKinnon continued working, extending her paper past 230 pages, which in midsummer 1977 she handed back to Emerson, who met with her to comment. Then to her amazement, following the suggestion by one of her political science professors, Robert Dahl, Yale University Press asked to see it. She walked it over and left it with a secretary. Soon after, an editor phoned to say that the secretary had taken the manuscript home and would not return it. When the secretary finally returned the manuscript to the editor, she did so by walking into the editor's office, closing the door, sitting down, and proceeding to tell the editor her own experiences with sexual harassment. MacKinnon's paper seemed to be a page-turner. In the last weeks of 1977, MacKinnon signed a contract with the press. As soon as she could get them the final manuscript, they would rush it out—in three months, they told her—in both hardcover and paperback.

WHEN BARRY BOUGHT MACKINNON'S *Sexual Harassment of Working Women*, she found a blueprint for the partly built law of sexual harassment. Thanks to the clarity of MacKinnon's book, Vinson's case could look like an easy case—perhaps even what Barry was coming to think of as "the big case in the sky," the one that might actually earn her some money. Not that piling up money dominated her life. A year would pass before she asked Mechelle Vinson to put a retainer agreement in writing.

MacKinnon's book made Vinson's case look winnable partly because its blueprint for litigating sexual harassment no longer rested on *no law*. After the early defeats in lower courts, a few crucial victories had followed, which the book analyzed. As Barry drafted her pretrial statement for Vinson, she cited three cases that had partial success. Furthermore, two of the three victories had come in the same federal courthouse in Washington, DC, where Barry would argue Vinson's case. In April of 1976, Diane Williams had won *Williams v. Saxbe* in the DC district court. For the first time, Barry could read in MacKinnon's book, "a federal judge held that sexual advances coupled with retaliation for their refusal constituted actionable sex discrimination."

The book's discussion of *Williams* did not mention an experience of MacKinnon's with that judge, Charles R. Richey. One day that April, when she was at her father's chambers, as she later recalled, "Judge Richey called up and had me come down and talk to him." He said that he had heard she was working on the problem of sexual advances at work and asked what she thought. MacKinnon told him she believed that unwelcome sexual pressure at work was a form of sex discrimination. He said, as she recalled, "Well that's a big relief, because that's what I just decided." He pointed to his just-finished *Williams* opinion on his desk.

Williams' victory came only at the lowest federal level. At the Court of Appeals for the District of Columbia in July of 1977, the decision in *Barnes* finally arrived, nineteen months after it was argued, carrying ninety footnotes and authored by Spottswood Robinson. Since the day in late 1975 when Catharine MacKinnon handed her paper to a young woman who said she worked with Judge Robinson, as MacKinnon recalled, *Barnes* had followed a long path.

After oral argument before Judges Robinson, MacKinnon, and Bazelon on December 17, 1975, the panel split. Listening to the lawyer who argued against Paulette Barnes, Judge MacKinnon made notes on the argument that "discrimination here is not because she is a woman but because she is a non-consenting female." A bit later, concerning the claim that such discrimination was "only imposed on some women," he wrote *"Geduldig v. Aiello"*—the case in which the Supreme Court had ruled that discriminating against some women (pregnant ones) differed from discriminating against all women. "I question," wrote Judge MacKinnon as his final note on the oral argument, "whether it is sex discrimination."

Although Chief Judge Bazelon rarely agreed with MacKinnon, whose nomination by Richard Nixon was widely said to represent an effort to resist the liberalism of judges like Bazelon, he too was inclined against Paulette Barnes. She had alleged, he wrote to his two colleagues, "nothing more than that a single supervisor who happened to be male, was attracted to a single employee who happened to be female" and who was then fired for refusing his advances. Although her sex was surely a cause for the firing, he continued, so too may have been "her hair color, eye color, perfume scent, marital status, etc." To describe her problem as sex discrimination would open "floodgates," he said, for claims that women were discriminated against if fired after they refused to do sewing or babysitting for their boss.

Robinson alone, noted Bazelon, seemed inclined to support Barnes. Following Bazelon's note, Judge MacKinnon sent a memo restating his belief that Barnes had not suffered sex discrimination. But he suggested he might be swayed if "a better job of legislative and statutory analysis can be done than has been done by the litigants." Challenged by his colleagues to do work that the *Barnes* litigators had not, in late March of 1976 Robinson replied that he was beginning research and "hopefully" would reply within two weeks. But Robinson was famously the slowest opinion writer among judges on the court—slow, his clerks came to believe, because his years litigating race cases made him believe that a black lawyer could not afford to leave gaps in a case. This draft would need nine months.

Fortunately for Paulette Barnes, 1975–76 was an unusual year in the chambers of Bazelon and Robinson. Of their five clerks, three were women. Judge Bazelon, one clerk would recall years later, asked the women whether they believed sexual harassment really did affect women in their work. They replied *yes*.

During the same months Judge MacKinnon had only male clerks, but he conferred with his secretary. He asked, for example, whether sexual harassment happened at the courthouse. Yes it does, she told him, and I can tell you who's being harassed. That answer, he let one clerk know, hit Judge MacKinnon as a revelation: a secretary whom he trusted thought sexual harassment was affecting women right around him in his court. Her answer added credence to what his daughter Kitty was coming up with.

In contrast, if Judge Robinson had doubts that sexual harassment amounted to sex discrimination, his clerks could not recall hearing them. Robinson seemed, they noticed, particularly sensitive to the impact of discrimination. One of his female clerks recalled that Robinson, although he worried about the safety of any of his clerks walking home alone at night in the capital, would not give her a ride home when she was the only one working late with him. He would, however, give her a ride when he was also driving one of the male clerks home. Growing up as he had in 1920s Richmond, she understood he feared the harassment he might subject her to and himself to, as a black man seen driving a white woman home. Making that hard choice—better for a woman he cared about to risk harassment alone in nighttime streets than to risk harassment as part of a mixed-race couple in a nighttime car—suggested that Judge Robinson felt the weight of discrimination in his daily life.

That clerk, Ellen Semonoff, found herself playing what she saw as an odd role on behalf of *Barnes* once she began working for Robinson in the summer of 1976. She already knew Bazelon, for whom her husband had clerked the previous year. While Judge Robinson labored to complete his *Barnes* draft, he gave her permission to, as she recalled, "go sit with" Bazelon and "work with" him to help him understand the case.

WHEN JUDGE ROBINSON'S "PROPOSED OPINION," as he called it, arrived in late 1976, it rejected the lower court's view that Paulette Barnes had been discriminated against "not because she was a woman, but because she refused to engage in a sexual affair with her supervisor." The allegations gathered by the district court, once restated by Judge Robinson, showed clear sex discrimination. They included these: Paulette Barnes had continually resisted sexual overtures from her boss at the Environmental Protection Agency. She advised him that "notwithstanding his stated belief that many executives 'have affairs with their personnel,' she preferred that their relationship remain a strictly professional one." After her rebuff, the director began a conscious campaign "to belittle" Barnes, "to harass" Barnes, and "to strip her of her job duties." This campaign "culminated in the decision" to abolish Paulette Barnes' job "in retaliation" for her "refusal to grant him sexual favors."

Applying the law of discrimination to the story of Paulette Barnes, Judge Robinson set a battle-weary tone. "It is much too late in the day," he wrote, "to contend that Title VII does not outlaw terms of employment for women which differ appreciably from those set for men." Finding that Barnes would never have been victimized "but for her womanhood," he ruled that she had suffered illegal discrimination. His analysis won over Judge Bazelon, who wrote back that "your eloquent opinion has at last persuaded me that gender-based discrimination can encompass sex." Judge MacKinnon did not align so easily. Early in his marginal scribbling on the proposed opinion he wrote, concerning the alleged harasser, "Abuse of his *position* but not sexual *discrimination*."

Judge MacKinnon instructed his clerk to draft a separate opinion, narrower than Robinson's. Earlier, in oral argument and in handwritten notes, he had suggested that Paulette Barnes' supervisor should be charged with attempted rape rather than her employer be charged under Title VII with sex discrimination. After his two colleagues agreed that Barnes had suffered sex discrimination, he turned his attention to protecting companies from unfounded claims. Influenced by what he later called his "long association with business" as general counsel for Investors Diversified Services, one of the first mutual fund companies, he told his clerk, Tom Campbell, to outline a set of preventive measures for employers.

Judge MacKinnon's opinion, intended to "narrowly limit" the situations in which Barnes would have a legal claim, became a detailed discussion of when an employer should face "vicarious liability"—be legally liable—for "sexual harassment imposed on an employee by a supervisor." MacKinnon's analysis, vastly different from his clerk's first draft, led into an extended discourse on the legal concept of *respondeat superior*. Rooted in ancient common law, *respondeat superior* governed when a master is responsible for the "torts" of his servant. Tort law, from the Latin *tortus* or twisted, applied primarily to actions in which one person hurt another. If an errant coach-driver hurt a milkmaid by running her down (perhaps causing her to twist her ankle) while he was driving the master's coach, the coachman had committed a tort. Was the coachman's master responsible? In the legal Latin of British common law, *respondeat superior* translated to an imperative: "Let the master respond."

In *Barnes*, the master was the EPA. If its employee made a sexual advance to Paulette Barnes, was the master responsible? Seeking to address this question, Judge MacKinnon devoted most of his analysis to occasions when the master (the EPA or a bank, for example) need not respond. He began by detailing what could be called the master's escape clause, as promulgated by the American Law Institute: A Master (capitalized by the institute) could escape responsibility by asserting that his servant (not capitalized) had behaved badly (run down a milkmaid or fired a reluctant lover) while acting outside the scope of his employment.

For a woman who lost her job owing to reluctance to sleep with her boss, as Paulette Barnes claimed, Judge MacKinnon saw "no suggestion that the sexual harassment was even arguably within the scope of employment." And that conclusion might have meant that even though she was discriminated against based on her sex, her employer could not be compelled under Title VII to offer her any relief, such as restoration of her job or lost pay.

To see whether she might be entitled to some relief, Judge MacKinnon continued probing the law of *respondeat superior*. The escape clause—the servant acted outside the Master's employment—was not ironclad. It had four exceptions, any of which could make the Master legally responsible. And in the fourth of those, after dismissing the first three, Judge MacKinnon found a narrow possibility for helping

Barnes. Exception four stated that the Master might be liable if the servant purported to act for the Master. So, if Barnes could prove that her boss purported to act for the EPA—in making his advance, perhaps, or eliminating her job—she might have a case.

After explaining the fourth exception, the weak spot in the Master's defense, Judge MacKinnon moved beyond concern for Barnes to concern for future employers. He spelled out four procedures by which employers could insulate themselves from liability. "At the least," he said, an employer should be free from liability if it

> 1) posts the firm's (or government's) policy against sexual harassment by supervisors, and 2) provides a workable mechanism for the prompt reporting of sexual harassment, which mechanism 3) includes the rapid issuance of a warning to the supervisor complained of, or the mere notation of a rejected sexual advance for possible future reference in case an issue is made of voluntariness, and 4) affords the opportunity of the complainant remaining anonymous.

Having provided those four steps to protect employers, Judge Mac-Kinnon turned back finally to Paulette Barnes. Did her case have a chance? He concurred that it did.

Barnes, in his view, could assert her employer was responsible if she could prove that her boss pressured her to have sex and *all* of the following four facts: Other management personnel at EPA harassed her. Other management personnel at EPA misled her when she filed her complaint against her boss. Her supervisors at EPA retaliated against her for filing her complaint. The EPA, with knowledge of the facts alleged by her, "ratified the discrimination that her supervisor improperly imposed upon her."

If she can prove all that, Judge MacKinnon concluded, she would have made her case "that the Environmental Protection Agency knew or should have known of the harassment involved" and the EPA would indeed be legally liable. He was giving the employer multiple protections, he made clear, because he believed *Barnes* involved "social patterns that to some extent are normal and expectable." Overcoming those protections for employers would amount to a major challenge for Barnes or any employee.

At least MacKinnon did not dissent—important, because most of his dissents eventually gained the support of majorities at the Supreme Court. In *Barnes*, however, focusing on the arcana of *respondeat superior* and the law of torts for companies, he concurred with Robinson and Bazelon on the pivotal question of whether sexual harassment could legally be considered sex discrimination.

Catharine MacKinnon never publicly criticized her father for his argument in *Barnes*. They never discussed the decision privately. Years later she would say that he "just took a tort approach," following "a more traditional way of thinking" that addressed harassment of women as an individual difficulty rather than as group-based discrimination. When her *Sexual Harassment of Working Women* appeared a year and a half after her father concurred in *Barnes*, it analyzed the shortcoming of tort law for understanding sexual harassment. Discussing efforts by judges to see sexual harassment as merely *tortious* (as merely the twisting of one person by another), she quoted from the concurrence in *Barnes* by "one appellate judge"—her father—left unnamed. Efforts by judges to apply tort law to sexual wrongs against women, she concluded, are partly helpful but "fundamentally insufficient."

JUDGE ROBINSON, HOWEVER, HAD SEEN THE LIGHT—a light that Catharine MacKinnon may have helped to shine. He seemed ready to scrutinize disadvantage, as MacKinnon urged in her law school paper, and subordination. Long before, in one of the few sections of her law school paper that dealt directly with *Barnes*, she had contended that "sexual harassment in virtually all cases is an employment practice which but for the woman's sex would be different, a showing which makes out a prima facie case of sex discrimination."

Robinson, repudiating the district court analysis that Barnes "was discriminated against, not because she was a woman, but because she refused to engage in a sexual affair with her supervisor," responded as follows (with emphasis added):

We cannot accept this analysis. . . . *But for her womanhood*, from aught that appears, her participation in sexual activity would never have been solicited. To say, then, that she was victimized in her employment simply because she declined the invitation is to ignore the asserted fact that she was invited only because she was a woman *subordinate* to the inviter in the *hierarchy* of agency personnel. . . . Thus gender cannot be eliminated from the formulation . . . , and that formulation advances a *prima facie case of sex discrimination* within the purview of Title VII.

The opinion seemed to share key terms of MacKinnon's paper, including the focus on a *subordinate* within a *hierarchy*, integral to Mac-Kinnon's concluding argument that women's place at work has been "separate and subordinate, not equal." The opinion overlapped with hers in several citations, including some relatively obscure cases. And it found that Barnes had suffered—as a result of her gender and in comparison to the men who worked for her agency—what Judge Robinson called "marked disadvantage." The *disadvantagement* approach proposed by MacKinnon, based on her extended analogy of race discrimination to sex discrimination, seemed to have met a judge who, as she would later say, "got it."

After the opinion appeared, MacKinnon was given a direct report of the effectiveness of her law school paper in an account by her father. During a preliminary discussion of *Barnes* in 1975, Judge MacKinnon told her that Robinson had expressed doubt that the case involved discrimination—a view that might explain why he initially relegated it to the court's summary calendar. Judge MacKinnon said that Robinson thought it was a travesty of civil rights to consider that the facts in *Barnes* were a civil rights violation. When the judges next discussed *Barnes*, apparently after Catharine MacKinnon handed over her paper in the Lexis room, Robinson said *Barnes* did indeed raise an important issue of civil rights and he wanted to write the opinion. Judge MacKinnon told his daughter he had never seen such a turnaround.

Further evidence that Judge MacKinnon believed his daughter's work affected the *Barnes* opinion comes from an oral history interview he recorded about a year before his death. In it he mentions her arrival at his courthouse on a day when he had "just walked out of a conference on *Barnes*." He praises her for reviewing "every case in the United States" to make her argument "against every court" in the country. "Kitty's book," he continues, "was then accepted worldwide. In the interim, prior to publication, Judge Robinson had come to the same conclusion and we followed his draft." Left unstated in the oral history is how Robinson in 1977, prior to publication of her book, came to "the same conclusion."

Although Catharine MacKinnon that year told two friends in confidence that her paper had been circulated in *Barnes*, for decades she avoided public discussion. Eventually in 1998 she mentioned to a reporter for the *New Yorker* that a clerk had asked for her paper and it became, as he reported in one sentence quoting her, "the basis" of the court's decision in *Barnes*. MacKinnon never conferred with Judge Robinson about her paper, and later that year he died. By then, neither of the women who had worked as his clerks in the autumn of 1975 could recall borrowing a paper from a law student at the court's Lexis terminal. Faith Shapiro, the clerk that year whose appearance best fits MacKinnon's recollection (and who was assigned to *Barnes* according Judge Robinson's other clerk), is now Judge Faith Hochberg of the United States District Court for the District of New Jersey. Although she does not remember working on *Barnes*, she does recall Judge Robinson "teasing me about being so tenacious about something in connection with that case." She recalls nothing more, as she puts it, "except the vague sense that he was giving me too much credit for work done only partly by me."

Whether or not Judge Robinson ever saw Catharine MacKinnon's paper, apparently their thoughts aligned. Soon their work would converge to provide support for Pat Barry in the case of Mechelle Vinson.

FOR PAT BARRY, THE *BARNES* DECISION was pivotal. Following it, courts ruled for women in a series of cases whose facts, like those in *Barnes*, fit the term Catharine MacKinnon had introduced in her law school paper and then her book: *quid pro quo* sexual harassment. In legal Latin, it meant "this for that," denoting the exchange of one valuable thing for another. As applied to sexual harassment, it often meant sex for salary or, in effect, "sleep with me and you get to keep your job."

Legal condemnation of *quid pro quo* sexual harassment seemed almost perfect for Vinson's case. Like Barnes, Vinson said she had been sexually pursued by a supervisor. She had been warned by him, she recalled, that he could fire her. Unfortunately, Vinson's story inverted the familiar *quid pro quo*. Whereas Barnes said she rebuffed her boss and lost her job, Vinson said she failed to repel him and kept her job. No woman had ever won a sexual harassment case in which she admitted to having slept with her boss.

Barry worried that a male judge would be hostile to a woman who, even if worried she would be fired, said she gave in to sex and now wanted damages. Barry worried the judge would see whatever happened as a "personal relationship between Taylor and Vinson"—rather than, as Barry viewed it, "coercive power, using the workplace, by the boss." And Barry worried that a judge would hear Vinson's story as merely her word against her boss's word.

When Barry opened her case on January 21, 1980, she sought to show that it was not a he-said-she-said argument about one "inharmonious personal relationship" (in the words of the lower court that Judge Robinson had overturned in *Barnes*). In her opening presentation to Judge John Garrett Penn in the United States District Court for the District of Columbia, Barry began by introducing other women who had suffered similar treatment from Sidney Taylor. She planned to introduce evidence concerning what MacKinnon's *Sexual Harassment of Working Women*, which Barry took with her to court, had analyzed in detail as a second form of sexual harassment, *condition of work*. In MacKinnon's definition, it was

> the situation in which sexual harassment simply makes the work environment unbearable. Unwanted sexual advances, made simply because she has a woman's body, can be a daily part of a woman's work life. She may be constantly felt or pinched, visually undressed and stared at, surreptitiously kissed, com-

mented upon, manipulated into being found alone, and generally taken advantage of at work—but never promised or denied
anything explicitly connected with her job.

Fortunately for Barry's plan to depict an unbearable "work environment," John Meisburg during his few months as attorney for Vinson
had found two women willing to testify that Sidney Taylor had created such an environment at the bank for themselves and for Vinson.
Confident that introducing multiple women who had been sexually
imposed on by Sidney Taylor at the bank would both depict the environment of the bank and corroborate Vinson, Barry called her first
witness: Christine Malone. Little of her potentially powerful testimony, however, became admitted as evidence.

Malone stated that when she was first employed, she saw that
Mr. Taylor "disrespected" the other teller then working at the bank.
But when Malone began explaining how he showed that disrespect
("he would put his hands . . ."), an objection by the bank's attorney
cut her off. Almost as soon as she took the witness stand, the bank's
attorneys began attacking her testimony as irrelevant. The first objection came in the second minute of her testimony, when Barry asked
Malone how old she had been when Sidney Taylor offered her a job
in August of 1973. Before she could say she was nineteen, one bank
lawyer interrupted with, "Objection. What's her age got to do with
anything, your Honor?" Barry's response set the tone for her future
claims: she intended to prove, she explained to Judge Penn, that "the
environment was ripe for the exploitation that went on; that is he had
a pattern and practice—he being Sidney Taylor—of hiring very young
women in desperate need of a job."

When asked whether Mr. Taylor made comments about her as a
woman, Malone stated—only after another objection, this one overruled—that Taylor said she "had big hairy legs and he would like to
get between them." Also, she went on, "he would put his hands on
my breasts and he would put his hands on my backside and it was just
disrespectful. That just tore me down. I couldn't stand it."

Steadily Barry tried to make her argument about what she referred
to as the workplace *pattern and practice* (from the Civil Rights Act

of 1964) or the workplace *environment* (from MacKinnon's book). But since *pattern and practice* traditionally referred to suits alleging discrimination against a class of women (as when law firms would not hire women attorneys) and since MacKinnon had not convinced a court, Barry's argument put her ahead of existing law.

As objections came relentlessly, Malone often could not finish a sentence. Even her fragments, however, sounded damning. When asked what statements Taylor had made about her job performance, she said, "To get anywhere in the bank you had to . . . go to bed with him." The bank's attorney objected; Judge Penn sustained the objection.

When asked if Vinson were ever present when Taylor tried to put his hands on Malone against her wishes, Malone said, "Yes." Before she could elaborate, the bank's attorney objected on the grounds that "what Mr. Taylor did with this witness has nothing to do with what Mr. Taylor did with Miss Vinson." Judge Penn sustained.

When asked if Taylor had ever been violent with her, Malone said, "Yes." Again before she could elaborate, the bank's attorney objected, claiming irrelevance. Barry insisted that Sidney Taylor's violence toward women was relevant, that it showed his "pattern and practice," showed that "this is the way he treats women in general." Judge Penn responded that "even if he treats them violently, I'm not sure that is sexual discrimination necessarily." He sustained the objection.

Pat Barry called two more witnesses who testified, often in similarly fragmentary fashion, around the objections of the bank's attorney and another attorney representing Sidney Taylor. Their fragments added to Barry's narrative of a sexually charged environment at the bank. A part-time employee, Wanda Brown, who was a student at Boston College, testified that while she worked at the bank, Taylor made "suggestive comments" about how her body was maturing, that he would read *Penthouse* at the bank and would invite the women employees to look at the magazine's nude pictures. Mary Levarity, a former employee, testified that Taylor had "been touching me, fondling my breasts and feeling me on my butt." She said she believed she was terminated by the bank because she "did not go to bed with Mr. Taylor."

To Barry, these other women's stories went to the heart of the case: "Mechelle was not the only victim." But over and over, Barry failed in her efforts to inject depictions of the bank's environment. When Barry asked Christine Malone to describe her response to Taylor putting his hands on her breasts, Judge Penn interrupted, not waiting for a new objection. What mattered, he said, was what Vinson experienced directly, whether Vinson "had a chance to observe this or not."

In hours of interrupted or rejected testimony, Barry lost her argument that she was entitled to depict the bank's working environment with the help of Vinson's coworkers. (Judge Penn offered Barry the possibility to call her witnesses back to testify in rebuttal to bank witnesses, a chance Barry eventually would not take. The bank said it would object to testimony that did not meet the rules for rebuttal, which can challenge earlier testimony but not initiate new testimony about, for example, a harassing environment or pattern and practice. Barry was also influenced by low money and morale. She and Vinson had run out of funds to pay witness fees, she would later say, and their witnesses felt "so humiliated" in their first attempts to testify that they "didn't want any part of the lawsuit at that point. Who wants to go and face another bloodbath?")

Underlying Barry's evidentiary struggle with Judge Penn lay a profound gap. No law supported the case she wished to make about the harassing *environment* for women at the bank. The only cases that gave grounds for considering workplace environment were cases concerning racial harassment. When judges thus far had considered harassing sexual environments, they had seen no illegality. In the same district court where Barry was now arguing for Vinson, a judge recently had considered a sexual harassment claim from Sandra Bundy, who worked for the District of Columbia Department of Corrections. Where Bundy worked, as the court put it,

> the making of improper sexual advances to female employees [was] standard operating procedure, a fact of life, a normal condition of employment.

The judge also found that Bundy had been pursued by several supervisors. One pushed her to spend workday afternoons at his apartment; another urged her to join him at a motel. To Judge George L. Hart Jr., none of this affected (in the words of Title VII) Bundy's "terms, conditions, or privileges of employment." She had been promoted, he said, as fast as anyone. Since Bundy had held onto her job, as had Vinson, sexual harassment in her work environment did not amount to illegal discrimination.

JUDGE PENN'S REFUSAL TO HEAR EVIDENCE about the environment at the bank left Vinson to make her case on her own. She discussed seeing "Mr. Taylor touching Christina on her back—rear end, touching her breasts and chasing her in the back where the typewriters were kept." She recalled the scene when Malone quit after Taylor called her a bitch. She described the evening weeks later, in May of 1975, when Taylor took her to dinner, told her he wanted to go to bed with her, warned her he could fire her, and drove her to a hotel. She said she went with him to a room and then, with Barry asking questions, described what followed.

In court a week later, Taylor denied that he ever "indulged in sex with Ms. Vinson." Taylor did not, however, insist that the bank environment lacked a sexual charge. He received significant corroboration from two bank employees. One, a teller named Dorethea McCallum, said she guessed a relationship might exist between Vinson and Taylor because they "did work pretty close together day by day and her dresswear was very exposive." McCallum also testified, over Barry's objections, that Vinson had "a lot of sexual fantasies" including one about a "deceased grandfather" who, restored to youth, would return to have sex with her. Another employee, Yvette Peterson, testified that she had seen Vinson "sexually fondling" Taylor and that Vinson worked at the bank wearing "low-cut dresses, low-cut blouses," and "extremely tight pants."

Immediately following Taylor's denial that he had taken Vinson to a hotel, his lawyer asked, "Did there come a period of time in May of 1975 when Ms. Vinson made sexual overtures to you?" Taylor answered in some detail:

> Well, that has happened several times. Really since I have had to have Ms. Vinson and Ms. Malone go back home and change clothes because their form of dress was really wrong for the type of atmosphere that we were working under.

Taylor did not get the chance to explain why, when asked about sexual overtures made by Vinson, he talked about clothes worn by Vinson. Rather than draw forth what Taylor thought had happened "several times," his lawyer changed the subject.

THE TRIAL ENDED ON FEBRUARY 4, 1980, and within four weeks Judge Penn issued his opinion. Neither Barry nor Vinson could retain any illusion they had brought an easy case. Judge Penn acknowledged "without question that sexual harassment of female employees" is forbidden by Title VII if "they are asked or required to submit to sexual demands as a condition to obtain employment or to maintain employment or to obtain promotions." Reading Judge Penn's opinion, Barry could see that he had defined sexual harassment in words that left her with no law. Scribbling in the margins and blank spaces in Judge Penn's printed opinion, Barry scrawled, in oversized letters, "WHAT PENN RECOGNIZED WAS QPQ"—*quid pro quo* harassment, that is, such as sleep with me or I fire you. After drawing double lines alongside "condition to obtain employment or to maintain employment," Pat Barry added in scrawl, "NO REFERENCE TO ENVIRONMENTAL HARASSMENT CLAIM."

Fortunately for Barry, however, Judge Penn did, in a footnote, mention his refusal to allow her to present what he called "wholesale evidence of a pattern and practice relating to sexual advances to other employees in her case in chief." His footnote would prove crucial in years to come. With environmental harassment omitted from consideration, Judge Penn went on to conclude that Vinson "was not the victim of sexual harassment or sexual discrimination."

On route to that conclusion, Judge Penn made a series of other findings, two of which would also prove critical in future years. First, after lengthy discussion, he concluded that the bank had not received notice that Sidney Taylor was engaged in harassing his workers. Without notice, the judge continued, the bank "cannot be held liable for the alleged actions of Taylor"—a ruling that would haunt later legal discussion.

Second, in an unusual "finding of fact," Judge Penn ruled as follows:

> If the plaintiff [Mechelle Vinson] and Taylor did engage in an intimate or sexual relationship . . . , that relationship was a voluntary one by [Vinson] having nothing to do with her continued employment at Capital or her advancement or promotions at that institution.

This "finding of fact" would haunt Barry. How, she wondered, could a fact begin with *IF*? A voluntary sexual relationship contradicted the testimony of *both* Vinson and Taylor—it would mean that both Vinson and Taylor had lied in court. Indeed, the court's indecisiveness about whether Vinson and Taylor engaged in a sexual relationship, which Taylor consistently denied, would inevitably leave ongoing uncertainty about most of Vinson's allegations and mean that Taylor's denial would need to be kept fully in mind by any future reader—judicial or otherwise—of her narrative.

Judge Penn's "hypothetical finding of fact," as Barry called it, felt unforgivable and unforgettable. Her friends disagreed: Forget about Vinson's case, they told her. You did your best. From her boyfriend, Barry heard over and over: You're throwing good time after bad.

And Barry had thrown away her own money. Barry was broke. Her friends had seen her slip before into a pattern: Take a case that she believed in but that would never pay. Get energized and then get irritated. Bitch and complain that, as she later put it, "Why do I have to be in on time . . . I'm not gettin' paid." Say "the hell with it." Sleep in. Go play. Then get energized again and go back to work, digging herself deeper into a lost cause.

Just this once, friends said to Barry, give it up. Mechelle Vinson couldn't pay for an appeal. But Barry obsessed on Judge Penn's words *if* and *voluntary*. She told a friend, "That judge didn't do his job." She announced to Vinson that they would appeal. Somehow, Barry would reverse Judge Penn's conclusion that Vinson "was not the victim of sexual harassment."

18

Appeal to a Higher Court

Pat Barry went back to her one-room apartment—she could no longer afford to rent her office in the National Press Building—and began typing. To meet one requirement for an appeal, Barry requested that the district court provide a copy of the trial transcript—and at no charge, since Mechelle Vinson was verging on bankruptcy and entitled to appeal *in forma pauperis*, as a pauper. Judge Penn denied the request for a transcript on the grounds that he "cannot find this appeal presents a substantial question."

Here was judicial power. By ruling that his decision had resolved all significant questions, he could prevent issuing the transcript by which his decision could be appealed to a higher court. Barry believed he feared being "exposed for what that trial showed."

Just as Barry was despairing that she would be unable to appeal, in a remarkable exception, the court of appeals ruled that she could proceed to appeal without the transcript. The exception came at a wretched time for Barry, then almost penniless. On outdated Press Building stationery, she wrote to Vinson asking her to borrow money to order a few bits of the transcript and then followed with a plea: "Unless you can get me $300, I'm afraid I will have to withdraw from the case. . . . I have hit rock bottom."

At bottom or not, Barry kept typing. She submitted her brief to the court of appeals. She got it in late, with a typo here and an omission there, but she got it in. It contained, particularly on the topic of Barry's attempt to introduce evidence concerning the bank's sexually hostile environment, an odd mix of legal argument and personal memoir. "Prior to trial," she wrote, Judge Penn's court

> gave no hint that it would not permit such evidence. . . . Thus, the plaintiff was taken completely by surprise when the Court ruled . . . that no pattern and practice would be permitted.

Testimony by Christine Malone and others, Barry told the court of appeals, "would have established the poisoned atmosphere created by Taylor . . . because of his acts of sexual harassment against all women employees repeated over and over."

Barry then added, in a mostly autobiographical paragraph,

> We concede that this evidence [of an atmosphere filled with acts of sexual harassment] did come in, but it came in a disorganized, unplanned fashion. Vinson and her counsel were demoralized. Vinson had no money to pay for witness fees in order to recall her witnesses for rebuttal.

Although still disorganized and soldiering on with no money, Barry at least was no longer working completely alone.

Back when she was beginning her appeal, she wrote for help to the legal director of Working Women's Institute, the new name for the group that coined the term *sexual harassment* at Cornell five years earlier. Although now moved to a rich-sounding address in Manhattan, Working Women's Institute remained poor—cubby-holed in the basement of a church on Park Avenue. But it had a legal director, Joan Vermeulen, who turned for help to the wealthier Women's Legal Defense Fund in Washington, which found another attorney, Ronald Schechter, who helped Barry after she won the chance to appeal. As well as writing a short brief, he teamed with her to argue Vinson's case before a three-judge panel of the United States Court of Appeals for the District of Columbia Circuit, on February 16, 1982. In oral argument, Barry thought he did a great job. She wished she had done as well.

Now she could do nothing more. She and Mechelle Vinson settled in to await an opinion. They would wait, in part, because one of the judges on the three-judge panel was Judge Spottswood Robinson.

BARRY'S ARGUMENT CAME AT THE START of bad days for Robinson. His decision in *Barnes* had set him on track to become his court's expert on sexual harassment, and in 1982 he was about to become chief judge of the circuit. Then, in the spring after the argument in *Vinson*, he fell ill. When doctors discovered a benign growth on his colon, they ordered surgery. Complications followed, forcing more surgery. For much of the next two years, Judge Robinson could not go to court. His opinion writing, never rapid, slipped into a deep backlog.

As months passed, Barry's life got harder. Giving up her one-room office-apartment in Washington, she moved home to California to start her legal practice anew. As before, however, she seemed to specialize in defending people without money. Meanwhile, Vinson couldn't find bank jobs and wound up delivering newspapers and working as a cashier in a food store. Neither had enough money to stay in touch by phone. A year passed. Vinson enrolled in nursing school but had to drop out for lack of funds. Once in a great while, she called Barry to ask what was happening. "Well," Barry would say, "call the court of appeals, Mechelle. I don't know." Barry did not say what she believed: the court of appeals would never rule.

In early 1985, some three years after Barry had argued before Judge Robinson, Mechelle Vinson received a call at her parents' home from a journalist, asking if she had heard "the decision." When Vinson asked what decision, the journalist said, You've won.

Vinson said, as she later recalled, "Oh come on, you're playing, just playing around." She "just felt that, after all these years, they'd forgotten, nothing's going to happen, and if it comes out it's going to be another negative decision." But the journalist insisted, so Vinson turned on the news, and there it was. And then Barry called and was crying out, as Vinson would later recall, "WE DID IT WE DID IT WE DID IT WE DID IT." And Vinson said "Yes, it's great!" But what was it?

To decide the case of Mechelle Vinson, Chief Judge Robinson began with a problem that can shackle any court of appeals: the appeals judge must accept the "facts" that have been found by a trial judge. After Vinson's trial, Judge Penn had declared, among his findings of fact, that Vinson "was not required to grant Taylor . . . sexual favors as a condition of either her employment or in order to obtain promotion." Following apparently from that "fact," Judge Penn then found that Vinson "was not the victim of sexual harassment and was not the victim of sexual discrimination."

Robinson had to find a route to steer around these problematic legal facts. To do so, he suggested that Judge Penn had been ruling on a too-narrow definition of harassment. And, Robinson was able to say, in effect, no wonder: mere weeks after Penn's decision against Vinson, the law had begun to acknowledge the existence of a new form of sexual harassment: "environmental" harassment.

The breakthrough came in March of 1980 when a set of sexual harassment guidelines emerged from a part of the federal government that, following early fears it would become a "sex commission," had done little to help women: the Equal Employment Opportunity Commission. Development of sexual harassment guidelines had emerged there thanks to Eleanor Holmes Norton, appointed director in 1977, who wanted to encourage women to bring complaints and wanted to educate courts and employers. The guidelines opened by defining the most familiar form of sexual harassment, *quid pro quo.*

From this now-illegal harassment, the EEOC guidelines turned to another type, the second form discussed in MacKinnon's *Sexual Harassment of Working Women.* Unwelcome sexual advances, requests for sexual favors, and so on also become illegal sexual harassment when the

> conduct has the purpose or effect of unreasonably interfering with an individual's work performance or creating an intimidating, hostile, or offensive working environment.

Whereas MacKinnon had said that "condition of work" harassment "simply makes the work environment unbearable," the EEOC under Eleanor Holmes Norton added specificity. (MacKinnon had not heard about the guidelines until they were drafted. She generally liked what she saw.)

The EEOC guidelines became public, as "interim interpretive guidelines," on March 11, 1980—two weeks too late to help Barry and Vinson, who lost her case before Judge Penn on February 26.

ENVIRONMENTAL HARASSMENT got its day in court two weeks after publication of the EEOC's interim guidelines. On March 26, 1980, three judges of the Court of Appeals for the District of Columbia Circuit, including Spottswood Robinson, heard the appeal for Sandra Bundy.

As the lower court had found fully legal, Sandra Bundy's workplace maintained a standard operating procedure—"the making of improper sexual advances to female employees." One of Sandra Bundy's supervisors had pressed her to spend the afternoon in his apartment looking at sexual literature and pictures, which he said could not be bought in bookstores. Another, who told her he had "a pocketful of money," suggested she go with him to the Bahamas or just "lay up in a motel." When Bundy complained to a higher supervisor, he urged her to begin a sexual relationship with him and added that "any man in his right mind would want to rape you."

Such "improper sexual advances," ruled the district court, amounted to no more than "a game played by the male superiors— you won some and you lost some." The decision depicted a boy's playground, a working world in which boys will be boys. Within the game, such advances amounted to not just standard procedure but also, as the judge said, "a fact of life, a normal condition of employment." This boy's game, he continued, was "not a matter to be taken seriously."

This game theory evidently appalled Robinson and two of his colleagues on the court of appeals. Writing for their three-judge panel, Judge J. Skelly Wright pounced on the district court's view that "Bundy's supervisors did not take the 'game' of sexually propositioning female employees 'seriously.'" "To state the all too obvious," the court of appeals observed, a supervisor might avoid investigating "precisely because" he realized that proof of sexual harassment would seriously indict his personnel.

The suspicion that sexual harassment constituted more than a game led the court of appeals to question "whether the sexual harassment of the sort Bundy suffered amounted by itself"—even if she suffered no tangible losses in income or opportunity—"to sex discrimination with respect to the 'terms, conditions, or privileges of employment.'" Put another way, the court asked whether a woman forced to suffer through this so-called game had lost any privilege guaranteed by the discrimination-fighting language of Title VII. To answer what it called this "novel question," the court of appeals turned to two primary sources: the abundant litigation history concerning race discrimination and the scant legal literature concerning sexual harassment. In an extensive review of race discrimination cases, the court of appeals found ample ammunition to support Bundy. It relied at length on a key race-discrimination case from another circuit, which concluded, regarding the key language of Title VII, that

> "terms, conditions, or privileges of employment" is an expansive concept which sweeps within its protective ambit the practice of creating a work environment heavily charged with ethnic or racial discrimination. . . . One can readily envision working environments so heavily polluted with discrimination as to destroy completely the emotional and psychological stability of minority group workers.

The concept of hostile environment abounded in cases declaring that Title VII was violated by a pattern of racial, ethnic, or religious slurs, or by segregated employee eating clubs—all situations involving not lost jobs or lost promotions but a discriminatory *environment*. Yet when the court of appeals turned to sexual harassment, it found no cases to support its novel stance. But it did find two sources from outside the courts: the EEOC's new guidelines and Catharine Mac-Kinnon's *Sexual Harassment of Working Women*.

The *Bundy* court cited EEOC rulings from the past decade, which held that Title VII "grants an employee a working environment free of discrimination." Furthermore, the Bundy court could cite the new EEOC guidelines on sexual harassment, which defined sexual harassment to include conduct that created "an intimidating, hostile, or offensive work environment."

More remarkable than the Bundy court's deference to the EEOC was its deference to *Sexual Harassment of Working Women*. "Should women be required to counterattack," MacKinnon's book asked about condition-of-work harassment,

> in order to force the man into explicit employment retaliation so she has something to complain about? The problem here is . . . analogous to a problem within the rape laws: a victim who resists is more likely to be killed, but unless she fights back, it is not rape, because she cannot prove coercion. With sexual harassment, rejection proves that the advance is unwanted but also is likely to call forth retaliation, thus forcing the victim to bring intensified injury upon herself in order to demonstrate that she is injured at all. . . . [T]o require a rejection amounts to saying that no series of sexual advances alone is sufficient to justify legal intervention until it is expressed in the *quid pro quo* form. In addition, it means that constant sexual molestation would not be injury enough to a woman or to her employment status until the employer retaliates against the job for a sexual refusal. . . . And this, in turn, means that so long as the sexual situation is constructed with enough coerciveness, subtlety, suddenness, or one-sidedness to negate the effectiveness of the

woman's refusal, or so long as her refusals are simply ignored while her job is formally undisturbed, she is not considered to have been sexually harassed.

Reprinting the long last sentence without quotation marks, the court of appeals transformed MacKinnon's opinion into judicial opinion. It ruled not only that Bundy had shown that she was a "victim of a pattern or practice of sexual harassment" but that such harassment was illegal sex discrimination "even if it does not result in loss of tangible job benefits." Now, at least within the federal courts of the District of Columbia, sexual harassment included the creation of an "intimidating or hostile or offensive work environment." Thus the concept of hostile environment—developed by the efforts of Working Women United for Carmita Wood, of Catharine MacKinnon in her law school paper that became *Sexual Harassment of Working Women*, and of Eleanor Holmes Norton at the EEOC—entered the law of sexual harassment.

BUNDY GAVE JUDGE ROBINSON NEW LAW to apply in the case of Mechelle Vinson. Reviewing her case in district court, he read about Pat Barry's fruitless efforts to focus her case-in-chief on the hostility in Vinson's work environment. Mostly missing from the official record were details such as Christine Malone's allegations that she was torn down by Sidney Taylor's comments about getting "between" her legs, Mary Levarity's claim that she was told she would have to "pay up" sexually, and Wanda Brown's surprise that her boss wanted to rub her feet and show her *Penthouse* nudes.

Robinson read Judge Penn's findings of fact, to which Robinson had to defer: Vinson "was not required to grant Taylor . . . sexual favors as a condition of either her employment or in order to obtain promotion," and she "was not the victim of sexual harassment and was not the victim of sexual discrimination." The combination of Barry's discussion of environment—which Penn had mostly banned from her case-in-chief—and Penn's finding of no harassment led Robinson straight to *Bundy*. Judge Robinson was able to say that Judge

Penn's finding was flawed: the new decision in *Bundy*, indeed the legal concept of environmental harassment, had not existed when Judge Penn ruled. Thus Penn had been able to judge only in terms of what Robinson called "*Barnes*-type" harassment (*quid pro quo*). Now, it was possible to consider "*Bundy*-type" harassment. And surely, on the new legal ground created by Judge Robinson and his two colleagues in *Bundy*, Mechelle Vinson had a legal claim.

Judge Robinson ruled that Vinson's "grievance" was clearly of the *Bundy*-type and thus demanded an "inquiry as to whether Taylor," in the language of *Bundy*, "created or condoned a substantially discriminatory work *environment*." This would require asking whether Vinson was subjected (again in the language of *Bundy*) to "sexually stereotyped insults" or "demeaning propositions" that illegally poisoned the "psychological and emotional work environment."

Robinson's new focus on environment gave him leeway to steer away from another of Judge Penn's findings of "fact": the hypothetical finding that *if* Vinson and Taylor had a sexual relationship, it was voluntary and had nothing to do with Vinson's job or promotions. Like Pat Barry, Judge Robinson worked to discredit the hypothetical. "This finding leaves us uncertain," he wrote, "as to precisely what the court meant." (Because the finding also left its origins uncertain, Robinson guessed it might originate in Penn's attention to testimony regarding Vinson's style of dress and alleged fantasies about men—fantasies that omitted her boss and whose existence she mostly denied. Such testimony, Judge Robinson ruled, "had no place in this litigation.") As to the finding's meaning, Judge Robinson suggested one possibility: "because Vinson's employment status was not affected," there "was no Title VII violation." This Robinson dismissed as an obvious error, overturned by the *Bundy* ruling that sexual harassment could be created by a hostile environment that need not have led to the loss of "tangible job benefits."

Robinson could not resist subjecting Penn's hypothetical to another possible interpretation: "Because the relationship was voluntary there was no sexual harassment." Because she didn't refuse, that is, she has no claim. Robinson attacked that interpretation with the *Bundy* holding that "a woman employee need not prove resistance to sexual overtures" in order to claim sexual harassment. "From that point," Judge Robinson continued, "we take what is hardly a major step by recognizing that a victim's capitulation to on-the-job sexual advances cannot work a forfeiture of her opportunity for redress. If capitulation were dispositive," he went on, a woman who once gave in to her boss's pressures "would thereby lose all hope of legal redress for being put in this intolerable position in the first place."

Thanks to *Bundy*, Robinson made clear, as of 1985 Mechelle Vinson had a chance. The district court, he ordered, must take Vinson's case afresh; Judge Penn must hear Pat Barry's argument about hostile-environment harassment. That was the news that led Barry to tell Vinson that "WE DID IT."

PATRICIA BARRY DID NOT EXPECT what hit next: a powerful dissent written by a judge who had played no part in earlier court decisions. Following a standard procedure that brings success only rarely (probably less than one chance in 250), the bank challenged Judge Robinson's opinion by requesting a rehearing by all the judges of the court of appeals sitting together—sitting *en banc*. The judges refused, by a vote of 10 to 3.

One of the losing judges, in a rare move, wrote a dissent. He was Judge Robert Bork, formerly a professor at Yale Law School, formerly the solicitor general of the United States (a position sometimes referred to as the Supreme Court's "tenth justice," a post that led to his firing of special prosecutor Archibald Cox, at the behest of Richard Nixon, in what became known as the "Saturday Night Massacre"), and soon to be nominated himself to the Supreme Court (and to see his nomination defeated in a controversial battle that would establish him, before a national television audience, as one of the most formidable legal figures in the nation). Judge Bork's dissent was joined by two eminent colleagues: Judge Antonin Scalia, who himself would be elevated to the Supreme Court, and Judge Kenneth Starr, who as special prosecutor in the late 1990s would impeach President Bill Clinton. This dissenting trio had an evident goal: catch the interest of the Supreme Court.

Bork's dissent pounced on Robinson's effort to assure that a victim's "capitulation to on-the-job sexual advances" would not cost her "all hope of legal redress." In his attack, seizing on the notion that Vinson had taken part in a sexual relationship that was *voluntary*, Bork utterly rephrased what he claimed Robinson had *explicitly* stated. Robinson's depiction—with apparently ironic quotation marks—as a "victim's 'voluntary' submission to unlawful discrimination" became, in Bork's un-ironic rephrasing, a "plaintiff's voluntariness in participating in a sexual relationship."

Bork's rephrasings—from " 'voluntary' submission" to "voluntariness," from "unlawful discrimination" to "sexual relationship"— helped him to raise a fearful specter: "sexual dalliance, however voluntarily engaged in, becomes harassment whenever an employee sees fit, after the fact, so to characterize it." Bork, drawing on testimony about Vinson that Judge Penn had not used against her in his opinion but that the bank had raised on appeal, related that

> evidence was introduced suggesting that the plaintiff wore provocative clothing, suffered from bizarre sexual fantasies, and often volunteered intimate details of her sex life to other employees of the bank.

Bork did not claim that Vinson had directed the alleged fantasies or details or even styles of dress toward her boss. Gathered together, Bork's implications offered a coherent specter: bad women can turn voluntary sex into federal lawsuits.

Bork's claim that such lawsuits would be impossible to defend led him to a related issue—one that had been present but became more dramatic now that, following Robinson's decision, a lower court was going to reconsider whether Taylor's actions had created a hostile work environment: Should the bank be liable for harassment, if any, by Taylor? Or should an employer like the bank perhaps be insulated, as Judge MacKinnon worried in *Barnes*, from "vicarious liability"?

In Bork's reformulation, Robinson's opinion meant "that the employer is virtually converted into an insurer that all relationships between supervisors and employees are entirely asexual." Since insurance can't stop sex, Bork made clear, the employer would make heavy payouts: "Though the employer has no way of preventing sexual relationships, he is defenseless and must pay if they occur and are then claimed to be harassment."

Bork's dark revision predicted ugly spawn: every sexual relationship can go bad; every bad relationship involving a supervisor can damage an office "environment"; every bad environment can generate a federal suit; every federal court, to the highest level, can be forced to sort out the subtleties of inharmonious personal relationships. The consequences for the courts might well be, as one lower court judge had suggested in an earlier sexual harassment case, needing "4,000 federal trial judges instead of some 400." Concluding his portrayal of the defenseless employer, Bork added, lest his point be missed by the nine justices in his audience, "The Supreme Court has never addressed the question of an employer's vicarious liability under Title VII."

"Oh boy, here we go," Pat Barry thought, when she saw Bork's dissent. Five months later, in October of 1985, the Supreme Court agreed to review Judge Robinson's opinion. The first case of sexual harassment to reach the Supreme Court would be Mechelle Vinson's.

Barry was worried. In the decade since Vinson found her first job at the Capital City bank, most of America's eleven federal court circuits had come to accept what courts at first denied: sexual harassment was sex discrimination, prohibited by Title VII of the Civil Rights Act of 1964. Vinson's case, because it had moved so slowly, now seemed largely in step with the law—except for the crucial concept of hostile-environment harassment, which at least had support in the guidelines of the EEOC and in *Bundy*. With all circuits and the EEOC apparently in agreement, Barry wondered why the Supreme Court would want to hear Vinson's case. Would it turn back years of advances in the law of sexual harassment?

Barry worried also because she had argued before the Supreme Court once and lost. By a vote of 5 to 4, Barry failed to extend the right of jury trial to federal employees who brought cases under the Age Discrimination in Employment Act. Although Barry liked to tell herself she had lost with dignity, she blamed herself for making what she called "bad law."

Barry was now in the thick of her legal practice in Grover City on the mid-coast of California. She knew she needed help. As she sat in her office typing her argument (already late) to the Supreme Court that it should not accept an appeal of Judge Robinson's decision, she expected to lose that argument. With Bork's dissent on her mind, she sent out a letter to ask for assistance from the person whose writing had already done the most to help her: Catharine A. MacKinnon.

FOR CATHARINE MACKINNON, Barry's letter of August 1985 came at a bad time: she was more or less unemployed and feeling financially desperate. Beginning with her earliest attempts at admission to Yale Law School, MacKinnon continued a complex relationship with legal academia. While a graduate student in political science, beginning in the spring of 1974 she began teaching courses to undergraduates that led to her creation of the first course in the Women's Studies Program at Yale. When MacKinnon's undergraduates heard details from her law school paper, some of them began describing what sounded like sexual harassment by faculty members at Yale, and the students then conferred with a lawyer's collective that MacKinnon had founded with other Yale law students. The collective, with one of its partners, Anne Simon, as lead counsel, filed the first sexual harassment case in education. None of the Yale students won. Some claims were declared moot because students had graduated. The trial judge apparently did not believe the account of the student whose case was permitted to go to trial. But MacKinnon's collective and students could claim a major victory: the first decision in federal court affirming that sexual harassment claims could be brought by students as sex discrimination claims against universities.

In 1979, following publication of MacKinnon's *Sexual Harassment of Working Women*, law students at Yale began pressing to have MacKinnon hired to teach, and she became a lecturer in law at Yale in the spring term of 1980. But this position would not lead to a full-time job. Years afterward one of her colleagues, Professor (and later

Judge) Guido Calabresi, would say that MacKinnon's work on sexual harassment was so original that law faculties did not understand its significance, and MacKinnon "didn't have the patience to write the kind of busy-work that we would have understood," through which she could have won tenure "with the left hand."

MacKinnon's teaching at Yale began a string of such untenured appointments, which would eventually take her for short-term teaching to a list of major American law schools including Stanford, Harvard, Chicago, and the University of California at Los Angeles, and also to a junior faculty position at the University of Minnesota. She traveled from job to job in an increasingly battered Isuzu pickup truck. When she received Pat Barry's letter in late summer, MacKinnon was living in a rented cabin north of San Francisco and had no job. Without office, library, computer, secretary, research assistant, or salary, she agreed to work on *Vinson*.

19

✦

To the Supreme Court

As soon as the Supreme Court decided in early October of 1985 to hear the case of Mechelle Vinson, Pat Barry began asking for more help, and attorneys around the country responded. Many thought *Vinson* was an awful case—plagued by factual voids (no transcripts) and factual confusions (hypothetical facts)—with which to introduce the issue of sexual harassment to the Court. They sought to avert disaster.

The attorneys needed someone to coordinate their efforts. The task went to Sally Burns, who, from her base as assistant director of the Sex Discrimination Clinic at the Georgetown University Law Center, could bring together a wide range of important attorneys working on women in law. Burns' boss at the clinic, for example, was Susan Deller Ross, who had been drawn to the law center by one of her closest friends, Wendy Webster Williams, now professor of law at Georgetown. Further, Burns had been friends with Catharine MacKinnon since their days as law students.

In Burns' view, Bork's dissent represented his deliberate choice to hook the Court with a case that could seem to involve a "bad woman"—one whom a trial judge seemed to have found was lying about at least her *willingness* to have sex (if not about having had sex at all). In choosing a bad-woman case, Burns supposed, Bork was choosing a case that exemplified his "world view": Here was a woman who voluntarily engaged in sex and then, when it went bad, sought vengeance. And, thanks to the existence of important federal law against discrimination, this vengeful woman had (in Burns' view of Bork's dissent) "been afforded the opportunity to make a federal case out of a failed relationship."

Burns began holding meetings with allies who could assist by writing supporting briefs as *amici curiae*—Latin for "friends of the court," but really legal friends of Vinson and Barry. Since the bank would also have its *amici* (Latin plural, masculine), Pat Barry began to think of her allies as the *amicae* (Latin plural, feminine).

JUDGE ROBINSON HAD RELIED HEAVILY on the guidelines of the Equal Employment Opportunity Commission in deciding for Mechelle Vinson. In October of 1985, word reached Barry and her *amicae* that the EEOC leadership was preparing to attack Judge Robinson's opinion.

The EEOC seemed divided. First, its general counsel, Johnny J. Butler, prepared the groundwork for what the EEOC could be expected to do: support Robinson's opinion and reject the claims of the bank. But Robinson's opinion was quickly countered by one of the EEOC's five commissioners, Rosalie Gaull Silberman. In a long memo to the commission, chaired by Clarence Thomas (who would join the Supreme Court in 1991), she argued that the EEOC should have "one overriding objective: to support our guidelines and their fundamental proposition that sexual harassment is a violation of Title VII." Silberman then made explicit a considerable fear: if the Supreme Court repudiated the claim of Mechelle Vinson, it might simultaneously repudiate the EEOC guidelines. Silberman offered a crisp strategy: attack Judge Robinson's opinion to save a limited version of the guidelines.

Robinson's opinion, Silberman argued, "relies upon what I believe is a misconstruction of our guidelines." As part of her strategy to "clarify" the guidelines, Silberman urged a variety of special protections for the employer—particularly in what she called "private, one-on-one 'environment' cases." Word spread quickly that the EEOC might, in a striking departure from its norms, support the employer against the employee. One headline, in the *Daily Labor Report* of October 29, 1985, read, "Controversy Builds at EEOC over Upcoming Sexual Harassment Case."

Silberman's willingness to defend employers in "environment" cases aligned with little-known work by Clarence Thomas before he became EEOC chair. As a member of a transition team created in 1980 by President-elect Ronald Reagan, Thomas coauthored a report criticizing the sexual harassment guidelines created by Eleanor Holmes Norton. Focusing on environmental harassment, his report argued that "the elimination of personal slights and sexual advances which contribute to an 'intimidating, hostile or offensive working environment' is a goal impossible to reach. Expenditure of the EEOC's limited resources in pursuit of this goal is unwise." It added that environmental harassment "undoubtedly led to a barrage of trivial complaints against employers around the nation."

One attorney at the EEOC who apparently tried to defend the guidelines in discussion with Clarence Thomas was his special assistant, Anita Hill. Soon after she joined the EEOC in 1982, unaware of Thomas' work for Reagan's transition, she was asked to review the EEOC's official stance on sexual harassment. The subject resonated (as the nation would learn in 1991 from her testimony during Thomas' hearings for confirmation to the Supreme Court). In earlier work as his assistant in another government post, according to Hill, he had pressed her to have a social relationship, and she declined. Her working relationship, she would testify,

> became even more strained when Judge Thomas began to use work situations to discuss sex. . . . His conversations were very vivid. He spoke about acts that he had seen in pornographic films involving such matters as women having sex with animals and films showing group sex or rape scenes. . . . On several occasions, Thomas told me graphically of his own sexual prowess. . . . My efforts to change the subject were rarely successful.

According to Hill, whose testimony was mostly denied by Thomas, such pressure stopped before they both moved to work for the EEOC.

Nonetheless, Hill would later recount in *Speaking Truth to Power*, preparing to defend the guidelines concerning environmental harassment to Clarence Thomas made her feel "as though I had been dipped in a vat of scalding water. . . . I was flooded with embarrassment at my own experience." Culminating her review, in 1982 Hill met with Thomas. Not mentioning vivid conversations from the past, she urged him to support long-standing EEOC policy and guidelines. Thomas "grumbled and muttered," Hill recalled. Nonetheless, she understood that he was accepting her recommendation.

Years of the Reagan administration sniping at claims of sexual harassment apparently found, in 1985, a precise target in the case of Mechelle Vinson. At the end of October, the EEOC's five commissioners, chaired by Clarence Thomas, met in closed session. In a vote said to be 3–2 by the *Daily Labor Report*, the EEOC decided to support the bank and oppose Vinson. For longtime watchers of the gyre of gender discrimination law, such as Donna Lenhoff of the Women's Legal Defense Fund, the decision seemed part of the administration's long-expected attack. Lenhoff heard that staffers for both Silberman and Thomas had lobbied other commissioners to support the bank. For Vinson's case, the commissioners' vote meant that the EEOC, on whose guidelines Vinson's slight success had rested, would now oppose her.

THE BRIEF OF THE UNITED STATES and the EEOC against Vinson tracked much of Bork's dissent. First, it treated the relationship between Vinson and Taylor as consensual and praised the lower court for seeking to "ensure that sexual harassment charges do not become a tool by which one party of a consensual sexual relationship may punish the other." Second, the government brief sought to minimize the impact of a hostile-environment complaint by insulating employers from responsibility. Speaking of "the naturalness, the pervasiveness, and what might be called the legal neutrality of sexual attraction (as opposed to racial prejudice)," it praised Judge Bork for seeking to limit employer liability. It quoted Judge MacKinnon, in his concurrence from *Barnes*, that it is not always easy to discern "the distinction between invited, uninvited-but-welcome, offensive-but-tolerated, and flatly rejected sexual advances."

Pat Barry, reading the government brief for the EEOC, grew livid. Where the government began to explain how the term *agent* technically (based on the common-law history of tort law) might not apply to Sidney Taylor, she wrote in the margin, "I really despise this intellectual dishonesty."

Writing the brief for Mechelle Vinson became, at Barry's request, MacKinnon's task. Working in early 1986 in her rented cabin, affiliated professionally with only a study center at Stanford University called the Institute for Research on Women and Gender, which gave her stationery but not money, MacKinnon began writing the Supreme Court brief on the law she had begun trying to define in law school.

As MacKinnon drafted, she remained hamstrung by the lack of a transcript, which Judge Penn had denied on the grounds that Vinson's appeal did not raise a "substantial question." Worse for MacKinnon, money could talk. Fragments of transcript, dramatically incomplete, had been created for the bank at the court of appeals. They contained, for example, what Vinson said when she was being grilled, on cross-examination, by the attorneys for the bank and Sidney Taylor. But they omitted what she said before that in her direct testimony—an omission that undercut Vinson along with the context for her cross-examination.

MacKinnon insisted to Sally Burns and other *amicae* that they needed all the testimony. A full transcript would cost up to $3,000, which a well-paid lawyer might have earned in three days. Vinson's underfunded *amicae* held a benefit concert at a club called Tracks, with contributors chipping in a dollar at the door. Burns tossed in more from her own pocket, getting the total to $650—enough to pay a typist for another batch of fragments. As MacKinnon's deadline loomed, many of those fragments still hadn't arrived. With about two weeks to go and still low on transcripts, MacKinnon kept typing.

In mid-January of 1986, Barry received an almost-full draft one day and then a day later, before she had time to respond, another draft, utterly revised. MacKinnon's emerging brief, to Barry's delight, flashed with outrage. Barry read with glee the draft's attack on her *bête noire*, Judge Penn's hypothetical finding that *if* there was sex it was *voluntary*. How might one know, MacKinnon's brief asked, "that, if a sex act which may or may not have occurred, occurred, the woman did consent to it"? The doubling of *occurred* was vintage MacKinnon, mixing classical rhetoric (*parenthesis* and *epistrophe*) with sass. Penn's hypothetical, MacKinnon continued,

> is a metaphysical riddle, not a factual finding. It is nothing other than a ruling that this is a woman who *would* have wanted it, whether it happened or not. As such it is not a finding of fact, it is an assassination of character.

While the hypothetical expresses Judge Penn's point of view about Vinson, MacKinnon continued, "it fails to enlighten reviewing courts about what Mr. Taylor did or did not do to her." Barry was delighted. In the space beneath the words *did or did not do* she wrote, "Yea!" and then, doubly underlined "Catharine!"

As new bits of transcript reached her, MacKinnon strengthened her brief's evidence that Barry had indeed argued a case of environmental harassment to Judge Penn. And indeed, here and there within the emerging transcript, MacKinnon found Barry's fruitless efforts to convince Judge Penn to consider "acts of discrimination against other women in the environment," as Barry put it, or "the daily environment . . . encountered whenever Mr. Taylor was . . . in that office."

Barry pushed MacKinnon to use the transcript to "hit the court with the facts of the case" in order to break down what she called, in a hand-scrawled note of February 1, "everyone's (bank & friends) cavalier treatment of case as 'love-affair-gone-sour-let's-get-even' case." A few sentences later, along similar lines, Barry continued:

> Don't you think we need a powerful *fact* statement and then rant & rave in our argument portion? I realize and acknowledge chauvinism of Bench, but they surely want to know what happened—actually happened—to Vinson.

She added in closing, "I remain optimistic."

In mid-February, MacKinnon's brief reached the Supreme Court. It began indeed, as Barry had urged, by using new bits of transcript to hit hard with the "facts of the case" as told by Vinson and several co-workers:

> 40 or 50 episodes of undesired and traumatic sexual intercourse . . . , bleeding and infections, inability to eat or sleep normally, loss of hair . . . , [bleeding] from the vagina for weeks . . . , threats of reprisals, including against her job . . . , [coworkers' testimony that] they had seen Mr. Taylor sexually accost, abuse, and handle Ms. Vinson at work, that she repeatedly asked him to stop, and that she appeared upset by it.

At the same time that she hit with the facts, MacKinnon hit with the absence of facts. She argued that the Supreme Court should, even at this late date, simply send the case back to a lower court for fuller findings of fact. To buttress this argument, MacKinnon offered a catalog of uncertainties, including the hypothetical finding of fact (*if* there was sex it was *voluntary*) that, she charged, "finds no facts at all." MacKinnon sought to turn Judge Penn's vexing "fact," which Judge Robinson strove to swerve around in order to justify a review, into a *non-fact*—a reason for the Supreme Court to send the case back down.

MacKinnon also attacked the bank's concluding efforts to limit employer liability and thus to turn sexual harassment into second-class discrimination. Trying to distance the realm of sexuality from the realm of discrimination, three times in its two concluding paragraphs, the bank's brief had spoken of sexual activity as *special* in nature. Sex, insisted the bank, was special because it was "generally secretive" and often "welcomed, desirable, and proper." The bank asked, Did sexual harassment have any place in the law of Title VII? Based on the same *specialness*, the bank said no.

MacKinnon excoriated the bank for claiming that "sexual activity is special" in order to "render sexual harassment an injury especially difficult for victims to prove." And she pounced on the effort to blur forced sex with welcome sex.

> Whatever specialness inheres in sex, it inheres in sex freely chosen. To the degree that freely chosen sex is special, forced sex violates that specialness. Sexual harassment by definition is never wanted. If it may be said to be special at all, it is especially abusive. Yet both the bank and their amici conflate unwanted forcible sexual initiation with welcome friendly suggestions. They equate forced sex with all sex, implying that if wanted sex has value, forced sex must also, a value to be recognized by special legal exemption. The value of something freely done, like philanthropy, does not undermine the culpability of the same act when it is forced, as with theft.

One deep fear, MacKinnon continued as her brief neared conclusion, "seems to be that if a woman can sue for forced sex at work, there will be no voluntary sex at work. . . . In this view, if women are given legal backing to decline unwanted advances, the only future will be an 'entirely asexual' workplace." The end of sex, she told the court, was not imminent. Ironically, in challenge to the bank, she asked,

> If an employer can be sued for culturally biased acts and epithets, can cultural holidays not be celebrated and discussed? With all respect, it is difficult . . . to believe that if forced sex is actionable, voluntary sex will become too big a risk to take.

MacKinnon then turned to a problem that had worried Pat Barry from her first days on the case: Mechelle Vinson may have said no to sex, and Mechelle Vinson may have resisted. But finally, she said, she had failed to make her refusal effective.

What made this case unusual, Catharine MacKinnon continued, was that Vinson differed from most women who,

> once forced to have sex, are too humiliated and intimidated to complain. The result is that most reported cases of sexual

harassment involve victims who were able successfully to resist. Unless rectified, this can mean that if a perpetrator can render a working situation sufficiently coercive to force the woman to have sex, by whatever means, he can then get away with anything.

Stigmatized for having yielded to coerced sex, women such as Mechelle Vinson suffered what MacKinnon called "the vicious paradox that some of the least of sexual harassment's victims are the most likely to sue, leaving some of the most injured of women effectively outside the ambit of judicial relief." Privately, Catharine MacKinnon had a shorter phrase for this vicious paradox: "if you're fucked, you're fucked."

WITH UNDER THREE WEEKS LEFT before oral argument, scheduled for March 25, Pat Barry arrived at Georgetown law school to face two days of "moot court," a practice session familiar to most law students and appellate advocates. In what amounted to a dress rehearsal for a major drama, Barry's role was to play herself, making her oral argument to the Supreme Court. Acting the roles of justices—set to probe and test and interrupt her, to push her argument in all its weakest places—were some of the nation's smartest analysts of sexual harassment law, including MacKinnon, and many of her *amicae*: Carin Clauss of the University of Wisconsin and formerly of the Department of Labor, Debra Katz of the Conference of Labor Union Women, and Sally Burns and Wendy Webster Williams of Georgetown University Law Center.

Hovering over many of the *amicae* was the awful Rehnquist decision in *Gilbert*, which had declared that under Title VII one could legally discriminate against pregnant women without discriminating against women in general. What if Rehnquist built on that ruling? What if he declared that sexual harassment, like pregnancy discrimination, was not illegal sex discrimination? What if he suggested that amorous men, following Stewart's template, distinguished attractive women from unattractive persons? Would Barry be ready to handle a tricky inquisition from Rehnquist and his allies?

As Barry began her presentation, a shock hit her assembled *amicae*. Barry had prepared no argument. She had been "doing a lot of self-sabotaging," as she said later, "like I didn't have an oral argument ready when I went to moot court." This approach came partly from her sense that some of the *amicae* wanted a more experienced advocate to take the lead at the Supreme Court. Months earlier she had declined an offer from Professor Laurence Tribe of Harvard to assist with her brief, saying in a letter to him that she would write it herself, although she eventually handed that responsibility to MacKinnon.

Barry began her moot-court argument before the simulated justices. She cited one case as precedent, and the justices asked her to distinguish it from other cases. She couldn't. She tried arguing on the basis of California law—but this was a federal court. They fired more questions. To some of the assembled *amicae*, Barry's performance was terrifying.

Vinson understood that the rehearsals were awful. She heard that the experts were pushing Pat to surrender the argument. Pat's "mannerisms" weren't appropriate for the Supreme Court, Mechelle Vinson recalled hearing, and Pat wasn't able to "present herself." As a consequence, recalled Vinson, Pat "was paranoid, and I was paranoid. I was calling her and she's uptight and there's no money, and, you know, a lot of things going on. . . . Then I say, my camp is falling all around me again, all falling down."

After the moot court, some *amicae* urged that Laurence Tribe should argue the case. Another suggestion was Professor Carin Clauss of Wisconsin. Barry, unsure whether to cling to arguing before the Supreme Court, talked to her mother. She asked friends, Should she give up the case? She asked another lawyer, and he told her, Look Pat, if you think you can do it, you can do it. Did she think she could do it? Well, she *wanted* to do it—partly for the glory and excitement—to stand up there, all alone, before the Supreme Court justices, trying to defend her client and to shape the law. She thought to herself, she would recall later, that the *amicae* wanted Tribe to do the oral argument and wanted themselves to sit at the Supreme Court counsel table, and then they wanted finally that "Mechelle and

I would be eternally grateful to them. And I said, 'No, noo, noo, I want to argue it.'"

Unnerved after the grilling at Georgetown, Barry got help from an attorney who had helped her before her earlier Supreme Court appearance. They staged another moot court to ensure that Barry was better prepared to face the justices.

20

✦

At the Supreme Court

Still preparing on the morning of the oral argument, readying herself for a question about environmental harassment that she had decided the justices would surely ask, Pat Barry arrived almost late for her Supreme Court argument, the first of the day on March 25, 1986. MacKinnon, who had arrived earlier to assist in the role of co-counsel, was being told by a clerk how to proceed with the argument. Arriving just in time, and bringing her mother to join the audience in the crowded courtroom, Barry did not see Vinson, whom she knew would be there to watch. At the counsel table, along with MacKinnon, was Sally Burns, ready to assist.

Oral argument began, soon after ten o'clock, with Robert Troll speaking for the bank. Following the track laid by Judge Bork's dissent at the court of appeals, he began,

> The primary question in this case is whether a corporate employer is automatically liable under Title VII for a supervisor's sexual advances toward a subordinate even though the employer did not know about the advances and never had a chance to stop them.

The bank seemed unworried about any implication that its male branch manager had made advances. Troll asserted that Mechelle

Vinson had claimed she "consented" to beginning a "sexual affair" and that her participation in any such affair had been ruled "voluntary" by Judge Penn. Troll continued to attack the court of appeals opinion along Bork's lines, warning that owing to Judge Robinson, "an innocent employer is liable automatically for a supervisor's sexual conduct."

Responding to those words, at that moment for the first time in a sexual harassment case before the Supreme Court, a woman entered the debate. She was Justice Sandra Day O'Connor—formerly a state judge from Arizona until President Ronald Reagan appointed her to the Supreme Court in 1981. At the time of the appointment, O'Connor was one of a few women judges who were sufficiently conservative to gain the president's nomination to the Court. Her reputation benefited from a longtime friendship with a classmate whom she had dated at Stanford Law School, Associate Justice William Rehnquist, a conservative powerhouse since his appointment to the Supreme Court in 1971 and by the 1980s a likely candidate to become the court's next chief justice. Despite her conservative bent, O'Connor knew well some types of employment discrimination suffered by women. After graduation from law school in 1952 near the top of her class, like Ruth Ginsburg at her own graduation a few years later from Columbia Law, O'Connor was denied work with private law firms because she was a woman.

But if Justice O'Connor knew employment discrimination, did she know sexual harassment? "Mr. Troll," she began, "do you concede that the trial court simply didn't handle the case as one involving a . . . hostile environment type claim?" Troll conceded. Immediately, O'Connor pressed for more: Concede that hostile environment is a valid claim. Concede that—even without what the bank called a "tangible job detriment" (being fired, for example)—hostile environment might be a valid claim. Concede, further, that if Mechelle Vinson had brought a case of racial harassment, no court would require such "tangible" effect as loss of a job. Concede, even further, that the same principle should apply in a sexual harassment case as in a racial harassment case.

Troll, speaking for the bank and on the defensive, backpedaled.

To the last demand that he concede, all he could answer, weakly, was, "Yes, we do." The odds that a male lawyer would face such cross-examination from a woman judge on a federal bench may have been tiny—women in 1986 constituted fewer than 7 percent of all federal judges. But the lone woman who represented 11 percent of the Supreme Court had tough questions about sexual harassment. And through the rest of Troll's half hour, Justice O'Connor continued to ask the strongest and hardest questions.

Troll concluded by offering little more than what he began with, that "there is something, we submit, very unfair about hailing an innocent employer into court for a problem that it was unaware of and would have corrected voluntarily." Thanks to Justice O'Connor, Pat Barry's voice would not stand alone. But would it stand better than it had three weeks before, when Barry's *amicae* had torn her argument to bits?

BARRY BEGAN HER ORAL ARGUMENT by urging the Supreme Court to send Vinson's case back to a lower court for new findings of fact and new rulings based on the new legal understanding of hostile-environment harassment. Within moments, Barry was pushed into new territory by Justice O'Connor. Had Barry six years ago, O'Connor asked, made it clear to Judge Penn that she was "proceeding on a hostile environment theory"? Had Barry, that is, managed to argue on the basis of a theory that in 1980 had not yet been endorsed by courts or the EEOC?

The question came as a gift, and Barry embraced it. Yes indeed, she had argued "pattern and practice" and had introduced evidence to show "the poison environment in which Ms. Vinson found herself." Following immediately, Justice Powell insisted on knowing what section of Barry's complaint to the court supported environmental harassment. Barry saw MacKinnon, sitting beside her, flipping pages to find the answer, but Barry didn't wait. Getting prepared for this question had made her almost late this morning, but now she could answer instantly that, in a set of documents submitted to the Court, the section was paragraph 14 of page 5:

Defendant Taylor has also sexually harassed numerous other
female employees of the defendant association, and said conduct constitutes a well-known pattern of behavior.

But that section, Powell remarked, made "no mention of environment."

"That's correct, Your Honor," responded Barry, herself suddenly
backpedaling. Her long-ago use of workplace *pattern and practice*
(associated for years with class-action claims) as a proxy for workplace *environment* (associated more recently with hostile-environment
claims) seemed about to undercut her in the high court. MacKinnon
caught her. She pointed to page 20 of their brief, which drew on new
transcripts for Vinson's trial. Barry, reading aloud to the Supreme
Court, confirmed that she had indeed attacked "the daily environment" that Mechelle Vinson "encountered whenever Mr. Taylor was
in that office." Thanks to smooth teamwork, the crucial concept now
stood firmly before the Supreme Court: Vinson had suffered daily
from a hostile and harassing *environment*.

Until that moment, Vinson had been suffering quietly. Seated far
back in the Supreme Court, with her former attorney John Meisburg
and her longtime boyfriend, Bactuu Wilson, Vinson felt agony while
listening to the bank's lawyer suggest she might have *consented* to an
affair. Vinson later recalled that Troll's words started to

> conjure up inside the courtroom my rapes, the abuse, going to
> the doctors to try to stop the female problems I was having. And
> everything, it just seemed like everything was going on inside.

And then Troll had sat and Pat had stood and Justice O'Connor had
helped and Pat had answered well. Slowly, Vinson began to notice a
change among the justices. While Troll had talked, she thought, they
looked a bit inattentive. But when Barry stood, "they stopped their
fidgeting, and they listened, and they looked, and they took in what
she was saying. And I said, My gosh, look at her! She was marvelous.
There was a different Pat that day." And Vinson thought, "The angels
are certainly blessing us."

For that moment at least, Barry was loving her work. No question from the justices seemed too hard to turn to her purpose. What if, one justice asked, the Supreme Court agreed that some "voluntariness" on the part of Mechelle Vinson might give the bank a defense? Barry steered the Court smoothly to Judge Penn's unwillingness to consider environmental harassment and the need to consider the environment before judging what behavior could be deemed voluntary. And then as mild pressure on Barry mounted, in again came Justice Sandra Day O'Connor: "It's been suggested that an element in a sexual harassment claim is that the conduct complained of be unwelcome." *Unwelcome* was the key term from the EEOC guidelines. O'Connor was acting almost as Barry's prompter, calling for the lines that Barry needed to speak.

At the next moment, in jumped a different voice. With Barry in midsentence, Justice Rehnquist interrupted to assert that determining whether advances were unwelcome required precisely the sort of evidence that both Barry and Judge Robinson for the court of appeals had wanted to exclude: what clothes Vinson wore to work. Barry remained smooth. Evidence of dress without anything more, she told him, did not make it more or less likely that Vinson welcomed the advances of her boss.

"Well now," he responded, turning to the sort of Socratic question favored by law teachers, "is that for you as a lawyer to say"— is it for you to decide what a judge can find relevant? Barry tried to respond, and suddenly she was debating Justice Rehnquist at the Supreme Court.

She said that a district court has authority to reject such evidence.

He said the district court admitted the evidence.

She said the court of appeals suggested the evidence prejudiced the district court.

They struggled onward:

REHNQUIST: "So you say, then, that evidence of the complaining employee's work place dress and voluntary conduct is not admissible . . ."?

BARRY: "Justice Rehnquist, what I'm saying to you—"

REHNQUIST: "Are you or are you not?"

BARRY: "No, I'm not saying that. Okay, what I am saying, Justice Rehnquist, is . . ."

How had Barry fallen into this he-said, she-said mess? Flailing, she began thinking like a state lawyer from California, defending herself with "the California Rules of Evidence—I think it's 1103 or 1105." She had tried almost the same move back at the moot court. The *amicae* had pounced, telling her that the United States Supreme Court demanded not California rules but federal rules of evidence. Before Justice Rehnquist could pounce again, another voice entered, saying calmly, "Miss Barry."

"May I ask," Justice O'Connor continued, "whether the Court of Appeals found that any of the findings of fact by the district court were clearly erroneous?"

Another gift! Again, O'Connor had steered Barry toward lines she knew well: the district court's findings of fact were difficult to review because Judge Penn had refused to grant a free transcript to Mechelle Vinson, Barry replied, on the grounds that "this case would not make any substantial law." Laughter burst out in the courtroom, friendly and cheering to Barry, and she was sailing again on smooth waters. Further, Barry explained, now that Judge Penn was instructed to think about environmental harassment, he might come to different findings. And on the recently raised topic of Vinson's clothing and behavior, she continued, if a transcript had been printed, the Court would have seen that attorneys for the bank never even asked Vinson "whether she wore these kinds of clothing."

"Well," she heard, in the distinctive voice of Justice Rehnquist interjecting, "you don't have to use that sort of evidence as impeaching evidence." Suddenly they were back in their old debate.

She said no one claimed that evidence of Mechelle Vinson's dress or even her fantasies was linked to her boss.

He said judges have great latitude in admitting evidence.

She said evidence on how Mechelle Vinson dressed should be as inadmissible in a sexual harassment case as evidence of how a victim dressed in a rape case.

He said, "I'm not sure the cases support you."
They continued:

BARRY: Well, Justice Rehnquist, the evidence of dress is so
subjective. . . .
REHNQUIST: This may be a good argument to make. . . . But
after the district court has resolved it against you . . .
BARRY: Well, Justice Rehnquist, just once more, just alluding
to the California Rules of Evidence.

How, Pat Barry wondered later, could she make this dumb mistake
twice? This time Justice O'Connor did not intervene to save her. Justice Rehnquist jabbed, "We're not governed by the California Rules
of Evidence."
Barry: "Yes, Justice."
Rehnquist: "We're practicing under federal rules of evidence."
Pat Barry was reeling now. What could she do? Moving out of the
dread debate, she insisted that Mechelle Vinson's dress and conduct
would be relevant if they indicated how she conducted herself toward
her supervisor, which they did not. Judge Penn himself, during the
trial, kept insisting he wanted to hear only "what happened between
Ms. Vinson and Mr. Taylor," an insistence that he seemed to forget
when presented with tales of lewd dress and fantasy.
Now Barry returned to the oddest of all the findings of "fact,"
the hypothetical finding that if there was sex, it was voluntary—or
more precisely, as Judge Penn had put it, any intimate relationship was
"voluntary by" Mechelle Vinson. The bank, Barry suggested, seemed
partly to hope that evidence of Vinson's attire and fantasies would
support the conclusion that her sex with her boss was *voluntary*. And
if so, Barry declared triumphantly, "then what they're saying, Justice
Rehnquist, is that their own supervisor committed perjury in a court
of law."
Barry had now slipped past the worst of Rehnquist's questions. A
moment later, when Justice Marshall surprised her by asking whether
Sidney Taylor was Vinson's supervisor "when he was out at the motel"
and was asking her to have sex, she thought, more or less, as she put it

later, "It was OK, it's Justice Marshall. He's an old-time guy." These old men now seemed little problem to Barry. Yes, Taylor could boss Vinson all the way to the hotel, Barry explained to Justice Marshall, because he could say, "Like I have the power to hire you, I have the power to fire you."

As Barry's half hour was about to expire, Chief Justice Burger attacked her claim (and Judge Robinson's) that the bank was liable for harassment by Taylor on the grounds that an employer is liable for actions by its employees. "Suppose," began the chief justice's hypothetical, that "Mr. Taylor was embezzling money from the bank." If the bank later made a claim to an insurance company, could the insurance company similarly hold the bank liable for Sidney Taylor's embezzlement?

Again unflappable, Barry brushed aside this last effort, stating that at least under the employer-employee relationship in Title VII law, the supervisor was legally indistinguishable from the employer and so, in this case, "Mr. Taylor was the bank."

Pat Barry's case was closed; Mechelle Vinson's case was set. Dazzled by Barry's performance, Vinson recalled, "I thought: the divine Father has answered our prayers, because Pat was a different person." Barry's *amicae* agreed. MacKinnon, who had left the moot-court session terrified, called Barry's argument "excellent." Others said to each other that Barry must have great short-term memory. One compared her to Eliza Doolittle in *My Fair Lady*, taking a crash course on deadline and then speaking the King's English. But would Barry's splendid performance suffice?

How THE JUSTICES WOULD VOTE seemed hard to predict. Justice O'Connor had helped Barry; numerous justices had probed deftly; the chief justice's closing hypothetical hinted he would oppose Barry; and Barry had been debated and forced into error, as if she were still a law school truant, by Justice Rehnquist.

In late June of 1986, newspapers announced a unanimous decision. Its author was Rehnquist. "Without question," he wrote for the Court, "when a supervisor sexually harasses a subordinate because of the subordinate's sex, that supervisor 'discriminate[s]' on the basis of sex." He condemned both *quid pro quo* harassment and harassment that creates a "hostile, or offensive working environment."

The *New York Times* and *Washington Post* made the decision front-page news. Under a headline reading "A Surprise from Justice Rehnquist," the *Post* quoted from one of his speeches, years earlier, saying that times change and judges may seem unpredictable. His opinion, it continued, "came as a pleasant surprise to civil rights advocates who have seldom found him in their corner."

Both papers hinted at a reason. The decision, said the *Post*, "was written by Justice William H. Rehnquist, President Reagan's choice as the next chief justice." When the *Post* quoted an attorney for the NOW Legal Defense Fund who called this the first time Rehnquist had "issued an opinion on our side," the *Post* added that the opinion was "written long before his nomination" but did not report on how long Chief Justice Burger's resignation had been anticipated. Rehnquist's nomination for chief justice preceded Rehnquist's presentation of Vinson's victory by only two days.

Barry was clearer than the newspapers. "We all know why Rehnquist wrote the decision," she said later. "He wanted to be approved as Chief Justice, and he didn't want all the women's groups on his back, right?" To be approved, Justice Rehnquist needed a confirmation vote from the Democrat-controlled Senate. Were women's rights attorneys like Barry right to suspect that Justice Rehnquist wanted strongly to write that decision?

No one may ever know for sure, but the process that led to Rehnquist's surprise emerges partly from conversations and memos among the justices. At their private conference three days after oral argument, Rehnquist spoke third from last in the order of seniority. From the comments of the first six justices, according to notes taken by Justice Brennan, Vinson seemed to be winning. Early support for Judge Robinson's opinion came from four justices: Brennan, Marshall, Blackmun, and (at least in part) White. Chief Justice Burger, sounding noncommittal about whether to reverse or affirm, thought that Vinson should have complained formally to the bank; he called strict liability the "core question." Only Powell seemed ready to reverse Judge Robinson. The findings of the district court were against Vinson, Powell said, and—choosing a metaphor that evoked a fallen Eve—"I wouldn't give her a second bite at the apple."

When his turn came, Rehnquist spoke against Robinson's opinion with more vehemence than anyone but Powell, according to Brennan's notes on Rehnquist's comments:

Finding of voluntariness (if took place, were voluntary) doesn't answer environmental theory. On strict liability, if there's a system for complaining can't hold bank liable. Her voluntariness is admissible. I'd let it go back for retrial with understanding I don't agree with much of Ct of Ap.

Rehnquist's disagreement with much of Robinson's opinion was not echoed by the last two speakers in the conference. Justice Stevens wanted to send the case back for a retrial on the "hostile environment theory." Justice O'Connor, apparently disagreeing with Rehnquist on a key point, said that "adequate complaint system is significant but not conclusive—depends on whether it's one employee would use." She supported a new trial that would need to determine "whether conduct unwelcome, not voluntary." Following this conference in which most voices aligned significantly (though far from completely) with Judge Robinson, Chief Justice Burger assigned the opinion to one of Robinson's strongest critics, Justice Rehnquist. He would be writing to affirm an opinion that had support from a majority of the court, which he and the chief justice elected to join.

When Justice Rehnquist's draft reached the court on April 22, 1986, it divided what had seemed, with only Powell in dissent, a nearly unanimous court. When Justice Marshall saw the draft opinion, he scrawled in large letters: "Join??? but wait!!"

Objection arose not to Rehnquist's acceptance that sexual harassment was sex discrimination but to what followed. Concerning what evidence could be heard, he ruled that Mechelle Vinson's dress and behavior were admissible as evidence, a view that may have suited numerous justices. Brennan's notes on comments by both Burger and White, though not mentioning clothes, said that "voluntariness" was relevant, and O'Connor had said that Vinson's "conduct was relevant."

The main objection came to the last part of Rehnquist's opinion. Was the bank, he asked, "strictly liable" for a hostile environment created by a supervisor's sexual advances, even though the employer neither knew nor reasonably could have known of the alleged misconduct? Here Rehnquist avoided a definitive ruling, citing problems that Pat Barry and Catharine MacKinnon had pointed to: the confused "state of the record" created by absence of a transcript and by Judge Penn's hypothetical finding of fact. Nonetheless, he held definitively that "the Court of Appeals erred in concluding that employers are always automatically liable for sexual harassment by their supervisors." And he stated agreement with the EEOC, which had chosen to turn against Mechelle Vinson. The justices of the Supreme Court, he declared, "agree with the EEOC that Congress wanted courts to look to agency principles for guidance in this area."

As a source for these principles, Rehnquist offered the same work by the American Law Institute on which Judge MacKinnon had drawn in his limited concurrence in *Barnes*. This was the work that declared that a Master (a bank, for example) could escape responsibility by asserting that its servant (a bank supervisor) had behaved badly (succumbed to a bank teller's sexually provocative speech or dress) while acting outside the scope of his employment as supervisor ("when he was out at the hotel," in the words of Justice Marshall). Much as Judge MacKinnon offered a series of tests that might have freed Paulette Barnes' employer from liability, Justice Rehnquist seemed to be charting an escape route for the bank.

Two days after the arrival of the draft, Justice John Paul Stevens expressed strong reservations about Rehnquist's move to limit the bank's liability. "As I understand the cases," wrote Justice Stevens,

the Courts of Appeals are unanimous in holding that there is strict liability in the "quid pro quo" type of case, as in other Title VII cases, but the rule is less certain in a "hostile environment" type of case. It would seem to me to make a good deal of sense to have the same rule apply to both kinds of cases

because as a matter of statutory construction, it seems doubtful
that Congress would have intended different rules to apply to
the two Title VII claims.

Justice Stevens' proposal that strict employer liability apply equally
in all sexual harassment cases quickly won the support of Brennan.
Both Marshall and Blackmun were inclined to follow. With one more
vote, Stevens would have a majority.

The day that Stevens expressed his reservations, Rehnquist replied
with a memo circulated to all the justices. For Stevens' position advocating absolute liability for hostile-environment cases, Rehnquist
replied that he was "willing to make a sixth vote, but not a fifth one."
Rehnquist was saying that if Stevens could gather a majority of five
votes, Rehnquist would join as Stevens' sixth (and unneeded) vote.
Rehnquist would not risk falling into a minority. But if Stevens could
gather only a minority of four, Rehnquist would stay with his old
majority and his old opinion. For whatever reason, perhaps including
the one suggested by Pat Barry, Rehnquist was willing to sacrifice a
legal view in order to stay in the majority on all points.

Soon after Rehnquist parried Stevens' objection, another indicator
arrived that Rehnquist's draft did not give strong support to Vinson's case. Justice Powell, who as the lone dissenter in conference had
opposed giving her another "bite," became the first justice to join
Rehnquist's full opinion.

For Stevens, the best chance for a fifth vote was apparently Sandra
Day O'Connor, and for weeks she did not join Rehnquist's opinion.
But on May 8 she wrote Rehnquist saying (in a familiar shorthand
of the court), "Please join me." A majority of votes soon followed,
with Chief Justice Burger joining on May 27, the day he told President
Reagan that he wished to resign.

Justice Stevens' reservation became a rebuke by Justice Marshall—
sufficiently strong that at first he said he would "circulate a dissent,"
technically impossible so long as he still voted with the judgment for
Vinson. Marshall's first draft, labeled a "concurrence" by his clerks,
criticized Rehnquist for refusing to "apply in this case the same rules
we apply in all other Title VII cases"—for refusing to hold the bank

strictly liable in a case of environmental harassment. After Marshall saw that his clerks had called his draft "concurring," he gave it a narrower label—"concurring in the judgment" only—in order to signal that he joined the judgment for Vinson but not the reasoning of Rehnquist. When insisting on this label, Marshall let his clerks know that he was angry at Rehnquist. Joining his narrow concurrence were Blackmun, Brennan, and Stevens.

Divisions and outrage within the court remained hidden, as did the twists on the road to the published decision: A chief justice who had a reputation for adjusting his vote in order to control assignment of decisions, and whose conference comments seemed doubtful about Vinson's case, voted for Vinson and then assigned the opinion to one of the two justices most skeptical of her case. Rehnquist, drafting his opinion supposedly to follow an 8-to-1 vote for Vinson in conference, diverged so far that his draft immediately gained the lone vote that had gone against Vinson, quickly alienated four votes that had supported her, and for many days did not get the pivotal fifth vote of O'Connor. When Stevens challenged that draft, Rehnquist stated his intention to stay in the majority, no matter which side of a legal position he needed to take. Thus he remained author of and aligned fully with a decision that made him seem, surprisingly, supportive of civil rights at the moment when the nation was considering his nomination to become chief justice of the United States.

With such complications far from public view, on June 20, 1986, the Supreme Court announced the opinion by Justice William Rehnquist. In a front-page headline about what it called a unanimous ruling, the New York Times announced that "Sex Harassment on Job Is Illegal." More than a decade of debate and judicial resistance had apparently ended.

MECHELLE VINSON RECEIVED A SETTLEMENT payment from the bank in 1991, after a return to district court. She used part of the money to pay some of her tuition for nursing school. The settlement required that she never disclose the dollar figure, and she has mostly avoided discussing the case. By 1993, she had found a job she loved, as a nurse treating incarcerated teenagers in the District of Columbia. More than a decade later she continued work as a nurse, helping victims of abuse, as reported by *Glamour* magazine in an article titled "These Women Changed Your Life."

Sidney Taylor went to jail in 1988 for embezzling from one of his bank's depositors. The *Washington Times* headline read, "Man Gets Prison Term for Bilking Elderly Woman." Pat Barry went bankrupt in 1988. Within a few years, she had revived her practice, continuing to defend women with little money and, when necessary, maxing out her credit cards to pay for court costs such as trial transcripts. Catharine MacKinnon in 1990 became a tenured professor of law at the University of Michigan. William Rehnquist became chief justice of the United States Supreme Court.

Part Five

VIOLENCE
(1990–2000)

21

———◆———

A Challenge for a Young Lawyer

One day in the spring of 1990, a new staffer in the offices of the Senate Judiciary Committee, just off the marble halls of the Dirksen Building and a short walk from the marble dome of the Capitol, received a surprise project from her boss, Senator Joseph Biden. He wanted her to figure out what Congress should do to reduce violent crimes against women.

Victoria Nourse, the new staffer, was thirty-one years old and six years out of law school. Except for being the only woman lawyer in her section of the Judiciary Committee, she wondered what in her background prepared her for this job. After law school at the University of California at Berkeley, Nourse had moved to New York to clerk for Edward Weinfeld, a revered trial judge known for working his clerks to exhaustion. Most nights before motions were due, Nourse worked so late she fell asleep in the courthouse. After she had worked on one of his opinions, to check for minor errors Nourse forced herself to re-read the whole opinion backward.

The clerkship led to offers from New York law firms, which tended to trust someone who could cut it with Judge Weinfeld. Nourse accepted an offer from one of the most prestigious, Paul, Weiss, Rifkind & Garrison, because she had heard Paul, Weiss was a firm that, if you worked hard and billed the hours, would promote you whether you were, as she put it, "green or purple." Except for hard work, Nourse had to admit she didn't really know much about where a law firm or the law itself would lead her.

Law was not part of her parents' plan for Victoria. From the time she was young in Marblehead, Massachusetts, Nourse's father, a small-town banker, had mapped her route through his alma maters, Andover, Princeton, and Harvard Business. Nourse went along for the first step.

But Andover ended the game of follow-the-father. She jumped coasts to go to Stanford. After graduating, she stayed in California to work for a year—crunching numbers at a think tank by day, waitressing by night—to become a state resident. What really annoyed her father came next: Victoria spurned business school. Without his blessing or money, she went to law school. And since she was now a state resident, she could attend one of the great law schools in the country, Boalt Hall of the University of California at Berkeley, for under $500 a semester.

Boalt Hall remained legendary for its influence on women and the law. Its women's group had given crucial help in 1970 to Wendy Webster Williams when she needed a legal brief for the path-breaking *Sail'er Inn*. Boalt Hall remained home to Professor Herma Hill Kay, who with Ruth Bader Ginsburg and Professor Kenneth Davidson of the State University of New York had created the first textbook on women in the law and who in 1992 would become Dean Kay, presiding over the entire law school. But Nourse, arriving at Boalt in 1981, didn't take Professor Kay's course or any courses on women and the law. Nourse did not go to law school to study women's issues.

Nourse liked research. At Paul, Weiss, after working for a few partners including one of the most revered, Arthur Liman, she received an unusual assignment. The firm had agreed to provide attorneys to the Senate to investigate what President Reagan knew about what became known as the "Iran Contra" affair—secret dealings in which the American government sold weapons to Iran and then diverted profits to fund the right-wing Nicaraguan rebels known as the Contras. Liman with two other partners and other attorneys went to assist individual senators. As the work started, Nourse became the young lawyer on the spot, staffing the senior lawyers and doing fast work for long hours.

As the Iran Contra investigation was winding down, Liman proposed her next job—a plum that could give her a chance at becoming partner, at a time when only one woman was a partner in the litigation division of Paul, Weiss. Liman wanted her to take charge of the research half of the insider trading case against Michael Milken. Nourse could imagine the trajectory. If she worked hard and beat the odds, she might emerge in the coveted position of partner with income approaching half a million dollars per year.

Nourse told him no. She decided that Liman was offering the chance, albeit for enormous amounts of money, to sit in a document room for what sounded like the rest of her life. She wanted to be a real lawyer like him, someone who argued cases in court. He had learned by working as a U.S. attorney, and she wanted to do the same. So, she joined the appellate staff of the Justice Department, flying to federal courts of appeals around the country, arguing cases about, for example, failed federal elevators and failed federal garage doors.

At about the time that Nourse decided she was not moving the law into new territory, in late 1989 she heard from a friend about a new job at the Senate Judiciary Committee, which was trying to forge a major crime bill. The Democrats, who controlled the Senate, and the committee needed to convince Americans that although the Republicans under President George H. W. Bush might want to look tough on crime, the Democrats were smart on crime.

Nourse interviewed with the chief counsel of the Senate Judiciary Committee, Ronald A. Klain, who made the job sound like no plum. Crucial to any crime bill would be the death penalty; crucial to the death penalty would be the law of *habeas corpus*. The ancient right to seek writs of *habeas corpus*, guaranteed in the Constitution (and perhaps originating in Magna Carta in the thirteenth century), gave advocates for death-row prisoners numerous opportunities to delay executions. The Senate Judiciary Committee needed a *habeas* specialist. Here was a job that fused the skills of Nourse-the-researcher with

Nourse-the-litigator. She would need to study up and become a *habeas* expert overnight in order to prepare for countless arguments with Republican staffers intent on out-toughing her on the death penalty. She took the job.

After Nourse had been on the job a few weeks, Klain had an extra task for her: figure out what Congress should do about violent crimes against women. Senator Joseph Biden of Delaware, their boss and the chair of the Senate Judiciary Committee, for years had wanted to do something about women and crime. On that committee in 1981, for example, he had pushed for a provision opposing laws that treated rape within marriage as a lesser crime than other rapes. He was rebuffed by a senator from Alabama, Jeremiah Denton, who replied, "Damn it, when you get married," as Biden later recalled, "you kind of expect you're going to get a little sex." In 1990, reading through crime statistics, Biden noticed an uptick in violent crimes against young women, which led him to studies suggesting that such violence was an accepted part of American culture. In early May of 1990, Klain read an article in the *Los Angeles Times* that he thought Biden should see. Written by Lisa Heinzerling, who had clerked at the Supreme Court with Klain the year before, the article described a mass murder of women:

> Last December, a man walked into the engineering school at the University of Montreal armed with a hunting rifle. He entered a classroom and divided the students he found there into two groups: women and men. Shouting at the women, "You're all a bunch of feminists," he picked them off as if they were ducks in a shooting gallery. By the time he had finished his deadly stalk, he had killed 14 women and injured many others. A note found in his pocket after he had killed himself declared that women had ruined his life.

Heinzerling's article then made an argument against current American law: Although some states and the federal government were enacting laws aimed at so-called hate crimes, none concerned hatred against women. A new federal law mandating the collection of information tracked only hate crimes targeting a "victim's race, ethnicity, religion or sexual orientation." Thus, argued Heinzerling, "if a woman is beaten, raped or killed because she is a woman, this is not considered a crime of hate."

To ignore hate crimes aimed at women, she concluded, "is to signal that crimes committed against women because they are women do not trouble us very much. That is a message welcome to no one but the misogynist."

Klain showed the article to Senator Biden, who responded immediately that he wanted to do something. "This wasn't a hard sell," recalled Klain. He went to Nourse with a challenge: what should Congress do?

It did not occur to Klain, who himself had taken a course on women and the law at Harvard, to ask Nourse what she studied in law school. Since the early years of such courses at New York University and Rutgers, students of both sexes had been probing the law of rape and violence against women. Nourse, who had skipped that kind of course at Berkeley, decided to begin some research.

GOING TO THE LIBRARY, Nourse took one of the most inspiring walks of American urban life: out of the marble-halled Senate office building, down Independence Avenue, past the towering Capitol dome, and into the Law Library Reading Room of the Library of Congress. Only its name had grandeur. It lacked the oak of law schools and the chrome of corporate law libraries. The library seemed not to trust its readers: from beneath the low acoustical-tile ceiling, video surveillance cameras peered down the narrow rows of legal books.

As she began, Nourse was looking for what she thought of as a *hook*. It had to be a problem in the law today. It had to catch senators, mostly old men. And it had to make those male senators think that millions of voters would thank them for figuring out what to do about violence against women.

Nourse started moving from casebook to law journal to practitioner's manual, back and forth across the Law Library Reading Room. Starting from scratch, she was giving herself a course on women in the law. Nourse glanced at the book she would have read if she had studied with Professor Kay at Berkeley: *Texts, Cases, and Materials on Sex-Based Discrimination*, the 1,001-page third edition of a textbook whose first edition Kay had begun planning with Ginsburg in 1971 and that appeared for the first time in 1974. Nourse read through back issues of early women's law journals, particularly the first, the *Women's Rights Law Reporter*, started by Ginsburg's students at Rutgers in 1971. There she could read about early gender battles as described by their litigators: Ginsburg on *Reed* and *Frontiero*, Wendy Williams on *Geduldig v. Aiello*.

Multiple articles traced the descent of American rape law from seventeenth-century formulations of British Common Law. Often the law harked back to a comment by Britain's Lord Chief Justice Matthew Hale, who died in 1676. A rape accusation, said Hale, is "easily to be made and hard to be proved, and harder to be defended by the party accused, tho never so innocent."

This seventeenth-century fear for the defenseless male struck a chord in the men who shaped American law. Through the nineteenth century, state courts embraced versions of what became known as the "Lord Hale instruction." Courts ordered that Lord Hale's worry become more than mere commentary; they ordered that some version of his warning be given by judges as an instruction to juries in rape trials. It became, as Judge David L. Bazelon remarked in the early 1970s, "one of the most oftquoted passages in our jurisprudence."

Other forms of modern American law had roots in Britain. Some state laws held that a man who sexually assaulted his wife had not committed rape—a legacy of the common-law doctrine that in marriage man and woman became one or of the elaboration (again conceived by Hale) that a married woman cannot be raped by her husband because by marrying she consented to all his demands for sex. Some local authorities as late as the 1970s did little to protect women from being beaten by their husbands, a practice whose roots may have grown from common-law rules that permitted a husband to control his wife through corporal punishment and perhaps from judicial opinions about the permissible size of a stick ("a switch no larger than his thumb" was one nineteenth-century American judge's view) that the law let husbands use for thrashing wives.

Nourse also looked to more current journals. In the *Yale Law Journal* of 1986, she found a major article written by Professor Susan Estrich of Harvard. For somebody working toward tenure, as Estrich had been, the article's opening sentences looked risky:

> Eleven years ago, a man held an ice pick to my throat and said: "Push over, shut up, or I'll kill you." I did what he said, but I couldn't stop crying. A hundred years later, I jumped out of my car as he drove away.

That story from Estrich's days as a college student at Wellesley resembled no opening in the history of the *Yale Law Journal*. Estrich continued, "I ended up in the back seat of a police car. I told the two officers I had been raped by a man who came up to the car door as I was getting out in my own parking lot."

The officers asked Estrich his race (black) and if she knew him (no). Those answers, she decided, had positive effect:

> Now they were on my side.
>
> They asked me if he took any money. He did; but while I remember virtually every detail of that day and night, I can't remember how much. But I remember their answer. He did take money; that made it an armed robbery. Much better than a rape. They got right on the radio with that.

The police never found the rapist and never got back in touch with Estrich. When Estrich wrote her article, a decade after the attack, she was not assailing the two cops who failed to find her unidentified rapist. She wrote to assail the legal system's handling of all forms of rape, and particularly a far more common rape: rape by men whom their victims can easily identify. Her article probed the system that, precisely when a rapist is most clearly known, most often fails to find that he has committed "rape."

For Nourse, Estrich's long article—longer than Ruth Bader Gins-burg's 116-page textbook from 1974, *Text, Cases, and Materials on Constitutional Aspects of Sex-Based Discrimination*—offered much of value: a link from rape law's early embarrassments to its modern ones. Estrich devoted the longest sections of her article to showing the continuity from Lord Matthew Hale to America's "Model Penal Code." The American law of rape focused on two tangled issues: the victim must prove that her attacker used force and that she did not consent.

For one example of the law's view of force, Estrich turned to a case from the 1890s. In Arkansas, according to Estrich, a man "seized his victim at gunpoint, told her he was a notorious train robber named 'Henry Starr,' threatened to kill her, and proceeded to have intercourse with her twice." At his trial, the jury convicted Henry Starr of rape. The attacker's lawyers appealed. They said Henry Starr had not used sufficient "force" to have committed rape.

The United States Supreme Court in 1897 agreed with Henry Starr's lawyers. The woman, after being abducted at gun point and told she might die, did not resist the rape *itself*. "More force is necessary" during the actual sex, the Supreme Court decided, for intercourse to become rape. Using a gun and threatening murder did not mean that Starr had used *impermissible* force in demanding sex.

Lest she be accused of making easy attacks on century-old cases, Estrich turned quickly to a 1974 case in which a man named Martin Evans convinced a college sophomore that he was

> a psychologist conducting a sociological experiment, took the woman to a dating bar to "observe" her, and then induced her to come to an apartment he used as an "office." When she rejected his advances, he said to her: "Look where you are. You are in the apartment of a strange man. . . . I could kill you."

Scared, the sophomore gave in. The New York Supreme Court found the man innocent of rape. The court then proceeded (in language Estrich did not quote) to give advice to men:

So bachelors, and other men on the make, fear not. It is still not illegal to feed a girl a line, to continue the attempt, not to take *no* for a final answer, at least not the first time.

Seducers should worry, the judge continued, if they crossed the line to force or threat—did more, apparently, than say, "I could kill you." Dismissing Evans as an "Abominable Snowman," the New York Supreme Court in 1976 decided that he had committed not illegal rape but legal "conquest by con job."

In her survey of permitted force, Estrich related other dark stories. In North Carolina in 1981, a man named Edward Alston had, as Estrich put it, "been involved in a 'consensual' relationship with a woman he often would hit if she 'refused to give him money or refused to do what he wanted.'" After six months of enduring him, she fled and "moved in with her mother." A month later, Alston pursued her to her school and

> blocked her path, demanded to know where she was living and, when she refused to tell him, grabbed her arm and stated that she was coming with him. The victim told the defendant she would walk with him if he released her arm. They then walked around the school and talked about their relationship. At one point, the defendant told the victim he was going to "fix" her face; when told that their relationship was over, the defendant stated that he had a "right" to have sex with her again.

They went to a friend's house. He then

> asked her if she was "ready," and the victim told him she did not want to have sexual relations. The defendant pulled her up from the chair, undressed her, pushed her legs apart, and penetrated her. She cried.

A trial court convicted him of rape and an appeals court agreed.

The North Carolina Supreme Court, however, disagreed. It conceded that, in Estrich's words, "her testimony provided substantial evidence that the act of sexual intercourse was against her will." So far so good. But the court was not satisfied about the level of force. As Estrich put it,

> The victim did not "resist"—physically, at least. And her failure to resist, in the court's evaluation, was not a result of what the defendant did before penetration. Therefore, there was no "force."

Or at least there was no evidence for the type of force that, the court believed, turns consensual sex into rape. For Edward Alston to cross the line from consensual sex to rape, hitting her—or threatening to change the look of her face—had to be part of actually forcing sex.

As Estrich made clear, the women's decisions not to fight back was one she could grasp.

> Hers is the reaction of "sissies" in playground fights. Hers is the reaction of people who have already been beaten, or who never had the power to fight in the first instance. Hers is, from my reading, the most common reaction of women to rape. It certainly was mine.

Estrich's response was an extraordinary identification of a law review author with a victim of what the law had ultimately decided not to call "rape."

As Estrich also made clear, the problem of proving force can mesh with a problem that she did not have when she was raped: the problem of proving non-consent. The law's worry that she had consented explained why the two policemen quickly asked Estrich if her attacker was black and if she knew him. Estrich's answers signaled to the officers, she later realized, non-consent; that's what got the policemen "on her side."

Dramatic proof of non-consent could make a woman's case easier. Henry Starr's victim could have resisted until he used his gun, Martin Evans' victim could have resisted until he "hurt her physically," and

Edward Alston's victim could have resisted until he fixed her face. That is, a woman could usually get evidence of non-consent by getting hurt as well as raped. But what if she, as Estrich put it, is "afraid enough, or intimidated enough, or, frankly, smart enough, not to take the risk of resisting physically"?

For the law's classic understanding of what a rape victim must do to prove she did not consent, Estrich turned to a case in Wisconsin in the early 1900s. A sixteen-year-old girl was walking across the fields to her grandmother's house when she was, she said, accosted by a neighbor. He grabbed her, knocked her legs out from under her, and forced her to have sex. The girl testified,

> I was trying all the time to get away just as hard as I could. I was trying to get up; I pulled at the grass; I screamed as hard as I could, and he told me to shut up, and I didn't, and then he held his hand on my mouth until I was almost strangled.

The jury believed her: he was guilty of rape.

The Wisconsin Supreme Court disagreed; it declared her attacker innocent of rape. He was innocent because, the supreme court ruled, the sixteen-year-old girl had done too little to warn her attacker that she did not consent. "Not only must there be entire absence of mental consent," ruled the supreme court, but there also

> must be the most vehement exercise of every physical means or faculty within the woman's power to resist the penetration of her person, and this must be shown to persist until the offense is consummated.

The supreme court, insisting on seeing marks of resistance, seemed to demand injury. But it went beyond injury, adding insult. "Medical writers insist," the court explained, that a woman who wishes to resist "is equipped to interpose most effective obstacles"—hands, for example, and pelvic muscles. Unless the man is much bigger and stronger than the woman, the court continued, "these obstacles are practically insuperable." The Wisconsin court evidently believed that a sixteen-year-old girl with strong pelvic muscles was immune from rape. The court ruled that she had consented to sex, making it legal.

THE CONSENT STANDARD FOR RAPE SHIFTED, at least in theory and mostly due to pressure from women beginning in the 1960s and 1970s, from demanding *utmost* resistance to *earnest* or sometimes *reasonable* resistance. But, as Estrich demonstrated, the law's fundamental distrust of women remained. In Hawaii in 1981, in a case of rape in an open field that echoed the Wisconsin case of 1906, a man convicted of raping his wife's fourteen-year-old cousin after offering to drive her home was declared legally innocent by an appeals court. It ruled that the girl had not shown what her state's law demanded: "earnest resistance." The court was not satisfied by what it called "the victim's pleas to appellant to stop and an attempt to push appellant off of her."

Hawaii was not alone in demanding such resistance. In 1979 in Maryland, a court acquitted a man who lured a high-school student to a deserted place by claiming he was an agent who could help her get work as a model. After insisting she did not want to have sex, she gave in because, she said, she was afraid: she was in an isolated house, where no one would hear if she screamed or help if she resisted. Again a jury found the attacker guilty, but a court of appeals freed him. The court explained the victim did not demonstrate sufficient physical resistance—which must reach "the extent of her ability at the time."

Yet by 1980, as Estrich found, most states had made some attempt to reform their rape laws. The most influential reforms began in the Model Penal Code. Begun in the 1950s by the American Law Institute—a members-only assembly of judges, lawyers, and scholars—the Code sought to provide a model for all state legal systems to consider and possibly adopt. Throughout the 1970s, comments kept being added, often to explain the rationales behind the Code—rationales that emerged in published form in 1980. Estrich's discussion of the Code became an important reference for Victoria Nourse.

The Code's drafters and commentators, all male for its section on "Sexual Offenses," aimed to provide a systematic approach to issues of force and consent or, as they put it, aimed to "avoid making the imposition-consent inquiry entirely on a subjective basis." To do so, the Code created three rules.

Rule 1 stated that the woman's testimony must be corroborated—a remarkable demand since rape rarely has witnesses. Here, the Code stepped beyond the British Common Law, which had not explicitly required that a woman's word be buttressed with other evidence.

Defense of the corroboration requirement placed the Model Penal Code's commentators under evident strain. After reminding readers that rape charges involve often-conflicting stories, they tried to make the corroboration requirement sound like a familiar part of all law—"only a particular implementation of the general policy that uncertainty should be resolved in favor of the accused." The corroboration requirement, that is, was only another of the law's time-honored attempts to "skew resolution of such disputes in favor of the defendant." Running hidden beneath such commentary was pressure on the drafters to protect rapists who may be, in the words of Morris Ploscowe, a New York magistrate and adjunct associate law professor at NYU who helped shape the Code's view of sex, "simply following" patterns of "behavior with which they are familiar." Ploscowe, the Code's expert on criminal sentencing, argued for the corroboration requirement lest a man find himself "at the mercy of revengeful, spiteful, blackmailing, or psychopathic complainants" or be convicted on the "uncorroborated testimony of a strumpet."

As Estrich made clear, the Model Penal Code demanded corroboration *only* for rape and sexual assault. By introducing for the first time an explicit corroboration requirement into rape law, the Code introduced a law that gave favor to men and costs to women.

Rule 2 demanded that any victim of rape file her complaint within three months. This new rule had rapid effect. Although no state law had required prompt complaint, soon a number of states were following it—or, in the case of Hawaii, outdoing it by demanding a complaint within one month of any sexual assault.

The Code's commentators offered multiple reasons for demand-

ing a speedy complaint, but most seemed to originate in fear. "The
requirement of prompt complaint springs in part," they explained,
from

> fear that unwanted pregnancy or bitterness at a relationship
> gone sour might convert a willing participant in sexual relations
> into a vindictive complainant.

Greater than their fear of the mercurial woman was their fear of
the scheming woman. "Perhaps more importantly," they continued, the
prompt complaint rule "limits the opportunity for blackmailing another
by threatening to bring a criminal charge for sexual aggression."
Rule 3 added nothing new. It looked straight back to the seventeenth century. Juries must be warned

> to evaluate the testimony of a victim or complaining witness
> with special care in view of the emotional involvement of the
> witness and the difficulty of determining the truth with respect
> to alleged sexual activities carried out in private.

This call for "special care" resurrected—now linked to women's
"emotional involvement"—Hale's suspicion that women could easily charge rape but men could not easily defend themselves. Estrich
quoted the Model Penal Code commentators' conviction that often

> the woman's attitude may be deeply ambivalent. She may not
> want intercourse, may fear it, or may desire it but feel compelled
> to say "no." Her confusion at the time of the act may later
> resolve into non-consent. . . . The deceptively simple notion of
> consent may obscure a tangled mesh of psychological complex-
> ity, ambiguous communication, and unconscious restructuring
> of the event by the participants.

Estrich noted that they felt "no need to cite any authority whatsoever
in support of their understanding of how women behave and think in

sexual encounters." This failure to cite such sources may have origins in either respect for or embarrassment about its most obvious source: "Dean Wigmore."

In 1904, Professor John Henry Wigmore, soon after becoming dean of Northwestern University School of Law, published the first volumes of what would become the dominant American law book on the crucial subject of evidence. Throughout the twentieth century, the dean and his topic became fused in his book's title and in the minds of American law students. During more than eighty years of required reading, he became *Wigmore on Evidence*.

Wigmore shared Lord Hale's fear that women would charge innocent men with rape. As a partial protection, Wigmore instructed that courts should admit evidence about the prior experiences with sex—the "unchastity"—of women who brought rape charges. He seemed unworried about women who might hesitate to bring an honest charge if the price meant opening themselves to cross-examination about every previous experience of consensual sex.

Fortunately for women, one of the first efforts of feminists beginning in the 1970s had been to counter Wigmore's urging that courts probe rape victims' sexual past. By the 1980s, when Estrich was writing, most states had taken action to modernize their rape laws. Still, the rise of Freudian psychiatry at the turn of the century had apparently given Wigmore a few ideas. Of women who complained of rape, said *Wigmore on Evidence*, their

> psychic complexes are multifarious, distorted partly by inherent defects, partly by diseased derangements or abnormal instincts, partly by bad social environment, partly by temporary physiological or emotional conditions.

Since such a woman might wrongly accuse a man, Wigmore had a solution: no rape case should go to trial until after the victim had been examined by a psychiatrist, who should then testify at trial about her mental health and sexual history. (Wigmore did not suggest that the possible rapist's psyche and sexuality be similarly examined.)

Wigmore's schema endured in law books throughout the century, even through a partial revision of *Wigmore on Evidence* in 1970 by Professor James H. Chadbourn of Harvard. They had also spawned elaboration in law journals, particularly during the 1950s and early 1960s. Perhaps the classic elaboration, cited by the Model Penal Code and courts of law, came in a 1952 article in the *Yale Law Journal*, "An Exploration of the Operation and Objectives of the Consent Standard." Its author, writing anonymously, as was the custom for law students writing in a university law review, explained that

> woman's need for sexual satisfaction may lead to the uncon-
> scious desire for forceful penetration, the coercion serving
> neatly to avoid the guilt feelings which might arise after will-
> ing participation.

A woman who wanted sex, the article continued, might act as if she did not want it. Worse, her actions might create evidence: crying, or scratching, or attempting to run away from a forceful man. So long as the man's sexual attack was not clearly contrary to the woman's wishes, the student author contended, "fairness to the male suggests a conclusion of not guilty."

In 1966, the *Stanford Law Review* weighed in on the law's classic demand in cases of sexual assault: utmost resistance. The anonymous writer thought he knew enough about women to explain why their resistance needed proof :

> Although a woman may desire sexual intercourse, it is custom-
> ary for her to say, "no, no, no" (although meaning "yes, yes,
> yes") and to expect the male to be the aggressor.

This Stanford law student wanted protection from a complaint that might arise if a woman gave in to sex out of "unconscious compliance." He wanted the resistance standard set high but still "low enough to make death or serious bodily injury an unlikely outcome."

In 1967, the *Columbia Law Review* insisted on the need for a witness because, said the student author, women's "stories of rape are frequently lies or fantasies."

Estrich responded by asking, in effect, Whose fantasy? Men had written for decades, she noted,

> about women's rape fantasies. But perhaps the better explanation for the law, as reflected in the Code and commentaries, lies in the fantasies of men.

Men had a fear, the "nightmare of being caught in the classic, nontraditional rape":

> A man engages in sex. Perhaps he's a bit aggressive about it. The woman says no but doesn't fight very much. Finally, she gives in. It's happened like this before, with other women, if not with her. But this time is different: She charges rape.

However unsupported by evidence, this male fear became encoded in law. As Estrich put it, "To examine rape within the criminal law tradition is to expose fully the sexism of the law."

By the time Victoria Nourse turned to Estrich's article on rape, Estrich had become one of the most prominent law professors in America. After becoming the first woman president of the *Harvard Law Review* in the mid-1970s and clerking at the Supreme Court, she returned to teach at Harvard while also becoming active in politics. She assisted with Ted Kennedy's presidential attempt in 1980, and then helped run Walter Mondale's presidential campaign in 1984. Soon after, her influential article on rape helped Estrich win tenure at Harvard Law.

But to Nourse's disappointment, Estrich proposed little that could help the United States Senate. As Estrich approached the hundredth page of her article, she made clear what she hoped for: "in a better world," men and women would tell each other that they wanted sex. In that better world, Estrich evidently wondered, if a woman merely submitted silently to pressure for sex, from her silence could the law

"presume nonconsent"? Estrich had shared this idea—silence beto-
kens non-consent—before publication. She heard criticism: we had not
achieved the world of vocal compliance that Estrich sought.

So in her published article Estrich offered what amounted to a
fallback position. At the very least, she insisted,

> the criminal law ought to say clearly that women who actu-
> ally say no must be respected as meaning it; that nonconsent
> means saying no; that men who proceed nonetheless, claiming
> that they thought no meant yes, have acted unreasonably and
> unlawfully.

And, she elaborated, in the difficult cases when women seemed to
yield to threats or extortion, the law of sex could simply mirror the
law of money:

> For the present, it would be a significant improvement if the
> law of rape in any state prohibited exactly the same threats as
> that state's law of extortion and exactly the same deceptions as
> that state's law of false pretenses or fraud.

That is, the New York man brought up on rape charges in the 1970s
would not be freed on the grounds that he had achieved "conquest by
con job." Instead, his fraud—his *con job*—would be as prohibited by
New York law as if he had gone after the college student's money.

The law could follow a simple rule, Estrich concluded: "I am arguing that 'consent' should be defined so that 'no means no.'"

What was Nourse to do? The most significant article on rape written by a female law professor in the 1980s argued that "no means no."
Could she return to the offices of the Senate Judiciary Committee,
ask for a meeting, and announce to Biden that we need a national law
saying "no means no"?

Furthermore, imbedded in Estrich's recommendations and evident
to any Senate staffer was a second problem. Estrich was making recommendations for *state* laws, because traditionally states, ever since
they began adopting Britain's national law, had governed rape law.

Pushing change through all fifty states could take decades. And each state remained free, at the end of that long process, to go its own way in how it prosecuted various types of sexual assault.

NOURSE REMAINED STUCK where she had begun, in the law library, looking for a hook. An article by a student in the *Duke Law Journal* of 1988 revealed that the cautionary instruction to juries based on Lord Hale's writing still echoed in the country's courts:

Arkansas in 1973: "Such a charge is easily made and hard to contradict or disprove."

California in 1974: "A charge such as that . . . is easily made and, once made, difficult to defend against, even if the person accused is innocent."

Idaho in 1978: "A charge such as that . . . is easily made, but difficult to disprove even though the defendant is innocent."

Beyond those echoes, the *Duke Law Journal* delivered a twist. In 1975, the California Supreme Court had unearthed the long-neglected context for Lord Hale's famous instruction. Although judges in the United States echoed Hale year after year, questioning the veracity of women of all ages and intellects, Hale seems to have devised his instruction when considering a special circumstance: a rape charge brought by a girl who was younger than twelve years, legally an infant.

Hale's question had been whether a girl so young, legally not competent to testify in most cases, should be allowed to testify at all—and he believed she *should*. Only then did Hale write what became his famous warning:

> It is true rape is a most detestable crime, and therefore ought severely and impartially to be punished with death; but it must be remembered, that it is an accusation easily to be made and hard to be proved, and harder to be defended by the party accused, tho never so innocent.

In other words, Hale was warning that although a jury must be cautious, it could choose to trust even a young girl. Since then, during hundreds of years of rape cases, states across America had trans-formed Hale's nuanced trust of one little girl into stark distrust of women.

The sleuthing into Hale conducted by the California court led a few other states to eliminate the cautionary instruction—but only a few. As of 1988, Nourse read in the *Duke Law Journal*, "over half of the states allow the cautionary instruction to be issued at the con-clusion of a rape trial." The *Duke Law Journal* proposed a solution similar to Estrich's: since state courts seemed unwilling to move, activ-ists should go after state legislatures, a slow process at best.

Nourse's tour through law journals took her to volumes too obscure to be reprinted in electronic services (which the Judiciary Committee did not have available in any event). In a 1990 volume of the *Florida Law Review*, she found a series of talks prepared for the official release of the findings of the "Florida Supreme Court Gender Bias Study Commission," and these looked promising. Nourse had never heard about any such commission and knew nothing about its origi-nators: the National Judicial Education Program and the National Association of Women Judges. Nor had she known that, as the law review said, Florida was the ninth state

> in which a state supreme court task force on gender bias had documented irrefutably that gender-based biases are distorting the justice system and that the victims of this distortion are overwhelmingly women.

What Nourse also saw in this just-published journal was an article that, finally, might offer what she needed to catch the attention of senators: a *hook*.

The article, by Robin West, a prominent law professor at the Uni-versity of Maryland, focused on the marital rape exemption—the law's ancient rule that a man is exempt from being charged with rap-ing his wife. That exemption, defended on the Senate Judiciary Com-mittee in 1981 by Senator Denton on behalf of getting "a little sex" in marriage, was so strong that it composed part of the definition of rape, as typified by the modern Model Penal Code: "A male who has sexual intercourse with a female not his wife is guilty of rape if . . ." The legal concept that a man cannot rape his wife was imbedded so firmly in law that it spawned an infamous joke: "If you can't rape your wife, who can you rape?" As the joke darkly implied, if the woman was the man's *wife*, no amount of force or threats or injury or pain could turn his sexual attack on her into *rape*.

West's article invoked *federal* law—the United States Constitution and its Fourteenth Amendment guarantee of equal protection under the law. "The so-called marital rape exemption," she argued, "constitutes a denial of a married woman's constitutional right to equal protection under the law."

West went further to argue that state statutes made a distinction between married victims and unmarried victims that was not *rational*:

> the marital rape exemption denies married women protection against violent crime solely on the basis of gender and marital status. What possibly could be less rational than a statute that criminalizes sexual assault, and punishes it severely, unless the victim and assailant are married.

For all the resistance of the supreme court to scrutinize discrimination, resistance so frustrating to Ruth Bader Ginsburg in the early 1970s, the court had remained willing to invalidate distinctions in state law that were clearly not rational. The Supreme Court had not yet, however, held unconstitutional this particular irrational distinction.

State courts were moving slowly, if at all. In 1984, a New York judge invalidated that state's marital rape exemption. Turning to the analysis by Judge Sol Wachtler of the court of appeals of New York, Nourse found yet another trail leading back to the seventeenth century.

Judge Wachtler's opinion began with the case at hand. In 1981 a man, who had been told to stay away from his wife in a legal order of protection, lured her to the motel where he was living by saying that he wanted to see their baby son. At the motel he attacked her, threatened to kill her, and forced her to perform fellatio on him and to engage in sexual intercourse with him. She charged him with rape.

A trial judge dismissed her charge because her husband was protected by the "marital exemption."

In order to reverse, Judge Wachtler's opinion had to travel back from the case at hand to address the history of the marital rape exemption. And back down the track, he found the words of Lord Matthew Hale from the 1600s:

> [The] husband cannot be guilty of a rape committed by himself upon his lawful wife, for by their mutual matrimonial consent and contract the wife hath given up herself in this kind unto her husband, which she cannot retract.

Did *in this kind* include, in the words of the Model Penal Code, the use of "force" or "extreme pain" or the "threat of imminent death"? In much of American law, the answer was apparently *yes*. Many American states and courts had turned Hale's opinion into law.

By ruling unconstitutional his state's marital exemption for rape, Judge Wachtler moved New York into a progressive minority. As of 1990, Nourse discovered as she sat reading in the Library of Congress, the majority of states continued, by a wide variety of legal means that West detailed, to permit husbands to, in effect, rape wives. A number of states, recognizing new American lifestyles, had extended the marital rape exemption to become what might be called live-in rape protection: if a man merely cohabited with a woman, he could gain protection from charges of rape.

Following similar logic and the language of the Model Penal Code, a few states had also created a form of date-rape protection that downgraded a rape charge if a woman was a man's "voluntary social companion." The most persistent of these states, with the only such law in force in the 1990s, was Delaware. Nourse realized that Delaware's denial of equal protection from date rape—unequal to the protection afforded by law to a woman attacked in another state—could indeed hook the attention of senators, including one who had a young daughter and was Nourse's boss: Senator Joseph Biden of Delaware.

Along with providing a new hook, West's article urged Nourse toward a new tactic: Forget going after the federal courts and the nine justices of the Supreme Court. Forget the Court's inadequate scrutiny of inequality and irrationality. Instead, said West, in search of true equality, go after the United States Congress. For Victoria Nourse, Robin West seemed to be speaking directly to her task. West offered a plan:

> Whether or not the U.S. Supreme Court or state supreme courts ever rule on the unconstitutionality of marital rape exemption, Congress has the power, the authority, and arguably the duty, to do so, under section five of the Fourteenth Amendment.

The Fourteenth Amendment itself was the law that had done little for women ever since the case in 1873 of Myra Bradwell, which denied her the right to practice law on grounds that included, as Justice Joseph P. Bradley made clear, restrictions on women that were ordained by "the law of the Creator."

Yet the Fourteenth Amendment guaranteed, in its section 1, that a state could not "deny to any person within its jurisdiction the equal protection of the laws." The resistance of the Supreme Court to extend this promise of equality to women had created many of the problems encountered by litigators, up to and beyond Ruth Bader Ginsburg's first victories in the 1970s.

The promise of the Fourteenth Amendment—its guarantee in section 1 of equality, of "equal protection of the laws"—remained unfulfilled. West's article, however, urged Nourse to think of section 1 as the goal but section 5 as the means. Section 5, the amendment's so-called enforcement clause, granted power to Congress to draft and pass legislation needed to deliver the Fourteenth Amendment's promise of equality. Drawing on this clause soon after its enactment, Congress had passed the powerful Civil Rights Act of 1871, which succeeded in halting the worst depredations of the Ku Klux Klan, and passed the ambitious Civil Rights Act of 1875, which attempted to combat discrimination against blacks in multiple locations including hotels, trains, and theaters. Both acts gave the federal government the power to prosecute private individuals who infringed the civil rights of others, and in cases involving conspiracy the 1871 Act gave power to any person deprived of a legal right to bring suit against private individuals (the conspirators) in federal court.

Nourse, still aiming for legislation to reduce violent crimes against women, turned again to West, who had sketched a proposal aimed at Congress: A Married Women's Privacy Act. It would "guarantee protection to all women against violent sexual assault" and would "prohibit irrational discrimination against married women" by rape laws.

· · ·

THE RIGHT TO PRIVACY HAD ORIGINS linked oddly to sex. In the long string of largely failed efforts to gain constitutional rights for women, one area had provided significant victories: the battles for access to birth control and then to abortion that became known collectively as battles for "reproductive freedom" or the "right to choose." Those battles, which began to take legal shape in the late 1950s, took a track quite different from most later efforts for women's rights. Reproductive freedom did not make a Fourteenth Amendment argument about *equality*. Rather, it began with a Fourteenth Amendment argument about *liberty*. Section 1 of the Fourteenth Amendment ended with two clauses:

> . . . nor shall any State deprive any person of life, liberty, or property, without due process of law; nor deny to any person within its jurisdiction the equal protection of the laws.

Rather than argue for equality, the attorneys who crafted the constitutional arguments for birth control argued for liberty—for, in a sense, what would become known as sexual liberation. They sought the liberty to have sex or, as the first jurisdictional statement to the Supreme Court put it in 1959, in an early case called *Poe v. Ullman*, "the right to engage in normal marital relations" and the related "freedom or privilege to procreate or not procreate."

The pursuit of this liberty led its author, Yale law professor Fowler Harper (who would eventually play a leading role in a more-famous successor case, *Griswold v. Connecticut*), to conjure the specter of the "long arm of the law" reaching into the bedroom to regulate "the most sacred relations between a man and his wife." This image of the invaded bedroom led directly to notions of invaded "rights of privacy." Professor Harper made no pretense that these new rights were "directly protected by the Fourteenth Amendment." Nonetheless, he raised several times the specter of the invaded marital bedroom and the countervailing right of privacy.

Also working with Harper in 1957, writing a brief that expanded the discussion of privacy, was a young lawyer at the ACLU named Mel Wulf—who, as ACLU legal director in 1971, would work with Ruth Bader Ginsburg. Wulf argued more strongly than Harper that "the Fourteenth Amendment protects persons from invasion of their privacy by the states." And Wulf's brief made clear that what he was arguing for was a right to sex, or at least sexual liberation. What he called the "invasion of privacy" included the law's presenting men and women a difficult choice that could lead to their "abstaining entirely from sexual intercourse." Years later, speaking to David Garrow for his monumental chronicle of the "right-to-choose" effort, *Liberty and Sexuality: The Right to Privacy and the Making of* Roe v. Wade, Wulf was characteristically candid. He remembered how his brief-writing on behalf of the right to privacy was made compelling by his personal sex life at the time: "I was then a single man, living in the Village, and sexually active if not promiscuous," he said. "I had a personal commitment to birth control." Wulf may have been more frank than other men about going to court for the freedom to have sex. In the process he had, as he later put it, "invented the right to privacy."

Lawyers were not ready to argue that the Constitution guaranteed sex, however, and the obvious replacement—a Fourteenth Amendment guarantee of liberty—ran into technical, legal problems. The Fourteenth Amendment guaranteed not liberty itself. Rather, it guaranteed that liberty should not be taken away "without due process of law." Lawyers were unwilling to argue that the Supreme Court return to the aggressive review that had in recent years been disparaged as "substantive due process" and that the Court was unlikely to revive.

But the Court's unwillingness to engage in substantive due process did not keep some of its members from responding positively, perhaps viscerally, to "the right to engage in normal marital relations." What began to take hold in the Supreme Court was support for the new idea of a right to privacy.

Tracing the path of an idea as it emerges may be impossible, but David Garrow's *Liberty and Sexuality* brilliantly tracks the development of legally protected *privacy*. In the Supreme Court in 1961, Charles Fried, fresh out of Columbia Law School (and later to become solicitor general), was clerking for Justice John Marshall Harlan. Although Fried hated Harper's "execrable" jurisdictional statement in the *Poe* case, he wrote ringingly in support of a married couple's freedom to "follow their inclinations and consciences without interference," with that freedom protected by a constitutional "right to privacy."

Soon afterward, in private conference after oral argument, Justice Harlan spoke of a "right to be let alone"—but was frustrated when a majority of Supreme Court justices preferred to dismiss this early case on a technicality. Harlan then directed Fried to write a dissent, which ran to sixty typed pages. To Fried's relief, Harlan did not rebuff his verbosity. With little change, Harlan made Fried's dissent his own, extolling at length the right to be let alone and the Constitution's protection of the privacy of the home. Printed alongside Harlan's vast dissent was a shorter one by William O. Douglas, stating that a guarantee of privacy "emanates from the totality of the constitutional scheme under which we live."

Although that early case went down to defeat, a right to privacy was rising. Both Harper and Wulf strengthened their privacy arguments in their next birth control case in the Supreme Court, the landmark *Griswold v. Connecticut*. And this time birth control won. The decision was assigned to William O. Douglas.

Within ten days, Douglas wrote his opinion. It rejected substantive due process. Then it created something new in Supreme Court law. Of marriage, he proclaimed that "we deal with a right of association as old as the Bill of Rights . . . a coming together for better or worse, hopefully enduring, and intimate to the degree of being sacred." And he concluded with a flourish:

> The prospects of police with warrants searching the sacred
> precincts of marital bedrooms for telltale signs of the use of

contraceptives is repulsive to the idea of privacy and association that make up a goodly part of the penumbra of the Constitution and the Bill of Rights.

Around the Supreme Court, clerks giggled. Justices turned jocular. Justice Tom Clark wrote to William O. Douglas that "I like all of it—it emancipates femininity and protects masculinity." Clark, Douglas, and Justice Byron White joked together: Birth control cases involved rights as fundamental as voting cases. With voting it was "one man one vote." With birth control, they all agreed, it was "one man one child."

Nourse knew that for years feminists had critiqued the male-driven rise of the right to privacy. Catharine MacKinnon's critique connected the law's protection of privacy to the law's failure to protect wives who are battered and wives who are raped. An indicator of this failure came in police policies that led officers, if called to homes to investigate assault charges, to choose not to arrest men for attacks that, if perpetrated outdoors in the street, would have led to arrests for assault. Another came in legal arguments defending the marital rape exemption as a defense against intrusion by government into the private lives of married couples. Thus private wife batterers found impunity not offered to the public batterer. "In this light," argued MacKinnon, a "right to privacy looks like an injury got up as a gift."

Aware of the widespread feminist condemnation of the substitution of privacy for equality, Nourse did not know what to make of Robin West's embrace of privacy. Nourse could not tell that West was playing a game—was being (as West would later say) perhaps "too cute."

West had thought, Why not try to reappropriate this tarnished notion of privacy? Why not try to use it to help women by proposing a law called the "Married Women's Privacy Act"? West was writing an imaginative talk to be given at a low-profile law school. As she brought her article to this ironic close, West never envisioned her article would be picked up, within a few weeks of publication, by a Senate staffer with instructions to create new legislation for women.

Nourse knew that the heart of a legislative effort should not rely on privacy. Thanks to West, she could state that women who were assaulted sexually received unequal protection, varying from state to state. Thanks to West, though indirectly, Nourse also had a concept for the right law. She could tell that West had based her "Privacy Act," enabling a legal suit for violation of a Fourteenth Amendment right, on legislation proposed earlier by Catharine MacKinnon, who in turn had based hers on the part of the Civil Rights Act of 1871 that permitted a person deprived of a legal right to bring suit.

MacKinnon, working with feminist theorist Andrea Dworkin and a coalition in Minneapolis, where both were teaching in 1983, had contended that pornography should be understood as a form of subordination of women that often included or incited violence against women. She described their proposed ordinance as "a law that recognizes pornography as a violation of the civil rights of women" and that "gives victims a civil action," a chance to sue, "when they are coerced into pornography, when pornography is forced on them, when they are assaulted because of specific pornography." The most controversial right to sue was against people who trafficked in pornography. Defending that provision, contained in a version of the ordinance passed by the city of Indianapolis, MacKinnon insisted it was tailored narrowly so that, as she put it, "we're talking rape, torture, pain, humiliation: we're talking violence against women turned into sex."

When the Indianapolis ordinance proceeded to a test in federal court in 1985, a three-judge panel of the United States Court of Appeals for the Seventh Circuit focused on the law's potential impact not on violence but on speech. They ruled unanimously that pornography was a form of speech, protected by the First Amendment of the Constitution. MacKinnon's ordinance lost, but the idea of a legal suit against violence remained.

MacKinnon's theories were familiar to Nourse, who had heard about them on frequent trips to Yale to visit a law student, Rick Cudahy, class of '87, whom she would later marry. During Cudahy's law school years, MacKinnon's work had high prominence. Her attack on sexual harassment, prominent ever since she wrote *Sexual Harassment of Working Women* while enrolled at Yale Law, had won affirmation at the Supreme Court in 1986 in the case of Mechelle Vinson. Her attack on pornography had generated legislative efforts in a number of cities and also congressional legislation, including the Pornography Victims Protection Act, introduced in 1984 but never passed. During those years, MacKinnon traveled widely to give lectures, compiled in 1987 as *Feminism Unmodified*. Also, through Rick Cudahy, Nourse had an unusual connection to MacKinnon's work. When the Indianapolis version of her antipornography ordinance was struck down by the Seventh Circuit Court of Appeals in 1985, one of the three judges voting against it was Judge Richard Cudahy, Rick's father.

Putting family aside, and without disputing the judgment of her eventual father-in-law, Nourse saw the potential for creating a strong law. It could directly target "violence against women" (MacKinnon's words) as a "violation of the civil rights of women" by giving "victims a civil action"—a chance to sue. Drawing on a long history of civil rights legislation, Nourse had found her course of action.

22

✦

Using Civil Rights to Combat Violence

S enator Joseph Biden introduced the "Violence Against Women
Act" on June 19, 1990, followed by a one-day hearing. The proposed bill contained more than just the civil rights section that Nourse
had pondered at the law library. The Violence Against Women Act—
VAWA, as everyone came to call it—opened with Title I, "Safe Streets
for Women." It introduced numerous provisions to increase penalties for sexual assaults, and to require assailants to pay victims for
losses such as medical costs and lost income. It also offered grants to
states and cities to assist training police and others to prevent violence
against women, and it provided funding to improve safety in public
transit. Title II, "Safe Homes for Women," focused on domestic violence and created a new federal criminal offense for batterers whose
attacks involved crossing state lines.

Title III, "Civil Rights," was both the shortest and the most
ground-breaking of VAWA's three sections. Nourse drew on past civil
rights law, imbedding language such as the Fourteenth Amendment's
guarantee of *privileges or immunities* and the congressional discussion of discriminatory *animus* during passage of the Civil Rights Act
of 1871. VAWA's civil rights section sought to guarantee to women
"equal protection of the laws" and "equal privileges and immunities
under the laws" to be "free from crimes of violence motivated by

the victim's gender." Such crimes were defined as "any rape, sexual assault, or abusive contact, motivated by gender-based animus." For the victim of such gender-based crime, the civil rights section created a new right to bring a lawsuit in federal court—a right with century-old origins and a complicated history.

In the late nineteenth century, right after the Civil War, many states put laws on their books that promised equality of treatment for citizens; nonetheless, numerous states failed to give black citizens protection against attacks. Across wide regions of the South, violent gangs, often with names like the White Brotherhood and the Ku Klux Klan, began killing blacks and their white supporters in acts of race-motivated violence. The attackers sought, beyond mere terror, the destruction of northern efforts to give civil rights to southern blacks and the restoration to southern whites of what became known as "home rule." Such attacks found their epitome in the late 1860s in Georgia when a gang of four hundred whites, including the local sheriff, fired guns into a group of blacks walking to a polling place to vote. When the blacks scattered, the whites pursued them, killing and wounding more than twenty.

To combat the violence, Congress passed the Civil Rights Act of 1871, which became widely known as the Ku Klux Klan Act. Legislating to enforce the Fourteenth Amendment's promise of equal protection, Congress gave federal prosecutors the authority to arrest private individuals if they conspired to deprive anyone of the "equal protection of the laws." Under the direction of a committed attorney general, the U.S. government by 1872 had indicted hundreds of Klansmen, put thousands to flight, and, according to Eric Foner in *Reconstruction*, his massive history of the years after the Civil War, broken the back of the Klan and reduced violence throughout the South. Along with its empowerment of federal prosecutors, the 1871 Civil Rights Act also empowered victims of race-motivated violence. It gave victims the power to sue their attackers in federal court if those attackers had conspired to deprive citizens of "the equal protection of the laws."

In 1875, a new civil rights act responded to less dramatic but more pervasive deprivations of rights. It established legal penalties against "any person" who tried to deny to blacks a wide range of rights—

including equal access to accommodation such as inns, to entertainment such as theaters, and to transportation such as trains. (In a compromise meant to make the bill easier to pass, an early revision stripped the bill of a clause that would have created multiracial schools and could have made unnecessary the legal battles that culminated in 1954 with *Brown v. Board of Education* and its condemnation of "separate but equal" public education.) Under the Civil Rights Act of 1875, blacks won the support of the federal government as they moved to desegregate such bastions as the Grand Opera House in New York and the Memphis & Charleston Railroad.

The great civil rights acts of the nineteenth century apparently arrived too soon. The 1871 Act went before the Supreme Court in 1883 when the federal government tried to bring to justice a white lynch mob led by a man known as R. G. Harris. The mob of twenty men had burst into a jail in Tennessee, pulled four blacks away from a deputy sheriff, and killed one. In response, in *United States v. Harris*, the Supreme Court in 1883 sided, in effect, with the lynch mob. The Court concluded that the Fourteenth Amendment did not empower Congress to resist discriminatory "action of private individuals." Drawing on an earlier opinion by Justice Joseph P. Bradley—the justice who had invoked the "law of the Creator" in 1873 to explain why women could not practice law—the Court in *Harris* ruled that the Fourteenth Amendment authorizes Congress to create laws against "the exertion of arbitrary and tyrannical power on the part of the government and legislature of the State" but not laws against "the commission of individual offences." *Harris* permitted federal prosecutors to combat only a lynch mob that received support from state officials—support from what the court called "state action."

The Civil Rights Act of 1875 got less time to achieve its goals. Writing in what ironically became known as the *Civil Rights Cases*, also in 1883, Justice Joseph P. Bradley stopped cold the Act's intent to open America's hotels, theaters, and railway cars to blacks. Bradley delayed America's movement toward civil rights by continuing his argument that the Fourteenth Amendment permitted the federal government to attack only state action. Bradley's opinion for the Supreme Court meant that train conductors could expel blacks from trains cars of the Memphis & Charleston Railroad, for example, though Tennessee could not legislate the expulsion. It meant that a theater owner could refuse blacks a seat and a hotel owner refuse blacks a place to sleep, though no state could legislate such refusals.

In a lone dissent, Justice John Marshall Harlan attacked Bradley's claim that Congress could not grant blacks the right to be free from race discrimination unless a state law assailed that right. Harlan also attacked other suggestions from Bradley, including that the former slave should cease to be the "special favorite of the laws" and that the Civil Rights Act of 1875 had sought to protect not civil rights but mere "social rights."

The Supreme Court's destruction in 1883 of the civil rights acts of 1871 and 1875 followed current events and Court decisions. In 1876, the Republican Party, after leading the struggle for emancipation of slaves, found itself unable or unwilling to resist attacks on black voters in the South during the presidential election of 1876. Losing southern states that he could have won, Republican Rutherford Hayes wound up with at best a one-vote victory in the electoral college. As he clung weakly to the presidency, Hayes yielded to the so-called Compromise of 1877, which permitted much-sought southern "home rule." Withdrawing many federal troops from the South, the Hayes administration seemed desperate "to conciliate the white men of the South," wrote one Kansas politician in February 1877, and to send others a message that included, as he put it, "Niggers take care of yourself."

The triumph of home rule and states rights had already received aid from the Supreme Court. The *Slaughter-House Cases* of 1873, which had interpreted the Fourteenth Amendment so narrowly that it could not help Myra Bradwell win the right to practice law, had also defined the rights of blacks in narrow terms. By enumerating in the aftermath to *Slaughter-House* only such federal rights as running for federal office, traveling to seats of government, and entering navigable waterways, the Supreme Court offered little to just-freed slaves. It also offered little to a federal government that wished to defend blacks from attack by individual whites—unless those blacks were, for example, trying to enter a waterway.

The Supreme Court's 1883 destruction of the civil rights acts of

1871 and 1875 rippled far into the twentieth century. The Court left Congress powerless, as argued by Professor Laurence Tribe of Harvard, "to prevent the emergence of 'Jim Crow' apartheid in the South." Justice Bradley's dismissal of blacks as "the special favorite of the laws," as argued by Professor Jack Balkin of Yale, helped inform the infamous 1896 decision, *Plessy v. Ferguson*, in which the Supreme Court created the "doctrine of 'separate but equal' facilities that would be used to justify segregation for decades." After the Court's evisceration of the civil rights acts of the 1870s, no major civil rights legislation passed Congress for nearly a century. Even then, the so-called state-action requirement that was elaborated in 1883 to limit the federal government's capacity to fight discrimination would weaken the grounding for the Civil Rights Act of 1964. It also had the potential to undercut an effort such as VAWA.

FORTUNATELY FOR VICTORIA NOURSE as she began drafting the civil rights section of the Violence Against Women Act for Senator Biden, she could rely on a provision of the 1871 Civil Rights Act that had survived: the right of citizens to bring a private lawsuit or civil action against individuals who have attacked them.

Drawing on the 1871 Act and *Griffin v. Breckenridge* of 1971, in which two white men who threatened to kill a group of black men in Mississippi were sued, Nourse worded VAWA to grant a woman attacked as a result of her sex the right to sue her attacker for gender-based deprivation of her civil rights. Nourse grounded VAWA's challenge to gender-based violence, as Congress had grounded the 1871 law's challenge to race-based violence, on the Fourteenth Amendment.

Though founded on the Constitution, Nourse's civil rights section had the potential to attract political attack. Senator Biden's staff decided to test it by having Nourse debate a staff member to see how it held up. The other staffer, a woman who had served as legal director, argued— not vociferously, as Nourse recalled—that the civil rights section could be dangerous politically. Nourse discussed legal wrongs. She focused on the problem of battering: assaults in the home were treated differently than assaults in the streets. She focused on inequities from state to state in the marital rape exemption: a man who raped a woman in Biden's home state would face a reduced charge if she was a social companion. Nourse's goal was to argue that many states were doing something wrong. She knew she had no weight on the staff, was a "nobody" in only her second meeting with Biden. But he was someone who believed in fighting, as she saw it, against "things that are wrong." After the mock debate, Biden decided to commit to the civil rights section.

Once she had Biden's go-ahead, Nourse began calling around Washington for input, but she found her greatest ally was in New York City: the NOW Legal Defense and Education Fund. "NOW Legal Defense," as everyone called it, had been created by the National Organization for Women in 1970 as a separate advocacy organization. (In 2004, the organization changed its name to "Legal Momentum.") Over the years, NOW Legal Defense had taken the lead in many women's legal battles. Nourse's call went to a 1982 graduate of Yale Law named Sally Goldfarb. Goldfarb had developed a specialty in working to expand and improve existing civil remedies for sexual abuse, such as easing the statute-of-limitations barriers that kept adults who had been abused as children from taking legal action against their abusers.

Nourse's phone message reached Goldfarb when she was in Washington for a meeting of the so-called Feminist Legal Strategies Project, which gathered legal advocates from as far away as California. Soon Goldfarb was standing in Nourse's office at the Senate Judiciary Committee. As Nourse described her concept of a civil rights law to oppose violence against women, Goldfarb's response was amazement: she thought, she later recalled, "Wow—where did this woman come from?"

To Goldfarb, Nourse's idea felt strikingly familiar. Goldfarb had traveled a different route to the same place. The valedictorian of her class at Princeton High School in New Jersey, she had gone to Yale College, where she majored in English and played viola in the Yale Symphony Orchestra. Graduating Phi Beta Kappa, she went on to Yale Law School. During her first year, in early 1980, she stepped into the first law course ever taught by Catharine A. MacKinnon, who was analyzing rape as a violation of the civil rights of women.

"First time she taught," Sally Goldfarb mused years afterward, smiling. "She later told me that she didn't know what she was doing. Of course she transformed my life completely. After that, I knew I wanted to specialize in women's rights."

After Goldfarb graduated, she clerked for a federal judge in Wisconsin, held a fellowship at Georgetown University Law Center run by Susan Deller Ross (who years before had created the Pregnancy Discrimination Act in concert with Ruth Weyand, Wendy Williams, Ruth Ginsburg, and others), and then went back to Wisconsin as an assistant state attorney general. In 1985 she moved to New York to become staff attorney with NOW Legal Defense. After talking to Nourse, Goldfarb called MacKinnon, who said, as MacKinnon later recalled, "If Biden wants to do something for women, he should recognize rape and battering as federal sex-discrimination claims."

THE COMBINATION OF SALLY GOLDFARB and NOW Legal Defense gave Victoria Nourse a crucial ally for the introduction of VAWA on June 19, 1990. Goldfarb drafted testimony to be delivered by her boss, Helen Neuborne. Nourse began preparing witnesses who could tell stories of having their lives altered by violence.

When Senator Biden convened the hearings in mid-June, he introduced VAWA's civil rights section as perhaps the bill's most important section. For too long, he said,

> we have ignored the fight of women to be free from the fear of attacks based on their gender. For too long, we have kept silent about the obvious—97 percent of all sex assaults in this country are against women.
>
> We know this; indeed, we assume it, but we ignore the implication: a rape or sex assault should be deemed a civil rights crime, just as "hate beatings" aimed at blacks or Asians are widely recognized as violations of their civil rights.

To capture how fear of sex-based violence alters women's lives, Goldfarb's language made the fundamental argument for VAWA:

> Just as a democratic society cannot tolerate crimes motivated
> by the victim's membership in a minority racial group and must
> pass special laws to combat such oppression, so too we must
> put into place effective laws to prevent and redress violent crime
> motivated by the victim's sex.

She also made sure the argument remained grounded in women's everyday lives. The testimony by Neuborne, speaking as executive director of NOW Legal Defense, opened with the story of a law professor at the University of Kentucky who began the discussion of rape in her criminal law class by asking each male student to tell the class what he does on a daily basis to protect himself from sexual assault. The men typically looked a bit blank. She then asked her female students, who filled in the blanks. One avoided a particular shopping mall because it lights its parking lot badly. One avoided the campus library at night when other students would be few. One locked all her windows shut at bedtime no matter how hot the weather. One, for fear of assault, carried a loaded gun.

In preparing the NOW Legal Defense testimony for her boss, Goldfarb was able to follow the lead, begun by Robin West and picked up by Nourse, of pointing to failures of justice that originated in state courts. Task forces on gender bias in the courts—like the one whose launching conference provided a forum for West to deliver her study on the enduring marital rape exemption—had originated in the work of NOW Legal Defense along with the National Association of Women Judges. Those task forces, operating in half the states, had encountered dramatic evidence of judicial mishandling of violence against women.

From a judge testifying to the New York task force about rape cases: "There are still all too many instances of the woman victim being put on trial with an underlying insensitivity permeating the courtroom."

From a judge chairing the Minnesota task force: " 'Acquaintance rape' promises to be one of the major upcoming issues with which the legal system must learn to deal effectively and with fairness to the victim."

From a judge whose comments were reported by the Maryland

task force: "I don't believe that anything like this could happen to me," said when explaining why he did not believe a woman's claim that her husband held a gun to her head.

The hearings led to an outpouring of support, hundreds of letters and telephone calls from around the country, far more than Senator Biden's office expected. With them came pressure to hold additional hearings on domestic violence and acquaintance rape. Nourse began to organize more hearings for late summer.

"DON'T YOU PEOPLE ALWAYS HAVE coalitions for everything?" Sally Goldfarb's husband, Joe Straus, asked her that summer after the hearings. They were taking their usual vacation, hiking in the high peaks of the Adirondack mountains of New York. The hearings had left Goldfarb energized, telling her husband—a music professor whom she had met when they were both students at Yale—that the VAWA was the embodiment of the feminist vision. But she worried that, without wide support, it might go nowhere.

In Joe's view, Sally always seemed to be heading off to multihour meetings with a coalition—on family leave, on childcare, and so on. One of her jokes was that in order to sit through all those coalition meetings, you had to have a strong bladder. So, asked Joe, why not create a new coalition? Yes, Sally thought, VAWA needed a coalition. But she told Joe she wasn't sure anyone was committed enough to start one—except, perhaps she was. Would anyone join?

Once she had approval from her boss, Goldfarb sent a letter to organizations that NOW Legal Defense had worked with, inviting them to help create a "task force with committees to work on law and policy, and grassroots action." The letter went out in late August. By the first week of September, Goldfarb was directing the task force's first gathering. Those present at the cramped and file-filled headquarters of NOW Legal Defense in New York included, as noted by Sally in her minutes, representatives of the ACLU Women's Rights Project; American Jewish Congress Committee for Women's Equality; Center for Battered Women's Legal Services Coalition Against Domestic Violence; National Center on Women and Family Law;

National Council of Jewish Women; National Federation of Temple Sisterhoods; National Organization for Women; New York City Commission on the Status of Women; New York State Office for the Prevention of Domestic Violence; New York University Law School Criminal Defense Clinic; Pennsylvania Coalition Against Domestic Violence; and Women in Criminal Justice.

These potential task force members learned that twenty senators were already sponsoring VAWA and that thirty-eight congressmen, led by Barbara Boxer, were sponsoring a House version. In her minutes of the meeting, Goldfarb recorded many participants' worries: Was Senator Biden "trustworthy"? Would he "sell out" civil liberties, perhaps even take steps toward restoring the death penalty for rape? Would civil rights groups not support VAWA because the civil rights section's inclusion of women might dilute the civil rights of racial and religious groups? Could a "racist and sexist" criminal justice system be trusted to address issues of violence? The participants discussed what a task force should do *if* it chose to endorse VAWA. As Goldfarb could tell, she didn't yet have a coalition. But she had a group that was ready to meet again and ready to agree that VAWA was a good idea.

The next three meetings, two in Washington and one in New York, brought in many new groups: the Anti-Defamation League; Center for Constitutional Rights; Center for Women Policy Studies; Coalition to Stop Gun Violence; Friends Committee on National Legislation; Kansas Coalition Against Sexual and Domestic Violence; Mennonite Coalition Committee; Mexican American Legal Defense and Education Fund; NAACP Legal Defense Fund; National Battered Women's Law Project; National Education Association; National Federation of Temple Sisterhoods; National Women Abuse Prevention Project; National Women's Law Center; Native American Rights Fund; New York City Task Force Against Sexual Assault; United Methodist Church; United States Student Association; Violence Against Women and Children Task Force; and Women of Reform Judaism.

Not every group had a participant at every meeting. Some attended one meeting and never returned. Many came again and again. Whether they came or not, Sally sent them meeting minutes, running often to ten typed pages, full of debate. By the November meeting, Goldfarb had a subcommittee able to agree that creation of a civil rights section for VAWA was worth considering. Goldfarb pushed for debate about what VAWA should cover, asking the group to discuss whether the civil rights section should reach the following crimes (as her minutes noted):

1) The homicide case in Canada in which a man separated the male and female students and killed only the women after announcing his hatred of women in a note and orally.

2) a domestic violence assault between adults in a home

3) stranger rape outside the home

4) Central Park Rape type crime—series of attacks by a group of men on both men and women, but the men are assaulted and robbed whereas the woman is far more severely beaten and is also raped.

Goldfarb was running a task force meeting as if it were a law school seminar, full of hypotheticals. The task force members dove into debates that would surface often: Were women attacked because they were small or because they were women? Did an attacker have to shout "bitch" to show bias? If an attacker said he hated blacks, hated gays, and loved women, and for those reasons attacked all three repeatedly, were women's civil rights untroubled—since women faced not hate crimes but love crimes? Running her task force meetings, Goldfarb was not getting agreement on all issues. But by the end of 1990 she was getting a task force that had dozens of members ready to argue and organize about VAWA.

A BIG GAP REMAINED. Goldfarb and her boss, Neuborne, knew that Goldfarb was organized but no organizer. She knew law but not lawmakers. Who could help? Neuborne called Pat Reuss. Reuss was the longtime legislative director for the legendary Women's Equity Action League, WEAL, the organization created by Bernice Sandler that in 1970 had discovered Executive Order 11246—the executive order that made law schools realize they could no longer have all-male faculties. Neuborne knew Reuss as one of the country's great grassroots feminist organizers, somebody who built ties and then kept those ties, with people all over the country.

Also, Neuborne knew Reuss was running out of money. WEAL had folded. Then the Women's Political Caucus, which hired Reuss as its legislative director, ran low on money and fired Reuss along with five other staffers. Reuss was suddenly an unemployed and divorced mother with three sons in college—"good kids," she would say, willing to keep college cheap by sleeping on friends' couches instead of sleeping in dorms. Organizing for women's rights could be a bit like sleeping on couches: a life, not a living. Since NOW Legal Defense was also running low on money and had closed its offices in DC, hiring Washington-based Pat Reuss was a steal. For $1,600 a month, Neuborne could hire Reuss to work twelve-hour days for love of VAWA.

Reuss did love VAWA. The last fun for grassroots women, Reuss thought, was winning the vote in 1920. To Reuss, *grassroots* meant women all over the country—women who cared about issues and maybe even got organized into groups, but women who rarely came to Washington. The grassroots, Reuss thought, had been getting a few losses and a few victories but no fun. Losing the equal rights amendment after years of work was no fun. Losing legal cases like *Geduldig v. Aiello* meant losing pregnancy benefits, and that was no fun. But even the victories weren't fun for the grassroots. Winning cases like *Reed* and *Wiesenfeld* was fun mostly for Ruth Ginsburg and her law students. Winning congressional passage of Title VII in 1964—partly thanks to the southern congressman who thought suggesting equality for women might kill the whole civil rights act—was fun mostly for a few smart congresswomen who beat him at his game. Unearthing Executive Order 11246 and getting women more places in universities was fun mostly for Bernice Sandler and WEAL. And now, from around the country, from the grassroots, Reuss was hearing that women hated violence against women and wanted VAWA and its civil rights section. You know why women are so excited about this? Reuss asked members of Goldfarb's budding task force: It's the first time since the equal rights amendment that they have the chance to work for a civil rights law that they perceive as their own.

So Goldfarb suddenly had an ally and a buddy. Montana-tawny in

her skin and hair color, tending toward fuschia and lime in her clothing choices, Reuss teased Goldfarb relentlessly: Couldn't Sally wear
some color besides navy blue? Couldn't Sally wear a little makeup on
that porcelain skin? Couldn't Sally attend a few more meetings? Reuss
started dragging Goldfarb around Washington from eight o'clock in
the morning to eight at night. When Goldfarb looked peaked, Reuss
would pull a granola bar from her purse and tell her to "eat this" and
keep working.

After Reuss joined the fight for VAWA in February of 1991, the
coalition got bigger and bigger. Groups endorsing VAWA ran down
the East Coast from Orono in Maine and Troy in New York to Wyn-
cote in Pennsylvania and on to Columbia in South Carolina. They ran
across the continent through Sutton in West Virginia, Saint Louis in
Missouri, Eau Claire in Wisconsin, and on to Winona in New Mexico.
They reached Seattle in Washington, Lake Oswego in Oregon, Culver
City in California, and branched out to Juneau in Alaska and Hilo
in Hawaii.

VAWA's endorsers had names that could seem predictable, or
not. Bronx Women Against Rape; Chicago Catholic Women; East
Hawaii Alternatives to Violence; American Nurses Association;
Maine Coalition for Family Crisis Services; No More Nice Girls;
Pennsylvania Coalition Against Domestic Violence; Women in Film;
Hispanic Health Council; Dominican Women's Caucus; American
Home Economics Association.

Groups were calling and writing their congressional representatives.
They were requesting copies of Senate hearings from the Judiciary
Committee. One day as copies of a new VAWA report headed off the
shelves into the mails, the longtime staff member in charge of com-
mittee publications looked archly at Nourse and said, as she recalled,
"Another one of your best-sellers, Victoria?"

Or, as Reuss liked to say, the grassroots were going berserk, and
Congress got the message. By early 1992, VAWA's list of cosponsors included 40 percent of the representatives and 50 percent of the
senators.

To an extent, VAWA's national support was perfectly matched to its
national concerns. By the time Nourse began to produce the Senate's

report on VAWA in late October of 1991, she had received invaluable evidence from judicial gender-bias task force reports emerging all across America. She used the reports to remind her readers of the sort of legal treatment of women that had created the need for VAWA:

> In Georgia, a judge reported that one of his colleagues, in a case of repeated domestic abuse, "mocked," "humiliated," and "ridiculed" the victim and "led the courtroom in laughter as the woman left. . . ." Subsequently, the woman was killed by her estranged husband.

> In Vermont, a probation officer questioned whether a 9-year-old girl was a "real victim," since he had heard she was a "tramp."

> In California, a judge commented at a hearing that a domestic violence victim "probably should have been hit."

> A Connecticut prosecutor badgered a 15-year-old: "Come on, you can tell me. You're probably just worried that your boyfriend got you pregnant, right? Isn't that why you're saying he raped you?"

> A Florida judge commented during sentencing that he felt sorry for a confessed rapist because his victim was such a "pathetic" woman.

This litany of judicial embarrassments had moved from presentations among judges, including the one in Florida, where Robin West proposed a federal law attacking the marital rape exemption, to the deliberations of the U.S. Congress. The work of one legal researcher in early 1990 had become, by late 1991, a broadly popular piece of legislation, supported by half the Senate, dozens of Congress members, and scores of grassroots women's organizations from coast to coast. The prospects for VAWA seemed too good to be true.

23

✦

Judges Strike Back

On the last day of 1991, the chief justice attacked the Violence Against Women Act. Victoria Nourse and her allies were shocked.

Then again, attacks by Justice William Rehnquist on women's rights could not be called rare. In 1970, while working as assistant attorney general under Richard Nixon, he had charged that equal rights amendment supporters showed "a virtually fanatical desire to obscure not only legal differentiation between men and women, but insofar as possible, physical distinctions between the sexes." Right after Ruth Ginsburg's first oral argument in 1972, soon after his appointment to the Court, Rehnquist had joined Chief Justice Warren Burger as one of only two immediate votes against the case of Sharron Frontiero. Rehnquist's early opposition to women's rights had set a pattern that he would rarely break. He authored *Gilbert*, the pregnancy fiasco in which he contended that Congress intended sex discrimination to exclude pregnancy discrimination. (Congress corrected him by passing the Pregnancy Discrimination Act.) His surprising decision in *Vinson*—that Mechelle Vinson's victimization by her boss, if true, constituted sexual harassment—could be viewed as a move to help make acceptable to women his nomination, announced two days earlier, to become chief justice.

These previous attacks by Justice Rehnquist took the familiar form of judicial opinions in legal cases. He waited until laws or interpretations of law reached him in his court before attacking either the law or its interpretation. Now, in a rare departure for any judge, let alone a chief justice, he decided to attack proposed legislation before it could become law.

Rehnquist's attack on VAWA came in the form of the chief justice's official "year-end report on the federal judiciary." Rehnquist was following a tradition introduced by his predecessor, Chief Justice Burger, who in 1970 initiated a series of "State of the Judiciary" addresses, on the model of the president's State of the Union address. Over fifteen years of these speeches, Chief Justice Burger referred at least glancingly to women on six occasions. Sometimes he even addressed concerns specific to women, as in 1983 when he spoke of "difficult and complex cases arising out of long overdue recognition of the rights of women and of minorities."

When Rehnquist rose to chief justice in 1986, he reduced the addresses to "year-end reports" and reduced the presence of women to almost nil. Five years of the chief justice's reports showed no concern for women's issues, and three omitted any mention of women.

The end-of-1991 report marked a dramatic change. In it, the chief justice attacked VAWA, particularly its civil rights section: The bill's "broad definition of criminal conduct is so open-ended" and its "new private right of action so sweeping," he contended, that VAWA "could involve the federal courts in a whole host of domestic relations disputes." Congressional addition of VAWA to what he called "the caseload crisis" could result in "degradation in the high quality the nation has long expected of the federal courts." He opposed all congressional additions unless "critical to meeting important national interests." Put another way, providing a legal remedy for violence against women was not of national importance. Finally, dramatically, the chief justice had managed in a year-end report to raise a women's issue.

Nourse wondered where this attack had come from. Who would have thought, she puzzled, that the chief justice knew anything about VAWA? Nonetheless, Nourse had encountered numerous hints of an approaching attack from large segments of America's mostly male judiciary. She just never imagined that it might involve America's chief justice.

THE GENDER DISPARITY in America's judiciary in 1991 stood roughly where the gender split of America's law schools had stood two decades earlier—back when the first law students came to Professor Ginsburg and asked her to teach them about women and the law. In those days, the proportion of women in American law schools was just breaking past 10 percent, and male professors were able to tell students that, as one had reportedly said at NYU, the idea of teaching a course on women in law was no better than teaching the law of the bicycle.

To many Americans in 1991, the nation's gender disparity on the courts was epitomized by the United States Supreme Court, where only one woman—Sandra Day O'Connor—sat alongside eight men. Her presence made the Supreme Court roughly 11 percent female. No citizen could see (and no report by the federal courts made clear) that lower levels of the federal judiciary lay further beneath gender parity. At the next level down stood the courts of appeals, with 230 judges, of whom 19 were women: below 9 percent. At the trial level, of the 753 judges on America's federal district courts, the number of women was 51: below 7 percent.

A woman in 1991 who took her case to the Supreme Court might feel she was facing considerable gender imbalance: eight to one. But the lower a woman's case stayed in the court system, the lower her chance that women judges would hear her case. At the lowest level— the ninety-four federal district courts where a woman might first tell her story to a judge—more than half the district courts in the nation had not a single woman: 0 percent.

Although Nourse knew women were rare in the judiciary (in her time as a lawyer for the Department of Justice, only once had she argued before a woman judge), she failed to realize that judges might try to influence legislation. Assuming that judges would be wary of intruding in the domain of legislators, Nourse did not see the early attacks on VAWA as auguries of a concerted action. The first official responses to VAWA had come not from judges but attorneys general, and those responses had diverged. In late 1990, the Department of Justice opposed significant parts of VAWA and offered a detailed critique of the civil rights section. In contrast, also in late 1990, the National Association of Attorneys General, representing all the state offices responsible for prosecuting violent crimes against women, voted unanimous support for VAWA. This disparity seemed to pit the inexperienced against the experienced. Federal attorneys who had largely avoided the problem of violence against women sought continued avoidance. State attorneys who had grappled with the problem sought help.

The first judicial response to VAWA emerged from a meeting of state chief judges in early 1991. In a page-long document titled "Resolution X," the Conference of Chief Justices of the state courts resolved that drafters of VAWA should eliminate the civil rights section. The state chief justices' objections included the following:

> WHEREAS, spousal and sexual violence and all legal issues involved in domestic relations historically have been governed by state and criminal law . . .

To Nourse, the sad story of how states and their courts had behaved "historically"—urging jurors to disbelieve women, for example, or ruling that a woman's rape became a non-rape if her attacker was her husband—amounted to good reasons for creating VAWA and its civil rights section.

Another significant objection came at the seventh point of the state chief justices' resolution:

> WHEREAS, the most regularly enforced federal civil rights statute (42 USC 1983) limits its jurisdiction to deprivation of civil rights by state action . . .

Goldfarb thought the chief justices were misinterpreting by attacking VAWA with an insistence on *state action*. VAWA was based not on the statute they mentioned but on the Civil Rights Act of 1871 (technically 42 USC 1985(3) in law books), which, as the Supreme Court had affirmed in 1971 in *Breckenridge*, permitted lawsuits against private individuals without requiring state action.

In their ninth objection, the state justices turned to logistics:

> WHEREAS, the federal cause of action created by [VAWA's civil rights section] would impair the ability of state courts to manage criminal and family law matters traditionally entrusted to the states . . .

To understand this *WHEREAS*, Nourse and Goldfarb needed to turn to the cover letter sent by the president of the conference of state justices to Senator Biden. There the chief justice of Maine, Vincent L. McKusick, explained that his colleagues worried particularly that the civil rights section would "add a new count to many if not most divorce and other domestic relations cases," thus making the cases harder to settle peacefully. To Goldfarb, this claim was the most troubling. The judges implied that *many if not most* women seeking a divorce might add a claim of violence, perhaps as a bargaining chip. As Goldfarb wrote in response, "The implication that vengeful wives will routinely file frivolous claims, in an effort to extort larger settlements, reflects a pernicious sexist stereotype."

The attack from the state chief justices, however troubling, seemed unsurprising. They might understandably be offended by a federal law that suggested state judges were making wrong judgments in cases of violence against women. Their objections had to be expected.

Less expected was the second judicial attack, from the federal courts in the spring of 1991. Nourse did not know its originating source, but it seemed to come less from judges than from accountants. In April, the Administrative Office of the U.S. Courts, whose director is an appointee of the chief justice, had subjected VAWA to a "judicial impact assessment"—a new idea, begun that year. An apparent model included environmental impact statements, which sometimes killed developers' plans by revealing that new construction would damage the environment.

Similarly, the new judicial impact assessment suggested that VAWA would damage the judiciary. To assess how many women would bring federal lawsuits under the civil rights section, the impact statement started with the number of American rape victims who knew their attacker's identity: more than 15,000 per year. For other assaults against women, it utilized a poll that estimated the number of victims who wished to "punish" their attackers—a number that added 38,000 more possible bringers of suits. Of that large number of assaulted women, it assumed that one-quarter, totaling 13,450 per year, would use the civil rights section to bring federal lawsuits. It thus estimated an enormous demand on the federal courts, with an estimated annual cost for the civil rights section alone of 450 work-years and $43.6 million. That cost was roughly triple the annual estimate for the Civil Rights Act of 1991—ambitious legislation that provided victims of intentional discrimination with a chance to sue for damages and provided victims of discriminatory seniority systems with extra time to challenge them in court.

Among the assumptions about VAWA's cost, a major one went unexplained. Why did the assessment suggest that of all assaulted women, the number suing would be as high as one-quarter? Although the first judicial impact statement did not answer that question, a later one did. Because three-quarters of the alleged attackers in criminal rape and assault trials were represented by public defenders, the assessment team assumed that those attackers would not be worth suing. But the remaining quarter, represented by private attorneys, might be men with money. For these attackers, the judicial impact statement assumed a lawsuit rate of 100 percent, an astonishingly high estimate. That assumption made possible the claim that VAWA would add more than 14,000 suits to the federal caseload, an increase of about 4 percent of all cases pending in federal courts—a specter, potentially scary to congressmen interested in VAWA, that would grow larger in the next attack.

IN AUGUST OF 1991, Chief Justice Rehnquist appointed four judges to an "ad hoc committee on gender-based violence." Their task became preparation of a resolution, in about a month, for an organization that he headed, the Judicial Conference of the United States, a group of twenty-seven judges, including the chief judge of each circuit, that sets policy for America's federal courts. Although the conference like the judiciary was more than 90 percent male, for this purpose Rehnquist appointed the conference's one gender-balanced committee: Judge Thomas M. Reavley, chair, from Texas; Judge John F. Gerry from New Jersey; Judge Barbara Rothstein from Washington State, and Judge Pamela Rymer from California. They were "charged with coordinating the Conference's views" on VAWA.

In early September the four judges gathered in Washington, DC, where they met with congressional staff, including Nourse, who insisted VAWA would not flood the courts and said she would consider proposed language from judges to provide assurance. (A day after the committee's meetings, on September 7 at the annual convention of what naval aviators call their Tailhook Association, a group of Navy men arrayed in a gantlet apparently assaulted Navy women who walked within their reach—giving the federal government new reasons to consider violence against women.) Soon after meeting Nourse, the committee reported to the chief justice and the Judicial Conference that "Senator Biden's staff expressed a willingness to consider how the bill might be tightened" and that the committee thus had "some cause to hope" for helpful changes.

The four-judge committee recommended that the Judicial Conference adopt a resolution that opened by stating support "in part" for VAWA, followed by opposition "in part" and then, immediately, more support for the "underlying objective of the bill." The proposed resolution commended "Congress and the authors of the legislation" and expressed the judges' desire to "play a constructive role" in helping Congress "fashion an appropriate response to violence directed against women."

After this opening affirmation, the draft resolution stated that it "reluctantly opposes" parts of VAWA, including the civil rights section. And although expressing concern that the civil rights section "is so broadly drafted as to make precise quantification of its target impossible," the draft noted that "the authors of the bill disagree"— affirming that Nourse and the other drafters did not intend to flood the courts. The draft resolution, designed to go for approval to a September 23 meeting of the conference, and carrying the signature of Judge Reavley and the names of all four judges, affirmed that the "Conference is prepared to work with Congress" on the Act.

Not all four judges seemed so prepared. "I have to tell you," Judge Gerry told the *Newark Star-Ledger*, for an article that appeared September 16, "this Congress is scary." He explained that the chief justice had appointed the committee to try to convince Congress that VAWA would have negative effects on the courts. Warning the newspaper that passage of VAWA "has the potential to turn the federal courts into a domestic relations court," the judge predicted "chaos," a "disaster"—hardly the affirmative phrasing offered by his committee's draft resolution.

During the late-September meeting of the Judicial Conference, most of the affirmative language above disappeared. Although the conference retained the phrase about preparedness "to work with Congress," its new resolution cut support for VAWA. It cut commendation of VAWA's authors. It cut acknowledgment of Nourse's intent to avoid overbroad drafting. Replacing the cuts, the conference repeated and extended the earlier attack of the state chief justices who "point out," said the conference's new resolution,

> that over three million domestic relations cases were filed in state courts in 1989. If a party to one-tenth of those suits were to seek collateral recourse under S. 15 [VAWA, Senate bill number 15], those cases alone would exceed the total of all cases now pending in the district courts and courts of appeals of the federal judiciary.

The Judicial Conference of the United States, under Chief Justice Rehnquist, was now claiming that VAWA could double the federal court caseload. The revisers managed to magnify the earlier judicial impact assessment more than twenty times. To do so, the mostly male federal judges ignored the reassurance, brought to them by their only gender-balanced committee, that VAWA's drafters seemed willing to make revisions to keep from overloading the courts.

• • •

FROM NOURSE'S VANTAGE, the attacks from judges seemed uncoordinated. First state judges attacked. Then the federal court impact statement made high caseload estimates, which the Judicial Conference outdid with fantastic caseload estimates. At each point, Nourse tried to respond, usually with a letter that she and Senator Biden composed together. Biden's response to the Judicial Conference of the United States, as it prepared to launch its attack on VAWA, was strong. Writing to Judge Reavley, chair of both the committee on gender-based violence and the all-male committee on Federal-State Jurisdiction, he stood firm:

> I will not mince words: As author of the legislation, I have stated that Title III [the civil rights section] of the bill does not federalize divorce law or domestic relations cases any more than any other civil rights law does.

Biden also answered the assertion that what the Judicial Conference called "domestic relations cases" did not belong in federal court. VAWA's civil rights section, like the Civil Rights Act of 1871, insisted Biden,

> is a civil rights provision. Like the 1871 law on which it is based, this bill protects persons from violent attacks leveled against them because of their membership in a particular group. As I am sure you know, while judges agree that current laws protect racial and political minorities, some argue that these laws do not protect women from similar attacks motivated by gender or sexual prejudice. My intent in Title III is simply to clarify that women deserve protection from any attack motivated by gender.

Beyond clarifying the bill's intent to the federal judges, Biden suggested judges were overstepping proper bounds with their inquiry into VAWA:

It is one thing for the Conference to conclude that "*if* the statute covers divorce actions, it is not a proper subject of federal jurisdiction," but it is quite another thing for the Judicial Conference to conclude that "the statute does *in fact* cover divorce cases," when the law's sponsor insists that it does not.

Biden was pointing to an unusual judicial opposition. Judges were not merely lobbying about legislation. In this unusual case, as Biden argued, judges were trying to interpret a piece of legislation in opposition to the stated intention of its drafters and in advance of its consideration by the full Congress.

In September of 1991, Biden was also holding confirmation hearings for a new nominee to the Supreme Court. To replace Justice Thurgood Marshall, a great civil rights leader, President George H. W. Bush had nominated the former chair of the Equal Employment Opportunity Commission, Clarence Thomas. Despite controversy over Thomas' lack of support for affirmative action, Thomas seemed guaranteed of confirmation as the hearings of the Senate Judiciary Committee opened on September 10. At around that time, however, Biden heard the first hint that Thomas might have put sexual pressure on a former employee, Anita Hill. On September 23, as the chief justice of the United States presided over the Judicial Conference at which judges voted to oppose VAWA's civil rights section, Biden learned the extent of Hill's allegations: Thomas had urged her to date him and had detailed his sexual interests to her, which included watching pornographic films that showed "group sex or rape scenes." The senator who was proposing VAWA in order to help women who had suffered from such crimes as rape was directing the confirmation of a judge who seemed possibly to enjoy watching films portraying rape.

When he first learned of Anita Hill from a staffer, Biden asked two questions: Was Hill credible? The staffer believed yes. Would Hill let her name and claims be used to confront to Thomas? The staffer believed no. In deciding not to contact Hill himself or send a staff member to confer with her, Biden may have been restrained by his memories of early VAWA hearings in which rape victims appeared to testify. Nourse had not wanted to press victims to make their experiences into a spectacle for the press. Biden did not want to pressure Anita Hill to appear at the Thomas confirmation hearings unless she wished to do so. "It was immoral," he told the authors of *Strange Justice*, the best history of the Hill-Thomas confrontation, "to push her in any way."

Anita Hill eventually did testify. Her allegations led to a nationwide discussion of sexual harassment and the ways that men in power have imposed sexually upon subordinate workers. Pat Reuss and others tried to get Ron Klain, Nourse's boss and Biden's chief of staff, to put experts on the stand to explain the dynamics of sexual harassment. The effort failed. In the process, Biden's inability to help a woman who was under attack—albeit verbal rather than physical—would shock women who had worked with him. As Biden was ending the Thomas hearings, he received a letter from the Judicial Conference. It had voted to condemn significant parts of VAWA, particularly the civil rights section. At least as important for VAWA would be the Senate confirmation vote of 52 to 48, the narrowest in a century, which replaced Thurgood Marshall with Clarence Thomas.

CHIEF JUSTICE REHNQUIST'S ATTACK ON VAWA, as presented in his year-end report of 1991, seemed to emerge from two directions. He stated that opposition to VAWA had been voiced by the Judicial Conference of the United States—though he did not say that he chaired the conference. More enduringly, he embedded his attack on VAWA within a discussion of what he called "long-accepted concepts of federalism." With *federalism*, Chief Justice Rehnquist raised one of the goals of his judicial career: to tilt the nation's balance of power toward the states. For Rehnquist, as for others, *federalism* was a code word that supplanted and revised earlier language such as *states' rights*, which had supplanted *home rule*. Calls for *federalism* thus called not for strengthening the national government but for limiting its strength.

Many of America's historic transformations have engaged issues of *federalism*—issues of how to apportion power within a federal system that includes both national and state governments. When the

Supreme Court in the *Dred Scott* decision of 1857 held that Congress lacked the constitutional authority to forbid the expansion of slavery into new territories that would eventually become states, it made a decision regarding federalism. The Civil War represented a contest over *federalism*—whether states' rights included the right to secede from the nation.

In his attack on VAWA, Rehnquist built his argument around the balance between state and federal courts, arguing that "the federal courts' limited role" should be "reserved for issues where important national interests predominate." Press coverage, including an editorial supporting Rehnquist in the *Washington Post*, did not ask why the issue of violence against women was not important and not national.

The chief justice's next salvo came a month later in Dallas at the mid-year meeting of the American Bar Association (ABA), the nation's leading association of lawyers. Invited to address the ABA membership, the chief justice again attacked VAWA. Again he recalled the opposition (but not the machinations) of the Judicial Conference to it. Again he alleged (without mentioning Senator Biden's words to the contrary) that the civil rights section was "so sweeping that it could involve the federal courts in a whole host of domestic relations disputes." He made clear that he was pressuring Congress and added, to the ABA, "I urge your attention to this issue also." Few listeners could doubt what the legal press duly reported: the chief justice was lobbying the ABA to undercut VAWA.

One of the ABA's associations of judges, the Conference of Federal Trial Judges, voted at that mid-year meeting to oppose VAWA's civil rights section. What none of VAWA's drafters anticipated was that these judges and others, in concert with the strong urging of the chief justice, were beginning to push for condemnation of VAWA by the entire ABA.

WITH ATTACKS MOUNTING, Victoria Nourse needed some "train time" with Senator Biden, and she got it two days after the chief justice's speech to the ABA. On most mornings, Biden caught an early-morning

Amtrak train to Washington from his home in Wilmington, Delaware. If a Washington-based staffer had something important to discuss with him, he or she would have to get up around five o'clock to catch the first northbound Metroliner out of Washington. That northbound train would drop the staffer on the platform in Wilmington a few minutes before Biden arrived to catch the southbound one. The reward: an hour or more of unbroken train time with the senator.

When Nourse met Biden on the Wilmington platform, they knew the topic included whether to answer the chief justice's attacks two days earlier. They had only a few hours to decide. At ten o'clock that morning, Biden was scheduled to speak at a hearing on VAWA arranged by his Democratic colleague and friend in the House of Representatives, Charles Schumer of New York.

Schumer, the chair of the House Subcommittee on Crime and Criminal Justice, had not moved instantly to support VAWA. Months earlier, Goldfarb had begun discussions with the powerful congressman from New York on a day when they happened to catch the same flight from Washington to New York. While the plane was still on the ground, Goldfarb had realized she didn't know the ethics of talking with a congressman. She called Reuss from her seat on the plane and whispered, "Chuck Schumer's two rows behind me." She whispered so softly that Reuss had to yell back into the phone: I can't hear you, I can't hear you! So Goldfarb whispered louder, and Reuss gave her marching orders: talk to him about VAWA.

As they talked, Schumer offered her a ride home since they lived only two blocks apart in Brooklyn's Park Slope neighborhood. Worried it might be unethical to accept a ride from a congressman, Goldfarb picked up the phone on the plane and called Reuss again. "You bet your booty," said Reuss. "You get in that car!" Reuss felt like she was advising a pre-teen on her first date: "First you thank him. And it wouldn't hurt to praise him unctuously about something." During the drive home, Goldfarb finally managed to ask Schumer what he thought of VAWA's civil rights section.

"I don't know that much about it," she remembered him saying. "But the federal judges don't seem to like it. If it's really controversial, don't expect me to stick my neck out for something that I don't really see the value of." Even if he weren't an ally, that was valuable information.

Later, Reuss and Goldfarb would meet with one of Congressman Schumer's new staff members, whom Reuss would come to think of as "that cute, young, smart David Yassky." She would never forget what happened in Schumer's offices when Goldfarb met Yassky. The pair started talking about Yale Law School, where it turned out Yassky had enrolled eight years after Goldfarb. To Reuss, it all sounded lovey-dovey: "I'm sitting in while they're doing their Yale love songs, or whatever," she recalled, not able to follow the names of the professors or the courses. "But I knew we were in." Yassky, she thought, would return their phone calls.

What Reuss did not realize was that the conversation had started with Yassky, after hearing about Biden's proposed civil rights section, blurting out more or less, "Oh yeah, like Catharine MacKinnon's theories!" While Goldfarb had attended the first of MacKinnon's Yale classes, Yassky had taken MacKinnon's last in her final term as a visiting teacher at Yale.

When it came to the civil rights section, Yassky did not need convincing. Soon after he joined Schumer's staff in September of 1991, the congressman had asked him to review a version of VAWA that Schumer's colleague and friend, then-Representative Barbara Boxer, had introduced in the House. When Yassky read the civil rights section, he became enthusiastic. The civil rights section took Yassky right back to the spring of 1990 and MacKinnon's course at Yale Law School, where she had argued that rape and other violence against women should be treated as an equality issue. Under the Fourteenth Amendment, women ought to be able to use civil law to get around the weaknesses of criminal law: women ought to be able to bring civil suits to defend their civil rights.

At Yale, Yassky and his law school friends often went after class to the school's dining hall and pondered what to do about the problem of violence against women. A few of them hit on a notion: they should set up a law clinic that would bring suits, under the 1871 Civil Rights

Act, for women who had been victims of sexual violence. Yassky and his friends got quite enamored of the idea but didn't do anything and soon graduated.

A year and a half after graduation, Yassky found he could do something about the issue after all. He responded to the bill with what he knew was an overly long memo, explaining that the civil rights section was the bill's "centerpiece" and that Congressman Schumer's office should get on board. "Conceptually," wrote Yassky,

> this bill is absolutely on target. The argument for it is that (1) women face pervasive and systematic violence and (2) they face obstacles in seeking legal redress through currently available channels. Women do not need new statutes forbidding violence against them—on paper, of course, they have plenty of rights. Their problem has been making those rights effective.

To help women defend those rights, Yassky added, women's rights groups should create legal clinics—pretty much what he and his friends had pondered creating as law students.

Yassky then outlined and answered three main objections to VAWA, putting each imagined objection in quotation marks:

> "It would burden the federal courts." True, but worth it—the problem is serious enough to merit the attention of federal judges.

> "This area should be left to the states." Again, it is true that the bill would significantly expand federal intervention in this area, but expanded intervention is appropriate. The model for this proposal is the Ku Klux Act of 1868 [sic]. When a broad segment of the population is being victimized by brutality, and the state governments fail inadequately to protect the victims, federal action is called for.

> "It would bring every divorce case into federal court." . . . If you believe that spouse abuse is involved in every divorce case, then you certainly ought to be in favor of this bill.

No wonder Reuss thought Yassky combined cute with smart. Few answers to the chief justice's fear of flooding the courts could cut to the chase better than Yassky's: if the problem was as big as the chief justice implied, then Congress truly needed to enact VAWA.

Congressman Schumer had asked Yassky to review VAWA because Biden and Boxer were urging his subcommittee to hold hearings on crime and criminal justice. Schumer quickly agreed, and Yassky began planning the hearings, which would include a rape victim from New York, a state attorney from Florida, a county prosecutor from Ohio, a number of the congressman's colleagues in the House, and also Senator Biden. Yassky scheduled the hearings for Thursday, February 6, 1992, two days after Rehnquist's attack on VAWA at the meeting of the ABA.

Meeting Biden for train time reminded Nourse of one of her first trips with him to the University of Delaware, where he was giving a talk on VAWA. As they were getting to their seats, they ran into another politician who lobbied Biden: "Oh, Joe," he said, "let me sit next to the pretty girl." Although Nourse had heard of far worse in Congress, Biden looked offended, she thought, and a bit perplexed. "She's my chief aide on the Violence Against Women Act," he responded, "and we're going to Delaware to give a speech."

Biden's speech at the University of Delaware, to a packed house, drew an overwhelming response. Nourse would always recall the women, after that speech, who walked up to Biden to tell him about their experiences as victims of incest or rape, or to tell him that they'd been battered by lovers or husbands. Biden was profoundly affected by their thanks for authoring VAWA. Those women and others he met later, Nourse came to believe, had a lot to do with Biden's decision to take on whomever he must in order to make VAWA succeed.

The attacks in early 1992 by the chief justice surely turned up the heat. When Nourse sat down with Biden on the train, Nourse realized that Biden had decided to take on the chief justice. He wanted to go over the Judicial Conference's objections, the legal issues involved, and what was happening with the chief justice. Late in their conversation, as an offhand comment, she remarked that she thought that in Rehnquist and his allies Biden was dealing with "true believers from the federalist pantheon." The true federalist believed, thought Nourse, that a bright line divided federal and state law.

Just after ten in the morning on February 6, 1992, the hearings began with a brief welcome from the chair and host, Congressman Schumer. Next some of his congressional committee members made brief statements indicating that they cared about violence against women. Then Schumer introduced Senator Biden.

Biden, listeners quickly realized, would not be brief. He announced that he would not beat around the bush: "We have got a Chief Justice who," said Biden, "does not know what he is talking about, when he criticizes this legislation." Lying before him on the table as he testified was his planned statement, drafted by Nourse and other staffers. Its large type said only that the chief justice's *"speech writers* have not done their homework." But Biden, ignoring his own speech writers, had evidently decided that the problem lay not with Supreme Court speech writers but with the chief justice who does "not know what he is talking about." The decision to take on the chief justice was pure Biden. Nourse worried about Yassky. When a senator goes to the House and takes over a congressman's hearing, "going on and on about his favorite topic," as she would say later, "this is what is known as a bad hearing."

From his frontal attack on the chief justice, Senator Biden moved to defend VAWA's civil rights section. It was broadly supported: by the National Association of Attorneys General, by fifty cosponsors in the Senate, and by his judiciary committee unanimously, with the support now of what he called "the ultimate odd couple, Strom Thurmond and Joe Biden." The civil rights section would not flood the courts with all crimes that victimize women. As he put it, a woman "cannot establish a cause of action under this bill by saying that, 'I am a woman; I have a bruise; ergo, I have a civil rights claim'—as the Chief Justice would lead you to believe."

Biden then moved back from his impromptu response to his prepared text. He argued that the Rehnquist's speech writers "failed to read" VAWA, which "specifically says in title III that the civil rights section he opposes does not cover random crimes or crimes not motivated solely by discrimination." And Rehnquist had "forgotten 120 years of civil rights history"—the use of civil rights laws to fight discriminatory violence that began in 1871 with the first antilynching laws.

But even as Biden turned toward his prepared text, he paused to recall one of the most surprising challenges he had heard—not just to VAWA but to traditional civil rights law.

> I find it interesting, as Ms. Nourse, who is the lead person for us on the Judiciary Committee meeting with the Federal Judges appointed by the Chief Justice to discuss this bill with us, asked one of the judges, "Well, this is no different than standard civil rights laws making it a crime to act this way against black folks," and one of the judges said, "Yes, that is right. That is the problem; I wouldn't do it for black folks either."

Obviously speaking off the cuff, Biden had compressed his story sharply, but a few moments later a congressman asked for elaboration, and Senator Biden told more fully the story that had led Nourse to opine that Biden was dealing with "true believers from the federalist pantheon."

That story was based on an exchange a few weeks earlier with members of the ad hoc committee chaired by Judge Reavley and appointed by the chief justice. Nourse had contended that VAWA had analogs among existing civil rights remedies. One of the two male judges, either Reavley or Gerry she recalled, then asked her, Which analogs?

Nourse responded by citing the Civil Rights Act of 1871, particularly the section that gave victims of discriminatory treatment an "action for the recovery of damages"—that is, a right to sue their attackers. Furthermore, she added, the Supreme Court held that victims of race discrimination were entitled to bring private legal action under that 1871 law. The case she had in mind was *Griffin v. Breckenridge*, decided by the Supreme Court in 1971.

But the judge who had been challenging her answered, as Nourse recalled, Well, I'm not so sure that was the right decision at the time. The judge went on to suggest that private lawsuits might be inappropriate for dealing with racial discrimination.

Nourse was shocked. Here was a lower-court judge who, in opposition to a Supreme Court decision, seemed to assert that a law permitting you to sue for lynching is dangerous because it allows you to sue for an offense also covered by state law. Here was a judge, she felt, who was a true believer in federalism. Here was a judge who saw such a bright line between state and federal law that he was willing to undo both a recently affirmed and a century-old component of civil rights law. And this judge had been appointed by the chief justice to probe VAWA.

Sitting beside Biden at the hearing Nourse thought, I knew he was going to take on the chief justice, but I didn't know he was also going to take on the Reavley Committee. At the same time, it struck her that Biden was getting to the core issue: If gender discrimination is different from racial discrimination, he seemed to demand, tell me why it's different? Don't keep saying it's all about domestic relations as Rehnquist did when he contended to the ABA that VAWA would "involve the federal courts in a whole host of domestic relations disputes." Take gender discrimination seriously as discrimination, Biden was saying, and then tell me how it's different from race discrimination.

By using a congressional hearing to take on the chief justice and one of the federalist faithful from his ad hoc committee on gender-based violence, Biden might have created a bad hearing for his friend Chuck Schumer, thought Nourse. But Biden was doing good for VAWA. He was saying VAWA is not the idea of some interest group or some staffer. He was saying that VAWA was his bill and that he was fighting for it. Biden was drawing, she thought, his line in the sand.

24

Seeking Equal Judicial Firepower

What good was a line in sand? Could Biden win? Three days after his dramatic challenge to the chief justice, Sally Goldfarb chaired a meeting of the NOW Legal Defense task force to discuss VAWA's chances. Goldfarb or Reuss announced that, as reported by Nourse, Senator Biden was willing to hold hearings that would involve judges directly. Was that a good idea?

Pat Reuss announced that she wasn't afraid of testimony by judges—especially if the judges' old-fashioned assumptions were rebutted by a panel of distinguished law professors. Goldfarb, however, worried that senators might not see the weakness of the judges' position and that press coverage might help judges carry the day against VAWA. Someone remarked that judges seem to have little respect for Joe Biden.

Then Eleanor Smeal, president of the Fund for the Feminist Majority, made a strong and obvious statement: VAWA needed its own judges. VAWA's supporters, she said, can't counter judges with only professors, and certainly can't counter Chief Justice Rehnquist. "Fight fire with fire," she said, according to notes from the NOW Legal Defense meeting: Fight their judges with "judges that support us."

We do have judges on our side, responded Goldfarb, but they aren't willing to speak against Rehnquist.

Then, said Smeal, You don't have equal firepower. Among state judges, men outnumbered women by a ratio of 10 to 1, and among federal trial judges men outnumbered women almost 14 to 1.

Goldfarb could think of only one group, however unlikely, that might provide a counterbalance to the weight of male judicial attack. That group, only a dozen years old and far from radical, was the National Association of Women Judges (NAWJ). It had helped create gender-bias task forces, themselves so useful for documenting the inequity that VAWA sought to address. Its newsletter was called *Counterbalance*.

The NAWJ had its origins in 1979, when two women judges from California decided the time had come to meet with peers across the country, many of them working as the only female judge in a court district or region. No official listings existed of women judges in America. The two organizers, Justice Joan Dempsey Klein and Justice Vaino Spencer, both of the California Courts of Appeal, found help from Professor Beverly Blair Cook of the University of Wisconsin. In the process of writing a history of pioneering women judges, Cook had compiled a partial list of names.

Starting from the professor's list and adding other names they found, the two judges came up with an estimate: America had perhaps three hundred women judges. Fifteen states had not a single woman judge. The entire federal court system had only twenty-eight women judges—a number that had more than doubled from 1976 to 1979 thanks to President Jimmy Carter. Working from their partial list, Klein and Spencer issued invitations for the first meeting of women judges in America. Approximately one hundred women decided to fly to California for a meeting at a hotel in Westwood, right opposite UCLA, from which women law students volunteered to assist.

AT THIS FIRST MEETING of the NAWJ in October of 1979, judges laughed and cried and stayed up late and drank jugs of wine and told what Justice Klein called "war stories." For starters, it seemed to Klein that almost every woman had a story of being chased around a judge's desk. Klein had been chased too, by male judges, first when she was a lawyer and later when she was a young judge—not that she dwelled on it. She was, as she later recalled, "a good-lookin' kid—nice legs. I was a little hotshot, and there I was: fair game."

The meeting's war stories went beyond sexual pursuit. Almost all the judges had stories of women in court being called "honey" or "dear." One judge from the Midwest had colleagues who, when they started talking "streety," as she put it, liked to call women "bitches." And behind the war stories lurked some clear discrimination, perhaps none more telling than Justice Klein's experience, a year earlier in 1978 when she was named administrative presiding justice for the entire second appellate district of the California Courts of Appeal. That position meant that she oversaw hiring decisions, including staff for the court clerk's office. She would never forget her early dealings with the court's longtime clerk. Meeting him in his office, she immediately saw that he liked having what she called "girly pix" with "women's bare breasts on the walls." But pictures aside, what struck Justice Klein most was that the clerk's office employed not a single woman and not a single member of a racial minority group. She suggested to the clerk that it was time to change. "There will be no women clerks here," she would always recall him saying, "Over my dead body."

How could the clerk of the court say this to his boss? Here was a state employee telling a state judge that her court systematically and invidiously discriminated against women. Here was a "state actor" (in the language of constitutional law) announcing that he violated the equality protection guarantee of the Fourteenth Amendment of the Constitution. Did the partial victories of Ruth Bader Ginsburg and others, beginning in 1971 with the case of Sally Reed, mean nothing in the California courts? What, for that matter, of Wendy Webster Williams' 1970 victory in *Sail'er Inn* in the California Supreme Court? California women had won the chance to work as bartenders, but nine years later California women still had no chance to work as court clerks? Justice Klein told her clerk that his job was getting beyond him. Then she appointed a new administrator to take over the hiring.

The mood at this first meeting was summed up a few years later by one of the women who flew west, Judge Gladys Kessler, then on the Superior Court of the District of Columbia. Kessler had, a few years out of Harvard Law, teamed up with Susan Deller Ross to teach one of the earliest courses on women in the law. Kessler recalled the first gathering:

> As more than 100 women judges gathered—at their own expense, on their own time, not knowing the sponsors or the tone of the meeting, but acknowledging their own heartfelt need for such an organization, it readily became apparent that an historic event was occurring.

As the women talked, many came to realize that the tone and motive for gathering originated at least partly in what one of the founders later called the "very lonely, very isolated lives of those women judges."

In the three days of their first meeting, the founding judges of the NAWJ moved fast. They elected officers, created a statement of purpose, adopted three initial resolutions, and chose Washington, DC, as the site for their first convention. For officers, the choice of leader was both natural and emblematic. As president, they elected Justice Joan Dempsey Klein, who was descended from California's first judge but had been discouraged from practicing law by her parents and by her counselors at school—who had urged her to become a teacher because, she recalled, "That's what girls do." As a statement of purpose, the women judges composed a fairly moderate list of intentions, which included

> to promote the administration of justice; to discuss legal, educational, social and ethical problems mutually encountered by women judges and to formulate solutions; to increase the number of women judges so that the judiciary more appropriately reflects the role of women in a democratic society; and to address other important issues particularly affecting women judges.

Adding precision to that somewhat-vague statement of purpose, the founders voted to adopt three concrete resolutions: the NAWJ supported the equal rights amendment, opposed membership by judges in clubs and other organizations that refused to admit women, and urged the U.S. president to appoint the first woman to the Supreme Court.

Approximately fifty judges who could not attend that first gathering in October of 1979 asked to join the NAWJ, and they too became founding members. One was then a county judge from Arizona, Sandra Day O'Connor. Most NAWJ judges could not have guessed how effectively she had been working toward a Supreme Court appointment, for which NAWJ colleagues would soon support her. Back in October of 1971, from her position then as a state senator, she had written President Richard Nixon to urge him to appoint a woman to the Supreme Court. At the time, Nixon was looking at two vacancies on the Court and weighing competing pressures. In favor of a woman were his wife, his daughters, and, he believed, the chance to win votes in the next election. Opposed was the chief justice of the United States, Warren Burger. Burger had already sent word that, as Nixon put it (captured then by tape but not made public until 2000), the chief justice "couldn't work with" a woman justice. Burger threatened to resign.

A week after that threat, Nixon made a choice that surprised O'Connor: he nominated her close friend, William Rehnquist. O'Connor had dated Rehnquist when both were students at Stanford Law School in the 1950s, and she had taken him home during a law school holiday to her family's Arizona ranch. Later, when both had married and settled in Arizona, their two families gathered on weekends for hiking trips into the mountains. They were such good friends that on one occasion a few years before Rehnquist's nomination, the families planned a two-week pack trip together. When an illness for one O'Connor child forced the parents to cancel, the Rehnquists took the mother of Sandra Day O'Connor on their long trek along the Gila River. In 1969 he joined the Justice Department.

As soon as O'Connor learned that Nixon was nominating her longtime friend, she began organizing allies. As thanks, he wrote back that the organization supporting him seemed to have emerged primarily as "a result of your doing." After attending his swearing in and seeing the Supreme Court for the first time, O'Connor stayed in Washington for the next few days and visited with the new justice and his family.

As the NAWJ met in October of 1979, with the goal of advancing a woman to the Court, they were unaware that another social connection had just developed between O'Connor and an important justice. That August, O'Connor had met for three days with Chief Justice Burger, entertaining him on a houseboat on a remote Arizona lake. Serendipity, as Joan Biskupic reports in her 2005 biography of O'Connor, had created opportunity. A relative of friends—John and Gail Driggs, the mayor of Phoenix and his wife—was the chief justice's assistant. He and Burger were traveling to Arizona in August of 1979 for a judges' conference. The Driggs invited them to cruise the red-rock beauties of Lake Powell. To add to the depth of lawyering and camaraderie, the Driggs asked the O'Connors if they would like to go boating with the chief justice. "Would we ever," replied O'Connor's husband. Sandra Day O'Connor and Gail Driggs began buying food to cook. During bright days on shipboard, through breakfasts and dinners and watersports, the chief justice warmed to O'Connor. That November, Burger invited her to join him on a trip to Britain, for a conference on Anglo-American law, as a representative of America's judges.

About two weeks after the first official convention of the NAWJ in Washington in 1980, and in the closing weeks of that year's presidential campaign, Ronald Reagan made a surprising announcement: if elected president, he would nominate a woman to the Court. Soon after winning election, Reagan had his chance. Possible nominees mentioned by the press included Joan Dempsey Klein, who was said to have Republican connections.

But the nomination went to O'Connor, who seemed to come from nowhere. Apparently unknown to outsiders and the press was that she had dated a future justice and later fought for his approval to the Court, and that she had entertained the current chief justice for days on shipboard in the Arizona wilds. After the chief justice worked to plant her name with Reagan, she then charmed the president with talk of her cattle-ranching past. O'Connor's exceptional nomination, albeit mysterious in origin, won the support of the NAWJ.

The exceptional nomination proved far from the rule for Reagan. To other courts, he appointed few women. During a gathering of the NAWJ in 1982, Dennis F. Mullins, a low-level official in the Justice Department office that was reviewing judgeship candidates, explained the problem to the *New York Times*: "A large number of women who have the required experience," he said, "do not share the President's strict constructionist political philosophy." He added that these women and their supporters did not know how to get a judge nominated: they had been insufficiently "aggressive or successful" in currying the support of powerful senators.

Currying could engender honeying. In 1985, in her role as president of the NAWJ, Judge Martha Craig Daughtrey led a delegation to Washington to urge President Reagan to appoint women judges. When one of the most powerful senators, Strom Thurmond of the Judiciary Committee, entered the room, he started honeying. The room was a "bachelor's paradise," he announced. "I want to congratulate you lady judges," he said, according to the *Washington Post*. "You really don't look like judges, you look like young ladies."

Old Strom had pulled an old trick: say something that sounds flattering, and if women complain, they sound bitchy. One woman in the room whispered to the woman next to her that "I just want to know what a lady judge looks like." Whispering, not bitching, went with currying. "Honey stories" might tell something about the powerlessness of women judges, but they created a case of damned if you complain and damned if you don't.

THE MOVE BEYOND THE TELLING of honey stories by individual judges, to the creation of bias reports by judicial task forces, began partly thanks to a decision made by Judge Marilyn Loftus of New Jersey to attend meetings of the NAWJ. This move had the potential to show the wide-ranging problems that women encountered in courts, the benefits of appointing women judges at all levels, and the difficulty of male-dominated courts in addressing violence against women.

In 1961, Marilyn Loftus graduated from law school and began rising in law so quickly that, as she later recalled, she was too busy for feminist activism. She went straight from school to the state attorney general's office, and by 1969 she had become first assistant attorney general for New Jersey. Then in the early 1970s women's groups began pushing to have women named to the bench, as she later recalled, and soon after, she became Judge Loftus of the Superior Court of New Jersey—which brought more hard work, far from the realm of women's issues. When Judge Klein in 1979 gathered the names of three hundred judges to invite to Los Angeles, she missed Loftus, who received no invitation.

In the summer of 1980, Judge Loftus got a surprise call from a friend, Judge Sonia Morgan of the New Jersey appellate division, who had gone to LA the year before. Morgan told Loftus about the next conference and invited her. "We're all judges," Loftus remembered telling Morgan. "We don't need to be in a women judges group." To her surprise, after she arrived in Washington for the 1980 conference, Loftus had a marvelous time. At the next annual conference, in Detroit in the autumn of 1981, Loftus walked into a program on gender bias in the courts offered by Judge Hortense Gabel of the New York State Supreme Court and Professor Norma Wikler of the University of California.

The study of gender bias in the courts had spent most of the past decade failing to begin. The concept had its origin one day in 1969 soon after an attorney from Louisiana named Sylvia Roberts had won one of the earliest sex discrimination cases brought under Title VII of the Civil Rights Act of 1964. Roberts then met with a judge, Griffin Bell, who was empowered to give Roberts' client the job that her victory entitled her to: "switchman" for a telephone company with the genteel-sounding name Southern Bell. To Roberts' horror, the judge worried aloud whether her client, Lorena Weeks, could do that job. A switchman, he said, would have to know a lot about electricity, and he "didn't even know how to fix his own air conditioner." How could a woman, he seemed to worry, handle a male job that befuddles a male judge? Roberts proffered that Weeks' husband was an electrician—hoping the judge believed that man and woman in marriage are legally one, or at least that husbands tell wives what to do. Weeks got the job. (Judge Bell later, after serving as attorney general of the United States, became a partner in the law firm that lost at the Supreme Court in 1984 after arguing that the Constitution's right to freedom of association permitted it to refuse to elect women to partnership.) "I realized then and there," Roberts later recalled, "that if we did not help judges to get past their own preconceptions about men and women, Title VII and all the other laws we were passing and changing would just be words on paper."

A year later, at the founding of NOW Legal Defense, Roberts became its first general counsel. Her proposal for a program to train judges about gender bias won support from her organization. The proposal also aligned with a 1971 study by two professors at NYU, John A. Johnston Jr. and Charles L. Knapp, who concluded that "'sexism'—the making of unjustified (or at least unsupported) assumptions about individual capabilities, interests, goals and social roles solely on the basis of sex differences—is as easily discernible in contemporary judicial opinions as racism ever was." Support from potential funders did not come, however; some insisted that judges were unbiased by definition.

NOW Legal Defense persisted. Students at NYU went into courtrooms as "court watchers" who then reported examples of judicial bias. From well-publicized cases, the organization culled odd judgments. From Colorado: after a man broke into a woman's trailer, hurled her to the floor, and pushed his hands into her clothes and vagina, a judge, dismissing a sexual charge, called the attack an "attempted seduction." From Wisconsin: a judge gave only probation to a teenage rapist on grounds that, within our modern and permissive society, the boy was responding "normally." From Connecticut: dismissing an indictment in an attempted rape, a judge said, "You can't blame someone for trying."

Finally in 1980, NOW Legal Defense managed to initiate what it called its National Judicial Education Program to Promote Equality for Women and Men in the Courts, with Professor Wikler as its founding director—taking a leave of absence from her teaching as a tenured professor of sociology. Wikler soon afterward asked the NAWJ to join as a cosponsor. She encountered brief debate. One judge suggested that the association should focus on the needs of children.

Another countered that NAWJ would lack purpose if it failed to assist women who appear in America's courts. Soon NAWJ joined in formal cooperation.

The first presentation on gender bias before a formal judicial education program came in November of 1980, at the National Judicial College in Reno, Nevada. Professor Wikler, speaking at the invitation of a judge who taught there often, titled her presentation "Sexism in the Courts." Some judges apparently objected. Wikler later heard, she told a friend, that in the back row three state supreme court justices had been throwing spitballs toward her.

A year later, in November of 1981, following some successful presentations to judges and shortly before her return to full-time teaching in California, Professor Wikler addressed the conference of the NAWJ in Detroit. With her was her successor as director, a 1974 graduate of Columbia Law School named Lynn Hecht Schafran.

Schafran had a fine background for a job educating judges about bias. In her last year at Smith College in the early 1960s, she had planned to apply to law schools until she learned that Harvard Law only a decade earlier had refused to admit women. Appalled, she turned to another interest, art history, and earned a master's degree at Columbia. Drawn still to legal issues, in 1971 she enrolled at Columbia Law, a year ahead of the arrival of its first woman professor, Ruth Bader Ginsburg—whose course on women in the law Schafran took in the fall of 1972. The next term Schafran took Ginsburg's Equal Rights Advocacy Seminar and then in the summer worked for her at the Women's Rights Project of the ACLU. There Schafran focused on efforts to eliminate discrimination in private clubs that refused to admit women—clubs to which judges sometimes belonged.

When Schafran expressed interest in clerking, Ginsburg sent her to the judge who had welcomed her when other judges refused to hire a woman clerk. During that clerking year, Ginsburg invited Schafran to the victory party to celebrate Justice Brennan's opinion in *Wiesenfeld*. In reply, Schafran told Ginsburg the story about Brennan's first woman clerk, who became his crucial drafter for *Wiesenfeld*. He had at first refused to hire her on the grounds she was a woman; only after her law school pushed did he concede. As Schafran's story to Ginsburg made clear, both of them knew, from their earliest days as lawyers and clerks, that judges discriminate against women.

After her clerkship, Schafran moved to litigating for a large New York firm but managed to find time to help Ginsburg on a case designed to challenge sex-segregated high schools. Responding to that use of time in a formal review before colleagues, one of whom had approved Schafran's work with Ginsburg, the chairman of the firm's litigation department berated her. "If you think that's what the law is all about," he said looking at Schafran, "you don't belong here." Schafran agreed. She *did* think that was what the law was about, and she *did not* belong there.

In 1978, a new opportunity led Schafran toward work with judges and discrimination. A former colleague at her firm, who had become legal director for NOW Legal Defense, asked her to serve as the first national director of what became known as the Federation of Women Lawyers Judicial Screening Committee. Designed to assess possible judicial nominees and to find qualified women, it set out to evaluate a range of qualities including what it called demonstrated commitment to equal justice under law. In 1979 when Professor Norma Wikler (who said that in her academic life she had "never met a judge") agreed to help NOW Legal Defense create its judicial gender-bias education program, Schafran began advising her. As Wikler prepared to return to teaching, Schafran agreed to take her place as director shortly before Wikler was scheduled to speak at the 1981 annual conference of the NAWJ in Detroit. At that meeting, when Judge Marilyn Loftus heard a presentation on gender bias by Professor Wikler and Judge Gabel, she realized that, as she put it later, women were "not being treated equally" in courtrooms. For Judge Loftus that was the moment, as she said later, "when the light went off in my head."

AFTER RETURNING TO HER CHAMBERS in the superior court in New Jersey, Judge Loftus contacted Robert Lipscher, the administrative director of the Administrative Office of the Courts. Courts have a problem with gender bias, she told him. He responded with openness, urging her to create a program for the next New Jersey Judicial College, the three-day annual meeting at which the state's judges gather for study and discussion of important issues.

Judge Loftus agreed, but she had a concern suggested by Wikler and Schafran in their presentation: could he set up a study for New Jersey? The administrative officer said he needed to discuss the idea with the New Jersey chief justice, Robert N. Wilentz. With his broad powers, Chief Justice Wilentz did something neither Judge Loftus nor Lynn Hecht Schafran had dreamed of: he decided that gender bias demanded a "task force." Draft a task force mandate, he told Loftus, and come back with a list of good members.

But when she returned with a draft stating that the task force would investigate "whether gender bias exists in the New Jersey judicial branch," he objected. "What," Judge Marilyn Loftus would always remember him asking, "do you mean *whether?*" He crossed off *whether* and wrote in that the task force would investigate "*the extent to which* gender bias exists" in the courts of the state of New Jersey.

The New Jersey task force gathered thirteen state judges and another twenty members including a prosecutor, two deputy attorneys general, some officials of the New Jersey State bar association, and five law professors including Nadine Taub from Rutgers law school. The only member of the committee not from New Jersey was Lynn Hecht Schafran, who was now director of the National Judicial Education Program to Promote Equality for Women and Men in the Courts.

In the fall of 1982, one committee designed a survey including questions asking members of the court system to state whether they had seen incidents of sexist behavior, had seen women given less credibility than men, or had seen differences in the impact of judicial decisions on women and men. More than 850 attorneys responded. During the winter of 1983, Judge Loftus sent working subcommittees of attorneys and judges to seven different regions of the state to invite attorneys to speak candidly. They gathered another two hundred attorneys' opinions.

Back came variants on the "honey" stories, some adding new insight: a woman attorney recalled the story of a colleague who informed a judge that she had "problems" with her case, only to hear him respond that "women are the problem."

Greater than problems with judges were those with fellow attorneys. Compared to judges, one woman attorney reported, "the conduct of male counsel is unquestionably more outrageous." She had, she reported, needed to "deal with everything from comments on my clothing and appearance to outright propositions." Another added that "most sexism and resentment seems to come from male attorneys."

Such stories might have merely added to the great anecdotal pile of legal sexism, had Judge Marilyn Loftus not made sure that the task force had a statistician to direct its surveys. Thus anecdotes became data. To the survey's question whether they had seen judges appear to treat women litigants or witnesses disadvantageously, the response was *yes* from 71 percent of women but only 30 percent of men. Revealing was the difference in their responses and therefore their perceptions.

Beyond the sexism of judges, the survey elicited stronger condemnation of attorneys. To the nearly identical question—whether they had seen *legal counsel* appear to treat women litigants or witnesses disadvantageously because they were women—the response was yes from 83 percent of women and 47 percent of men.

Always women seemed to see more discrimination than men. Did judges view women's expert testimony as less credible than men's? *Yes*, said 41 percent of women and 9 percent of men. Did judges view female attorneys as less credible? *Yes*, said 61 percent of women and 15 percent of men. Did judges make jokes demeaning to women? *Yes*, said 69 percent of women and 40 percent of men.

In November of 1983, the New Jersey Supreme Court Task Force on Women in the Courts prepared to present its findings as the final event in that year's New Jersey Judicial College. A summary had been prepared in case the press showed interest, and seven committee members had prepared to speak in what Judge Loftus saw as "very very careful" presentations. No one wanted the New Jersey courts to seem benighted. As Judge Loftus was walking to the presentation, she asked Chief Justice Wilentz if he would add a brief comment, which she saw him hastily scribble on a sheet of yellow paper.

When time for the gender-bias task force's presentation finally came, at the end of three days of judicial educating, judges looked ready to leave. A few stood up to depart early. Chief Justice Wilentz cut them off. "You sit down," Judge Marilyn Loftus recalled him saying. "You need this."

After that rough start, the presentation went smoothly. "Gender bias is a national problem," Lynn Hecht Schafran explained, reassuring New Jersey judges that they were not being singled out for criticism. Others discussed the group's summary, which stated, in part,

> Stereotyped myths, beliefs and biases appear to sometimes affect decision-making in certain subject areas, e.g. damages, domestic violence, juvenile justice, matrimonial and sentencing. Additionally, it appears that there may be inequality of treatment of men and women in the legal and judicial environment (courtroom, chambers and professional gatherings).

To follow the presentations and distribute the careful press summary, the court's public information officer had scheduled a press conference—to the great surprise of Schafran, who had seen that most courts want only judges present during judicial education sessions. What task force members did not know was that a reporter from the *New York Times* had been sitting throughout the main presentations, unobtrusive and not exactly invited, in the back of the room; he then skipped the press conference.

"PANEL IN JERSEY FINDS BIAS AGAINST WOMEN IN THE STATE COURTS" was the next day's headline on the front page of the *New York Times*. After quoting the summary about "stereotyped myths, beliefs and biases," it credited Chief Justice Wilentz for creating the task force and then reprinted his hastily scribbled remarks:

> "There's no room for gender bias in our system," Chief Justice Wilentz told the assembled judges. "There's no room for the funny joke and the not-so-funny joke, there's no room for con-

scious, inadvertent, sophisticated, clumsy, or any other kind of gender bias, and certainly no room for gender bias that affects substantive rights.

"There's no room because it hurts and it insults. It hurts female lawyers psychologically and economically, litigants psychologically and economically, and witnesses, jurors, law clerks and judges who are women. It will not be tolerated in any form whatsoever."

The *New York Times* article created a ripple effect. In New York, Chief Judge Laurence H. Cooke—at the behest of Supreme Court Judge Betty Ellerin—created a task force for his state. New York's report hit hard in its overview:

> The Task Force has concluded that gender bias against women litigants, attorneys and court employees is a pervasive problem with grave consequences. Women are often denied equal justice, equal treatment, and equal opportunity. Cultural stereotypes of women's role in marriage and in society daily distort courts' application of substantive law. Women uniquely, disproportionately and with unacceptable frequency must endure a climate of condescension, indifference and hostility. Whether as attorneys or court employees, women are too often denied equal opportunities to realize their potential.

Where New Jersey surveyed almost 900 attorneys and court personnel, New York surveyed almost 1,800. Where New Jersey created a rather slim report, New York produced a phone book–sized document of more than three hundred pages. Further extending beyond the lead of New Jersey, which devoted modest space to the issue of how courts respond to domestic violence, New York gave the fullest treatment in its report—its first and largest subsection, sixty-six pages—to "The Court's Response to Violence against Women."

Regarding violence against women, New York judges set a high standard for candor. Judge Richard D. Huttner, the administrative judge of the New York City Family Court, for example, testified that he had heard a colleague make a statement, with which Judge Huttner at first agreed, concerning victims of domestic violence:

> Why don't they just get up and leave? They have been taking these beatings all these years and now they want me to intercede. All they have to do is get out of the house. What do they want from me?

Only later, Judge Huttner said, did he come to dispute that colleague's view.

On the subject of rape, the New York task force proved particularly strong. It opened with the statement that "rape is a violent crime that until recently was virtually unprosecutable in New York" because the law "provided more quarter for the accused than protection for the victim." New York law had tilted against victims, said the task force, in most areas. Corroboration: as late as 1972, New York had the strictest requirement in the country, demanding that corroboration of a victim's testimony "extend to every material fact essential to constitute the crime." Resistance: as late as 1982—during years in which some New York law enforcement officials were urging victims in rape attempts to submit rather than resist and thus risk injury— New York law required that a victim prove her "earnest resistance." Marital rape exemption: in 1984, the year the New York task force began operation, the New York Senate failed to repeal the state law that restricted a wife from charging her husband with rape.

As in New Jersey, the New York task force gathered statistics that assisted the transformation of anecdote into data. To determine whether acquaintance rape was judged as "real rape," as Susan Estrich asked in her book of that title, New York surveys asked whether judges demonstrated less concern about rape cases in which the parties had some acquaintance. The response was *yes*—judges seemed less concerned—from 74 percent of women and 53 percent of men.

Because of New Jersey and New York's lead, other states followed. In 1985, the NAWJ established the National Task Force on Gender Bias in the Courts, with Judge Loftus as its first chair. By 1988, the Conference of Chief Justices of state courts adopted a resolution urging every state to create a task force on gender bias in the courts and, building beyond that model, a task force on gender and ethnic bias as well. By 1990 states publishing reports of gender-bias task forces included California, Colorado, Florida, Illinois, Maryland, Massachusetts, Michigan, Minnesota, Nevada, Rhode Island, Utah, and Washington.

Federal courts proved far more resistant than states to examining gender bias. Not until 1987 did a federal court invite a presentation by the National Judicial Education Program, and the invitation came from a former NOW Legal Defense board member, Marilyn Patel, who had by then become judge of the United States District Court for the Northern District of California. In 1990 the Federal Courts Study Committee continued the resistance, considering but rejecting a proposal to encourage task forces on problems of gender bias and race bias. The reason, said the committee: "the quality of the federal bench and the nature of federal law keep such problems to a minimum." Despite that resistance, two of America's eleven federal circuits decided, without the Study Committee's recommendation, to begin their own task forces in the 1990s. First, in response to urging from local lawyers, came the DC Circuit Judicial Council. It appointed as its chair Judge Clarence Thomas. (Nothing happened for two years, until after Thomas joined the Supreme Court and left the task force.) Second, again responding to regional attorneys, came the Ninth Circuit Task Force on Gender Bias in the Courts. That task force would quickly involve federal judges from all across the western states—Arizona, California, Oregon, and Washington—in a process that led to a far-reaching report and to a climactic launching of its report, which would have profound effects on VAWA.

And so, starting in the state courts and moving toward the federal courts, reports from the gender-bias task forces accumulated, most of them thick as urban phone books. Aligned on a shelf, they made an impressive display: reams and reams of documentation of gender bias, historic and current, permeating American courts.

Most attorneys, judges, and law professors never saw that impressive display. Libraries at major law schools received copies, but they usually shelved the reports by state, scattering them through the stacks. Not until Victoria Nourse of the Senate Judiciary Committee began in 1991 to receive copy after copy in the mail from Lynn Hecht Schafran, and to recognize their value for VAWA, did the task forces' reports as a unified body of work gain a significant audience. Nourse may have been the first person beyond the leaders of the National Judicial Education Program at NOW Legal Defense or the NAWJ who had ever seen the potential power of almost a decade of surveys and investigations into judicial gender bias led by America's National Association of Women Judges.

25

✦

Women Judges to the Rescue

The judge-created reports of judicial gender bias that helped shape the Violence Against Women Act had some power. But by February of 1992, that power seemed far from adequate. Twice already Chief Justice William Rehnquist had attacked VAWA. And even though Senator Biden was ready to fight for VAWA, the bill seemed besieged by judges. Dominoes were falling. Rehnquist's side had won over most identifiable contingents of judges—state chief justices, federal trial judges—and his lobbying at the American Bar Association suggested that he was committed to winning the ABA itself. Victory at the ABA House of Delegates would extend his condemnation of VAWA beyond all the judges in America to, in effect, all the lawyers in America. If Rehnquist could win the ABA, Victoria Nourse and Senator Biden believed, congressional support for VAWA might evaporate.

The one group of judges who might have the power to stop the dominoes was the National Association of Women Judges. Two months earlier, before Rehnquist showed his hand, Sally Goldfarb had sent a memo to a few officers of the NAWJ, at Lynn Hecht Schafran's suggestion, asking for their support. Goldfarb added that even if the NAWJ were unable to endorse VAWA, the judges' willingness to speak publicly about the inadequacy of current state remedies for women victims of sexual assault—as documented by the task force reports—would provide "much-needed perspective."

In attendance at the same ABA meeting at which Rehnquist attacked VAWA was the almost-ubiquitous Schafran. Conversing with the NAWJ's president, Judge Cara Lee Neville of Minnesota, Schafran asked whether the NAWJ might formally support VAWA—even though support meant opposing the chief justice. Because the NAWJ members would not be gathering again until October, the Board of Directors agreed to consider Schafran's request at its mid-year meeting in March.

Also in March, Nourse got word, which she quickly passed to Goldfarb, that some ABA judges were aiming to convince the entire ABA to oppose the bill. Goldfarb quickly sent out a memo, with emphasis: "*LYNN*, could you please help with this?" Suddenly, the future of VAWA seemed to rest on the women judges of America and Schafran.

As the NAWJ Board of Directors prepared for their annual March meeting, a packet arrived from Schafran asking for the association's endorsement. The packet made clear the strife over the civil rights section. It included Nourse's memo describing the "unexpected controversy" that VAWA "would swamp the federal courts with unimportant 'domestic relations' cases." It included Senator Joseph Biden's challenge that VAWA's critics needed to "consider why they believed acts of domestic violence with an 'interstate' nexus too unimportant to merit federal jurisdiction when current federal law bars 'interstate' theft of a car or a cow."

The packet also included a detailed rebuttal by Goldfarb of claims from both state and federal judges. Goldfarb, like Biden, did not mince words. The resolution of the state chief justices, for example, was both sexist and legally faulty. By suggesting that vengeful wives would file frivolous claims, the chief justices were projecting a "pernicious sexual stereotype." Further, by ignoring the section of the 1871 Civil Rights Act on which VAWA was based, the state chief justices misconstrued civil rights precedent in a manner that amounted to "legal error." Goldfarb's critique flayed Rehnquist as well. In rushing to protect the federal judiciary from any increase in their workload, she alleged, he "misread the proposed legislation and betrayed a tragic insensitivity to the needs of American women who are victims of assault, rape, and other acts of violence."

WHEN THE NAWJ BOARD OF DIRECTORS convened in March, they met at a point of imminent collision. Hurtling down a track from one direction came many of the nation's judicial groups and all the nation's chief justices including Chief Justice Rehnquist. Hurtling from the opposite direction came VAWA and its idealistic young women lawyers. And between the women and the judges stood the NAWJ.

At the board meeting, debate became spirited. Some judges argued that NAWJ should step aside. One judge reportedly told her colleagues that if they supported VAWA, they would be seen as an adjunct for the National Organization for Women. Another argued that if the NAWJ voted in favor of VAWA, a member might be forced to recuse herself in a VAWA case—to disqualify herself as biased in VAWA's favor. Still others argued that NAWJ should not engage in "lobbying." And no judge seeking to rise within the federal system would gain by opposing Chief Justice Rehnquist.

Other judges insisted that the NAWJ could not step aside. Two judges galvanized the meeting by saying, in different ways, What's the point of having a women judges association if all we do is have social gatherings and can't vote our consciences? They were two leaders of the association, soon to be presidents: Judge Betty Ellerin, who had persuaded Chief Judge Cooke to establish the New York State Task Force on Women in the Courts, and Judge Cindy Lederman of Florida, who more recently, while still working as an attorney in Miami, had helped initiate the Florida Supreme Court Study Commission. Though Lederman had no idea that Florida's task force had played any role in VAWA, she well remembered the process of convincing the state's chief justice to create it. After he insisted there was no gender bias in his state courts, Lederman and her colleagues gathered $10,000 and conducted a pilot study, returning to show the chief justice that yes, indeed, there was.

When she returned with the pilot study, Florida's chief justice told a story against himself that Lederman would recall with a smile long afterward. Before he had been appointed a supreme court justice, he told the assembled women attorneys, the only thing he had ever judged was the Miss Opa-locka contest.

Soon Florida had a gender-bias task force, and soon Lederman was appointed a judge in the court system of Dade County. To her it was important that the NAWJ, above all, stand up for other women in America and fight against injustice. Responding to the arguments of Lederman and Ellerin, the board voted to present a resolution supporting VAWA to its full membership. The NAWJ would defend VAWA.

BUT WHAT WOULD THE ABA DECIDE? The showdown would come at its August 1992 annual meeting in San Francisco. The growing opposition of America's mostly male judges seemed likely to convince the mostly male house of delegates of the ABA to oppose the civil rights section of VAWA. If so, as Victoria Nourse observed, the message would be clear: if America's lawyers would not defend VAWA, who would? VAWA's civil rights section might face lengthy redrafting or slow withering.

For Nourse, the judges' attack at the ABA came at a bad time. Ever the quick study, Nourse had risen in responsibility on Biden's staff. By mid-1992, she had become the staffer with primary responsibility for coordinating the entire crime bill. She had little time to think of VAWA.

Goldfarb at NOW Legal Defense was Nourse's key ally in refining language for VAWA, which now had 51 cosponsors in the Senate and 182 in the House. Anticipating the showdown at the ABA, she produced detailed responses to the judges' attacks, which had been coordinated within the Judicial Administration Division, the ABA's section concerned with issues surrounding the judiciary. Because the Division's critique of VAWA offered little new, Goldfarb could say little new in response.

The division again raised the specter that VAWA would add costs to the federal courts of $43.5 million. That huge estimate, Goldfarb replied, assumed that every woman who was raped or assaulted would sue her attacker—so long as she knew who he was and he had any money. The division repeated arguments of the Judicial Conference and the chief justice that VAWA would disrupt state and federal courts by creating the risk that domestic relations cases would be drawn into federal courts. Goldfarb countered that VAWA's language and recent Supreme Court precedent were allied in limiting VAWA's role in cases of "divorce or other domestic relations matters." The division criticized the term "crime of violence" as overbroad, detailing possible discrepancies among different Senate documents. Rather than parse such details, Goldfarb reiterated VAWA's larger goal in a document for distribution at the ABA convention:

> Just as prior civil rights statutes were part of an effective response to pervasive racial violence, Title III is an integral part of the long-overdue national response to violence against women.
>
> Not only are state criminal laws alone an incomplete solution to the problem, the response within the state criminal system itself has sometimes been discriminatory. An important purpose of the post-Civil War era statutes was to provide redress when state court remedies failed to ensure justice to the newly protected class of racial minorities. Similarly, the current climate of discrimination against women has often affected state court systems in such a way as to deprive women of the right to the equal protection of the laws. State gender bias studies have concluded that crimes disproportionately affecting women are often treated less seriously than comparable crimes against men. ... The post-Civil War era civil rights laws were instrumental in the change in the racial climate of the country. They declared, for the first time, a national commitment against racially motivated violent attacks.

VAWA, Goldfarb insisted, "will play a similarly important role in our national response to gender-based violent attacks." All salvos had been fired. Goldfarb and Nourse were talking civil rights. The chief justice and his allies were talking dollars and logistics.

Not only had Goldfarb, Nourse, and their colleagues said all they had to say; they had also taken VAWA as far as they could. In this head-on collision with America's mostly male judges, the women leading the push for VAWA seemed likely to lose. On first reading the Judicial Administration Division's resolution and realizing the force of its attack, Schafran informed Goldfarb and others that "we are way behind." Pat Reuss added a concern about its drafters: "Did these people go to law school or the Tailhook convention?" Reuss and Schafran could sense that their younger allies, opposing the mostly male Judicial Administration Division, did not have "equal firepower."

WITH THE YOUNG WOMEN OF VAWA OUTGUNNED, a more established cohort stepped in to save VAWA. Moving from the wings to center stage were two influential women with strong roots in the legal profession: Judge Mary Schroeder and Professor Judith Resnik.

From the United States Court of Appeals for the Ninth Circuit came Judge Schroeder. A judge of open and direct style with the physical presence of a raptor—alert to each movement in a complex conversation or crowded room—Schroeder had the respect of her fellow members of the NAWJ. She also had enough experience with discrimination to have experienced the value of civil rights legislation. After beginning law school at the University of Chicago in 1962, she found that searching for summer jobs produced almost nothing. But after passage of the Civil Rights Act of 1964, she later recalled, federal agencies began "beating a path to the doors of the major law schools looking for women and minorities, of which there were, naturally, almost none. As a result, I had the pick of the best of the government jobs, and I owe my career to the enactment and the enforcement of Title VII." In 1978, President Jimmy Carter moved Schroeder up to the ninth circuit from her position as a state judge on the Arizona Court of Appeals—opening a post to which the governor, Bruce Babbitt, appointed a judge from a lower-level state court, Sandra Day O'Connor.

A federal judge with life tenure, Schroeder had no fear of speaking her mind. She had played no part in the NAWJ board's decision to

draft a resolution supporting VAWA, and her only earlier involvement with the legislation had been to confer briefly with Schafran
about some early drafting for what would become a section of the
bill that sought congressional funding for studies of gender bias in
the federal courts. Schroeder knew the value of federal gender-bias
task forces directly, as convener of the ninth circuit's working group
in the state of Arizona. But Judge Schroeder had no prior involvement with VAWA's civil rights section, and she had doubts about its
language.

From the University of Southern California Law School came Professor Judith Resnik, a specialist in the federal courts and a member
of the NAWJ and its Judicial-Academic Network, which brought
judges in contact with leading scholars. Prolific in publication and
astonishing in energy, Resnik could seem ubiquitous—faxing comments on VAWA to Schafran from Jerusalem, gathering hard-to-find
data on the numbers of women judges in America, and occasionally
arguing crucial cases herself. Resnik in 1987 had successfully argued
a Supreme Court case defending the decision of a local Rotary Club
to break the rules of Rotary International by admitting women. Like
Judge Schroeder, Professor Resnik had taken a lead in working with
the ninth circuit's gender-bias task force, on which she served as one
of eight official members. Uniting Schroeder and Resnik, beyond
their commitment to federal court studies of gender bias and their
membership in the NAWJ, was a shared view of VAWA's civil rights
section: it was appropriate for the federal courts to be engaged in
litigation that responded to the national problem of violence against
women.

Judge Schroeder's work on VAWA began with a phone call from
NAWJ's president-elect, Judge Brenda Murray. A self-effacing administrative law judge with the Security and Exchange Commission in
Washington, Brenda Murray would say of her stature that her sort of
judge lies at the "bottom of the judicial heap." What Brenda Murray
suggested, as Judge Schroeder understood her, amounted to a vision
of NAWJ's role: the organization was perhaps the only one that could
talk to all involved with VAWA. The NAWJ could talk to VAWA's
feminist supporters, talk to its legislative drafters, and talk to its

judicial opponents. And Murray knew that Schroeder was not just at the top of the judicial heap, with only the Supreme Court above her, but also respected by judges throughout the nation.

Schroeder accepted from Brenda Murray what would become a two-part challenge: First, chair a committee, including NAWJ members who had argued for and those who had argued against supporting VAWA, to create a resolution backing VAWA. Second, become the voice of the NAWJ: negotiate among opposed forces to direct VAWA toward a form that would meet the needs of American women and the American Constitution.

The first challenge could not wait because in August, at the ABA's annual meeting, the Judicial Administration Division would make its final push for condemnation of VAWA's civil rights section. Rushing to be ready, Schroeder's committee agreed on its resolution by the end of July:

> BE IT RESOLVED THAT THE NATIONAL ASSOCIATION OF WOMEN JUDGES endorses the provisions of Title I—Safe Streets for Women, Title II—Safe Homes for Women, Title IV—Equal Justice for Women in the Courts Act and Title V—Equal Justice for Women in the Courts Act of the Violence Against Women Act of 1991, S.15 as reported. The National Association of Women Judges supports in principle the provisions of Title III creating a federal remedy for those whose civil rights have been violated by violent attacks motivated by the victim's gender, provided that the provisions of Title III are narrowly tailored to create such a federal form of action in those cases in which a federal forum is both necessary and appropriate.

The committee supported Title III, the civil rights remedy, only "in principle." At least one member of Judge Schroeder's committee, Judge Lederman of Florida, had pushed for a resolution to support Title III as written. But other judges hesitated, including Norma Shapiro, a federal district court judge from Philadelphia, whose role was crucial and partly beyond her control. Years before, she had taught one of the early law school courses on women in law, in 1971 at the University of

Pennsylvania. Now Judge Shapiro was both a member of the Judicial Administration Division and its official delegate to the ABA House of Delegates. Her position was awkward: as a member of the Judicial Administration Division, she was well placed to urge alteration of its resolution before submission to the ABA House of Delegates. But once a resolution was submitted, as the Judicial Administration Division's delegate she would be *instructed* to present not her own view but the Judicial Administration Division's to the other assembled delegates of the ABA.

In part to give Judge Shapiro a chance to sway the Judicial Administration Division, the NAWJ committee agreed on a multistep compromise: First, NAWJ's resolution would support Title III not as written but "in principle." Second, Judge Shapiro would work to convert the Judicial Administration Division's condemnation of Title III into similar support in principle—but with insistence that its civil rights remedy be "narrowly tailored." Third, if needed, NAWJ would offer, as an appropriate tailor, the chair of its own VAWA committee: Judge Schroeder, moderate and trusted by all, who would go to work with Senator Biden's drafters. Judge Schroeder would undertake to show them how to make Title III acceptable to the judges who would review it in court.

IMMEDIATELY BEFORE THE CLIMACTIC MEETING at the ABA came a gathering of federal judges in Idaho—one that would have significant impact on VAWA. In the first week of August in 1992, Schroeder, Resnik, and Schafran were gathering with federal judges from all over the west for the Ninth Circuit Judicial Conference in Sun Valley, made far from idyllic by smoke spreading overhead from summer fires. On August 5, for the first time, a federal court circuit would follow where, beginning with Marilyn Loftus' work in New Jersey, some thirty states had led. Members of the federal judiciary were meeting to discuss a drafted report on gender bias in their courts.

Giving a history of gender-bias task forces, Professor Barbara Babcock of Stanford—who had cowritten the textbook that grew from the first sex discrimination courses at New York University, Georgetown, and Yale—linked the training of women lawyers to the later creation of task forces on gender bias in the courts.

> The task force movement has many links with legal education. On the most basic level, it was not until law schools graduated significant numbers of women that their experiences became, in a sense, statistically significant enough to translate into the findings found in task force reports.

Put another way, until significant numbers of women lawyers appeared before judges, even deep judicial bias against women remained statistically invisible—remained anecdote, not data. And just as the education of women created the need for gender-bias task forces, Babcock added, the task forces were sharpening the way law teachers and law students perceived the influence of gender on the courts and the law.

Following Babcock came Judith Resnik. For months she had labored with the other seven members of the Ninth Circuit Gender Bias Task Force and in consultation with dozens of judges and attorneys associated with the ninth circuit. What they had produced, in the familiar phone-book shape, was an essentially finished analysis of gender bias—albeit labeled "preliminary" to invite commentary. Resnik opened with recollection of advice she received early in her teaching career from a well-meaning colleague. "Be careful," he said,

> Don't teach in any areas associated with women's issues. Don't teach family law; don't teach sex discrimination. Teach the real stuff, the hard stuff: contracts, torts, procedure, property. And be careful—don't be too visible on women's issues.

Working on articles about judges, federalism, and habeas corpus, Resnik had a reputation based on the "hard stuff." But she also was engaged in making clear to the nation's law teachers and judges that, as she told the assembled judges in Sun Valley, "all areas of federal law are connected to and affect 'women'—and, unfortunately, can provide occasions for gender bias."

The Ninth Circuit Task Force found, Resnik told the judges, that women and women's concerns pervaded the federal courts. Despite the fact that federal judges had crafted a "domestic relations" rule that gave them license to hand many family-related cases to judges in the states, family issues ran through federal courts. Indeed, she argued, legislation before and after the New Deal had created what amounted to "federal laws of the family"—though federal judges thought of them as the federal laws of pension, tax, immigration, welfare, and bankruptcy. In many of these areas, women were involved in half or even a majority of cases.

Yet federal courts resisted considering women as a group. Women had been ignored not just in speeches on the "state of the judiciary" but also, she told the judges of the ninth circuit, in all of the reports since the 1940s of the Administrative Office of the United States Courts. Most evidently, federal courts chose to ignore women and the possibility of bias against women by choosing not to follow their state court brethren in creating gender-bias task forces, which by 1992 had published reports in twenty-one states. About this failure and the attitude that sanctioned such federal failure, Resnik spoke strongly:

> Women are everywhere in the federal courts, but no one—until this study—paid much attention. This silence is a form of gender bias, and the work of the Ninth Circuit begins a process of ending that form of discrimination.

Lest her listeners doubt that the ninth circuit report had found discrimination, Resnik offered examples from the marginalia scribbled on its surveys, some of which sounded "pretty angry" and ranged

> from telling us that this activity was stupid and wasteful ("a complete waste of time and money!"; "a pile of garbage"; "much ado about nothing") to telling us that we were doing something harmful by asking questions about gender. One comment, by a male lawyer, summed up many: "Why the Ninth Circuit should focus on gender bias is beyond me when there are real legitimate problems within the Ninth Circuit which are not being addressed."

Resnik's scholarship amounted to a sustained, multiyear response to what Chief Justice Rehnquist, in his 1991 report that condemned VAWA, had called the "long-accepted concepts of federalism" with, as he put it, "the federal courts' limited role reserved for issues where important national interests predominate." Resnik presented women's issues as imbedded within the federal courts, though apparently unseen by judges seeking to identify "important national interests."

Discussions of what mattered to the federal courts, including bias against women, linked the launching symposium for the Ninth Circuit Gender Bias Report to the Violence Against Women Act, although Resnik did not mention VAWA in her speech.

VAWA was nonetheless on Resnik's mind: half the members of the "ad hoc committee on gender-based violence" appointed a year earlier by Chief Justice William Rehnquist were in the audience at Sun Valley: Judge Barbara Rothstein (U.S. District Court for the Western District of Washington) and Judge Pamela Rymer (U.S. Court of Appeals for the Ninth Circuit), who had assisted the work of the task force.

During the conference at Sun Valley, both judges spent time in conversation with Resnik or Schafran, discussing and reconsidering judicial opposition to VAWA. (Resnik had already spent hours discussing VAWA at Rymer's home in Los Angeles. Separately, at her home in Washington State, Rothstein would wind up talking for hours about VAWA with a former sorority sister from thirty years before at Cornell University: Helen Neuborne, head of NOW Legal Defense and thus colleague and boss to Goldfarb and Schafran.) In conversations with Rymer and Rothstein, Resnik heard their worries that VAWA's Title III needed to be narrowed. Further, Rothstein and Rymer expressed interest in sending a note to Biden to reopen dialog so long, Schafran gathered, as Biden would welcome their effort. Nourse quickly responded that Biden would be pleased to hear from them.

The launching ceremony for the report of the Ninth Circuit Gender Bias Task Force at Sun Valley offered a particularly fine opportunity for creating a unity of purpose among women involved in federal courts. The day after Resnik's speech, judges at the conference assembled to hear a speaker whom, though a founding member of the NAWJ, no one saw as a radical feminist. Supreme Court Justice Sandra Day O'Connor, after praising the task force report as comprehensive and well supported, told a brief story:

> A couple of years ago, I gave a speech in which I discussed the existence of a glass ceiling for women. The next day, headlines and newspaper articles trumpeted my statements as if I had made a surprising new discovery. But it is now 1992, and I don't think most of us were surprised to learn that the Task Force found the existence of gender bias in a federal circuit.

Continuing, she spoke of the disparities in percentages between women lawyers and women judges. She spoke of the difficulty attorneys have in imagining a woman as "partner" and went on to suggest that judicial images of an "effective advocate" or "credible litigant" or even "judge" may all act to exclude women. And, pushing further, she explained to the mostly male judges who had gathered to hear her that the task force report "asks us to take seriously claims that may not bother us personally." Like Resnik, Justice O'Connor challenged federal judges to think more expansively than usual about the reach and responsibility of the federal courts in addressing discrimination against women.

THE SHOWDOWN AT THE ABA occurred in early August of 1992. Although conciliation with Judges Rymer and Rothstein, and thus with half the Judicial Conference's committee, seemed suddenly possible, such belated conciliation would do nothing to help VAWA if the ABA condemned its civil rights section. As Resnik and Schafran headed west from Sun Valley to San Francisco for the ABA meeting, their hope for compromise rested in the work of the NAWJ. Judge Shapiro, as agreed with her fellow members of NAWJ's committee on violence against women, would try to convince her fellow members of the Judicial Administration Division to shift from its attacking resolution to NAWJ's cautious, supporting resolution.

Despite some worries about what the new compromise language

might be, Nourse was thankful for the NAWJ. She had heard that the judges opposing VAWA would be hard to beat, and she saw that NAWJ's compromise might be the best that she and Senator Biden could hope for.

As the showdown approached, neither Biden nor Nourse were well positioned to play a role. Biden was tied up in Senate discussions about war in Bosnia, although he did manage to make a call to Judge Shapiro. And Nourse would be hard to reach on the weekend before the ABA showdown. She and her fiancee, Rick Cudahy, were flying to Chicago for his sister's wedding. Nourse told Schafran that she could be reached "in an emergency c/o Judge Richard Cudahy in Winnetka." Also at the wedding, Nourse expected she might see one of Rick's aunts, Judge Rya Zobel of the first circuit. (She had been chair of the Conference of Federal Trial Judges in February of 1992 when it voted to attack VAWA.) In Nourse's world, judges abounded. With Rick, her future had become a running joke: she would never again find work as a federal litigator, they agreed, because Victoria would always be branded as that woman who forced the federal courts to take domestic relations cases.

But if Judge Shapiro could convince the Judicial Administration Division to support all of VAWA, at least in principle, the worst opposition between VAWA's drafters and its opponents could be averted. A route would open to compromise. Alas, bad news about Shapiro's efforts kept reaching Schafran, who was attending the ABA convention.

Saturday, August 8: NAWJ's supporting resolution would not replace the Judicial Administration Division attack. Shapiro was now encouraging the Judicial Administration Division to defer.

Monday, August 10: One of Biden's staff members had several conversations with Norma Shapiro about a deal with the Judicial Administration Division—the division would defer its attack if Biden would defer the bill for six months. Biden told his staff he was willing to confer with Shapiro herself but not with the Judicial Administration Division because it was being controlled by people who really wanted to defeat the civil rights section.

Later on August 10, more information: Shapiro had mentioned

language that could amend the Judicial Administration Division's opposition to qualified opposition. In an amended resolution, the Judicial Administration Division might oppose VAWA's civil rights section "unless the legislation creates federal offenses and causes of action narrowly defined and specifically tailored to the need for a federal forum." Conferring by phone, Schafran, Goldfarb, and Nourse decide that Goldfarb should call Shapiro and urge a shift from qualified opposition to qualified support. Could Shapiro convince the Judicial Administration Division—if the legislation is "narrowly defined and specifically tailored to the need for a federal forum"—to support VAWA's civil rights section in principle?

Tuesday, August 11, about 9:00 a.m.: Goldfarb heard from Shapiro that support was impossible. Shapiro had tried but failed to get the Judicial Administration Division to accept NAWJ's phrasing. Goldfarb left the conversation feeling that Judge Shapiro had her hands tied.

The showdown that Norma Shapiro and many others in the NAWJ had worked so hard to avoid was now less than thirty hours away. Could VAWA's supporters, after weeks of trying for compromise, gather the votes to stave off the well-planned attack of the Judicial Administration Division?

The task of marshaling opposition fell to Schafran. What she needed were women of stature and fire who were willing to speak against federal judges on the floor of the House of Delegates. Where could she turn for firepower? Shapiro had done her best and now, as an instructed delegate of the Judicial Administration Division, had no choice but to argue its side. Schroeder, after the ninth circuit conference, had not traveled to San Francisco for the ABA. Schafran knew where to turn—back to allies in some of her earliest work to end gender imbalances in the federal judiciary. She found those allies ready to step forward.

ON AUGUST 12, 1992, hundreds of ABA delegates gathered in a grand room of the San Francisco Hilton. Beginning at 2:25 p.m., Lynn Hecht Schafran sat taking notes as the drama unfolded. First rose Judge Norma Shapiro, always dignified and precise, to argue for the Judicial

Administration Division position: the ABA should oppose VAWA's civil rights section. The chair asked the position of the Board of Governors. As Schafran expected, the board opposed the Judicial Administration Division—which meant support for VAWA.

The Board of Governors' support for VAWA had a hidden history, stretching back several months. In May, the Judicial Administration Division had tried to push the Board of Governors for hasty condemnation of VAWA. Seeking help, Schafran turned to women who had already played a crucial role in advancing the cause of women in the judiciary. She spoke to Brooksley Born, whom she had first worked with when they both testified before Congress in 1981 on behalf of Ronald Reagan's nomination of Sandra Day O'Connor to the Supreme Court. Born was then the first woman member and chair of the ABA's Standing Committee on Federal Judiciary, which evaluated potential judges. In that role, she had rewritten long-standing ABA rules that had excluded women by requiring prospective judges to have compiled fifteen years of experience as litigators—a requirement that, as of the early 1980s, few women could meet.

Speaking from her vantage as a member of the ABA's Board of Governors, Born made her view clear to Schafran: whatever the merits of the Judicial Administration Division's attack on VAWA, the division should not circumvent the usual debate in the House of Delegates. But when Born arrived a few days later for the division's presentation, she began to hear a very different view. First, one judge supported the Judicial Administration Division attack as an effort to limit the work of federal judges. A prominent member of the Board of Governors followed, saying that efforts not to burden judges so evidently aligned with ABA policy that the Judicial Administration Division should feel free to oppose VAWA. "All the men," Brooksley Born told Schafran, concurred.

By the time Born finally was called on to speak, she was furious. She gave it to them, as she later put it, "with both barrels." VAWA's civil rights section, she told them, does not create a new federal crime. It creates a civil action for civil rights in federal court. She was surprised to hear, she continued, that opposition to such a civil right was

ABA policy. The problem of gender-based violence was serious, she continued, and she felt sure that the other women in the room had been victims of it, as she had. The resolution, she insisted, should not avoid full debate in August in the House of Delegates. Voting a few minutes later, the Board of Governors supported her almost unanimously (except for the resolution's proponent). Recalling her meeting later, Born told Schafran that it made her realize something afresh about gender-based violence: how deeply into denial are many men of goodwill.

Despite losing the support of the ABA's Board of Governors at the May meeting, at the August annual meeting Judge Shapiro proceeded to say that the Judicial Administration Division opposed VAWA for its expansion of federal jurisdiction and some of its language, such as "crimes of violence" and "motivated by gender." She mentioned high cost estimates. As she concluded, Schafran noted, she received a smattering of applause.

To rebut rose Brooksley Born. Born's many roles in the ABA only began to suggest her reputation. Perhaps the most-often-told story concerned her rise to partner in the prestigious Washington firm Arnold & Porter. After graduating first in her class at Stanford Law in 1964, she held a federal clerkship and soon after became a lawyer at Arnold & Porter. Three years into the job, she gave birth to her first child. After returning to full-time work she quickly found herself, as she told a *Washington Post* reporter in 1980, an "absolute wreck." She eventually announced her resignation, only to receive a counterproposal from a senior partner: work three days a week but don't expect to make partner. She agreed, raised two children, made uncountable calls from home to clients who assumed she was phoning from the office at Arnold & Porter, and developed into one of the firm's most able tax lawyers.

Several years later, on the night before Brooksley Born's fellow associates at the law firm were scheduled to be voted on for partnership, one of the firm's partners called her at home. "A considerable body of thought" at Arnold & Porter, the *Post* story quoted the partner saying, held that "a mistake had been made" in ruling her out for partnership, and could she tell them when she would be ready to return to work full time?

"I don't know," Born recalled saying, "if I'll ever be able to go back full time."

The next day, Arnold & Porter made her a partner. A few years later, with both her children enrolled in school, she returned full time.

When Born rose to address the House of Delegates, she made clear the gravity of their vote. If they passed the resolution, for the first time they would put the ABA on record as opposing federal civil rights legislation. Violence against women, she continued, is epidemic and impairs all aspects of women's lives. She praised the bill for its innovative remedies and suggested that if federal courts feel flooded, they may need to fill vacant judgeships. She concluded that the ABA must not urge federal courts to close their doors.

In response, a Judicial Administration Division supporter insisted VAWA must be narrowed to preserve the federal courts' ability to function. Another VAWA defender asked the ABA to look beyond issues of efficiency and to help ensure women the same sort of federal remedies available to victims of racial and ethnic violence. Another Judicial Administration Division supporter worried that VAWA would lead to fights between federal and state courts over who would handle prominent cases. Another VAWA defender, speaking on behalf of the National Conference of Women's Bar Associations, stated that her board opposed the Judicial Administration Division's first resolution and had never seen today's amended resolution.

The debate felt too close to call. As Schafran expected, the first motion was that the resolution be deferred. Norma Shapiro spoke in opposition and won: no deferral.

A voice vote was called. The response was loud and clear: defeat for the Judicial Administration Division.

But raising a point of order, Shapiro insisted that the chair had failed to permit her, as the resolution's proponent, to make the division's closing argument. She was right. The chair voided the vote.

Shapiro insisted that judges do not oppose VAWA because of their workload. VAWA, she insisted, was confusing to the concept of federalism. Speaking with her characteristic dedication and pride in her court system, she added that the federal courts would take whatever Congress assigned and do their best with it. But, she continued, the Administrative Office of the Courts is concerned about the impact of new federal civil actions.

Applause was mild. The chair called for the final vote.

Aye? "More votes this time," noted Schafran.

No? The no's, scribbled Schafran, underscoring in a zorro-like slash, *"have it."* VAWA's civil rights section would *not* be opposed by the ABA. It would not be opposed by American lawyers. The time was 2:53 *p.m.* (also underscored), August 12, 1992. VAWA had survived its worst moment on route to Congress.

STAVING OFF DEFEAT AT THE ABA led to the next challenge: how to eliminate the opposition of the heavily male Judicial Conference, which had challenged VAWA's language far more forcefully than recommended by its gender-balanced committee on gender-based violence. Fortunately, although the full conference in late September of 1991 had cut much of the committee's affirmative language about VAWA, the conference had permitted its committee to continue dialog with VAWA's sponsors. On that committee, which still included Judges Pamela Rymer and Barbara Rothstein, a new chair had arrived, Judge Stanley Marcus. A graduate of Harvard Law and a former federal prosecutor from Florida, appointed district judge by Ronald Reagan in 1985, Marcus had won the esteem of lawyers who practiced before him. Professor Resnik, speaking to him at length about VAWA, came to admire him and to sense that, as a former prosecutor, he understood some of the problems women encountered in courts. At his invitation, she spoke not just to him and to members of his four-member ad hoc committee but also to the larger committee of the Judicial Conference that he chaired: the Committee on Federal-State Jurisdiction. Judge Schroeder also spoke to Marcus regularly. Through late 1992, after the ABA declined to condemn

VAWA's civil rights section, and into early 1993, as VAWA still sat in limbo in Congress, Schroeder sometimes felt she was speaking to him daily. They discussed new language. She felt that he began to grasp what lay behind VAWA and the entire concept of its civil rights section. Resnik similarly felt that Marcus was beginning to see that federal judges harmed themselves and their courts when they seemed to lobby, as Chief Justice Rehnquist had, against women who were knocking on the federal door.

In March of 1993, Judge Marcus achieved a breakthrough that Schroeder saw as a "miracle." He achieved it at the Judicial Conference of the United States, the twenty-seven-judge body convened by the chief justice that eighteen months earlier had opposed VAWA's civil rights section. Despite the fact that VAWA's drafters had made no new concessions, Judge Marcus convinced the conference to end opposition to VAWA's civil rights section. Reversing the early direction of the chief justice, the conference shifted from opposition to no position, opening the way for moderate judges on Marcus' committee to push for an acceptable and constitutional civil rights law for women.

A LAST TRANSFORMATIVE MEETING lay ahead for VAWA's civil rights section, on April 26, 1993. Far from the brightly lit ballroom full of ABA delegates, this meeting was private and essentially unknown. It gathered most of the key judges and drafters in the battle over VAWA in what Victoria Nourse and Sally Goldfarb came to think of as "the dark room." Coming as chair of the Judicial Conference committee on violence against women was Judge Stanley Marcus, along with one of the original committee members, Judge Barbara Rothstein. With them, they brought two lobbyists from the Administrative Office of the Courts. Judge Mary Schroeder came as representative of the NAWJ. Meeting with the judges were what Judge Schroeder saw as "the feminists." From NOW Legal Defense came Pat Reuss, legislative organizer, and Sally Goldfarb, legal brains. Hosting the gathering and representing the Senate Judiciary Committee was VAWA's original drafter, Victoria Nourse—who, as host for the gathering, had not planned to meet in a dark room.

When the group gathered at her office, Nourse expected to adjourn to one of the Senate Judiciary Committee's meeting areas, probably the committee's grand conference room with its brown-leather chairs beneath walnut-toned wood and a ceiling about thirty feet high. To Nourse's surprise, senators were meeting there. Because all nearby meeting areas were taken, Nourse had nowhere to take the judges.

Along the marble halls of the Dirksen Building they walked, then down two flights in an elevator, looking for an empty room and eventually pushing through doors marked only SD G19: *Senate Dirksen Building, ground floor, room 19.* Dull turquoise walls contrasted with scuffed cranberry carpets. Metal chairs sat stacked along a wall of floor-to-ceiling cabinets that seemed designed to store volleyballs or badminton nets. "Rumpus room," thought Nourse, but this was the best meeting place she could find. In the dim room, Nourse could see small gilt chandeliers hanging from a low ceiling but giving little light. (The room was used, rarely, for overflow from formal dinners.) The judges and the feminists gathered chrome chairs into a circle and began deciding the future of VAWA.

If deciding VAWA's future was the judges' agenda, however, the feminists had not known that agenda in advance. Goldfarb arrived at the meeting, she would later recall, thinking the judges "would try to bully us" or would try to bully Nourse in order to bully Biden. Nourse went into the dark room thinking "nothing is going to happen." To this point, Nourse's meetings with judges had felt heated but unproductive. This time, she hoped to sit quietly and let Judge Marcus listen to Pat Reuss and Sally Goldfarb. Nourse wanted him to hear from NOW Legal Defense, which represented a coalition of real live people.

Soon Nourse realized this would be an unusual meeting in the Senate building. Almost immediately it became, she thought, a "lawyer's lawyer meeting." On one side were the judges. On the other, speaking for the feminists, was essentially one young lawyer, Sally Goldfarb. First, the judges raised a couple of issues that Nourse had heard about in an odd way. For months at the office of the Senate Judiciary Committee, faxes had been arriving with anonymous drafts that proposed language for VAWA. Although Nourse couldn't tell whom they came from, they led her to believe that some judges out there wanted to find common ground. As the meeting began in the dark room, she decided that some of those judges were sitting before her.

Two topics came up so briefly they seemed compressed into code. Goldfarb scribbled in her notes "felony." OK said Nourse. Goldfarb scribbled "pendent jurisdiction." OK said Nourse. So two issues were settled instantly: One, the Senate would amend its bill to apply VAWA only to crimes that had the seriousness of a felony. Two, VAWA would not give jurisdiction to federal courts over claims based in state laws, such as a woman's claims concerning divorce, alimony, or child custody. To Nourse, her OKs seemed less than concessions. They seemed reassurances that Joseph Biden meant what he had already said in public hearings.

Next, however, came the big discussion: How broad was VAWA's sweep? How, Judge Marcus asked, do you define "crime of violence"? Do you want to include every violent crime against women?

No, said the feminists.

Judge Schroeder insisted that VAWA's language needed sharpening beyond Senator Biden's oft-repeated comment that VAWA does not cover "random" crimes. VAWA now said that it covered crimes of violence committed "because of or on the basis of gender." The language had been adopted by Nourse long ago, from the language of Title VII of the Civil Rights Act of 1964. But judges kept insisting that "because of . . . gender" was too general.

Earlier, before the meeting, both Judge Schroeder and Judge Marcus had pushed to limit VAWA to crimes that occurred not just *because of* gender but because of "animosity" or "hatred" toward a gender. In a late 1992 phone conversation, Schroeder had pushed Sally Goldfarb to consider language that, as Sally Goldfarb transcribed it, went more or less as follows:

> . . . Motivated by gender means any crime committed because
> of or on the basis of sex due to animosity against the gender
> as a class as distinguished from animus against a particular
> individual.

Goldfarb, speaking for NOW Legal Defense, refused to accept that language. The distinction between animosity toward one woman and all women *as a class*, she wrote back to Schroeder, assumed wrongly that there exists

> a clear distinction between misogyny directed at all women and misogyny directed at one woman. In fact, the two are often blurred; many men (for example, batterers) take action against one woman that expresses their contempt for all women as symbolized by that one woman.

This was the sort of argument that led Nourse, long ago, to respect Goldfarb as a lawyer—a fearless one, it seemed, willing to take on a federal judge who was also one of VAWA's only judicial friends.

An urging that VAWA contend only with "hatred" had been handed out as part of a memo with suggestions by judges when Judge Marcus met earlier in the year with congressional staff members. The memo, containing neither letterhead nor name of author, began, "You have asked for thoughts about how the bill's language might be more tightly focused." This anonymous *thoughts* memo proposed that VAWA cover a "gender-based crime of violence" only if it was "motivated by hatred for the gender of the victim." This was phrasing that Goldfarb and NOW Legal Defense could not accept.

Since January, both judges had thought in detail and conferred often about VAWA's language. Judge Schroeder now brought up the phrase "invidiously discriminatory animus." Goldfarb and Nourse recognized it immediately as the language in *Griffin v. Breckenridge*, the case that Nourse had found herself defending at her first meeting with the Judicial Conference of the United States committee that Judge Marcus now chaired. *Griffin* relied on the same anticonspiracy section of the 1871 Civil Rights Act that helped inspire VAWA. It said that *if* African-Americans could show an attack was motivated by "some racial, or perhaps otherwise class-based, invidiously discriminatory animus," they could sue a group of white attackers for conspiracy to violate their civil rights.

The language of *invidiously discriminatory animus* had strong appeal: it linked VAWA, at least via court decisions, to its roots in early civil rights law and its still-deeper roots in the Fourteenth Amendment's promise of equality. Though *animus* did not appear in the Civil Rights Act of 1871 itself or the amendment from which it sprang, a congressman named Shellabarger had used it during the 1871 debates on that Act. The Act, he said, covered a violation of a citizen's right to equality if the "animus and effect" of that violation is "to strike down the citizen, to the end that he may not enjoy equality of rights as contrasted with his and other citizens' rights." Though archaic in phrasing, the congressman's goal made modern sense for VAWA: if a woman is struck down, to the end that she may not enjoy equality of rights with men, she deserves protection of the law. In the words of Congressman (later President) James A. Garfield concerning the 1871 Act, it responded to the complaint that states, even when their laws are "just and equal on their face," were guilty of "systematic maladministration" or "a neglect or refusal to enforce their provisions" as a result of which "people are denied equal protection" of the law.

Nourse, in her earliest drafting of VAWA, had included the term *animus* in its old sense of purpose or motive. In June of 1990, she had defined a "crime of violence motivated by the victim's gender" under VAWA as "any rape, sexual assault, or abusive sexual contact motivated by gender-based animus." *Animus* had dropped out of VAWA months later during haggling over how broadly or sharply to define the sort of violence that VAWA covered.

Restoring the word *animus*, as suggested by the judges, could link VAWA to its origins in nineteenth-century law. That linkage also fit a belief in the twentieth-century viability of those civil rights laws. Although the civil rights acts of 1871 and 1875 had been nearly destroyed by retrograde Supreme Court cases of 1883, recent decisions like *Griffin v. Breckenridge* suggested readiness to reject those cases.

More optimistically, in a case called *Guest* in 1966, six justices of the Supreme Court combined in two opinions—though neither was the majority opinion—to suggest that they no longer felt bound by the *Civil Rights Cases'* insistence in 1883 that the Fourteenth

Amendment permitted the federal government to attack only state action. Three justices agreed that Congress had the power to punish private conspirators who infringed rights guaranteed by the Fourteenth Amendment. Three other justices, going further in an opinion written by Justice William J. Brennan Jr., suggested that the *Civil Rights Cases* were wrongly decided in 1883. Summing up the views of the six members of the Court, Brennan's opinion stated that "a majority of the Court today rejects" the state action requirement of the *Civil Rights Cases*. The justices' suggestion in 1966 that the *Civil Rights Cases* were wrong seemed to step beyond an oddity from two years before—and to step around a difficulty with which William Rehnquist had been associated since his first year working at the Supreme Court, as a clerk in 1952.

In two 1964 cases, the Supreme Court considered the constitutionality of the public accommodations provisions, officially Title II, of the Civil Rights Act of 1964. Those provisions resembled the ban on discrimination in hotels and trains attempted by the Civil Rights Act of 1875, which was eviscerated in 1883 by Justice Joseph P. Bradley's decision that the Fourteenth Amendment permitted the federal government to attack only state action. Both Congress and the Kennedy-Johnson administrations grounded the 1964 Civil Rights Act on two sources of constitutional authority. One was the Fourteenth Amendment's guarantee of equal protection, which seemed intuitively strong but remained technically weak from the 1883 evisceration. Second was the commerce clause, which had been expanding in power since at least 1937. That year the Supreme Court used the commerce clause to sustain the National Labor Relations Act, and in 1942 the Court upheld an agricultural act in *Wickard v. Filburn*, the case that said congressional power to regulate interstate commerce extended even to wheat grown at home for home consumption.

Considering those two sources of constitutional authority—protection of equality, roadblocked since the 1880s by the *Civil Rights Cases*, and protection of commerce, affirmed since the 1930s by multiple decisions—the Supreme Court in 1964 swerved. Dodging the roadblock, it affirmed the civil rights act using only the commerce clause.

Such swerves had a history. When the Supreme Court in *Brown v. Board of Education* ruled that separate but equal schools were unconstitutional, after hearing oral arguments in both 1952 and 1953 (by, among others, Thurgood Marshall and Spottswood Robinson) the Court swerved around deciding whether the Fourteenth Amendment guaranteed equality in public education. The Court swerved also around reversing the original case, *Plessy v. Ferguson*, that created the "separate but equal" doctrine. Instead, the Supreme Court in *Brown* ruled only that the doctrine had "no place" in the area of "public education."

The swerve around *Plessy* dodged opposition of the sort that surfaced in a memorandum prepared in 1952 by one of Justice Robert H. Jackson's law clerks, recently graduated from Stanford Law School, William Rehnquist. "I think *Plessy v. Ferguson* was right and should be reaffirmed," wrote Rehnquist in 1952, although his memo acknowledged that it was making "an unpopular and unhumane proposition for which I have been excoriated by 'liberal' colleagues." When the Rehnquist memo became public years later, Rehnquist insisted that it represented his drafting of Justice Jackson's views—an insistence opposed by the secretary of the deceased justice, who charged that Rehnquist had "smeared the reputation of a great justice." Still later, Rehnquist admitted that he might have defended *Plessy* among fellow clerks, strengthening the belief that Rehnquist had sought in 1952 to affirm *Plessy* and its doctrine of "separate but equal." Suggestions that Rehnquist did not oppose segregation appeared again in the 1960s. Writing in the *Arizona Republic*—apparently playing against Lincoln's famous lines in the Gettysburg Address that America is "dedicated to the proposition that all men are created equal"—Rehnquist suggested that "we are no more dedicated to an 'integrated' society than to a 'segregated' society." At about the same time that he articulated such openness to segregation, according to an Arizona legislator, Rehnquist stated that he was "opposed to all civil rights laws."

Swerves left problems. By not "confronting and overturning the racist *Civil Rights Cases*," as Professor Balkin of Yale puts it, "the Warren Court effectively performed an end-run" around those cases when it affirmed the Civil Rights Act of 1964 on the foundation of only the commerce clause. That little-discussed dodge created an embarrassment: the Supreme Court of the United States seemed to view civil rights law as merely economic law, grounded not in equality but in commerce. The dodge also created a weakness: if a later Court chose to point out the obvious—not all civil rights are economic rights—that later Court could begin to cut away civil rights.

The 1966 assertion by Justice Brennan in *Guest*, claiming that six justices saw the *Civil Rights Cases* as wrongly decided, thus had the potential to correct both an embarrassment and a weakness in civil rights law that stretched from 1883 through 1964. Brennan in *Guest* was reasserting Supreme Court support for equality. Not until 1992, however, did a majority of the Supreme Court state that *Plessy* had been "wrong the day it was decided."

The suggestion to add the word *animus* to VAWA thus had the advantage of echoing *Griffin v. Breckenridge* and, through that case from 1971, aligning with the Supreme Court's apparently belated move to reaffirm the promise of equality created by the Fourteenth Amendment. Adding *invidiously discriminatory animus* could bring disadvantages, however. It could seem to root VAWA in judicial decisions interpreting merely the Civil Rights Act of 1871, whereas VAWA's true roots were broader, in the Fourteenth Amendment and its promise of equal protection of the law. Worse, *invidiously discriminatory animus* would link VAWA tightly to a decision called *Bray v. Alexandria Women's Health Clinic*, delivered for the Supreme Court on January 13, 1993, by one of its most conservative justices, Antonin Scalia. And *Bray*'s ugliness, from the vantage of feminists, was hydra-headed.

In *Bray*, Scalia ruled that the 1871 Civil Rights Act did not apply to conspiracies that obstruct women from gaining access to abortion clinics, a ruling that overturned two lower courts. Those courts (and others, less directly) had ruled that obstruction of women by a nationwide group called Operation Rescue was indeed covered by the Act. Many judges believed Operation Rescue so analogous to the Ku Klux Klan that Justice Sandra Day O'Connor, opposing Scalia, described Operation Rescue's obstruction of women as "a modern-day paradigm" of the situation the 1871 Act (also called the Ku Klux

Klan Act) was "meant to address." Finally, in explaining why the 1871 Civil Rights Act did not apply to women obstructed from reaching abortion clinics, Scalia relied on the old embarrassment of *Geduldig v. Aiello* and the early pregnancy cases.

APPARENTLY *GEDULDIG V. AIELLO* LIVED. Nineteen years had passed since Wendy Williams had argued, before the Supreme Court in *Geduldig*, against government health insurance plans that refused to cover women who became pregnant. "Nowhere is the economic discrimination against women," she told the Court, "more apparent than in the rules and practices surrounding the reality that women are the bearers of children." From that reality had emerged the "stereotyped notions that women belong in the home with their children, that women are not serious members of the work force, and that women generally have a male breadwinner in their families to support them." And from those notions had emerged a body of law which, as she said, forces

> able-bodied women off the job, which denies them unemployment insurance once they've gone on mandatory maternity leave, denies them sick leave when their disability results from pregnancy, . . . which does not permit them to return to work at the time when they become physically able, often denies them seniority and other benefits which accrue to workers normally disabled, and finally—when they try to return to the job—often the jobs themselves are denied.

Williams had made the argument that pregnancy discrimination was unconstitutional sex discrimination. Writing against her for the Court, Justice Potter Stewart ruled that pregnancy discrimination constituted not illegal discrimination against women but legal discrimination between "pregnant women and nonpregnant persons."

The embarrassment was so obvious that a year later, when Justice Rehnquist tried to extend the argument to say that Title VII of Congress's Civil Rights Act of 1964 permits similar discrimination against pregnant women, Congress quickly passed the Pregnancy Discrimination Act to correct the Court's error and state the obvious: discriminating against the pregnant was discriminating against women.

But the victory of the obvious over the embarrassing did not undo *Geduldig v. Aiello*, which had interpreted not a law drafted by Congress but the Constitution drafted by the founding fathers. Despite congressional repudiation of its illogic, *Geduldig* lived on quietly, ready to do damage. *Bray* gave Justice Scalia the chance to trot out part of Justice Stewart's embarrassing *Geduldig* footnote: "While it is true that only women can become pregnant, it does not follow that every legislative classification concerning pregnancy is a sex-based classification." What that meant in *Bray* for obstruction of women from reaching abortion clinics was evident: only *pregnant* women are suffering—not all women. And in response to a dissent by Justice Stevens pointing out that Congress in the Pregnancy Discrimination Act had repudiated this logic, Scalia answered waggishly but precisely: "Congress understood *Geduldig* as we do." Congress understood, he seemed to say, that it can undo our misunderstandings of Congress but not our misunderstandings of the Constitution.

Scalia went one step further in refusing to acknowledge that the objects targeted for discrimination were women. The "characteristic that formed the basis of the targeting here was not womanhood, but the seeking of abortion." It drew a line not between women and men, but between women seeking an abortion and all other persons who were not. Such sophistry became possible only thanks to what Scalia called the "continuing vitality of *Geduldig*."

IF THE PHRASE *INVIDIOUSLY DISCRIMINATORY ANIMUS* conjured Scalia's hydra-like decision in *Bray*, of which one coil wrapped around *Geduldig v. Aiello*, why would the judges in the dark room raise that phrase? Perhaps they still hoped all three words might become accepted for use in VAWA. But Goldfarb and Nourse were unwilling, partly because in *Bray* Scalia had sought to define *invidiously discriminatory animus* by focusing on *invidious*. The word, his Webster's dictionary told him, meant "tending to excite odium, ill will, or envy;

likely to give offense; esp., unjustly and irritatingly discriminating."
As defined thus by Scalia, this *animus* seemed a hateful animus, and
perhaps even verged on *hatred*—precisely what Nourse and Goldfarb
had refused to accept as a requirement for invoking VAWA.

But the judges insisted that they turned to *animus* and *Bray* for
good reason. Thinking "we need proper historical sources here,"
Schroeder later recalled, she re-examined all the important civil rights
cases from after the Civil War through *Bray*, in which she saw remarkably appealing language concerning *animus*.

In the middle of *Bray*, as Scalia was rejecting the claim that opposition to abortion reflects an animus against women in general, he made
what seemed a concession:

> We do not think that the "animus" requirement can be met
> only by maliciously motivated, as opposed to assertedly benign
> (though objectively invidious), discrimination against women.

Scalia seemed to be saying that *animus* (in the sense of purpose)
against women might not stem from hatred (not be *maliciously motivated*) yet still be hateful (be *objectively invidious*). He continued that
such animus, though not demanding malice,

> does demand, however, at least a purpose that focuses upon
> women by reason of their sex—for example (to use an illus-
> tration of assertedly benign discrimination), the purpose of
> "saving" women because they are women from a combative,
> aggressive profession such as the practice of law.

Just as *Bray* revived one of law's great embarrassments regarding
women (*Geduldig*, 1974), it seemed to revile another: *Bradwell* from
1873. States could prohibit Myra Bradwell and other women, *Bradwell*
had said, from practicing law—a ruling that brought forth, from a
group of justices in 1873, the contention that the "law of the Creator"
limited women to marriage and motherhood. Further, *Bray* seemed
to offer a definition of *animus* that could bridge civil rights efforts
from the Civil Rights Act of 1871 to the Violence Against Women

Act of the 1990s. Sitting in the dark room with the judges and the feminists, Judge Marcus read aloud Scalia's expansive-seeming concept of discriminatory *animus*: "a purpose that focuses upon women by reason of their sex."

These judges, Nourse was coming to believe, were constructively trying to find a way to meet the concerns of the judiciary yet still to achieve something for women. For a time, she listened quietly as the three judges debated with Goldfarb over technicalities of existing civil rights law—section 1983, section 1985(3)—and heard Goldfarb lay out the argument that a legal problem existed because whole categories of violent crimes against women fall between the cracks of American civil rights law. At a certain point, Nourse would later say, "I really think I saw a light go off in Marcus's head." The light came when "Sally convinced him that there was a real problem. And before, he thought it was a fraud, he thought it was a *fake*, there was no real problem."

Discussion moved to possible language. A few days before, Judge Schroeder had suggested that VAWA might cover acts "motivated at least in part by animus against the gender of the victim." At one point, Judge Marcus said something that Goldfarb, after months of drafts and redrafts, found heartening. He said that the bill's "language won't be perfect," and she jotted that down in her notes. Some questions will remain, she understood him to mean, until cases are litigated and judges have the opportunity to apply the law to specific facts. She appreciated that. She felt he was easing her burden as a drafter by not forcing her to spell out the answer to every question that might arise.

THE JUDGES AND THE FEMINISTS left the dark room with a mood of mutual respect. Talking to Sally Goldfarb as they left, Pat Reuss called Judge Stanley Marcus *professorial*. Goldfarb called him *avuncular*, and Reuss teased her because Reuss had to go to a dictionary to find out that Goldfarb thought the judge acted like an uncle. For months after, Reuss would work her new word into conversations and correspondence: "Dear Sally, have an *avuncular* birthday." Even if silly, *avuncular* caught some qualities shared by the judges in the dark room: concern that was somehow familial, and a relation in which age and experience could both influence and be influenced by the perceptions of the young.

Concerning the meeting, Judge Marcus later reported in a formal letter to the House Judiciary Committee on some of the language that had been hammered out. Judge Schroeder reflected later on that meeting with warmth, as a gathering in which

> the feminists, for lack of a better word, were able to understand and articulate the concerns of the judges, and the judges were able to understand and articulate the concerns of the feminists.

Nourse, Judge Schroeder felt, was a "brilliant young woman" who could grasp the problems the judges were having with VAWA. And she was someone who, "unusual for a legislative aide," had put her heart into this legislation. But she also seemed, to Schroeder, primarily a lobbyist: "not out to create legislation so much as to get the legislation passed." As for the real lobbyist, Sally Goldfarb, Schroeder thought her "extremely knowledgeable about problems that women are experiencing." Goldfarb, she believed, had the qualities of a "first-rate lawyer": the ability to understand the other side and to adjust to its views. And Schroeder realized that Goldfarb also represented a coalition—that "she could not go out on a limb by herself. So she always had to go back to get consensus, and she did that brilliantly as well."

Reflecting on her months of debate and negotiation with both women on the shape of VAWA, and on the pivotal last meeting in the dark room, Judge Schroeder came to feel that dealing with young attorneys, "each so brilliant and so articulate," makes you "feel good about the legal profession, that there are people like that in it." Schroeder "worked so hard," she later explained

> because I wanted the federal government to realize the importance of this problem of violence against women in our country.

And it's something that has been kind of thought of as a state problem. And yet the resources of the federal government are so great that it needs to share them with the states.

Narrowed language for VAWA emerged from the dark room. Phrasing added by Nourse, which Judge Marcus mentioned with apparent approval months later in writing to a member of the House Judiciary Committee, included a tightened definition of crimes that VAWA covered. They must be not only "committed because of gender or on the basis of gender" but also must be "due, at least in part, to an animus based on the victim's gender."

Not long after the meeting, Nourse reported she was leaving government to accept a position as law professor at the University of Wisconsin. Soon afterward, Goldfarb won appointment as a professor at Rutgers School of Law in Camden, New Jersey—sister school to the law school in Newark that first appointed Ruth Bader Ginsburg a professor. Soon after Goldfarb joined the Rutgers faculty, Ginsburg became the second woman on the United States Supreme Court.

VAWA in late 1993, long protected by a no-amendment policy of Senators Joseph Biden and Orrin Hatch, itself became a late amendment to the vast congressional crime bill. On September 13, 1994, the Violence Against Women Act became law.

26

Reckoning at the Supreme Court

The Violence Against Women Act reached the Supreme Court in January of 2000, with a case brought by Christy Brzonkala, who said she had been raped in her first days as a college freshman. Her case arrived with a dramatic narrative that the Court was obligated, legally, to "accept as true." Opposing lawyers were making their primary legal challenge not against the veracity of Christy Brzonkala but against the law on which her case relied: the civil rights section of the Violence Against Women Act.

The facts before the Supreme Court were presented most clearly by the judge who wrote the majority opinion for a three-judge panel of the United States Court of Appeals for the Fourth Circuit. The story of Christy Brzonkala, as told at length by Judge Diana Gribbon Motz, began as follows. "On the evening of September 21, 1994," in the first weeks of Christy Brzonkala's first term as a freshman at Virginia Polytechnic Institute, known as Virginia Tech,

> Brzonkala and another female student met two men who Brzonkala knew only by their first names and their status as members of the Virginia Tech football team. Within thirty minutes of first meeting Brzonkala, these two men, later identified as Antonio Morrison and James Crawford, raped her.

Brzonkala and her friend met Morrison and Crawford on the third floor of the dormitory where Brzonkala lived. All four students talked for approximately fifteen minutes in a student dormitory room. Brzonkala's friend and Crawford then left the room.

Morrison immediately asked Brzonkala if she would have sexual intercourse with him. She twice told Morrison "no," but Morrison was not deterred. As Brzonkala got up to leave the room Morrison grabbed her, and threw her, face-up, on a bed. He pushed her down by the shoulders and disrobed her. Morrison turned off the lights, used his arms to pin down her elbows and pressed his knees against her legs. Brzonkala struggled and attempted to push Morrison off, but to no avail. Without using a condom, Morrison forcibly raped her.

Before Brzonkala could recover, Crawford came into the room and exchanged places with Morrison. Crawford also raped Brzonkala by holding down her arms and using his knees to pin her legs open. He, too, used no condom. When Crawford was finished, Morrison raped her for a third time, again holding her down and again without a condom.

When Morrison had finished with Brzonkala, he warned her "You better not have any fucking diseases." In the months following the rape, Morrison announced publicly in the dormitory's dining room that he "liked to get girls drunk and fuck the shit out of them."

Brzonkala at first told no one what happened. She withdrew from friends. She cut her hair short. She skipped classes.

Eventually she told a roommate she had been raped. Later she filed a complaint against both football players under the college's sexual assault policy. The complaint stayed internal partly because sexual assault, as Judge Motz noted, "is the only violent felony that Virginia Tech authorities do not automatically report to the university or town police."

During Tech's taped investigation, as Motz recounted, Morrison admitted that he had sexual intercourse with Christy Brzonkala even though she said "no." Although Tech decided it lacked evidence against Crawford (who denied the charge and was backed by a suitemate), it found Morrison guilty of sexual assault. It suspended him for two semesters.

Morrison's attorney threatened to sue Tech on procedural grounds: Morrison had been found guilty under a sexual assault policy that, though released for dissemination to students months before Brzonkala reached campus, had not yet been printed in the student handbook. Tech's dean of students went to Brzonkala's house, a four-hour journey from campus, to ask her to participate in a second hearing—"a mere technicality to cure the school's error," as Judge Motz put it.

Brzonkala learned later that she could not merely resubmit previous testimony from her witnesses. The university wanted sworn affidavits, which she lacked time to get. "In contrast," wrote Judge Motz, Tech gave Morrison "ample time to procure the sworn affidavits" of his student witnesses, and Tech "exacerbated this difficulty by refusing Brzonkala or her attorney access to the tape recordings of the first hearing, while granting Morrison and his attorney complete and early access to those tapes." Despite these limits, the committee found Morrison had "violated the University's Abusive Conduct Policy" and again imposed suspension for two semesters. When Morrison reappealed, a Tech provost reaffirmed that he had indeed violated Tech's policy on abusive conduct.

But comparing Morrison's offense to other cases involving abusive conduct, the provost judged his suspension "excessive." The Tech provost eased the penalty to a novel form of suspension—"deferred" until after Morrison graduated. He would lose no time away from Tech. The provost, as Judge Motz remarked later, "did not elaborate on the 'other cases'" that led Tech to devise nonexcessive penalties.

Tech did not tell Brzonkala that the man she said had raped her would return to campus with her for the fall of 1995. She learned from a sports page in the Washington Post. It said Morrison's "return to school also means a return to football," as linebacker on Tech's powerhouse team. (It went to that year's Sugar Bowl. By then Mor-

rison and Crawford had each been charged with new criminal violence—breaking the door of a bar; hit-and-run involving a car—and
so missed Tech's big game.)

Reading Christy Brzonkala's narrative of those facts, no judge
doubted that they met VAWA's definition of gender-motivated violence. The first federal judge to hear Brzonkala's case, Judge Jackson
L. Kiser of the United States District Court for the Western District
of Virginia at Roanoke, found against her in 1996 even though he
spent much time affirming that her case met the much-debated *animus* test—that the "crime of violence" she suffered be due at least in
part "to an animus based on the victim's gender." A gang rape, he
said, "indicates a conspiracy of disrespect." Further, by gang-raping
a woman they had met only a few minutes earlier, the judge said,
the rapists showed they "had little if any knowledge of Brzonkala's
personality." In a rape not based on personality, said the judge, "an
inference of gender animus is more reasonable."

A gang rapist's statement to his victim that she "better not have
any fucking diseases," the judge said, gave further evidence of the
"disrespect that Morrison had for Brzonkala." And even "more relevant to gender animus," the judge ruled, was that Morrison had
stated, in the presence of at least one woman, "I like to get girls drunk
and fuck the shit out of them." A rapist need not say "I hate women,"
added the judge, in order to be sued under VAWA.

But finally, Judge Kiser ruled, the details of any attack on Christy
Brzonkala in this case did not matter. On grounds of federalism—"if
our federal system is to survive," as he said—Congress lacked authority, under either the commerce clause or the Fourteenth Amendment,
to pass the Violence Against Women Act. Congress, he said, cannot
"cure all of the ills of mankind"—phrasing that made violence by
men seem, like sin or slavery, biblically ancient. Judge Kiser ruled
unconstitutional the civil rights section of VAWA, beginning its route
to the Supreme Court.

FOUR DAYS BEFORE ORAL ARGUMENT at the Supreme Court, Christy
Brzonkala stood awkwardly at a podium for a press conference orga-

nized by NOW Legal Defense. She looked like the athlete she had been in high school, the center on a basketball team that reached the finals of the Virginia state championships. But now, shoulders slumping, she looked as if she had been brought before the press to describe a bad loss. "It's too traumatic for me to recall the details of that night," she began. "I don't want to keep reliving it. But I can tell you this: rape is like having your soul torn out." As for VAWA, she continued, its passage declared that "rape is a brutal form of discrimination. Women are raped because they are women."

When reporters asked what she was doing now, she said she had become a "local Washingtonite," working in a restaurant. She said she planned to go back to college, but when a reporter asked how soon, she said she had no idea: "I don't try to plan any more." A reporter asked her to speak on an "emotional level" about setbacks in her case. "It's been tough," she said. "My whole take on the thing is that, you know, I should go as far as I can go so that I don't look twenty years down the line and say: I could have done something else"

In earlier rounds in district courts, VAWA had posted seventeen wins and only two losses (including Brzonkala's before Judge Kiser). Further, following that loss, Brzonkala's case had won before the panel of three judges at the court of appeals, giving VAWA a victory in its first test in an appeals court.

The route to the Supreme Court took a sharp turn soon after that victory. On the three-judge panel was a dissenter, Judge Michael Luttig, who had been appointed to the court of appeals in 1991 (it then had no women). In the weeks before joining the court, while he was still employed by the Justice Department, Luttig had given Clarence Thomas, then a nominee to the Supreme Court, what amounted to a crash course in constitutional law to assure Thomas could pass tests thrown at him by Biden's committee on the judiciary. A former clerk to Antonin Scalia (before he joined the Supreme Court) and to Warren Burger (when he was chief justice), Luttig continued working to prepare Thomas to respond to charges by Anita Hill and the ensuing debate about sexual harassment—helping Thomas through times when he wailed, as Luttig recalled, "These people have destroyed my life." In Luttig's judicial chambers hung a photo of Justice Thomas in judicial robes that is inscribed to Luttig: "This would not have been possible without you! Thanks so much, buddy!"

Luttig's dissent succeeded against the case of Christy Brzonkala: his colleagues on the court of appeals agreed to rehear the case as a full court, *en banc*. He emerged with a victory of seven judges (including one woman) to four judges (including one woman, Judge Motz). Opening his triumphal opinion, he wrote in the voice of men who framed the Constitution, "We the people, distrustful of power," he began, "provided that our federal government would be one of enumerated powers, and that all power unenumerated would be reserved to the several States and to ourselves." Here was the voice of a true believer, as Nourse once imagined, in the federalist pantheon. Here was an echo to an era when "we the people" could refer merely to males.

Judge Luttig's triumph at the court of appeals meant that the future of VAWA—which had been upheld in every court decision except the ones written by Kiser and Luttig—would be settled at the Supreme Court. In the years after Congress passed VAWA and after two football players allegedly attacked Brzonkala, however, two important cases arrived at the Court. It would use them to shift the foundations underlying the Violence Against Women Act.

THE FIRST FOUNDATION-SHIFTING CASE was called *Lopez*, for the twelfth-grader, Alfonso Lopez Jr., who carried a pistol into his school and was subsequently prosecuted under a federal law known as the Gun-Free School Zones Act of 1990. Since *Lopez* concerned regulating guns, which the federal government had done for years, what seemed unusual was that the Act had been ruled unconstitutional by a court of appeals. That court opposed the Act based on what seemed merely a procedural lapse: Congress did not make findings that the law was based on the commerce clause—did not engage in hearings like those organized by Nourse before the Senate Judiciary Committee, which had located both the national need and the constitutional grounding for VAWA. Despite this lapse, which seemed correctable by hearings, Congress's power to make such a law seemed solid. The

Supreme Court had upheld congressional authority under the commerce clause in all cases for more than half a century.

At oral argument before the Supreme Court in *Lopez*, Solicitor General Drew Days began by asserting that the lower court's "extraordinary step of invalidating an act of Congress as beyond its power under the Commerce Clause" had emerged from that lower court's misreading of Supreme Court precedent. Justice Scalia, asking the morning's first question, suggested that precedent could change. The Court, Scalia suggested, might be "concerned that the original understandings and structural theories that underlay the Federal system have been so eroded that that whole system is in danger."

Following Scalia came Justices O'Connor and Rehnquist. Years earlier, after losing a case that might have limited the commerce clause, they had written together that "this Court will in time again assume its constitutional responsibility" to limit congressional action. Their questions in *Lopez* suggested that time had arrived.

Returning the Constitution to a limited role was part of what O'Connor had been put on the Supreme Court to accomplish. Her nomination in 1981 culminated an effort by Republican presidents to nominate not just a woman but a conservative one. This endeavor to appoint what Richard Nixon called a "strict constructionist" had involved William Rehnquist since 1969. At the Justice Department, Rehnquist had the job of creating a list of potential conservative appointees. In the process, he presented the White House with his own definition of strict constructionist: a judge who "will generally not be favorably inclined towards claims of either criminal defendants or civil rights plaintiffs."

Nixon had the chance from 1969 to 1971 to appoint four such justices, in two pairs. Within the second pair he sought to score political points by appointing a woman, he said, "if she's a conservative. Now if she's a liberal, the hell with it." Rehnquist told a reporter that he himself could not be nominated because "I'm not a woman, and I'm not mediocre." To his inner circle, Nixon joked that maybe Rehnquist could "get a sex change." Soon Nixon concluded he could "never," according to his assistant H. R. Haldeman, "find a conservative enough woman for the Supreme Court." Nixon then appointed

Rehnquist, sending to the Supreme Court a justice who knew that his power followed from an aborted attempt at affirmative action.

At the start of his presidency in 1981, President Reagan shared Nixon's problem. Most women who could become judges failed to align, as a Justice Department official put it, with Reagan's "strict constructionist political philosophy." Seeking a Supreme Court justice, Reagan found an exception—Justice Rehnquist's longtime friend since their days in law school and Chief Justice Burger's new acquaintance since their houseboat vacation on Lake Powell—Sandra Day O'Connor. In the months before her nomination in 1981, O'Connor had added to her conservative credentials. At a high-powered conference on federalism, she gave a talk that became a law review article. She proposed tactics to keep civil rights cases out of federal courts and affirmatively quoted Justice Rehnquist. She suggested leaving many such cases to the states, much as opponents of VAWA's civil rights section years later would argue that states should handle women's claims. O'Connor's article, appearing soon before her nomination, signaled she was unlikely to disagree often with Rehnquist. In the decade following the passage of VAWA in 1994, they would agree in 70 percent of non-unanimous cases, making her Rehnquist's second-most-reliable ally. During his entire career, he voted more often with her than with any other justice. Rehnquist and O'Connor both reached the Court thanks to presidents who hoped to nominate a conservative woman and restrain the liberalism of courts and Congress.

During oral argument in *Lopez*, O'Connor and Rehnquist asked what Congress could not do. Days declined to speculate. Scalia asked Days if Congress could enact a "Federal domestic relations law" that would govern such disputes as divorce. Scalia's language echoed Rehnquist's 1991 charge that VAWA could involve "federal courts in a whole host of domestic relations disputes." As Solicitor General Days began to offer areas in which Congress had already legislated, Justice Scalia interrupted and named the area on his mind: "Domestic violence." Apparently referring to VAWA while considering *Lopez*, he added with vehemence: "I'm aware." VAWA had become law eight weeks before.

The end arrived for a half-century of congressional authority under the commerce clause when the chief justice announced the majority

Lopez decision on April 26, 1995. For a 5–4 court, he declared that the Gun-Free School Zones Act violated the Constitution. After the chief's brief announcement, Justice Breyer made the rare move of reading aloud from his dissent, joined by Justices Stevens, Souter, and Ginsburg. Speaking at greater length than the chief justice, Breyer argued that upholding the act would have been "consistent with, if not dictated by, this Court's prior precedent" and would "simply recognize that Congress had a 'rational basis' for finding a significant connection between guns in or near schools and (through their effect on education) the interstate and foreign commerce they threaten."

To justify ending the Court's deference to Congress, Rehnquist went back to "first principles," as he put it, and indeed to James Madison, writing in *The Federalist* to say that "the powers delegated by the proposed Constitution to the federal government are few and defined." Key to Rehnquist's analysis was his claim that the Gun-Free School Zones Act had "nothing to do with 'commerce'"—regardless of government arguments about economic and commercial losses caused by increases in crime or decreases in educational attainment.

Rather than deny that a weakened educational system could weaken commerce, Chief Justice Rehnquist leapt beyond *Lopez*. He raised the twin specters that Congress might try to regulate "all violent crime" and "family law," including disputes involving divorce and child custody. In deciding *Lopez*, the chief justice evidently aimed at the nascent Violence Against Women Act and what he had called, while lobbying against it in 1991, its potential to involve the federal courts in a whole host of disputes about domestic relations. His newest ally, Clarence Thomas, added that *Lopez* only began the Court's backward push toward "the original understanding of that Clause." Looking for rational findings from Congress should yield to looking two centuries back for "first principles." If Rehnquist wanted a trap for VAWA, he now had one.

In the wake of Chief Justice Rehnquist's decision in *Lopez*, Linda Greenhouse of the *New York Times* noted that "the Federal judiciary's policy-making arm, which Chief Justice Rehnquist heads," had opposed recent congressional action against crime, including what she called "household violence." She suggested the likelihood of upcoming collisions between the Court and Congress: the "stunning decision" in *Lopez*, she said, offered "a forceful reminder not only of the Court's raw power—nine people, divided 5 to 4, invalidated a law that two houses of Congress and the President of the United States approved five years ago—but also of its [the Court's] inevitable role in shaping the country's ongoing political dialogue." In contrast to other commentators including the head of the Office of Legal Counsel in the Justice Department—who construed *Lopez* as a "relatively narrow decision"—Greenhouse linked *Lopez* back to past attacks on VAWA and forward to future ones.

A SECOND FOUNDATION-SHIFTING CASE, *City of Boerne v. Flores*, reached the Supreme Court in 1997, when congressional power under the Fourteenth Amendment met its attack in another case that seemed remote from VAWA. The case began after two members of the Native American Church, who used peyote as a sacrament, were fired from their jobs at a "private drug rehabilitation agency." When they applied to their state government for unemployment benefits, Oregon would not pay them because they lost their jobs after breaking the law. Those laws made no exception for using a drug as a religious sacrament.

When the peyote case went to the Supreme Court in 1990, the Court sided with Oregon against the Native Americans. Writing an opinion for a 5–4 majority, Justice Scalia diverged from a long-standing test that required states to show a "compelling interest" in order to justify limits on the free exercise of religion as guaranteed by the Constitution. Widespread outrage led Congress to respond. Its response partly resembled creation of the Pregnancy Discrimination Act in 1978 after the Supreme Court declared that Congress had not intended the Civil Rights Act of 1964 to outlaw discrimination against the pregnant. What Congress drafted in response, the Religious Freedom Restoration Act in 1993, explicitly restored the compelling-interest test. No law, said the Act, may substantially burden the exercise of religion unless that law serves a "compelling governmental interest." Congress relied on the Fourteenth Amendment's section 5, the same section that partly supported VAWA and, earlier, such civil rights laws as the Voting Rights Act of 1965. Congressional support was nearly unanimous, with support from all but three senators and unanimity in the House. Unlike the Pregnancy Discrimination Act, however, which told the Supreme Court how to interpret an act of Congress, the Religious Freedom Restoration Act told the Supreme Court how to interpret the Constitution. Congress claimed to be exercising its Fourteenth Amendment power to "enforce" guarantees of the Constitution.

When the Religious Freedom Restoration Act reached the Supreme Court in 1997 in *Boerne*, the justices rejected Congress's claim to tell the Court how to interpret the Constitution. Writing for a solid majority, Justice Kennedy rebuffed Congress's power to define what test the Court should use to judge constitutionality.

To differentiate a law that Congress could not adopt from one that it could, such as the Voting Rights Act of 1965, Justice Kennedy in *Boerne* added a new test to the Supreme Court's review of congressional efforts to enforce constitutional guarantees. When Congress legislates under the Fourteenth Amendment in order to prevent constitutional harm—such as harming the exercise of religion—there must be "a congruence and proportionality between the injury to be prevented or remedied and the means adopted" to address the injury.

The Supreme Court's 1997 action to limit congressional power under the Fourteenth Amendment, partly by assessing "congruence and proportionality," meant that the Supreme Court had dramatically altered American law in the three years since Congress enacted VAWA. VAWA had left Congress in 1994 with two foundations: the Constitution's commerce clause and the Constitution's Fourteenth Amendment. Within three years, the Supreme Court had battered both.

The undercutting of constitutional support for VAWA gave Judge Luttig grounds for both *we-the-people* triumphalism and an assertion that the attorneys for Christy Brzonkala knew their VAWA case had become a loser. The decisions in *Lopez* and *Flores*, he trumpeted for his court of appeals majority, had "all but preordained" their defeat. So confident was Judge Luttig that he ventured a defense of states' powers to create a "marital rape exemption." He defended states' rights to protect rapist-husbands on the grounds that, although a rape exemption may represent "regrettable public policy," such policy choices "have traditionally been made not by Congress, but by the States." The grim joke regrettably remained: If you can't rape your wife, who can you rape?

THE MORNING FOR THE SUPREME COURT to hear oral arguments on Christy Brzonkala's case and VAWA began with temperatures just above freezing and a chill wind blowing. Visitors hoping to hear the argument, scheduled to begin at 10:00 a.m., arrived before 6:00 a.m. to line up on the marble plaza in front of the Court. By dawn the number of would-be spectators standing in frigid wind on the Supreme Court plaza passed sixty people. Police officers began telling new arrivals that they were too late to hear the case. Around the corner from the plaza, another line of spectators was growing inside the Court building. In this line, open only to attorneys admitted to practice in the Supreme Court, stood Sally Goldfarb. Victoria Nourse, now pregnant with her second child, could not manage the trip east from her new job as a law professor at the University of Wisconsin. Just ahead stood Goldfarb's colleague from NOW Legal Defense, Julie Goldscheid, who would make the first of the day's two arguments for VAWA. Goldscheid, whose efforts for women's rights went back to the early years of sexual harassment law when she worked for Working Women's Institute in the basement of a church, was listening closely to last-minute thoughts from another attorney waiting in the spectator line, Professor Judith Resnik of Yale Law School. Near the line's front stood Lynn Hecht Schafran. After the line moved and she entered the courtroom, Schafran found herself seated in the Court's front row and facing her former professor, Ruth Bader Ginsburg. More prominently positioned in the front row was another attorney who had played a pivotal role in the creation of VAWA. Dressed in a dark suit and turning to talk with friends and allies before argument began, placed almost precisely opposite the chief justice, was Senator Joseph Biden.

To open oral argument, Goldscheid stepped forward to take the first ten minutes, to be followed by the solicitor general of the United States, Seth Waxman, also supporting VAWA. "Congress enacted the civil rights remedy of the Violence Against Women Act," Goldscheid began, "to remove one of the most persistent barriers to women's full equality and free participation in the economy: discriminatory gender-based violence." With this connection of equality to economy, Gold-scheid put VAWA on both of its constitutional supports: its origin in discrimination (linked to the Constitution's Fourteenth Amendment) and its impact on the economy (linked to the Constitution's commerce clause). She did not get far.

Justice Scalia broke in with questions: a Congress that could enact VAWA, he suggested, could also enact a "general criminal statute" against violence such as "a federal rape law or a federal robbery law, right?" The attack, echoing his earlier strategy in *Lopez*, met a well-prepared reply from Goldscheid. Each VAWA case, she pointed out, must show discriminatory motivation—the much-discussed *animus* requirement—which was typified in Christy Brzonkala's case by her attacker's proclamation that he "liked to get girls drunk and fuck the shit out of them."

The animus requirement, Julie Goldscheid argued, meant that VAWA's power under the commerce clause found limitation as well as support in the Fourteenth Amendment's protection against discrimination. Far from a general criminal statute, VAWA was both noncriminal (it enabled a civil suit) and nongeneral (only discriminatory animus, of the sort the Fourteenth Amendment empowered Congress to combat, could permit a lawsuit).

Scalia, without acknowledging discrimination or limitation, pressed the point that VAWA might allow Congress to enact "general Federal criminal laws on all subjects because all crime affects interstate commerce" and even to "sweep away all State laws." Far from worrying they would be swept away, Goldscheid countered, states had showed strong support for VAWA. Not only had attorneys general from thirty-eight states supported VAWA in a letter to Congress, but thirty-six had submitted a brief on its behalf to the Supreme Court. Furthermore, she argued, Congress should retain power to fight discriminatory gender-based violence because discrimination is "uniquely and traditionally an area of Federal concern."

At this point, seven minutes into the argument, another justice entered: Sandra Day O'Connor. Her vote was one Goldscheid needed.

Although attuned to arguments about discrimination, O'Connor as far back as 1981, in the law review article published shortly before her nomination, had tried to keep federal courts from taking civil rights cases that could be left to state courts. Now questioning Goldscheid, and pointing out that gender bias might be documentable in inadequate alimony for women, O'Connor wondered if Goldscheid's theory would allow Congress to legislate in such areas as divorce— allowing new sorts of discrimination claims to reach federal courts.

As Goldscheid tried to work through O'Connor's question, another justice broke in: what would make unconstitutional the passage, by Congress, of a general murder statute? Back in stronger territory, Julie Goldscheid drew what seemed a clear line: Without a showing of discriminatory animus, a federal murder law would fail the animus test set by the Court in *Griffin v. Breckenridge*. Ten minutes into the argument, her time was up. The chief justice interrupted her in mid-sentence. She ceded the floor to her ally in argument, Solicitor General Seth Waxman.

Almost as soon as Waxman began, a question from the chief justice stopped him: was the government arguing not just on the basis of the commerce clause but also on the basis of the Fourteenth Amendment? Indeed we are, said the solicitor general. Justice Kennedy stepped in to urge the solicitor general to please confine himself to the commerce clause.

Trying to save both VAWA and future congressional legislation, Waxman told the Court that its *Lopez* majority had authored a four-part test for future legislation by Congress under the commerce clause. Deferentially, the justices gave the solicitor general two almost-uninterrupted minutes to portray their opinion in a way that might help his case. Just as he reached his climactic point four, with which he hoped to tie VAWA to a truly federal concern—and tie back elegantly to Julie Goldscheid's best point, that discrimination is "uniquely and traditionally" a federal worry—the solicitor general faced an interruption that he could not ignore. Sandra Day O'Connor interjected that she, too, wanted VAWA tied to a federal concern. She offered a way to make the tie: Congress could give the justices a jurisdictional hook. If justices are trying to find that legislation is constitutional under the commerce clause, she said, "the Court has been helped many times" by legislation that contains "some kind of jurisdictional hook that the conduct that took place" did so "in interstate commerce. There is no such hook here."

She wanted a hook that VAWA could have possessed. VAWA already had a hook, attempted at least, to the Fourteenth Amendment: an attack must show discriminatory *animus*. Justice O'Connor apparently wanted a comparable hook to the commerce clause: an attack must, for example, make its victim unable to enter the labor market as she planned, perhaps because the attack made her unable to continue at college. Christy Brzonkala's story embodied such hooks. Unable to study after an attack, she said, she stopped attending classes and needed to withdraw from Virginia Tech. When she learned her alleged rapist had been readmitted to the university for the start of the 1995 football season, she left the school and then moved out of state to get a job (thus moving in interstate commerce) in a bar—a lower level in the labor market than many college graduates aspire to.

Although Christy Brzonkala's case would have attached to a hook under the commerce clause, no drafter of VAWA anticipated a need in the years before the Supreme Court used *Lopez* to change the rules. The solicitor general tried to argue that Congress had deliberately omitted such a hook, but his explanations opened the way to counterattacks. Justice O'Connor argued that his approach could justify creating "a federal remedy for alimony or child support." Justice Scalia suggested that VAWA assumed the states were "bad actors." Chief Justice Rehnquist added that problems encountered by women in state courts with "archaic stereotypes" could appear also in federal courts.

The solicitor general, forced to parry one challenge after another from the same justices whose votes in *Lopez* had undercut VAWA's footing on the commerce clause, barely managed to return to the original grounding of VAWA: an effort to deliver equality that had its basis in the Fourteenth Amendment's guarantee of "equal protection of the laws." As the solicitor general began to discuss equality, the chief justice informed him that time had run out for his defense of VAWA.

Outdoors on the steps of the Supreme Court minutes after the end of oral argument, standing in light rain beneath an umbrella that carried the seal of the Senate, Senator Biden made (as the solicitor general could not) an argument for equality: "Men don't choose not to take jobs" for fear of gender-motivated violence, he said, but "women do alter their life patterns." And by countering states that fail to protect women against gender-based violence, he continued, this law "empowers my daughter and granddaughters." The key to the survival of VAWA, he predicted, were Justices Kennedy and O'Connor. Within that building, he said, gesturing to the marble steps behind him, the justices were engaged in a "titanic struggle" to see if a bare majority would dramatically shrink the authority of the legislature elected by the people.

Less publicly, as they walked away from the Court, supporters of VAWA worried about the key question raised by Justice Sandra Day O'Connor: What about adding an explicit hook to the commerce clause in order to give the Court what she called *help*? The inference seemed clear. If the drafters of VAWA could help O'Connor with a hook, she could help them with a vote. But the hook and her vote could come only at some future point with a rewritten VAWA. As Sally Goldfarb rushed to catch a train from Washington back to her home in New Jersey, she wondered aloud whether VAWA's drafters would have wanted to craft a bill narrow enough to win with this Supreme Court. She wasn't sure.

As the day turned from drizzle back to damp wind, Christy Brzonkala stood opposite a side door of the Supreme Court and next to the Washington headquarters of NOW Legal Defense, where some attorneys and reporters had gathered. She wore a gray jacket over black pants and blouse, purchased after a friend told her that she should try to dress well for her day at the Court. Preparing to take final questions from a television reporter, she tried to draw warmth from a cup of cold coffee. With the camera off, she said she felt as if she had stayed awake for the past three nights, ever since the press conference when she had been asked to talk on an "emotional" level.

As Christy Brzonkala shivered, an NBC reporter told her that an attorney for one of her alleged assailants had suggested that she brought charges because the men allegedly involved were black. No, she said, "when a woman is raped, she doesn't see a color. She sees an animal."

Would Brzonkala, the reporter asked, talk about her current boy-friend? Wasn't he an African-American? A staffer at NOW Legal Defense stepped forward saying, "You don't have to answer that."

"It's OK," Brzonkala reassured her. "I was brought up in a fam-ily," she said to the NBC camera, where race was "no problem." Yes, she explained, she and her boyfriend had been together two years; she had wanted him to come today, but he preferred to stay away. As she spoke, her father and mother stood within earshot. Brzonkala contin-ued that now, living away from home with a job she liked, she felt her life had moved on.

But for a while earlier you were, the reporter asked as the cam-era ran, "suicidal"? Again the staffer moved to intervene, and again Brzonkala waved her off. For a "brief time," she said, she had been suicidal. She had been trying to "figure out who I was."

Then the newsman asked his toughest question: did Brzonkala ever feel she was a pawn? She pondered, looking taken aback. No, not really like a pawn, she said. She paused and then added, More "like a queen." Again she looked like a tired athlete, struggling to find words after a loss.

In closing, the reporter asked, did she have anything she wanted to add? No, she said first, but then, looking game, she raised her right hand. To the camera she said, "Women rule."

CHRISTY BRZONKALA WAS WRONG. Chief Justice Rehnquist, fearing the loss of O'Connor's vote, had lobbied her. After a late-afternoon phone call in which she told him he had her support, he said, "Well, we got it"—his fifth vote.

In the opening paragraph of his opinion, for a 5–4 majority, Chief Justice Rehnquist named the three cases that doomed VAWA: *Lopez* (1995), together with *Harris* (1883) and the *Civil Rights Cases* (1883). With these cases as precedent, Christy Brzonkala and VAWA had little chance. Rehnquist buried, in mid-paragraph, a single sentence about an attack: "Brzonkala alleges that, within 30 minutes of meeting Mor-rison and Crawford, they assaulted and repeatedly raped her."

As for words that showed *animus*, Rehnquist cut them. What Mor-

rison allegedly said to Brzonkala became "You better not have any
. . . diseases." Dots replaced *fucking*. What Morrison allegedly said
later became "that he 'liked' to get girls drunk and . . ." The dots, said
Rehnquist, replaced "boasting, debased remarks about what Morrison
would do to women, vulgar remarks that cannot fail to shock and
offend." Thanks to Rehnquist, readers could stay unoffended. The
dots replaced "fuck the shit out of them." The chief justice had cut
animus—and animosity—against women.

What mattered most was Rehnquist's *Lopez* decision, written after
VAWA passed Congress. VAWA, Rehnquist now wrote, flunked the
tests he had prepared in *Lopez*: The gender-motivated crimes of violence that VAWA fought are not "economic activity." Congressional
findings, even as numerous as VAWA's, may be judged insufficient by
the Court. Congressional drafting of VAWA provided no jurisdictional
hook to the commerce clause.

Regarding the lack of that hook, the chief justice seemed to chide
Congress. "Although *Lopez* makes clear that such a jurisdictional element would lend support to the argument that [the Violence Against
Women Act] is sufficiently tied to interstate commerce," he wrote,
"Congress elected" to create a remedy for such violence that might
not reach beyond state lines. Leaving unstated that he wrote *Lopez*
after Congress wrote VAWA, Rehnquist left readers guessing whether
he had designed *Lopez* to trap VAWA. In stopping VAWA, he held
together the same bloc of Justices (Kennedy, O'Connor, Scalia, and
Thomas) that had aligned in *Lopez* to cut back, after five decades, the
Court's consistent record of deferring to Congress in its enforcement
of the commerce clause.

Four dissenting justices opposed the chief justice. The Violence
Against Women Act, wrote Justice Souter, "would have passed
muster" under the commerce clause in the Supreme Court at any
time between 1942 (when the Court ruled that interstate commerce
included growing food at home to eat at home) and 1995, when *Lopez*
changed the rules. Noting that homegrown food had been ruled by
the Court to affect interstate commerce because it could potentially
affect the market for food beyond state lines, Justice Souter pointed
to more direct effects of VAWA: "Supply and demand for goods in

VIOLENCE (1990–2000)

interstate commerce will also be affected by the deaths of 2,000 to 4,000 women annually at the hands of domestic abusers, and by the reduction in the work force by the 100,000 or more rape victims who lose their jobs each year or are forced to quit." A cost estimate by Congress for 1993, he said, reached $5 billion. He pointed to four years of congressional hearings that produced detailed findings, to the support of state attorneys general, and to evidence from twenty-one state gender-bias task forces that, he said, gave Congress a rational basis to believe that "crimes of violence motivated by gender have a substantial adverse effect on interstate commerce" that justifies creating "a federal civil rights remedy aimed exactly at violence against women." Justices Stevens, Ginsburg, and Breyer joined Justice Souter in his failed effort to use the commerce clause to save VAWA. Until thirty years earlier, the Court had employed no more than rational-basis scrutiny in assessing legislation that hurt women. Now it was giving harsher scrutiny—asking Congress to have more than a rational basis—to reject laws passed by Congress to help women.

CHIEF JUSTICE REHNQUIST'S UNDERCUTTING of the commerce clause left VAWA with a last leg to stand on, its inspiration from the days in 1991 when Victoria Nourse began her research in the Library of Congress. Her earliest drafting grounded VAWA on the Fourteenth Amendment, passed soon after the Civil War, which guaranteed that a state could not "deny to any person within its jurisdiction the equal protection of the laws."

As if toying with Nourse's inspiration, Chief Justice Rehnquist began by recalling the broad power granted to Congress by the Fourteenth Amendment to enforce that guarantee of equality. He then recalled the two civil rights acts of the 1870s against which the Supreme Court ruled in 1883: the Civil Rights Act of 1871, the so-called Ku Klux Klan Act, enacted by Congress to end the widespread slaughter and intimidation of black citizens by white gangs across wide regions of the South; and the Civil Rights Act of 1875, enacted to overcome white resistance to granting blacks equal access to accommodation such as inns and to transportation such as railroads.

Rehnquist aligned the origins of the civil rights acts in the 1870s with the origins of VAWA in 1991. "There is abundant evidence," he wrote, "to show that the Congresses that enacted the Civil Rights Acts of 1871 and 1875 had a purpose similar to that of Congress in enacting [VAWA]: There were state laws on the books bespeaking equality of treatment, but in the administration of these laws there was discrimination." Rehnquist aligned also with Nourse's argument, which she had drawn from studies of gender bias: when it came to violence against women, some state laws and some state courts delivered inequality of treatment.

Adding historical depth, Chief Justice Rehnquist quoted congressmen who in the 1870s had supported civil rights. Representative James A. Garfield argued for federal civil rights legislation on the grounds that some states—even those "where the laws are just and equal on their face"—deny citizens equality through a mix of "systematic maladministration" of the laws or a "neglect or refusal to enforce" those laws. Senator Charles Sumner, author of the Civil Rights Act of 1875, which he died fighting for, condemned state courts for failure to enforce state legislation that mimicked federal civil rights laws but amounted to merely "a dead letter."

The alignment of VAWA with these civil rights acts, said Chief Justice Rehnquist, did not help VAWA. It hurt VAWA. The 1871 Act reached the Court in 1883 when R. G. Harris challenged it for empowering federal law enforcement officials to arrest "private persons" for "conspiring to deprive any one of the equal protection of the laws enacted by the State." Chief Justice Rehnquist, without explaining that Harris had led a lynch mob, which killed a black man after pulling him from custody in a Tennessee jail, said that "we concluded" in 1883 that the Fourteenth Amendment did not empower Congress to resist the discriminatory "action of private individuals." (Perhaps only a justice of the Supreme Court can say, without irony, that *we* reached our conclusion twelve decades ago.)

"We reached a similar conclusion," continued the chief justice, in repudiating the effort by the Civil Rights Act of 1875 to desegregate America's hotels, theaters, railway cars, and similar places where people gather. The so-called *Civil Rights Cases* of 1883, he said, removed authority from Congress, under the Fourteenth Amendment, to attack "purely private" discrimination. He did not say that those later cases gave support to the anti-black laws of the Jim Crow era. Both cases of 1883 helped establish the view that the Fourteenth Amendment, as Rehnquist stated, "prohibits only state action."

Briefly he raised a contrary view, expressed by optimistic legal analysts and some of his fellow justices, that a consensus had emerged on the Supreme Court that its anti-civil-rights cases of the 1880s had been wrongly decided: that its wrongful crippling of the civil rights acts and thus of the Fourteenth Amendment could be viewed as one of its nineteenth-century errors, committed in a time of racism and national depression. Despite the lingering of the so-called *state-action requirement*, epitomized by the Court's 1883 ruling in *Harris* that federal prosecutors could combat only a lynch mob that received support from the action of state officials, those old cases seemed moribund. By one measure of currency, the legal citation service known as Shepard's, not since 1913 had a majority of the Supreme Court explicitly followed either *Harris* or the *Civil Rights Cases*.

Going directly against assertions that the decision in "the *Civil Rights Cases* is no longer good law," in his VAWA opinion of 2000 Chief Justice Rehnquist re-entered a legal battle in which he had earlier made the case—in his 1952 memo defending the 1896 *Plessy* case and its separate-but-equal doctrine—for what seemed the losing side of segregation. To redefine that battle, he now sought to divide and conquer the six justices who had sought, in the *Guest* case of 1966, to inter those embarrassing cases of 1883.

Attacking Justice Brennan while he attacked VAWA, Chief Justice Rehnquist worked against Brennan's 1966 argument that, as Rehnquist put it, "the *Civil Rights Cases* were wrongly decided" and that Congress thus retained the power under the Fourteenth Amendment to "prohibit actions by private individuals." Rehnquist countered that Brennan had the support of only three justices. The other three whom Brennan claimed as supporters, said Rehnquist, agreed on mere *dicta*—a judge's opinion that is not a legal opinion. Rehnquist did not quote at length from their opinion, written by Justice Clark on behalf also of Justices Black and Fortas. Clark, after noting that the

Court in *Guest* had avoided the question whether Congress has the power to punish private action, and after opposing the inference that avoidance signaled agreement, went on to conclude with "no doubt" that the Fourteenth Amendment "empowers the Congress to enact laws punishing all conspiracies—with or without state action—that interfere with Fourteenth Amendment rights."

Although the combined writings of Brennan and Clark had produced what observers of the Court including Brennan saw as a majority of six votes in support of civil rights, now Rehnquist chose to portray them as merely two groups of three votes that failed to total six. With his five votes, Rehnquist resurrected the almost-buried judgments of the Supreme Court of 1883. That old Court's decisions to eviscerate the civil rights acts of 1871 and 1875 were "correct," he said. Those decisions doomed the civil rights section of VAWA.

As he revived the ill-named *Civil Rights Cases*, Rehnquist made no effort to inter the language of their author, Justice Joseph P. Bradley. Writing in 1883, Bradley demeaned recently freed blacks as "the special favorite of the laws." Blacks should be protected, said Bradley, not specially but only by "ordinary modes." He did not mention that lynching of blacks had become, itself, an ordinary mode.

Justice Bradley, a decade before he suggested how to protect blacks, had suggested how to protect women: men would protect women. Before terminating the Civil Rights Act of 1875, Bradley had written the following as he helped terminate a different quest, that of Myra Bradwell to become a lawyer:

> Man is, or should be, woman's protector and defender. The natural and proper timidity and delicacy which belong to the female sex evidently unfits it for many of the occupations of civil life.

Man *should* protect woman, Bradley helped determine for a unanimous Supreme Court, from occupations such as practicing law. This was the decision that Ruth Bader Ginsburg, in her first Supreme Court brief of 1971, had referred to as "old debris"—overdue for clearing away by the Court but too petty to merit critique. Man should defend woman, Bradley added, because the "paramount destiny and mission of woman are to fulfil the noble and benign offices of wife and mother. This is the law of the Creator."

So ended the decade-long quest to create a civil rights law prohibiting violence against women—impaled on an opinion by a long-dead justice who had invoked his Creator to close the profession of law against women. So ended also what Joseph Biden viewed as the most important section of a bill that represented his "single most important legislative accomplishment." Although a nineteenth-century justice's stricture on women seemed mere debris to Ruth Ginsburg in her younger days, now his restriction on civil rights loomed large.

For Christy Brzonkala, some vindication came, but only in small forms. Even before her case reached the Supreme Court, she learned that one of the men whom she said attacked her, James Crawford, had been arrested with another football player on the charge that they raped a female student in their apartment and had been suspended by the college. He later, though denying guilt, accepted a one-year suspended sentence and admitted the prosecution had sufficient evidence to convict him for aggravated sexual battery. Soon after oral argument at the Court, Brzonkala settled a case for discrimination against Virginia Tech, which paid her $75,000 while denying all wrongdoing. For VAWA, however, vindication was scant, except in a few regions that began drafting local laws modeled on VAWA's civil rights section.

States' rights, refashioned as federalism, had trumped women's rights. National commerce had trumped women's safety. Chief Justice Rehnquist, who had once written in support of segregation—of *Plessy* and its separate-but-equal doctrine in his early days at the Supreme Court when just a clerk—now as a chief justice managed to revive cases from before *Plessy* that had helped keep blacks less than equal to whites. Resurrecting those cases with a one-vote majority, he stripped away congressional power to protect women from violence and perhaps do other work for the nation. The Supreme Court, as ever mostly male, closed the twentieth century by reaffirming a nineteenth-century justice who claimed blacks were the law's favorites and women were protected, thanks to the Creator, by men.

POSTSCRIPT

———✦———

Toward Equality
(Twenty-first Century)

This history of women's work to reshape male-formed law has relied on many documents. None illumine how, during a few months beginning in the summer of 2005, the Supreme Court rolled back to a ratio of eight men to one woman, a disproportion unseen in entering classes of law schools since 1971.

As yet we have no equivalent of the presidential tapes, first available in late 2000, which document that President Richard Nixon proposed nominating Judge Mildred Lillie in 1971 as what he called a sort of "screen," a form of "playing around" to push aside obstacles (his wife had urged he choose a woman, as had many other women, including Sandra Day O'Connor, then a state senator in Arizona) before naming his real nominees: Lewis Powell and William Rehnquist.

We do know that in 2005 President George W. Bush, when he had Supreme Court openings to replace Rehnquist and O'Connor, felt pressure from his wife and also from O'Connor to nominate a woman. Apparently worried that the few conservative women judges he could find might drift to the left if elevated to the Supreme Court, he found a woman to nominate whom he could announce had "devoted her life" to law, as he saw it: Harriet Miers. She had worked for him as his personal attorney, his campaign attorney, his White House staff secretary, and then his White House counsel.

Miers' few weeks as a nominee, ending in her withdrawal under fire, produced the result that she and much of the president's staff originally sought. Justice Samuel Alito, named the day her nomination fell apart, became the second of two new conservative male justices appointed by Bush, along with John Roberts, a former Rehnquist clerk.

We do not know if President Bush's staff failed to vet Miers fully, or if they vetted sufficiently to anticipate a failed nomination. Perhaps they did not gather the public information that she had given money to Al Gore's presidential campaign in 1988—data sure to worry Republicans. Perhaps neither staffers nor the president knew that in 1989, as a candidate for Dallas City Council, she had endorsed a constitutional amendment banning abortion—likely to alienate Democrats and some moderate Republicans. Perhaps no one knew that she would, conversing with at least one Republican senator after her nomination, leave him convinced that she believed the Constitution contained a right to privacy—a key grounding for court decisions to permit abortion. Perhaps staffers did not know she would have trouble, as they later suggested, studying up on constitutional law for confirmation hearings before the Senate Judiciary Committee. And no documents explain why Miers, famous as a perfectionist when sending information to the president, failed to include accurate dates when sending information about her legal career to that committee—a failure that led to her public excoriation by its Republican chair three weeks before she was due to testify.

No memos from staffers have come to light that contain such commonplace phrases as "win-win" situation or "can't lose" scenario to describe nominating Miers, the one woman who had done the president's legal bidding for years, while holding Alito as the next option.

As soon as the president's men told her that her confirmation seemed impossible, Miers withdrew. She chose not to test the possibility, far from foreclosed, that she might have won enough votes in the Senate to become a Supreme Court justice. We may never find White House documents saying that Miers served as a sort of screen, or as a defense guaranteeing that neither the president's wife nor anyone else could claim he had refused to nominate a woman. Such documents may not exist. The fact remains that when two openings appeared on the Supreme Court in 2005, no woman had a serious chance to become a justice.

From within the Supreme Court, we may not find records similar to those from Chief Justice Burger in the 1970s when he threatened to resign in order to block the appointment of a woman to his court. We do understand, however, that Chief Justice Rehnquist maneuvered O'Connor out of the Court ahead of him, creating the opening that was filled by one of his former clerks, John Roberts (after whose nomination O'Connor quickly commented that he was "good in every way, except he's not a woman").

We also know that male justices, on a court with only one woman, seem to feel free to speak for and about women. One instance came in the spring of 2007 when Justice Anthony M. Kennedy invoked "the bond of love the mother has for her child" in declaring constitutional a ban on an abortion procedure, as if he had experienced that maternal bond. He was, as Ruth Bader Ginsburg replied in dissent, echoing "ancient notions" such as those of Justice Bradley in 1873 that (as she quoted) "the paramount destiny and mission of woman are to fulfil the noble and benign offices of wife and mother." Such ideas "about women's place in the family and under the Constitution," she contended, "have long since been discredited." But with Justice Rehnquist in 2000 affirming an 1883 opinion by Bradley (calling blacks "the special favorite of the laws") while rejecting the Violence Against Women Act, and with Justice Kennedy in 2007 seeming to affirm Bradley's views while rejecting forms of abortion, ancient law seems to have gained new credit—or to have at least gained the necessary five votes, all male.

The twenty-first century may yet bring a move toward a time of equality in the Supreme Court. In the century's first decade, American law schools are alive with women: 47 percent of students and 35 percent of faculty. Membership of women in the American Bar Association has reached 30 percent. Women hold 23 percent of judgeships in federal courts. Only the Supreme Court of the United States remains overwhelmingly male, atop a system of top-down rulings.

One might suppose that the gender of judges no longer shapes judgments about gender. But during the last three decades of the twentieth century, that supposition proved often false. Men in law fought to avoid looking closely at discrimination. Men in law fought to penalize pregnant women at work. Men in law fought to permit their firms to discriminate against women. Men in law saw sexual harassment as a normal condition of employment. Men in law cut away the legal power of Congress to curtail violence against women. Men in law then gained an increased majority on the Supreme Court.

Mostly outside the scope of this book have been the presidents who have contrived to appoint male justices, and outside it also are the mostly male senators who have ratified so many male appointments. Every four or six years, however, presidents and senators look to the nation. Voters can vote for equality.

ACKNOWLEDGMENTS

Early on a series of mornings in January of 1995 at the Supreme Court, I unlocked a massive door leading to a ground-floor corridor. Ahead stretched doors with names including Ginsburg, O'Connor, Rehnquist, Souter, and Scalia. These were rooms where justices could store documents. I walked to the door marked "Ginsburg," unlocked it using a key that I had borrowed from the justice's chambers, and entered a windowless room. Nine paces long and five paces wide, with dim fluorescent lights suspended from high ceilings, it resembled an abandoned squash court.

Documents from some of Justice Ginsburg's earlier court cases filled some of the seventeen file cabinets along the far right wall, I understood. Justice Ginsburg had told me not to look in them.

Each morning I turned instead to the near left corner and a mustard-colored cabinet, full of letters and briefs that Ginsburg had saved from her days as an attorney trying to improve the law for women. To take notes, I had brought a Macintosh Powerbook 100. The room had one table and one electrical outlet, both far away. Each morning, I moved the table to the files. From my briefcase I pulled out two extension cords, which combined to give me electricity to type.

Each day, I also brought a sandwich for lunch and snacks for dinner. I could continue to work, we had agreed, so long as I did not impose on Justice Ginsburg's chambers, far upstairs. My key, needed to enter the room but not to lock it closed, was on loan to me each day from one of the justice's staff members, Gerald Lowe, who usually left the building by six o'clock in the evening. So long as I had his key, I could leave and re-enter the room, and I did occasionally, because the restrooms were a few corridors away. After he retrieved his key around six, I was permitted to stay in the room as long as my stamina lasted. I usually left near midnight.

The research in that Supreme Court cell, like many other moments of privileged research that made this book possible, I owe to generosity that I will always find remarkable and impossible to express adequate thanks for. A few months earlier, in the chambers of Justice Ginsburg at the Supreme Court, as part of an interview, we had been talking in the late afternoon after her staff had gone home. I had already interviewed former students and friends of hers from the days when she was Professor Ginsburg at Columbia, and I had read many files from the archives of the American Civil Liberties Union, kept at Princeton. Late in our conversation, Justice Ginsburg said, more or less: for you to do this book as well as you seem to wish, you need access to my files. And so I wound up working late on many nights in her storage room, often with a ravenous appetite.

Similar early conversations led to time in some of the most fascinating repositories of memory I have entered: A long night in Pat Barry's law office south of Los Angeles. Long study in Catherine East's basement in suburban Virginia. Days with Catharine MacKinnon's files, some of which had become nests for mice. Laptop note-taking in Wendy Williams' files in a caged space within Georgetown University Law Center's parking facility, where exhaust fumes filled my head with pain.

Sometimes I had to ask people if they would ship their files to me so that I could copy them. Sometimes I simply drove away with files. I had heard about the files of Ruth Weyand, hero of the pregnancy cases, from everyone who ever saw her Washington office. Her friends recalled myriad file cards describing strategies for each injustice Weyand hoped to attack. But a few years before I started reporting, Weyand had driven off a road in Colorado, and people supposed that her files were lost. With the help of her daughter, Sterling Weyand Perry, I finally found them in a shack near the Maryland shore, in a summer community begun in the 1800s by descendants of Frederick Douglass.

Just after Sterling Perry and I arrived, and before I could get a look at the files, Ruth Weyand's grandchildren announced to their mother that the crabs were running, and all four of us—Perry, her two children, and I—wound up barefoot in a creek that drains from a backwater marsh into the Chesapeake Bay. Swinging nets, next to about a dozen of the Weyand family's neighbors, we loaded up with crabs. Back at the shed, I loaded up with Weyand's pregnancy files, packing them into cardboard boxes from a nearby food market and filling my station wagon—except for space on the front floor, where I put a brown paper bag holding a few delicious-looking Maryland crabs. As I was starting the car to drive six hours north to New Haven, Connecticut, I tried to thank Sterling Perry enough for her generosity. What she said was, roughly (in a rare instance, I was not taping or taking notes): Well, you know, Harvard asked for those files, and Columbia asked for those files. But you're from Yale, and you came to the door. (Months later, I shipped all the files back to her.)

Help for this book started, chronologically, with Catharine MacKinnon, before I imagined writing the magazine article for the *New York Times Magazine* from which this book eventually began. At Yale Law School in 1990, when MacKinnon came to offer her last course in her wandering years as a visiting professor before she was finally offered tenure by the University of Michigan, I walked a couple of blocks from my office to check out the first class in her thirteen-week course. As I entered the room, I could feel a buzz of anticipation.

MacKinnon began speaking, and class time flew. She talked about the course's expectations: Anyone who raises a hand gets called on. You can write "about your own life, as it pertains to this course, as it will." You can write in your own voice; don't act "like you're nobody, from nowhere." About the law, she added, "I remain unreconstructed in the view that law is about the world."

It was one of the best opening classes I had heard, and I returned for the next session. The buzz had grown louder. This time I sat with an old friend, a former English professor who had shifted to the study of law. She leaned toward me, just as MacKinnon was about to speak, and said, "I love her hair." My jaw dropped, no word came, MacKinnon's voice filled the room, and class accelerated.

As it ended, I decided I should ask MacKinnon's permission to keep attending. Anyone can listen, she said, but who are you? I said I taught writing at Yale and also reported for magazines, and that one reason I wanted to visit her course was that I might try to write something about what she was teaching. She said that I was always welcome in the classroom, and that everything she said was public, but that she would probably not help me. She said she was particularly uninterested in any writing that was primarily about her rather than about her work. Eventually she helped a great deal as I reported an article that became "Defining Law on the Feminist Frontier" in the *New York Times Magazine* of October 6, 1991. It received a small award from the American Bar Association and a critique from some attorneys, particularly Professor Nadine Taub of Rutgers, who said that women's fight to redefine law was a bigger battle than the article showed. This book is partly an acknowledgment of her challenge.

At an early stage in this reporting, a magazine editor who had sent me on assignments that involved different challenges—dodging soldiers at Tiananmen Square in China shortly after the shootings there, sitting atop a scared humpback whale off the eastern shore of Canada, hiking across miles of Russian wilderness—asked me a question about this book. "Shouldn't they," he asked, "get a broad to write that book?" In the months that followed, as I worked with litigators, arranged interviews, and hunted for documents, it struck me that only one guy ever asked a question like that. I owe many people thanks for welcoming me as I worked on this project.

One of the great pleasures of this book came from times when I had the chance to hire one of the students I had taught at Yale— usually for five or ten hours to look for a few documents, sometimes at the Library of Congress. I'm truly honored to have known those students (some of them now journalists or attorneys) in a classroom and beyond: Vanessa Agard-Jones, Karen Alexander, Ellen Barry, Allison Battey, Emily Bazelon, Katherine Bell, Abigail Deutsch, Jodie

Esselstyn, Eve Fairbanks, Alison Henyey, Karen Jacobson, Suzanne Kim, Katherine McCarron, Catherine Olender, Jennifer Pitts, Megan Pugh, Ann Sledge, and Jada Yuan. Two of my former students, Josh Civin and Margo Schlanger, clerked for Justice Ginsburg while this book was in progress; although I never asked them for information, their presence made me feel a bit less of an outsider at the Court, and I want to thank them.

For guiding me toward understanding about the legal issues covered by this book, I am indebted to the many attorneys and others whom I interviewed. They are listed in this book's endnotes, our hundreds of hours of interviews remain vivid to me, and I cannot thank them enough.

I also benefited from many other guides who helped me understand the work of women to reshape the law, and they include Barbara Babcock, Guido Calabresi, Deborah Cantrell, Beverly Blair Cook, Karen Davis, Nancy Davis, Norman Dorsen, Christine Durham, Catherine East, Betty Ellerin, Cynthia Fuchs Epstein, Brenda Feigen, Linda Garbaccio, Lillian Garland, Tita Gratwick, Sandra Grayson, Marcia D. Greenberger, Kent Harvey, Ann Branigar Hopkins, Phineas Indritz, Marian M. Johnston, Rhoda Karpatkin, Linda Krieger, Brian Landsberg, Cecilia Lannon, Jane Larson, Donna Lenhoff, Judith Lichtman, Karen Malkin, Linda Marchiano, Deborah L. Markowitz, Douglas McCollam, Margaret Moses, Donna Murasky, Colleen Patricia Murphy, Aryeh Neier, Helen Neuborne, David Oppenheimer, Kathleen Peratis, Charles L. Reischel, Deborah Rhode, Spottswood Robinson IV, Bernice Sandler, Patricia Schroeder, Joseph Sellers, Reva B. Siegel, David Silberman, Anne E. Simon, Nancy Stanley, Nancy Stearns, Gloria Steinem, Nadine Taub, James A. Thomas, Gerald Torres, Laurence Tribe, Jim Turner, Barbara Underwood, Eileen Wagner, Rosalie Wahl, Mary Roth Walsh, Jonathan Weinberg, Sarah Wilson, and Diane Zimmerman. In Justice Ginsburg's chambers I appreciated enormously the help of Gerald Lowe, Linda O'Donnell, and Cathy Vaughn. All the excellent guidance that I have requested and received may not have averted all error, I fear, and I would like to give thanks in advance to readers, many of them far more expert in the law than I will ever be, who are willing to write me to correct any factual errors that may linger in the text; my email address is strebeigh@aya.yale .edu, and paper mail may be sent via the publisher.

I received invaluable help at libraries and document collections, and I wish to thank the following: at the Barnard Center for Research on Women, Alison Cummings; at Boalt Hall Library, Alice Youmans; at Harvard Law School Library, David Warrington; at Howard University's Moorland-Spingarn Research Center, Joellen ElBashir; at New York University, Deb Ellis and Carole Sparkes; at the Minnesota Historical Society, Tracey Baker; at the National Archives and Records Administration in New York City, Martin Rosenberg; at the Seeley G. Mudd Manuscript Library of Princeton University, Paula Jabloner; at the Supreme Court Library, Sara Sonet; at the Supreme Court public information office, Kathy Arberg, Yolanda Sanders, and Ed Turner; at the United States District Court in Washington, DC, Vernell Marshall and Ted Raymond; at University of Pennsylvania libraries, Cynthia Arkin; at Yale University libraries, Gene Coakley, Jo-Anne Giammatei, Sarah Prown, Ken Rudolf, Fred Shapiro, and Lisa Spar.

When parts of this book appeared in magazines, I was helped enormously by the generous editing of Katherine Bouton at the *New York Times Magazine,* Lincoln Caplan at *Legal Affairs*, and Kate Marsh and Dayo Olopade at the *New Republic.*

For the editing of this book, I've had the great good fortune to work with Amy Cherry at W. W. Norton, whose insights and ongoing commentary played a role in shaping every page. In working with Norton I've also gained from the guidance of Erica Stern and the copy editing of Mary Babcock. I've been fortunate to have as my agent Liz Darhansoff, of Darhansoff, Verrill & Feldman, an agent who reads and comments at all stages of a project including, in the case of this book, suggesting what became its title.

My start on this book may have begun earlier than I know, when my father, a graduate of Columbia Law School, died before I was born. My mother then left the only place she knew well, New York City, to move the two of us to a twelve-family town in New England where she could find work as a teacher in a nearby grade school that would welcome us both, with me enrolling at age three. The school let me repeat for two years in its first-year class, called nursery school, so that my mother could begin a teaching career. That special education, and my mother's boldness on an unfamiliar path, influenced me to a depth that I probably can't convey or comprehend.

My greatest good fortune has been the chance to live for decades with one of the best readers and minds I know, Linda Peterson, who has taken moments away from such tasks as chairing Yale's English Department to engage in fine battles over this book's diction and direction. I love her totally.

—Fred Strebeigh,
New Haven, Connecticut, Spring 2008

NOTES

Prologue: Toward Equality (1968)

For more extensive notes, visit www.wwnorton.com and www.equalwomen .com.

ix If you entered Harvard Law School before 1950: Ruth Bader Ginsburg, "Remarks on Women's Progress in the Legal Profession in the United States," 33 *Tulsa Law Journal* 13 (1997), p. 13.

ix By 1967 . . . about 5 percent . . . In 2001, . . . more than 49 percent: "First Year and Total J.D. Enrollment by Gender 1947–2005," available at www. abanet.org/legaled/statistics/charts/enrollmentbygender.pdf (visited 5/19/07). Harvard Law School, *Alumnae Directory, 1953–2003* (Cambridge: Harvard Law School, 2003), pp. 793–796, and David Warrington, Librarian for Special Collections, Harvard Law School Library, email to author, 8/31/07.

ix "reduced by close to a half" . . . "a policy of admitting women, the halt, and the lame" . . . "the foreign born": House Committee on Education and Labor, Special Subcommittee on Education, *Higher Education Amendments of 1968: Hearing on H.R. 15067*, 90th Cong., 2d sess., 1968, held 2/9/68, p. 179. See detailed note online.

x fastest advance in the history of America's elite professions: For comparison to physicians, see Mary Roth Walsh, *"Doctors Wanted: No Women Need Apply"* (New Haven: Yale University Press, 1977), p. 245 (women in 1947 for the first time accounted for more than 9% of medical students in the United States, a level women did not reach in law schools until 1971). For comparison to university professors, see Martha S. West and John

W. Curtis, *AAUP Faculty Gender Equity Indicators 2006*, available at
www.aaup.org/AAUP/pubsres/research/geneq2006 (visited 2/6/08), figure
1, which shows that women in 1960 were earning more than 10% of doc-
torates, the usual entry degree for a professorship; as of 2000, that figure
had had risen to approximately 45% (see U.S. Department of Education,
Digest of Education Statistics 2005 (Table 246), available at http://nces
.ed.gov/programs/digest/d05/tables/dt05_246.asp?referrer=report (visited
2/6/08)). For comparison to architects, see Nicolai Ouroussoff, "Keeping
Houses, Not Building Them," *New York Times*, 10/31/07, which reports
that, according to the American Institute of Architects, its membership in
2006 was less than 14% women.

x "a game played by the male superiors": *Bundy v. Jackson*, 19 Fair Empl.
Prac. Cas. (BNA) 828. Decided 4/25/79, United States District Court for
the District of Columbia.

Part One
SCRUTINY (1970–1975)

In this part, I rely on the personal papers of, and interviews with, Ruth Bader
Ginsburg and Stephen Wiesenfeld, her client in *Weinberger v. Wiesenfeld* at the
Supreme Court. I am grateful for their generosity and for the care with which
they reviewed my narrative for possible errors. Important primary sources,
particularly interviews and collections of documents, are listed below, with
the abbreviations used in the endnotes that follow. Other primary sources
and important secondary sources appear with full citations in the endnotes.
More detailed endnotes can be found at www.wwnorton.com and www.equal
women.com.

Berzon interview	Interview with Marsha Berzon, San Francisco, 5/16/95
Blackmun papers	Papers of Justice Harry A. Blackmun, Library of Congress
Brennan papers	Papers of Justice William J. Brennan Jr., Library of Congress
Commentator	*The Commentator: The Student Newspaper of the New York University Law Center*
Douglas papers	Papers of Justice William O. Douglas, Library of Congress
Freeman interview	Interview with Mary Elizabeth (M. E.) Freeman, New York City, 3/22/94
Ginsburg files	Personal files of Justice Ruth Bader Ginsburg, consulted August 1994 and January 1995, in the justice's storage room at the Supreme Court

Ginsburg interview	Interview with Ruth Bader Ginsburg, Washington, DC, 8/24/94
Goodman interview	Interviews with Janice Goodman, New York City, by phone, 4/13/94 and 8/16/05
Kelly interview	Interview with Mary F. Kelly, White Plains, New York, 3/29/01
Markowitz interview with Ginsburg	Interview with Ruth Bader Ginsburg conducted by Deborah L. Markowitz with Susan Deller Ross and Wendy Webster Williams, Washington, DC, 2/24/86, as preparation for Deborah L. Markowitz, "In Pursuit of Equality: One Woman's Work to Change the Law," 11 *Women's Rights Law Reporter* 2 (Summer 1989), pp. 73–98. Although Markowitz's article at p. 75n22 says that the interview is available at the Schlesinger Library for Women's History at Radcliffe College, the library apparently does not have the tapes (I conferred with Schlesinger librarians including Ann Engelhart on 2/1/94 and Jacalyn Blume on 8/17/05). In the summer of 1994, Markowitz permitted a Yale student, Jody Esselstyn, to visit at her home in Vermont in order to make duplicate tapes of this fascinating interview; I am indebted to them both.
Marshall papers	Papers of Justice Thurgood Marshall, Library of Congress
Martin Ginsburg interview	Interview with Martin D. Ginsburg, Washington, DC, 2/7/95
Princeton ACLU papers	American Civil Liberties Union papers, Box 679, Seeley G. Mudd Manuscript Library, Princeton University
Root-Tilden files	Files of Root-Tilden-Kern Scholarship program at New York University School of Law, as of 10/27/05
Wiesenfeld files	Files of Stephen Wiesenfeld, as of 3/13/94
Wiesenfeld interview	Interview with Stephen Wiesenfeld, Tamarac, Florida, 3/11–13/94
Wulf interview	Interview with Mel Wulf, New York City, 3/4/94

1: The Story of Paula Wiesenfeld

3 Late in 1972: Ruth Bader Ginsburg, letter to Stephen Wiesenfeld, 12/27/72, in Ginsburg files. They had first spoken the day before, by phone.

3 Immediately she knew: Ginsburg, letter to Phyllis Zatlin Boring, 12/27/72, in Ginsburg files.

3 the legal case she needed: "*Wiesenfeld* was going to be the ... perfect case,"

in Ginsburg interview. In Markowitz interview with Ginsburg, Ginsburg said, "If ever there was a case to attract suspect classification for sex lines in the law, [*Wiesenfeld*] was the one." For a fine article that focuses on *Wiesenfeld*, see Ruth Cowan, "Women's Rights through Litigation: An Examination of the American Civil Liberties Union Women's Rights Project, 1971–1976," 8 *Columbia Human Rights Law Review* 373 (1976). Further references will be cited as Cowan, "Women's Rights."

3   greatest professional goal: Confirmed by Ruth Bader Ginsburg, letter to author, 8/7/03.

3   "gender lines in the law": Ruth Bader Ginsburg, "Responses to ABA Personal Data Questionnaire," 6/18/93, p. 8, in Ginsburg files.

3   When Paula Polatschek first met: Biographical information and quotations are from Wiesenfeld interview and Wiesenfeld files (including photos), unless otherwise indicated. See detailed notes online.

7   difficulties faced by single fathers: Richard Gorman, "Benefits War Began with Letter to Home News," *New Brunswick Home News*, 3/21/75, p. 19, in Wiesenfeld files. Gorman reports that the article to which Wiesenfeld replied was "written by a news service, appeared on Nov. 16, 1972, and outlined the plight of single fathers raising young children."

8   He calculated his potential return: Wiesenfeld interview. He said, "Why would anybody spend hundreds of thousands of dollars to recover $206 a month?" For a similar calculation (using a later rate of payment) and narrative of Stephen's decision, see Cowan, "Women's Rights," p. 385.

8   Professor of Spanish . . . and founder of the New Jersey branch: Records for New Jersey Women's Equity Action League of Phyllis Zatlin Boring, description available at www.scc.rutgers.edu/wild/browse_coll.cfm (visited 8/14/05).

9   Boring: Quotations from Boring's letter are from Phyllis Zatlin Boring, letter to Stephen Wiesenfeld, 11/27/72, in Wiesenfeld files. See note online.

9   ally in pushing Rutgers to admit women: Correspondence of Phyllis Zatlin Boring and Ruth Bader Ginsburg, letters of December 1970 through September 1971, in Ginsburg files.

9   board member of WEAL . . . Ginsburg: Ruth Bader Ginsburg, letter to author, 8/7/03.

9   December 26, 1972: Ruth Bader Ginsburg, letter to Stephen Wiesenfeld, 12/27/72, in Ginsburg files.

9   Ginsburg called Stephen Wiesenfeld: "He wrote that letter, and Phyllis Zatlin Boring read it, and she called me; that's how it all began." Ginsburg interview.

9   Three "facts": Wiesenfeld interview.

9   To the last he replied, "My son is in my care": Stephen Wiesenfeld, letter to Ruth Bader Ginsburg, 1/1/73, in Wiesenfeld files.

10   the case she had been seeking: Ruth Bader Ginsburg, letter to Phyllis Zatlin Boring, 12/27/72, in Ginsburg files. She wrote, "It's a great case and we certainly will take it if Mr. W agrees. . . . If you come across any other gems like this, please let me know." Confirmed by Ruth Bader Ginsburg, letter to author, 8/7/03.

10   "double-edged sword": Brief for Petitioner-Appellant by Ruth Bader Ginsburg and Martin D. Ginsburg, in *Charles E. Moritz v. Commissioner of Internal Revenue*, 469 F.2d 466 (10th Cir. 1972), undated typescript in advance of argument on 10/28/71, p. 20, in Ginsburg files.

11   Joan Ruth Bader: This biographical narrative for Ruth Bader Ginsburg relies on numerous sources, of which the best include articles written following her nomination to the Supreme Court. Most valuable are a three-part series by David Von Drehle, "Ruth Bader Ginsburg: Her Life and Her Law," *Washington Post*, 7/18–20/93; and a two-part series by David Margolick, "Ruth Ginsburg: Her Life and Her Law," *New York Times*, 6/25/93 and 6/27/93. A fine early biography is by Eleanor H. Ayer, *Ruth Bader Ginsburg: Fire and Steel on the Supreme Court* (New York: Dillon Press, 1994). These sources include many details (including stories of Flatbush, meningitis, the Go-Getters, the Chinese restaurant, cancer, and bank accounts) about which I did not reinterview Justice Ginsburg when we spoke. Further references will be cited as Von Drehle on Ginsburg; Margolick on Ginsburg; and Ayer, *Ginsburg*; see also detailed endnotes online.

11   "with the smell of death": Von Drehle on Ginsburg, 7/18/93, p. A1.

12   "scary smart": Margolick on Ginsburg, 6/25/93, p. A1.

12   various campus bathrooms: Ruth Bader Ginsburg, letter to author, 8/7/03.

12   boyfriend from . . . camp: Von Drehle on Ginsburg, 7/18/93, p. A1.

12   "New England grandmother type": Ruth Bader Ginsburg, letter to author, 8/7/03.

13   Ruth collected notes taken by students . . . keep the family together: Ruth Bader Ginsburg, letter to author, 8/7/03.

13   Eva Hanks, was asked by a male colleague: Tracy Schroth, "At Rutgers, Ginsburg Changed," *New Jersey Law Journal* , 6/21/93, p. 1.

14   Until the last months of 1969: Barbara Allen Babcock, Ann E. Freedman, Eleanor Holmes Norton, and Susan C. [later Susan Deller] Ross, *Sex Discrimination and the Law: Cases and Remedies* (Boston: Little, Brown, 1975), p. v. Further references will be cited as Babcock and others, *Sex Discrimination* (1975).

14   two law students: Ginsburg interview; the two were Janice Goodman and Mary F. Kelly.

14   PATH train: Kelly interview.

14   September of 1968 . . . bookstore . . . Ross said, Don't you think: Good-
     man interviews; confirmed by Susan Deller Ross, letter to author, 8/8/05.
     See also *Women at NYU Law School, 1892–1992* (New York: New York
     University School of Law, 1992), p. 20; published by NYU law school for
     "our celebration of 100 years of women graduates."

14   Root-Tilden Scholarship . . . package worth about $10,000 a year: House
     Committee on Education and Labor, Special Subcommittee on Education,
     Discrimination against Women: Hearings on Section 805 of H.R. 16098,
     91st Cong., 2d sess., 1970, "Statement of Women's Rights Committee of
     New York University Law School," p. 588. See also Diane Schulder, "Does
     the Law Oppress Women," in Robin Morgan, ed., *Sisterhood Is Powerful*
     (New York: Random House, 1970), p. 142, with citation to The Women's
     Rights Committee, "Fair and Equal Treatment for Women at New York
     University Law School" (1969).

15   *women's liberation*—a phrase coined . . . male mockery and heckling:
     Susan Brownmiller, *In Our Time: Memoir of a Revolution* (New York:
     Dial Press, 1999), p. 16. Further references will be cited as Brownmiller, *In
     Our Time*. Women's Liberation groups were forming in Chicago and then
     New York (pp. 18–21); the New York group became New York Radical
     Women. For "Shit. I asked for volunteers" . . . "assumption of male supe-
     riority" . . . "The position of women in SNCC is prone," see pp. 12–14.

15   When Holmes volunteered for SNCC in the summer of 1963: Joan Steinau
     Lester (as authorized by Eleanor Holmes Norton), *Fire in My Soul* (New
     York: Atria Books, 2003), p. 111ff. Further references will be cited as
     Lester, *Fire in My Soul*.

16   "let me tell you" . . . "I go to the Yale Law School": Lester, *Fire in My Soul*,
     p. 112.

16   "future public leaders": House Committee on Education and Labor, Special
     Subcommittee on Education, *Discrimination against Women: Hearings
     on Section 805 of H.R. 16098*, 91st Cong., 2d sess., 1970, "Statement
     of Women's Rights Committee of New York University Law School," p.
     588.

16   in 1968, all law schools received an incentive: House Committee on Educa-
     tion and Labor, Special Subcommittee on Education, *Higher Education
     Amendments of 1968: Hearing on H.R. 15067*, 90th Cong., 2d sess.,
     1968, held 2/9/68, p. 166, and R. Drummond Ayres, "Colleges Attack
     New Draft Rules," *New York Times*, 1/30/68, p. 30.

16   NYU . . . twenty for every hundred: Paul Sobell, "Class of '71 Rated
     Good despite Draft Call Blues," *Commentator*, 9/12/68, p. 1; Dennis
     Stern, "Admissions Director Says '72 Best on All Counts," *Commenta-
     tor*, 10/1/69, p. 3.

17   "too strong": Bernice Sandler, " 'Too Strong for a Woman': The Five

Words That Created Title IX," *About Women on Campus* (newsletter of the National Association for Women in Education), Vol. 6, No. 2, Spring 1997, p. 1. See also Bernice Sandler, "A Little Help from Our Government: WEAL and Contract Compliance," in Alice C. Rossi and Ann Calderwood, eds., *Academic Women on the Move* (New York: Russell Sage Foundation, 1973), partly reprinted in Babcock and others, *Sex Discrimination* (1975), pp. 525–534.

17 taught her how to file complaints: Interview with Bernice Sandler, Washington, DC, by phone, 3/19/98. See note online.

17 When the NYU Women's Rights Committee began: Narrative comes primarily from Goodman interviews; interview with Susan Deller Ross, Washington, DC, 8/25/94; and Ross and Goodman, emails and phone calls with author, August 2005.

17 Niles . . . in 1951 helped create the scholarship: "Faculty Tables Root Study," *Commentator*, 4/29/70, p. 3.

18 "It is the sense of the faculty": Daniel Collins, memo to Jan Goodman, 10/18/68, in Root-Tilden files.

18 Professor Niles had visited . . . Foundation, evidently hoping it would oppose . . . Niles' reasons . . . "encourage bright young women": Russell Niles, letter to Daniel Collins, 12/15/66, in Root-Tilden files. Niles wrote, in part, "I regret to have to report that it was his [executive director's] opinion that . . . we could admit women if we wanted to. I am still opposed to admitting women."

18 Niles had insisted . . . inappropriate . . . "administrative action": "Memo Urges Root Opening for Women," *Commentator*, 11/20/68, p. 1.

18 faculty had already voted . . . But it never followed: Administrative delay from 1966 to 1968 seems likely to have emerged in part from concern for Professor Niles. After the faculty voted again in 1968, a colleague wrote to the dean of the law school urging delay by yet another year before letting women get the Root-Tilden Scholarship. He said delay would be "more gracious toward Dean Niles." Ralph F. Bischoff, "Memorandum to Dean McKay," 12/10/68, in Root-Tilden files.

18 "nobody cared enough": Interview with Susan Deller Ross, Washington, DC, by phone, 7/29/05.

18 Women's Rights Committee would take legal action . . . would sue their own law school: Susan Deller Ross, letter to author, 8/8/05: "I threatened litigation in the faculty meeting."

19 Within days, outgoing mail: "Faculty Meeting Approves Root Openings for Women," *Commentator*, 12/4/68, p. 3.

19 Jan Goodman and a friend named Mary F. Kelly headed for Rutgers . . . two tenured women law professors: Ginsburg interview, Goodman interviews, and Kelly interview.

19   "proved not to be a burdensome venture": Ruth Bader Ginsburg, "Some Reflections on the Feminist Legal Thought of the 1970s," 1989 *University of Chicago Legal Forum* 9 (1989), p. 11.

19   "land, like woman, was meant to be possessed": Curtis J. Berger, *Land Ownership and Use: Cases, Statutes, and Other Materials* (Boston: Little, Brown, 1968), p. 139, cited in Ruth Bader Ginsburg, "Some Reflections on the Feminist Legal Thought of the 1970s," 1989 *University of Chicago Legal Forum* 9 (1989), p. 9n2.

19   "How have people": Ginsburg, quoted in Margolick on Ginsburg, 6/25/93, p. A1.

19   responding to the urging of her Rutgers students and the emissaries from NYU: Markowitz interview with Ginsburg. See also Deborah L. Markowitz, "In Pursuit of Equality: One Woman's Work to Change the Law," 11 *Women's Rights Law Reporter* 73 (Summer 1989), p. 75fn22. Further references will be cited as Markowitz, "In Pursuit."

20   spring of 1970, Ginsburg taught her first course on women and the law: Ruth Bader Ginsburg, letter to author, 8/7/03. Although Justice Ginsburg seems sure that she taught her seminar on women and the law for the first time in the spring of 1970, Rutgers Law School–Newark does not have a record of the course in that term. According to the law school's registrar, Linda Garbaccio, assistant dean for academic services, the law school's class rosters show Ruth Bader Ginsburg teaching her seminar in the spring of 1971. Dean Garbaccio says she "can't guarantee" that class rosters are accurate; also, the catalogs for 1970–71 are missing from both the law library and the registrar's office. (The course does not appear in course catalogs for 1968–69 or 1969–70; if Ginsburg added the course in the middle of the 1969–70 academic year, a catalog would not list it.) A student transcript for Diana Rigelman (on file with author) shows that she took Professor Ginsburg's "Women & the Law Sem," Course No. 446, in the spring of 1971, and Rigelman believes that the course was being offered for the first time. The course catalog for 1971–72 shows the course taught again in the spring of 1972, Ginsburg's last term teaching at Rutgers. Interview with Dean Linda Garbaccio, Registrar's Office, Rutgers Law School–Newark, by phone, 5/4/06; transcript for Diana J. Rigelman, Rutgers Law School–Newark, dated 6/4/72, copy provided to author by Diana Guza-Wells (formerly Rigelman).

20   phone call from a stranger: Ginsburg interview. The date of the call evidently came between the following two letters: Nora Simon, first letter to New Jersey ACLU, 7/23/70, and Ruth Bader Ginsburg, letter on behalf of Simon to L. Howard Bennett (director of Equal Opportunity for the Armed Forces), 7/29/70, both in Ginsburg files.

20   bounced around by ACLU offices: Nora Simon, letter to Washington

ACLU, 1/8/70, and Clara L. Breland (secretary, Legal Department, national ACLU in New York City), letter to Nora Simon, 3/26/70, both in Ginsburg files.

20 wondered why Nagler called her: Ginsburg interview.

20 Working at the New Jersey ACLU that summer . . . Diana Rigelman: Nora Simon's first contacts with the New Jersey ACLU seem to be two letters, both dated 7/23/70, one of which is addressed to Diana Rigelman. Nora Simon, letter to Rigelman, 7/23/70, in Ginsburg files. Most details of Nora Simon's case come from Ginsburg files and Ginsburg interview.

20 just taken Ginsburg's first-year course: Interview with Diana J. Guza-Wells (formerly Rigelman), Bellingham, Washington, by phone, 2/22/06; Diana J. Guza-Wells, email to author, 3/31/06; transcript for Diana J. Rigelman, Rutgers Law School–Newark, dated 6/4/72, copy provided to author by Diana Guza-Wells.

20 "ice woman" . . . "a female lawyer with clout": Diana J. Guza-Wells (formerly Rigelman), emails to author, 3/06.

21 sad story: Nora Simon, letter to "Dear Miss/Sir" at New Jersey ACLU, 7/23/70, in Ginsburg files.

21 letter to the director for Equal Opportunity: Quotations from the letter are from Ruth Bader Ginsburg, letter to L. Howard Bennett, 7/29/70, in Ginsburg files.

22 "zippy" legal complaint: Ruth Bader Ginsburg, letter to Marc Adams Franklin, 10/6/70, in Ginsburg files.

22 simply mailed her original letter to the offices: Ruth Bader Ginsburg, letters to Melvin Laird, Stanley Resor, and others, 9/17/70 and 9/24/70, in Ginsburg files.

23 Two weeks after the Army relented: John G. Kester (Office of the Army), letter to Ruth Bader Ginsburg, 10/15/70, in Ginsburg files.

23 Martin walked into her office . . . "You've gotta read this," . . . case of Charles E. Moritz: Martin Ginsburg interview and Martin Ginsburg letter to author, 8/12/03.

23 "Marty" . . . "you know I have no time to read tax cases": Ginsburg interview.

23 "household help for invalid mother": Brief for Petitioner-Appellant by Ruth Bader Ginsburg and Martin D. Ginsburg, in *Charles E. Moritz v. Commissioner of Internal Revenue*, 469 F.2d 466 (10th Cir. 1972), undated typescript, p. 3, in Ginsburg files (copy to author, 1/20/95).

23 Moments after . . . crank calls . . . best stationery . . . 100 percent concession: Martin Ginsburg interview.

24 at her office door appeared: Wulf interview.

24 remembered her as "Kiki" Bader: See Ruth Bader Ginsburg, letter to Mel Wulf, 10/11/71, in Princeton ACLU papers. She signs the letter "Kiki."

25 helped develop the legal concept of a right to privacy: Wulf interview. See also David Garrow, *Liberty and Sexuality: The Right to Privacy and the Making of Roe v. Wade* (New York: Macmillan, 1994), pp. 167–172. Further references will be cited as Garrow, *Liberty and Sexuality.*

25 "plucked Ruth Ginsburg from obscurity": Wulf interview.

25 "some down and dirty women's rights work" . . . "the lofty aeries": Wulf interview.

25 male-female pair, each as irrational as the other: Ginsburg interview.

26 *Moritz* would be "as neat a craft": Ruth Bader Ginsburg, letter to Mel Wulf, 11/17/70, in Ginsburg files; elaborated in Ruth Bader Ginsburg, letter to author, 8/7/03.

26 "docketing statement": in Ginsburg files.

26 "Dear Ruth/Kiki": Mel Wulf, letter to Ruth Bader Ginsburg, 2/2/71, in Ginsburg files.

26 offered to settle for a dollar: Martin Ginsburg interview.

26 she immediately wrote Wulf: Ruth Bader Ginsburg, letter to Mel Wulf, 3/2/71, in Ginsburg files and in Princeton ACLU papers.

26 "I am the lawyer": Mel Wulf, letter to Ruth Bader Ginsburg, 3/9/71, in Princeton ACLU papers.

27 As she read the jurisdictional statement . . . shortcomings: Ginsburg interview.

27 "Dear Mel": Ruth Bader Ginsburg, letter to Mel Wulf, 4/6/71, in Ginsburg files.

27 "one of the very best presentations" . . . Dorsen sent a copy of his letter to Wulf: Norman Dorsen, letter to Ruth Bader Ginsburg, 4/12/71, in Ginsburg files.

27 Within three days, Wulf called: Ruth Bader Ginsburg, letter to Leo Kanowitz, 4/15/71, in Ginsburg files.

27 seeking a role in *Reed* was one of the key decisions: Panel discussion at Columbia Law School, 11/19/93.

27 "Damn, maybe I didn't pluck her from obscurity": Wulf interview. Wulf said this after the author showed him the text of Ginsburg's letter to Wulf, 4/6/71, quoted above.

2: Old Law Meets a New Case—*Reed*

29 "should not admit any person": This and subsequent quotations from the Illinois Supreme Court decision, unless otherwise indicated, are from *Bradwell v. Illinois*, 83 U.S. 130 (1872).

30 *Slaughter-House Cases*: Quotations from the decision in this case, unless otherwise indicated, are from *In Re Slaughter-House Cases*, 83 U.S. 36 (1872). For a discussion of their impact, see Pamela Brandwein, *Recon-*

structing Reconstruction: The Supreme Court and the Production of Historical Truth (Durham: Duke University Press, 1999), pp. 62–68.

30 Justice Samuel Freeman Miller declared: Quotations from Miller's and his colleagues' opinions, unless indicated otherwise, are from *Bradwell v. Illinois*, 83 U.S. 130 (1872). See note online.

31 "standards of review": For contemporary discussion, see Note, "Developments in the Law—Equal Protection," 82 *Harvard Law Review* 1065 (1969), p. 1076ff.

31 case of Sally Reed: Details of *Reed* are from In the District Court of the Fourth Judicial District of Idaho, In the Matter of the Estate of Richard Lynn Reed, Clerk's Transcript on Appeal, filed 1/30/69, in Princeton ACLU papers. See also Brief for Appellant (Sally Reed), by Melvin L. Wulf and Ruth Bader Ginsburg to Supreme Court, filed 6/25/71, in *Reed v. Reed*, 404 U.S. 71 (1971). Further references will be cited as Wulf-Ginsburg Brief for Sally Reed.

31 "tender years" doctrine: Markowitz interview with Ginsburg.

32 "males must be preferred to females": *Reed v. Reed*, 404 U.S. 71 (1971), p. 73.

32 ACLU volunteer attorney: Markowitz interview with Ginsburg. Marked-up copy of *Law Week* of 3/10/70 [38 LW 2481] is in Princeton ACLU papers.

32 "nature itself has established the distinction": Wulf-Ginsburg Brief for Sally Reed, p. 54.

32 "rational basis" . . . "irrational classification" of women's role: Jurisdictional Statement for Sally M. Reed, by Melvin L. Wulf and Allen R. Derr (with acknowledgement on last page to "Miss Eve Cary, third year law student at New York University Law School") to Supreme Court, pp. 6 and 10, dated 7/1/70, in *Reed v. Reed*, 404 U.S. 71 (1971).

32 she saw that his strategy was less radical: Ginsburg interview.

33 Florida law that failed this test . . . "one racial group" . . . "overriding": *McLaughlin v. Florida*, 379 U.S. 184 (1964).

33 start of a larger strategy: The creation of this strategy is explained superbly in Markowitz, "In Pursuit," pp. 73–98, and in Cowan, "Women's Rights," p. 384ff. I drew also on Markowitz interview with Ginsburg and my interview with Ginsburg, when she explained that strict scrutiny was "an idea that I wanted to plant" in *Reed* and *Moritz* and that she thought the Supreme Court justices "were going to inch their way to the idea" during multiple cases.

34 Wulf had failed to convince Reed's lawyer, Allen Derr: See Mel Wulf, letter to Allen R. Derr, 6/4/71, Princeton ACLU papers.

34 Ann E. Freedman . . . spreading the idea of legal courses: Interview with Ann E. Freedman, Philadelphia, by phone, 5/17/98.

34 calling out, "BOO": Goodman interviews.

34 "educate the court on everything" and Brandeis: Goodman interviews.

34 "kinship between race and sex discrimination" . . . "In the earlier common law": Brief for Appellant (Sally Reed) by Mel Wulf and Allen R. Derr (but author names crossed off by hand) to Supreme Court, undated draft of c. 6/9/71, typescript p. 12 (numbered by Princeton library as 44618–16), in *Reed v. Reed*, 404 U.S. 71 (1971), in Princeton ACLU papers. This draft, containing marginalia by many different hands, is a fascinating artifact of the work on a major case. Quotations from Madison, *New York Herald*, and Myrdal appear at (in library pagination) 44618–26 and 28.

35 they presumed, she would fix their footnotes . . . "We just dumped it on her": Goodman interviews.

36 A needy male married to a wealthy woman . . . "Nobody could see anything wrong": Martin Ginsburg interview.

36 "what better place to catch a man?": Markowitz interview with Ginsburg; confirmed by Ruth Bader Ginsburg, letter to author, 7/8/03.

36 Frankfurter . . . "I can't stand girls in pants!": Margolick on Ginsburg, 6/25/93, p. A1.

37 Learned Hand, a judge she revered: Ruth Bader Ginsburg, "Interpretations of the Equal Protection Clause," 9 *Harvard Journal of Law and Public Policy*, 41 (1986), p. 45.

37 strong language . . . inhibited: Markowitz interview with Ginsburg.

37 Edmund L. Palmieri . . . balked . . . trial basis: Gerald Gunther, "Ruth Bader Ginsburg: A Personal, Very Fond Tribute," 20 *Hawaii Law Review* 583 (1995), p. 584.

37 Hand . . . "Young lady": Margolick on Ginsburg, 6/25/93, p. A1.

37 justices were men . . . "What is this sex discrimination?": Ginsburg interview.

37 ranging from 1908 . . . to as recent as 1961: Wulf-Ginsburg Brief for Sally Reed, p. 41.

38 "a sharp line between the sexes": Justice Frankfurter in *Goesaert v. Cleary*, 335 U.S. 464, 465 (1948).

39 "about a merry old alewife": Ginsburg interview. See also Ruth Bader Ginsburg, "Some Reflections on the Feminist Legal Thought of the 1970s," 1989 *University of Chicago Legal Forum* 9 (1989), p. 13.

39 "Sex, like race and lineage": This and subsequent quotations from the *Reed* brief are from Wulf-Ginsburg Brief for Sally Reed), p. 20, citing *Sail'er Inn v. Kirby*, 3 CCH Employment Practices Decisions 8222 (5/27/71), pp. 6756–6757.

40 Ginsburg had no expectation of winning strict scrutiny: Ginsburg interview. See note online.

40 deception here, as Ginsburg knew: Discussion of tactical deceptions in this brief draws on Ginsburg interview.

41 work that had reached back decades: Ginsburg recalls how she and her husband found *F. S. Royster Guano Co. v. Virginia*, 253 U.S. 412 (1920): "I know how we got to *Royster Guano*. We looked up every old equal protection case and took the one with the best language." Ginsburg interview. The Ginsburgs may have also encountered this case and its fine language in Note, "Developments in the Law—Equal Protection," 82 *Harvard Law Review* 1065 (1969), p. 1076.

41 "must be reasonable, not arbitrary": *F. S. Royster Guano Co. v. Virginia*, 253 U.S. 412, 415 (1920).

41 rightly repudiated . . . *Royster Guano* became a joke: Ginsburg interview.

41 "never before been questioned": This and other quotations from Stout's brief, unless otherwise indicated, are from Brief for Respondent (Cecil R. Reed) by Charles S. Stout to the Supreme Court, c. 7/9/71, In *Reed v. Reed*, 404 U.S. 71 (1971), available at www.yale.edu/lawweb/avalon/curiae/html/404-71/006.htm (visited 3/26/03).

42 Ginsburg immediately realized that the Court might dismiss: Markowitz interview with Ginsburg.

42 "Have you given any thought": Mel Wulf, letter to Allen R. Derr, 9/17/71, in Princeton ACLU papers.

42 series begun half a year before: Mel Wulf, letter to Allen R. Derr, 3/8/71.

42 letters not just to Derr: Mel Wulf, letter to Sally Reed, 9/29/71.

42 On his mind, as on Ginsburg's . . . what Wulf called "the kind of locker-room humor": Mel Wulf, letter to Allen R. Derr, 6/4/71; Ginsburg interview.

42 "a lady law clerk": Supreme Court transcript of *Phillips v. Martin Marietta Corporation*, 400 U.S. 542 (1971), argued 12/9/70.

42 in private conference: Douglas papers.

43 he had told some of his own clerks that he would never hire a woman as clerk: Bob Woodward and Scott Armstrong, *The Brethren: Inside the Supreme Court* (New York: Simon and Schuster, 1979), p. 141. Further references will be cited as Woodward and Armstrong, *Brethren*.

43 not to nominate a woman as justice: John W. Dean, *The Rehnquist Choice: The Untold Story of the Nixon Appointment That Redefined the Supreme Court* (New York: Free Press, 2001), pp. 91, 179–180, and 287 (Nixon tapes were not made public until 2000). Further references will be cited as Dean, *Rehnquist Choice*.

43 He believed, she pointed out, that *wives* have children but fathers don't:

Ruth Bader Ginsburg, "Sex and Unequal Protection," 11 *Journal of Family Law* 347 (1971), p. 352.

43   Ginsburg believed, his banter might not have sunk so low: Ginsburg interview.

43   "going into the big leagues with a big league brief" . . . "damn fool" . . . Wulf urged Derr to cede oral argument: Mel Wulf, letter to Allen R. Derr, 7/21/71, Princeton ACLU papers.

43   "The ACLU underestimated her": Goodman interviews.

43   Derr stood his ground, with the support of Sally Reed: Allen R. Derr, letter to Sally Reed, 12/9/71, in Princeton ACLU papers.

43   opening analogy: Markowitz interview with Ginsburg.

43   Derr began by telling the Court that "we are here today": This and subsequent quotations from Derr's oral argument are from Supreme Court transcript of *Reed v. Reed*, 404 U.S. 71 (1971), argued 10/19/71; audio recording available at www.oyez.org/cases/1970–1979/1971/1971_70_4/argument (visited 7/29/07).

44   Ginsburg was appalled: Markowitz interview with Ginsburg.

44   one justice, asking about the Michigan case: Anonymity of justices speaking in oral argument was preserved in official Supreme Court transcripts prior to October 2004; see "Supreme Court of the United States Argument Transcripts," available at www.supremecourtus.gov/oral_arguments/argument_transcripts.html (visited 8/16/06). Where I write "one justice," I have found no clues that make possible a positive identification of the justice.

44   "may have been one of the worst" . . . Wulf believed all hope hung on Ginsburg's brief: Mel Wulf, letter to Allen R. Derr, 10/21/71, in Princeton ACLU papers.

44   "perhaps the worst argued": Justice Blackmun, oral argument notes, 10/19/71, in Blackmun papers.

44   Burger's decision . . . "The question presented": This and subsequent quotations from the *Reed* decision are from *Reed v. Reed*, 404 U.S. 71 (1971). See detailed notes online.

45   Wulf and Ginsburg had never doubted the Court would invalidate Idaho's preference: Mel Wulf, Letter to Allen R. Derr, 10/21/71, in Princeton ACLU papers; Markowitz interview with Ginsburg.

45   "the bland and very narrow opinion": Mel Wulf, letter to Allen R. Derr, 12/20/71, in Princeton ACLU papers.

45   Ginsburg, in contrast, was delighted . . . first step she needed: Ginsburg interview.

45   "more liberal bunch" . . . "giant step" . . . "turning point case": Markowitz, "In Pursuit," p. 80. See note online.

46   Ginsburg presented the ACLU board with a proposal to create the "Wom-

en's Rights Project" . . . $50,000: Ginsburg interview. See also Susan M. Hartmann, *The Other Feminists: Activists in the Liberal Establishment* (New Haven: Yale University Press, 1998), p. 83 (which says budget was $30,000).

46 $5 million . . . Playboy Foundation: Cowan, "Women's Rights," p. 384.

46 "I knew when I was outclassed": Wulf interview.

46 "the year of *the* woman": Ginsburg interview.

46 Columbia, fearful: Ginsburg interview; see also Cowan, "Women's Rights," pp. 384–385. See note online.

3: *Frontiero* Brings Hopes

48 case of Susan Struck: For most details of *Struck*, see Markowitz, "In Pursuit," pp. 80–81.

48 serving in Vietnam in 1970 . . . automatic rule required discharge: Brief for Captain Susan R. Struck by Ruth Bader Ginsburg, Melvin L. Wulf, Joel M. Gora, and Brenda Feigen Fasteau to Supreme Court, pp. 3–4, in *Struck v. Secretary of Defense*, No. 72–178, cert. granted, 409 U.S. 947, vacated, 409 U.S. 1071 (1972). Further references will be cited as Struck brief.

48 government encouraged her to have an abortion: Markowitz, "In Pursuit," p. 81; Struck brief, pp. 54–56.

48 "moral or administrative reasons": Ginsburg, in Markowitz interview with Ginsburg; quoted in Markowitz, "In Pursuit," p. 81.

49 "Captain Struck indulged in": Ginsburg, in Markowitz, "In Pursuit," p. 81.

49 more arguments before the Supreme Court than any man alive: Lincoln Caplan, *The Tenth Justice: The Solicitor General and the Rule of Law* (New York: Knopf, 1987), pp. 33, 52. Further references will be cited as Caplan, *Tenth Justice*.

50 extra pay for their housing . . . both Frontieros were thrifty: Appendix to Brief for Sharron A. Frontiero and Joseph Frontiero by Joseph J. Levin, Jr., and Morris S. Dees, Jr., to Supreme Court of the United States, p. 11, undated, in *Frontiero v. Richardson*, 411 U.S. 677 (1973) available at www.yale.edu/lawweb/avalon/curiae/html/411–677 (visited 8/24/05).

50 $8,200: Supreme Court transcript of *Frontiero v. Richardson*, 411 U.S. 677 (1973), argued 1/17/73.

50 "rational basis": *Frontiero v. Laird*, 341 F. Supp. 201, 209 (M.D. Ala. 1972).

50 Levin . . . asked Mel Wulf for ACLU help . . . understanding that the ACLU would have primary responsibility for *Frontiero* . . . any oral argument would be handled by Ruth Ginsburg: Ruth Bader Ginsburg, letter to Joseph

J. Levin Jr., 10/24/72, and Joseph J. Levin Jr., letter to Ruth Bader Ginsburg, 10/27/72, both in Ginsburg files. See also Markowitz, "In Pursuit," p. 82, particularly notes 116–118.

51   first chance to argue . . . "grown very attached": Joseph Levin, letter to Mel Wulf, 10/17/72, in Ginsburg files.

51   "not very good at self-advertisement": Ruth Bader Ginsburg, letter to Joseph Levin, 10/24/72, in Ginsburg files.

51   agreed . . . that Ginsburg would handle the oral argument . . . "chauvinistic": Joseph Levin, letter to Ruth Bader Ginsburg, 10/27/72, in Ginsburg files.

51   an *amicus* brief . . . parent briefs: Ginsburg interview. For analysis of how the *Frontiero* brief diverged, see Markowitz, "In Pursuit," p. 82.

52   The split . . . called attention to disagreement even among *Frontiero*'s supporters: Markowitz interview with Ginsburg.

52   his [Levin's] argument: Details and quotations from Levin's oral argument for *Frontiero* are from Supreme Court transcript of *Frontiero v. Richardson*, 411 U.S. 677 (1973), argued 1/17/73, beginning at 1:28 p.m.

52   her first argument before the Supreme Court . . . At lunchtime she had been so nervous she had not eaten: Ayer, *Ginsburg*, p. 52, citing Elinor Porter Swiger, *Women Lawyers at Work* (New York: Messner, 1978), p. 52.

53   "Mr. Chief Justice": Details of and quotations from Ginsburg's oral argument for *Frontiero*, unless otherwise indicated, are from Supreme Court transcript of *Frontiero v. Richardson*, 411 U.S. 677 (1973), argued 1/17/73.

54   Brenda Feigen began to wonder: Interview with Brenda Feigen, Beverly Hills, California, by phone, 6/14/94.

54   Martin Ginsburg began to worry: Martin Ginsburg interview.

54   radicals from NYU . . . sound utterly logical: Goodman interviews.

55   insist they were mesmerized: Interview with Brenda Feigen, Beverly Hills, California, by phone, 6/14/94.

55   C+ . . . "very precise female": Blackmun notes on oral argument, 1/17/73, in Blackmun papers. Blackmun gave Levin a B–.

55   strict scrutiny apparently played no part . . . "nothing to do with" *Reed* . . . "has the right to draw lines": Details and quotations from justices' conference are from conference notes, 1/19/93, by Justices Blackmun, Brennan, and Douglas, in Blackmun papers, Brennan papers, and Douglas papers.

56   when the justices considered whether to hear Frontiero's case: tally of votes on jurisdictional statement in *Frontiero*, undated, in Brennan papers.

56   feinted toward nominating a woman . . . resisted fiercely by Chief Justice Burger: See Dean, *Rehnquist Choice*, including pp. 91 ("Poor old Burger couldn't work with the woman"), 179–180 (Burger threatens to resign),

181 (Nixon tells his attorney general that "I don't think any of those women are worth a damn"), and 287 (tapes released for public listening on 11/16/00).

56 merely a "screen": Joan Biskupic, *Sandra Day O'Connor: How the First Woman on the Supreme Court Became Its Most Influential Justice* (New York: Ecco, 2005), p. 41. Further references will be cited as Biskupic, *O'Connor*.

57 Douglas had been scribbling: Conference notes in Douglas papers. (Conference notes by Blackmun also show no mention of "suspect classification" or "strict scrutiny." Blackmun papers.)

57 Douglas assigned the opinion to his frequent ally, Brennan: Document headed "October Term A. D. 1972," dated 1/22/73, in Marshall papers. See note online.

57 Brennan had been strongly influenced by Ginsburg's argument: Martin Ginsburg interview.

57 Brennan had been counting votes . . . one more vote . . . Potter Stewart: Brennan memorandum to all justices, 2/14/73, says "perhaps there is a court"—enough votes—for strict scrutiny, and see Brennan memorandum to all justices, 2/28/73, in Marshall papers.

57 "We hold today": This and details of Brennan's revision are from Justice William J. Brennan Jr., "3rd DRAFT," circulated 2/28/73, in Brennan papers.

58 "You have now gone all the way": Lewis F. Powell, memo to Justice William J. Brennan Jr., 3/2/73, in Marshall papers.

58 "on account of sex": Babcock and others, *Sex Discrimination* (1975), p. 129.

58 Some legal experts opposed . . . argument made by William Rehnquist: See Robert C. Post and Reva B. Siegel, "Legislative Constitutionalism and Section Five Power," 112 *Yale Law Journal* 1943 (2003), p. 2003.

58 majority of state legislatures by 1973 supported the ERA, as did Ruth Bader Ginsburg . . . Jefferson: Ruth Bader Ginsburg, "The Need for the Equal Rights Amendment," 59 *American Bar Association Journal* 1013 (1973), pp. 1013 (Jefferson), 1018 (majority), and 1019 ("sharp legislative lines").

58 "My principal concern" . . . "Women certainly": Lewis F. Powell, letter to Justice William J. Brennan Jr., 3/2/73, in Marshall papers.

59 Stewart's long-awaited memo . . . agreed generally with Powell: Potter Stewart, letter to Justice William J. Brennan Jr., 3/5/73, in Marshall papers.

59 a strong response to Powell . . . "will of the people": Justice William J. Brennan Jr., letter to Lewis F. Powell Jr., 3/6/73, in Marshall papers.

60 Stewart . . . failed to talk Brennan into a compromise: Woodward and Armstrong, *Brethren*, pp. 301–303. See note online.

60   Stewart . . . not step beyond the decision in *Reed*: Potter Stewart, letter to
      Justice William J. Brennan Jr., 3/7/73, in Marshall papers.
60   "shuttlecock" . . . "The author of *Reed*": Warren Burger, letter to Justice
      William J. Brennan Jr., 3/7/73, in Marshall papers.
60   so Ginsburg supposed: Markowitz interview with Ginsburg. Ginsburg
      says, "I would say that Stewart was lost to strict scrutiny because Brennan
      moved too soon."
60   "the will of the people": *Frontiero v. Richardson*, 411 U.S. 677, 692
      (1973).
60   could tell how close . . . heard rumors that Stewart had wavered: Ruth
      Bader Ginsburg, "Gender and the Constitution," 44 *University of Cincin-
      nati Law Review* 1 (1975), p. 19.
60   "the female of the species": Ginsburg interview; see also Ruth Bader Gins-
      burg, "The Need for the Equal Rights Amendment," 59 *American Bar
      Association Journal* 1013 (September 1973), p. 1017, quoting Stewart from
      Harvard Law School Record, 3/23/73, p. 15.
61   labeled a "concurrence" . . . "the Court" . . . "has assumed" the respon-
      sibility: *Frontiero v. Richardson*, 411 U.S. 677, 691, (1973) (Powell, J.,
      concurring).
61   *Wiesenfeld* was the perfect case: Ginsburg interview.
61   disaster . . . Kahn: Ruth Bader Ginsburg, letter to Stephen Wiesenfeld,
      5/3/74, in Wiesenfeld files.
62   "ripe for change": Cowan, "Women's Rights," p. 392.
62   ACLU rules forbade bringing a case to the Supreme Court: Ginsburg inter-
      view; Markowitz, "In Pursuit," p. 85; interview with Kathleen Peratis,
      New York City, 3/8/94.
62   shocked her. "You're from the ACLU?": Ginsburg interview ("Well," she
      said, "you could have picked me up off the floor").
62    $15 . . . sought only to help men: Ruth Bader Ginsburg, "Gender in the
      Supreme Court: The 1973 and 1974 Terms," 1975 *Supreme Court Review*
      1 (1976), pp. 4–5.
62   A few days later . . . Hoppe, sent: Bill Hoppe, letter to Mel Wulf, 10/31/73,
      in Ginsburg files.
62   "Egad!" . . . "Today a woman is fully emancipated": Bill Hoppe, jurisdic-
      tional statement to Supreme Court, dated 6/29/73, in Ginsburg files.
62   His enclosed letter . . . "would appreciate any help": Bill Hoppe, letter to
      Mel Wulf, 10/31/71, in Ginsburg files.
63   "large leeway" . . . Douglas was unlikely: Ruth Bader Ginsburg, "Gender
      in the Supreme Court: The 1973 and 1974 Terms," 1975 *Supreme Court
      Review* 1 (1976), pp. 5–6.
63   Douglas saw his mother left destitute . . . "often meant the difference":

William O. Douglas, *Go East, Young Man: The Early Years* (New York: Random House, 1974), p. 21.

63 She decided not to discuss sex as a suspect classification: Ruth Bader Ginsburg, memo to Brenda Feigen and Marc Fasteau, 11/13/73, in Ginsburg files.

63 her oral argument for Kahn: Details and quotations of Ginsburg's oral argument are from Supreme Court transcript of *Kahn v. Shevin*, 416 U.S. 351 (1974).

64 the votes quickly went against Ginsburg . . . Scribbling notes . . . "women as widows are largely destitute": Conference notes, 3/1/74, in Douglas papers.

64 his opinion for the Court: Details and quotations from Douglas' opinion are from *Kahn v. Shevin*, 416 U.S. 351 (1974). See detailed notes online.

64 The lone consolation for Ginsburg: Markowitz, "In Pursuit," p. 86.

64 backward: Ruth Bader Ginsburg, "Supreme Court Back on Track," 1 *Women Law Reporter* 203 (May 1975), p. 203, in Wiesenfeld files.

4: *Wiesenfeld* Brings Reality

65 "bad precedent": Ruth Bader Ginsburg, letter to Stephen Wiesenfeld, 5/3/74, in Wiesenfeld files. Calling *Kahn* a "keen disappointment," she told Wiesenfeld that "bad precedent has been set and we will have to do our best to overcome it."

65 "if ever there was a case": Markowitz, "In Pursuit," p. 84. This discussion of *Wiesenfeld* is indebted to Markowitz and to parts of Cowan, "Women's Rights."

65 *Wiesenfeld* . . . "presents no possibility of settlement": Cowan, "Women's Rights," p. 397, and see pp. 395–399 for fine discussion of Ginsburg's strategy in *Wiesenfeld*.

65 media was beginning to call "men's lib": "Landmark for Male Liberation," *Family Circle*, June 1974, p. 14, in Wiesenfeld files.

66 the route to the Supreme Court would run . . . via district court: Ruth Bader Ginsburg, letter to Stephen Wiesenfeld, 12/27/72, in Wiesenfeld files.

66 "breaking new ground": Interview with Sandra Grayson, Manhasset, New York, by phone, 2/25/94.

67 a student would write; Professor Ginsburg would rewrite . . . manna . . . "I mean" . . . "to pick a man" . . . "Ruth" . . . would cut and polish . . . "OH, YES YES" . . . part of students' lives: Freeman interview.

67 "Having gone through more helpers and housekeepers": Ruth Bader Ginsburg, letter to Stephen Wiesenfeld, 1/10/73, in Wiesenfeld files.

67   Ginsburg's vision of an ideal society . . . "illustrative of what Ruth has been saying her whole life": Freeman interview.

68   Ginsburg challenged her ERA seminar: Cowan, "Women's Rights," p. 385.

68   "natural basis": "Widower Bids for Equal Aids on Benefits," *Newark Star Ledger*, 6/21/73, in Wiesenfeld files.

68   Wiesenfeld heard the government make an argument: Wiesenfeld interview.

68   "mother's insurance benefits" of just under $250 per month . . . could not exceed $200 per month: *Weinberger v. Wiesenfeld*, 420 U.S. 636, 641 (1975).

68   Stephen worried . . . without describing his scheme to Ginsburg . . . gave up his job at Cyphernetics: Wiesenfeld interview. He said, "She was the kind of person you knew would not ask you to alter your lifestyle or what you want to do in order to keep her going. But once I knew that these things might have an effect on the outcome, I chose to make it as simple as possible—to not disqualify myself by earning too much money." For "give up his job," see also Affidavit of Stephen Wiesenfeld, dated 9/28/73, in Appendix, filed 12/9/74, in *Weinberger v. Wiesenfeld*, 420 U.S. 636 (1975), p. 19.

70   "back in the situation" . . . affidavit: Ruth Bader Ginsburg, letter to Jane Z. Lifset, 9/12/73, in Ginsburg files; Ruth Bader Ginsburg, letter to Stephen Wiesenfeld, 2/7/93, and Jane Z. Lifset, letter to Stephen Wiesenfeld, 6/5/73, both in Wiesenfeld files.

70   never told Ginsburg: Ginsburg interview and Wiesenfeld interview.

70   "She was the kind of person": Wiesenfeld interview.

70   "strong argument for dismissal" . . . "inherently suspect": *Wiesenfeld v. Secretary of Health, Education & Welfare*, 367 F. Supp. 981, 986, 990 (D. N.J. 1973).

70   somewhat obscure position: Caplan, *Tenth Justice*, p. 3.

70   Bork . . . Cox . . . "Saturday night massacre": For narrative, see Bob Woodward and Carl Bernstein, *The Final Days* (New York: Simon and Schuster, 1976), pp. 66–72; Woodward and Armstrong, *Brethren*, pp. 339–341; Caplan, *Tenth Justice*, pp. 36–38.

71   Paula Wiesenfeld . . . "contributed to Social Security": Brief for Stephen Wiesenfeld by Ruth Bader Ginsburg and Melvin L. Wulf to Supreme Court, p. 10, filed 12/20/74, in *Weinberger v. Wiesenfeld*, 420 U.S. 636 (1975).

72   oral argument: Details and quotations of Ginsburg's oral argument, unless otherwise indicated, are from Supreme Court transcript of *Weinberger v. Wiesenfeld*, 420 U.S. 636 (1975), argued 1/20/75. See detailed notes online.

72 sat him directly beside her . . . "this was as genuine as any case" . . . "this sort of sex stereotyping" . . . see themselves: Ginsburg interview.

73 "presents a classic example": Brief for Stephen Wiesenfeld by Ruth Bader Ginsburg and Melvin L. Wulf to Supreme Court, p. 23, filed 12/20/74, in *Weinberger v. Wiesenfeld*, 420 U.S. 636 (1975).

73 Wiesenfeld was sitting at home. . . . Ginsburg was calling: Wiesenfeld interview.

74 "The Government seeks to characterize": This and subsequent quotations of the Court's opinions are from *Weinberger v. Wiesenfeld*, 420 U.S. 636 (1975). See detailed notes online.

74 "This was Justice Brennan's year": Lynn Hecht Schafran, letter to Ruth Bader Ginsburg, 4/4/75, in Ginsburg files.

75 Schafran had the story basically right: Berzon interview. When I related Schafran's narrative to Berzon, she exclaimed, "Who told you that? Who knows it?"

75 Another rumor . . . curse in chambers . . . "an older gentleman": Berzon interview.

75 Burger, Rehnquist, and apparently Blackmun planned to vote against: Blackmun papers.

75 "had to be the perfect case": Ginsburg interview.

76 Gone, as if forgotten . . . "strict scrutiny" . . . knew Brennan could not muster the votes . . . " 'heightened scrutiny' without further labeling": Ruth Bader Ginsburg, letter to Professor Elizabeth Defeis, 8/18/75, in Ginsburg files; quoted partly in Markowitz, "In Pursuit," p. 88.

76 "skeptical scrutiny": *United States v. Virginia*, 518 U.S. 515, 531 (1996).

76 Wiesenfeld . . . wanted the victory to be not just principled . . . "I wanted to make sure that I qualified for the benefit for a while" . . . entrepreneurial venture: Wiesenfeld interview.

76 $22,000 profit . . . 1975 to 1982 on Social Security benefits: Stephen Wiesenfeld, letter to author, 10/1/03.

Part Two
PREGNANCY (1972–1978)

In this part, I rely on the personal papers of Ruth Weyand (courtesy of her daughter) and interviews with a number of plaintiffs and attorneys including Sally (Augustina) Armendariz, Linda Dorian, Mary Dunlap, Ruth Bader Ginsburg, Jacqueline Jaramillo, Herma Hill Kay, Stanley Pottinger, Susan Deller Ross, Peter Weiner, and Wendy Webster Williams. Important primary sources, particularly interviews and collections of documents, are listed below, with the abbreviations used in the endnotes that follow. Other primary sources and

important secondary sources appear with full citations in the endnotes. More
detailed endnotes can be found at www.wwnorton.com and www.equalwomen
.com.

Armendariz interview	Interview with Sally (Augustina) Armendariz, Gilroy, California, 5/16/95
Blackmun papers	Papers of Justice Harry A. Blackmun, Library of Congress
Brennan papers	Papers of Justice William J. Brennan Jr., Library of Congress
Dorian interview	Interview with Linda Dorian, Olviedo, Florida, by phone, 9/18/95
Dunlap interview	Interview with Mary Dunlap, San Francisco, by phone, 6/6/95
East files	Files of Catherine East as of 2/8/95
East interview	Interview with Catherine East, Arlington, Virginia, 2/8/95
Fuentes interview	Interview with Sonia Pressman Fuentes, Potomac, Maryland, by phone, 6/14/95
Ginsburg interview	Interview with Ruth Bader Ginsburg, Washington, DC, 8/24/94
Greenberger interviews	Interviews with Marcia Greenberger, Washington, DC, by phone, 6/13/95 and 6/28/95
Jaramillo interviews	Interviews with Jacqueline Jaramillo, Colorado Springs, by phone, 6/9/95 and 6/14/95
Kay interview	Interview with Herma Hill Kay, Berkeley, California, 5/10/95
Marshall papers	Papers of Thurgood Marshall, Library of Congress
Pottinger interview	Interview with Stanley Pottinger, South Salem, New York, by phone, 9/15/95
Ross and Williams interview	Interview with Susan Deller Ross and Wendy Webste Williams, Washington, DC, 8/25/94
Weiner interview	Interview with Peter Weiner, driving in California, by phone, 5/2/95
Weyand files	Files of the late Ruth Weyand (courtesy of her daughter, Sterling Perry) as of 5/21/95
Weyand interview	Thomas J. Moore, "Interview with Ruth Weyand," 3/25/77, Part 4, p. 38, in "Monograph, *General Electric Company v. Gilbert*, Professor Park, April 28, 1977," in files of the late Ruth Weyand (courtesy of her daughter, Sterling Perry) as of 5/21/95

5: What Happened to Sally Armendariz Could Not Happen to a Man

81 "happen to a man": Ruth Bader Ginsburg, "From No Rights, to Half Rights, to Confusing Rights," 7 *Human Rights* 13 (1978).

81 rear-ended by another car . . . mother . . . woke up blind: Armendariz interview.

81 twenty-nine years earlier: Consolidated Complaint for Injunctive and Declaratory Relief (Civil Rights) by Roland C. Davis, Joel Gomberg, Cecilia D. Lannon, Joseph C. Morehead, Peter Hart Weiner, and Wendy Webster Williams to United States District Court for the Northern District of California, dated 12/26/72, in Civ. No. C-72–1402 SW [*Carolyn Aiello v. Sigurd Hansen*] and C-72–1547 SW [*Augustina D. Armendariz, Elizabeth B. Johnson, Jacqueline Jaramillo v. Sigurd Hansen*], reprinted in Brief for the State of California to the Supreme Court, Appendix, dated 2/9/74, in *Geduldig v. Aiello*, 417 U.S. 484 (1974). Further references will be cited as *Aiello* complaint.

82 miscarriage . . . not even wash dishes: *Aiello* complaint.

82 Her doctor told her to stay away: *Aiello v. Hansen*, 359 F. Supp. 792, 795 (N.D. Cal. 1973).

82 Disability Insurance . . . "arising in connection with pregnancy": *Geduldig v. Aiello*, 417 U.S. 484, 486, 489 (1974).

82 Young Christian Workers . . . demanded an appeal . . . voluntary? . . . "all the time": Armendariz interview.

83 "the guys": Armendariz interview.

83 One of the first guys . . . one of his fellow clerks: Weiner interview.

83 federal fellowships . . . poverty law: Wendy Webster Williams, letter to author, 6/10/05.

84 talk to him about his work: Dunlap interview.

84 few women law students: Sandra Pearl Epstein, "Law at Berkeley: The History of Boalt Hall" (PhD dissertation, University of California, Berkeley, 1979), p. 426. Further references will be cited as Epstein, "Law at Berkeley."

84 belonged at home . . . wasting spaces: Dunlap interview.

84 "strict scrutiny" . . . "not in our lifetimes": Ross and Williams interview.

84 fourteenth woman appointed . . . Armstrong, had been appointed at Berkeley in 1922: Herma Hill Kay, "The Future of Women Law Professors," 77 *Iowa Law Review* 5 (1991).

84 Barbara Nachtrieb Armstrong . . . not fall to zero: Epstein, "Law at Berkeley," pp. 410, 421–425.

85 "rife with discrimination" . . . liberalizing abortion: Harriet Chiang, "Crusader Leads Boalt Hall," *San Francisco Chronicle*, 8/7/92, p. A12.

85   inspired by Amelia Earhart, she flew: Wendy Webster Williams, letter to author, 6/10/05.

85   no organization at Boalt Hall . . . discuss the status of women: Kay interview.

85   Boalt Hall Law Wives Club . . . served coffee: "An Informal Introduction to Boalt Hall," 1970, p. 20, typescript in library of Boalt Hall.

85   no group gathered university women . . . someone in the president's office . . . "Dear Boalt Hall Girl": Kay interview.

85   new breed: not passive consumers: Herma Hill Kay, "The Future of Women Law Professors," 77 *Iowa Law Review* 5 (1991).

86   On the spot, the women decided: Wendy Webster Williams, speaking during interview with Ruth Bader Ginsburg conducted by Deborah L. Markowitz with Susan Deller Ross and Wendy Webster Williams, Washington, DC, 2/24/86, as preparation for Deborah L. Markowitz, "In Pursuit of Equality: One Woman's Work to Change the Law," 11 *Women's Rights Law Reporter* 73 (Summer 1989), pp. 73–98. Further references will be cited as Markowitz interview with Ginsburg.

86   Boalt Hall Women's Association . . . plan a course . . . "rooting out of anti-woman discrimination": "An Informal Introduction to Boalt Hall," 1970, p. 20, typescript in library of Boalt Hall.

86   "Wanted by the Law: Women!": Wendy Webster Williams, "The Gifts of Mary Dunlap (1949–2003)," 19 *Berkeley Women's Law Journal* 12 (2004), pp. 12–13.

86   tall woman stood out . . . urgency and energy . . . "Question Authority!": Kay interview.

86   "deny review" . . . "scooting right in to my judge" . . . sex discrimination!: Williams, in Ross and Williams interview.

86   Justice Peters . . . write me a memo . . . "killed myself" . . . "Well": Williams, in Ross and Williams interview.

87   "sprightly and ribald": *Goesaert v. Cleary*, 335 U.S. 464 (1948), quoted in Ruth Bader Ginsburg, *Text, Cases, and Materials on Constitutional Aspects of Sex-Based Discrimination* (St. Paul: West Publishing, 1974), p. 17; and see Part 1 in the book.

87   Sail'er Inn was a topless bar . . . topless bartenders: Kay interview and Dunlap interview.

87   rely on that brief in her draft: Wendy Webster Williams, letter to author, 6/10/05.

87   a bit improper . . . "An *amicus* brief HAS TO COME IN." And Professor Kay said: Williams, in Ross and Williams interview.

87   Kay . . . called on the students: Kay interview.

88   "the smarmiest thing": Dunlap interview.

88   Women's Association resolved . . . Kay gave guidance: Kay interview.

88 Mary Dunlap and Margaret Kemp, wrote the brief: Dunlap interview. Quotations from the *Sail'er Inn* brief are from Brief for Sail'er Inn, a California Corporation, doing business as The Classic Cat, by Herma Hill Kay, Sponsor of the Boalt Hall Women's Association, to the Supreme Court of the State of California, dated 12/1/70, in *Sail'er Inn v. Kirby*, 5 Cal.3d 1 (1971); copy in files of Herma Hill Kay as of 8/1/97.

88 Sail'er Inn lawyers . . . used the Boalt Hall brief . . . "Hi! This is Ray Peters": Williams, in Ross and Williams interview.

89 first decision . . . sex discrimination violated the Constitution: Wendy Webster Williams, letter to author, 6/10/05.

89 decision in *Sail'er Inn*: Quotations from the *Sail'er Inn* decision are from *Sail'er Inn v. Kirby*, 5 Cal.3d 1 (1971). See detailed notes online.

89 No one reading . . . naked women: The *Sail'er Inn* opinion makes no reference to such words as *naked, nude,* or *topless.*

6: The First Pregnancy Case: *Aiello*

90 Williams heard . . . worked together: Ross and Williams interview.

90 Elizabeth Johnson, a single mother with a five-year-old child: Most details of Johnson's story are from *Aiello* complaint and from interview with Cecilia Lannon, attorney for Elizabeth Johnson, San Rafael, California, by phone, 5/5/95.

91 Jaramillo, from Oakland: Most details of Jaramillo's story are from Jaramillo interviews and *Aiello* complaint.

91 Williams . . . last vacation: Wendy Webster Williams, letter to author, 6/10/05.

91 Williams . . . filed suit as planned in state court . . . California . . . requested that her cases be removed to federal court: Williams, in Ross and Williams interview. See also Jurisdictional Statement by Evelle J. Younger, Elizabeth Palmer, and Joanne Condas to Supreme Court, p. 5n4, in *Geduldig v. Aiello*, 417 U.S. 484 (1974). Further references will be cited as California Jurisdictional Statement in *Geduldig v. Aiello*.

91 Aiello, whose original lawyer soon decided to leave the case: Wendy Webster Williams, letter to author, 6/10/05.

92 The shock waves from *Aiello*: Greenberger interviews.

92 In nine arguments . . . had not lost: Paul Bogas, "Patience, Planning Pay Off for Equal Pay Act Counsel," *National Law Journal*, 12/23/85, p. 1. Further references will be cited as Bogas, "Patience."

92 In the first half of 1971 . . . groundwork: Equal Employment Opportunity Commission, "Failure to Include Pregnancy under Disability Insurance Plan Was Sex Bias," Decision No. 71–1474, 3/19/71, in Weyand files. This EEOC decision initiated the case that Weyand argued as *General Electric*

Company v. Gilbert, 429 U.S. 125 (1976). See also Weyand interview, p. 4-38; Weyand explains that the case began in response to a report on the EEOC decision of March 19 that she published in the May–June 1971 issue of her union's publication, *Keeping Up with the Law.*

92   nephew to a famous feminist . . . tried to get him disqualified . . . met when he refused to hire her as his clerk . . . He started muttering . . . secretary didn't want to work with female law clerks: Williams, in Ross and Williams interview.

93   "classifications based upon": Brief for Appellees (Carolyn Aiello et al.) by Wendy Webster Williams and Peter Hart Weiner to Supreme Court, p. 24, dated 3/13/74, in *Geduldig v. Aiello*, 417 U.S. 484 (1974).

93   breakthrough . . . new lawyer: Susan Deller Ross, letter to author, 8/8/05, and see Part 1 in the book.

93   Wendy did a great job: Armendariz interview.

93   May 31, 1973, . . . opinion, written by Alfonso Zirpoli: Quotations from *Aiello* opinions, unless otherwise indicated, are from *Aiello v. Hansen*, 359 F. Supp. 792 (N.D. Cal. 1973). See detailed notes online.

95   *Supremes* . . . men on the high court: Williams, in Ross and Williams interview.

95   another California woman: *Rentzer v. Unemployment Insurance Appeals Board*, 32 Cal. App. 3d 604, 108 Cal. Rptr. 336 (1973).

95   compensate "in part" for wage loss . . . "abnormal pregnancy with involuntary implications" . . . "normal pregnancy and delivery": California Jurisdictional Statement in *Geduldig v. Aiello*, pp. 8, 41, 49.

95   Armendariz, for example, received $84: Armendariz interview.

96   When Jacqueline Jaramillo's IUD failed: Jaramillo interviews and *Aiello* complaint.

96   "cradle Catholic" . . . worry that abortion might be her only chance: Jaramillo interviews.

97   Center for Law and Social Policy . . . imperfect case: Greenberger interviews.

98   As oral arguments began: Details of and quotations from oral arguments, unless otherwise indicated, are from Supreme Court transcript of *Geduldig v. Aiello*, 417 U.S. 484 (1974), argued 3/26/74. Further references will be cited as Supreme Court transcript of *Geduldig v. Aiello*. See detailed notes online.

98   "redhead" and "B+": Blackmun's oral argument notes in Blackmun papers.

99   On crutches . . . None asked: Ross and Williams interview.

99   Blackmun scribbled "B-" . . . "long stringy hair": Blackmun's oral argument notes in Blackmun papers.

100   not until 1971 had two women . . . right to abortion: Clare Cushman, ed.,

Supreme Court Decisions And Women's Rights: Milestones to Equality (Washington, DC: CQ Press, 2001), p. 272. Further references will be cited as Cushman, *Supreme Court*. *Doe v. Bolton* is discussed in Garrow, *Liberty and Sexuality.*

101 In the conference for discussion of *Geduldig v. Aiello:* Tally sheet in Blackmun papers and memos in Brennan papers.

101 Stewart's draft: Quotations from Stewart's draft opinion in *Geduldig v. Aiello* are from Justice Potter Stewart, "2nd DRAFT," circulated 5/15/74, in Brennan papers.

102 "skirted discussion of sex discrimination": RR [apparently Robert I. Richter], memo to Justice Harry A. Blackmun, 5/15/74, in Blackmun papers.

102 Brennan circulated a draft of his answering dissent: Quotations from Brennan's draft are from Justice William J. Brennan Jr., circulated in typescript 6/10/74, in Brennan papers, dissent in *Geduldig v. Aiello,* 417 U.S. 484 (1974).

102 twenty-four-line footnote: Quotations from the footnote are from Justice Potter Stewart, "3rd DRAFT," circulated 6/12/74, in Brennan papers.

7: The Second Pregnancy Case: *General Electric*

104 most successful women lawyers in the history of Supreme Court: Some women who, unlike Weyand, were not undefeated at the Supreme Court had argued more often there, with the record going to thirty cases argued by Bea Rosenberg. See Cushman, *Supreme Court*, pp. 228–229.

104 By the time she was seven years old, Ruth Weyand: This and other details of her life are from Bogas, "Patience," p. 1; "Courage, Patience, and Driving Energy: A Portrait of Ruth Weyand," *Law School Record* (University of Chicago Law School), Spring 1986, pp. 14–15; "Ruth Weyand Resume," typescript in files of the late Phineas Indritz as of 9/17/95; and Bart Barnes, "EEOC Counsel Ruth Weyand Identified as Crash Victim," *Washington Post*, 11/20/86, p. B10. See detailed notes online.

105 "I wanted to go right out" . . . "If I could" . . . "the faculty was not keen": Bogas, "Patience," p. 1.

106 "I kept submitting briefs": Bogas, "Patience," p. 1.

106 late 1940s . . . with Thurgood Marshall: Interview with Phineas Indritz, Silver Spring, Maryland, by phone, 9/15/95, and see *Shelley v. Kraemer,* 334 U.S. 1 (1948), argued by Thurgood Marshall and Loren Miller, with Ruth Weyand "with them on the brief."

106 another NAACP lawyer, Leslie S. Perry: "Lobbyists: Four Negroes Working behind the Scenes to Influence Congress on Civil Rights," *Ebony*, July 1950, pp. 25–28.

106 married in 1949 . . . 1950, when word of their marriage became public:

"Perry Swears He's Wed to Miss Weyand," *Washington Post*, 2/4/50, p. B7.

106 alienating her husband's affections: "Miss Weyand, NLRB Attorney, Sued by NAACP Man's Wife," *Washington Post*, 1/10/50, p. 13.

106 Interracial marriage remained illegal . . . "a successful negro male": "Famous Negroes Married to Whites," *Ebony*, December 1949, pp. 20–30.

106 Weyand chose not to use anesthesia: Greenberger interviews.

107 "was reported to feel that Miss Weyand's value": "Ruth Weyand, NLRB Lawyer, Who Married Negro, Is Fired," *Washington Post*, 1/19/50, p. 1.

107 Weyand played a major role . . . "comparable worth" . . . Equal Pay Act of 1963: Judy Mann, "A Gentleman and a Lawyer," *Washington Post*, 7/8/94, p. E3.

107 "take-it-or leave-it" . . . *Boulwarism*: Bart Barnes, "EEOC Counsel Ruth Weyand Identified as Crash Victim," *Washington Post*, 11/20/86, p. B10.

107 ideal case for Ruth Weyand: Details on the case and its origins are from Weyand interview. I am indebted to this fine interview, saved by Ruth Weyand and her daughter, for much of the narrative of Ruth Weyand's early work on the *General Electric* case. See also Susan M. Hartmann, *The Other Feminists: Activists in the Liberal Establishment* (New Haven: Yale University Press, 1998), p. 44.

108 Barbara Hall . . . "felt good": Joint Appendix, dated 11/24/75, in *General Electric v. Gilbert*, 429 U.S. 125 (1976).

108 in a flip: Photograph of Martha Gilbert (and others) for *AFL-CIO News*, 4/20/74, in Weyand files.

108 Erma Thomas . . . Emma Furch: Brief for Martha V. Gilbert et al. by Winn Newman, Ruth Weyand, and Seymour DuBow to Supreme Court, dated 12/31/75, in *General Electric v. Gilbert*, 429 U.S. 125 (1976), pp. 23–29, 32–35. Further references will be cited as *Gilbert* brief. See further notes online.

109 Sherrie O'Steen . . . "put me out without pay": Joint Appendix, dated 11/24/75, in *General Electric v. Gilbert*, 429 U.S. 125 (1976).

109 "women did not recognize the responsibilities of life": Appendix Vol. III, p. 958, dated 11/24/75, in *General Electric v. Gilbert*, 429 U.S. 125 (1976), quoting Gerard Swope in David Loth, *Swope of GE* (New York: Simon and Schuster, 1958).

109 "long-standing differentials between rates for women's jobs and men's jobs": Decision of the War Labor Board in *General Electric Company*, 28 War Labor Rep. 666 (1945), reprinted in Appendix Vol. III, pp. 996–1003, dated 11/24/75, in *General Electric v. Gilbert*, 429 U.S. 125 (1976).

110 Title VII was the employment section of the landmark Civil Rights Act of 1964: Narrative of events leading to Title VII relies significantly on Richard

Kluger, *Simple Justice: The History of* Brown v. Board of Education *and Black America's Struggle for Equality* (New York: Vintage Books, 1975), p. 755ff. Further references will be cited as Kluger, *Simple Justice.*

111 Equal Pay Act of 1963: History of Equal Pay Act relies on Cynthia Harrison, *On Account of Sex: The Politics of Women's Issues, 1945–1968* (Berkeley: University of California Press, 1988). See also Jo Freeman, *The Politics of Women's Liberation* (New York: McKay, 1975), and Catharine MacKinnon, *Sex Equality* (New York: Foundation Press, 2001), p. 17ff. Further references will be cited as Harrison, *On Account of Sex* and Freeman, *Politics of Women's Liberation.* See further notes online.

112 "a seniority system": The language of Equal Pay Act of 1963 is from 29 U.S.C. section 206(d) (1) (1964), quoted in Caruthers Gholson Berger, "Equal Pay, Equal Employment Opportunity and Equal Enforcement of the Law for Women," 5 *Valparaiso University Law Review* 326 (1971), p. 327.

112 "race, color, religion, or national origin" . . . nothing about sex . . . "would not even give protection": The quotations and narrative of the campaign to add "sex" to Civil Rights Act of 1964 are from Harrison, *On Account of Sex*, p. 176.

112 equal rights amendment . . . opposed by the Kennedy administration: Pauli Murray, *Song in a Weary Throat: An American Pilgrimage* (New York: Harper and Row, 1987), pp. 348–349.

112 party sent every member of Congress a resolution: Caruthers Gholson Berger, "Equal Pay, Equal Employment Opportunity and Equal Enforcement of the Law for Women," 5 *Valparaiso University Law Review* 326 (1971), p. 332.

112 If civil rights legislation had to pass, Smith had been arguing . . . lacked the votes: Jo Freeman, "How Sex Got into Title VII," 9 *Journal of Law and Inequality* 163 (1991), pp. 171, 181. Further references will be cited as Freeman, "How Sex."

113 two congresswomen decided: Harrison, *On Account of Sex*, p. 177; see also Freeman, "How Sex," and, for role of Martha Griffiths, see Flora Davis, *Moving the Mountain: The Women's Movement in America since 1960* (New York: Simon and Schuster, 1991), pp. 39–40 and 504–505. Further references will be cited as Davis, *Moving the Mountain.*

113 On February 8, 1964, Smith rose on the House floor to propose an amendment . . . "real grievances" . . . "yes, dear": *Civil Rights Act* of 1964, 88th Cong., 2d sess., *Congressional Record* 110 (2/8/64): H 2577.

113 eleven of the twelve women members: Harrison, *On Account of Sex*, pp. 178–179.]

113 "if a colored woman shows up": *Civil Rights Act* of 1964, 88th Cong., 2d sess., *Congressional Record* 110 (2/8/64): H 2579.

114   all but one of the men . . . voted against the full bill: Harrison, *On Account of Sex*, p. 179.

114   according to Griffiths, Smith told her that he had offered his sex amendment "as a joke": Davis, *Moving the Mountain*, p. 45, based on interview of Griffiths by Davis, 12/3/85.

114   many women lobbied aggressively: Strong support came from the National Federation of Business and Professional Women, with 150,000 members; see Freeman, "How Sex," p. 178.

115   a third of all complaints, far more than expected, came from women: Equal Employment Opportunity Commission, Fifth Annual Report (1971), p. 30, cited in Freeman, "How Sex," p. 164. See also Sonia Pressman Fuentes, *Eat First—You Don't Know What They'll Give You, the Adventures of an Immigrant Family and Their Feminist Daughter* (Philadelphia: Xlibris, 1999), p. 131. Further references will be cited as Fuentes, *Eat First*.

115   "boredom" to "virulent hostility": Aileen Hernandez, quoted in Harrison, *On Account of Sex*, p. 187.

115   first executive director . . . "the Commission is very much aware": Harrison, *On Account of Sex*, p. 187.

115   "fluke" that had been "conceived out of wedlock": Herman Edelsberg, at NYU 18th conference on labor, 61 *Labor Relations Reporter* (8/25/66), pp. 253–255, quoted in Freeman, *Politics of Women's Liberation*, p. 54n26.

115   In one of its earliest decisions, the EEOC . . . "no blacks need apply" . . . segregated by sex: Harrison, *On Account of Sex*, pp. 188–190.

115   Pregnancy seemed the toughest issue: Fuentes interview. See note online.

115   first woman lawyer . . . "sex maniac": Fuentes, *Eat First*, pp. 129–132.

115   two theories . . . "disability due to pregnancy" . . . terminate a woman when her pregnancy started to show . . . Did seniority accumulate during pregnancy leave?: Sonia Pressman Fuentes and Cruz Reynoso, "Prohibition in Sex Discrimination on the Basis of Pregnancy" (law review article draft), undated but c. 1968, in files of and courtesy of Sonia Pressman Fuentes, 6/14/95, pp. 1–4, 16, 23. See note online.

116   At the start of the 1970s . . . Sonia Fuentes . . . leaned personally toward special treatment . . . pregnant with her own daughter in 1971, six weeks sounded about right: Fuentes interview.

116   In the fall of 1970 . . . believed was the best place: Ross and Williams interview.

117   two of the ACLU's women board members were hopping mad: Interview with Susan Deller Ross, Washington, DC, 8/25/94. For related narrative, see also Susan M. Hartmann, *The Other Feminists: Activists in the Liberal Establishment* (New Haven: Yale University Press, 1998), pp. 71–81.

117   Ross took on . . . special-treatment laws: Ross and Williams interview; Susan Deller Ross, letter to author, 8/8/05; and see Susan Deller Ross, "Sex

Discrimination and 'Protective' Labor Legislation," reprinted in House Committee on Education and Labor, Special Subcommittee on Education, *Discrimination against Women: Hearings on Section 805 of H.R. 16098,* 91st Cong., 2d sess., 1970, pp. 592–603.

117 As Ross's critique of protective labor laws became known: East interview.

118 "Disabilities caused or contributed": Equal Employment Opportunity Commission, "Guidelines on Discrimination Because of Sex," Part 1604.10b, Title 29 of the *Code of Federal Regulations, Federal Register* 37 (4/5/72): 6837; quoted in *Gilbert v. General Electric,* 375 F. Supp. 367, 380 (E.D. Va. 1974).

118 "equal treatment" . . . advantages: Wendy Webster Williams, "Equality's Riddle: Pregnancy and the Equal Treatment/Special Treatment Debate," 13 *New York University Review of Law and Social Change* 323 (1984–85), p. 328.

119 She chose . . . Robert R. Merhige Jr.: Weyand interview, p. 4-42.

119 Judge Merhige's opinion . . . "The maternity policy": *Cohen v. Chesterfield County,* 326 F. Supp. 1159 (E.D. Va. 1971), 1161.

119 General Electric trial in district court . . . "serious doubts that costs mean anything": Details are from excerpts of transcripts of proceedings of *Gilbert v. General Electric,* 375 F. Supp. 367 (E.D. Va. 1974), argued 7/24–26/73, reprinted in Appendix Vol. I, p. 308, through Vol. II, p. 717, dated 11/24/75, in *General Electric v. Gilbert,* 429 U.S. 125 (1976).

120 "friendly judge": Weyand interview, p. 4-43.

120 Then in early 1973 the entire court of appeals . . . "can relieve females from all of the burdens": *Cohen v. Chesterfield County,* 474 F.2d 395, 397 (4th Cir. 1973).

120 Three months later, the Supreme Court said it would hear: *Cohen v. Chesterfield County,* 411 U.S. 947, certiorari granted, 4/23/73.

120 within three months, Judge Merhige issued his long-delayed *General Electric* opinion: Quotations of Merhige's opinion are from *Gilbert v. General Electric,* 375 F. Supp. 367 (E.D. Va. 1974), decided 4/13/74. See detailed notes online.

122 Weyand felt doomed: Weyand interview, p. 4-44.

122 Beatrice Rosenberg . . . more cases than any other woman: Cushman, *Supreme Court,* pp. 228–229.

122 Then in 1972, she moved to join the EEOC: "Beatrice Rosenberg; Prominent Attorney for the U.S. Was 81," *New York Times,* 12/2/89, p. 1:15.

122 Rosenberg sent Linda Dorian . . . Dorian found Weyand . . . piles of documents . . . least wanted to face Clement Haynsworth: Dorian interview.

122 "relieve females": *Cohen v. Chesterfield County,* 474 F.2d 395, 397 (4th Cir. 1973).

123 GE's lawyers appeared jubilant: Dorian interview.

123 To Weyand, the *Liberty Mutual* case had terrible shortcomings . . . very few details: Weyand interview, pp. 4–60–61; Theophil C. Kammholz, Stanley R. Strauss, John S. Battle Jr., J. Robert Brame III, Winn Newman, Ruth Weyand, and Seymour DuBow, "Joint Petition of All Parties for a Writ of Certoriari to the United States Court of Appeals for the Fourth Circuit," p. 7, filed 6/17/75, in *General Electric v. Gilbert*, 429 U.S. 125 (1976).

123 no "evidentiary facts that could arguably give rise to a defense": *Wetzel v. Liberty Mutual*, 511 F.2d 199, 208 (3rd Cir. 1975).

124 GE's lawyers wrote to the court of appeals to ask for a quick decision . . . appeals court . . . would delay . . . One of GE's attorneys then went to Weyand with a suggestion: Interview with Stanley R. Strauss, counsel for General Electric, by Samuel J. Malizia, Washington, DC, 4/6/77, p. 14, in Weyand files. Further references will be cited as Strauss 1977 interview by Malizia.

124 Bea Rosenberg at the EEOC agreed: Dorian interview.

125 "a well-recognized difference" . . . "need only be 'rationally supportable'": *Gilbert v. General Electric*, 519 F.2d 661, 666–667 (4th Cir. 1975).

125 Supreme Court argument: Quotations from oral arguments are from Supreme Court transcript of *Liberty Mutual v. Wetzel*, 424 U.S. 737 (1976), argued 1/19/76; Supreme Court transcript of *General Electric v. Gilbert*, 429 U.S. 125 (1976), argued 1/19–20/76 (first oral argument). See detailed notes online.

128 "didn't want the government to participate": Dorian interview.

128 "tighten your brief again": Dorian interview.

129 *General Electric* would be "restored to calendar for reargument": *General Electric v. Gilbert*, 425 U.S. 989 (1976).

129 rearguments were uncommon: David J. Fitzmaurice, "Memorandum," 6/23/76, in Weyand files.

129 school desegregation cases . . . lengthy questions: Kluger, *Simple Justice*, p. 615.

129 attorneys received no guidance . . . Speculation among attorneys: Dorian interview, and Strauss 1977 interview by Malizia, pp. 15–16.

129 Blackmun's notes . . . "pass": Conference notes in Blackmun papers; conference notes are thin in Brennan papers.

129 "Do I recuse"?: Justice Harry A. Blackmun, handwritten note to self, 9/18/76, in Blackmun papers.

129 "4 to 4" . . . "a bit of strong-arming in typical PS fashion": Justice Harry A. Blackmun, dictated note to self, 8/31/76, in Blackmun papers.

130 "male-oriented" . . . "oh, come now?" . . . "so—" . . . "I have no idea"

. . . "Donna overstates": Donna Murasky, typed memo to Justice Harry A. Blackmun, 8/14/76, in Blackmun papers. Justice Harry A. Blackmun's handwritten marginalia is on pp. 10, 26.

130 Rosenberg . . . sought to assure Weyand . . . "OK, Linda, here's the deal": Dorian interview.

130 reputation for making sex discrimination a priority in the Civil Rights Division: Brian K. Landsberg, email to author, 5/7/03.

130 He had pressed to end discrimination against women in universities: Ginsburg interview.

130 Baffled when invited to join the reargument . . . "doomed mission": Pottinger interview.

131 opening the reargument: Details and quotations from the reargument, unless otherwise indicated, are from Supreme Court transcript of *General Electric v. Gilbert*, 429 U.S. 125 (1976), reargued 10/13/76 (second oral argument).

132 turning red in the face: Dorian interview.

132 "Boy this is just exactly": Pottinger interview.

133 Weyand had lost her poise but Pottinger had kept his . . . "Linda" . . . "he didn't want the government involved": Dorian interview.

133 Blackmun . . . remained a hope: Interview with Seymour DuBow, by Thomas J. Moore, Washington, DC, 3/23/77, in Weyand files.

133 "pretty bad": Justice Blackmun, handwritten notes during oral argument, 10/13/76, in Blackmun papers.

133 *General Electric* decision: *General Electric v. Gilbert*, 429 U.S. 125 (1976).

133 justices' conference in October . . . "still not firm" . . . "still is correct": Justice Blackmun, conference notes in Blackmun papers.

133 Brennan, preparing to dissent: Justice William J. Brennan Jr., letter to Justices Marshall and Stevens, 10/20/76, in Marshall papers.

133 "culminated" in the 1972 EEOC guidelines: *General Electric v. Gilbert*, 429 U.S. 125, 156 (1976) (Brennan dissenting), identical text to first draft of dissent, circulated 11/23/76, p. 12, in Brennan papers.

134 Stewart urged Rehnquist to follow Blackmun's: Potter Stewart, letter to William Rehnquist, 11/22/76, in Blackmun papers.

134 In his opinion, Rehnquist: Details and quotations are from *General Electric v. Gilbert*, 429 U.S. 125 (1976).

134 letters (dug up by GE) . . . same general counsel, Charles Duncan . . . "sex maniac": Testimony of Charles Duncan, in excerpts from transcript of proceedings of *Gilbert v. General Electric*, 375 F. Supp. 367 (E.D. Va. 1974), argued 7/24–26/73, reprinted in Appendix, p. 666, dated 11/24/75, in *General Electric v. Gilbert*, 429 U.S. 125 (1976); "Opinion Letter of General Counsel, October 17, 1966," in Appendix, pp. 720–722, quoted

in *General Electric v. Gilbert*, 429 U.S. 125, 142 (1976); Fuentes, *Eat First*, pp. 129–132.

135 Stevens . . . "Of course": *General Electric v. Gilbert*, 429 U.S. 125, 161 (1976).

8: The Final Pregnancy Battle: Beyond the Supreme Court

136 "Women's Rights Movement Is Dealt Major Blow" . . . "shock and anger": Lesley Oelsner, "Supreme Court Rules Employers May Refuse Pregnancy Sick Pay," *New York Times*, 12/8/76, p. A1.

136 Weyand . . . did not mope. She laid a plan: Bogas, "Patience," p. 1.

136 the lone dissenter on the court of appeals had started a pattern . . . "legislate in favor" . . . "legislatures have made less rational classifications for centuries": *Gilbert v. General Electric*, 519 F.2d 661, 669 (4th Cir. 1975).

136 "the folks" in Congress: Supreme Court transcript of *General Electric v. Gilbert*, 429 U.S. 125 (1976), argued 1/19–20/76 (first oral argument).

137 "if we are wrong, Congress can change": Justice Harry A. Blackmun, handwritten note to self, 9/18/76, in Blackmun papers, which contains both "if we are wrong, Congress can change" and (as its last words) "Congress can change if we are wrong." See also Justice Harry A. Blackmun, dictated note to self, 8/31/76, in Blackmun papers, pp. 5–6, which says, "If we are wrong, Congress could change the Act" and "There is one comfort, and that is that Congress may cure the situation if our guess is not in accord with their desire."

137 As she read Justice Rehnquist's *General Electric* opinion . . . "did not intend": *General Electric v. Gilbert*, 429 U.S. 125, 140 (1976).

137 hastily typed press release . . . "move to get Congress": "For Immediate Release," carbon copy dated 12/7/76, in Weyand files.

137 An Associated Press wire story . . . gave half its space: Richard Carelli, "Court-Pregnancy," Associated Press (typescript), 12/8/76, in Weyand files.

137 long-term planning: Dorian interview.

137 took a "dive": Pottinger interview.

137 Within days . . . "Feminist Leaders Plan": UPI, "Feminist Leaders Plan Coalition for Law Aiding Pregnant Women," *New York Times*, 12/15/76, p. 2:14.

138 op-ed article . . . "If it is not sex discrimination": Ruth Bader Ginsburg and Susan Deller Ross, "Pregnancy and Discrimination," *New York Times*, 1/25/77, p. 33.

138 Ross and . . . Williams . . . testifying: Quotations from the bill and the committee hearing are from House Committee on Education and Labor,

Subcommittee on Employment Opportunities, *Legislation to Prohibit Sex Discrimination on the Basis of Pregnancy: Hearing before the Subcommittee on Employment Opportunities of the Committee on Education and Labor, House of Representatives, Ninety-fifth Congress, First Session, on H.R. 5055 and H.R. 6075 . . . Held in Washington, D.C., April 6 [–June 29], 1977*, 2 vols. (Washington, DC: U.S. Government Printing Office, 1977).

138 stayed up most of the night: Ross and Williams interview.
139 "overturn" . . . "I know that when I cast my vote for Title VII" . . . 376 to 43 in the House . . . won in all the courts of appeals . . . eighteen district courts: Senate Committee on Labor and Human Resources, *Legislative History of the Pregnancy Discrimination Act of 1978: Public Law 95–555* (Washington, DC: U.S. Government Printing Office, 1980), pp. 2, 11–12, 137, 191, 211.

Part Three
LAWYERING (1968–1984)

In this part, I rely on the personal papers of and interviews with Diane S. Blank and Mary F. Kelly, and on interviews with, among others, Judge Constance Baker Motley, Eleanor Holmes Norton, and Harriet Rabb. Important primary sources, particularly interviews and collections of documents, are listed below, with the abbreviations used in the endnotes that follow. Other primary sources and important secondary sources appear with full citations in the endnotes. More endnotes can be found at www.wwnorton.com and www.equalwomen .com.

Blackmun papers	Papers of Justice Harry A. Blackmun, Library of Congress
Blank files	Files of Diane S. Blank as of 3/23/01
Blank interviews	Interviews with Diane S. Blank, New York City, 3/16/01 and 3/23/01
Commentator	*The Commentator: The Student Newspaper of the New York University Law Center*
Cooper interview	Interview with George Cooper, Key West, Florida, by phone, 4/3/01
Dolkart interview	Interview with Jane Dolkart, Dallas, Texas, by phone, 4/04/01
Kelly files	Files of Mary F. Kelly as of 5/22/01
Kelly interviews	Interviews with Mary F. Kelly, White Plains, New York, by phone, 3/29/01 and 4/4/01
Kohn interview	Interview with Margaret Kohn, Washington, DC, by phone, 3/12/01

Moss interviews	Interviews with Sara Moss (formerly Sara Steinbock), New York City, by phone, 5/9/02 and 5/24/02
Motley interview	Interview with Judge Constance Baker Motley, New York City, 6/20/02
NARA files	National Archives and Records Administration (NARA), New York City, as of 3/18/02
Norton interview	Interview with Eleanor Holmes Norton, driving from New Haven to Hartford, Connecticut, 5/22/05
Rabb interview	Interview with Harriet Rabb, Washington, DC, by phone, 2/26/01

9: A Problem in the Profession

143 wanted to be a lawyer: Blank interviews.

143 fall 1968 issue . . . "furnished with castoffs" . . . "since he was" . . . "never be satisfied": "Success as a Student's Wife," *Bride's*, August/September 1968, p. 187.

144 business and constitutional law . . . easier than at Barnard . . . "finite": Blank interviews.

144 dean's list in her first year . . . "law clerk": "Resume of Diane S. Blank third year," in Preston David, the City of New York Commission on Human Rights, "Determination after Investigation: D. Blank against Sullivan & Cromwell," dated 1/28/74, in Blank files. Further references will be cited as Commission on Human Rights, "Determination."

144 "wrong side of the tracks": Blank interviews.

144 out of commission five days: Blank interviews; for similar narrative, see Douglas McCollam, "Taking It to the Street," *American Lawyer*, March 1999, pp. 122–123. I am indebted to McCollam for giving me copies of some of his reporting files. Further references will be cited as McCollam, "Taking It."

144 Did her husband . . . want her to be a lawyer: Diane Blank, personal journal entry, 6/11/73, in Blank files.

145 Kelly began encountering odd reactions: Kelly interviews and Mary F. Kelly, letter to author, 5/13/05.

145 "valiant Christian women": Kelly interviews.

145 "ladies day" . . . abortion and rape and sexual imagery: Kelly interviews.

146 Blank requested an interview with the firm Shearman & Sterling: Narrative is from Blank interviews; Diane Blank, letter to Joan Graff at Equal Employment Opportunity Commission, 2/4/70, in Blank files; further references will be cited as Blank letter to Graff, 2/4/70. See also Cynthia Fuchs Epstein, *Women in Law*, 2nd ed. (Urbana: University of Illinois Press, 1993), pp. 184–187.

147 "equivocal" . . . "whole situation looked equivocal" . . . "small numbers involved" . . . meet a Shearman & Sterling interviewer: These quotations as well as others from, and much of the narrative of the meetings with, Shearman & Sterling are from Blank letter to Graff, 2/4/70. See detailed notes online.

147 pages of charts: Diane Blank, chart of men and women, "interviewed and not interviewed" c. 10/2/69, in Blank files.

148 "this emissary role could best be filled by a single (not married) male" . . . "a woman would never have to appear in court" . . . "But" . . . "the ladies have their own little luncheon party": Blank letter to Graff, 2/4/70.

150 "the prejudice encountered by girl students": "Group Meets with McKay to Demand Women's Rights," *Commentator*, 11/6/68, p. 1.

150 In the fall of 1969 . . . no one knew: Cooper interview; see also McCollam, "Taking It," pp. 122–123.

150 Nancy Grossman . . . memo . . . "have an opening": Nancy Grossman, "memorandum re interview with Shearman & Sterling," 10/27/69, in Blank files.

150 Nicholas J. Bosen . . . letter . . . "when do you plan": Nicholas J. Bosen, assistant dean and director of placement, University of Chicago, letter to Shearman & Sterling, 10/29/69, in Blank files.

151 "female activists" . . . "the charge of discrimination": Hamilton Hadden Jr., letter to Nicholas J. Bosen, 11/5/69, in Blank files.

151 Chicago's placement dean quickly backed down . . . letters saying that "allegations in this case" . . . "most vocal": Nicholas J. Bosen, letter to Placement Office, Columbia University School of Law, 11/19/69, in Blank files.

151 Chicago students sent Nancy Grossman's memo: Law Women's Caucus, University of Chicago Law School, letter to Placement Office, New York University, 12/19/69, in Blank files.

151 filed a charge of discrimination . . . "a patently discriminatory": Marjorie Gelb, "Charge of Discrimination," 1/5/70, and Marianne O'Brien and Kathy Soffer, letter to Law Women's Caucus of University of Chicago, 2/23/70; both in Blank files.

151 1969 in Diane Blank's kitchen: Blank interviews.

152 April 1970 . . . NYU School of Law: Diane Blank and Janice Goodman, memo to National Conference of Law Women, 4/13/70, in Blank files.

152 Dean Robert McKay of NYU urged . . . Association of American Law Schools refused . . . Women's Rights Committee decided to conduct its own study: Women's Rights Committee of New York University School of Law, "Proposals," undated but apparently December 1969, and Women's Rights Committee of New York University School of Law, "Pilot Study of Sex Based Discrimination in the Legal Profession," 12-page typescript,

undated but apparently February 1970, both in Blank files. Further references will be cited as NYU Women's Rights Committee, "Pilot Study".

152 700 questionnaires: Details of and quoted responses from the questionnaire are from NYU Women's Rights Committee, "Pilot Study." See detailed notes online.

154 "needed to do group therapy": Norton interview. Excellent narratives of the *Newsweek* case appear in Brownmiller, *In Our Time*, pp. 140–146, and Lester, *Fire in My Soul*, pp. 149–150.

10: Taking Action

155 as far west as Berkeley and as far south as Duke: "Statement of Mrs. Diane Blank and Mrs. Susan D. Ross, Women's Rights Committee of New York University Law School," House Committee on Education and Labor, Special Subcommittee on Education, *Discrimination against Women: Hearings on Section 805 of H.R. 16098*, 91st Cong., 2d sess., 1970, pp. 584–592.

155 For two days they discussed issues affecting women law students . . . series of resolutions . . . "worst offenders" . . . "join a Title VII action": Diane Blank and Janice Goodman, memo to National Conference of Law Women, 4/13/70, in Blank files.

156 Isn't motherhood the greatest goal . . . "politically educated": Dolkart interview.

157 Another Columbia student, Margaret Kohn . . . "For some reason women": Kohn interview. Part of Kohn's complaint is reprinted in Babcock and others, *Sex Discrimination* (1975), pp. 376–377.

157 more than 130 attorneys . . . three were women . . . decided not to interview five women: Complaint of Diane Serafin Blank, dated 6/28/71, attached to Commission on Human Rights, "Determination"; see also Harriet Rabb, Howard J. Rubin, and George Cooper (of counsel), "Complaint Class Action," 1/15/75, in *Blank v. Sullivan & Cromwell*, 75 Civ. 189 (S.D. N.Y. 1977).

157 learned that three were women . . . jotted down immediately after on a note card, "some of the partners have prejudices against women": Transcript of deposition of the plaintiff (Diane Blank) conducted 4/24–25/75, 221-page typescript in *Blank v. Sullivan & Cromwell*, 75 Civ. 189 (S.D. N.Y. 1977), pp. 137–139; in NARA files. Further references will be cited as Blank 1975 deposition.

157 why a nice lady like you: Kelly interviews.

158 teamed up with Professor Daniel Collins . . . seventy-six schools: Daniel G. Collins and Mary F. Kelly, letter attaching "preliminary statistical compilation of the responses to a questionnaire sent to law school deans by

the AALS Special Committee on Women in Legal Education," 12/22/70, in Kelly files.

158 response to NYU's urging: Jacob Laufer, "AALS Finds Sex Discrimination," *Commentator*, 2/2/71; Women's Rights Committee of New York University School of Law, "Proposals," undated but apparently December 1969, in Blank files.

158 Within weeks, at age thirty-two and pregnant with her first child, Norton became chair of the city's Commission on Human Rights: Lester, *Fire in My Soul*, p. 160. See also Robin Morgan, ed., *Sisterhood Is Powerful* (New York: Random House, 1970), p. 598.

158 excited that students wanted to engage in rigorous study of sex discrimination . . . Root-Tilden . . . presumed it was reserved for men by a bequest . . . "almost no feminist consciousness": Norton interview. See also Lester, *Fire in My Soul*, p. 146.

159 symposium on the equal rights amendment . . . "the 'Women's Rights Amendment' and Kindred Matters": Association of the Bar of the City of New York, "Has 'Women's Liberation' Liberated Anyone?" 3/25/71, invitation in Kelly files.

159 "to make feminists look like idiots" . . . told Ellie Norton . . . meeting soon after, which included both Norton and Steinem: Blank interviews.

159 Gloria Steinem rose to address an audience of some fifteen hundred: Details of and quotations from the symposium, unless otherwise indicated, are from "Women's Lib Uses a 'Trojan Horse'," *New York Times*, 3/26/71, p. 45; Timothy Ferris, "The Gals Find the Bar Guilty," *New York Post*, 3/28/71; Jan Pawlak, "Women Demonstrate at Bar Symposium," *Commentator*, 3/30/71, p. 1. See detailed notes online.

159 Mary Kelly . . . "Has the anti-defamation league": Quotations from talk are from Kelly's notes for talk to Association of the Bar of the City of New York, 3/25/71, in Kelly files.

161 race discrimination case: *Griggs v. Duke Power*, 401 U.S. 424 (1971).

161 contributed to the brief: Cooper interview.

161 "the effects of employment practices" . . . "startling breakthrough": George Cooper, "Introduction, Equal Employment Law Today," 5 *Columbia Human Rights Law Review* 263 (1973), p. 265.

161 Cooper had another idea . . . "peanuts grant" . . . "the old-boy network" . . . "the balls for the job" . . . "I had enough awareness": Cooper interview.

161 family friend of the dean: Rabb interview.

162 high-school hopes to become a cheerleader: Lindsey Van Gelder, "Harriet Rabb, Scourge of Corporate Male Chauvinism," *New York*, 6/26/78, pp. 38–40. Further references will be cited as Van Gelder, "Harriet Rabb."

162 "the idea of having a Jewish cheerleader" . . . "Harry, it's that nigger girl calling": Nan Robertson, *The Girls in the Balcony: Women, Men and*

the New York Times (New York: Random House, 1992), p. 161. Further references will be cited as Robertson, *Girls in the Balcony.*

162 "Valentine's Day massacre": Cynthia Fuchs Epstein, *Women in Law*, 2nd ed. (Urbana: University of Illinois Press, 1993), p. 66.

162 Embarrassing questions: Alan Kohn, "The Ms. Who Keeps Picking on the 'Boys'," *New York Law Journal*, 5/10/77, p. 1. Further references will be cited as Kohn, "Picking on the 'Boys'."

162 similar questions aimed at her friends: Harriet Rabb, letter to author, 5/10/05.

163 "saving the world from reactionaries": Rabb, quoted in Robertson, *Girls in the Balcony*, p. 162.

163 she phoned Bruce . . . neither of their employers would totally trust: Harriet Rabb, letter to author, 5/10/05; for a similar narrative, which Rabb partly disputes, see Van Gelder, "Harriet Rabb," p. 40, and Robertson, *Girls in the Balcony*, pp. 162–163.

164 Republicans in the capital . . . Democrats do not hire: Van Gelder, "Harriet Rabb," p. 40.

164 only a week . . . "contact the White House": Harriet Rabb, letter to author, 5/10/05;

164 "My dear": Bazelon, quoted in Robertson, *Girls in the Balcony*, p. 163.

164 caught George Cooper by surprise: Cooper interview.

164 "was like a gift": Dolkart interview.

165 Norton . . . introduced Blank to Rabb: Jonathan Kwitny, "Law Firm Is Stung by Hiring-Bias Suit Filed by Woman Lawyer and Heard by Woman Judge," *Wall Street Journal*, 8/8/75, p. 26. Further references will be cited as Kwitny, "Law Firm Is Stung." See online note.

165 For Norton, the students' suits fit the sort of cases she wanted: Norton interview.

165 Margaret Kohn's . . . "women are really good at": Complaint of Margaret Kohn, dated 5/27/71, partly reprinted in Babcock and others, *Sex Discrimination* (1975), pp. 376–377. But see also Affidavit of John B. Loughran, 11/6/72, in *Kohn v. Royall, Koegel & Wells*, 59 F.R.D.515, 515 (S.D. N.Y. 1973), in NARA files.

165 "anti-female bias" . . . "prejudiced against women": Complaint of Diane Serafin Blank, dated 6/28/71, attached to Commission on Human Rights, "Determination."

166 9 women among 1,409 partners . . . "We would give you": "Statement for the Press" beginning "Complaints are being filed against 10 New York City law firms for discrimination against women lawyers in recruitment, hiring, conditions of employment, and promotion," apparently July 1971, in Blank files.

166 "strong advocate" . . . "did not like to hire women": "13 Women Law Students Here Accuse 10 Large Firms of Bias," *New York Times*, 7/1/71, p. 59.

166 New York State Bar Exam . . . single test location: This and most details are from Mary F. Kelly, "Affidavit," July 1971 (day not stated), in Kelly files. See also Alan Kohn, "Bar Examiners to Abolish Separate Areas for Women," *New York Law Journal*, 7/21/71, p. 1; Bruce Drake, "Fem Students Sue the Bar Examiners," *New York Daily News*, 7/20/71; Mary Connelly and Marvin Smilon, "Testing Board Invites Gals: Join Men at Bar (Exams)," *New York Post*, 7/21/70.

167 "one female matron": Mary F. Kelly, "Affidavit," July 1971 (day not stated), p. 4, in Kelly files.

167 "We want to be sure . . . statistically better than men": Bruce Drake, "Fem Students Sue the Bar Examiners," *New York Daily News*, 7/20/71.

167 "character and fitness": Mary F. Kelly, "Affidavit," July 1971 (day not stated), p. 3, in Kelly files.

167 Kelly called Rabb . . . "administrative convenience": Kelly interviews. See note online.

168 as a "cooperating attorney" . . . Rabb initiated a federal suit: Alan Kohn, "Bar Examiners to Abolish Separate Areas for Women," *New York Law Journal*, 7/21/71, p. 1; Bruce Drake, "Fem Students Sue the Bar Examiners," *New York Daily News*, 7/20/71; Mary Connelly and Marvin Smilon, "Testing Board Invites Gals: Join Men at Bar (Exams)," *New York Post*, 7/21/70.

168 agreement produced unsatisfactory results . . . Rabb took Norton's place: Rabb interview.

169 "always one woman" . . . "Shit may hit the fan": Cooper interview.

169 Rabb found that Dean Sovern backed her: Harriet Rabb, letter to author, 5/10/05.

169 tossing out five for lacking "probable cause": Alan Kohn, "Court Lauds Pattern in Settling Rogers & Wells Sex-Bias Suit," *New York Law Journal*, 2/9/76, no page number evident. See also McCollam, "Taking It," pp. 122–123.

169 Reporting in April of 1972 . . . "was the second best applicant" . . . "probable cause" . . . "permission to sue": Preston David, the City of New York Commission on Human Rights, "Probable Cause Decision: Margaret [Kohn] against Respondent [name omitted], Complaint No. 5207-JS," dated 4/27/74, reprinted in Babcock and others, *Sex Discrimination* (1975), pp. 378–380, 382 ("permission to sue").

170 Reporting in January of 1974: Quotations from the report are from Commission on Human Rights, "Determination."

171 EEOC did not see "probable cause" . . . "right to sue": Arthur W. Stern, "Determination," *Blank v. Sullivan & Cromwell*, Equal Employment Opportunity Commission Case No. YNY 5–138, 10/16/74, in NARA files.

II: A Young Woman Takes an Old Wall Street Firm to Court

172 Harriet Rabb submitted . . . "pattern and practice of sex discrimination": Harriet Rabb, Howard J. Rubin, and George Cooper (of counsel), "Complaint Class Action," 1/15/75, in *Blank v. Sullivan & Cromwell*, 75 Civ. 189 (S.D. N.Y. 1977), in NARA files.

172 family of progressive lawyers . . . London had never lost: Glenn Fowler, "Ephraim London, 78, a Lawyer Who Fought Censorship, Is Dead," *New York Times*, 6/14/90, p. B13.

172 one of a few Socialist Party congressmen . . . defended the rights of garment workers: American Jewish Historical Society, "An 'Entirely Different' Jew in Congress," *Chapters in American Jewish History*, available at www.ajhs.org/publications/chapters (visited 2/21/07).

173 Constance Baker Motley had been winning race discrimination cases (she won nine out of ten): Constance Baker Motley, *Equal Justice under Law: An Autobiography* (New York: Farrar, Straus and Giroux, 1998), p. 218. Further references will be cited as Motley, *Equal Justice*, which is the source for most biographical details and quotations, unless noted otherwise. See detailed notes online.

173 chef for . . . Skull and Bones: Douglas Martin, "Constance Baker Motley, 84, Civil Rights Trailblazer, Lawmaker and Judge, Dies," *New York Times*, 9/29/05, p. B1.

176 probably (Supreme Court historians remain unsure) the first black woman: Cushman, *Supreme Court*, p. 224.

176 case concerning the right to adequate counsel . . . "intent" to ravish: *Hamilton v. State of Alabama*, 368 U.S. 52 (1961); see Motley, *Equal Justice*, pp. 192–194, 271n1.

176 allowing Motley to remark: Motley interview.

177 "seeks a declaratory judgment": Harriet Rabb, Howard J. Rubin, and George Cooper (of counsel), "Complaint Class Action," 1/15/75, in NARA files.

177 "affirmative defenses" . . . "unclean hands" . . . urged other women to lie: Ephraim London, "Answer," 4/7/75, in NARA files.

177 "ugliest case": Diane Blank, personal journal entry, 4/8/75, in Blank files.

177 "ask to be relieved" . . . "Unconscious feelings": Ephraim London, letter to the Hon. Constance Baker Motley, 4/16/75, in NARA files.

178 she had expected lawyers to "misbehave" . . . no lawyer had ever tried to get her to leave a case: Motley interview.

178 "there would not be any judge": Harriet Rabb, letter to the Hon. Constance Baker Motley, 4/17/75, in NARA files.

179 legal deposition . . . London began: Quotations from and details on the deposition of Blank, unless indicated otherwise, are from Blank 1975 deposition.

179 "I feel like this horrible inevitable thing": Diane Blank, personal journal entry, 4/23/75, in Blank files.

182 Blank's case looked not great . . . "mindset" . . . "a kid" . . . "lion of the bar": Moss interviews.

183 In a letter . . . "yahoo": Ephraim London, letter to Harriet Rabb, 4/30/75, in district court transcript of *Blank v. Sullivan & Cromwell*, 75 Civ. 189 (S.D. N.Y. 1977), pretrial conference, 6/2/75, p. 19, in NARA files. Further references will be cited as *Blank* transcript 6/2/75.

183 Motley replied to London's letter . . . "timely and sufficient affidavit": Constance Baker Motley, letter to Ephraim London, 5/8/75, in NARA files.

183 June 2, 1975 . . . pretrial conference: Unless otherwise noted, conference details and quotations come from *Blank* transcript 6/2/75. See detailed notes online.

184 "A suit for violation of Title VII": *Kohn v. Royall, Koegel & Wells*, 59 F.R.D.515, 522 (S.D. N.Y. 1973), quoting *Bowe v. Colgate-Palmolive*, 416 F.2d 711, 719 (7th Cir. 1969).

184 Steinbock was shocked: Moss interviews.

184 risen from about 1.4 to 12.5 percent: Arthur W. Stern, "Determination," *Blank v. Sullivan & Cromwell*, Equal Employment Opportunity Commission Case No. YNY 5–138, 10/16/74, in NARA files.

185 "Oh my god": Moss interviews.

185 "job was to stall": Motley interview.

186 "some of the partners have prejudices against women": Blank 1975 deposition, pp. 137–139.

186 *barrator* . . . "frequently exciting" . . . *champerty* . . . "pests of civil society": William Blackstone, *Commentaries on the Laws of England* (Oxford: Printed at the Clarendon Press, 1765), Vol. 4, Chap. x, Sect. 11, pp. 134–135; *Black's Law Dictionary*, 6th ed. (St. Paul: West Publishing, 1990), pp. 151, 230–231. (*Black's* uses the spelling *barretor*.)

186 To Motley, they echoed her recent past: Motley interview.

186 Southern states responded . . . *barratry* and *champerty*: Motley, *Equal Justice*, p. 126; Mark V. Tushnet, *Making Civil Rights Law: Thurgood Marshall and the Supreme Court, 1936–1961* (Oxford: Oxford University Press, 1994), pp. 272–282 (further references will be cited as Tushnet,

Making Civil Rights Law); and Susan D. Carle, "From Buchanan to Button: Legal Ethics and the NAACP," 8 *University of Chicago Law School Roundtable* 281 (2001), p. 297.

186 "runner" . . . "capper" . . . "individual or organization": Susan D. Carle, "From Buchanan to Button: Legal Ethics and the NAACP," 8 *University of Chicago Law School Roundtable* 281 (2001), p. 300.

186 Virginia's highest court ruled . . . violating the state's new antibarratry statute . . . "valid police regulation": *NAACP v. Harrison*, Supreme Court of Virginia, 202 Va. 142, 160 (1960). See also Tushnet, *Making Civil Rights Law*, pp. 275–276.

187 Writing the decision in early 1962 for a 5–4 majority: This narrative of the two decisions relies on the superb research in Tushnet, *Making Civil Rights Law*, pp. 275–282.

187 "to discriminate as partisans in favor of Negroes": Felix Frankfurter, letter to Hugo Black, 2/19/62, quoted in Tushnet, *Making Civil Rights Law*, p. 277.

187 "moved not by financial gain but by public interest": Felix Frankfurter, draft opinion, January 1962, *NAACP v. Button*, 371 U.S. 415 (1963), quoted in Tushnet, *Making Civil Rights Law*, pp. 278, 363n16.

188 *puerile* . . . "may now be applied to a woman's conduct": Ephraim London, "Affidavit in Support of Motion," dated 5/12/75, p. 3, in NARA files.

188 She had doubts he would try such tactics before a male judge: Motley interview.

188 "You know how everybody talks" . . . knew was improper . . . contempt of court: Motley interview.

189 "identified with those who suffered discrimination": Ephraim London, "Affidavit in Support of Disqualification," 7/24/75, in NARA files.

189 Motley went looking for courage . . . Judge Leon Higginbotham: Motley interview.

189 Only the year before, in a case: Quotations from Higginbotham's response are from *Commonwealth of Pennsylvania v. Local Union 542*, 388 F. Supp. 155 (E.D. Pa. 1974). See detailed notes online.

190 "no President had ever appointed a black": *Commonwealth of Pennsylvania v. Local Union 542*, 388 F. Supp. 155, 177 (E.D. Pa. 1974).

190 answer to London's challenge: *Blank v. Sullivan & Cromwell*, 418 F. Supp. 1, 75 Civ. 189 (S.D. N.Y. 1977), 8/4/75, denying motion for disqualification.

191 "to make its victims social and economic cripples" . . . "I hasten to add": Ephraim London, "Affidavit in Support of Disqualification," 7/24/75, p. 12, in NARA files.

191 not be "objective": Ephraim London, "Petition for a Writ of Mandamus Directing Judge Constance Baker Motley to Disqualify Herself as Judge of This Case," 8/5/75, in NARA files.

191 "offers as support for this 'identification'": This and subsequent quotations from Motley's response are from *Blank v. Sullivan & Cromwell*, 418 F. Supp. 1, 4 (S.D. N.Y. 1977), 8/4/75, denying motion for disqualification. See note online.

192 embodying "bias": Ephraim London, "Affidavit in Support of Disqualification," 7/24/75, in NARA files.

192 "not so strong" . . . "stronger each time he showed up" . . . Steinbock's favorite line: Moss interviews.

193 "wasn't so all-fired important" . . . Commission on Human Rights, "before which many of the complaints were filed": Kwitny, "Law Firm Is Stung."

193 Rabb was upset, calling the article scurrilous . . . "talk of Wall Street" . . . "a law firm that can't win its own lawsuit": Diane Blank, personal journal entry, 8/9/75, in Blank files.

193 "a sort of second string law review": Kwitny, "Law Firm Is Stung."

194 "Title VII does not require an offer of partnership": Ephraim London, "Affidavit: Objections to Report of Magistrate Harold J. Raby, made March 15, 1976," dated 4/1/76, p. 2, in NARA files.

194 fourteen-page affidavit . . . "I personally": John F. Cannon, "Affidavit of a Partner of Sullivan & Cromwell Regarding Report of United States Magistrate," dated 4/1/76, in NARA files.

195 "partners and partnerships are not within the purview" . . . "choosing to do business in the partnership form": Brief for the Equal Employment Opportunity Commission by Abner W. Sibal, Joseph T. Eddins, Beatrice Rosenberg, and Charles L. Reischel to District Court, pp. 2–4, dated 6/15/76, p. 4, in NARA files.

195 "Title VII did not make it unlawful": Defendant's Brief in Opposition to Motion for Rehearing and Modification of the Court's Order of 5/24/76, by Ephraim London, p. 2, dated 7/9/76, in NARA files.

195 "unnecessary" . . . "to reach the difficult issue": *Blank v. Sullivan & Cromwell*, 75 Civ. 189 (S.D. N.Y. 1977), order defendants to respond to interrogatories, 11/22/76.

196 "It is difficult to conceive of anything more telling": Order of 1/7/75, by Judge Morris Lasker, in *Kohn v. Royall, Koegel & Wells* (S.D. N.Y. 1973), quoted in *Blank v. Sullivan & Cromwell*, 75 Civ. 189 (S.D. N.Y. 1977), order defendants to respond to interrogatories, 11/22/76.

12: Time to Settle

197 By late spring of 1977, a proposed settlement: Agreement, signed by Diane Blank, Harriet Rabb, Sullivan & Cromwell, and Ephraim London, dated 4/11/77, in NARA files.

197 press reported: "Details Disclosed of Settlement by Sullivan & Cromwell

of Bias Suit," *New York Law Journal*, 5/6/77, p. 1; Arnold H. Lubasch, "Top Law Firm Agrees to Bar Sex Discrimination in Jobs and Promotions," *New York Times*, 5/8/77; Jonathan Kwitny, "New York Law Firm Accepts Conditions in Hiring-Bias Case," *Wall Street Journal*, 5/9/77; Kohn, "Picking on the 'Boys'," p. 1.

197 "Two women lawyers and a woman judge": Jonathan Kwitny, "New York Law Firm Accepts Conditions in Hiring-Bias Case," *Wall Street Journal*, 5/9/77.

197 not discriminate in the future, as it "has not certainly in the past several years": District court transcript of *Blank v. Sullivan & Cromwell*, 75 Civ. 189 (S.D. N.Y. 1977), settlement hearing 6/28/77.

198 *Recruiting women*: This and other elements of the agreement are from Agreement, signed by Diane Blank, Harriet Rabb, Sullivan & Cromwell, and Ephraim London, dated 4/11/77, in NARA files.

199 $30,000 as fees: Agreement, signed by Diane Blank, Harriet Rabb, Sullivan & Cromwell, and Ephraim London, dated 4/11/77, in NARA files.

199 Blank received $2,000: Blank interviews.

199 "Obviously": Jonathan Kwitny, "New York Law Firm Accepts Conditions in Hiring-Bias Case," *Wall Street Journal*, 5/9/77.

13: The Chief Justice's Second Draft

200 known to her friends as Betsy . . . graduating in 1972 . . . Harlan Fiske Stone Scholar: William G. Blair, "Woman in the News; Victor in Bias Case: Elizabeth Anderson Hishon," *New York Times*, 5/23/84, p. D27.

200 She saw herself as someone who did not wear armbands or march in demonstrations: Connie Bruck, "The Case No One Will Win," *American Lawyer*, November 1983, pp. 101–106.

201 "fair and equal" . . . papers in federal court: Chief Justice Warren E. Burger, "1st DRAFT," *Hishon v. King & Spalding*, 467 U.S. 69, 71–72 (1984), circulated 12/28/83, pp. 3, 8, in Blackmun papers.

201 "Title VII does not apply to decisions regarding partnership": *Hishon v. King & Spalding*, 678 F.2d 1022, 1024 (11th Cir. 1982).

201 "nine of the twelve active judges of the Eleventh Circuit": Emmet J. Bondurant, quoted in Connie Bruck, "The Case No One Will Win," *American Lawyer*, November 1983, p. 105.

201 For a summer outing, King & Spalding . . . "the body we'd like to see more of": James B. Stewart, "Fairness Issue; Are Women Lawyers Discriminated against at Large Law Firms?" *Wall Street Journal*, 12/20/83, p. 1.

202 Oral argument on Halloween: Quotations from the oral argument are from Supreme Court transcript of *Hishon v. King & Spalding*, 467 U.S. 69 (1984), argued 10/3/83.

202 "get over" the pain of injustice: Connie Bruck, "The Case No One Will Win," *American Lawyer*, November 1983, p. 102.

202 all nine justices voted against King & Spalding: Conference notes, dated 11/2/83, in Blackmun papers.

202 apparently in favor of applying Title VII to partnerships: Justice John Paul Stevens, letter to Chief Justice Warren Burger, 12/30/83, in Blackmun papers.

202 Burger—during oral argument in a Title VII case—had sought reassurance . . . "as a matter of general policy": Supreme Court transcript of *Phillips v. Martin Marietta Corporation*, 400 U.S. 542 (1971), p. 7, argued 12/9/70, and see Part 1.

203 His draft opinion: Quotations from the draft opinion are from Chief Justice Warren E. Burger, "1st DRAFT," *Hishon v. King & Spalding*, 467 U.S. 69 (1984), circulated 12/28/83, in Blackmun papers. See note online.

203 Blackmun scrawled . . . "Do not Destroy": For comparison of handwriting, compare the word "Do" to same word in oral argument notes, 10/31/83, in Blackmun papers.

203 "novel theory of Title VII": Justice William J. Brennan Jr., "1st DRAFT," *Hishon v. King & Spalding*, 467 U.S. 69 (1984), circulated 12/30/83, p. 4n3, in Blackmun papers.

204 "there seems to be considerable feeling" . . . Justice Blackmun penciled, "*Of course!*": Chief Justice Warren E. Burger, memorandum to the conference, 12/30/83, in Blackmun papers.

204 After again discussing the alleged "contract," in a footnote he conceded . . . "private discrimination": *Hishon v. King & Spalding*, 467 U.S. 69, 74–75, 75n6 (1984).

204 press reported . . . "ruled unanimously" . . . "advertising agencies": Linda Greenhouse, "High Court Rules Rights Law Covers Law Partnerships," *New York Times*, 5/23/84, p. A1; Fred Barbash, "Partnerships at Issue; Law Firms Held to Anti-Bias Rule," *Washington Post*, 5/23/84, p. A6.

205 "Give me a break": George F. Will, "Put 'er There, Partner," *Washington Post*, 5/27/84, p. C7.

Part Four

HARASSMENT (1974–1986)

In this part, I rely on the personal papers of and interviews with Patricia J. Barry, Catharine A. MacKinnon, and Karen Sauvigné, and on interviews with, among others, Mechelle Vinson. I also learned a great deal from the files of Working Women United, the papers of Judge George E. MacKinnon, and the 1980 trial transcript of *Vinson v. Taylor*, which was unavailable to Supreme Court litigators and justices. Important primary sources, particularly interviews and collections of documents, are listed below, with the abbreviations used in the endnotes that follow. Other primary sources and important secondary sources appear with full citations in the endnotes. More detailed endnotes can be found at www.wwnorton.com and www.equalwomen.com.

Barry files	Files of Patricia J. Barry as of 3/19/93
Barry interviews	Interviews with Patricia J. Barry, Los Angeles, 3/17–19/93
Blackmun papers	Papers of Justice Harry A. Blackmun, Library of Congress
Brennan papers	Papers of William J. Brennan Jr., Library of Congress
Burns interviews	Interviews with Sarah E. Burns, New York City, by phone, 2/11/93 and 6/15/93
Catharine MacKinnon files	Files of Catharine A. MacKinnon as of 5/11/95
Catharine MacKinnon interview(s)	Interviews with Catharine A. MacKinnon on multiple dates including Washington, DC, 10/5/90; Ann Arbor, Michigan, 10/21–24/90; Washington, DC, 12/16/90; California, by phone, 2/15/95; California, 5/11/95; California, 10/18–21/95; California, by phone, 3/14/98; and New Haven, Connecticut, 4/2/04
George MacKinnon papers	George E. MacKinnon Papers, Minnesota Historical Society
Katz interview	Interview with Debra Katz, Washington, DC, by phone, 8/20/93
Lenhoff interviews	Interviews with Donna Lenhoff, Washington, DC, by phone, 8/17/93 and 8/18/93
Ludwic interview	Interview with Judith Ludwic, Washington, DC, 4/6/93
Marshall papers	Papers of Thurgood Marshall, Library of Congress
Meisburg interviews	Interviews with John Marshall Meisburg Jr., Orlando, Florida, by phone, 5/28/93 and 6/2/93
Meyer interview	Interview with Susan Meyer, New York City, by phone, 2/25/98
Nemy interview	Interview with Enid Nemy, New York City, by phone, 6/22/05
Sauvigné files	Files of Karen Sauvigné as of 6/7/93
Sauvigné interview	Interview with Karen Sauvigné, New York City, 6/7/93
Semonoff interview	Interview with Ellen Semonoff, Cambridge, Massachusetts, by phone, 5/6/98
Singer interview	Interview with Linda Singer, Washington, DC, by phone, 2/6/98

Vinson DC transcript   District court transcript in *Vinson v. Taylor*, 23 Fair
Empl. Prac. Cas. (BNA) 37 (D.D.C. 1980). For this
transcript, I am indebted to the Washington Lawyers'
Committee for Civil Rights Under Law, including
Joseph M. Sellers and Eloise Kehler, who in June 1993
permitted Katherine McCarron, who had recently
graduated from Yale, to copy their approximately
1,500-page transcript of proceedings on Civil Action
No. 78–1793, for the dates of the trial, 1/21–2/1/1980,
in the United States District Court for the District of
Columbia. In an earlier effort, I found only fragments
of the transcript available at the courthouse. Many
attorneys working on this case during its route from
district court to the Supreme Court, including Patricia
J. Barry and Catharine MacKinnon (see later narrative), never had access to full transcripts; nor have other
reports of which I am aware.

Vinson interview   Interview with Mechelle Vinson, Washington, DC,
4/17/93

Working Women files   Files of Working Women United (and its successor
Working Women's Institute) at the Barnard Center for
Research on Women, Columbia University

14: No Law

209 Mechelle Vinson: Biographical details and quotations about Vinson's life,
and details and quotations about Sydney Taylor and his behavior, are from
Vinson interview and *Vinson* DC transcript, unless indicated otherwise.

209 nineteen-year-old Mechelle Vinson: *Vinson* DC transcript, 1/22/80,
p. 16.

209 between railway lines: Author visit, 3/25/95, to 13th Place, NE, Washington, DC.

209 "a very small, black bank" . . . "be something": Vinson interview.

210 One day in September of 1974: *Vinson* DC transcript, 1/22/80, pp. 16–19;
Vinson v. Taylor, 23 Fair Empl. Prac. Cas. (BNA) 37 (D.D.C. 1980).

210 marriage that was now having problems . . . bank as her chance finally to
advance: Vinson interview.

210 "outstanding" . . . head teller and assistant branch manager simultaneously: Pretrial Statement of Defendant, Sidney L. Taylor, to United States
District Court for the District of Columbia, filed 1/3/80, p. 2, in *Vinson
v. Taylor*, 23 Fair Empl. Prac. Cas. (BNA) 37 (D.D.C. 1980).

210 "9 plus": Sidney L. Taylor, letter to George J. Boyce, President, Capital

City Federal Savings and Loan Association of Washington, DC, 9/29/77, attached to Answer for Plaintiff's Request for Production of Documents, by Karen Smith Woodson, to United States District Court for the District of Columbia, filed 12/18/79, in *Vinson v. Taylor*, 23 Fair Empl. Prac. Cas. (BNA) 37 (D.D.C. 1980).

210 "go far": *Vinson* DC transcript, 1/29/80, p. 25.

210 dapper: Meisburg interview.

210 gentlemanly: *Vinson* DC transcript, 1/22/80, p. 18, and 1/24/80, p. 33.

210 first black assistant manager for any major savings association: *Vinson* DC transcript, 1/28/80, p. 16.

210 proud . . . create jobs for young black employees: *Vinson* DC transcript, Sidney Taylor, 1/28/80, p. 16–19.

210 Mr. Taylor, as she always called him: Ludwic interview.

210 even during her initial ninety-day probationary period . . . began to wonder: *Vinson* DC transcript, 1/22/80, p. 33.

211 "prettying up": Vinson interview.

211 Chinese restaurant: *Vinson* DC transcript, 1/22/80, p. 50.

211 "You all have worked so good . . . gave you the overtime": *Vinson* DC transcript, 1/22/80, p. 47.

211 "Oh Christina . . . just don't know": Vinson interview.

211 Christina's bottom . . . breasts: *Vinson* DC transcript, 1/22/80, p. 33.

211 "Your eyes may shine": Vinson interview.

211 ladies' bathroom . . . shake it at Christina . . . "Excuse me": *Vinson* DC transcript, 1/22/80, pp. 33–35.

211 "you see and you don't say": Vinson interview.

212 "You're gonna settle this goddamn sheet" . . . stormed out the door: *Vinson* DC transcript, 1/22/80, p. 41, and 1/24/80, p. 21; Vinson interview.

212 Next week, Christina didn't have a job: *Vinson* DC transcript, 1/21/80, pp. 84–90; Vinson interview.

212 Sidney Taylor would deny most of it: *Vinson* DC transcript, 1/29/80, pp. 13–14.

212 stories have never been verified: This has been well stated by Augustus B. Cochran III in his fine history, *Sexual Harassment and the Law: The Mechelle Vinson Case* (Lawrence: University Press of Kansas, 2004), p. 3: "The reader is strongly advised to suspend judgment about the particular facts of this case and to treat all disputed facts as unproved." In this case, "a series of rulings, appeals, and remands left the factual issues ultimately unresolved; the truth or falsity of the parties' various versions of events was never definitively established by a court of law. The Supreme Court did not rule on the veracity of any version of the facts." See also Cochran's "cautionary note to the reader" on p. 57, which says, in part, "Readers

should not assume that any particulars of this story are verified truth and should be aware that the facts of this case, by and large, have never been authoritatively established." Further references will be cited as Cochran, *Sexual Harassment.*

212 giving her $120: *Vinson* DC transcript, 1/22/80, p. 48.

212 join him for dinner: *Vinson* DC transcript, 1/24/80, p. 45.

212 "Mechelle, I have been good to you": *Vinson* DC transcript, 1/22/80, p. 49.

212 bed with him: *Vinson* DC transcript, 1/22/80, p. 50.

212 "just like he hired me, he would fire me": *Vinson* DC transcript, 1/24/80, p. 47.

212 "he put his penis in": *Vinson* DC transcript, 1/22/80, p. 53.

212 "there was never a time that I indulged in sex": See *Vinson* DC transcript, 1/29/80, pp. 13–14, with questions by one of Sidney L. Taylor's attorneys, Karen Smith Woodson, and answers by Taylor: "Q: Now, did there come a time in May of 1975 that you indulged in sexual intercourse with Ms. Vinson? A: No. There was never a time that I indulged in sex with Ms. Vinson. Q: Did there come a time in May of 1975 that you had dinner at a Chinese restaurant with Ms. Vinson? A: Not Ms. Vinson. Maybe with Ms. Vinson and Ms. Malone, but never with Ms. Vinson alone. I do remember taking—having dinner with them at a restaurant on Rhode Island Avenue, but we were all there together and it wasn't dinner. They were going to eat Chinese food. I eat in the area, so I stopped by and had a beer and I went on home. Q: Did you purchase this dinner for them? A: No, I did not. Q: Now, did there come a time when you, in May of 1975, took Ms. Vinson to a hotel in or around New York Avenue? A: No, I never have. Q: Did there come a period of time in May of 1975 when Ms. Vinson made sexual overtures to you? A: Well that has happened several times. Really since I have had to have Ms. Vinson and Ms. Malone go back home and change clothes because their form of dress was really wrong for the type of atmosphere that we were working under."

213 "I felt I didn't owe him anything": Vinson interview.

213 next morning at work . . . do what he wanted: *Vinson* DC transcript, 1/22/80, pp. 58–59.

213 sex many times: *Vinson* DC transcript, 1/22/80, pp. 64–75.

213 "the vault door closed": *Vinson* DC transcript, 1/22/80, pp. 77–78.

213 put his hands on her body: *Vinson* DC transcript, 1/22/80, pp. 68–70.

213 "dick sucked" . . . "You are going to fuck me" . . . "I give you a paycheck": *Vinson* DC transcript, 1/22/80, pp. 68–70, 77–78.

214 "outside women": *Vinson* DC transcript, Mechelle Vinson, 1/22/80, pp. 59–61.

214   "tired of Mr. Taylor touching them" . . . "relaxing" . . . "get the hell out": *Vinson* DC transcript, 1/23/80, 11:00 a.m., p. 48.

214   "Because he had told me": *Vinson* DC transcript, 1/24/80, p. 47.

214   "low-cost divorces": Ludwic interview and Vinson interview.

214   hair was falling out . . . "I have a boss that's bothering me" . . . never intended to divulge . . . "What locked in my mind" . . . "On what legal ground": Ludwic interview.

215   "sexual favors": *Barnes v. Costle*, 561 F.2d 983, 985 (D.C. Cir. 1977); and *Barnes v. Train*, 13 Fair Empl. Prac. Cas. (BNA) 123, decided 8/9/74 by Judge John Lewis Smith Jr., United States District Court for the District of Columbia.

216   "verbal and physical sexual advances": *Corne v. Bausch and Lomb*, 390 F. Supp. 161 (Arizona 1975).

216   "wanted to lay me" . . . "working relationship" . . . "restrained me": Adrienne Tomkins, "Sex Discrimination," *Civil Liberties Review*, September–October 1978, pp. 19–22.

216   early 1970s . . . teller named Margaret Miller: Mary C. Dunlap, "Are We Integrated Yet? Pursuing the Complex Question of Values, Demographics and Personalities," 29 *University of San Francisco Law Review* 693 (1995).

216   "cooperative" . . . "felt this way about a black chick": *Miller v. Bank of America*, 418 F. Supp. 233 (N.D. Cal. 1976); *Miller v. Bank of America*, 600 F.2d 211 (9th Cir. 1979).

216   Justice Department: *Williams v. Bell*, 587 F.2d 1240 (D.C. Cir. 1978).

216   "Seldom a day goes by" . . . "harassment and humiliation": *Williams v. Saxbe*, 413 F. Supp. 654 (D.D.C. 1976).

216   but "the subtleties": *Barnes v. Train*, 13 Fair Empl. Prac. Cas. (BNA) 123.

216   "every time any employee": *Corne v. Bausch and Lomb*, 390 F. Supp. 161 (Arizona 1975).

216   "if an inebriated approach": *Tomkins v. Public Serv. Elec. & Gas*, 422 F. Supp. 553 (D. N.J. 1976).

217   "a natural sex phenomenon": *Miller v. Bank of America*, 418 F. Supp. 233 (N.D. Cal. 1976).

217   "gal" clerks: Mary C. Dunlap, "Are We Integrated Yet? Pursuing the Complex Question of Values, Demographics and Personalities," 29 *University of San Francisco Law Review* 693 (1995), p. 703.

15: Naming Sexual Harassment

218   events in early 1975: This section draws on Meyer interview, Sauvigné interview, Sauvigné files, Working Women files, and Lin Farley, *Sexual*

Shakedown: The Sexual Harassment of Women on the Job (New York: McGraw-Hill, 1978). Further references will be cited as Farley, *Sexual Shakedown*. It also gained from an excellent history that appeared as this book was going to press: Carrie N. Baker, *The Women's Movement against Sexual Harassment* (Cambridge: Cambridge University Press, 2008). Further references will be cited as Baker, *Women's Movement against Sexual Harassment*.

218 a letter of late March in 1975 . . . "Dear Sisters": Lin Farley, Susan Meyer, Karen Sauvigné, letter to "Dear Sisters," undated (apparently March 1975), in Catharine MacKinnon files. MacKinnon may have saved the only copy still in existence; with it in her files, which she generously allowed me to sort through for days, sometimes discarding the remains of nests made by mice, is a note to her teacher at Yale Law School, Barbara Underwood, saying, "Attached is the original letter I got about the Cornell sexual harassment problem." (See also later discussion of MacKinnon's suggestion to Underwood about how to use this letter to create an exam question for Underwood's course, Sex Discrimination, at Yale Law School in the spring of 1975.) I did not find a copy of this letter in the Working Women files or Sauvigné files.) Date of late March in 1975 is inferred from phrase "two weeks ago" combined with three sources: 3/7/75 decision against Carmita Wood (Robert B. Hardy, Referee, New York State Department of Labor, "Decision and Notice of Decision," 3/7/75, in Working Women files), which this letter follows; statement that it was "about this time" (3/7/75) that Carmita Wood came to the Human Affairs Program (in Lin Farley, "Special Disadvantages of Women in Male-Dominated Work Settings," p. 8, in testimony given before the Commission on Human Rights of the City of New York, in "Hearings on Women in Blue-Collar, Service, and Clerical Occupations," 4/21/75, typescript in Working Women files; further references will be cited as Farley, "Special Disadvantages"); and Human Affairs Program, "For Immediate Release: Working Women Join to Fight Sexual Exploitation," 4/3/75, in Working Women files, press release announcing the creation of Working Women United. Catharine MacKinnon, in *Sexual Harassment of Working Women: A Case of Discrimination* (New Haven: Yale University Press, 1979), credits Working Women United as the first to use *sexual harassment* as "anything approaching a term of art" (p. 250n13) and gives the date of 10/6/75 (p. 253n61). Further references will be cited as MacKinnon, *Sexual Harassment* (1979). MacKinnon also gives credit for development of the concept to the Alliance against Sexual Coercion of Cambridge, Massachusetts. Date of late March in 1975 for term *sexual harassment* is slightly earlier than implied by Susan Brownmiller's excellent chapter, "Its Name Is Sexual Harassment," in *In Our Time*, pp. 279–294, in which Karen Sauvigné links the choice of the term *sexual harassment*

to preparation for the speak-out of 5/4/75 (p. 281), and earlier than suggested in Jeffrey Toobin, "The Trouble with Sex," *New Yorker*, 2/9/98,
p. 50, which says that the "first use of that precise term [sexual harass-
ment] seems to have been at a 1975 conference at Cornell when a group of
feminists based in Ithaca held a 'Speak-Out on Sexual Harassment.'" The
earliest use of "sexual harassment" [spelled "harrasment"—an indicator
of its novelty] in a non-public letter may occur in Karen Sauvigné, letter to
Maurie E. Heins, 3/28/75, in Working Women files; another indicator of
novelty is that Heins, the attorney who agreed to represent Carmita Wood,
is addressed as "Dear Mauri"; see also Baker, *Women's Movement against
Sexual Harassment*, pp. 30–31, 207n17.

218 Human Affairs Program: Sauvigné interview; Meyer interview; Brownmiller, *In Our Time*, p. 279ff.; Baker, *Women's Movement against Sexual
Harassment*, p. 28ff.

219 "consciousness-raising" . . . "a remarkable tool" . . . "Each one of us had
already quit": Farley, *Sexual Shakedown*, pp. xi–xiii.

219 Farley began asking: Farley, "Special Disadvantages," p. 6 ("we have been
searching for more than six months"). And see Farley, *Sexual Shakedown*,
p. xi.

220 Wood's story . . . legal documents: Working Women files and Catharine
MacKinnon files. See further notes online.

220 never be able to prove conclusively: No court ever ruled on these allegations; they are not legally proved.

220 "Good evening" . . . hand on her bottom . . . Wood quickly stepped away:
Brief on Behalf of Claimant-Appellant [Carmita Wood], In the Matter
of the Claim of Carmita Wood for Unemployment Insurance benefits
pursuant to Article 18 of the Labor Law, case no. 75–92437, New York
State Department of Labor Unemployment Insurance Appeals Board,
by Maurie E. Heins, Susan K. Horn, attorneys for Claimant-Appellant;
Ellen Yacknin on the brief, undated but apparently c. June 1975, pp.
1–2, in Catharine MacKinnon files. Further references will be cited as
Wood brief.

220 "stand with his hands shaking": Affidavit of Carmita Wood, In the Matter of Carmita L. Wood, Ref. 75–92437, New York State Department of
Labor Unemployment Insurance Appeal Board, undated but apparently
c. May 1975, p. 3, in Catharine MacKinnon files; further references will
be cited as Wood affidavit. See also affidavit of Pamela Henderson, In the
Matter of Carmita L. Wood, Ref. 75–92437, New York State Department
of Labor Unemployment Insurance Appeal Board, undated but apparently
c. May 1975, p. 3, in Catharine MacKinnon files; further references will
be cited as Henderson affidavit. And see affidavit of Connie M. Korbel, In
the Matter of Carmita L. Wood, Ref. 75–92437, New York State Depart-

ment of Labor Unemployment Insurance Appeal Board, dated 4/29/75, p. 3; further references will be cited as Korbel affidavit.

221 "he grabbed my arms" . . . "During the course of the dance": Wood affidavit, p. 4.

221 "about to cry" . . . "nerve": Korbel affidavit, p. 2.

221 "looked at her and made her feel uncomfortable" . . . "dismissed" . . . "a diversion she enjoyed": Affidavit of Henry E. Doney, In the Matter of the Claim for benefits under Article 18 of the labor law made by Carmita L. Wood, Case No. 75–92437, New York State Department of Labor Unemployment Insurance Appeal Board, dated 7/28/75, pp. 8–9, in Working Women files. In this affidavit, Doney also stated that he believed Carmita Wood's allegations against their boss were "complete fabrications" (p. 7); he also said that his comments at Wood's unemployment hearing of 2/18/75 were badly transcribed but that he had not submitted corrections (p. 7).

221 hockey practice . . . "very capable women" . . . "capable of taking care of themselves, so to speak" . . . "try not to get into those situations": Henry E. Doney, in Hearing before Referee Robert Hardy, Jr., 2/18/75, In the Matter of the Claim for benefits under Article 18 of the labor law made by Carmita L. Wood, Case No. 75–92437, New York State Department of Labor Unemployment Insurance Appeal Board, pp. 33–34, in Working Women files. Further references will be cited as Wood unemployment hearing.

222 "for health reasons" . . . "didn't sell a thing": Carmita Wood, "Summary of Interview, New York State Department of Labor," 12/16/74, two handwritten pages, in Working Women files.

222 "You quit your job without good cause": New York State Department of Labor (signature not legible), "Notice of Determination to Claimant," 12/30/74, in Working Women files.

223 "So you're saying, in effect": Wood unemployment hearing, pp. 14–15, 19.

223 "personal non-compelling reasons": Robert B. Hardy, Referee, New York State Department of Labor, "Decision and Notice of Decision," 3/7/75, in Working Women files.

223 "not a bra burner": Meyer interview. See note online.

223 Seeking a name: Sauvigné interview; Meyer interview; Brownmiller, *In Our Time*, p. 281. The question of who created the phrase *sexual harassment* has led to controversy. Meyer and Sauvigné, when interviewed, credit the group at the meeting. Farley, who has been quoted that "it hit me—it's harassment!" (interview in Peter Wyden, "Sexual Harassment," *Good Housekeeping*, July 1993, p. 121), has taken some individual credit. Eventually the three had "an unfortunate falling-out,"

according to Susan Brownmiller, "an escalation of their long-running quarrel over who actually named sexual harassment." Brownmiller, *In Our Time*, p. 285.

224 "We understand": This and subsequent quotations from the letter are from Lin Farley, Susan Meyer, Karen Sauvigné, letter to "Dear Sisters," undated (apparently March 1975), in Catharine MacKinnon files.

224 "girl Friday": Meyer interview.

225 names of these "Dear Sisters" had been gathered: Sauvigné interview.

225 only one lawyer wrote back: Sauvigné interview.

225 "just exploded in my mind": Catharine MacKinnon interview, 10/5/90.

226 public school that was good enough . . . "life's work" . . . "that women were real" . . . took her to the offices where he worked: Catharine MacKinnon interviews.

227 "put Kid Cann in jail" . . . run for governor: David Chanen, "U.S. Appeals Judge George MacKinnon, of St. Paul, Dies at 89," *Minneapolis Star Tribune*, 5/3/95, p. 6B.

227 "he took me seriously": Catharine MacKinnon interviews.

227 study both law and politics: Catharine MacKinnon, letter to author, 4/2/04.

227 "By the time you applied" . . . B at Smith College in graphic arts . . . black women and to men returning from Vietnam: Catharine MacKinnon, email to author, 6/17/05.

228 "it's in opposition to the whole purpose" . . . her previous applications had not received a full review: Catharine MacKinnon interview, 4/2/04; Catharine MacKinnon, email to author, 6/18/05; interview with James A. Thomas, Madison, Connecticut, by phone, 5/17/06.

228 met once a week for dinner . . . issue of *Rat* . . . "first feminist anything" . . . mimeographed copies: Catharine MacKinnon interviews. For more on *Rat*, see Brownmiller, *In Our Time*, p. 75ff.

16: Women and the Law

231 "similarly circumstanced": *F. S. Royster Guano Co. v. Virginia*, 253 U.S. 412, 415 (1920).

231 "similarly situated": *Reed v. Reed*, 404 U.S. 71, 77 (1971). The legal use of "similarly situated" extends back in U.S. law to the early nineteenth century; see *Mutual Assurance Society v. Faxon*, 19 U.S. 606 (1821).

231 MacKinnon believed . . . "disadvantagement" because of sex: MacKinnon interviews; Catharine MacKinnon, letter to author, 2/25/04.

231 "about everything the situation of women was really about": Catharine MacKinnon interviews.

231 copy . . . to Underwood . . . "How is this sex discrimination?" . . . "con-

ditions of work": Catharine MacKinnon, letter to Barbara Underwood, undated but apparently the spring of 1975, in Catharine MacKinnon files.

231 group calling itself: Working Women United, "Who Are We," 5/4/75 (but undated), in Catharine MacKinnon files.

231 folding chairs . . . basketball hoops: snapshots in Working Women files.

232 no agreement for making their testimony public . . . half a year to complete a transcript: Karen Sauvigné, letters to Catharine MacKinnon, 1/5/76 and 3/8/76, in Catharine MacKinnon files. The 68-page transcript of the speak-out for years was not readily available. (In June 1993, for example, Karen Sauvigné generously permitted me to read those pages from her copy that contained testimony by women whom she knew had spoken publicly on other occasions.) The transcript is "Speak-Out on Sexual Harassment of Women at Work," Ithaca, New York, 5/4/75, Karen Sauvigné Papers, Brooklyn, New York, Private Collection; reprinted online as document 5 in "How Did Diverse Activists in the Second Wave of the Women's Movement Shape Emerging Public Policy on Sexual Harassment?" in Kathryn Sklar and Thomas Dublin, eds., *Women and Social Movements in the United States, 1600–2000*, Vol. 2 (Binghamton, State University of New York at Binghamton, Center for the Historical Study of Women and Gender, 1998), at www.alexanderstreet6.com/wasm/wasmrestricted/DP71/doc5 .htm (visited 3/31/06). Further references will be cited as Sklar and Dublin, *Women and Social Movements*.

232 "continually but peripherally" . . . "penalties you paid for being a woman in the workplace": Nemy interview.

232 "you aren't in any position": Subsequent quotations from Nemy's article are from Enid Nemy, "Women Begin to Speak Out against Sexual Harassment," *New York Times*, 8/19/75, p. 38.

233 "become a public figure" . . . "It's rough" . . . "Inside myself there was fear": Carmita Wood, "Woman Alone," *Labor Pains* 1, no. 1 (August 1975), p. 5, reprinted online as document 6I in "How Did Diverse Activists in the Second Wave of the Women's Movement Shape Emerging Public Policy on Sexual Harrassment?" in Sklar and Dublin, *Women and Social Movements*, Vol. 2 at www.alexanderstreet6.com/wasm/wasmrestricted/ DP71/doc6I.htm (visited 3/31/06).

234 MacKinnon called Karen Sauvigné: Letter of 1/28/78, Catharine MacKinnon to Karen Sauvigné, in Catharine MacKinnon files.

234 MacKinnon penned . . . "not energy to appeal": *Labor Pains* 1, no. 1 (August 1975), p. 3, with MacKinnon's marginalia, in Catharine MacKinnon files.

234 paper that she titled: All quotations from MacKinnon's "Sexual Harassment" paper, unless otherwise indicated, are from Catharine A. MacKinnon,

"Sexual Harassment of Working Women: A Case of Sex Discrimination," typescript with cover page notation "Catharine A. MacKinnon, Yale Law School, Supervised Analytic Writing [for] Professor Thomas Emerson, Supervisor, Spring, 1976"; this copy, with Emerson's handwritten comments, is in Catharine MacKinnon files. (MacKinnon generously let me review this version of her drafting, marked on its title page as "Tom's copy"; the library of Yale Law School has a copy without Emerson's notes.) Completion date for this draft, based on footnotes (e.g. to *New York Times* of 8/22/76), seems to have been late summer or early fall 1976. Further references will be cited as MacKinnon, "Sexual Harassment," typescript, 1976. See detailed notes online.

235 MacKinnon juxtaposed three legal opinions: MacKinnon, "Sexual Harassment," typescript, 1976; cases are quoted on p. 38. Full citations appear in MacKinnon, *Sexual Harassment*, p. 278.

238 "must be reasonable": *Royster Guano v. Virginia*, 253 U.S. 412, 415 (1920).

239 "not because she was a woman" . . . "evidence an arbitrary barrier": *Barnes v. Train*, 13 Fair Empl. Prac. Cas. (BNA) 123. Decided 8/9/74 by Judge John Lewis Smith Jr., United States District Court for the District of Columbia.

239 "formal equality": MacKinnon, *Sexual Harassment* (1979), p. 33.

241 term *sexual blackmail:* Jack Wheeler, bench memo to George E. MacKinnon, 12/16/75, for *Barnes v. Costle*, 561 F.2d 983 (D.C. Cir. 1977), in George MacKinnon papers.

242 perhaps the Friday after Christmas in 1975: Most details come from Catharine MacKinnon interview, 4/2/04; from her subsequent review of her 1975 date book; from her emails to author of 4/9/04 and 6/9/05; and from her annotations on fact-checking drafts of 2/25/04 and 8/4/05. In her email of 4/9/04, she said she believed her father recommended the Friday after a holiday as a day when few people would want to use the Lexis machine; in 1975 both Thanksgiving and Christmas came on Thursdays. Her date book shows that she arrived in Washington to visit her parents on the Wednesdays before both holidays and that possible dates for her visits to the courthouse include Friday 11/28/75 and Friday 12/26/75 (as well as Wednesday 12/24/75 and Monday 12/29/75). A week before Thanksgiving Judge Spottswood Robinson, as screening judge, had assigned *Barnes* to the court's "summary calendar" for argument on 12/17/75; see "Confidential Screening Memorandum," of Judge Robinson for *Barnes*, 11/20/75, in George MacKinnon papers. A likely date for a private conference of the three judges, according to an oral history by George E. MacKinnon, is 12/24/75, a date when he recalls the following: "Kitty . . . came down from

Yale, and she came in at noon on the last day before Christmas vacation [in 1975]. She was going to stay with us for the holidays. And as she came in, I had just walked out of a conference on *Barnes v. Costle*, which is a sex discrimination case, and we hadn't really settled on the case at the conference." (See George E. MacKinnon interview for the District of Columbia Circuit Oral History Project, 2/18/94. Final copy available from Library of Congress. Raw transcript with annotations by George E. MacKinnon available from Minnesota Historical Society.) Catharine MacKinnon apparently had not seen her father's papers at the Minnesota Historical Society before the author sent her some copies while checking facts for this book. See author's letter to Catharine MacKinnon, 6/9/05, and MacKinnon, email to author, 8/6/05: "wow, this is really fascinating!"

242 screened in advance and assigned to the court's summary calendar: "Confidential Screening Memorandum," of Judge Robinson for *Barnes*, 11/20/75, in George MacKinnon papers.

242 "that was all he knew": Catharine MacKinnon interview, 3/14/98.

242 Suddenly a young woman in a dark suit: The narrative of MacKinnon's interaction with this woman comes from recollections of Catharine MacKinnon in the form of interviews (particularly 4/2/04), follow-up emails, and annotations by Catharine MacKinnon on fact-checking drafts of 2/25/04 and 8/4/05. Confirming this narrative of MacKinnon handing her law school paper to a young woman who said she worked with Judge Robinson has proved fascinating but difficult. The two women who were Judge Robinson's only clerks in the fall of 1975 are Susan Low Bloch, now a law professor at Georgetown, and Faith Hochberg, now judge at the United States District Court for the District of New Jersey. In interviews, they could recall neither this meeting in the Lexis room nor working on *Barnes*. (For Hochberg's recollection, see text below at "being so tenacious.") The one woman clerking for Judge Robinson the next year, Ellen Semonoff, believes that either Bloch or Hochberg did some drafting on *Barnes*. By phone, Judge Robinson declined to comment, saying that there was "no harm in asking" but that he made a "firm policy not to discuss work for the court." Efforts to check this narrative—which may never be fully confirmed—included interviews with the following: Judge Spottswood W. Robinson III, Richmond, Virginia, by phone, 6/14/93; Susan Low Bloch (Robinson clerk, 1975–76), Washington, DC, by phone, 3/19/98 and 5/14/98; Faith Hochberg (Robinson clerk, 1975–76), New Jersey, by phone, 3/31/98, with follow-up emails, April 1998; Ellen Semonoff (Robinson clerk, 1976–77), Cambridge, Massachusetts, by phone, 5/6/98; John P. (Jack) Wheeler III (MacKinnon clerk who worked on *Barnes*, 1975–76), New York City, by phone, 8/18/98; Tom Campbell (MacKinnon clerk who

worked on *Barnes*, 1976–77), San Jose, California, by email, 6/21–27/05; Barbara Childs Wallace (MacKinnon clerk, 1979–80), Jackson, Mississippi, by phone, 5/5/98; Lynn Bregman (Bazelon clerk, 1975–76), Washington, DC, by email, 3/25–28/98; E. Donald Elliott (Bazelon clerk, 1975–76), New Haven, Connecticut, and Washington, DC, by phone, 4/1/98 and 5/4/98; and David Silberman (Bazelon clerk, 1975–76), Washington, DC, by phone, 3/31/98.

243 Do you have anything written . . . I don't have a copy: Catharine MacKinnon interview, 3/14/98, and Catharine MacKinnon, email to author, 8/6/05.

243 (in words MacKinnon would long recall as verbatim), "it's got to be more than we've got" . . . "This is my shot": Catharine MacKinnon interview, 3/14/98; MacKinnon, letter to author, 4/2/04.

244 "to learn how to bend the law to the needs of blacks": Kluger, *Simple Justice*, p. 128. I am indebted to *Simple Justice* for much of the background on Judge Spottswood W. Robinson III.

244 turning point in his life . . . idol . . . highest grade-point average: Laura A. Kiernan, "The Fire Still Burns," *Washington Post*, 5/27/81, p. A1.

245 extraordinary scholarship . . . "Mr. Footnote": Susan Low Bloch, quoted in Kenneth Karpay, "Waiting for Robinson; Circuit Judge Toils to Clear Backlog," *Legal Times*, 6/22/87, p. 1. When Robinson left active duty on the court, Judge MacKinnon wondered whether he "took all his footnotes with him." Letter of 12/11/91, in George MacKinnon papers.

17: Mechelle Vinson Goes to Trial

246 another feminist lawyer: Most biographical information on and quotations from Barry, unless otherwise indicated, are from Barry interviews and Patricia J. Barry, letter to author, 9/24/05. See detailed notes online.

246 "Born a feminist": Ludwic interview.

247 "cavalierly" . . . "much less cavalier toward *Hoyt*": Supreme Court transcript of *Edwards v. Healy*, 421 U.S. 772 (1975), argued 10/16/74.

248 chemist from India: *Kulkarni v. Alexander*, 662 F.2d 758 (D.C. Cir. 1978).

248 Meisburg, who had spent most of his career in government: Meisburg interview.

248 "He had said" . . . lawyer with a totally different style: Vinson interview.

249 only law book on the subject—*Sexual Harassment of Working Women*: In Farley, *Sexual Shakedown*, pp. 125–146; Chapter 7 is called "The Law: Civil Remedies." After describing the few existing cases, it relies on a law professor named John J. Pemberton Jr. to predict briefly (pp. 145–146)

where the law will go. He says that a long-range solution will occur when there are "a lot more women lawyers to take these cases."

249 "the big case in the sky": Barry interviews.

250 "a federal judge held that sexual advances": MacKinnon, *Sexual Harassment* (1979), p. 63.

250 "Judge Richey called up" . . . "Well, that's a big relief": Catharine MacKinnon interview, 4/2/04, and Catharine MacKinnon, letter to author, 4/24/06. See note online.

250 *Barnes* had followed a long path: Most of the narrative of *Barnes* comes from interviews with clerks and from documents preserved in the George MacKinnon papers. The Bazelon papers in the Biddle Law Library of the University of Pennsylvania Law School apparently do not contain information on *Barnes* (phone request by author, 3/17/98). Judge Robinson's papers are not available, although Howard University has requested them in the past, according to Joellen ElBashir, Curator of Manuscripts, Howard University (phone request by author, 6/8/06). For extensive references to George MacKinnon papers, see note online.

250 "discrimination here" . . . "only imposed on some women" . . . "*Geduldig v. Aiello*" . . . "I question . . . whether it is sex discrimination": Handwritten notes of Judge MacKinnon dated 12/17/75, written during oral argument that day for *Barnes v. Costle*, 561 F.2d 983 (D.C. Cir. 1977). George MacKinnon papers.

251 "nothing more than": Judge Bazelon, memo to Judges MacKinnon and Robinson, 1/28/76, in George MacKinnon papers.

251 a memo restating his belief . . . "a better job": Judge MacKinnon, memo to Robinson and Bazelon, 3/17/76. In a letter of 5/29/85, MacKinnon recalled that because he and Bazelon were having doubts that "any theory could support a finding of gender based 'sex discrimination'" in *Barnes*, "we assigned the opinion" to Robinson. Letter of George E. MacKinnon to Prof. Kenneth Culp Davis, 5/29/85. All are in George MacKinnon papers.

251 "hopefully" would reply within two weeks: Memo from Judge Robinson, 3/19/76, in George MacKinnon papers.

251 clerks came to believe: Semonoff interview.

251 Of their five clerks, three were women: Clerking for Robinson were Faith Hochberg and Susan Low Bloch; for Bazelon were Donald Elliott, Lynn Bregman, and David Silberman (whose wife, Ellen Semonoff, clerked the next year for Robinson). The clerk who recalls Bazelon asking about clerks' sexual harassment is Elliott. Interviews with E. Donald Elliott, New Haven, Connecticut, and Washington, DC, by phone, 4/1/98 and 5/4/98.

251 MacKinnon had only male clerks: Clerking for him were Jack Wheeler and

Mark Peterson. Interview with John P. (Jack) Wheeler III, New York City, by phone, 8/18/98. Although Wheeler could not recall working on *Barnes*, his bench memo of 12/16/75, the day before oral argument, is in George MacKinnon papers. That memo expressed doubt that what Wheeler called "sexual blackmail" was covered by Title VII, but urged further analysis of the legislative history.

252 he conferred with his secretary . . . let one clerk know: Interview with Barbara Childs Wallace, Jackson, Mississippi, by phone, 5/5/98.

252 One of his female clerks . . . not give her a ride home . . . she understood: Semonoff interview.

252 what she saw as an odd role . . . "go sit with" . . . "work with": Semonoff interview. "I wouldn't have done it [talked to another judge about a case] without Judge Robinson knowing about it," she recalled. "I was pretty straight."

252 "proposed opinion": Quotations from this opinion are from "Proposed opinion" by Judge Robinson, 12/16/76, in George MacKinnon papers.

253 "your eloquent opinion": Memo from Judge Bazelon to Judges Robinson and MacKinnon, 1/17/77, in George MacKinnon papers.

253 "Abuse of his *position* but not sexual *discrimination*": Italics here represent underlining in Judge MacKinnon's handwriting. Written in margin of p. 6 of "proposed opinion" by Judge Robinson, 12/16/76, in George MacKinnon papers.

253 Judge MacKinnon instructed his clerk to draft a separate opinion, narrower than Robinson's: Memo from Tom Campbell to Judge MacKinnon, 4/13/77, in George MacKinnon papers.

253 "long association with business": George E. MacKinnon interview for the District of Columbia Circuit Oral History Project, 2/18/94, p. 52 in final copy available from Library of Congress.

253 MacKinnon's opinion: Quotations from this opinion, unless indicated otherwise, are from *Barnes v. Costle*, 561 F.2d 983, 995, 999–1001 (D.C. Cir. 1977) (MacKinnon concurrence). Further references will be cited as Judge MacKinnon *Barnes* concurrence; see detailed notes online. Language in the published opinion of 7/27/77 is narrower than in the memo from Tom Campbell to Judge MacKinnon, 4/13/77.

254 "Let the master respond": *Black's Law Dictionary*, 6th ed. (St. Paul: West Group, 1990), pp. 1311–1312.

256 They never discussed the decision privately: Catharine MacKinnon, email to author, 8/6/05.

256 "just took a tort approach": Catharine MacKinnon interview, 12/16/90.

256 "one appellate judge" . . . "fundamentally insufficient": MacKinnon, *Sexual Harassment* (1979), p. 165; Judge MacKinnon is named in an endnote, p. 283.

256 "sexual harassment in virtually all cases": MacKinnon, "Sexual Harassment," typescript, 1976. Because the draft of the paper that I rely on for
this narrative carries the date "Spring, 1976" and seems to have received
revisions as late as September of 1976, it evidently predates Judge Robinson's opinion of 7/27/77 but would not be the version handed to a clerk in
late 1975.

257 "We cannot accept this analysis": *Barnes v. Costle*, 561 F.2d 983, 990
(D.C. Cir. 1977).

257 "marked disadvantage": *Barnes v. Costle*, 561 F.2d 983, 991 (D.C. Cir.
1977).

257 judge who, as she would later say, "got it": Catharine MacKinnon interview, 3/14/98.

257 direct report of the effectiveness of her law school paper in an account by
her father: Catharine MacKinnon, emails to author, 8/6/05 and 4/29/08.

257 in 1975, . . . Robinson had expressed doubt: This preliminary discussion
could have occurred on or near 11/20/75 when Judge Robinson assigned
Barnes to the summary calendar (for less important cases). It might have
occurred before oral argument (12/17/75) and presumably before discussion in conference (apparently 12/24/75, according to Judge MacKinnon's interview for the District of Columbia Circuit Oral History Project,
2/18/94), at which Robinson apparently contended that Barnes had been
subjected to sex discrimination. This timing suggests that a handover of
Catharine MacKinnon's paper might have needed to occur not on the
Friday after Christmas (12/26/75) but on the Friday after Thanksgiving
(11/28/75), a possible date according to her date book: Catharine MacKinnon interview, 4/2/04, and her email of 4/9/04 after she checked her date
book.

257 travesty of civil rights: Catharine MacKinnon, email to author, 6/9/05.

257 believed his daughter's work affected the *Barnes* opinion . . . "just walked
out of a conference" . . . "the same conclusion": George E. MacKinnon
interview for the District of Columbia Circuit Oral History Project,
2/18/94. Final copy available from Library of Congress. He recalls the
day that he "just walked out of a conference on *Barnes*" as the "last
day before Christmas vacation"; her date book shows that she arrived in
Washington from Yale and went to his chambers on the last day before
Christmas, Wednesday, 12/24/75. Although I have found no documents
showing that *Barnes* (argued 12/17/75) was the subject of a conference a
week later (12/24), the dates seem reasonable. A former clerk who recalls
hearing the story that Catharine MacKinnon's paper influenced the court
on sexual harassment is Barbara Childs Wallace, clerk to Judge Mac-
Kinnon in 1979–80. She says, "I have heard a version of that story, and I
always have understood that his [Judge MacKinnon's] understanding of

sexual harassment and some of the understanding of the District of Columbia Circuit came from something that Kitty had done early on. I can't do anything else other than to confirm that I had heard that story way back in 1979." Interview with Barbara Childs Wallace, Jackson, Mississippi, by phone, 5/5/98.

258 "the basis": Jeffrey Toobin, "The Trouble with Sex," *New Yorker*, 2/9/98, p. 50. He writes, "MacKinnon gave a copy of her paper to a law clerk on the case in the federal appeals court, and, she claims, 'it became the basis of the decision'" in *Barnes* at the Court of Appeals.

258 later that year he died: Eric Pace, "Spottswood W. Robinson 3d, Civil Rights Lawyer, Dies at 82," *Washington Post*, 10/13/98, p. B11.

258 neither of the women who had worked as his clerks: Susan Low Bloch recalls that the clerk on *Barnes* was Faith (Shapiro) Hochberg. Interviews with Susan Low Bloch, Washington, DC, by phone, 3/19/98 and 5/14/98.

258 "teasing me about being so tenacious" . . . "except the vague sense": Interview with Faith Hochberg, New Jersey, by phone, 3/31/98, and follow-up email of 4/6/98.

259 No woman had ever won . . . admitted to having slept with her boss: Catharine A. MacKinnon, *Feminism Unmodified: Discourses on Life and Law* (Cambridge: Harvard University Press, 1987), p. 109 and p. 254n18. Further references will be cited as MacKinnon, *Feminism Unmodified*.

259 "personal relationship" . . . "coercive power": Barry interviews.

259 Barry opened her case: Quotations from Barry's opening statement and witnesses' testimony during the trial, unless otherwise indicated, are from *Vinson* DC transcript, 1/21/80. See detailed notes online.

259 "the situation in which sexual harassment": MacKinnon, *Sexual Harassment* (1979), p. 40.

260 John Meisburg . . . found two women willing to testify: Meisburg interviews; Cochran, *Sexual Harassment*, pp. 60, 66.

260 Malone stated . . . saw that Mr. Taylor "disrespected": *Vinson* DC transcript, 1/21/80, p. 15.

260 "Objection. What's her age" . . . "the environment was ripe": *Vinson* DC transcript, 1/21/80, p. 5.

260 "had big hairy legs" . . . "he would put his hands on my breasts": *Vinson* DC transcript, 1/21/80, p. 21.

261 "To get anywhere in the bank you had to . . . go to bed with him": *Vinson* DC transcript, 1/21/80, p. 30.

261 Malone said, "Yes" . . . "what Mr. Taylor did with this witness": *Vinson* DC transcript, 1/21/80, p. 52.

261 "pattern and practice" . . . "even if he treats them violently": *Vinson* DC transcript, 1/21/80, p. 79.

261 "suggestive comments" . . . read *Penthouse* . . . nude pictures: *Vinson* DC transcript, 1/23/80, 3:50 p.m. session, pp. 15, 16–17, 39, 44–45.

261 "been touching me": *Vinson* DC transcript, 1/28/80, p. 38.

261 "did not go to bed": *Vinson* DC transcript, 1/28/80, p. 8.

262 "Mechelle was not the only victim": Barry interviews.

262 "had a chance to observe this or not": *Vinson* DC transcript, 1/21/80, p. 21.

262 "so humiliated": Barry interviews.

262 "the making of improper sexual advances" . . . "terms, conditions, or privileges of employment": *Bundy v. Jackson*, 19 Fair Empl. Prac. Cas. (BNA) 828, decided 4/25/79, United States District Court for the District of Columbia.

263 Penn's refusal to hear evidence about the environment: In one exchange, he limited testimony from Christine Malone about what he called "the environment" at the bank. See *Vinson* DC transcript, 1/21/80, p. 21. He described such limitations as his refusal to "allow plaintiff to present wholesale evidence of a pattern and practice relating to sexual advances to other female employees in her case in chief." *Vinson v. Taylor*, 23 Fair Empl. Prac. Cas. (BNA) 37 (D.D.C. 1980), fn1.

263 "Mr. Taylor touching Christina on her back": *Vinson* DC transcript, 1/22/80, p. 33.

263 bitch: *Vinson* DC transcript, 1/22/80, p. 41.

263 drove her to a hotel: *Vinson* DC transcript, 1/22/80, p. 51–53.

263 "indulged in sex": *Vinson* DC transcript, 1/29/80, p. 14.

263 "did work pretty close . . . very exposive": *Vinson* DC transcript, 1/30/80, p. 14.

263 "a lot of sexual fantasies": *Vinson* DC transcript, 1/30/80, p. 23.

263 "sexually fondling": *Vinson* DC transcript, 1/31/80, 1:45 p.m., p. 19.

263 "low-cut dresses" . . . "extremely tight pants": *Vinson* DC transcript, 1/31/80, 1:45 p.m., p. 14.

263 "Did there come a period" . . . "Well, that has happened": *Vinson* DC transcript, 1/29/80, p. 14.

264 Judge Penn issued his opinion: Quotations from the opinion are from *Vinson v. Taylor*, 23 Fair Empl. Prac. Cas. (BNA) 37 (D.D.C. 1980), decided 2/26/80. See detailed notes online.

264 Barry scrawled, in oversized letters: This and what she scrawled are from Barry's annotated copy of opinion by Judge Penn, *Vinson v. Taylor*, 2/26/80, in Barry files.

265 Taylor's denial would need to be kept fully in mind by any future reader: See Cochran, *Sexual Harassment*, p. 3 ("The reader is strongly advised to suspend judgment about the particular facts of this case and to treat all disputed facts as unproved") and p. 57 ("Readers should not assume

that any particulars of this story are verified truth and should be aware that the facts of this case, by and large, have never been authoritatively established").

265 "hypothetical finding of fact": Patricia J. Barry, letter to Joan Vermeulen, 6/6/80, in Barry files, including "[Judge Penn] made an inappropriate finding of fact. . . . hypothetical finding of fact." Barry interviews: " 'If there was sex it was voluntary'—that's what drove me to the court of appeals."

265 Barry was broke: Patricia J. Barry, letter to Mechelle Vinson, 5/20/81, in Barry files.

265 Her friends had seen her . . . "Why do I have to be in on time" . . . give it up . . . "That judge didn't do his job": Barry interviews.

18: Appeal to a Higher Court

267 one-room apartment—she could no longer afford to rent her office: Barry interviews.

267 "cannot find this appeal presents a substantial question": *Vinson v. Taylor*, 27 Fair Empl. Prac. Cas. (BNA) 948 (D.D.C. 1980), decided 6/10/80, motion to appeal *in forma pauperis*.

267 "exposed for what that trial showed": Barry interviews.

267 court of appeals ruled that she could proceed to appeal without the transcript: Patricia J. Barry, letter to Mechelle Vinson, 5/8/81, in Barry files.

267 "Unless you can get me $300": Patricia J. Barry, letter to Mechelle Vinson, 5/20/81, in Barry files. As of the end of 1981, according to Barry's records, Vinson's total payment to Barry was $170. Letter, 7/21/91, in Barry files.

268 She got it in late: Barry interviews.

268 "Prior to trial": This and subsequent quotations from Barry's brief are from Brief for Mechelle Vinson by Patricia Barry to Court of Appeals, dated 8/14/81, in *Vinson v. Taylor*, 753 F.2d 141 (D.C. Cir. 1985), pp. 39–40.

268 Back when she was beginning her appeal, she wrote for help: Patricia J. Barry, letter to Joan Vermeulen, Working Women's Institute, 593 Park Avenue, New York City, 6/6/80, in Barry files.

269 Barry thought he did a great job. She wished she had done as well: Barry interviews.

269 fell ill . . . surgery: Kenneth Karpay, "Waiting for Robinson; Circuit Judge Toils to Clear Backlog," *Legal Times*, 6/22/87, p. 1.

269 Vinson couldn't find bank jobs . . . enrolled in nursing school but had to drop out: Vinson interview.

269 "Well," . . . "call the court of appeals, Mechelle": Barry interviews.

269 Vinson received a call ... "the decision" ... "Oh come on, you're playing" ... "WE DID IT" ... "Yes, it's great": Vinson interview.

270 "was not required to grant Taylor" ... "was not the victim of sexual harassment": *Vinson v. Taylor*, 23 Fair Empl. Prac. Cas. (BNA) 37 (D.D.C. 1980).

270 Eleanor Holmes Norton ... who wanted to encourage women: Interview with Eleanor Holmes Norton, driving to Hartford, Connecticut, 5/22/05. See also Lester, *Fire in My Soul*, pp. 206–207.

270 "conduct has the purpose": "EEOC Interim Interpretive Guidelines on Sexual Harassment," *Daily Labor Report*, 3/11/80, p. E-1, in Working Women files.

271 "condition of work": MacKinnon, "Sexual Harassment," typescript, 1976, p. 15; MacKinnon, *Sexual Harassment* (1979), p. 32.

271 "the making of improper sexual advances": This and subsequent quotations from the district court's *Bundy* case and ruling are from *Bundy v. Jackson*, 19 Fair Empl. Prac. Cas. (BNA) 828, decided 4/25/79, United States District Court for the District of Columbia.

272 "Bundy's supervisors did not take": These and other quotations from the court of appeals ruling, unless otherwise indicated, are from *Bundy v. Jackson*, 641 F.2d 934 (D.C. Cir. 1977). See detailed notes online.

272 "'terms, conditions, or privileges'": *Rogers v. Equal Employment Opportunity Commission*, 454 F.2d 234 (5th Cir. 1971). See also MacKinnon, *Sexual Harassment* (1979), pp. 210–211.

273 "Should women be required" ... "in order to force" ... Reprinting the long last sentence: MacKinnon, *Sexual Harassment* (1979), pp. 46–47; *Bundy v. Jackson*, 641 F.2d 934, 945–946 (D.C. Cir. 1977).

274 "was not required to grant Taylor": This and subsequent quotations of the court's opinions are from *Vinson v. Taylor*, 753 F.2d 141 (D.C. Cir. 1985).

276 success only rarely (probably less than one chance in 250): See Micheal W. Giles, Virginia A. Hettinger, Christopher Zorn, and Todd C. Peppers, "The Etiology of the Occurrence of En Banc Review in the U.S. Court of Appeals," *American Journal of Political Science* 51, no. 3 (July 2007): 449–463. The authors report that throughout the 1980s the court of appeals for the District of Columbia never reheard more than 10 cases *en banc* in a year. Nationwide in 1999 (the only full year reported in the article), the authors report that "while the Courts of Appeals decided nearly 27,000 cases after oral argument or submission of briefs in 1999, only 94 cases, less than 1%, were decided en banc in that year." (To be precise, 94 of 27,000 would be .35%.)

277 a "plaintiff's voluntariness": This and subsequent quotations from Bork's dissent are from *Vinson v. Taylor*, 760 F.2d 1330 (D.C. Cir. 1985), 5/14/85,

dissent by Judge Bork, circuit judge, with whom Circuit Judges Scalia and Starr join, dissenting from the denial of rehearing *en banc.*

278   "4,000 federal trial judges instead of some 400": *Tomkins v. Public Serv. Elec. & Gas*, 422 F. Supp. 553 (D.C. N.J. 1976), decided 11/22/76.

278   "Oh boy, here we go": Barry interviews.

278   By a vote of 5 to 4, Barry failed to extend the right of jury trial: *Lehman v. Nakshian*, 453 U.S. 156 (1981), decided 6/26/81.

279   lost with dignity . . . "bad law": Barry interviews.

279   With Bork's dissent on her mind, she sent out a letter . . . MacKinnon: Patricia J. Barry, letter to Catharine MacKinnon, 8/23/85, in Barry files.

279   financially desperate: Catharine MacKinnon interviews, 10/21–24/90, and Catharine MacKinnon, letter to author, 4/2/04.

279   Some claims were declared moot because students had graduated . . . trial judge apparently did not believe: *Alexander v. Yale University*, 631 F.2d 178, 183–184 (2d Cir. 1980).

279   first decision in federal court affirming: *Alexander v. Yale*, 459 F. Supp. 1, 8–9 (D. Conn. 1977), citing *Barnes v. Costle*, 561 F.2d 983 (D.C. Cir. 1977), including Judge MacKinnon's concurrence (pp. 1000–1001). See also MacKinnon, *Sexual Harassment* (1979), p. 34.

279   law students at Yale began pressing: Catharine MacKinnon interview, 10/18/95, supplemented by Catharine MacKinnon, letter to author, 4/2/04.

280   "didn't have the patience": Interview with Guido Calabresi, New Haven, Connecticut, 11/20/90.

280   agreed to work on *Vinson*: At some point a controversy developed about who would assist Barry as co-counsel at the Supreme Court. Although MacKinnon says that she "took the case as co-counsel" (Catharine Mac-Kinnon, letter to author, 4/2/04, comments on fact-checking draft dated 3/31/04, p. 102), Barry believes she did not ask MacKinnon to be co-counsel (Patricia J. Barry, letter to author, 9/24/05, comments on fact-checking draft dated 8/5/05, p. 23). See note online.

19: To the Supreme Court

281   asking for more help: Patricia J. Barry, letter to Judith Kurtz of Equal Rights Advocates, 10/24/85, in Barry files.

281   awful case: Burns interviews, Lenhoff interviews, and Katz interview.

281   "bad woman" . . . "been afforded the opportunity": Burns interviews.

282   prepared the groundwork: "Memorandum of EEOC General Counsel Johnny J. Butler, October 24, 1985," *Daily Labor Report*, 10/30/85.

282   Silberman . . . "one overriding objective": "Memorandum of Commis-

sioner Rosalie Gaull Silberman, October 28, 1985," *Daily Labor Report*, 10/30/85, p. E-1.

282 attack Judge Robinson's opinion to save . . . the guidelines: In her memo of 10/28/85, Commissioner Rosalie Gaull Silberman described her strategy as designed to "strongly support our guidelines on strict liability, explaining that the facts of this case do not fall within the guidelines." She characterized Vinson as someone "engaged in a private relationship that the trial court found to be voluntary until the plaintiff [Vinson] opted out." She argued that "under the narrow set of facts in Vinson . . . the employer should not be held strictly liable."

282 "relies upon what I believe is": "Memorandum of Commissioner Rosalie Gaull Silberman, October 28, 1985," *Daily Labor Report*, 10/30/85, p. E-1.

283 "Controversy Builds At EEOC over Upcoming Sexual Harassment Case": *Daily Labor Report*, 10/29/85, p. A-4. The article reported that "Commissioner Ricky Silberman will be pushing her fellow panel members to adopt the defendant employer's position" and that "the EEOC general counsel's office will argue against Silberman's interpretation."

283 "the elimination of personal slights": Paul Taylor, "Thomas's View of Harassment Said to Evolve; His Record at EEOC Is Source of Dispute," *Washington Post*, 10/11/91, p. A10. According to Jane Mayer and Jill Abramson, *Strange Justice: The Selling of Clarence Thomas* (Boston: Houghton Mifflin, 1994), at p. 368 in an endnote for p. 73, "this transition memo was made available to the Judiciary Committee when Thomas was nominated to the Supreme Court." Further references will be cited as Mayer and Abramson, *Strange Justice*.

283 Thomas' hearings for confirmation to the Supreme Court . . . "became even more strained": Hearings before the Senate Committee on the Judiciary (Pt. 4), 102d Cong. 36–41 (1999). Available at http://gos.sbc.edu/h/hill .html.

284 "as though I had been dipped in a vat" . . . "grumbled and muttered": Anita Hill, *Speaking Truth to Power* (New York: Doubleday, 1997), pp. 77–78.

284 vote said to be 3–2: "Government Joins Employer's Side in Sex Harassment Case before Supreme Court," *Daily Labor Report*, 12/16/85, p. A-5.

284 Lenhoff heard that staffers . . . had lobbied: Lenhoff interviews.

284 "ensure that sexual harassment charges do not become a tool": This and subsequent quotations from the government's brief are from Brief for the United States and the Equal Employment Opportunity Commission as Amici Curiae by Charles Fried, Solicitor General, et al. to Supreme Court, dated 12/11/85, in *Meritor Savings Bank v. Vinson*, 477 U.S. 57 (1986),

p. 15. Further references will be cited as *Meritor* Brief for the United States. See detailed notes online.

285 "I really despise": Barry marginalia in *Meritor* Brief for the United States, pp. 22–23, in Barry files.

285 Writing the brief for Mechelle Vinson became, at Barry's request, MacKinnon's task: Patricia J. Barry, letter to author, 9/24/05; Barry interviews.

285 full transcript would cost up to $3,000 . . . total to $650: Sarah E. Burns, assistant director, Georgetown University Law Center Sex Discrimination Clinic, letter to Joseph F. Spaniol Jr., Clerk of the Court (Supreme Court), 2/10/86, in Barry files.

285 club called Tracks: Katz interview.

285 draft one day . . . another draft: Catharine MacKinnon, letters to Patricia J. Barry, 1/13/86 and 1/15/86, in Barry files.

286 "that, if a sex act" . . . "is a metaphysical riddle" . . . "Yea!" . . . "Catharine!": Barry marginalia on draft brief, 1/15/86, p. 32, in Barry files.

286 "acts of discrimination against other women in the environment" . . . "the daily environment": Brief for Mechelle Vinson by Patricia J. Barry and Catharine A. MacKinnon to Supreme Court, pp. 19–20, dated 2/11/86, in *Meritor Savings Bank v. Vinson*, 477 U.S. 57 (1986). Further references will be cited as Vinson Supreme Court brief.

286 "hit the court" . . . "Don't you think" . . . "I remain optimistic": Patricia J. Barry, letter to Catharine MacKinnon, 2/1/86, in Barry files.

287 MacKinnon's brief: Quotations from the brief, unless indicated otherwise, are from Vinson Supreme Court brief. See more detailed notes online.

287 "generally secretive" . . . "welcomed, desirable, and proper": Brief for Meritor Savings Bank by F. Robert Troll Jr., et. al. to Supreme Court, p. 37, dated 12/11/85, in *Meritor Savings Bank v. Vinson*, 477 U.S. 57 (1986).

289 "if you're fucked": Catharine MacKinnon, letter to author, 4/2/04.

289 Georgetown law school to face two days of "moot court": Burns interviews and Katz interview. And see Patricia J. Barry, letter to Catharine MacKinnon, apparently from early 1986, in Barry files: "are you coming to DC on 3/6 to assist me in preparation for oral argument?"

289 Hovering over many of the *amicae*: Karen Malkin, "*Meritor Savings Bank, FSB v. Mechelle Vinson*: A Tale of Litigation," unpublished paper written February 1987 for Gender and the Law Seminar, Professors Susan Deller Ross and Wendy Webster Williams, Georgetown University Law Center. See note 290 concerning "Strategy Tape #2, March 7, 1986" (taped by Sarah Burns at a meeting of *amicae*).

290 "doing a lot of self-sabotaging" . . . "like I didn't have an oral argument": Barry interviews.

290 declined an offer: Patricia J. Barry, letter to Professor Laurence Tribe, 10/25/85, in Barry files.

290 tried arguing on the basis of California law: Katz interview.

290 terrifying: Catharine MacKinnon, letter to Patricia J. Barry, 8/6/87, in Barry files; Katz interview.

290 "mannerisms": Vinson interview.

290 After the moot court, some *amicae* urged that Laurence Tribe should argue: Burns interviews, Katz interview, and Catharine MacKinnon, letter to Patricia J. Barry, 8/6/87, in Barry files: "I continue to be amazed that you do not realize that Larry Tribe's experience and qualifications to argue before the Supreme Court were obviously superior to yours. They were superior to mine. . . . We had a chance for the best possible."

290 talked to her mother . . . asked friends . . . glory and excitement . . . "Mechelle and I would be eternally grateful": Barry interviews.

291 Unnerved . . . another moot court: Patricia J. Barry, email to author, 8/19/05.

20: At the Supreme Court

292 readying herself for a question . . . Barry arrived: Patricia J. Barry, email to author, 8/19/05 ("I came in late with my mother"), and letter to author, 9/24/05 ("I was almost late for *Vinson* because I wanted to document my answer to a question MacKinnon's group had not asked me in moot court and I was certain would be asked").

292 MacKinnon . . . being told by a clerk how to proceed: Catharine MacKinnon, letter to author, 4/2/04.

292 Oral argument began, soon after ten o'clock: Quotations from oral arguments, unless indicated otherwise, are from Supreme Court transcript of *Meritor Savings Bank v. Vinson*, 477 U.S. 57 (1986), argued 3/25/86, p. 3. Further references will be cited as *Meritor* transcript. See detailed notes online.

294 women in 1986 constituted fewer than 7 percent of all federal judges: Judith Resnik, " 'Naturally' without Gender: Women, Jurisdiction, and the Federal Courts," 66 *New York University Law Review* 1682 (1991), Appendix III.

294 Getting prepared for this question: Patricia J. Barry, letter to author, 9/24/05.

295 "conjure up inside the courtroom" . . . "they stopped their fidgeting" . . . "The angels are certainly blessing us": Vinson interview.

296 one justice asked: Anonymity of justices speaking in oral argument was preserved in official Supreme Court transcripts prior to October 2004; see

"Supreme Court of the United States Argument Transcripts," available at www.supremecourtus.gov/oral_arguments/argument_transcripts.html (visited 8/16/06). Where I write "one justice," I have found no clues that make possible a positive identification of the justice.

299 "It was OK, it's Justice Marshall": Barry interviews.

299 "I thought . . . divine Father": Vinson interview.

299 "excellent": Catharine MacKinnon, letter to Patricia J. Barry, 8/6/87, in Barry files.

299 "Without question" . . . "when a supervisor sexually harasses": *Meritor Savings Bank v. Vinson*, 477 U.S. 57, 65 and 67 (1986), decided 6/19/86.

300 "came as a pleasant surprise" . . . "issued an opinion on our side" . . . only two days: "A Surprise from Justice Rehnquist," *Washington Post*, 6/20/86, p. A18: "This week, only two days after he [Justice William Rehnquist] was nominated to head the court, an opinion he had written was handed down that gives approval to a broad definition of sexual harassment."

300 "We all know why Rehnquist wrote the decision": Barry interviews. Reasons for women's groups to oppose Rehnquist included his critique of the equal rights amendment in 1970 while he was working as assistant attorney general under Richard Nixon: the ERA could turn "holy wedlock" into "holy deadlock," and ERA supporters seemed to have "a virtually fanatical desire to obscure not only legal differentiation between men and women, but insofar as possible, physical distinctions between the sexes." William Rehnquist, "ERA Would Threaten Family Unit," reprinted in *Legal Times*, 9/15/86, p. 4, as cited in Robert C. Post and Reva B. Siegel, "Legislative Constitutionalism and Section Five Power: Policentric Interpretation of the Family and Medical Leave Act," 112 *Yale Law Journal* 1943 (2003), p. 1992n146.

300 Vinson seemed to be winning . . . "core question" . . . "I wouldn't give her a second bite at the apple": Brennan papers. For an almost complete transcription, see Cochran, *Sexual Harassment*, pp. 110–113, and see p. 117 for observation that Rehnquist's draft "split the court."

301 "Finding of voluntariness" . . . Justice Stevens . . . "hostile environment theory" . . . Justice O'Connor . . . "adequate complaint system": Brennan papers.

301 Rehnquist's draft reached the court on April 22 . . . "Join??? but wait!!": Chief Justice William Rehnquist, "1st DRAFT," 4/22/86, in Marshall papers, with handwritten date and Marshall's annotation on first page.

301 Burger and White . . . "voluntariness" was relevant . . . O'Connor . . . "conduct was relevant": Brennan papers.

302 "strictly liable" . . . "state of the record" . . . "the Court of Appeals erred"

... "agree with the EEOC" ... same work by the American Law Institute:
Meritor Savings Bank v. Vinson, 477 U.S. 57, 70–72 (1986).

302 "As I understand the cases" ... "the Courts of Appeals": Justice John Paul
Stevens, letter to Chief Justice William Rehnquist, 4/24/86, in Marshall
papers.

303 Marshall and Blackmun were inclined to follow: Justice William J. Brennan Jr., letter to Chief Justice William Rehnquist, 4/24/86, and Justice
Thurgood Marshall, letter to Chief Justice William Rehnquist, 5/1/86,
both in Marshall papers.

303 "willing to make a sixth vote, but not a fifth one": Justice William Rehnquist, letter to John Paul Stevens, 4/24/86, in Marshall papers.

303 Rehnquist was willing to sacrifice a legal view in order to stay in the majority: For an argument that Rehnquist made a similar sacrifice that kept him
in control of an opinion concerning women's rights a few years later, see
the comment of Professor Akhil Amar of Yale Law School concerning a
case that protected the Family and Medical Leave Act (*Nevada Department of Human Resources v. Hibbs*, 536 U.S. 938 (2002)). "Rehnquist was
willing to be the sixth vote, but it's not clear that he would have been the
fifth," said Amar, as quoted in Jeffrey Rosen, "Is Rehnquist a Feminist?
Sister Act," *New Republic*, 6/16/03. Rosen goes on to argue that control
of the opinion allowed Rehnquist, although forced to join the five other
colleagues including Sandra Day O'Connor and Ruth Bader Ginsburg
who supported the Family and Medical Leave Act, to steer the opinion in
a way that would permit curtailment of Congress's future ability to enact
civil rights legislation. Rosen notes that Rehnquist's opinion, if accepted
in 1978, might have given the Court grounds to overturn the Pregnancy
Discrimination Act—a law that (as Rosen does not mention; see Part 2
in this book) had overturned an earlier decision by Rehnquist. Tweaking Rehnquist, Rosen suggests that he "seemed to be channeling Betty
Friedan" in his opinion with language that attacks outdated "stereotypes
about women's domestic roles" that are "reinforced by parallel stereotypes
presuming a lack of domestic responsibilities for men." Rosen does not
suggest that the channeling of Friedan might have been part of an effort
to keep his voting aligned with O'Connor's on women's issues where he
could not win her to his side. Nor does he speculate what language in support of civil rights might have entered a decision written by Ruth Bader
Ginsburg, for example, had Rehnquist joined his frequent allies—Scalia,
Thomas, and Kennedy—as a losing fourth vote. For discussion of similar
tactical maneuvering employed by Chief Justice Warren Burger to control
opinions, see Woodward and Armstrong, *Brethren*, p. 70. For brief mention by Chief Justice John Roberts of Rehnquist's willingness to become a
sixth vote joining opinions with which he disagreed, see Jeffrey Rosen, *The*

Supreme Court: The Personalities and Rivalries That Defined America
(New York: Times Books, 2007), p. 233.

303 "Please join me": Sandra Day O'Connor, letter to Chief Justice William
Rehnquist, 5/8/86, in Marshall papers.

303 May 27 . . . told President Reagan that he wished to resign: David Hoff-
man, "Reagan Relied on His Instincts," *Washington Post*, 6/18/86, p. A1:
"Chief Justice Warren E. Burger's plans to retire came to the attention of
the White House late last month when, using former White House counsel
Fred F. Fielding, he arranged a meeting with Reagan for May 27, officials
said." Thus Rehnquist almost surely knew the chief justice was resigning
about a month after he offered to be "a sixth vote" but "not a fifth one"
and thus stay in the majority of all components in the decision regarding
Mechelle Vinson; Rehnquist may have known far earlier that the position
of chief justice was about to become open.

303 "circulate a dissent": Justice Thurgood Marshall, letter to Justice William
Rehnquist, 5/28/86, in Marshall papers.

303 technically impossible so long as he still voted with the judgment for Vinson. Marshall's first draft, labeled a "concurrence" by his clerks . . . "concurring in the judgment" only . . . clerks know that he was angry: Interview
with Jonathan Weinberg, Detroit, by phone, 8/17/07.

304 In a front-page headline: Stuart Taylor Jr., "Sex Harassment on Job Is
Illegal," *New York Times*, 6/20/86, p. A1.

304 settlement: For discussion of the route to settlement, 8/22/91, see Cochran,
Sexual Harassment, pp. 122–127.

304 tuition for nursing school . . . never disclose the dollar figure: Vinson
interview.

305 nurse, helping victims of abuse: Sheila Weller, "These Women Changed
Your Life," *Glamour*, September 2005, pp. 267–268.

305 Sidney Taylor went to jail in 1988 for embezzling: Jay Mallin, "Man Gets
Prison Term for Bilking Elderly Woman," *Washington Times*, 4/20/88.

305 Pat Barry went bankrupt in 1988: Barry interviews.

305 MacKinnon in 1990 became a tenured professor: Fred Strebeigh, "Defining Law on the Feminist Frontier: Prof. Catharine A. MacKinnon," *New
York Times Magazine*, 10/6/91, p. 28.

Part Five

VIOLENCE (1990–2000)

In this part, I rely on the papers of and interviews with Sally Goldfarb, Victoria
Nourse, and Lynn Hecht Schafran, including documents in the files of Legal
Momentum in New York City and Washington, DC, and on interviews with
members of the National Association of Women Judges, many conducted during

the association's twentieth annual conference in St. Louis, 10/10/98. Important primary sources, particularly interviews and collections of documents, are listed below, with the abbreviations used in the endnotes that follow. Other primary sources and important secondary sources appear with full citations in the endnotes. More detailed endnotes can be found at www.wwnorton.com and www.equalwomen.com.

Brennan papers — Papers of William J. Brennan Jr., Library of Congress

Brzonkala interview — Interview with Christy Brzonkala, Washington, DC, 1/11/00

Ellerin interview — Interview with Judge Betty Ellerin, New York City, by phone, 8/13/97

Emerson interview — Interview with Ruth Emerson, New Haven, Connecticut, by phone, 8/26/97

Goldfarb interviews — Interviews with Sally Goldfarb, New Jersey, by phone, 3/11/97, and New York City, 5/13/97

Goldfarb-Nourse-Reuss interview — Interview with Sally Goldfarb, Victoria Nourse, and Pat Reuss, Washington, DC, 4/17/97

Jobes interview — Interview with Judge Clarice Jobes, Washington, DC, by phone, 2/4/99

Klain interview — Interview with Ronald A. Klain, Washington, DC, by phone, 6/14/06

Klein interviews — Interviews with Justice Joan Dempsey Klein, St. Louis, Missouri, 10/10/98, and Los Angeles, by phone, 5/3/06

Lederman interview — Interview with Judge Cindy Lederman, St. Louis, 10/10/98

Legal Momentum DC files — Files of Legal Momentum (formerly NOW Legal Defense), Washington, DC, as of 4/18/97

Legal Momentum NY files — Files of Legal Momentum (formerly NOW Legal Defense), New York City, as of 5/13/97

Loftus interview — Interview with Judge Marilyn Loftus, New Jersey, by phone, 7/29/98

MacKinnon interviews — Interviews with Catharine MacKinnon, California, 10/18–21/95

Murray interview — Interview with Judge Brenda Murray, St. Louis, 10/10/98

Neuborne interview — Interview with Helen Neuborne, New York, by phone, 8/6/97

Nourse files — Files of Victoria Nourse as of 8/8/97

Nourse interviews — Interviews with Victoria Nourse, Maryland, by phone, 3/21/97; Washington, DC, 6/4–6/6/97; Maryland, by phone, 9/20/97

Resnik interviews	Interviews with Judith Resnik, New Haven, Connecticut, by phone, 7/18/97, and driving in Massachusetts, by phone, 7/15/06
Schafran files	Files of Lynn Hecht Schafran as of 6/2/97
Schafran interview	Interview with Lynn Hecht Schafran, New York City, 7/6/97
Schroeder interview	Interview with Judge Mary Schroeder, Phoenix, by phone, 7/7/1997
Shapiro interview	Interview with Judge Norma Shapiro, St. Louis, 10/10/98
West interview	Interview with Robin West, New Haven, Connecticut, 9/12/97
Wulf interview	Interview with Mel Wulf, New York City, 3/4/94
Yassky files	Files of David Yassky as of 6/2/97
Yassky interview	Interview with David Yassky, Washington, DC, by phone, 6/2/97

21: A Challenge for a Young Lawyer

309 new staffer: Nourse interviews and Goldfarb-Nourse-Reuss interview.

310 "green or purple": Nourse interviews.

310 first textbook: First textbook by publication date is Kenneth Davidson, Ruth Bader Ginsburg, and Herma Hill Kay, *Text, Cases, and Materials on Sex-Based Discrimination*, 1st ed. (St. Paul: West Publishing, 1974). The second is Babcock and others, *Sex Discrimination* (1975). See note online.

312 Klain had an extra task: Nourse interviews and Klain interview.

312 On that committee in 1981 . . . "Damn it" . . . "you kind of expect" . . . part of American culture: Joe Biden, *Promises to Keep: On Life and Politics* (New York: Random House, 2007), pp. 239–240. Further references will be cited as Biden, *Promises to Keep*.

312 "Last December": Lisa Heinzerling, "So Rape Isn't Hatred?" *Los Angeles Times*, 5/4/90, p. B7.

313 "This wasn't a hard sell": Klain interview.

313 probing the law of rape and violence against women: For a history, much occurring outside of law schools and influential on them, see Brownmiller, *In Our Time*, p. 194ff.

313 Law Library Reading Room: Description and details of the room and Nourse's experience are from author visit, 6/6/97, and Nourse interviews.

314 rape law from seventeenth-century: Vivian Berger, "Man's Trial, Woman's Tribulation: Rape Cases in the Courtroom," 77 *Columbia Law Review*

1 (1977), p. 3n8, quoting Lord Coke (1628), and p. 10n69, quoting Lord Hale (1646). Further references will be cited as Berger, "Man's Trial."

314 "easily to be made": Matthew Hale, *The History of the Pleas of the Crown* (1736), Vol. 1, p. 635.

314 nineteenth century, state courts embraced . . . the "Lord Hale instruction": For California, see *People v. Rincon-Pineda*, 538 P.2d 247, 252 (1975); in general, see A. Thomas Morris, "Note: The Empirical, Historical and Legal Case against the Cautionary Instruction: A Call for Legislative Reform," 1988 *Duke Law Journal* 154 (1988), p. 155.

314 "one of the most oftquoted passages": *United States v. Wiley*, 492 F.2d 547 (D.C. Cir. 1973) (Judge David L. Bazelon, concurring). See note online.

314 1970s did little to protect women from being beaten by their husbands: S. Rpt. 101–545 on S. 2754, "Violence Against Women Act of 1990," 10/19/90, p. 36: "Up until as late as 15 years ago, many jurisdictions refused to arrest and prosecute spouse abusers, even though a comparable assault on the street by a stranger would have led to a lengthy jail term."

314 common-law rules that permitted a husband: Reva B. Siegel, " 'The Rule of Love': Wife Beating as Prerogative," 105 *Yale Law Journal* 2117 (1996), p. 2118.

314 "a switch no larger than his thumb": *State v. Rhodes*, 61 N.C. (Phil. Law) 453 (1868). See note online.

315 found a major article: All quotations describing Estrich's experience and analysis, unless indicated otherwise, are from Susan Estrich, "Rape," 95 *Yale Law Journal* 1087 (1986). Further references will be cited as Estrich, "Rape" (1986). See detailed notes online.

317 "So bachelors" . . . "Abominable Snowman": *People v. Evans*, 85 Misc. 2d 1088, 1095; 379 N.Y.S.2d 912, 922 (Sup. Ct. 1975), aff'd, 55 A.D. 2d 858, 390 N.Y.S.2d 768 (1976).

318 proving force . . . proving non-consent: Estrich, "Rape" (1986), p. 1121.

319 "afraid enough": Estrich, "Rape" (1986), p. 1101.

319 "I was trying all the time": Estrich, "Rape" (1986), p. 1122.

319 "Not only must there be" . . . "must be the most vehement": Estrich, "Rape" (1986), p. 1123, quoting *Brown v. State*, 127 Wis. 193, 199; 106 N.W. 536, 538 (1906).

319 "Medical writers insist": Estrich, "Rape" (1986), p. 1123, quoting *Brown v. State*, 127 Wis. 193, 199–200; 106 N.W. 536, 538 (1906).

319 The consent standard for rape shifted . . . to *earnest* or sometimes *reasonable* resistance: Estrich, "Rape" (1986), p. 1099.

320 "earnest resistance" . . . "the victim's pleas": Estrich, "Rape" (1986), pp. 1124–1125, citing *State v. Lima*, 2 Hawaii App. 19, 624 P.2d 1374 (1981), rev'd., 64 Hawaii 470, 643 P.2d 536 (1982).

320 isolated house: Estrich, "Rape" (1986), pp. 1116–1117.

320 "the extent of her ability at the time": Estrich, "Rape" (1986), p. 1125, citing *Goldberg v. State*, 41 Md. App. at 68, 395 A.2d at 1219.

320 by 1980 . . . most states had made some attempt to reform their rape laws: Estrich, "Rape" (1986), p. 1133.

320 Model Penal Code: See Estrich, "Rape" (1986), p. 1134. See also Berger, "Man's Trial," p. 7n44.

320 Model Penal Code. Begun in the 1950s: Roswell B. Perkins, "Herbert Wechsler December 4, 1909–April 26, 2000," *ALI Reporter*, Spring 2001, available at www.ali.org/ali/R2303_memorial.htm (visited 1/9/08). See also Linda R. Hirshman and Jane E. Larson, *Hard Bargains: The Politics of Sex* (New York: Oxford University Press, 1998), pp. 185–187.

320 American Law Institute—a members-only assembly of judges, lawyers, and scholars: American Law Institute, available at www.ali.org (visited 1/9/2008).

320 Estrich's discussion of the Code became an important reference: Nourse interviews.

321 drafters and commentators, all male for its section on "Sexual Offenses": The four members of the "Reportorial Staff for Model Penal Code" were Chief Reporter, Herbert Wechsler, Columbia University School of Law; Reporter, Louis B. Schwartz, University of Pennsylvania Law School; Associate Reporters, Morris Ploscowe, New York, New York, and Paul W. Tappan, New York University. Of the five members of the "Reportorial Staff for Revision of the Commentaries," one was a woman, Professor Malvina Halberstam, Cardozo School of Law, who did not work on the section on "Sexual Offenses." For guidance the American Law Institute also designated fifty-four more consultants and advisors, including physicians and a professor of English; all were male. See "Model Penal Code and Commentaries," available at www.ali.org/ali/stu_mod_pen.htm (visited 1/9/08).

321 pressure on the drafters . . . who helped shape the Code's view of sex, "simply following" . . . "uncorroborated testimony of a strumpet": Linda R. Hirshman and Jane E. Larson, *Hard Bargains: The Politics of Sex* (New York: Oxford University Press, 1998), pp. 187–191, 204; William M. Freeman, "Ex-Magistrate Ploscowe Dies; Criminal-Law Expert Was 71," *New York Times*, 9/22/75, p. 36.

321 demanded corroboration *only* for rape and sexual assault: Estrich, "Rape" (1986), p. 1137.

323 "Dean Wigmore": See, for example, Berger, "Man's Trial," p. 9n67.

323 Wigmore instructed . . . "unchastity": Berger, "Man's Trial," p. 16 (for three ways offered by Wigmore to prove "unchastity," including reputation).

325 first woman president of the *Harvard Law Review* . . . clerking at the

Supreme Court . . . Kennedy's presidential attempt . . . Mondale's presidential campaign: Mary Battiata, "Susan Estrich and the Marathon Call," *Washington Post*, 10/16/87, p. D1; Bella Stumbo, "Dukakis Aide Estrich," *Los Angeles Times*, 6/4/88, p. 1.

325 to Nourse's disappointment: Nourse interviews.

327 *Duke Law Journal* of 1988: A. Thomas Morris, "Note: The Empirical, Historical and Legal Case against the Cautionary Instruction: A Call for Legislative Reform," 1988 *Duke Law Journal* 154 (1988).

327 California Supreme Court had unearthed: *People v. Rincon-Pineda*, 538 P.2d 247 (1975).

327 "It is true rape is a most detestable crime": *People v. Rincon-Pineda*, 538 P.2d 247, 254 (1975), quoting Matthew Hale, *The History of the Pleas of the Crown* (1736), Vol. 1, p. 635.

328 The sleuthing into Hale conducted by the California court . . . "over half of the states allow the cautionary instruction" . . . activists should go after state legislatures: A. Thomas Morris, "Note: The Empirical, Historical and Legal Case against the Cautionary Instruction: A Call for Legislative Reform," 1988 *Duke Law Journal* 154 (1988).

328 "in which a state supreme court task force": Lynn Hecht Schafran, "Gender and Justice: Florida and the Nation," 42 *Florida Law Review* 181 (1990).

328 marital rape exemption—the law's ancient rule: Jill Elaine Hasday, "Contest and Consent: A Legal History of Marital Rape," 88 *California Law Review* 1373 (2000), p. 1392ff.

329 "If you can't rape your wife, who can you rape?": See, for example, Michael D. A. Freeman, " 'But If You Can't Rape Your Wife, Whom Can You Rape?': The Marital Rape Exemption Re-examined," 15 *Family Law Quarterly* 1 (1981).

329 "The so-called marital rape exemption" . . . "the marital rape exemption denies": Robin West, "Equality Theory, Marital Rape, and the Promise of the Fourteenth Amendment," 42 *Florida Law Review* 45 (1990) 45–51, 63–71. Further references will be cited as West, "Equality Theory."

330 "husband cannot be guilty": *People v. Liberta*, 64 N.Y.2d 152, 162 (1984), citing Matthew Hale, *The History of the Pleas of the Crown* (1736), Vol. 1, p. 629.

330 a few states had also created a form of date-rape protection: "Note: Acquaintance Rape and Degrees of Consent: "No" Means "No," but What Does "Yes" Mean?" 117 *Harvard Law Review* 234 (2004), at n15; the note lists Delaware, Hawaii, Maine, and West Virginia.

330 "voluntary social companion": Joseph R. Biden Jr., "Congress and the Courts: Our Mutual Obligation," 46 *Stanford Law Review* 1285 (1994), n102.

330   most persistent . . . law in force in the 1990s, was Delaware: Todd Spangler, "Senator Takes Aim at Out-of-Date Rape Statute Still on the Books," *Daily Record* (Baltimore), 9/24/97, p. 24; Deborah W. Denno, "Why the Model Penal Code's Sexual Offense Provisions Should Be Pulled and Replaced," 1 *Ohio State Journal of Criminal Law* 207 (2003), p. 210; "Note: Acquaintance Rape and Degrees of Consent: 'No' Means 'No,' but What Does 'Yes' Mean?" 117 *Harvard Law Review* 234 (2004), at n15.

330   hook the attention of . . . Nourse's boss: Nourse interviews.

331   Robin West seemed to be speaking directly: Nourse interviews.

331   "Whether or not the U.S. Supreme Court": West, "Equality Theory," p. 76.

331   "equal protection of the laws" . . . section 1 as the goal but section 5 as the means: West, "Equality Theory," p. 52.

331   Civil Rights Act of 1871: Eric Foner, *Reconstruction: America's Unfinished Revolution, 1863–1877* (New York: Harper and Row, 1988), p. 458ff. Further references will be cited as Foner, *Reconstruction*. See note online.

331   Civil Rights Act of 1875: Foner, *Reconstruction*, p. 555ff.

332   A Married Women's Privacy Act . . . "guarantee protection": West, "Equality Theory," p. 76.

332   right to privacy: Much of this narrative relies on Garrow, *Liberty and Sexuality*, which, unless otherwise indicated, is also the source of quotations in this discussion. For take legal shape in the 1950s, see p. 145ff. See detailed notes online.

332   Rather than argue for equality: A woman attorney who worked on an early case, Ruth Calvin Emerson (see Garrow, *Liberty and Sexuality*, p. 170), recalls no one making an argument about equality. Emerson interview. In addition to Garrow's history, for later discussion see MacKinnon, *Feminism Unmodified*, pp. 250–251, and Ruth Bader Ginsburg, "Some Thoughts on Autonomy and Equality in Relation to *Roe v. Wade*," 63 *North Carolina Law Review* 375 (1985).

333   ACLU legal director in 1971: Samuel Walker, *In Defense of American Liberties: A History of the ACLU* (New York: Oxford University Press, 1990), p. 186, and see Part 1.

333   "invented the right to privacy": Wulf interview.

335   defending the marital rape exemption as a defense against intrusion by government: *People v. Liberta*, 64 N.Y.2d 152, 165 (1984).

335   "In this light": MacKinnon, *Feminism Unmodified*, p. 100.

335   "too cute": West interview.

336   West had based her "Privacy Act" . . . legislation proposed earlier by Catharine MacKinnon: West interview.

336   MacKinnon, working with feminist theorist Andrea Dworkin: Catharine

MacKinnon interviews, and interview with Andrea Dworkin, Brooklyn, 11/14/95.

336 "a law that recognizes pornography" . . . "we're talking rape, torture": MacKinnon, *Feminism Unmodified*, p. 210. See also Catharine MacKinnon and Andrea Dworkin, *In Harm's Way: The Pornography Civil Rights Hearings* (Cambridge: Harvard University Press, 1997), p. 426ff.

336 pornography was a form of speech: *American Booksellers Association v. Hudnut*, 771 F.2d 323 (7th Cir. 1985), affirmed 475 U.S. 1001 (1986).

336 MacKinnon's theories . . . Rick Cudahy: Nourse interviews.

337 "violence against women" . . . "violation of the civil rights of women" . . . "victims a civil action": MacKinnon, *Feminism Unmodified*, p. 210.

22: Using Civil Rights to Combat Violence

338 Biden introduced the "Violence Against Women Act" on June 19, 1990: Victoria F. Nourse, "Where Violence, Relationship, and Equality Meet: The Violence Against Women Act's Civil Rights Remedy," 11 *Wisconsin Women's Law Journal* 1 (Summer 1996). Further references will be cited as Nourse, "Where Violence."

338 Title III, "Civil Rights" . . . "equal protection of the laws": Wording in the bill is from Senate Committee on the Judiciary, *Women and Violence, Part 2: Hearings on Legislation to Reduce the Growing Problem of Violent Crime against Women*, 101st Cong., 2d sess., 1990, Serial No. J-101–80, pp. 221–223; Biden, *Promises to Keep*, p. 244. See note online.

339 after the Civil War, many states put laws: The following discussion relies on Foner, *Reconstruction*, particularly pp. 425–444 and 504–590. See further notes online. Also useful are the history sections of *Bray v. Alexandria Women's Health Clinic*, 506 U.S. 263 (1993).

340 great civil rights acts of the nineteenth century: In addition to Foner, *Reconstruction*, see Frank J. Scaturro, *The Supreme Court's Retreat from Reconstruction: A Distortion of Constitutional Jurisprudence* (Westport, CT: Greenwood Press, 2000), and Jack M. Balkin and Sanford Levinson, "Understanding the Constitutional Revolution," 87 *Virginia Law Review* 1045 (2001).

340 man known as R. G. Harris . . . Court concluded: Quotations on the *Harris* decision are from *United States v. Harris*, 106 U.S. 629, 638–639 (1883).

341 lone dissent . . . "special favorite of the laws": *Civil Rights Cases*, 109 U.S. 3 (1883).

341 In 1876, the Republican Party . . . "to conciliate the white men": See Foner, *Reconstruction*, pp. 504–587, for a narrative of the retreat from what Foner calls the "idea, born during the Civil War, of a powerful national

state protecting the fundamental rights of American citizens," and see p. 582, where Foner quotes the Kansas politician of 1877.

342 "to prevent the emergence of 'Jim Crow' apartheid in the South": Laurence H. Tribe, *American Constitutional Law*, 2nd ed. (Mineola, NY: Foundation Press, 1988), p. 1695n16.

342 "the special favorite of the laws": Jack Balkin, "History Lesson," *Legal Affairs*, July–August 2002, pp. 44–49. Further references will be cited as Balkin, "History Lesson."

342 a provision of the 1871 Civil Rights Act that had survived: *Griffin v. Breckenridge*, 403 U.S. 88, 92, 99 (1971).

342 The other staffer: Nourse interviews.

343 "NOW Legal Defense" . . . had been created: Lynn Hecht Schafran, "Educating the Judiciary about Gender Bias," 9 *Women's Rights Law Reporter* 109 (1986), p. 112. Further references will be cited as Schafran, "Educating."

343 "Wow—where did this woman come from?": Goldfarb-Nourse-Reuss interview.

343 analyzing rape as a violation of the civil rights of women: MacKinnon interviews; see also MacKinnon, *Feminism Unmodified*, p. 81 (reprinting a lecture of 11/16/81).

344 "First time she taught": Goldfarb interviews.

344 After talking to Nourse . . . "If Biden wants to do something": Interview with Catharine MacKinnon, New Haven, 9/16/2008.

344 Biden convened the hearings in mid-June: Biden's words, Goldfarb's language, and the judges' testimony to the state task forces are quoted from Senate Committee on the Judiciary, *Women and Violence, Part 1: Hearings on Legislation to Reduce the Growing Problem of Violent Crime Against Women*, 101st Cong., 2d sess., 1990, Serial No. J-101–80, p. 11. Further references will be cited as Judiciary hearings, *Women and Violence, Part 1*. See detailed notes online.

345 professor at the University of Kentucky: Sally Goldfarb, letter to author, 8/12/05.

346 "Don't you people" . . . strong bladder: Goldfarb interviews.

346 "task force with committees": Sally Goldfarb, letter to "Dear Friend," 8/23/90, in Legal Momentum NY files.

346 first week of September . . . "trustworthy": Sally Goldfarb, "Minutes from Task Force on Violence Against Women Act September 5, 1990," 9/13/90, in files of NOW Legal Defense, New York City, as of 5/21/97. For Goldfarb minutes from task forces, see further notes online.

347 November meeting . . . "1) The homicide case in Canada": Sally Goldfarb, "Minutes from Task Force on Violence Against Women Act November 19, 1990," 11/19/90, in Legal Momentum NY files. (For discussion of

homicide case in Canada, see Lisa Heinzerling, "So Rape Isn't Hatred?" *Los Angeles Times*, 5/4/90, p. B7.)

348 Goldfarb was organized but no organizer: Goldfarb interviews.

349 Reuss was running out of money: Neuborne interview.

349 "good kids": Goldfarb-Nourse-Reuss interview.

350 fuchsia and lime . . . granola bar . . . "eat this": Goldfarb interviews.

350 Groups endorsing VAWA: "List Of Organization Endorsements (as of 2/5/91), Violence Against Women Act," 2/5/91, typescript in Legal Momentum NY files.

350 "Another one of your best-sellers, Victoria?": Nourse interviews.

350 the grassroots were going berserk: Goldfarb-Nourse-Reuss interview.

350 By early 1992, VAWA's list of cosponsors: House Committee on the Judiciary, Subcommittee on Crime and Criminal Justice, *Violence Against Women*, 102d Cong., 2d sess., 1992, Serial No. 42, pp. 9 and 12. Further references will be cited as House Crime Hearings 1992, *Violence Against Women*.

351 "In Georgia": Senate Committee on the Judiciary, *The Violence Against Women Act of 1991*, 102d Cong., 1st sess., 1991, S. Rep. No. 197, p. 34. Further references will be cited as Senate Judiciary, *VAWA of 1991*.

23: Judges Strike Back

352 On the last day of 1991, the chief justice attacked: Rehnquist, "1991 Year-End Report," in Legal Momentum NY files; reprinted in *Third Branch: The Newsletter of the Federal Courts*, January 1992, and in *Congressional Record* 138, E746, 747 (3/19/92). Further references will be cited as Rehnquist, "1991 Year-End Report." See also Biden, *Promises to Keep*, p. 245.

352 "a virtually fanatical desire": Memorandum from William Rehnquist, assistant attorney general, to Leonard Garment, special counsel to the president, reprinted in "Rehnquist: ERA Would Threaten Family Unit," *Legal Times*, 9/15/86, p. 4, as quoted in Robert C. Post and Reva B. Siegel, "Legislative Constitutionalism and Section Five Power: Policentric Interpretation of the Family and Medical Leave Act," 112 *Yale Law Journal* 1943 (2003), p. 1992n146.

353 rare departure . . . attack proposed legislation before it could become law: See Judith Resnik, "The Programmatic Judiciary: Lobbying, Judging, and Invalidating the Violence Against Women Act," 74 *Southern California Law Review* 269 (2000), p. 271. Further references will be cited as Resnik, "Programmatic Judiciary."

353 "year-end report on the federal judiciary" . . . "State of the Judiciary"

addresses . . . "difficult and complex": Analysis of report and addresses can be found in Judith Resnik, " 'Naturally' without Gender: Women, Jurisdiction, and the Federal Courts," 66 *New York University Law Review* 1682 (1991), p. 1732. Further references will be cited as Resnik, "Naturally."

353 "broad definition of criminal conduct": Rehnquist, "1991 Year-End Report," p. 5.

354 in 1991, the nation's gender disparity on the courts: Resnik, "Naturally," p. 1705.

354 Nourse . . . failed to realize that judges might try to influence legislation: Victoria Nourse, letter to author, 9/27/05.

355 Department of Justice . . . detailed critique: Bruce C. Navarro, United States Department of Justice, letter to Joseph Biden, receipt stamped 10/9/90, in Nourse files.

355 Association of Attorneys General . . . unanimous support: Resolution dated 12/7/90, reprinted in Senate Committee on the Judiciary, *Violence Against Women: Victims of the System*, 102d Cong., 1st sess., Senate Hearing 369, 1991, p. 37.

355 "Resolution X" . . . "WHEREAS": Conference of Chief Justices, Resolution X [concerning] S. 15, Violence Against Women Act, "adopted as proposed . . . January 31, 1991," in Schafran files.

355 Goldfarb thought the chief justices were misinterpreting: Goldfarb interviews and NOW Legal Defense, "The Violence Against Women Act: Facts on the Impact on State and Federal Courts," undated but c. January 1992, in Schafran files.

356 "add a new count to many if not most": Vincent L. McKusick, president, Conference of Chief Justices, letter to Joseph R. Biden Jr., 2/22/91, in Schafran files.

356 "The implication that vengeful wives": NOW Legal Defense, "The Violence Against Women Act: Facts on the Impact on State and Federal Courts," undated but c. January 1992, in Schafran files.

356 director is an appointee of the chief justice: Judith Resnik, "Constricting Remedies: The Rehnquist Judiciary, Congress, and Federal Power," 78 *Indiana Law Journal* 223 (2003), p. 292.

356 "judicial impact assessment"—a new idea, begun that year: Resnik, "Programmatic Judiciary," p. 271n7, citing A. Fletcher Mangum, ed., *Conference on Assessing the Effects of Legislation on the Workload of the Courts: Papers and Proceedings* (Washington, DC: Federal Judicial Center, 1995).

357 15,000 per year . . . 13,450 per year: Office of Judicial Impact Assessment, Administrative Office of the U.S. Courts, Judicial Impact Statement: Violence Against Women Act of 1991, S. 15 (April 8, 1991), reprinted in

Senate Committee on the Judiciary, *Violence Against Women: Victims of the System*, 102d Cong., 1st sess., Senate Hearing 369, 1991, p. 8.

357 triple the annual estimate for the Civil Rights Act of 1991 . . . challenge them in court: Office of Judicial Impact Assessment, Administrative Office of the U.S. Courts, Judicial Impact Statement: Civil Rights Act of 1991, S. 1745 (Enacted) P.L. 102–166, March 19, 1992, pp. 1–4, in Legal Momentum DC files.

357 three-quarters of the alleged attackers . . . public defenders: Office of Judicial Impact Assessment, Administrative Office of the U.S. Courts, Judicial Impact Statement, Violence Against Women Act of 1991, S. 15 as reported (June 8, 1992), pp. 12–13, in Legal Momentum DC files. The first Judicial Impact Statement on VAWA on 4/8/91 assumed that 4% of civil cases would go to trial; by 6/8/92 it had raised that to 7%, raising its estimate of the cost of VAWA.

357 VAWA would add more than 14,000 suits to the federal caseload, an increase of about 4 percent of all cases: Administrative Office of the U.S. Courts, "Report of the Proceedings of the Judicial Conference of the United States," 9/23–24/91, under heading "Committee on Federal-State Jurisdiction, Violence Against Women Act," in Legal Momentum NY files.

357 August of 1991 . . . "ad hoc committee" . . . "charged with coordinating the Conference's views": Memorandum from L. Ralph Mecham, Director, Administrative Office of the United States Courts, 8/19/91, in Legal Momentum NY files.

358 conference's one gender-balanced committee: Resnik, "Naturally," p. 1711n143.

358 Tailhook Association . . . arrayed in a gantlet apparently assaulted: Eric Schmitt, "Military Court Assails Navy in Ruling on Tailhook," *New York Times*, 1/12/94, p. A16; Neil A. Lewis, "Officer Cleared in Main Tailhook Case," *New York Times*, 10/22/93, p. 12.

358 the committee reported to the chief justice: Quotations from the report are in "Special Report, Gender-Based Violence, September 1991, Report of the Judicial Conference Ad Hoc Committee on Gender-Based Violence," 7-page typescript, in Legal Momentum NY files.

359 "I have to tell you": Herb Jaffe, "Federal Judges Assail 'Disastrous' Crime Bills," *Newark Star Ledger*, 9/16/91, p. 1.

359 "point out" . . . "that over three million domestic relations cases": Administrative Office of the U.S. Courts, "Report of the Proceedings of the Judicial Conference of the United States," 9/23–24/91, under heading "Committee on Federal-State Jurisdiction, Violence Against Women Act," in Legal Momentum NY files.

360 seemed uncoordinated . . . tried to respond: Nourse interviews.

360 "I will not mince words" . . . "is a civil rights provision" . . . "It is one thing": Joseph Biden, letter to Judge Thomas M. Reavley, 9/20/91, in Legal Momentum NY files.

361 Judges . . . lobbying: For a discussion of the growth and mechanisms of judicial lobbying, I've benefited from Judith Resnik and Lane Dilg, "Responding to a Democratic Deficit: Limiting the Powers and the Term of the Chief Justice of the United States," a talk first presented at the symposium "The Chief Justice and the Institutional Judiciary" in November 2005, at the University of Pennsylvania Law School; typescript on file with author.

361 George H. W. Bush had nominated . . . Clarence Thomas: This narrative relies on, and unless otherwise indicated, the quotations are from Mayer and Abramson, *Strange Justice*. See detailed notes online.

362 Reuss and others tried to get Ron Klain . . . experts on the stand: Goldfarb-Nourse-Reuss interview and Klain interview.

362 Judicial Conference . . . condemn significant parts of VAWA: L. Ralph Mecham, letter to Joseph Biden, 10/10/91, in Nourse files.

362 "long-accepted concepts of federalism": Rehnquist, "1991 Year-End Report," p. 5.

362 *federalism* was a code word . . . not for strengthening the national government but for limiting its strength: See John T. Noonan Jr., *Narrowing the Nation's Power: The Supreme Court Sides with the States* (Berkeley: University of California Press, 2002), pp. 2–3. And see Mark Tushnet, *A Court Divided: The Rehnquist Court and the Future of Constitutional Law* (New York: W. W. Norton, 2005), p. 250. Further references will be cited as Tushnet, *Court Divided*.

363 "the federal courts' limited role": Rehnquist, "1991 Year-End Report," p. 3.

363 editorial supporting Rehnquist: "Federal Courts, Local Cases," *Washington Post*, 1/5/92.

363 "so sweeping": Chief Justice William Rehnquist, "Remarks before the House of Delegates at the American Bar Association's Mid-Year Meeting," Dallas, Texas, 2/4/92, pp. 12–13, typescript, in Legal Momentum NY files.

363 voted at that mid-year meeting to oppose VAWA's civil rights section: The Conference of Federal Trial Judges, "Resolution," 2/1/92, fax, in Legal Momentum NY files.

363 What none of VAWA's drafters anticipated: Victoria Nourse, memo to unnamed recipients, 2/13/92, in Schafran files; Sally Goldfarb, memo to Pat Reuss, Ruth Jones, and Lynn Hecht Schafran, 3/17/92, in Schafran files; Lynn Hecht Schafran, memo to Helen Neuborne, Deb Ellis, Sally Goldfarb, Ruth Jones, and Pat Reuss, 7/7/92, in Legal Momentum DC files.

363 "train time": Nourse interviews.

364 At ten o'clock that morning: House Crime Hearings 1992, *Violence Against Women*, held 2/6/92.

364 "Chuck Schumer's two rows behind me" . . . "You bet your booty": Goldfarb-Nourse-Reuss interview.

364 "I don't know that much about it": Goldfarb-Nourse-Reuss interview. (Quotations are Goldfarb's colloquial recollection and are not verbatim from Schumer.)

365 "that cute, young, smart David Yassky" . . . "I'm sitting in while they're": Goldfarb-Nourse-Reuss interview.

365 "Oh yeah, like Catharine MacKinnon's theories!": Goldfarb interviews.

365 Yassky had taken MacKinnon's last in her final term: Yassky interview; *curriculum vitae* for Catharine MacKinnon, email to author, 4/8/04, from Karym Koiffman, assistant to Prof. Catharine A. MacKinnon, University of Michigan Law School.

366 an overly long memo: Quotations from the memo are from David Yassky, memo to Charles Schumer, 9-page typescript, 10/21/91, in Yassky files.

367 "Oh, Joe" . . . "let me sit next to the pretty girl" . . . "She's my chief aide" . . . "true believers from the federalist pantheon": Nourse interviews.

368 "*speech writers* have not done their homework": Typescript in Nourse files.

368 "going on and on": Nourse interviews.

24: Seeking Equal Judicial Firepower

371 Three days after . . . Reuss announced that she wasn't afraid . . . "Fight fire with fire": Minutes of meeting of National Task Force on the Violence Against Women Act, NOW Legal Defense, 2/9/92, handwritten on lined paper, in Legal Momentum DC files.

372 by a ratio of 10 to 1 . . . almost 14 to 1: Resnik, "Naturally," p. 1705.

372 No official listings existed of women judges in America: Klein interviews, and Judge Gladys Kessler, "Foreword," Symposium Issue, National Association of Women Judges, 14 *Golden Gate University Law Review* 473 (1984), p. 474. Further references will be cited as Kessler, "Foreword."

372 At this first meeting: Videotapes of this meeting are available at the Schlesinger Library at Radcliffe; see Linda C. Morrison, "The National Association of Women Judges: Agent of Change," 17 *Wisconsin Women's Law Journal* 291 (2002), pp. 300–301.

372 laughed and cried and stayed up late and drank jugs of wine: Jobes interview.

372 "war stories" . . . chased around a judge's desk . . . "a good-lookin' kid": Klein interviews.

373 stories of women in court being called "honey" or "dear": Klein interviews; see also Michael Kernan, "For Her Honors; Sisterhood on the Bench; Joan Dempsey Klein & The Judges' Network," *Washington Post*, 10/4/80, p. F1 (style section), and David Margolick, "Women Find Bar to Bench a Far Journey," *New York Times*, 10/17/82, p. 16. Further references will be cited as Kernan, "For Her Honors," and Margolick, "Women Find Bar."

373 "streety" . . . "bitches": Jobes interview.

373 "girly pix" . . . "There will be no women clerks here": Klein interviews.

374 "As more than 100 women judges": Kessler, "Foreword," p. 474.

374 "very lonely, very isolated lives of those women judges": Karen Berger Morello, *The Invisible Bar: The Woman Lawyer in America, 1638 to Present* (New York: Random House, 1986), p. 245.

374 descended from California's first judge: Klein interviews.

374 "That's what girls do": Kernan, "For Her Honors," p. F1.

374 "to promote the administration of justice": Kessler, "Foreword," p. 475.

375 became founding members . . . Sandra Day O'Connor: Klein interviews.

375 county judge from Arizona . . . as a state senator, she had written President Richard Nixon: Biskupic, *O'Connor*, pp. 40, 65–68.

375 In favor of a woman were his wife, his daughters: Dean, *Rehnquist Choice*, pp. 63, 82, 157–158.

375 Burger . . . "couldn't work with" a woman justice . . . threatened to resign: Dean, *Rehnquist Choice*, pp. 91, 179–180. See Part 3.

375 O'Connor: The narrative of Sandra Day O'Connor's letter to Nixon, of the friendship of the O'Connor and Rehnquist families, and of O'Connor's work to support his nomination relies on the fine research in Biskupic, *O'Connor*, pp. 37–50.

375 O'Connor had dated Rehnquist . . . holiday to her family's Arizona ranch: William Rehnquist, interview with Mike Eagan, "One-on-One with the Chief," *Stanford Lawyer*, Spring 2005, p. 26, available at www.law .stanford.edu/publications/lawyer/issues/72/1on1Rehnquist.html (visited 3/25/06).

375 "a result of your doing": Biskupic, *O'Connor*, p. 47.

376 "Would we ever" . . . began buying food to cook: Biskupic, *O'Connor*, p. 68.

377 "A large number of women": Margolick, "Women Find Bar," p. 16.

377 Daughtrey led a delegation . . . "bachelor's paradise" . . . "I just want to know what a lady judge looks like": Elizabeth Kastor, "Courting Ritual: Women Jurists Salute Congresswomen," *Washington Post*, 3/27/85, p. B2 (style section).

377 decision made by Judge Marilyn Loftus . . . no invitation . . . "We're all judges": Loftus interview.

378 "didn't even know how to fix his own air conditioner" . . . "I realized then

and there": Sylvia Roberts, in conversation with Lynn Hecht Schafran, 3/6/1985, quoted in Schafran, "Educating," pp. 111–112.

379   train judges: Lynn Hecht Schafran, "Gender Bias in the Courts: An Emerging Focus for Judicial Reform," 21 *Arizona State University Law Journal* 237 (1989), pp. 242–243. And see Schafran, "California: First as Usual," 22 *Women's Rights Law Reporter* 159 (2001), p. 160. Further references will be cited as Schafran, "California."

379   " 'sexism'—the making of unjustified": John A. Johnston Jr. and Charles L. Knapp, "Sex Discrimination by Law: A Study in Judicial Perspective," 46 *New York University Law Review* 675 (1971).

379   "court watchers" . . . "attempted seduction" . . . "normally" . . . "You can't blame": Schafran, "Educating," p. 112, which cites Phyllis Segal, "Proposed Project on Judicial Attitudes toward Women: An Introductory Overview," NOW Legal Defense and Education Fund (1978), pp. 5–6.

379   Finally in 1980 . . . National Judicial Education: Norma J. Wikler, "On the Judicial Agenda for the 80s: Equal Treatment for Men and Women in the Courts," 64 *Judicature* 202 (1980), pp. 208–209; Schafran, "Educating," p. 111.

379   asked the NAWJ . . . brief debate: Lynn Hecht Schafran, letter to author, 8/10/05, p. 2.

380   three state supreme court justices . . . throwing spitballs: Schafran interview; confirmed by Schafran in letter to author, 8/10/05. For a report of the November 1980 meeting but not the spitballs, see Schafran, "Educating," p. 114.

380   Lynn Hecht Schafran: Story of Lynn Hecht Schafran and Norma Wikler draws on Schafran interview and Schafran letters to author, 8/8–10/05.

380   Schafran told Ginsburg the story: Lynn Hecht Schafran, letter to Ruth Bader Ginsburg, 4/4/75, in personal files of Justice Ruth Bader Ginsburg, consulted August 1994 and January 1995, in the justice's storage room at the Supreme Court; and see Part 1.

381   "If you think that's what the law is all about": Lynn Hecht Schafran, panel discussion at Columbia Law School, 11/19/93, videotape recorded by author.

381   "never met a judge": Schafran, "Educating," p. 113.

381   "not being treated equally": Loftus interview.

381   Judge Loftus contacted Robert Lipscher: Loftus interview. See also Schafran, "Educating," p. 117.

382   "What" . . . "do you mean *whether*?": Loftus interview.

382   thirteen state judges and another twenty members: "The First Year Report of the New Jersey Supreme Court Task Force on Women in the Courts— June 1984," 9 *Women's Rights Law Reporter* 129 (1986), p. 131. Further references will be cited as "First Year New Jersey Task Force."

383 "problems" . . . "women are the problem" . . . "the conduct of male counsel" . . . "most sexism and resentment": Schafran, "Educating," pp. 120–121, 137.

383 task force had a statistician: Loftus interview.

383 71 percent of women but only 30 percent of men: "First Year New Jersey Task Force," pp. 137–140. See notes online.

383 In November of 1983: Norma Juliet Wikler and Lynn Hecht Schafran, "Learning from the New Jersey Supreme Court Task Force on Women in the Courts," 12 *Women's Rights Law Reporter* 313 (1991), p. 369.

383 "very very careful" . . . "You sit down": Loftus interview.

384 "Gender bias is a national problem" . . . "Stereotyped myths": Robert Hanley, "Panel in Jersey Finds Bias against Women in the State Courts," *New York Times*, 11/22/83, p. A1.

384 scheduled a press conference: Schafran interview.

384 sitting throughout the main presentations . . . the back of the room . . . skipped the press conference: Loftus interview.

384 "Panel in Jersey" . . . "'There's no room for gender bias'": Robert Hanley, "Panel in Jersey Finds Bias against Women in the State Courts," *New York Times*, 11/22/83, p. A1.

385 "The Task Force has concluded": Huttner's testimony and words from the New York task force report are from "Report of the New York Task Force on Women in the Courts," reprinted in 15 *Fordham Urban Law Journal* 11 (1986–1987). See detailed notes online.

386 1985 . . . National Task Force: Lynn Hecht Schafran, letter to author, 8/10/05. See also Lynn Hecht Schafran, "Will Inquiry Produce Action? Studying the Effects of Gender in the Federal Courts," 32 *University of Richmond Law Review* 615 (1998), p. 619. Further references will be cited as Schafran, "Will Inquiry."

387 "the quality of the federal bench": Schafran, "Will Inquiry," p. 621n19, citing Judicial Conference of the United States, *Report of the Federal Courts Study Committee* (Philadelphia: Federal Courts Study Committee, 1990), p. 169.

387 begin their own task forces in the 1990s: Judith Resnik, letter to author, 3/23/06.

387 It appointed as its chair Judge Clarence Thomas. (Nothing happened . . .): Schafran, "California," p. 163.

25: Women Judges to the Rescue

389 VAWA might evaporate: Nourse interviews; Biden, *Promises to Keep*, p. 245. See note online.

390 "much-needed perspective": Sally Goldfarb, memo to Judges Cara Lee

Neville, Roslyn Bell, and Mary M. Schroeder, 12/11/91, in Legal Momentum DC files.

390 Judge Cara Lee Neville . . . Schafran asked: Schafran interview.

390 Nourse got word . . . *"LYNN,* could you please help with this?": Sally Goldfarb, memo to Pat Reuss, Ruth Jones, and Lynn Hecht Schafran, 3/17/92, in Schafran files.

390 packet arrived from Schafran: Lynn Hecht Schafran, letter to board of National Association of Women Judges, 2/28/92, in Schafran files.

390 "unexpected controversy": Victoria Nourse, memo to unnamed recipients, 2/13/92, in Schafran files.

390 detailed rebuttal by Goldfarb . . . "pernicious sexual stereotype" . . . "misread": NOW Legal Defense, "The Violence Against Women Act: Facts on the Impact on State and Federal Courts," undated but c. January 1992, in Schafran files.

391 At the board meeting: Lederman interview and Murray interview; Lynn Hecht Schafran, notes on phone conversation with board member of National Association of Women Judges, 5/1/92, in Schafran files.

392 appointed a judge . . . Dade County: Tristram Korten, "Courting Disaster: Judge Cindy Lederman, Champion of Justice and Advocate Extraordinaire, Bends the Rules on the Bench," *Miami New Times,* 3/23/00.

392 above all, stand up for other women: Lederman interview.

392 The board voted to present a resolution supporting VAWA: Lynn Hecht Schafran, letter to Barbara Mendel Mayden, 3/17/92, in Schafran files.

392 $43.5 million . . . every woman who was raped or assaulted would sue: National Task Force on the Elimination of Violence Against Women, "The Violence Against Women Act," undated but c. July 1992, 4 pages beginning "Violence Against Women has reached epidemic proportions . . . ," in Legal Momentum DC files, p. 3.

393 disrupt state and federal courts . . . "crime of violence" as overbroad: Theodore A. Kolb, chair, "American Bar Association Judicial Administration Division Standing Committee on Federal Judicial Improvements, Report to the House of Delegates," 6/25/92, in Legal Momentum DC files.

393 "divorce or other domestic relations" . . . "Just as prior civil rights statutes" . . . "will play a similarly important role": National Task Force on the Elimination of Violence Against Women, "The Violence Against Women Act," undated but c. July 1992, 4 pages beginning "Violence Against Women has reached epidemic proportions . . . ,"in Legal Momentum DC files.

394 "we are way behind": Lynn Hecht Schafran, memo to Helen Neuborne, Deb Ellis, Sally Goldfarb, Ruth Jones, and Pat Reuss, 7/7/92, in Legal Momentum DC files.

394 "Did these people go to law school": Pat Reuss and Kate Duba, letter to

Sally Goldfarb, Ruth Jones, and Lynn Hecht Schafran, 7/3/92, in Schafran files.

394 "beating a path to the doors": Mary M. Schroeder, "Judging with a Difference," 14 *Yale Journal of Law and Feminism* 255 (2002), p. 261.

394 no fear of speaking her mind: Schroeder interview.

395 earlier involvement . . . confer briefly with Schafran: Lynn Hecht Schafran, notes on phone conversation with Mary Schroeder, 6/5/91, discussing Lynn Hecht Schafran, "Proposed Draft," 5/31/91, in Schafran files.

395 Schroeder knew the value of federal gender-bias task forces directly . . . doubts about its language: Schroeder interview.

395 defending the decision of a local Rotary Club: *Rotary International v. Rotary Club of Duarte*, 481 U.S. 537 (1987).

395 appropriate for the federal courts . . . violence against women: Resnik interviews.

395 phone call from NAWJ's president-elect: Schroeder interview.

395 "bottom of the judicial heap": Murray interview.

395 Brenda Murray suggested . . . the only one that could talk to all: Schroeder interview.

396 two-part challenge: Schroeder interview.

396 "BE IT RESOLVED": "Re: NAWJ Resolution," 7/25/92, in Schafran files.

396 Lederman . . . support Title III as written: Lederman interview.

396 other judges hesitated, including Norma Shapiro: Lynn Hecht Schafran, handwritten notes, 7/13/92, in Schafran files.

397 delegate . . . *instructed*: Lynn Hecht Schafran, memo to Sally Goldfarb, 7/30/92, in Schafran files and Legal Momentum DC files.

397 multistep compromise . . . First . . . "in principle" . . . "narrowly tailored": "Re: NAWJ Resolution," 7/25/92, in Schafran files and Nourse files; Lynn Hecht Schafran, letter to Judge Norma Shapiro, 8/25/92, in Schafran files; Shapiro interview.

397 Third . . . Judge Schroeder: Schroeder interview and Murray interview.

397 far from idyllic by smoke spreading overhead from summer fires: Resnik interviews.

397 On August 5, for the first time: Judith Resnik, "Gender Bias: From Classes to Courts," 45 *Stanford Law Review* 2195 (1993), p. 2197. See note online.

397 from the first sex discrimination courses: Babcock and others, *Sex Discrimination* (1975), p. v.

398 "The task force movement has many links": "Report of the Ninth Circuit Gender Bias Task Force: Introduction: Gender Bias in the Courts and Civic and Legal Education," 45 *Stanford Law Review* 2143 (1993), p. 2143.

398 Ninth Circuit Gender Bias Task Force: Discussion Draft," title page, July 1992, in library of Yale Law School.

398 "Be careful" . . . "Don't teach": This and subsequent quotations from Resnik's speech are in Judith Resnik, "Gender Bias: From Classes to Courts," 45 *Stanford Law Review* 2195 (1993), pp. 2195–2196.

399 published reports in twenty-one states: Lynn Hecht Schafran, letter to author, 8/10/05.

400 half the members of the "ad hoc committee on gender-based violence": Judith Resnik, letter to author, 3/23/06.

400 both judges spent time in conversation: Resnik interviews and Judith Resnik, email to author, 7/11/06. See also Lynn Hecht Schafran, handwritten notes on phone conversation with Sally Goldfarb, 8/5/92, and with Victoria Nourse, 8/7/92; and Schafran, fax to Chris Schroeder and Victoria Nourse, 8/19/92, in Schafran files.

400 discussing VAWA at Rymer's home: Lynn Hecht Schafran, letter to Sally Goldfarb, 5/25/92, in Schafran files; Resnik interview, 7/18/97.

400 Rothstein would wind up talking . . . Helen Neuborne: Neuborne interview.

400 Nourse quickly responded that Biden would be pleased: Lynn Hecht Schafran, handwritten notes on phone conversation with Victoria Nourse, 8/7/92, in Schafran files.

401 "A couple of years ago": Quotations from O'Connor's talk are from "The Effects of Gender in the Federal Courts; the Final Report of the Ninth Circuit Gender Bias Task Force," reprinted in 67 *Southern California Law Review* 745 (1994).

401 Judge Shapiro, as agreed: "Re: NAWJ Resolution," 7/25/92, in files of Lynn Hecht Schafran at Legal Momentum as of 6/2/97.

401 Despite some worries . . . thankful for the NAWJ: Lynn Hecht Schafran, handwritten notes on phone conversation with Victoria Nourse, 8/7/92, in Schafran files.

402 Biden was tied up in Senate discussions: Victoria Nourse, fax to Lynn Hecht Schafran and Sally Goldfarb, c. 8/7/92, undated, in Schafran files.

402 "in an emergency c/o Judge Richard Cudahy in Winnetka" . . . running joke: Nourse interviews.

402 Saturday, August 8 . . . defer: Lynn Hecht Schafran, handwritten notes, 8/8/92, in Schafran files.

402 Monday, August 10 . . . Later on August 10 . . . "unless the legislation": Lynn Hecht Schafran, handwritten notes on conference call with Chris Schroeder, Victoria Nourse, and Sally Goldfarb, 8/10/92, and Lynn Hecht Schafran, handwritten notes, 8/12/92, all in Schafran files.

403 Tuesday, August 11, about 9:00 a.m.: Lynn Hecht Schafran, handwritten notes on two phone calls with Sally Goldfarb, 8/11/92, in Schafran files.

403 The task of marshaling opposition fell to Schafran . . . allies ready: Sally Goldfarb, fax to Lynn Hecht Schafran, 8/11/92, in Schafran files.

403 Schafran sat taking notes: Lynn Hecht Schafran, handwritten notes, 8/12/92, in Schafran files.

404 Brooksley Born, whom she had first worked with: Lynn Hecht Schafran, letter to author and email to author, 8/10/05.

404 Born was then the first woman member . . . rewritten long-standing ABA rules: "Legends in the Law: A Conversation with Brooksley Born," *Washington Lawyer*, October 2003, available at www.dcbar.org/for_lawyers/resources/legends_in_the_law/born.cfm (visited 2/20/05).

404 "All the men" . . . "with both barrels": Lynn Hecht Schafran, handwritten notes, phone conversation with Brooksley Born, 7/15/92, in Schafran files; confirmed by Brooksley Born, letter to author, 8/23/05.

405 Judge Shapiro . . . "crimes of violence" and "motivated by gender": Lynn Hecht Schafran, handwritten notes, 8/12/92, in Schafran files.

405 first in her class at Stanford Law in 1964 . . . calls from home to clients: Susan Wood, "My Job, My Self," *Washington Post Magazine*, 6/24/79, p. 10; Brooksley Born, letter to author, 8/23/05.

405 "absolute wreck" . . . "A considerable body of thought" . . . "a mistake had been made" . . . "I don't know": Born quoted in Laura A. Kiernan, "Lawyers Juggle Career, Family Demands," *Washington Post*, 9/29/80, p. 28.

406 Born rose to address the House of Delegates . . . "More votes this time" . . . *2:53 p.m.* (also underscored), August 12, 1992: Lynn Hecht Schafran, handwritten notes, 8/12/92, in Schafran files.

407 Resnik . . . came to admire . . . spoke not just to him . . . larger committee of the Judicial Conference: Resnik interviews.

408 Schroeder sometimes felt she was speaking to him daily . . . breakthrough that Schroeder saw as a "miracle": Schroeder interview. See note online.

408 shifted from opposition to no position: Judge Stanley Marcus, letter to Honorable Don Edwards, 11/16/83, reprinted in Hearing before the Subcommittee on Civil and Constitutional Rights of the Committee on the Judiciary, *Crimes of Violence Motivated by Gender*, 103d Cong., 1st sess., 1993, Serial No. 51, pp. 70–71. Further references will be cited as Judiciary hearing, *Crimes of Violence* (1993).

408 April 26, 1993: Sally Goldfarb, notes dated 4/26/93, in Legal Momentum NY files. Author reviewed these 5 pages of handwritten notes with Goldfarb, New York City, 5/13/97.

408 "the dark room": Goldfarb-Nourse-Reuss interview.

408 "the feminists": Schroeder interview.

409 meeting areas were taken: Nourse interviews.

409 room . . . SD G19. . . scuffed cranberry: Author visit, 6/6/97.

409 "Rumpus room": Nourse interviews.

409 "would try to bully us" . . . "nothing is going to happen" . . . "lawyer's lawyer meeting": Goldfarb-Nourse-Reuss interview and Nourse interviews.

410 "felony" . . . "pendent jurisdiction" . . . seriousness of a felony . . . not give jurisdiction to federal courts: In addition to Sally Goldfarb, notes dated 4/26/93, see also Judge Stanley Marcus, letter to Honorable Don Edwards, 11/16/83, reprinted in Judiciary hearing, *Crimes of Violence* (1993), pp. 70–71.

410 not cover "random" crimes: Senate Judiciary, *VAWA of 1991*, p. 69; House Crime Hearings 1992, *Violence Against Women*, p. 11.

410 "Motivated by gender means" . . . "a clear distinction between misogyny": Sally Goldfarb, fax to Judge Mary Schroeder, 12/1/92, in Legal Momentum DC files.

411 Judge Marcus met earlier in the year: Pat Reuss, draft memo to Violence Against Women Task Force, 2/24/93, in Legal Momentum DC files. Reuss' memo is cover sheet for memo beginning "You have asked for thoughts," which she describes as "Judges' suggestions for changes in the VAW (as passed out to House staff during visits by Judge Marcus, representing the U.S. Judicial Conference)."

411 "You have asked for thoughts": 5-page typescript (no author listed and no title), apparently from early 1993 (certainly later than 9/19/92 and before 2/24/93), in Legal Momentum DC files.

411 Since January, both judges had thought in detail and conferred often about VAWA's language: Schroeder interview.

411 "invidiously discriminatory animus" . . . "some racial": Sally Goldfarb, notes dated 4/26/93; *Griffin v. Breckenridge*, 403 U.S. 88, 102 (1971).

411 *Griffin* relied on the same anticonspiracy section of the 1871 Civil Rights Act that helped inspire VAWA: Sally Goldfarb, letter to author, 8/12/05; Nourse, "Where Violence," p. 8.

412 "animus and effect" . . . "to strike down the citizen": *Griffin v. Breckenridge*, 403 U.S. 88, 100 (1971).

412 "just and equal on their face": *Congressional Globe*, 42d Cong., 1st sess., App. 153 (Apr. 4, 1871) (remarks of Rep. Garfield), cited in *Carpenters v. Scott*, 463 U.S. 825, 845 (1983).

412 Nourse, in her earliest drafting . . . defined a "crime of violence" . . . dropped out of VAWA months later: Nourse, "Where Violence," pp. 7, 12.

412 case called *Guest* . . . "a majority of the Court today": *United States v. Guest*, 383 U.S. 745 (1966).

413 resembled the ban on discrimination in . . . Civil Rights Act of 1875: For language of Civil Rights Act of 1875, section 1, see *Civil Rights Cases*, 109 U.S. 3, 8 (1883): "all persons within the jurisdiction of the United States shall be entitled to the full and equal enjoyment of the accommodations, advantages, facilities, and privileges of inns, public conveyances on land or water, theatres, and other places of public amusement." For similarity

of provisions in the 1875 Act to those upheld under Civil Rights Act of 1964, see Catharine MacKinnon, "Disputing Male Sovereignty: On *United States v. Morrison*," 114 *Harvard Law Review* 135 (2000).

413 swerved . . . affirmed the civil rights act using only the commerce clause: Balkin, "History Lesson."

414 oral arguments in both 1952 and 1953 (by, among others, Thurgood Marshall and Spottswood Robinson): Kluger, *Simple Justice*, pp. 563–667.

414 "no place" in the area of "public education": *Brown v. Board of Education*, 347 U.S. 483, 495 (1954).

414 "I think *Plessy v. Ferguson* was right and should be reaffirmed": For the classic discussion of the Rehnquist memo of 1952, see Kluger, *Simple Justice*, pp. 606–609. Kluger concludes that Rehnquist's memo "was an accurate statement of his own views on segregation" (p. 609). For an analysis drawing on more recent evidence, see Tushnet, *Court Divided*, pp. 18–21, which argues that "Rehnquist took the opportunity provided by Jackson's ambivalence about judicial activism to put down on paper his own views about the Constitution and civil rights."

414 "smeared the reputation of a great justice" . . . "we are no more dedicated": Kluger, *Simple Justice*, p. 609.

414 Writing in the *Arizona Republic* . . . "opposed to all civil rights laws": Sue Davis, *Justice Rehnquist and the Constitution* (Princeton: Princeton University Press, 1989), p. 6. Further references will be cited as Davis, *Justice Rehnquist*.

414 "confronting and overturning" . . . begin to cut away civil rights: Balkin, "History Lesson."

415 "wrong the day it was decided": *Planned Parenthood v. Casey*, 505 U.S. 833, 863 (1992).

415 Scalia ruled: All quotations from the *Bray* case, unless otherwise indicated, are from *Bray v. Alexandria Women's Health Clinic*, 506 U.S. 263 (1993).

416 "Nowhere is the economic discrimination" . . . "able-bodied women": Supreme Court transcript of *Geduldig v. Aiello*, 417 U.S. 484 (1974), argued 3/26/74, pp. 29–30.

416 Potter Stewart . . . "pregnant women and nonpregnant persons": *Geduldig v. Aiello*, 417 U.S. 484, 497n20 (1974), and see Part 2.

418 hateful animus . . . Nourse and Goldfarb had refused to accept: Sally Goldfarb, "Possible Changes in the Violence Against Women Act," 4/22/93, in Legal Momentum DC files.

418 "we need proper historical sources here" . . . appealing language concerning *animus*: Schroeder interview.

419 Judge Marcus read aloud . . . "a purpose that focuses": Sally Goldfarb, notes dated 4/26/93, in Legal Momentum NY files.

419 These judges, Nourse was coming to believe . . . "I really think I saw a light go off": Goldfarb-Nourse-Reuss interview.

419 Goldfarb lay out the argument . . . cracks of American civil rights law: Sally Goldfarb, letter to author, 8/12/05.

419 A few days before, Judge Schroeder had suggested . . . "motivated at least in part by animus against the gender of the victim": Sally Goldfarb, "Possible Changes in the Violence Against Women Act," 4/22/93, in Legal Momentum DC files.

419 "language won't be perfect": Sally Goldfarb, notes dated 4/26/93.

419 She appreciated that . . . easing her burden: Goldfarb interviews.

419 *professorial . . . avuncular*: Goldfarb-Nourse-Reuss interview.

420 "the feminists, for lack of a better word" . . . "brilliant young woman" . . . "extremely knowledgeable" . . . "worked so hard" . . . "because I wanted the federal government": Schroeder interview.

421 "committed because of gender or on the basis of gender" but also must be "due, at least in part, to an animus based on the victim's gender": Nourse, "Where Violence."

421 no-amendment policy of Senators Joseph Biden and Orrin Hatch: Nourse, "Where Violence," p. 27.

26: Reckoning at the Supreme Court

422 Violence Against Women Act reached the Supreme Court: *United States v. Morrison*, 529 U.S. 598 (2000).

422 "accept as true": *Brzonkala v. Virginia Polytechnic Institute and State University*, 132 F.3d 949, 953 (4th Cir. 1997). Further references will be cited as *Brzonkala*, Fourth Circuit (1997).

422 The story of Christy Brzonkala: All information and quotations relaying the story told by Motz are from *Brzonkala*, Fourth Circuit (1997), pp. 953–956, unless otherwise indicated. See detailed notes online.

424 "return to school also means a return to football": "Virginia Tech LB Returns," *Washington Post*, 8/22/95, p. E03; *Brzonkala*, Fourth Circuit (1997), p. 955.

425 breaking the door of a bar: Richard Jerome and Mary Esselman, "No Justice, No Peace," *People*, 3/11/96, p. 45.

425 hit-and-run . . . missed Tech's big game: Associated Press, "Virginia Tech Aims to Raise Image to Level of Its Game," *New York Times*, 9/7/97, p. 3.

425 first federal judge . . . "indicates a conspiracy of disrespect": This and subsequent quotations from Judge Kiser's ruling are from *Brzonkala v. Virginia Polytechnic Institute and State University*, 935 F. Supp. 772, 784–785, 801 (W.D. Va. 1996). See detailed notes online.

426 athlete she had been . . . state championships: Sean Burke, "Virginia AAA Girls; Salem Outlasts Woodson in 2 Overtimes for Title," *Washington Post*, 3/12/94, p. D7.

426 "It's too traumatic": Quotations from and details of the press conference are from a transcript by author from videotape, "Gender-Based Violence: *Brzonkala v. Morrison*," 1/7/00, Washington, DC, C-SPAN ID 154583.

426 seventeen wins and only two losses: NOW Legal Defense and Education Fund, "Summary, *Brzonkala v. Morrison*," available at www.nowldef.org/html/courts/brzsumm.htm (visited 12/27/99).

426 Luttig . . . crash course in constitutional law . . . clerk to Antonin Scalia . . . and to Warren Burger: Mayer and Abramson, *Strange Justice*, p. 211.

426 "These people have destroyed my life": John C. Danforth, *Resurrection: The Confirmation of Clarence Thomas* (New York: Viking, 1994), p. 108.

427 "This would not have been possible": Deborah Sontag, "The Power of the Fourth," *New York Times Magazine*, 3/9/03, p. 40.

427 *en banc* . . . seven judges . . . to four . . . "We the people, distrustful of power": *Brzonkala v. Virginia Polytechnic Institute and State University*, 169 F.3d 820 (4th Cir. 1999). Further references will be cited as *Brzonkala*, Fourth Circuit *en banc* (1999).

427 *Lopez* . . . Gun-Free School Zones Act: *United States v. Lopez*, 514 U.S. 549 (1995).

428 authority under the commerce clause . . . half a century: Linda Greenhouse, "High Court Kills Law Banning Guns in a School Zone," *New York Times*, 4/27/95, p. 1.

428 "extraordinary step" . . . "concerned that the original understandings": Supreme Court transcript of *United States v. Lopez*, 514 U.S. 549 (1995), argued 11/8/94, pp. 1–2.

428 Years earlier . . . "this Court will in time again assume its constitutional responsibility": *Garcia v. San Antonio Metropolitan Transit Authority*, 469 U.S. 528, 579 (1985), and see Linda Greenhouse, "Justices Step In as Federalism's Referee," *New York Times*, 4/28/95, p. A1.

428 "strict constructionist" . . . "if she's a conservative": Dean, *Rehnquist Choice*, pp. xv, 5–6, 16, 45, 113, 295n51. See detailed notes online.

428 "I'm not a woman, and I'm not mediocre": "The President's Two Nominees," *Time*, 11/1/71; Dean, *Rehnquist Choice*, p. 191.

428 "never" . . . "find a conservative enough woman": Jack M. Balkin and Sanford Levinson, "Understanding the Constitutional Revolution," 87 *Virginia Law Review* 1045 (2001), p. 1072n115, citing David Alistair Yalof, *Pursuit of Justices: Presidential Politics and the Selection of Supreme Court Nominees* (Chicago: University of Chicago Press, 1999), pp. 55–61,

quoting H. R. Haldeman, *The Haldeman Diaries: Inside the White House* (New York: G. P. Putnam's, 1994), p. 365 (diary entry of 10/15/71).

429 "strict constructionist political philosophy": Margolick, "Women Find Bar," p. 16.

429 law review article . . . keep civil rights cases out of federal courts . . . quoted Justice Rehnquist: Sandra Day O'Connor, "Trends in the Relationship between the Federal and State Courts from the Perspective of a State Court Judge," 22 *William and Mary Law Review* 801 (1981), pp. 810, 815; for discussion of the article at the time of her nomination, see "Testimony of Lynn Hecht Schafran, Esq., National Director, Federation of Women Lawyers' Judicial Screening Panel" (Sandra Day O'Connor hearings in 1981), available at www.gpoaccess.gov/congress/senate/judiciary/sh-j-97–51/402–411.pdf (visited 1/27/08); see also Aric Press, "A Woman for the Court," *Newsweek*, 7/20/81, p. 16.

429 During oral argument in *Lopez*, O'Connor and Rehnquist . . . Scalia: Quotations from the oral argument are from Supreme Court transcript of *United States v. Lopez*, 514 U.S. 549 (1995), argued 11/8/94, which does not state which justices are asking questions. See detailed notes online. I have added names based on listening to recorded argument in Jerry Goldman, ed., *The Supreme Court's Greatest Hits 2.0* (Evanston: Northwestern University Press, 2002). CD-ROM. Anonymity of justices speaking in oral argument was preserved in official Supreme Court transcripts prior to October 2004; see "Supreme Court of the United States Argument Transcripts," available at www.supremecourtus.gov/oral_arguments/argument_transcripts.html (visited 8/16/06). According to the public information office of the Court, there is no way to identify justices speaking in oral argument prior to October 2004 except to read a transcript (hoping that an attorney addressed a justice by name), listen to an official audio recording such as those reproduced on *The Supreme Court's Greatest Hits* (hoping to identify a justice by tone of voice), or review press reports (hoping that some newspaper managed to report who was speaking); interview with Ed Turner, deputy public information officer, Supreme Court, Washington, DC, by phone, 8/18/06. In this book I have used all the methods suggested by Mr. Turner, hoping to avoid errors of the sort that the Court's change in policy has averted since 2004.

429 chief justice announced: Quotations from the *Lopez* decision, including the dissent, unless otherwise indicated, are from *United States v. Lopez*, 514 U.S. 549 (1995). See detailed notes online.

430 "the original understanding of that Clause": *United States v. Lopez*, 514 U.S. 549, 584 (1995) (Thomas dissenting).

430 "the Federal judiciary's policy-making": Linda Greenhouse, "Justices Step In as Federalism's Referee," *New York Times*, 4/28/95, p. A1.

431 "relatively narrow decision": Ann Devroy and Al Kamen, "Clinton Says Gun Ruling Is a Threat," *Washington Post*, 4/30/95, p. A1.

431 second foundation-shifting case: *City of Boerne v. Flores*, 521 U.S. 507 (1997).

431 The case began . . . peyote as a sacrament: *Employment Division, Department of Human Resources of Oregon v. Smith*, 494 U.S. 872 (1990).

431 fired . . . "private drug rehabilitation agency": John T. Noonan Jr., *Narrowing the Nation's Power: The Supreme Court Sides with the States* (Berkeley: University of California Press, 2002), pp. 23–27.

431 the Court sided with Oregon . . . "compelling interest": Joan Biskupic, "Supreme Court Overturns Religious Freedom Statute," *Washington Post*, 6/26/97, p. A1, and Linda Greenhouse, "Laws Are Urged to Protect Religion," *New York Times*, 7/15/97, p. A15.

431 Religious Freedom Restoration Act: Quotations from the Act and from the Supreme Court decision, unless indicated otherwise, are from *City of Boerne v. Flores*, 521 U.S. 507 (1997). See detailed notes online.

432 all but three senators and unanimity in the House . . . "enforce" guarantees: Linda Greenhouse, "Defending the Judiciary; High Court Voids a Law Expanding Religious Rights," *New York Times*, 6/26/97, p. A1.

432 "all but preordained": See *Brzonkala*, Fourth Circuit *en banc* (1999), p. 825: "As even the United States and appellant Brzonkala appear resignedly to recognize. . . ."

432 "marital rape exemption": *Brzonkala*, Fourth Circuit *en banc* (1999), p. 843. Judge Luttig pointed out that as of 1990, seven states still prohibited prosecuting a man for marital rape and thirty-three states restricted prosecution of marital rape.

433 temperatures just above freezing . . . sixty people . . . opposite the chief justice, was Senator Joseph Biden: Reporting by author, 1/11/00.

433 oral argument: Quotations from oral arguments, and descriptions, unless otherwise indicated, are from Supreme Court transcript of *United States v. Morrison*, 529 U.S. 598 (2000), argued 1/11/00, and author's reporting at oral argument. See detailed notes online.

435 a jurisdictional hook: For a discussion of such hooks or triggers, see Tushnet, *Court Divided*, p. 260, on "what constitutional scholars call a jurisdictional trigger." Tushnet describes the addition, after Supreme Court overrulings, of such a trigger or hook to the Gun-Free School Zones Act. And see Tushnet's p. 271 for discussion of the addition of a trigger in an effort restore part of the overruled Religious Freedom Restoration Act.

436 Unable to study after an attack . . . stopped attending classes . . . left the school: *Brzonkala*, Fourth Circuit (1997), pp. 953–955.

436 out of state to get a job . . . in a bar: Brzonkala interview.

436 Outdoors on the steps . . . "Men don't choose" . . . "women do alter"
. . . "empowers my daughter" . . . "titanic struggle": Reporting by author,
1/11/00.

437 As the day turned from drizzle . . . "when a woman is raped" . . . "Women
rule": Reporting by author, 1/11/00.

437 lobbied her . . . "Well, we got it": Jan Crawford Greenburg, *Supreme Conflict: The Inside Story of the Struggle for the Control of the United States Supreme Court* (New York: Penguin Press, 2007), pp. 16–17. Further references will be cited as Greenburg, *Supreme Conflict.* See note online.

438 In the opening paragraph of his opinion: Quotations from the majority and dissenting opinions, unless otherwise indicated, are from *United States v. Morrison,* 529 U.S. 598 (2000). See detailed notes online.

442 those later cases gave support to the anti-black laws of the Jim Crow era: Laurence H. Tribe, *American Constitutional Law,* 2nd ed. (Mineola, NY: Foundation Press, 1988), p. 1695.

442 not since 1913 had a majority of the Supreme Court explicitly followed either *Harris* or the *Civil Rights Cases*: According to Shepard's (visited 6/2/04 via Lexis), the Supreme Court had not followed the *Civil Rights Cases* since *Butts v. Merchants & Miners Transp. Co.,* 230 U.S. 126 (1913); it had not followed *Harris* since *United States v. Stanley,* 109 U.S. 3 (1883).

443 "the special favorite of the laws": *Civil Rights Cases,* 109 U.S. 3 (1883).

443 "Man is, or should be" . . . "paramount destiny": *Bradwell v. Illinois,* 83 U.S. 130, and see Part 1.

444 "old debris": Brief for Appellant (Sally Reed) to Supreme Court, filed 6/25/71, in *Reed v. Reed,* 404 U.S. 71 (1971), p. 46.

444 most important section: Biden, *Promises to Keep,* p. 244.

444 "single most important legislative accomplishment": Joe Biden, "The Fight Against Domestic Violence," *Huffington Post,* 10/18/07, available at www .huffingtonpost.com/joe-biden/the-fight-against-domesti_b_69000.html (visited 8/23/2008).

444 James Crawford . . . charge that they raped a female student . . . suspended by the college: Angie Watts, "Va. Tech Players Arrested; Edmonds, Crawford Deny Rape Charges," *Washington Post,* 12/17/96, p. E01; Angie Watts, "Va. Tech Players Suing Accuser; 2 Suspended from Team," *Washington Post,* 12/18/96, p. C01.

444 denying guilt . . . admitted the prosecution had sufficient evidence . . . aggravated sexual battery: Tony Ayala Jr., "Cases Involving Athletes and Sexual Assault," *USA Today,* 12/21/03, available at www.usatoday.com/ sports/03–12–22-athletes-assault-side_x.htm (visited 9/1/06).

444 paid her $75,000 while denying all wrongdoing: Brooke A. Masters, " 'No

Winners' in Rape Lawsuit; Two Students Forever Changed by Case That Went to Supreme Court," *Washington Post*, 5/20/00, p. B01.

444 regions that began drafting local laws modeled on VAWA's civil rights section: Sally Goldfarb, "No Civilized System of Justice: The Fate of the Violence Against Women Act," 102 *West Virginia Law Review* 499 (2000), p. 544n362.

Postscript: Toward Equality (Twenty-first Century)

445 disproportion unseen in entering classes of law schools since 1971: "First Year and Total J.D. Enrollment by Gender 1947–2005," available at www.abanet.org/legaled/statistics/charts/enrollmentbygender.pdf (visited 5/19/07).

445 presidential tapes, first available in late 2000: Dean, *Rehnquist Choice*, p. 287.

445 "screen" . . . "playing around": Nixon tapes, No. 11–1, quoted in Biskupic, *O'Connor*, pp. 41, 350n12.

445 in 2005 President George W. Bush, when he had Supreme Court openings: See Greenburg, *Supreme Conflict*, pp. 248–284; my postscript's narrative of the Miers' nomination follows Greenburg's chronology and supposes that future historians may learn still more than already appears in her invaluable reporting.

445 "devoted her life": Jeffrey Toobin, *The Nine: Inside the Secret World of the Supreme Court* (New York: Doubleday, 2007), p. 284. Further references will be cited as Toobin, *Nine*.

446 she might have won enough votes in the Senate: Toobin, *Nine*, p. 296.

447 Rehnquist maneuvered O'Connor out: Greenburg, *Supreme Conflict*, p. 20; Toobin, *Nine*, p. 252.

447 "good in every way, except he's not a woman": Dan Balz and Darryl Fears, "Some Disappointed Nominee Won't Add Diversity to Court: O'Connor Was among Those Hoping for a Woman or Minority," *Washington Post*, 7/21/05, p. A15.

447 "the bond of love" . . . "ancient notions" . . . "about women's place": *Gonzales v. Carhart*, 127 S. Ct. 1610, 1634, 1649 (2007).

CREDITS

Material from the American Civil Liberties Union Records, Box 679, Princeton University Archives, Department of Rare Books and Special Collections, reprinted by permission of Princeton University Library.

Material from the files of Patricia J. Barry reprinted by her permission.

Material from the files of Diane S. Blank reprinted by her permission.

Material from the files of Ruth Bader Ginsburg reprinted by her permission.

Excerpts from Susan Estrich, "Rape," 95 *Yale Law Journal* 1087 (1986), reprinted by permission of The Yale Law Journal Company, Inc., and The William S. Hein Company; volume 95, pages 1087–1184.

Material from the files of Mary F. Kelly reprinted by her permission.

Material from the files of Catharine A. MacKinnon reprinted by her permission.

Material from the George E. MacKinnon Papers reprinted by permission of the Minnesota Historical Society.

Material from the files of Victoria Nourse reprinted by her permission.

Material from the files of Karen Sauvigné reprinted by her permission.

Material from the files of Lynn Hecht Schafran reprinted by her permission.

Material from the files of Stephen Wiesenfeld reprinted by his permission.

Material from the files of Ruth Weyand reprinted by permission of her daughter, Sterling Perry.

INDEX

———————

abortion, 85, 100, 118, 145, 332, 447
  Bray and, 415–16, 417
  General Electric and, 120–21, 123, 126
  Jaramillo's opposition to, 91, 96–97
  right to privacy and, 25, 446
  Roe v. Wade and, 48, 121, 129
ACLU, *see* American Civil Liberties Union
Administrative Office of the U.S. Courts,
      356, 381–82, 399, 407, 408
adoption, 21–22, 48
affirmative action, 233, 361, 429
Age Discrimination in Employment Act
      (1967), 278
Aiello, 91–104, 119
  shock waves from, 92
  Supreme Court and, 95–98
  three-judge district court and, 92–95, 98
  see also Geduldig v. Aiello
Aiello, Carolyn, 91, 95, 98, 119, 132–33
Air Force, U.S.:
  Frontiero and, *see Frontiero*
  Struck and, 48–50
Alabama, 176
  civil rights in, 110, 175
  Southern Poverty Law Center in, 50, 51
alcoholism, 49
alien citizenship, 54, 57
alimony, 113, 410, 436
Alito, Samuel, 446
Alston, Edward, 18, 317, 319

American Bar Association (ABA), 247, 447
  Board of Governors of, 404, 405
  House of Delegates of, 389, 392, 397,
      403, 404, 405, 406
  Judicial Administration Division of,
      392, 396, 397, 401–6
  San Francisco meeting of, 392–93, 396,
      401–7
  Standing Committee on Federal
      Judiciary of, 404
  VAWA and, 363, 367, 370, 389–90,
      392–93, 396
American Civil Liberties Union (ACLU), 9,
      31–35, 41–62, 154, 333
  ERA opposed by, 117
  Frontiero and, 50–61
  Moritz and, 24–27
  Reed and, 25–28, 31–34, 41–46, 161
  Ross's internship at, 117
  Simon's letter to, 20–22
  Struck and, 48–50, 61
  Wiesenfeld and, 9–10
  Women's Rights Project of, 9, 46–47,
      48, 51, 127, 225, 247
American Law Institute, 254, 302
Americans for Democratic Action, 145
Amistad, 174
amniotic embolism, 6
Annual Survey of American Law, 147, 157,
      181

561

stories of, 156–58
Title VII and, 111
Environmental Protection Agency, U.S.,
215, 253, 254, 255
Equal Employment Opportunity
Commission, U.S. (EEOC), 93,
114–19, 139, 179
Blank's case and, 170–71, 177, 184,
195, 196
Columbia training clinic funded by, 161,
164
General Electric and, 119, 122–23, 124,
127–28, 130, 133–34, 137
Griggs and, 133
Kohn's case and, 170
Norton at, 270, 271, 274
pregnancy decisions of, 93, 107, 108,
115–16, 118, 119, 122, 124, 126,
131, 134
as sex commission, 115, 270
sex discrimination case against legal
firms planned by, 155–56
sexual harassment guidelines of, 270–
71, 273, 278, 282, 296
Vinson and, 270–71, 278, 282–85, 294,
296, 302
Equal Justice Under Law (Motley), 173
Equal Pay Act (1963), 20, 46, 107, 111–12,
126
equal protection:
in California Constitution, 89
Geduldig and, 98
see also Fourteenth Amendment, equal
protection in
ERA (equal rights amendment), 58–61,
112, 113, 349, 352
ACLU opposition to, 117
symposium on (1971), 159–61
Erlenborn, John, ix
espionage, 173, 226
estate administration, *Reed* and, 20, 25,
31–32, 42
Estrich, Susan, 325, 386
rape of, 315
Yale Law Journal article of, 315–26
Eval-U-Metrics, 5
Evans, Martin, 316–17, 318
Evers, Medgar, 15
Executive Order 11246, 348, 349
"Exploration of the Operation and
Objectives of the Consent Standards,
An" (anonymous), 324

Farley, Lin, 219–20, 223–25, 231, 232
fathers, 42–43, 68
single, 6–10
FBI, Rabb's file with, 163, 164
Federal Courts Study Committee, 387
federal funds, sex discrimination and, 17
federalism, 429, 444
VAWA and, 362–63, 368, 370, 400, 425
Federalist, 430
Federation of Women Lawyers Judicial
Screening Committee, 381
Feigen, Brenda, 54, 55
feminism, 14, 34, 116–17, 158–61, 163,
409, 420
Blank's law firm and, 179–80
of MacKinnon, 228, 229
Motley's limited contact with, 192
violence against women and, 312, 346
Feminism Unmodified (MacKinnon), 336
Feminist Legal Strategies Project, 343
fertilizer making, *Royster Guano* and, 41
Fifth Amendment, 195
film, free speech extended to, 172–73
First Amendment, 201, 202, 204, 227
pornography and, 336
Fisk University, 175
Florida, 33, 77, 351
gender-bias task force in, 391–92
widows' tax break in, 62–64, 73
Florida Law Review, 328
Florida Supreme Court Gender Bias Study
Commission, 328
Florida Supreme Court Study Commission,
391
Foner, Eric, 339
Fordham, 167
Fortas, Abe, 442
Fourteenth Amendment, 54, 88, 335,
431–32
due process clause of, 41, 194, 195,
332, 333, 334
equal protection in, 28–31, 44, 45, 50,
56, 66, 76, 87, 89, 93, 124, 135,
238, 329, 331, 332, 339, 365, 373,
412–15, 434, 440–43
Harris and, 340
liberty and, 332–33
state action and, 340–41, 412–13, 442,
443
VAWA and, 338, 342, 412–15, 425,
434–36, 440–43
Frankel, Marvin E., 168

Liberty and Sexuality (Garrow), 333, 334
Liberty Mutual, 123, 125–29, 136
Liberty Mutual, 123–29
Library of Congress, 313–14, 440
Lillie, Mildred, 445
Liman, Arthur, 310–11
Lincoln, Abraham, 110, 174, 414
Lindsay, John, 158
Lipscher, Robert, 381–82
litigation, women lawyers turned away
    from, 156, 157, 165
Loftus, Marilyn, 377–78, 381–84, 386, 397
London, Ephraim:
    as anticensorship lawyer, 172–73
    barratry charges of, 186, 187, 188
    Blank's deposition taken by, 179–82,
    187
    conspiracy probe of, 180–82
    Diane Blank and, 172–73, 177–95,
    197–98
    Motley's disqualification sought by,
    188–92
    Motley's letters from, 177–79, 182–83,
    192
    separate trial request of, 184–85, 190
    "yahoo" letter sent by, 183, 187–88,
    193
London, Meyer, 172
London & Buttenwieser, 172, 173
Lopez, 427–32, 434, 435, 436, 438, 439
Lopez, Alfonso, Jr., 427
"Lord Hale instructions," 314, 327–28
Los Angeles Times, 312–13
Louisiana, women excluded from juries in,
    247
Ludwic, Judith, 214–15, 248
Luttig, Michael, 426–27, 432–33
lynching, 105, 340, 370, 441, 442

McCallum, Dorethea, 263
McKay, Robert, 152
MacKinnon, Catharine Alice, 226–29,
    233–43
    Barry's letter to, 279–80
    book by, see Sexual Harassment of
    Working Women
    "Dear sisters" letter and, 225, 231
    education of, 225–31, 233, 279
    pornography attacked by, 336–37
    privacy rights critiqued by, 335
    teaching jobs of, 279–80, 305, 343–44,
    365

Vinson and, 279–80, 285–90, 292,
    294–95, 299, 302
    women's "disadvantagement" as viewed
    by, 231, 235
    Yale independent project of, see "Sexual
    Harassment of Working Women"
MacKinnon, George E., 226, 227, 241,
    242, 243
    Barnes and, 250–56, 277, 284–85, 302
McKusick, Vincent L., 356
MacWhorter, R. Bruce, 148, 149
Madison, Dolley, 34, 35
Madison, James, 430
Magna Carta, 311
Malone, Christine, 210–12, 260–64, 268,
    274
March on Washington, 111
Marcus, Stanley, 407–11, 419–21
marriage:
    interracial, 106–7
    rape within, 312, 314, 328–32, 335,
    343, 345, 355, 386, 432
Married Women's Privacy Act, proposed,
    331, 335–56
Marshall, Thurgood, 64, 101, 187, 204,
    361, 362, 414
    Frontiero and, 56, 57, 58
    General Electric and, 129, 133
    NAACP and, 40, 56, 106, 175, 176,
    227, 244
    Vinson and, 298–304
Marxism, 229
Maryland, 320, 345–46
master's escape clause, 254–55, 302
Meisburg, John Marshall, 248, 260, 295
Memphis & Charleston Railroad, 340, 341
Meredith, James, 175
Merhige, Robert R., Jr., 119–22
Meyer, Susan, 219, 223–25, 231
Michigan, female bartender ban in, 38, 44,
    87, 88
Miers, Harriet, 445–47
military, sex discrimination and, 46, 76
    Simon's case and, 20–23
    Struck and, 48–50
military, Sherman & Sterling interviews
    and, 148
Milken, Michael, 311
Miller, Margaret, 216, 217
Miller, Samuel Freeman, 30
Millett, Kate, 229
Minneapolis coalition, 336